Marcus Galdia

Lectures on Legal Linguistics

PETER LANG
EDITION

Bibliographic Information published by the Deutsche Nationalbibliothek
The Deutsche Nationalbibliothek lists this publication in the Deutsche Nationalbibliografie; detailed bibliographic data is available in the internet at http://dnb.d-nb.de.

Library of Congress Cataloging-in-Publication Data
A CIP catalog record for this book has been applied for at the Library of Congress

Coverabbildung: Marcus Galdia

ISBN 978-3-631-72582-5 (Print)
E-ISBN 978-3-631-72778-2 (E-Book)
E-ISBN 978-3-631-72779-9 (EPUB)
E-ISBN 978-3-631-72780-5 (MOBI)
DOI 10.3726/b11443

Peter Lang Edition is an Imprint of Peter Lang GmbH.

Peter Lang – Frankfurt am Main · Bern · Bruxelles · New York · Oxford · Warszawa · Wien

This publication has been peer reviewed.

www.peterlang.com

Contents in Brief

Detailed Contents

Abbreviations

ADA	Americans with Disabilities Act (US)
All E.R.	All England Law Reports
BGB	Bürgerliches Gesetzbuch (German Civil Code)
CC	Code Civil (French Civil Code)
CIC	Corpus Iuris Civilis
CISG	United Nations Convention on the International Sale of Goods
D	Digesta Iustiniani (Corpus Iuris Civilis)
ECJ	European Court of Justice
ECPA	Electronic Communication Privacy Act (US)
EU	European Union
HTS	Harmonized Tariffs Schedules (US)
INCOTERMS	International Commercial Terms
OSCE	Organization for Security and Co-operation in Europe
PECL	Principles of European Contract Law (EU)
PTO	Patent and Trade Office (US)
SEC	Securities and Exchange Commission (US)
UCC	Uniform Commercial Code (US)
UCITA	Uniform Computer Information Transactions Act (US)
UNCITRAL	United Nations Commission on International Trade Law
UNIDROIT	International Institute for the Unification of Private Law

Legal terms, with exception of terms expressed in the English language are provided an abbreviation relating to their origin, e.g. (FR) for French or (CN) for Chinese legal terms. In some contexts American legal terms are marked with (US) and English legal terms with (UK). An asterisk (*) indicates grammatically incorrect structures or constructed lexical units.

Preface

Why has this book been written? This book goes back to my *Legal Linguistics* that appeared 2009 at Peter Lang International Publishing. During several years I used the book and its follower *Legal Discourses* (2014) in my courses on legal linguistics and comparative law, mainly at Riga Graduate School of Law and at the International University of Monaco. As time went by, I have reshaped, updated and expanded the initial text. Gradually, a new book emerged as a result of a long process of improving and rewriting the text published in 2009. It seemed to me that its version expanded by more than one half can no longer be called a second edition of the previous book notwithstanding the fact that I basically tried to incorporate the initial argument into this text. Therefore, I decided to call this book *Lectures on Legal Linguistics*. This title clarifies that the text emerged as a result of my teaching experience and that it is also connected to my *Legal Linguistics*. In *Legal Linguistics* I tried to sketch the conceptual boundaries of a new branch of knowledge called legal linguistics and in *Legal Discourses* I attempted at describing the use of legal language toward a broader contextual background. Results achieved in both books allow now a new exposition of main legal-linguistic problems as they appear today in the pragmalinguistic perspective. This book is therefore also more explicative than the initial text that had been largely explorative. Also with this idea in mind, I thought that a new title imposes itself as this book addresses the problems from a readjusted angle. It covers the theoretical approaches from previous texts, yet also makes them more accessible and better readable. The tone used in the exposition of legal-linguistic problems that will follow is therefore close to lecturing, which had been the initial form of the texts compiled within the rewriting process of *Legal Linguistics*. I do not perceive it necessarily as a disadvantage, yet I have to admit that like all other techniques of text composition it also has some shortcomings such as repetitiveness and some length in the development of the argument due to the structure of the spoken word. However, I tried to counteract the irritations, which might come up through introducing into the current text some succinct paragraphs that cut short basic issues discussed in particular chapters. Thus, my intention to explore the relevant problems at length and readers' interest in getting useful information about legal linguistics in a form as short as possible compromise in a text acceptable to its author and hopefully also useful for readers receptive to the particular vision upon the subject matter adopted by the author. Equally, materials included in the last part of the book are now more fully commented than it has been the case in *Legal Linguistics* in order to contrast or to compare the findings that readers may reach with the perspective adopted by the author.

As mentioned, this book deals with the use of language in the area of law. This is a very general statement that allows different interpretations. Nowadays, questions related to linguistic aspects of law are dealt with in an interdisciplinary branch of knowledge that is frequently called legal linguistics. The number of material issues as well as theoretical problems discussed in legal linguistics is constantly growing. These problems are addressed by researchers from different points of view. At this stage of its development it seems to be worthwhile to focus on some fundamental issues in the research that may be helpful for the understanding of the scope of the discipline, its findings and its future tasks. Therefore, on the following pages, we will take a closer look at the theoretical foundations and the material achievements of legal linguistics as two main issues which determine its current and future standing among the interdisciplinary branches of knowledge. By doing so, we will clarify the question of what is the relation between law and language that has been traditionally identified as the focal point in all fundamental legal-linguistic research approaches. In other words, we will make plain what are the linguistic aspects of law. As a result of this step, prerequisites of the perception of legal linguistics as a particular legal theory will become understandable as well. Meanwhile, a broad definition of the subject seems to be appropriate because of the vast number of problems canvassed in the legal-linguistic research. In the theoretical part of this book, legal linguistics will be mainly understood as a subject dealing with two questions, namely how law is created and how it is applied with linguistic means. Both main legal-linguistic features of law, i.e. its creation and its application with the help of language, are fundamental to the appreciation of this phenomenon as one of the most efficient social institutions. Creation of law as well as its application in its different forms such as interpretation, argumentation or translation are complex linguistic operations. Their characterization has always been a challenge for the legal theory and it is equally a challenge for the contemporary legal linguistics. Therefore, in this book, I will try to explain how law is interpreted and translated, and use these exemplary facets of the legal practice in an attempt to better understand the legal discourse. This theoretical goal is approached through analyses of legally relevant linguistic materials, mostly court opinions and statutory provisions. The analyses have been carried out in order to demonstrate that the fundamentals of legal linguistics are well anchored in the legal practice.

How is this book structured? The book begins with an introduction into its main theoretical issues based on examples from the legal practice. It demonstrates also in a succinct form what law is actually about when it is seen from the jurists' perspective. This question is not without importance for the shaping of legal linguistics which deals with the linguistic manifestation of law and all too often presupposes that whoever engages in it masters perfectly the law. Neither is it realistic to assume that those who master law would also master linguistics. Therefore, in the introductory part some thoughts upon law and upon linguistics are presented in a way that should facilitate the understanding of what will follow. Needless to say that those few pages spent on the parent disciplines of legal linguistics cannot make up for thorough studies of both subjects. In fact, interdisciplinary studies have their inherent constraints and those courageous enough to deal with them will always suffer from a lack of sufficiently founded knowledge. The remedy against this shortcoming is constant awareness of the researcher about own limits rather than a timid reserve and resignation.

After the sketch of preliminaries, material issues of legal linguistics such as legal terminology and subsequently the linguistic operations that are characteristic of law, especially legal argumentation, legal interpretation and legal translation will be introduced and discussed. This is the main part of the book which also shows that the theoretical fundamentals, which were mentioned in the introductory part, are essential to the understanding of all linguistic operations that constitute the legal discourse. Broader aspects of discourse and textuality will also be dealt with in the context of Law and Literature. While keeping in mind the daily needs of professionals dealing with legal-linguistic issues, all over the book practical matters discovered in the research are discussed and, where possible, also suggestions are made for the practical use of the legal-linguistic research. Because the book aims to be of practical importance for jurists, linguistic issues relevant to the emergence of the global law as well as to the law of communication as examples of the most important already practiced areas of legal linguistics are characterized and restructured from the legal-linguistic perspective. Next to it, linguistic legislation is presented in the final part of the chapter on communicational legal regulation. The book ends, unsurprisingly, with conclusions. In the appendix the reader will find notes and commented materials which refer to issues and cases mentioned in the main text. They are commented and annotated in order to facilitate readers' orientation in the subject and draw their attention to the method of legal-linguistic text analysis. This is, in short, the general structure of the book.

What detailed knowledge is provided in this book? The exposition of the pragma-linguistic theory of legal linguistics incorporates reference to its practical application. Practically important for every professional of law is the mastery of the legal argumentation. Without understanding this topic no other linguistic operation in law, such as translation of legal documents or justification of court decisions can be conscientiously performed. Therefore, legal argumentation in its relation to all other linguistically relevant aspects of law is the central material topic of this book. The legal discourse, which is the overarching structure for the language used in law, is by its nature argumentative and law is in fact identical with this specific discourse. Therefore it is practically important to elaborate requirements for successful legal argumentation. Once the linguistically relevant essence of legal argumentation is understood, the rest of legal linguistics – with all respect for this fascinating discipline – could be equally well included in footnotes.

Before dealing with legal argumentation and other linguistic operations in law some time will be spent on scrutinizing legal terminology. The reason for this specific attention to legal terminology is that many people still approach the legal language through its terminology. I will therefore reflect upon this traditional approach and integrate it into our perspective that is dominated by argumentative features of the legal discourse. In fact, legal arguments are developed around legal concepts that manifest themselves in texts in the form of terms. Therefore, analyses of the legal language should not be reduced to terminological issues. When seen from the argumentative perspective the language used in law appears in its most illustrative context. What is more, in the broader perspective of the legal discourse the legal terminology will become operational in different speech acts. These speech acts will help determine what there is in law that might make it appear as being composed of mere words. Moreover, textual aspects of law are best understood in comparison with literature. We will therefore have a glimpse of the sister discipline Law and Literature to learn from it and benefit where possible. More specifically, I will ask why do lawyers speak and write differently than other people do and reflect upon their purportedly arcane language use. In this context, I will also ask why the language used by lawyers is often ambiguous and I will reflect upon the necessity for remedies. Finally, I will try to sketch out a retrospective upon the original legal language and look back to the times when the basic legal language was constructed as part of our efforts to describe its creation. Some knowledge of Latin is necessary to understand this part of our study. Equally, practical aspects of drafting legislation and textual alternatives to the Roman conception of law will be introduced as well. In consequence of all those detailed analyses, legal linguistics will emerge as a description of two already mentioned activities exercised by lawyers, i.e. creation and application of law with linguistic means. When this point in the argument is reached, these *Lectures on Legal Linguistics* will fulfil its objective that is to clarify the relation between law and language. Many other issues of legal linguistics that are sometimes mentioned in the text are reflected in particular research. I hope that readers interested in the fundamental legal-linguistic research, which is my main point of concern, will not underestimate particular research issues that the elaborate legal-linguistic literature is nowadays able to offer. These lectures should therefore incite readers to go further and in no way limit their legal-linguistic horizons to issues discussed in this book. Additional legal-linguistic research and the analysis of particular legal languages in provided in Heikki E.S. Mattila's books on *Comparative Legal Linguistics* (2002b, 2006, 2012a, 2013a), available in Finnish, English and French versions. They include further leading bibliographies for all those who use this book as an introductory book into legal linguistics. One can also read both books in the reverse order. One can start with *Comparative Legal Linguistics* and then read *Lectures on Legal Linguistics* that stresses more the methodology of legal-linguistic research and therefore can be perceived either as fundamental or as particular, depending on the point of view. Finally, no reader can nowadays complain that there is not enough literature to read about law and language. The abundance of writings and methodological approaches to the subject enabled even the establishing of a specialized Masters' program at the Riga Graduate School of Law where materials presented in this book have been regularly used.

What other practical consequences follow from this research? Legal linguistics has also a role to play in the comparative legal science. It can contribute to the solution of some problems which are discussed there by pointing out that the central legal-linguistic questions must be asked in the comparative law as well. This book is written in a time when global law as a coherent regulative body of generally accepted rules still does not exist. Therefore, a comparative approach to the legal diversity and the legal culture has been adopted here. However, I will not conceal my support to efforts undertaken by the legal science to overcome the legal diversity and to contribute to the development of the global law. Legal linguistics can contribute to the development of the language of the global law. This practical task may be perceived as urgent and be possibly even more relevant than the main theoretical aspects of legal linguistics upon which this book lays the main stress. Both issues are, however, interrelated. They can, therefore, be perceived as two sides of the same coin. Moreover, legal linguistics deals also with regulations concerning language use. Therefore, I included an overview of problems related to this specific area. I deal there with language use in multilingual societies and especially with the development of effective legal mechanisms which support the linguistic cohesion in modern societies. Also in this area legal linguistics shows again its practical impact upon the legal science. Next to it, issues concerning legislative drafting are included and discussed, especially focusing on the debate about plain language and the linguistic alternatives to it. Finally, the question whether future law could abandon the form of textuality typical of the Roman law, which until now has preconditioned it, is mentioned as one more practical issue to which legal linguistics should be able to provide some innovative ideas.

How can this book be used? This book is written for all professionals interested in linguistic aspects of law. It can become instrumental as a textbook introducing legal linguistics for everyone who is also interested in the theoretical fundamentals of the subject. Courses in legal linguistics which are now parts of curricula all over the world address very often the non-legal audience composed mainly of interpreters and translators of legal texts. Also this audience should be able to use this book with some benefit. This book does not contradict the tendency to perceive legal linguistics as a course in legal terminology for non-lawyers or a course in foreign legal terminology for lawyers. Yet, it addresses the issue from a broader perspective and aims explicitly to reach lawyers while being also accessible to non-lawyers who wish to acquire specific skills in order to exercise a profession that is related to law. However, this book cannot replace a course in comparative law or in jurisprudence. It has been construed as a complementary part of both disciplines. Despite all the inconveniences described, it seems to be well adapted to the needs of teaching law, and it can also serve as an introduction into legal reasoning against the background of comparative law. At least, the author was using the materials upon which this book is based in this sense during his teaching of courses on Legal Culture and Comparative Law, U.S. American Business Law and Principles of the E.U. Economic Law, Law of Communication and Internet as well as International Business Law and International Law.

From what theoretical perspective has this book been conceived? This book was developed in an interdisciplinary exchange between legal science and linguistics. Contrasting and combining methods of diverse disciplines or parts of them is an inevitable prerequisite of any work of this sort. Works from philosophical and linguistic pragmatics, analytical philosophy and French *épistémologie* form its main theoretical framework. This theoretical commitment has an additional practical consequence. The focus on one theoretical approach, which stresses the linguistic and philosophical pragmatics, means also that no exhaustive overview of publications and issues discussed in the legal-linguistic research could be undertaken here. First, publications by Heikki E. S. Mattila (2002b, 2006, 2012a, 2013a) provide a thorough overview of these issues and include broad if not the broadest available bibliography of legal linguistics. Second, no encyclopaedia of legal linguistics was planned by the author, but rather a very specific view upon the subject matter due to unresolved fundamental methodological issues of the subject itself. Readers interested in other conceptions of legal linguistics will find in the chapter *Language and Law* a critical commentary of existing currents in this domain. There, also a state of the art report is outlined for readers who prefer a problem-oriented rather than a methodologically founded approach to legal-linguistic issues. Meanwhile, opinions of jurists and linguists about issues discussed or to be discussed in legal linguistics rarely coincide. I am not necessarily focused on establishing harmony within the received and other opinions among jurists and linguists about the usefulness of legal theory or legal linguistics. I have also at another place (Galdia 1989: 329) expressed a pessimistic view about the possibility to establish a legal science that is not doctrinal but scientific, i.e. at least explicit in terms of its underlying theory. Meanwhile, the mainstream legal science still cultivates an implicit or at best positivist method that isolates it from other social sciences. I doubt that a fundamental change could occur soon in the legal science. Therefore, in the whole book I am rather optimistic about the development of legal linguistics, yet at the same time pessimistic about a possible and sustainable legal-linguistically founded influence upon the mainstream legal science. I can only recommend to readers and students to take this apparently marginal reflection seriously when reflecting upon particular thoughts expressed in this book.

How and where has this book been written? Legal materials used in this work mostly concern U.S. American and French law due to my involvement in teaching at the International University of Monaco between 2005 and 2017, i.e. in the time when the main part of this research was prepared. I used these materials also while teaching courses on Legal Linguistics and Comparative law at Riga Graduate School of Law between 2010 and 2015. Nevertheless, the general remarks in this book also aim at reflecting language use in the civil law of European provenance although this has not always been explicitly stated in the text. The reason for this approach is that legal linguistics is perceived here as uniform in its methodological setting; it does not depend on the specifics of laws in different jurisdictions. Parts of this study were written during professional assignments that I spent in Russia, Macedonia and Montenegro. Access to original publications of some classics there has been difficult. This is the reason why sometimes e.g. a German writer is quoted in the text in the Serbian language version of his work. Interested readers in countries where original editions of the books mentioned in the text are available should not encounter particular problems with the identification of right paragraphs in the original works.

Author's last word (in the preface) Legal linguistics in its contemporary shape is a fascinating but also a challenging enterprise. Both, readers and writers who wish to deal with this topic need a lot of enthusiasm and patience to accomplish their respective tasks. Let us therefore reiterate and linguistically reformulate some of the main thoughts of this preface in order to encourage the readers to deal with the chapters which will follow. For the author, law is a type of socially relevant argumentation, a discursive and predominantly institutionalized practice. Language is used in it in a specific way. Language use in institutional settings can be aptly characterized with the help of pragmalinguistic approaches. This broad understanding of law and language makes it possible to perceive legal linguistics (also) as a theory of law. Therefore, the entire book can be perceived as prolegomena to the pragmatic theory of law. This task makes it also necessary to focus extensively on basic paradigmatic and epistemological notions of such a theory, its preliminary questions and conceptual prerequisites. The time spent on this reflection is not lost, because the emerging legal linguistics needs a solid basis for its future development. Otherwise, it would risk disappearing in details and footnotes and would continue to be perceived as marginal in legal sciences as well as in linguistics proper. I, for my part, aim at preventing this discouraging scenario. Ultimately, the term legal linguistics is, unlike in my *Legal Linguistics* not spelled here anymore with initial capital letters in order to stress that it refers to an emerging and independent – although interdisciplinary – branch of knowledge. Legal linguistics developed considerably in the past years. Therefore, I think that it is possible to abandon this somehow programmatic and ideological, yet well-intentioned spelling.

This preface has been long. Meanwhile, it included also some preliminary considerations about legal linguistics that may encourage the reader to deal with the rest of the book. It would be preferable to start with the chapter *Introducing Legal Linguistics* that is however all but succinct.

Monaco, March 2017

Acknowledgments

My previous legal-linguistic publications as well as these *Lectures on Legal Linguistics* largely benefited from advice and criticism expressed by colleagues and by critics unknown to me personally. I am particularly grateful for advice and support provided by Prof. Heikki E.S. Mattila of the University of Rovaniemi. His pioneering research into legal linguistics was for me the basis and the incentive to engage in this expanding subject. I was introduced into legal linguistics by Prof. Edeltraud Bülow of the University of Münster. I am particularly indebted to Prof. Bülow for discussions concerning the draft of these lectures and for valuable and critical remarks. Prof. Bülow also read and commented upon an earlier draft of this book. I would also like to thank my colleagues Ms Irēna Lapsa, Mr Christopher Goddard and Mr Antonio Liaci of the Riga Graduate School of Law for their support, interest and encouraging words during my work on this book.

Prof. Maria Teresa Lizisowa, Prof. Tatiana Dubrovskaya and Dr. Milena Hadryan put their recent legal-linguistic publications at my disposal. This has greatly facilitated my research. I had also the pleasure to discuss legal-linguistic problems with Prof. Clara Hoyan Chan whose research helped me to understand better the Chinese legal linguistics. Prof. Grażyna Maria Mirecka and Mr. Serge Toumassian of the International University of Monaco helped me to solve problems with data processing. Prof. Jaakko Husa mentioned in his review of my previous book some problematic issues that are treated more extensively in this work. Prof. Juha Karhu drew my attention to Gaius's legal-linguistic remarks that are presented in this book in Notes and Commented Materials. Contacts with Prof. Aleksandra Matulewska and her team of legilinguists at the Adam Mickiewicz University in Poznań helped me to broaden and to systematize many issues that I tried to connect in order to establish a coherent legal-linguistic perspective upon law. I wish to espress my gratitude to all scholars mentioned above.

M. Galdia

Part 1: Introducing Legal Linguistics

In the introductory part I will reflect upon some theoretical questions that will be further elucidated in the main part of this book. First of all, I will try to establish what lawyers are actually doing when they create or apply law. This will help us to understand the law before we specifically approach legal linguistics. Furthermore, I will use some short narrative examples to illustrate different aspects of the language used in law. Moreover, in order to make my observations theoretically operational in subsequent chapters I will establish a conceptual framework based mainly upon linguistic and philosophical pragmatics which will be needed later in our case analyses. I will also show that the choice of the conception of language is fundamental to any reflection upon language and law. Finally, I will claim that language in legal contexts conveys moral values. Therefore, I will include some preliminary observations about the role ethics plays in law and in its language. The combination of linguistic pragmatics and ethics will enable us to engage in numerous analyses of court opinions and statutory provisions which will follow in the main chapters of this book. This chapter is relatively long, yet it can also be used as a short introductory course in legal linguistics as it shows, although only cursorily, the main topics of the subject without going into details.

1.1 Preliminary Questions

First things first: A sketch of a *mini-theory of legal language* may facilitate the understanding of some preconditions of a more fully fledged conception of legal linguistics that will emerge in subsequent chapters. Already in the preface the theoretical tendency of these lectures has been briefly indicated: law will be perceived on the many pages that follow as a *discursive practice.* This fundamental theoretical assumption has consequences: First, law as a discursive social practice is always made or *engendered by someone.* Law is not discovered in nature nor is it predetermined by whatever supernatural forces or phenomena. It also means that law *depends on discursiveness* for its creation and its application. Second, law that emerges in discursive practices can be good or bad because it is made by people under conditions of their limited knowledge and their volatile ethical attitudes. Therefore, law will be inevitably imperfect like all other social institutions that were created in the history of humankind. Third, law is created and applied with the help of *linguistic means,* i.e. discursively. Discursiveness that is constitutive of law is also critical to the *rationality of law,* i.e. to processes in which it meaningfully emerges. Therefore, it is necessary to understand how *meaning* emerges in law before law can be documented by legislative institutions or applied in courts. Fourth, the meaning of law is not encoded in legal materials, it is not deducted from them but *constructed.* This intricacy of legal semantics is caused by the *indeterminacy of meaning in language* and by constant changes in ethical attitudes of citizens. Meaning in law emerges in numerous *legal-linguistic operations* such as argumentation, justification or fact finding that steer the *legal discourse.* Legal discourse represents the network of our utterances about law; it can be institutionalized or informal. Fifth, legal discourse is further determined by non-optional *textual patterns* such as written judgments or printed statutory provisions that further stabilize it. Sixth, legal discourse transfers *legal regulation* that can be characterized as the subject matter of law. Seventh, regulation as an inherent part of the legal discourse is strictly speaking not the domain of jurists. Jurists participate in its setting, yet they are not masters of regulation. In democratic societies, citizens shape legal regulation in accordance with their knowledge, beliefs and ethical commitments. Where daily knowledge does not suffice, experts provide their part into the legislative discourse. Legal regulation is therefore the *dynamic* part of the legal discourse. In turn, legal-linguistic operations have been *stabile* over centuries and they are also geographically equally represented all over the planet. Finally, the textual patterns of law are relatively stable, yet they *evolve* unlike legal-linguistic operations.

From the above postulates and assumptions further consequences follow for law and legal linguistics. However, this introductory chapter is not the appropriate place to deal with them. At this point it is relevant to keep in mind that *discursiveness* and not something else is *constitutive of law* and that a *legal-linguistic theory* can be developed on the basis of the consequences that follow from the finding that law is a discursive practice. At this stage, especially my postulates four, five and six may be perceived as a *mini-theory of legal language.* An expanded version of this theory will appear step by step in the subsequent chapters of the book. The introductory part will deal in more detail with the conceptual prerequisites of the legal-linguistic theory that were sketched in this paragraph.

1.1.1 Are laws made with words?

Legal linguistics, into which these lectures should introduce the readers, deals with the language of law. Indubitably, the readers of the numerous pages that follow will not be particularly impressed by my initial remark that law and language are closely related. Most legal professionals and also many interested citizens realized this fact long ago without the help of a particular academic discipline. In fact, many citizens have equally experienced this very loosely formulated statement as a part of their biographies. How shall we react to this experience accumulated by professionals of law and laypersons? Shall we become trivial or ironical, or both, when talking about law? Some may wish it so, as they suspect sheer power behind the subtle construct of law. Others would find an ironical or sarcastic reaction more appropriate because for them law is nothing more than language, mere words. Could both of those observer groups of the legal practice be right, i.e. could it be that law is powerful and while being so it is empty and constitutes a risky analogy with the naked emperor in Andersen's tale? In this study about linguistic aspects of law which exposes explicit theoretical ambitions we cannot exclude such fundamental observations. Before approaching the language in law we will have to determine what actually law is and what the legal science is. How shall we explain law in terms of language without risking to appear naïve? How to avoid falling into the pitfalls of legal reasoning which were thoroughly constructed by generations of lawyers before us? We will try, first of all, to describe what lawyers are actually doing from the perspective of someone interested mainly in the linguistic part of their work. We will identify the aspects of their work which are linked to language and by so doing we will also show which parts of the lawyers' work are less dependent on language. In this way we will make plain that the question of whether there is something more in law than language is essential to any conception of legal linguistics. This procedure may seem cumbersome, but legal linguistics cannot be developed in a vacuum. To put it more specifically, there is no legal linguistics without law. Therefore, understanding law toward the background of the societal experience made with its complex mechanisms is a necessary precondition for its construction. And, there is even one more obstruction to the careless and rather nonchalant start with the legal linguistics without law. Legal linguistics is profoundly grounded in its parent disciplines, i.e. in legal sciences and in linguistics which as all modern branches of knowledge speak with different voices. Seen from these different perspectives, law emerges sometimes as a wordless fact and sometimes as an endless cascade of words. However, it also manifests itself regularly as a texture of both wordless facts and voiceful arguments. The legal linguist must be able to cope with all these disenchanting situations.

1.1.2 Interdisciplinary aspirations

As mentioned in the preface, the theoretical background of this book is interdisciplinary. The basic theoretical framework has been mentioned already. Yet, it has not been explained. I will therefore outline it on the pages which follow and subsequently apply it as a conceptual framework to legal texts. In the main part of the book these sketched ideas will be described in a more detailed way in combination with case analyses. These case analyses will help us to develop a material theory of law, i.e. a theory that starts with materials which it scrutinizes. This procedure is close to the interest in the daily experience made with law which was mentioned in the foregoing paragraph. Moreover, the material analyses will also show that legal linguistics provides not only some insight into linguistically relevant parts of legal mechanisms but is also capable of embracing law in a way that forms a fully-fledged theory of law. Thus, our goal is more ambitious than showing some pertinent relations between law and language. As said, our approach is material; it is based mostly on legal decisions issued by courts while applying statutory provisions and interpreting precedents. I will therefore regularly make reference to court decisions and sometimes even quote them extensively. It is important to show that linguistic aspects play always a decisive role in the application of law. Therefore, reference will be made also to routine cases which otherwise neither substantially nor procedurally represent any points apt to raise particular attention. As noted, this procedure is necessary to prove the ubiquitous character of law and language relations. Our analysis is therefore not limited to spectacular cases, sometimes referred to as hard cases. In legal linguistics all statutes and all court opinions and other documents with legal relevance such as contracts or last wills matter equally. They all show different aspects of the language used in legal contexts. Therefore, the reader of this book should not try to find out why these and not other legal cases or statutory provisions or quotes from administrative documents have been used for this research. With good reason other materials could have been used as well. Even more so, whatever linguistic sources that relate to law can be used for our purpose. Were legal linguistics selective in its sources, it could not function as a part of our theoretical knowledge about law or language. In consequence, it would not make much sense to study it, either. The interdisciplinary method that is used in this book can be illustrated with the help of some legal-linguistic narratives, textual samples that represent legal language as parts of the legal discourse.

1.1.3 Some legal-linguistic narratives

In order to engage in the discussion of problems analysed in this book I will scrutinize some short narratives taken from the legal practice:

I. A court has to determine the meaning of *chicken*, a word used in a contract on chicken delivery between two parties who disagree. The plaintiff pretends that it includes young birds only while the defendant insists upon all *fowls* being perceived in trade as *chickens* (cf. Frigaliment Importing Co. v. B.N.S. International Sales Corp. 190 F. Supp. 116, S.D.N.Y. 1960, quoted also in Notes and Commented Materials no. 45).
II. An accused in a common law country does not use the honorific form *Your Honor* when addressing the judge.
III. A British legal scholar introduces a chapter on the Law of the European Union in his text-book for law students writing: "The law relating to the European Community is now a wide ranging subject. European Community law **intrudes upon**, and affects, an ever increasing volume of domestic law and now represents an important source of law in the United Kingdom" (emphasis added).
IV. A court has to decide whether *protective gear* can be perceived as *accessory* to roller blades under U.S. Customs Regulations (cf. Rollerblade, Inc. v. U.S. 282 F. 3d 1349; Fed. Cir. 2002, quoted also in Notes and Commented Materials no. 48).
V. A court considers whether a foreign State can obtain the letter of administration in a case when an intestate decedent according to the provisions of this State inherits as heir. Yet, it may refuse to grant the letter of administration in the same case when the State according to its own provisions obtains the estate as *bona vacantia* (cf. In re Maldonado – State of Spain v. Treasury Solicitor, All ER 1953, vol. 2. p. 1579 sqq., quoted also in Notes and Commented Materials no. 61).

All of the five above cases refer to law and the legal practice. In all of them language has an important role to play. However, it seems that they represent different aspects of legal practice and reflect various facets of language use in law. Yet, how to grasp this difference? Is this difference a legal or a linguistic problem? The reader will intuitively realize that answers to such questions cannot be found in a law book. They are different from questions of structural character in law such as: In what statute is the rule of *anticipatory repudiation* in commercial contracts stated in the U.S. law? The right answer is: in Sec. 2–610 UCC. And the *right to inspection*? In Sec. 2–513 UCC. And the *mailbox rule*? In Sec. 2–206 UCC. These structural questions are not about the application of law. They simply refer to its inner structure and provide provisional, mechanical information about law which remains irrelevant to the propositional content of the quoted provisions. Moreover, the content of the few provisions mentioned here does not change through attributing numbers to them or through identifying them with the help of numerical reference. These quotations are doubtless also important for lawyers as they pertain to their activity of knowing how to determine sources of law, i.e. where to find law. However, they definitely will not dominate our investigation because they are accidental to problems of creation and application of law. Indeed, law is more than a mechanical system of references which link legal provisions to numbers. For many, law begins with its inner structure where issues and regulations (facts and rules) are interrelated in a specific order. This specific order is dressed in words. For instance, in the UCC provisions referred to above there is more than pure mechanics. Legal notions such as *anticipatory repudiation* or *mailbox rule* are created and used there. In the legal practice, lawsuits emerge about the application of such notions. Parties to lawsuits will try to convince the judges that their reading of the law is the right one, i.e. the one which society is ready to enforce with the help of competent authorities. In the lawsuit only one of the possible readings of the law will be determined by the judges as the right one, i.e. the one which will be enforced. If necessary, force will be used to provide full credit to a court decision that involves such a technical issue like the scope of the application of a legal notion, be it *anticipatory repudiation* or whatever other not particularly poetically sounding concept. In fact, law is power expressed with linguistic means. In our study we will therefore also have to show this process in the course of our material analyses. All other related problems, e.g. why it is necessary to introduce concepts such as *anticipatory repudiation* or *mailbox rule* into laws are dealt with in the legal science. The legal linguist takes such issues for granted.

Let us now come back to our short introductory cases. They shall illustrate that language use in law differs as the context of use is changing. They show situations of language use, i.e. the contexts in which speakers engage in legal discourses. The legal linguist works differently on materials that refer to those different situations. Here, it is decisive to establish the appropriate perspective upon language, both in the situation of use and in the situation of reflecting upon the use. Otherwise, language will not work properly. It will lead to confusion that expressed in terms of law means injustice. This being said, in case I the judge is dealing with identifying the meaning of the word *chicken* which belongs to the ordinary language. In the legal-linguistic perspective it is necessary to find out how the judge actually determines the meaning of a word that belongs to the ordinary language. As a second step, it is necessary to decide whether the interpretive strategy adopted by the judge corresponds to our knowledge about language and especially to our knowledge about the way we grasp the meaning of a word. Finally, the legal linguist may decide to make suggestions about the appropriate strategic choice in such situations. This, in short, is the way in which the legal linguist deals with our case I. Similarly, in case IV the judge analyzes a legal term *accessory* and determines its scope of application toward the background of a commercial transaction which involves also the use of words belonging to the ordinary language, in casu *protective gear*. Here again, the legal linguist scrutinizes the way in which the judge understands the ordinary language. Yet, in addition to it, she has to reflect upon professional strategies of language use in law in situations where legal provisions indicate the way in which a legal concept such as *accessory* shall be determined. The legal linguist follows here the instruction provided by the legislator and examines the way in which the judge reacted to it. Finally, she establishes whether the judge acted in accordance with the rules that determine the way in which legal language shall be understood. Additionally, she may also address critically the legislative regulation, should it not correspond to our professional knowledge of what is language. In case V the judge interprets the legal doctrine while reflecting upon the intricacies of language use in interpretation. For the legal linguist it is decisive to establish how the judge interprets legal provisions as a professional of law. The legal linguist first studies the techniques used by the legal professional and subsequently evaluates them in order to understand how legal professionals structure the use of language in legal contexts in which they used to act. Needless to say, she may also comment upon these techniques should she feel challenged by them as a professional of language. Finally, in case III a legal writer provides in an academic text a strategy for the interpretation of legal acts in that he posits that some of them *intrude* upon others. The legal linguist shows in such a case primarily that there is an intention in this contention. She has to prove it because this may not be evident to all language users and she has also to reflect upon the author's strategy to engage in the task of providing this sort of interpretive strategies to readers. And what about our case II? In common law countries judges are usually addressed as *Your Honor* (Mattila 2006: 49). This communicative implication is definitely a pragmatic issue (cf. Levinson 1983: 10, Leech 2014) because it is based on a linguistic convention of use. However, its legal implications remain unclear. What would happen if a party in litigation would omit the honorific address? Neither the substantive nor the procedural law in the common law tradition require that the parties address the judge in this way. The legislation prohibits the parties from offending the judge, but is the omission of the honorific an offence? The legal linguist has to clarify these and other questions which will be discussed in this book later.

In the subsequent chapters we will shed more light on the five short narratives which helped us to describe the way language works in legal contexts and the way the legal linguist tries to cope with these different situations. We will also establish a perspective for the theoretical reflection upon the distinctions which we have found out while studying them. The examples of language use illustrated with the above short narratives are far from being exhaustive in terms of legally relevant language use. However, they undeniably show the evolving variation of strategies in context-bound language use. In addition, they also demonstrate that the legal linguist's professional reflection upon this use depends on different contexts of use. This is the main result needed in the preliminary part of our *Introduction.* I will deal more precisely with details of the legal-linguistic method in subsequent chapters. This method is particularly important because it establishes a perspective upon law that is specific to a legal linguist as a professional who exercises in an area that is neither law nor linguistics but something between both. Therefore, the legal linguist is primarily a specialist in the legal-linguistic method. This method establishes his profession and makes a professional of him. Therefore, one cannot overestimate the importance of the discussion about the legal-linguistic method in legal linguistics proper.

1.1.4 Tasks of legal science

In order to perform her professional tasks the legal linguist needs to know what is the legal science. The utmost reason for this requirement is that the language use that she analyzes is dominated by the professionals of law. Those legal professionals learned their professional language simultaneously with their law studies (Mattila 2006: 19). Therefore, the legal linguist must be interested in finding out how the legal science works, i.e. how it provides linguistically relevant professional knowledge. It is evident from the material samples scrutinized above that the knowledge about the numerical reference to legal provisions or the knowledge of case names alone cannot be perceived as knowledge of law. The specific knowledge about the law which means predominantly knowledge about its content in a given moment is the task of the legal science. Popular interest in law reduces the matter to merchandizing legislative messages; its interest is directed toward a product. Therefore law in it is reduced to a rule. An exchange based on this kind of epistemic interest may look as follows: *What is the speed limit in town? Fifty kilometres per hour.* The dialogue describes an interest in law that excludes its most relevant feature, i.e. its legal-linguistic aspect. It focuses on a petrified rule that shows at best a facet of law. Valid law is not a question-answer exercise but the result of the application of legal-linguistic operations upon legal texts as parts of the legal discourse. Only within this framework the rule *Speed limit in towns is fifty kilometres per hour* will be understood properly. Driving as a legal term appears in such a framework as an action that sometimes does not allow to even approach the speed limit of fifty kilometres per hour, especially when sight is bad or road conditions are particularly challenging. Sometimes it may be allowed to exceed the limit. When for instance an emergency happens, particularly when life is in jeopardy, law makes an exception to the rule. It goes without saying that also for the fire brigade, police cars or emergency vans exceptions will have to be made to the stated rule according to the multiple circumstances that life may produce. Therefore, the right answer to the speed limit question would be: *it depends.* A statute may literally impose the fifty kilometres limit upon car drivers. This speed can however be legally exceeded or even further limited depending on the circumstances. The appropriate speed limit is found out by courts – when necessary – in the application of discursive mechanisms that make appear the totality of circumstances that must be considered in order to determine whether the speed limit in question has been appropriate, i.e. legal or not. This is law.

1.1.4.1 Systematization in law

In order to infer the content of law from statutes or cases, or both, the jurist may systematize or classify them according to the subject matter treated in them. Legal provisions or judicial opinions may be classified as belonging to *private* or to *public law*. Furthermore, a more precise differentiation can be made and private law provisions be divided into provisions relevant to *contracts*, *torts*, *property*, *family* and *succession*. They can also be divided into *substantive* and *procedural* provisions. The law of the European Union has been classified differently. Notions of *primary* and *secondary law* have been perceived as the most suitable framework for its classification. Enormously many possibilities for classification or systematization of legal provisions or rules exist. As of now, only a few possibilities have been used for this enterprise by the legal science. There is undoubtedly an inherent logic in these attempts to systematize legal provisions or court decisions. Thus far, the results of the traditional classification are mostly coherent and rational, although they may at times divide the social facts which form their background along formalistic lines. This is the case when social facts of a regulation or a case are seen first in the light of the *substantive law* and then in the light of the *procedural law*. In this perspective, the matter which forms a social fact is artificially split which may lead to problems of apprehension and application of the provisions in question (cf. MCC Ceramic v. Ceramica Nuova in Notes and Commented Materials no. 67). The systematization efforts are nevertheless based on tradition rather than on logic. However, this result is not surprising because the role of systematization or classification is to introduce some preliminary order into the subject matter which is studied. Without this methodological approach jurists would risk getting lost in the law that they try to apprehend. Meanwhile, legal provisions and court decisions are too numerous to be known or studied in the chronological order of their promulgation by the legislator or their issuance by the courts of law respectively. At this stage, we may maintain that in order to perform the task of systematization some concepts such as *private law*, *contracts* or *substantive law* had to be created with linguistic means in past times by those who first approached the challenging task of systematization. Systematization of the sort described above is a relatively simple thing. Legal doctrine developed much more complex methods of systematization that concern mainly legal concepts. I will deal with them later when trying to explain why the legal doctrine could be perceived as legal linguistics without linguistics. At this stage, the statement may remain enigmatic, yet it is actually quite rational.

Above remarks about law might seem marginal to the subject of the legal science. And indeed, positive law is based on linguistic conventions. Its systematization as well as other legal-linguistic operations can be properly understood when this simple thought is taken seriously. This finding is much more important than above reference to jurists' attempts at systematizing law because it might be misunderstood in an essentialist way saying that first there is law (an object that is there like a piece of wood) and only later systematic work begins on it. Law as whatever other linguistic convention can be questioned at any moment as to its validity. The reason for this challenging situation is that law like other linguistic conventions is made with words. Meanwhile, can a judge rely on words while deciding whether someone will spend several years in prison? When the knowledge that represents law consists only of words one cannot expect that results about the inquiry into law would emerge automatically and be unequivocal. This assumption concerns also the law as a set of rules applied in courts and the legal science that tries to understand law. Many questions asked in the legal science such as whether there really is a difference between *private* and *public law* do not make much sense when the above has been understood. As law is a linguistic construct it may make a difference between private and public law or it may neglect this topic and introduce other more efficient conceptual differences. Legal linguists have the advantage that they approach law from the linguistic perspective. We will see later that many confusing questions in the legal science disappear when law is scrutinized from the linguistic point of view. The knowledge of law is the mastering of legal-linguistic mechanisms, devices and procedures that will be called later legal-linguistic operations. For the time being, it may suffice to know that these operations comprise logical devices such as analogy, legal speech acts such as accusation or more complex speech samples such as legal argumentation. In these legal-linguistic operations meaning emerges in law. Thus, when we master these operations we also master law because we can react to challenges that emerge in disputes about the valid content of law in a professional way.

1.1.4.2 Other legal-linguistically relevant criteria

After the preliminary classification of textual samples has taken place it is possible to engage in broader proceedings that are equally relevant to legal linguistics. At this point, the question arises as to what proceedings suit best the study of law on a more advanced level. Historically, it has been proposed to deal with legal concepts and study their function in the provisions and their use in court decisions in order to elucidate and to systematize them (cf. Aarnio 2011). However, very soon it became plain that law deals not only with concepts, although it undeniably deals with them. Law also deals with evaluations along the established dominant views about right and wrong in society. Values which underlie the decision making process in establishing legal provisions by the legislator as well as in the process of their application in courts must also be taken into consideration. Otherwise, only a conceptual skeleton of law would emerge as a result of legal studies. What is needed instead is a multi-dimensional view of intertwined legal provisions, an analysis of rules inferred from them and from judicial decisions as well as values which determine the choices in operating them. Therefore, today, when law is studied, attention is drawn both to the complex legal structure composed of legal rules and to the values which control their application. Here, however, the additional question could be asked as regards the way in which these efforts could be generalized or finalized. I propose a linguistic point of view as the most suitable perspective for studying law. From the linguistic point of view, the legal argumentation is the basis of an advanced structure of law. For us, legal arguments as textual samples and patterns of the legal discourse are the most suitable elements of classification or systematization in law. The knowledge about this structure composed of legal arguments within the legal discourse is the knowledge of law. The legal linguist studies the use of these arguments and assists the jurist in his studies of legal argumentation that the jurist undertakes within the legal doctrine.

1.1.4.3 Knowledge of the subject matter and knowledge of law

The legal-linguistic analysis of the language used in legal texts (written as well as oral) requires substantial knowledge of law. This requirement can be fulfilled through diligent legal studies. More problematic is however the knowledge of the subject matter, i.e. the facts on which a judicial decision is based or those which form the background of a legislative initiative. Access to written sources (mostly court or administrative files) on which legal decisions are based is almost impossible in most countries. Sometimes, direct witnesses of the legislative actions, mostly politicians, mention unknown motives for legislative acts in their diaries. Moreover, facts reported in legal opinions may not correspond to the real course of events and this may be known to the issuers of a court decision and the parties or may remain hidden even for them. All this factual knowledge is however essential in the analysis of argumentative strategies used in court opinions and legislative acts. The lack of such reliable knowledge constitutes an impediment to the progress in the legal-linguistic research and threatens it by the assumption of naivity when official motivations for legal acts or court decisions are taken at face value (cf. Ross 1966: 57). This methodological problem of the legal-linguistic research is difficult to overcome. Analogously, in literary studies, the narration from the omniscient perspective (Rimmon-Kenan 1989: 95) is used in some types of narration. The omniscience is however easily accessible there because it mainly depends upon the author's intention. In dealings with law the omniscient view upon the subject matter is impossible to achieve because factual data is never available in its entirety even if the linguistic strategy of dealing with it in the public sphere, especially in court decisions, may signal complete factual knowledge. Hence, the only methodological tool which remains at the researchers' disposal is the general rationality test. It includes the coherence test for the motivations provided by the court or the legislative body, and the correspondence test in which information is evaluated along the experience based on the social practice. This rationality test – as imperfect as it may be – guarantees at least that the perspective taken in the research concentrated upon the language use in law will not be perceived as purely repetitive, and therefore also intentionally or unintentionally affirmative of the analyzed legal text. Furthermore, it prevents the use of a methodology unsusceptible of the risk that motivations provided for in some legal texts may differ from those which were decisive for the decision taken. For the legal linguist, therefore, dealing with language use means to be alerted to all possible contexts and conditions of use, explicit and implicit. In sum, understanding structural requirements imposed upon the lawyer's work, be they systematization of legal provisions and case law or the determination of facts toward the background of moral evaluations, is an essential precondition for any legal-linguistic approach. The corresponding linguistic stage to it is the knowledge about the creation of language and the underlying signification processes as well as the mechanisms of linguistic change that affects the language used in law and in all its other varieties.

1.2 Pragmatics for Lawyers

1.2.1 Pragmatic preferences

The legal linguist willing to assist the jurist must base her knowledge on a scientifically founded theory in order to be accepted by the jurist. She has constantly to compete with other professional views about law which can be challenged only with good arguments, i.e. those which convince due to their particular rationality. The legal linguist uses arguments based on legal linguistics. Her first methodological problem is that legal linguistics is in the stage of emergence and a lot of work will have to be done until it will be able to compete effectively with other branches of knowledge which also deal with law. How, then, will the legal linguist try to develop her recommendations for the jurist? We may use one of our short cases to understand how theory is developed in legal linguistics. It goes without saying that linguistic habits such as the use of honorifics, e.g. *Your Honor*, while addressing judges are part of the language use in courts of law. Our question must however be, are they also part of legal linguistics? Here, we would like to stress that we favor linguistic use which is relevant to the judicial decision making process. Equally, we are attracted by language use in the legal argumentation as far as it is relevant to the decision as well as to stylistic particularities as long as they matter for the decision taken. These aspects of language use are for us the predominant part of legal linguistics. It would be however unjustified to exclude communicative situations or other – even marginal – aspects of language use from legal linguistics simply because they seem not to influence directly the decision taken. In legal linguistics, we should try to get hold of all communicative situations in law and of their structures and mechanisms. Otherwise, legal linguistics would impoverish the legal science and be applicable only to some selected aspects of the legal culture. The legal culture embraces a vast area of social phenomena which are sometimes remote from the act of making a decision in a court of law such as the shape or decoration of court rooms or court buildings (Mattila 2006: 13). However, we should not forget that some of them might be more influential than others and we must mark it in our approach to legal linguistics.

In the approach adopted here inferences overtly and intentionally conveyed by speakers in a context (Levinson 1983: 24) are the criterion distinguishing language use which is primarily reflected in the legal-linguistic use and language use which is peripheral to it. This statement can be used in order to formulate a theory for the use of the legal linguist. This distinction is not in contradiction with the tendency in the linguistic pragmatics of the last decades to stress conversational analysis. It leaves enough room for this approach, and does not develop to the detriment of the conversational analysis because the role of the legal discourse remains essential, even if sometimes only parts of it are scrutinized in a different context than the discursive one. This holds true for some issues concerning the legal terminology that doubtless have a role to play in the legal discourse but may also be addressed in isolated surroundings. The later approach is even typical of the legal-linguistic research. It simply means that some approaches and results may be under specific circumstances more relevant than others. Which approach should be perceived as dominant in a case is a question of the case itself. Some discourse analysis research, e.g. concerning criminal law shows that this approach may be more prolific than others when fact finding is at stake and witness testimony must be evaluated by the judge (cf. Xu 1998, Fletcher 2007, Anesa 2009 and 2012). This approach is also instrumental in determining the role of the honorific address in our case II. Apparently, the omission of the honorific *Your Honor*, especially when done systematically, i.e. constantly and ostentatiously practiced by the speaker who personally depends on the decision taken by the judge may influence the decision making process. However, particular research would be necessary to find out under what circumstances the use or omission of the honorific is essential to the decision making. In turn, deciding whether goods are inherited by the State as *last heir* or whether they are *bona vacantia*, and only subsequently are incorporated into the treasury of the State (our introductory case V) is not dependent on social conventions used by speakers when approaching courts. Here, professional argumentation matters. The professional argumentation is not emotive as is the conversational practice of addressing a judge. Therefore, other aspects of linguistic use may be more relevant to understanding structures that dominate vertically structured discourses. Overall, dealing with the use of language as a starting point for building a theory suitable for the legal linguist leads to its scientific roots. They are for us, as indicated previously, pragmatics and general semiotics. Pragmatic and general semiotic approaches to law offer many examples of fruitful implementation within the legal theory (cf. Jackson 1985: 4, Dubouchet 1990, Cotterrell 2006). The range of practical applications of one and the same theory may cover some aspects of the Scandinavian legal realism, the American legal realism, the speech act theory and the legal semiotics of Algirdas J. Greimas (cf. Jackson 1985: 8–9). Some aspects within these theories, however, may not correspond or may underscore other than legal-linguistically relevant elements. We will therefore remain tolerant to other viewpoints because they may contribute to legal linguistics in a way methodically different from ours while we will be visibly favoring one approach. This specific tolerant approach concerns especially materials analyzed in the research that has been methodologically differently construed than ours.

The above preliminary remarks on theory building allow the first summary of requirements that are relevant to the dealing with legal linguistics. Legal linguistics builds its theory while keeping in mind the needs of the legal science. Methodologically, however, it is not grounded in the legal science but in linguistic and social theories. In this book a choice has been made between these theories and some have been preferred to the detriment of others. This means also that a differently founded legal linguistics is possible and this will be shown in the chapter on *Foundations of Legal Linguistics* where other approaches than the pragmatically oriented perspective will be discussed. Likewise, our initial short analyses of legal-linguistically relevant materials also brought first theoretically relevant results. They illustrate the first important shift in the modern reflection upon law from the inner-structural perspective of conceptual analysis and legal systematization to the problems of creation and application of law. In my approach I will show that both can be adequately integrated into a legal-linguistic theory of law based on pragmatics. Yet, first of all I will have to explain why I have chosen this approach and by selecting it I seem to prefer it to others. This preference has a personal background because I simply know this approach better than others. In addition, I also assume that it provides innovative insights into problems of the structure and the application of law. Indeed, as many theorists argue, legal and pragmatic reasoning display affinities that cannot be a coincidence.

1.2.2 What is pragmatics about?

I have already mentioned that linguistic pragmatics deals with language use, and that legal linguistics in the sense in which we are going to outline it deals with the language use in law. All of it may sound mysterious and the impression might come up that first there is language, then we take and use it and make for instance law of it. On the other hand, neither linguistic pragmatics nor legal linguistics are as trivial as this series of issues may suggest. In our preliminary thoughts about law and language many things are commingled. And our task will be to bring order into this amorphous amalgam. To begin with, distinguishing between language and its use is a metaphor (cf. Davidson 2001: 247). In fact, we cannot deal with language without using it. Moreover, distinguishing between law and language in the analysis of their supposed interrelation is another such metaphor. Here, again, the legal language does not exist outside its legal context of use. Seen from the pragmatic perspective, language is a mode of acting in the world, not just a mode of reflection upon it (Enos 1996: 54, Jaszczolt 2016). Therefore, using language means performing actions (Holtgraves 2002: 177). The minimal linguistic form of such actions is the *speech act*. The speech act may, for instance convey a promise or a threat, accuse someone of having committed a crime, and convince the hearer or not. In terms of the speech act theory, which deals with the systematization of speech acts and tries to understand how they function we undertake different actions when we use language. We may wish to introduce changes to the world around us while using *declarations* or *directives*. We may describe our set of mind with *assertives*; we can also describe our emotions with *expressives*. All these actions are social, because they involve also other people (Holtgraves 2002: 178). The actions which we named as examples of speech acts have a specific grammar and a criterion of correctness of use which is called *felicity* (Levinson 1983: 229). They may be performed in a successful way, but they may also fail. For instance, the speaker who is making a promise may as well convince the hearer as he may fail (Searle 2004: 66). Therefore, we have to know the preconditions for the successful performance of speech acts because we are not interested in performing them in order to fail. In other words, we have to know how to transform our intentions into successful social actions. In order to achieve this competence we need to know a lot about prerequisites of such actions. Some speech acts are rather simple daily routine that we perform without problems. For instance, asking the way from a person on the street. We acquire the knowledge necessary to perform them as we grow up in the community of speakers in which they are used. Other speech acts, such as making a judicial decision about somebody's criminal responsibility are more complex in their nature. They require additional formal (institutional) training and material (linguistic) competence. The exercise of these actions is analogous to games (Levinson 1983: 227). We play them with others, in society, where it is also determined who can play, who plays according to the rules, as well as who succeeds and who does not. Players may be on equal footing like two judges or two criminals. Their roles as players may also be differently distributed. Imagine a judge and a criminal playing according to the rules of the criminal procedure. Their distance in mastering the rules of successful game may be so big that they can only assume to play the same game as they play it on different procedural levels. Also, the grammar they use is often different. These legal games, and we can imagine them as legal discourses composed of legal speech acts, are played in a co-operative mood. Otherwise, they would quickly be terminated. Sometimes, however, the procedures of language use may impose rules upon players and oblige them to play even against their desires. They will then play an adversarial game but the game will continue due to its imposed structure. This is the way our judge plays with the criminal while using words. The criminal becomes involved in the game with own words structured according to the rules of his grammar which may also mean that he may remain silent. Our introductory case II, which concerns a person who addresses the judge as *Your Honor* or omits the honorific address, makes plain how the legal speech act functions, i.e. how it can succeed or fail. It goes without saying that some players are more skillful than others. Even in simple discourses of daily routine there is a difference in performance between players. In our example we will rather recommend to the accused to play according to the convention when he defends himself, i.e. when he performs speech acts that are qualified as defense. The defense discourse may be based on a very simple legal speech act, e.g. *It wasn't me, (Your Honor)* (cf. Galdia 2014: 323–324). It can, however, also include more sophisticated formulations such as *The charges raised against me are statute barred, (Your Honor).* We may additionally assume that the accused will probably be more successful when he includes the honorific *Your Honor* when specifically addressing the judge than when he systematically and ostentatiously omits it. Finally, it may prove that including or excluding the honorific address has been less decisive than we assumed. We have previously mentioned that specific research based on field work would be needed in order to determine this circumstance. However, another reason for this indeterminacy of results (felicity of the legal speech act) is that speech acts of defense exercised before the judge by the accused are part of a broader language game that we call legal discourse. Many players engage in them, for instance, during the trial, think of the public prosecutor, the defense lawyer, the panel of judges and the accused personally. Add to it emotional reactions from the public and newspaper reports about the case (cf. Dubrovskaya 2010 and 2014). All of them contribute to the legal discourse and influence linguistically the final result. In addition, complex games such as legal discourses include linguistic operations that require professional knowledge to be played successfully. This knowledge cannot be acquired in daily socialization processes, unless one is the child of a Supreme Court judge. They take place against the background of complex sets of performance rules defined in institutionalized processes. Therefore, law students first learn the law, then get practical training, and after this they are ready to participate in professional legal discourses. Legal linguistics that is based on linguistic pragmatics explains how language mediates the complexity of social interactions where legal discourses take place.

1.2.3 Pragmatic notions

Pragmatics has been frequently perceived as a complicated and a controversial academic concept by the pragmatists themselves as well as in the criticism advanced by its opponents (cf. Notes and Commented Materials no. 1). I will understand it as a tradition of scientific reasoning based foremost on Anglo-American analytical philosophy, especially its ordinary language streaming, and its recent transformations in American and European scientific reasoning. Central to our work will be the distinction between *sentence* as a semantic problem and *utterance* which invokes the actual context (Levinson 1983: 18, 19) that is characteristic of any pragmatic conception. Levinson (1983: 21) puts it as follows: "Pragmatics is the study of the relations between language and context that are basic to an account of language understanding." Indeed, both aspects of the pragmatic nature of utterance are decisive for legal-linguistic pragmatics because it deals with utterances in legal texts (mostly statutes or precedents) which are conceived as actual in the specific legal perspective, i.e. that law can change. Later on, we will reflect upon this dynamic element in law and we will also ask whether law is an aporetic phenomenon and what does this mean for the prediction of results in judicial decisions. Again, we will see that this is a problem of finding the appropriate way for the interpretation of legal texts. We have also noticed that *language usage* and *context* play a particular role in pragmatics. And indeed, many singular pragmatic approaches to language are based on these concepts. Pragmatics, like all other scientific disciplines, has its own method and its own set of issues upon which it used to concentrate. However, the characteristic feature of pragmatics is that the set of issues the researchers focus upon is still in the making. Some are already fixed, but many others can be discovered and added to it. Until now, the linguistic pragmatics concentrated on *deixis, anaphora, conversational implicatures, presuppositions, speech acts* and *conversational analysis.* The future will show which additional phenomena will be discovered and added to this list. Furthermore, legal pragmatics may display or analyse instantiations of certain pragmatic concepts in the language of law (cf. Kryk-Kastowski 2006: 14, Lizisowa 2017: Chapter V) or adapt a broader perspective and try to understand law while analysing the legal language with the help of the pragmalinguistic method. The first approach is more prolific in purely linguistic approaches to law while the other, which dominates our enquiry, enables not only to describe the language of law but also to understand law and the work of jurists. In these lectures I will mainly use *speech acts* and *discourse analysis.* Apparently, also all other named phenomena could be made operative in a pragmatically oriented legal linguistics. For example, deixis shows how utterances such as *Come here!* are understood in contexts in which they were pronounced. In law, it could make plain how time or place specifications contribute to the success or failure of legal speech acts. Anaphora refers to the structure of speech acts in a broader context (Levinson 1983: 86). It seems to have implications for legal linguistics as well because lawyers tend to use constructions in which referring expressions are more frequently or at least differently applied than in the ordinary language (Galdia 2008: 25). Speaker's status is marked in questions such as *Have you stopped beating your wife, yes or no?* as the question can be answered only by a "wife-beater". This feature has consequences for every institutional speech act in law. Those detailed questions will be discussed later after more pragmatically relevant general examples have been scrutinized. At this place, once again, it is important to maintain that the preponderance of some pragmatic issues in this book does not mean that others are irrelevant.

1.2.4 How pragmatics operates in legal contexts

As said, in this work I will propose to use pragmatic concepts while analyzing law. Pragmatics in this sense is the philosophical and linguistic theory dealing with specific aspects of language and its use by the speaker who is also an interpreter. In legal linguistics it is important to determine the role of the speaker because participation in the legal discourse is based mostly on professional (institutionally founded) competence, and not only on pure linguistic competence. This means in practice that it is not sufficient to speak like a judge; one must also have been appointed to exercise the function of a judge by the competent organ. Under these circumstances, only the person involved may pronounce the judgment while using his professional knowledge and his general linguistic competence. That the judge adjudicates does not mean that he simply speaks. It means first of all that in his legal speech acts he interprets the law. Therefore, legal linguistics does not reduce the judge to a simple speaker of a language. It approaches him as an interpreter of law. What does a simple act of interpretation look like? We will look at it first from the position of a non-professional speaker in order to avoid getting involved in complicated legal matters, in addition to pragmatic questions which are already intricate enough. The example that will be analyzed it therefore as illustrative as it is misleading. We may readily assume that our knowledge about language enables us to distinguish between logically possible meanings of labels such as *smoking* and *non-smoking* that can be defined as denoting premises which are reserved for activities rather than the specific groups of people, and where even hard smokers can use the premises for non-smokers provided they do not actually smoke there. Moreover, non-smokers can use premises for smokers but they will not be able to prevent the smokers from smoking there. The example may seem a little complicated and not so evident at all, at least linguistically. We have to admit that no one masters a language completely and therefore we sometimes have to test our knowledge by asking others what they mean with what they say. For instance, when we do not understand the expression *Welsh rabbit* we simply ask what is meant by it. We can do the same with the distinction *smokers* and *non-smokers* and easily establish a consensus about its use. Happily, under regular communicative circumstances we will not need to go that far because most such regulatory language is understandable to us without further consideration. Later I will ask why it is so.

At a stage, however, the professional legal competence is necessary to interpret legally relevant language use. The smoker example is particularly significant in our context of law and language because it includes a *legal position*, a *protection of a subjective right,* which – before it can be claimed and enforced – must be duly identified. We must understand exactly which actions are allowed and which are prohibited under the signs of *smokers* or *non-smokers* before we formulate a legal claim. But can we do it without knowing the law and rely only on our linguistic competence as English speakers? Strangely enough we cannot, because the linguistic use of captures for premises in which a legal position is protected is inherently linked to law as well as to language in which it has been formulated as a *right*. Therefore, we cannot understand one of the two captures while knowing language only, we understand them properly solely when we grasp the law inherent in the linguistic caption. Again, in life, we usually do not have such problems because the knowledge of social rules is integrated into our speaker competence.

1.2.5 Environment of pragmatics

Pragmatics is not an isolated science. General semiotics and hermeneutics accompany it in all analyses; the first being omnipresent and thus inevitable wherever signs are used. The other functions foremost as a tool for verifying whether we identify the right issues in the text analysis. We will therefore try to incorporate some of their concepts. In our attempt to synthesize, we will remain loyal to the conceptual realm of semiotics which seems mandatory for any science and is at least unavoidable in analyzing texts. M. Foucault (1966: 44) determined the relation between hermeneutics and semiotics in that he distributed the tasks between both:

> *Appelons herméneutique l'ensemble des connaissances et des techniques qui permettent de faire parler les signes et de découvrir leur sens ; appelons sémiologie l'ensemble des connaissances et des techniques qui permettent de distinguer où sont les signes, de définir ce qui les institue comme signes, de connaître leurs liens et les lois de leur enchaînement...*

As a matter of fact, semiotics which underlies the conceptional work of this research enables us to identify the relevant *legal signs* and shows which operations can be accomplished with them. We will concentrate on the practically most relevant ones, i.e. on argumentation, interpretation, and translation. First of all, semiotics draws our attention to the process of creation of signs in law (cf. Jackson 1985). This is essential to legal linguistics because other disciplines dealing with law such as legal theory and legal pragmatics focus mostly on the application of legal rules expressed in language and take the process of emergence of legal language for granted. The general semiotics and the semiotics of law teach us that legal-linguistic consideration actually begins at the point where legally relevant language use begins to emerge. Also linguistic pragmatics has been less interested in the process of emergence or constitution of language and concentrated rather on the use of the ready made language. Therefore, the creation of law is construed here as a point of reference for all other processes and operations with signs in law.

1.2.6 Pragmatic vs. semantic theories of legal language

I have stressed in 1.2.3 the distinction between utterances and propositions, and I am now trying to set up a theory which shall be distinct from semantic theories about language, and specifically about legal language. For a long time, legal language has been perceived from the perspective of traditional semantics alone and researchers used to concentrate upon legal terminology (Mattila 2006: 11). Semiotics and especially pragmatic analysis had to follow suit but they were as a matter of fact never fully integrated into what might be called jurisprudence or legal theory. For instance, traditional canons of legal interpretation (i.e. literal, systematic, historical, sociological or teleological interpretation) were recommended in the legal doctrine and it was argued that, if followed, they would ensure the appropriate interpretation of legal provisions (Lasarte 2006: 74–78, Wank 2015). Achievements of linguistically oriented legal theory have not been implemented there. As we will be dealing foremost with the language use in written texts (both in legal provisions and in judicial decisions) or in written quotes of spoken languages, one could question the central role of pragmatics in this undertaking. The critics of our approach would stress the semantic rather than pragmatic aspects of law and they would argue that those were central to a theory of law. However, pragmatic concepts expounded above and below show that pragmatics is not only a discipline dealing with what was left by semantics but a theory of communicative aspects of language par excellence. A theory of interpretation makes a part of it; it includes literal interpretation and a question as to whether this type of interpretation is productive in legal interpretation as a part of legal linguistics and legal theory.

Our problem has also a historical background. The theoretical development in semiotics opposed the *dyadic* (binary) and the *triadic* sign models (Jackson 1985: 3; Recanati 2008: 138). The evolution of the concept of sign in the semiotic research strengthened our view upon law as a complex sign that cannot cope without its interpreter. The search of meaning in the classical sense, supported by reference to the work of Ferdinand de Saussure based its views on a dyadic concept of *signifiant* and *signifié*. This concept was radically questioned by Jacques Derrida who challenged the space between the sign and the signified. Charles Sanders Peirce went even further and imagined already during F. de Saussure's lifetime a triadic sign model composed of *signs*, *objects* and *interpretants* (Sheriff 1989). The result of this distinction has been that not only the structural method was challenged but also our static view of a sign composed of two isolated elements had to be abandoned. The interpreter returned upon the semiotic scene and made theory more complicated but also more revealing. Why should this distinction matter to the legal linguist? In works such as G. Cornu's *Linguistique juridique* the dyadic sign model is adopted (Cornu 2005: 26). The focus upon *signifiant* and *signifié* in the sense of the terms introduced by Ferdinand de Saussure and later, in 1915, published in *Cours de linguistique générale* results in a perspective which stresses semantic implications of the legal language. Cornu (2005: 29) mentions pragmatics as *nom donné à l'étude des relations entre les signes et leurs usagers* and provides an impressive list of speech acts identified in the French legal language (Cornu 2005: 38). Nevertheless, he finally concentrates in his approach to legal linguistics on semantic aspects of legal terminology and of the legal discourse. Hence, the dyadic sign model prefigures the subsequent treatment of the legal language. It leads also to the preference of decoding of meaning in texts to the detriment of their interpretation (Jackson 1985: 20). As law is for me an argumentative practice, I will support here approaches to the sign structure that allow an adequate description of language use in law and that include all three pragmatically relevant components. I will also assume in the following that a semantic theory is truth-conditioned. With this in mind one could ask whether the truth-conditionality is a sufficient criterion to determine the meaning of a legal concept. Were it the case, then taking into account pragmatic implications in a legal analysis would be an unnecessary burden for lawyers. However, some theories of interpretation, such as R. Dworkin's, base the interpretation at least in hard cases on contextual assumptions and cannot infer their 'right contents' in that they apply procedures of formal logic to them. Here, I adhere to these views and therefore cannot support a conception of legal linguistics based on concepts and methods of traditional semantics that attempts to decode an allegedly unequivocal meaning in legal texts. In the following paragraph we will see that other researchers share my reservations.

1.2.7 Extension of the concept of semantics

The realm of semantics can also be defined broadly and include most if not all issues traditionally allotted to pragmatics (cf. Recanati 2008: 97). This extension of the concept of semantics would invade upon the realm of pragmatics even if defined very narrowly. Indeed, also the opposite operation is possible. At the current stage of discussion about semantics and pragmatics I still have an option and I will exercise it to the benefit of pragmatics. I feel encouraged to do so also by the ongoing discussion in the general linguistics about the overlapping areas in both pragmatics and semantics (cf. Pohl 2008, Cruse 2010). Nevertheless, I shall also mention that some researchers still insist upon the necessity to distinguish strictly between the semantic and the pragmatic domains (cf. Akmajian 2001: 264). Also in the contemporary legal-theoretical discussion many attempts have been undertaken to redefine the relation between semantics and pragmatics. Canale and Tuzet (2007: 33) identified the drift toward pragmatization of semantics as a consequence of the strengthening of the pragmalinguistic theory in law. In our view, this drift may also strengthen the overall position of the pragmalinguistic theory as it shows its general utility. When nowadays inferential conceptions of semantics can operate with concepts such as *context sensitivity*, *process sensitivity* or *contextual constraints* (Canale and Tuzet 2007: 40) so it is possible only due to the pioneering work done within the pragmatic research. Traditional semantics does not contribute much to issues which I perceive as central in legal linguistics. Its strength lies in the moment of incorporation of pragmatic concepts in its own theory which is accounted for by Canale and Tuzet (2007: 32, cf. also Canale 2015) who also admit that for legal interpretation the pragmatics of semantic content is useful. Here we may note that pragmatists even in the time when the classics of pragmatics J.L. Austin or L. Wittgenstein were at work never had doubts about this result. This can in part explain the reasons for our preferential treatment of the pragmatic perspective which in our view can better integrate traditional areas of language description.

1.2.8 Is there more than language in law?

Previously, different perspectives upon law, of which the legal and the linguistic ones are central, have been demonstrated in order to illustrate the specifics of the legal-linguistic point of view. We can now re-enter the discussion of a basic question in this introductory part that is whether laws are made only of words. This question is not a pure intellectual experiment. It concerns the essence of all activities in law and must therefore be approached also as a precondition to legal linguistics. In fact, were laws made of words only, which means that laws would be an amalgam of phrases, it would not make sense to study them as they would not provide any knowledge that could be generalized or systematized. Legal linguistics would still be possible but it would be practically useless because law would be based on arbitrary use of language. In fact, some critics of law discouraged legal studies referring to law as a bundle of sophisms. Others were suspicious about law as a subject of academic studies because for them law provided regularly several and contradictory answers to whatever legal question. Science, they claimed, had to deliver precise answers to precise questions as is allegedly the case in other branches of knowledge, for instance in natural sciences. These critics underestimated the complexity of language where no mechanism prevents engendering false or contradictory utterances. However, our language allows for the formulation of competing utterances in terms of truth or validity. This is one of the most interesting qualities of language for the legal linguist. Luckily, language has also the capacity to engender coherent worlds. This means that by using language we are able to construct worlds of words which are organized in more complex units such as speech acts. Some of those worlds created with words are quite complex. N. Goodman (1978) pointed out that many of our primary conceptions about the world such as our comprehension of the universe and the stellar bodies are structured around linguistic creations like *Morning Star* and the like. On the other hand, however, we are aware of the fact that there exists also a non-linguistic, non-verbal reality, a world composed of objects without words (Searle 1999: 14). Our interest in the issue is that we wish to position law on the scale between linguistic and non-linguistic worlds. We need to know the place law takes on this scale in order to be able to determine what matters in legal linguistics and what does not. Yet, first of all, the determination of the place law takes on the scale between linguistic and non-linguistic worlds determines the future of this discipline. Here, again, we will start with the analysis of some linguistic examples. In a text sample from the Wall Street Journal: *The Malacca strait links the Indian and the Pacific Oceans and carries half of the world's oil and a third of its commerce* we discover a purely linguistic reality – in an alleged link *Malacca strait* between *two* oceans, all this being a linguistic construct related to nature. The other part of it is metaphorical use. Equally, a sentence *The North Atlantic Ocean connects the New and the Old World* sets up a linguistic fiction that refers to a natural phenomenon that can be framed linguistically in a variety of ways. Its fictitious character is made plain when the formulation is used in a more precise context, e.g. *This map depicts the North Atlantic Ocean as connecting the New and thc Old World* in reference to a map that establishes a visual link between the two continents by the use of arrows. This linguistic construct structures nature in a specific way, many other structures (or none) would be thinkable as well. In its factual background there is solely water. Another example is the one of the *sun set.* We know even with our rudimentary knowledge of high school astronomy that in reality the sun neither rises, nor sets. Yet, we understand the motivation grounded in our unsophisticated daily experience which stands behind the lexicalization of this experience. We can therefore continue to speak about *sun sets* notwithstanding the admirable achievements of natural sciences that explain us reality behind images that we used to witness.

Cultural phenomena are constructed along the same principles. The famous orientalist Edward Said (1979: 6) stressed that the term *orientalism* was an occidental invention and as such has no role to play in cultural sciences. It is one more linguistic invention. We create such language because we create culture. Occasionally, someone, like E. Said in the debate about *orientalism*, is able to make clear that this sort of linguistic creation is empty, that is has no material content. Are legal utterances of the same type? Some legal materials may indicate a positive answer. Sometimes the linguistic character of law is explicitly invoked by jurists and one may therefore ask whether this fact is indicative of the nature of the phenomenon law or rather of a specific professional view jurists adopt when they approach legal problems. Let us now illustrate this issue with the help of an example. The Maldonado case, already quoted here among our introductory narratives as case V and known due to the decision of the House of Lords as State of Spain v. Treasury Solicitor (All ER 1953 vol. 2. p. 1579 sqq.) is in this respect a challenge. As far as the claim of the State of Spain to be granted a letter of administration for the estate of its intestate deceased citizen, Ms. Maldonado, is based on Spanish law where the estate is inherited by the State as last heir, the House of Lords might have considered it as in accordance with the laws of England. Were the claim based on the Spanish law understood as providing the right to the estate through an act of appropriation the House of Lords might have considered it as contrary to the laws of England. One of the Lord Justices while recognizing the linguistic dimension of the case put it this way:

> *the distinction between succession by a sovereign State and the appropriation of bona vacantia by a foreign State is said to be* ***a mere matter of words****. This argument is not without persuasive force, but I do not think the question can truly be said to be one of* ***distinction without difference****. The foreign State can only succeed under its own law of succession where the succession is governed by that law. On the other hand, where the case is not one of succession but of appropriation of ownerless property, the right applies to any ownerless property which may be reached by the law of the foreign State concerned, irrespective of the law by which its devolution is governed, provided only that by the relevant law it is in fact ownerless. Then it is said that the foreign State, being omnipotent so far as its own law of succession is concerned, can* ***constitute itself successor*** *in circumstances in which it could equally well rely on claim based on jus regale. But in accepting the foreign State's law of succession, English law recognizes the foreign State as arbiter of what the succession is to be.* (emphasis supplied)

Does the above quote convince us that there is more behind the legal issue at stake than words? The characterization of a legal problem as a *distinction without difference* or *a mere matter of words* clearly indicates that from the judge's point of view we have here to do with sophisms. On the other side, the judge also argues that a legal argument may also have a *persuasive force* and then it would not be a *distinction without difference,* i.e. a sophism. It would convince him, we may suppose, because it conveys a truth, i.e. an utterance which convinces the professional of law. The specific structure of this truth in terms of the legal profession is for the judge of argumentative nature because it has a *persuasive force.* Also Alf Ross (1957) supposed that in law we are able to speak significantly with meaningless words; only the context of use determined for him the meaning of legal notions such as *ownership.* We may therefore retain as a result of our introductory remarks that law appears here to the judge as a linguistic construct which transports a very specific truth. This truth is grounded in professional argumentation about the validity of propositions that state the law. The task of the legal linguist is to determine the linguistic constituents of this professionally defined truth. Consequently, when we ask whether law is in fact language and nothing more then we actually ask a fundamental question of legal linguistics. Negative answers would probably come from some branches of social sciences. Some would argue that law makes part of social sciences which analyze societies that fill law with content. But here, again, it seems that it is first of all the notion of language which stimulates the debate rather than the law itself. Language perceived in pragmatic terms cannot be viewed simply as a system of formally related signs outside society in which it has been created and in which it functions and evolves. Thus, language even as an abstract notion automatically reflects all social practices because it is grounded in them. In this narrower sense, law is very much about language. More precisely, law refers to and it comes about in acts of legal argumentation. Yet, opinions concerning the notion of *language,* its extension and its limits differ as well.

1.2.9 Which conception of language to choose?

Thus, in order to be able to deal with this intricate fundamental question the linguist must reflect upon linguistic elements in legal provisions. And this task, in turn, requires that the legal linguist as a professional of language has a clear conception of what language is actually about. The reflection upon language is at least as old as the reflection upon law. Therefore, while dealing with these phenomena and especially when dealing with both of them simultaneously a choice is necessary among various conceptions of law and of language. A further choice must be done among interdisciplinary conceptions of Law and Language. In these lectures I have constantly exercised choices but I have also justified my preferences. In the introductory part I deal with the theoretical framework of legal linguistics for which a conceptual network is necessary. While discussing different approaches I simply describe the way in which I am looking for this framework. Linguistics, however, does not provide for one coherent view of language. Therefore, the legal linguist cannot take the concept of language for granted in the hope that an implicit theory of language would manifest itself in due course of her research. When I pretend – and some may perceive it as truly pretentious – that I am developing here a theory of law which is in its heart linguistic, I will have to state what is language for me. Helpful in this sense are extreme views such as R. Rorty's formula "there is no such thing as a language" (Rorty 1992: 373). This means first of all that the concept of language depends upon the linguistic theory adopted for its description. We could use here as a frame of reference for the legal-linguistic research a classical conception of linguistics like the one presented in Jean Aitchison's *Linguistics* (1978: 18) or in J. Lyons' introductory work into theoretical linguistics (1968). Both feature phonetics, phonology, syntax, semantics and interdisciplinary areas in sequence. We could also adopt a circle of linguistic levels starting with a bigger unit such as text and ending with phonetics. Yet, by so doing we would have to prove that all these linguistic levels are equally relevant to the emergence of legal meaning that is central to our view of language use in law. The reader realizes that this cannot be the right answer. Heikki E.S. Mattila (2002a: 175) attempted a choice in this sense and stressed also its limits. Language clearly is not composed of words that are structured according to syntactic rules. It is much more than that. Formally, one could of course argue that without the physical act of uttering sounds – which we can localize at the lowest level of the traditional linguistic scheme – no legal meaning would come up. And this is right, but this is a very formal truth. We realize that a sincere answer to problems we are here dealing with cannot be simply reduced to sound emissions. On the other side, an approach which focuses exclusively on syntactic or semantic features of legal language is vulnerable because it is obviously incomplete. Language is a complex mechanism and it does not consist of philosophical traps and paradoxes as it does not consist exclusively of simple physical sound emissions. We therefore need a broader conceptual basis, but it should not be too broad. Too broad is a formal-logical analysis of legal language because it cannot explain the argumentative and interpretive moments in the legal language and especially in norm application (cf. Verschueren/Östman 1995: 60). It also remains incomplete – although on a very high level of abstraction.

For legal linguists, linguistic pragmatics – and especially the speech act theory and the discourse theory – has the advantage that it covers all levels of language description upside down or vice versa and provides their appropriate evaluation in terms of a pragmatic perspective. The speech act theory grounds its observations in the physical act of voice emitting. The *locutionary act* is the very beginning of the linguistic adventure without which no linguistic act would subsist. But the speech act theory also insists on the multilayered structure of *illocutionary* and sometimes *perlocutionary* acts which convey propositions and not only sounds and which produce meaning in the sense which interests us here. The basic unit remains the *speech act* and not the more or less indivisible phoneme and this is already a good beginning. These speech acts can be analyzed in isolation or as parts of broader units such as *discourses.* In terms of linguistics, a phenomenon that interests us can be perceived as described exhaustively when its role in a discourse has been identified. In legal linguistics, at least, no higher level of speech realization than *legal discourse* seems to exist (cf. Galdia 2014). Therefore, I favor pragmatic instruments for language description. Among them especially the speech act theory proved to be able to provide particularly innovative insights into the way how law functions through language. Yet, before speech acts emerge in the language complex signification processes must take place there.

1.2.10 Language in pragmatic perspective

I will explain those complex signification processes on a few examples. An English language speaker will easily be convinced by the enunciation that *strong* collocates with *coffee* in an expression *strong coffee,* but *powerful* does not. On the other hand, in the German language both collocations are effective provided they are transferred correctly. Why is it so? In the daily use of language speakers make choices from its vocabulary while constructing sentences according to syntactic rules. These choices are the basis for the pragmatic aspect of language next to its syntactic and semantic aspects. However, in language choice is limited. Linguistic rules determine the ambit of our linguistic creativity. Our example has a semantic connotation like the classical question *Is the Buckingham Palace a house?* which is perceived by many as a problem of semantics. While in both examples the semantic and the syntactic aspects are undeniably traceable, the preference of speakers can be explained only from the pragmatic perspective, i.e. from the daily use of language by the speakers. One can test the efficacy of this approach by analyzing the use of the expression *Good Morning!* that is applied only under definite conditions and can be shifted to other conversational situations dominated by irony or threat only with reference to the conventional use. Hence, the scope of application of this expression can be widened to include ironical greetings that mean exactly the opposite of the affirmative and benevolent aim of a *Good Morning!* To grasp this specific usage we definitely need pragmatics. We realize that speakers understand such ironical expressions without problems. They automatically determine the right context of their use. And this holds true also for a procedure that is necessary for speaking and understanding language: the context cannot be separated from the vocabulary and the syntax. Otherwise, an enunciation would be understandable only to those who understand it anyway; it is to the speakers but not to the hearers. As seen, language use involves an interpreter and it does not exist beyond the act of its usage by the speakers. The interpreter tries to identify intentions in speech acts. In our *Good Morning!* – example he will regularly be able to determine whether the speaker uses it as a formal greeting formula or whether he uses it informally, when the morning began really badly for him or for the hearer. The linguistic and especially the *pragmatic competence* enable the interpreter to figure out what is actually meant by an utterance. This is, in short, the way in which speakers and hearers cope with language. The approach which will be followed in this book is close to this experience because the act of identifying intentions is crucial to jurists' work with language in their daily practice. The legal linguist can also deal with language in its abstract form, as it is stated in a dictionary. In such a case, however, many legal-linguistic operations will be overlooked because they manifest themselves exclusively in the use of language under changing circumstances. Equally, one could deal with the utterance *Good Morning!* in the sense declared in most dictionaries and English primers. There, we would identify this expression as a *greeting*, but we would not understand that it may also mean an ironical greeting or even a threat. The legal linguist who works with a pragmatic method cannot simply look into dictionaries when she interprets legally relevant language. She would miss the point would she concentrate on the static and abstract form of language. When we deal with an abstract form of it we deal with linguistic remnants or certain selected aspects of it, but definitively not with *the* language.

Let us look at some additional examples which illustrate how the use determines meaning. Would we agree when a specialist analyzing the enunciations: *War is war, Paris is Paris* or *Children are children* would pretend that they express a logical relation of the propositional subject with itself, that they are tautologies? Almost certainly we would argue that our expert does not get the phrases right, although in terms of formal logic these enunciations are classical examples of tautologies (cf. Wierzbicka 1987). Yet, they say us much more than their logical form seems to indicate to our specialist because we are able to identify their metaphorical use. The same concerns enunciations formulated in a negative way, their logical sisters like: *The England of today is not the England of yesterday* which mean more than a simple negation of the subject. Still further, in *A child needs love* or in *A car must be insured* we instantaneously understand that not an individual child or a particular car is meant but rather a general concept embracing all children or all cars. We are able to infer the meaning from the syntactical form of the sentences only because we also understand the use which leads to the emergence of such syntactic structures. In language, levels analyzed by linguists in isolation, like syntax or semantics, are intertwined. They regularly also imply each other. For example, semantic and syntactic implications are manifest in *The news **is** good.* They are linked to the pragmatics of such an utterance. The pragmatic aspect in the utterance is that speakers form this sort of counter-systemic structures. The principles of their choice making are pragmatic although the linguistic mechanisms implied in the utterances are mainly morphologic and syntactic. A further example may make clearer this interdependence of linguistic levels in the language. How do we construe the difference between *rabbit* and *bunny* or *dog* and *doggie*, the later two words in each pair belonging to infantile language use? We are able to differentiate between the lexical variations because we know the context of their use, and therefore properly identify them as in essence equal but belonging to either adult or infantile language use. This essential knowledge seems to belong to the realm of semantics, the rest is pragmatics. Paradoxically, without the residual pragmatics the essential discovery would remain useless, it would be a pure formality. Therefore, these seemingly trivial examples make plain why we insist upon the eminent role of pragmatic reasoning in this book. Pragmatics and pragmalinguistics are not limited to speech acts, conversational implicatures etc., although they include all of those issues. Pragmatics is not only a modern but also an ambitious part of philosophy and linguistics. It aims at showing not only some particular pragmatic phenomena in linguistic use. Its main task and its most ambitious overarching idea is to demonstrate how language works in general. The scope of pragmalinguistic research is very broad and I will not be able to use it with all its potentialities in a research limited to preliminary questions of legal linguistics.

1.2.11 Linguistic turn in law

One more fundamental legal-linguistic issue has to be mentioned in the introductory part as an explanation of conceptual choices exercised in this book. In the history of thought this issue is called *linguistic turn*. The linguistic turn marked the development of philosophy in the last century. Its initial idea had been that fundamental philosophical problems were in essence linguistic problems. Therefore, the hope arose within the analytical philosophy that through the application of linguistic analysis upon philosophical concepts the main philosophical issues could be solved (Rorty 1992: 371). And, as a matter of fact serious progress has been achieved in the philosophical research by means of the linguistic analysis. Fundamentally, notions pertaining to metaphysics were identified as such and excluded from the scientific discourse (Engel 2000: 63). Later on, conceptions of formal scientific language were developed. In the consequence of these efforts the interest shifted toward the ordinary language and its use. This is also the stage which today might be perceived as most promising within the inheritance of analytical philosophy. Whether analytical philosophy led to the solution of the most pertaining philosophical problems has been an issue of controversial debates. Certainly, it is not up to me to determine the result of these debates. I am foremost interested in the linguistic turn because it did not take place in the legal science although the hypothesis that legal problems are at their bottom problems of language is within the reach of daily professional experience of jurists as well as of people concerned by their decisions (cf. Galdia 2014: 211). In law, the linguistic turn would accomplish a shift of interest from the isolated systematization of provisions and concepts in the civil law tradition and in the parallel also a shift from analyzing rules and principles in the common law with means perceived as logical toward a linguistic perspective. Law would be seen predominantly as a linguistic phenomenon because it is created and applied in linguistic operations. This shift in perspective is not really revolutionary because it mainly states the factual situation. It does not create any new law, but simply adjusts our perception of law. There is no reason why the fundamental operations in law, i.e. its creation and its application, should be perceived as something else than linguistic operations. But, surprisingly, they are even today approached from all but linguistic points of view.

As already demonstrated, systematization efforts in law concerned different linguistic aspects of emergence of legal rules and their application. As mentioned in 1.1.4.1, legal rules had been divided as representing *substantive* law, *procedural* law or *conflict of laws*. Branches of law, such as *contracts, torts, administrative, penal* or *constitutional* law had been developed upon the basic distinction traditionally made since the Roman times between *private* and *public* law which itself is a result of the systematization of legal rules. In the law of the European Union, the rules have been divided into *primary* and *secondary* law. These different perspectives ground in doctrines and dogmas used in the legal research and in the legal education. It would not be particularly realistic to wish that they disappear from the legal discourse, mostly because they form a substantial part of it. Systematization efforts in law led to a more transparent structure of law. They also improved the rationality of decisions that are made in the domain of law. But they also displayed limits of this approach. To be truly operative in law, systematization would have to focus on legal arguments as used in legal discourses and not on legal concepts and their prerequisites. Yet, the systematization of legal arguments did not take place in the legal science. However, it seems inevitable that issues pertaining to legal argumentation would be perceived as central to legal research and legal education. Still today, legal argumentation is treated mostly as a peripheral phenomenon belonging to legal theory and not to the core activities in legal research and in legal education. The linguistic turn in law that is supported in this book intervenes precisely at this point.

1.3 Morals for Lawyers

1.3.1 Law without morals?

Some eminent legal thinkers might have opposed this topic fundamentally while saying that law is not necessarily connected to morality (cf. Jackson 1985: 6) and that this negative relation is also true when reversed. Therefore, they would discourage us to deal with this topic in a book dedicated to legal linguistics. Moreover, they would stress that in law we deal with legal institutions and statements which provide us the basis for prediction of future judicial decisions and not about the evolution and the appraisal of values. They would also try to convince us that jurists do not need to deal with ethics because all decisions pertaining to morals in law have been taken already before the stage when jurists begin to work. They would shift the responsibility for the ethical content of the law to parliaments which debate and enact laws within political discourses that embrace all pertinent arguments, not only the legal ones. Therefore, for many specialists the relation between the legal language and the results it produces in law remains unclear. Some claim that bad legislation can emerge from the same legal language as well as good legislation, like a bad house or a good house can be constructed from bricks of the same quality (Pigolkin 1990: 8). In their view, the legal language should be perceived as an *ethically neutral tool* in the hands of the legislator. However, the existence of an ethically neutral language has never been proven with the necessary conviction (cf. also Aarnio 2014). Legal language, even the formal if not formalistic language of the Roman private law is value-laden and transports convictions and views about the social practice which are fundamental to society in which it emerged. The legal rules are not only a result of value-laden social debates; they are also a part of them (Hare 1952). Discourse about values is an ongoing debate. At times, we are not able to recognize its nature (Galdia 2014: 395–400). This happens also when we deal with the Roman law that is remote from the debates of our times and that provides us the form, i.e. concepts rather than their social background. The approach that strictly distinguishes between law and ethics belongs to legal positivism. Its most negative outcome is that it encourages obedience to immoral law (Minda 1995: 51). This result should be avoided in legal linguistics. Consequently, in the following paragraphs attention will be called to issues concerning ethics, especially ethics as perceived by lawyers who make decisions related to social values. The reflection upon these issues is necessary here because values manifest themselves in the legal language as an inherent part of it. The legal linguist cannot understand law and, in consequence, also the linguistic aspects of law without understanding the processes in which values enter law and also determine its application.

1.3.2 Some examples of morals in law

We may clarify the ethical residue in the law with the help of two additional introductory cases:

Case VI: Casey Martin, a successful professional golfer who won numerous competitions applied to the golf tournament organizers to permit him the use of a cart. The reason for Martin's request has been his progressing disease that has atrophied his right leg. This degenerative circulatory disorder called Klippel-Trenaunay-Weber syndrome caused Martin pain and fatigue during his walks and created a significant risk of haemorrhaging and fracturing his tibia. The tournament organizers refused to accommodate his request claiming that all competitors had to play on equal conditions. Martin sued the tournament organizers.

The U.S. Supreme Court had to deal with Martin's case. In PGA Tour Inc. v. Martin (532 U.S. 661, 121 S. Ct. 1879, 2001 U.S. LEXIS 4115) it had to decide whether the provisions of the Americans with Disabilities Act (ADA) guaranteed to a handicapped professional golf player the use of a golf cart during the tournaments which obligated the participants to walk during the play. One of the lower courts decided that using a golf cart in a situation where other participants had to walk would *fundamentally alter the nature of the tournaments.* The U.S. Supreme Court did not share this view and decided in favor of Martin. However, in the dissenting opinion, the decision is criticized for exercising *benevolent compassion* with the handicapped plaintiff instead of applying law. *Agility, strength, speed, balance, quickness of mind, steadiness of nerves, intensity of concentration* says the dissenting opinion *are not evenly distributed. No wild-eyed dreamer has ever suggested that the managing bodies of the competitive sports that test precisely these qualities should try to take account of the uneven distribution of God-given gifts when writing and enforcing the rules of competition.* Thus, according to the dissent the plaintiff would have to accept this situation as he had to accept his progressive handicap. The dissenting opinion develops an own rule for the application of the ADA. This rule postulates that in ordinary situations handicapped persons would have to accept their handicap unless the statute provides for explicit guarantees of equal treatment. However, this rule is nothing more than one of possible linguistic interpretations of the ADA. It does not replace the statute; neither does it discover a better law, a better meaning of the provision. Toward the background of social goals on which the ADA is based the majority decision is more convincing. It is better embedded in the ethical rules of the contemporary society which tries to limit the manifestation of physical inequalities and to integrate handicapped persons in all areas of social life.

The introductory case VII will further stress the value-load of law: Parents of a public middle school student sued the school in order to prevent prayers, benedictions and religious invocations during the graduation ceremony by a clergyman invited by the school. They relied on the establishment clause of the First Amendment of the U.S. Constitution that says: *Congress shall make no law respecting an establishment of religion, or prohibiting the free exercise thereof; or abridging the freedom of speech, or the press; or the right of the people peaceably to assemble, and to petition the Government for a redress of grievances.* The U.S. Supreme Court in its decision Lee v. Weisman (112 S.Ct. 2649, 1992) found that compelling students to participate in a religious exercise is prohibited by the Constitution. It referred to the generally accepted interpretation providing that the government may not coerce anyone to support or participate in religion or its exercise, or otherwise act in a way which establishes a state religion, or tends to do so. Again, in the dissenting opinion, a contrary view was expressed by pretending mainly that: (1) the establishment of religion clause should not have been interpreted so as to invalidate a long-standing American tradition of non-sectarian prayer at public schools graduation, (2) religious invocations and benedictions during the graduation ceremonies involve no psychological coercion of students to participate in religious exercises, (3) the only coercion that is prohibited by the clause is that backed by the threat of penalty, and (4) the school did not direct or control the prayers during the graduation ceremony so that no involvement of the government with religious activity could have been established.

Doubtless, deciding the two above cases without taking an ethical standing, i.e. exercising choices among values at stake is not possible. The application of law does not consist of a schematic or rigid use of preformulated linguistic templets or in decoding meaning in the concepts challenged before the U.S. Supreme Court. It involves constant decision making processes in a society where a debate about values is ongoing. Pragmatic aspects of the legal language are related to values which dominate the public discourse about the right content of law. The citizenry has its own opinions about what is right and what is wrong as well as what is just and what is unjust in society. Sometimes it also provides reasons for its choices. Jurists, too, have opinions about which values to support in society and which tendencies to combat. They use these opinions to solve legal cases as those illustrated above. The most important challenge for legal linguists is the circumstance that the legal discourse stresses, especially in its professional and institutionalized variety the discursive element of legality and neglects or conceals ethical elements in law. Legal linguists must be aware of this circumstance and reposition the elements of the legal discourse that they investigate when they are distorted by other participants. Professionalism in legal linguistics is based on this skill as it is based on the intellectual capacity to view law as a linguistic construct that emerges discursively.

1.3.3 What is the place of law in our life?

Now I will address one more possible misunderstanding that might have emerged after the reading of the previous paragraph. It stresses the ethical element in the legal discourse, yet it does not tend to overstressing it. Ethics is fundamental to law, yet the legal element in the legal discourse is not without importance for the legal linguist. When we study law we look at specific social mechanisms that steer human behavior. They have their specific institutional, textual and structural features that distinguish them from other socially relevant institutions. Therefore a special subject has been created in the academia in order to train people in these specific discursive practices. This measure is as such not necessarily bad, yet it caused by the negligence of the founding fathers of the legal science an unnecessary split between law as an object of academic study and other social sciences. Meanwhile, the specific features of law as research object and teaching subject cannot be underestimated. I would hope that the legal science would overcome in future the artificial boundary that it erected in order to protect itself against challenging developments in other social sciences. This hope may suffice for the academia. Yet, law unlike some other subjects is primarily a non-academic area of social interaction. In everyone's biography the presence of law is sensible at least to some extent. We know from our experience that law is neither almighty nor does it fill the room around us totally. In the rapidly changing world some wish rather more law forgetting that law is not omnipotent, while others wish rather less law and more spontaneous and collective decisions about what is right and what is wrong in society. The later refer to the alleged failure of law to establish sustainable peace in society and among nations. Both share the view that law matters although they weigh its impact differently. We shall therefore ask where law is particularly effective and why it is important to have it there. Law is obviously not as omnipresent as oxygen is in the air around us, nor is it our invisible companion like gravitation or radiation. Neither law nor its fundamental principles can be found in nature nor can nature help us to learn something about law when we have to create or to apply it. Yet still, we often notice and sometimes we are even forced to acknowledge that law exists. Of course, this is only occasionally the case. Law is an elusive companion, it appears in our lives from time to time and its importance varies – it is rather capricious like a cat and not faithful like a dog. But, still, it is domesticated enough to play a constant, although not decisive, role which is taken care of by natural phenomena or moral principles in our daily life. Therefore, law should not be overestimated in respect of the role that it plays in our lives and compared with oxygen, although it might occasionally function as oxygen for society or be seen as a tool of a sovereign who exercises power through it. Neither do we constantly need law nor are we its obedient slaves. The legal linguist realizes that law plays a different role in our life than language without which we cannot cope in our social sphere even for a moment. Law regulates only parts of our biography and structures only partly our societies. In structuring and regulating individual or social behavior law makes use of sets of values and becomes part of our behavior, i.e. of our *life form* which we used to call daily life. It may still be much less necessary in our life than oxygen or language. Yet, modern societies are abundantly regulated and become increasingly dominated by law as the language used in them becomes more and more legal. Law appears therefore to be an efficient mechanism of social regulation, possibly because it is expressed with linguistic means that allow conceptual complexity that otherwise could not be reached. Yet, as a social mechanism it clearly has its limits. It is worthwhile to dedicate a reflection to the issue of the limits of law because lawyers regularly tend to underestimate or overlook them. In this respect they resemble linguists for whom language is simply everything.

1.3.4 Why law matters although it is not omnipotent?

First of all, the limits of law manifest themselves in our daily experience. When we are asked by a policeman on the street to show our ID card although we are not able to understand the reasons for his demand, or when we are requested to follow him to the next police station we notice the importance of law. If we are employed by someone whom we progressively disgust and he/she feels exactly the same way about us, or when we are requested to pay tax advances in an amount which makes appear our daily striving futile, we again realize the importance of law. It matters of course on many other occasions as well, but when we sit on a bench in the municipal park or take a sunbath at the seaside, it often does not matter at all. However, if a bellicose person does not appreciate the way we used to sit on a bench or questions our way to make our skin smooth by sunshine and uses force to appear more persuasive, then law matters again, more than ever. Modern law is construed as a mechanism that protects citizens. The interest in studying it is linked to this task. Meanwhile, it also transports elements of control and constraint. What is more, in times of globalization the power of the national state and its law diminishes. The national law does not attract any more by its triumphant mechanisms of enforcement. Its subjects, who became citizens in the course of societal evolution and nowadays perceive themselves increasingly as citizens of the world, abandon realms they dislike. Thus, the legislator who wishes not to become alienated or lonely in the end will have to make laws palpable to the citizens concerned. Pampered and spoiled as they are, the citizens become gradually the real princes of law. Yet still, even if the legal catering does not always work out, it shows that law matters. In this context the legal-linguistic knowledge becomes useful. The legal linguist knows how to make better laws, i.e. how to use language in a way that the final product of legislative efforts would convince the citizens about the necessity of measures taken. The same holds true for court decisions. Our two initial cases VI and VII have probably proven to most readers that ethical problems can be solved by courts in a satisfying way. Therefore, there is generally no reason to show disrespect to or ignore the law in critical situations of life. In fact, as law can be a fine companion, our question will be how to find it and how to cope with it best, maintain its friendship, and construe it properly. As we appreciate friendship but disapprove obstinacy, we are ready to become its critical friends after we have found it. This question demands but also rewards concentration.

1.3.5 Material ethics and formal ethics

Our two introductory examples with ethical load have demonstrated that there is a way to solve such cases. They have shown also that opinions about the right solution of fundamental ethical questions in them may differ even among professionals of law. Indeed, the diversity of opinions about ethical issues dealt with in law is a social fact. Gender, racial or environmental issues, same sex marriage or pornography lead to controversies in societies. We have different opinions about what is right and what is wrong in the society we live in, and we even have views about right and wrong in societies to which we do not belong, and which we for instance visit as tourists. Values and opinions about them differ, and change with time. To date, all efforts to establish material provisions related to values which would be acceptable to all members of society have failed. For many values there is no common denominator which would unify the disparate views about them. Therefore, some were tempted by the idea to establish institutions which ruled authoritatively about what was right and what was wrong in a society. However, this idea is becoming less and less persuasive to most people nowadays. Some legal linguists may feel at a loss when exposed to the ethical jungle of modern societies. Therefore, following the debate about ethics is essential to any approach to law, i.e. also to the legal-linguistic perspective.

1.3.5.1 *Science shows the way?*

Science has been perceived by many as the last resort for establishing the right way to go in society. However, scientists have also been in the avant-garde to demonstrate the variety of possible views and opinions about society and its values. Economists, sociologists and psychologists deal with this variety which for them constitutes society and they are not inclined to reduce it along some obscure directives. Jurists or other scholars cannot know it better than other citizens whether pornography or prostitution in a society should be prohibited or legalized. We can assume that they have their own views on these issues as citizens, but these views are not professional opinions. Roughly the same could be assumed of other professionals. At best, science can show the material diversity of societal views about values but it cannot establish the right values for a society, neither can it provide instruments for distinguishing right from wrong (Mackie 1977: 35). We increasingly become aware of the circumstance that values in society are a question of debate and that this ongoing debate is unavoidable in every society. Where it does not take place, society becomes rigid and stagnates. Where it is prohibited, totalitarian, oppressive and inhumane rule puts down roots which are difficult to eradicate once they encroached upon society.

1.3.5.2 *Establishing rules for social dialogue*

As soon as we become aware of the circumstance that all societal issues are by their very nature subjected to deliberation, science can help. It can work on establishing methods for the efficient deliberation in society about the appropriateness of value-laden choices which are grounded in material ethics (cf. Steinvorth 1990: 48). It can show how is it possible to reach the most advanced solution in a societal debate about a value-related issue such as virtual child pornography, insider trading or tax evasion. The task to set up procedures in which the diverse ethical views could be discussed in society in the most appropriate way coincides with argumentative techniques and procedures. It is therefore crucial to grasp the importance and the place of moral issues in law. They are definitely not excluded from it. Instead, they make part of it; but they do it in a very specific way. Therefore, we can concentrate in this book upon issues relating to language and still remain in the center of the debate about values. Moreover, while talking about the language use in law we would not be able to avoid ethical issues. In sum, the relation between law and ethics can be perceived as a typical academic problem. Like language, ethics cannot be distilled away from law. Equally, language cannot be separated from ethical issues that it transfers. Thinking these issues together is a challenge for the legal science. Analyzing this challenge is the task of the legal linguist.

1.3.5.3 Professional ethics for lawyers

Jurists would however feel abandoned had they to cope with the diversity of opinions about moral values on their own. Therefore, law provides for its professionals some directives for the appropriate dealing with it. Legal morality is based on issues central to the strengthening of democracy and peace in the world. It is based on principles which with time were filled with substance and which constantly must be refined and modernized. Culture of peace, culture of human rights, cultural diversity and business ethics make part of this moral background of law (cf. Rorty 1993: 115). They make it possible to create general legal rules and to apply them in cases. The closer the jurist, and especially the judge, approaches the most convincing standards of legal morality in his decision the better is the law governing a society. One could contest this view by the contention that jurists do not need to endorse the law; they solely need to know it. Also this view is problematic as it has a clear positivist background. This approach enables, at best, the systematization of law; the application of law remains impossible without a defined opinion about values which shape the most convincing legal decision. Furthermore, all legal professions, for instance attorneys-at-law regularly set up rules for the exercise of their profession. Other corporate legal professions such as judges have also set up moral standards for their professional acting. This is by far not an exclusive attempt to define morals in terms of professional constraints. Also in business life a vivid discussion about business ethics is going on and issues relevant to corporate governance and codes of conduct are perceived as central within modern managerial structures.

1.3.5.4 Volatility in law

Ethical issues manifest a sort of sustainability in society. Society tends to debate about many such issues as assisted suicide or abortion over and over again. These issues and values discussed in discourses about them are regularly modified, yet the ethical discourse remains in its essence rather rigid. Legal regulation is much more volatile. Indeed, one of the most irritating aspects of legal regulation, especially for those dealing with this phenomenon professionally, is that it constantly changes. The formulation by Julius von Kirchmann (1938: 37) that three words of the legislator can convert whole juridical libraries into wastepaper became proverbial for generations of lawyers (cf. Jestaed 2012: 122). This is of course a practical problem to which lawyers have to adapt. They do not work on a construction of an edifice which is growing bigger floor by floor. Instead, they are rather engaged in reconstructing the building which should become more convenient for its inhabitants to live in. This element of volatility in law has consequences for the work with law which includes its setting, its study and its application. Legal science is a method rather than a set of provisions once established. Methodological skills make the jurist and distinguish him from the layperson. Methodological skills embrace a lot of disparate issues like working with definitions and legal terminology, establishing facts from the testimony of others, tracing the appropriate legal provisions at the moment of their application. All these skills are grounded in language use. Therefore, coping with the volatility in law means being able to use the language of law adequately.

1.3.6 How to trace ethics in law?

We were until now dealing with ethical issues in law as if they were unproblematically visible in legal texts. This is definitely not the case and frequently it is necessary to prove that a legal text, e.g. a legal act or a judicial opinion, displays problems which are relevant in terms of ethics. This is the case because ethically relevant issues in law are as a rule not discussed as problems of ethics but as problems of the application of law. In this situation, the sister discipline of legal linguistics, Law and Literature, provides some methodological advice as how to proceed. It analyzes an issue of law as a part of literature, mostly by focusing upon narrative fiction presented by a writer, e.g. Franz Kafka or Fyodor Dostoevsky. There, it can free itself from the boundaries of the rule-oriented legal system and try to focus upon the ethical problems in law in a safe isolation from the immediate boundaries of jurisdiction and its formal-procedural requirements. It can view the problems as such and by so doing it manifests that law does not only deal with the application of legal-technical rules and that it cannot be reduced to such simple activity (Weisberg 1992: 237). Furthermore, it makes plain the ethical dimension of law and prefers to reflect its ends rather than procedures (Weisberg 1992: 242). Legal linguistics can contribute to this method in that it concentrates on the issues of creation and use of language in ethically critical situations in law. When dealing with ethics in law we are confronted with hierarchical social structures and power issues which are expressed mostly with linguistic means. Here again, it is necessary to adjust the legal-linguistic method to this specific communicative situation where speakers do not talk to each other in a space determined by perfect equality of weapons, arguments and procedures. Scholars, such as James Boyd White, warned in their writings against this power-oriented language use which may rather seek domination instead of dialogue (Weisberg 1992: 237). R. Weisberg scrutinized three publications by White, *The Legal Imagination* (1973), *Heracles' Bow* (1987) and *Justice as Translation* (1991) in order to show that linguistic communication in law has very specific boundaries. Later on, we will focus upon procedural boundaries relevant to the language use as described by Jürgen Habermas and Robert Alexy. White, in turn, and also Weisberg, were rather interested in the ethical issue of the establishing of communicative boundaries in law. They came close to the classical perspective taken by Friedrich Nietzsche who viewed power-dominated communication rather skeptically. He insisted upon distance and distrust toward "*writers and institutions primarily centered around the word*" (Weisberg 1992: 302). Legal linguistics must learn the bitter lesson based on these findings. This makes any work on language use in law undoubtedly more challenging. But the effort is rewarded by results which explain the law and not only the language used in it.

1.4 An Introduction Must End

It would be tempting to continue in this introductory part into legal linguistics the list of its epistemological prerequisites which – when woven together – would provide a solid conceptual foundation for a coherent discourse about this new branch of legal sciences or linguistics. Above, we mentioned ethics as one of its pillars. Equally, also the deliberative nature of law, the tasks and methods of the legal sciences as well as the necessity to accomplish the linguistic turn in law have been touched upon. On the other side, general linguistics and also the specific perspective upon language that is called linguistic pragmatics or pragmalinguistics have been introduced as central to the vision of legal linguistics developed in this book. Certainly, we would also have to discuss additionally at least the anthropological parameters of law which ground in the circumstance that law is made by humans for humans and that it emerges toward the background of their culture. We will nevertheless not address this issue here. Instead, it must suffice to remind the readers that law with all its linguistic and ethical constraints is embedded in a broader practice which is our culture. It cannot, therefore, be studied or applied in isolation from other cultural phenomena. In this culture, law emerges in signification processes as an amalgam of legal signs. We have encountered already some of them, for instance statutes and court opinions. Legal semiotics scrutinizes the processes in which legal signs emerge and are applied. They are deeply hidden in the structure of our minds and in our culture. Legal linguistics covers only some of these processes. It concentrates on those parts of the legal culture which are expressed verbally. We must of course be aware of further implications of the semiotic domain, but we do not necessarily need to explore them here in all detail. Meanwhile, we have reached a perspective in our argument that enables us to look at how law is expressed with linguistic means which interests us most. This result enables us to end the introduction, and concentrate now on some more specific aspects of the metaphorical relation between law and language.

Part 2: Language and Law

Under the heading Language and Law I will defend the necessity to establish a discipline called by me and some others legal linguistics. I will look back at the achievements of a highly heterogeneous research into Law and Language and sketch possible developments, especially the pragmatically oriented legal linguistics. Legal linguistics will be characterized in its geographic and epistemological development. Subsequently, the borderline will be drawn between it and subjects which come close to it in order to better expose the legal-linguistic domain and mark the difference between this specific subject and the adjacent branches of knowledge. Once the subject of legal linguistics is characterized, the language use in legal contexts will be scrutinized, mostly referring to established (not always pragmatically oriented) research. Furthermore, I will accentuate specific features of language used in law in the light of pragmatics. Especially, I will closely look at the legal terminology and ask what terminology means in terms of pragmatics. After having read this chapter, the students will have a clearer view of legal linguistics. Some preliminary knowledge of the subject comes already from the introductory part. This part will provide a more professional and specific view upon legal linguistics as research object and teaching subject. Meanwhile, the main aim of this book is reached only when the reader begins to think like a legal linguist. This aim can realistically be reached only after the study of the third chapter that shows the theory and the practice of legal linguistics. Let us not precipitate the course of things and return to part two.

2.1 Foundations of Legal Linguistics

Conceptual foundations of legal linguistics are only partly rooted in pragmalinguistic reasoning. Currents, methods and approaches that are not explicitly pragmalinguistic or are even in opposition to the main intellectual tendency that underlies these lectures will have to be reflected at this stage of the exposition of the legal-linguistic argument. Reasons for this enterprise are at least twofold. First, frameworks of reference that reveal the origins of legal linguistics as well as issues discussed in it are understandable only toward the background of the historical development of the discipline. Second, the necessity to establish a pragmalinguistically founded legal linguistics becomes plain when its method is contrasted with other approaches and with the results achieved within the research based upon these approaches. Therefore, mentioning, discussing or even integrating non-pragmatically oriented research results makes sense. Pragmatics as a discipline that focuses upon language use in order to understand human communication is primarily interested in the emergence of meaning in language. This is not surprising because meaning is the most striking element of language that deserves utmost attention of researchers. In order to accomplish the pragmatic postulate I concentrate therefore in this book on communicative devices such as legal-linguistic speech acts which function within legal discourses. However, meaning constitution as a cognitive process is manifold. I assume that the traditional research provides some valuable input into the pragmatic discussion of the language of law, at least as far as issues discussed in it are concerned. Mentioning this research in these lectures appears to me as methodically acceptable. I adhere to the broader, integrative conception of pragmatics. In light of this conception, a pragmatic theory of language would have to integrate all levels of meaning constitution, not only semantics and the traditional, narrow pragmatics. Aspects of meaning manifest themselves on the phonetic, morphophonemic and syntactic levels of the structure of language. Future pragmatic theories of language will have to deal more intensely with the issue of integrating aspects of meaning present in pragmatically less relevant manifestations of language use. Finally, I doubt that the role of pragmatic legal linguistics in researching processes of meaning constitution in law could be seriously questioned in future research. Meanwhile, legal linguistics as a subject clarifies in the amalgam of approaches and views discussed in this part of the book. The reader should therefore approach with calm and patience the following pages that refer to pragmatic and non-pragmatic aspects of meaning in law that are often captured under the rubric *language of law*. Yet, before this issue will be addressed I will look at the discipline called *Law and Language* or *legal linguistics* that deals with it professionally.

2.1.1 Language and Law

The principal theoretical issue in the contemporary discussion about legal linguistics has been the long-standing relation between or rather the interrelation of language and law (Mattila 2006: 6) that we explore here mostly as a metaphor. In the terminology used in the English speaking countries, the caption *Law and Language* has been regularly used in order to characterize research into this particular interrelation. I have reversed the common order of words in the above heading for the needs of this chapter in which language analysis will dominate our perspective. Notwithstanding this change in the perspective I still hope that the analysis which follows can contribute essentially to the classical topic *Law and Language* in equal degree.

As previously mentioned, the very distinction between law and language or in the reverse order the distinction between language and law seems to be of stylistic rather than of substantial nature. Indeed, there is no law without language and to suppose it seriously would mean to fall into one of the numerous metaphysical traps existing both in the legal theory and in the more practically oriented legal reasoning. It seems that the conception of law existing independently of language has never been earnestly considered (Viehweg 1954: 54). Some exceptions could possibly be found in studies related to logical formalization of law which began with G. W. Leibnitz's (1646–1716) impressive but failed idea of law operating *more geometrico*. His fundamental works on this issue *Dissertatio de arte combinatoria* (1666) and *Nova methodus discendae docendaeque jurisprudentiae* (1667) show the limits of any attempt to formalize law, i.e. to make it work like a calculus. Leibnitz had been aware of the fact that law is structured by *topoi*, i.e. by certain common places which are recurrently used in the legal argumentation. However, he hoped to be able to control their use under an arithmetically founded *ars combinatoria.* Nowadays, the discursive nature of law is not questioned any more and a method controlling the use of legal arguments with formalized procedures appeals only to some researchers. Moreover, the research into possible formalization of law showed the deep logical structure of law functioning in language rather than the independence of both. Nevertheless, the failure of the formalization project should not be misunderstood. Although law will never function like a logical calculus, it will never function independently of logic either. Challenging in this respect is nowadays the way in which both aspects could be balanced in the research. The central role of language in law cannot be replaced by any other communicational mechanism. Hence, the distinction between law and language in the above caption – and not only there – is a question of convention in the developing research into this still unclear interrelation. It is, at best, of administrative importance in legal linguistics and it is typical of metaphorical language use that is acceptable provided one is aware of the metaphorical character of such language. Otherwise, it may give rise to problems that are metaphysical, i.e. caused by the language itself. Dealing with the question of law in the language or language in the law is nothing more than a – probable unavoidable – stage in the development of legal linguistics as a theory of law. To date, in the common law tradition that dominates the English speaking world *Law and Language* defines itself, like *Law and Literature* or *Law and Economics*, as an interdisciplinary field which is based upon both areas of social practice and scientific research, which are law and language respectively (Schauer 1993: xiv). It deals with the development of legal (mostly English) language and includes a panoply of perspectives with more or less explicit semiotic background. Especially, issues concerning the indeterminacy of legal language as contrasted with the language of literary works attracted the attention of writers in this area. Here again, it becomes obvious that the determination of what is law and what is language is essential to the debate about the metaphorical interrelation of both if a sterile or blurred debate should be avoided. A particular view of law or of language shapes the argumentative framework and the research results. This relation is undoubtedly an issue for a legal theory which also wishes to call itself linguistic. Otherwise, a somehow unproductive listing of situations in which language is used in legal contexts comes up and no further consequences follow from it. In fact, to maintain that law is both a product of and dependent on language (Schauer 1993: xi) demands further explanation. With Schauer we can underline that this simple claim already includes a methodically determined position in the legal theory. Further elaboration on the issue leads directly into the solved and unsolved problems of legal theory. According to Schauer, "the relationship between law and language seems in some ways special. To say why that is so, however, or even to maintain that it is so at all, is in itself to take a position on one or another position of legal theory." Schauer (1993: ix) deplores the "intrinsic messiness of the subject itself", and calls it therefore slippery. Indeed, it took two thousand years to reach the level of theoretical reflection on law and language or language and law that we now have at our disposal. The theoretical debate which begins with the Greek rhetoric (Wolf 1950/1952: 13) and continues in the Roman epoch and in the Middle Ages (Curtius 1996: 258), which passes through the tormented waves of the Enlightenment and all theoretical approaches which emerged in modern times (cf. Berman 1983) had produced an amalgam of ideas, perspectives and opinions. Again, it took time to separate the wheat from the chaff and lay foundations for the contemporary legal theory and to prove the necessity of legal linguistics. Therefore, when talking about language and law, we should bear in mind this unusual process of development, its aspects of continuity and discontinuity, turns and breaches in the debate about the conceptual relation we focus upon (Viehweg 1954: 29). Rare are disciplines which can refer to such an edifying past and even rarer are those which can directly benefit from research done into their subject by generations profoundly remote in time. It is worthwhile to ask about the possible reasons for this thematic continuity. First of all, it might be that practical needs of using language in courts, in negotiations with private parties or with authorities strengthened this continuity of reflection (Mattila 2006: 6). Yet, it could also be that the textual basis of law transferred in form and content from generation to generation imposed a view upon law as a social practice that manifests a stronger link to written texts and through it to language than any other socially relevant practice.

2.1.2 The search for the name

I have frequently mentioned here that legal linguistics is a relatively new discipline. This statement is true and it is false at the same time. It is false because the so-called relation between law and language as the historically first legal-linguistic question had occupied lawyers from time immemorial. It is true because until recently legal linguistics did not exist as an autonomous branch of legal science or linguistics. Furthermore, its status as an interdisciplinary field of research has not been particularly strong either. Not even the name of this new discipline is assured. H.E.S. Mattila (2002a: 170) and G. Cornu (2005: 10) refer to the French legal scholar François Gény who used the term *linguistique juridique* already in 1921 in his work *Science et technique en droit privé positif III*. In French-speaking Canada the term *jurilinguistique* and its English equivalent *jurilinguistics* are in use (Gémar/Kasirer 2005, Preite 2013), also Polish and Russian denominations *juryslingwistyka* (cf. Pieńkos 1999) and *pravovaya lingvistika (правовая лингвистика)* are in use respectively. The Polish legal theorist Eugeniusz Bautro used the term *lingwistyka prawnicza* in his philosophically founded outline of this new area of knowledge (Bautro 1935, Galdia 2014: 32). In the Czech research, Hlouch (2007/8: 42) uses the term *právni lingvistika* when talking about the development in Germany, in Ukrainian the term *juridichna lingvistika* (*юридична лінгвістика*) is in use (Pradid 2002). In Greek, νομική γλωσσολογία is used (cf. Gortych-Michalak 2013). In Latvian, the term *juridiskā lingvistika* is used, especially within the Legal Linguistics Study Programme at the Riga Graduate School of Law. In Italian, the term *linguistica giuridica* is occasionally applied (Veronesi 2000). In Spanish, the term *jurilingüística* is in use (Macías Otón 2015), in Catalan *llengua i dret* is used as well (cf. Revista de Llengua i Dret/Journal of Language and Law). In Norwegian *rettslingvistikk*, in Swedish *rättslingvistik*, in Danish *retsligvisitik* and in Finnish *oikeuslingvistiikka* are in use. In German, the term *Rechtslinguistik* is used for various theoretical approaches which cover also general philosophical and critical studies about the relation between the language used in law and the dominant ideology. For the German name usage E. Bülow (1985: 30) pointed to a publication by A. Podlech in 1976 where the concept of (D) *Rechtslinguistik* was developed in contrast to a programmatically narrower Law and Language studies. In Chinese, the term *falü yuyanxue* (法律语言学 / 法律語言學) is used both for legal linguistics and forensic linguistics as apparent equivalents (cf. Liu 2007, Du 2004). The English speaking world is problematic in the sense of name giving for our undertaking. There, mostly foreign authors apply in their works the term *legal linguistics* (Mattila 2002a: 171, 2013, Galdia 2009, cf. also Goodrich 1984: 178). The formulation *Law and Language* seems still to dominate the professional language usage in the English-speaking academia.

2.1.3 Legal linguistics in the world

It is therefore appropriate to justify the new general approach to Law and Language and several authors dealing with this issue such as G. Cornu or H.E.S. Mattila did it before me. They tried to legitimize the existence of the new discipline differently. They proceeded by focusing on selected topics in the societal and academic discourse which they perceived as decisive for the relation between language and law. We will start with a geographic approach that shall illustrate the spatial distribution in the process in which legal linguistics actually emerged. It is, by necessity, a sketch and cannot cover all geographical regions of the planet due to limited access to publication in Europe from e.g. Latin America (cf. Bulygin 1983) or Africa (cf. Opeibi 2008, Becker 2013) where legal-linguistic research develops as well. To date, the geographically oriented description of legal-linguistic research concentrates mostly on the development in the U.S., in France and in Russia. It focuses upon the achievements of some eminent scholars in this field such as Heikki E.S. Mattila in Finland who shaped the subject toward the background of the comparative law or Peter Tiersma in the U.S. who broadened the traditional historically oriented approach there, respectively. The overview that follows does not cover purely philosophical or legal-theoretical research which is not exclusively legal-linguistic but which has been fundamental to the development of modern legal linguistics like many publications by G. H. von Wright, A. Aarnio or J. Habermas. Instead, it concentrates on achievements which can be explicitly counted as belonging to legal linguistics. Fundamental philosophical and legal-theoretical research is taken into consideration here at places where particular legal-linguistic issues are described. Therefore, e.g. G.H. von Wright is mentioned in parts concerning the role of logic in law and A. Aarnio and J. Habermas in parts concerning the structure of the legal discourse.

2.1.3.1 *Some tendencies and developments in Europe*

(Germany) German speaking countries with a multitude of legal-linguistic approaches represented there could constitute a specific legal-linguistic area of research. Publications by E. Forsthoff, H. Dölle or H. Neumann-Duesberg relating to current legal-linguistic issues appeared already in the forties of the last century (Bülow 1981). Salas (2001: 209) ties the emergence of Law and Language studies in Germany to the analytic philosophy and refers especially to Eckmann (1969) and Koch (1976). J. Engberg (2013: 28) stressed particularly the importance of D. Busse's *Recht als Text* (1992). Elderly German legal-linguistic research comprises also works by G. Dilcher (1961), S. Sonderegger (1965), R. Leodolter (1975), B. Altehenger (1983), S. Becker (1972), B. Baum (1986), P. Kirchhof (1987), C. Fuchs-Khakhar (1987), F. Schönherr (1985), H. Hattenhauer (1987), G. Kocher (1992) and M. Heller (1992). B. Steinbauer (1989) dealt with pragmalinguistic aspects in diachronic perspective, T.M. Seibert (1981, 1989) analyzed German court files. More recently, W. Grasnich (2001) wrote about legal justification, A. Lerch (2004) dealt with the understandability of legal texts, L. Hoffmann (1987) wrote about communication in courts, D. Heller and K. Ehrlich (2007) edited a publication on communication in law, M. Galdia (1999) drafted an encyclopaedic note on the development of legal German, E. Lutz (1998), M. Rathert (2006) and C. Lüscher (2012) wrote about the relation of law and language, H.D. Fisher (2009) compiled a book on German law and its language, D. Stein, F. Olsen, R.A. Lorz (2009) wrote about theoretical aspects of law and language, D. Stein (2010) dealt with meaning in law and in linguistics, T. Fonsén (2011) researched the influence of legal German upon legal Finnish, J. Iluk (2014) edited a volume of research papers that deals also with legal German, the editors of the ÖJZ in Austria edited a publication about legal language (Redaktion der ÖJZ 2014). Recently, E. Felder (2003, 2012, 2013a, 2013b, 2016) focused on semiotic, textological and sociolinguistic aspects of legal communication in his numerous contributions. Among legal scholars, B. Grossfeld (2005) and T. Lundmark (1999, 2005, 2006, 2012) were particularly interested in legal-linguistic issues. In the German-speaking area the vast number of publications concerns various aspects of law and language that are difficult to synthesize. Detailed bibliography of German legal linguistics is provided in Lindroos (2015). At the University of Cologne the electronic journal *ZERL – Zeitschrift für Europäische Rechtslinguistik* is edited by the project European Legal Linguistics, (D) *Europäische Rechtslinguistik*. Furthermore, an e-publication *International Journal of Language and Law* appears under the editorial responsibility of German scholars. ***(Netherlands)*** In the Netherlands, G.R de Groot dealt with legal translation (Balkema/de Groot 1987), M. van Hoecke (2002) authored *Law and Communication*, J. Bos (1986) wrote about systemic legal language, C.J.W. Baaij (2012) wrote about legal translation. ***(Italy)*** Close to the German legal-linguistic tradition is the Italian perspective upon law and language that is dominated by works of legal theorists such as E. Pattaro, U. Scapelli, M. Jori, L. Gianformaggio and N. Bobbio (Pintore 1995). Nowadays, research in Italy benefits also from Anglo-American influence in works of M. Gotti (2011) and P. Anesa (2009,

2012). L. Luzzati (1990) dealt with the vagueness of legal norms, L. Peotta (1998) researched German and Italian court decisions, G. Benedetti (1999) wrote about *mute law* (cf. also Sacco 2010), D. Veronesi (2000) wrote about Italian and German legal linguistics, G. Rovere (2005) analyzed electronic corpora relevant to legal language, M. Timoteo and B. Pozzo (2008) edited a volume that provides descriptions of European legal languages and B. Pozzo (2014) edited a volume on non-European legal languages, A. Mariani Marini and F. Bambi (2013) edited a volume on the written and spoken legal language, M.V. Dell'Anna (2013) and J. Visconti (2016) dealt with the language in Italian court decisions. M. Lentano (2014) researched rhetoric and law, P. Pellegrino (2014) dealt with alternative models of legal communication while taking into account both prose and poetry. ***(Spain and legal Spanish/ Catalan)*** In Spain, legal argumentation constitutes the essential part of the legal theory developed by M. Atienza (2008) that is fundamental to the development of legal linguistics. Legal-linguistic research that reflects the issue of understandability of the legal language is represented in the works by J. Prieto de Pedro (1991) and C. Duarte i Montserrat (1985, 1995, 1998). A. Borja-Albi (2004, 2014), F. Prieto-Ramos (2011) and E. Macías Otón (2015) dealt with legal translation. J. Gandasegui (1998) dealt with the development of legal Spanish. R. Villa-Real and M.A. del Arco Torres (1999) published a dictionary of Spanish legal terms. J.J. Ponsoda Sanmartín (1996) dealt with elderly forms of legal Catalan and Aragonesian. M. T. Turell (2005) edited a volume on forensic linguistics. M. Xirinachs (2002) dealt with legal Catalan. Interesting is also the research by H.G. von Mutius (2003/2004) that refers to the Jewish tradition of interpretation in elderly Spanish legal texts. J. Nowak-Michalska (2012: 20–22) proposed an overview of the research into legal Spanish. The Catalan *Revista de llengua i dret* publishes legal-linguistic contributions. ***(Portugal)*** In Portugal, A.M. Cordeiro (2004) dealt with problems of translation of legal terminology. ***(Hungary)*** Hungarian legal linguistics is dominated by structuralist and pragmatic approaches. A detailed description of the development of the Hungarian legal language has been prepared by K. Kaczmarek (2011: 21–41) as a part of a monograph dedicated to problems of legal translation. Aspects of differentiation of language use in the area of law are introduced in the monograph based upon a distinction proposed by M. Szabó and contrasted with the approaches developed by A. Trosborg (1995) and B. Wróblewski (1948). F. Trimmel (1993) wrote about judicial rhetoric, M. Szabó (2001, 2002) dealt with the legal Hungarian, especially in the perspective of its communicative function. E. Vinnai (2010, 2011) introduced explicit pragmatic aspects into the Hungarian legal-linguistic research. ***(Romania)*** M. Saramandu (1986) dealt with legal-administrative terminology of elderly Romanian documents. ***(Bulgaria)*** D. Yankova (2004, 2008) dealt with legal language and legal translation. ***(Czechoslovakia/Czech Republic)*** In former Czechoslovakia, an attempt to compare legal terminology of Slavonic countries has been undertaken already 1933 (cf. Bařinka 1933). Later, in the Czech Republic, F. Kořenský et al. (1999) wrote about legal and linguistic analysis of legal texts from the point of view of legal informatics, R. Kuchar (1998) dealt with diachronic aspects of law, L. Hlouch (2007/8) wrote about theory and reality of legal interpretation. ***(Bosnia-Herzegovina)*** E. Mešanović-

Meša (2011) analyzed the use of Bosnian, Croatian and Serbian in the legislation of Bosnia-Herzegovina. ***(Croatia)*** J. Babić (2013) edited the proceedings of the round table on law and language. ***(Ukraine)*** J.F. Pradid (2002) wrote an introduction into legal linguistics, the Italian legal linguist L. Goletiani (2011, 2016) regularly includes data on legal Ukrainian in her research into legal Russian. ***(Latvia)*** K. Klava (1989) dealt in a research prepared in Sweden with Latvian documents of the 17th century, A. Kuzmins (2015) reviewed Latvian linguistic legislation since the beginning of the 20th century.

For some countries and languages I am able to provide broader overviews in paragraphs below.

2.1.3.2 Legal terminology and discourse in France

Legal-linguistic research in France has been traditionally dominated by the issues related to legal terminology that has been scrutinized from the diachronic and from the synchronic perspective. It started with the idea of distinguishing between the properly legal vocabulary and the non-legal terminology. J.-L. Sourioux and P. Lerat published in 1975 *Le language du droit* that is until today perceived as one of the fundamental works on the subject. G. Cornu approached problems of legal linguistics through the analysis of legal terminology in his *Linguistique juridique* that is currently available in its third edition. One of the most significant epistemological discoveries revealed in Cornu's *Linguistique juridique* is the step taken by the author from purely lexicological analyses to an overarching idea of legal discourse (FR *discours juridique*). According to Cornu, the legal discourse unites the terminology into a coherent entity (Cornu 2005: 15). Since Cornu's analysis of the legal discourse based on legal terminology the area of legal linguistics is no more limited to purely lexicological scrutiny. Another important step for the development of the new scientific domain was the introduction of the linguistic legislation (FR *droit linguistique*) into the realm of legal linguistics. Cornu's broadening of the legal-linguistic domain can be characterized as paradigmatic due to his particularly convincing justification for the introduction of the subject matter which regulates the use of language with legal means (Cornu 2005: 2, 36, 421). As a result, one can maintain that legal terminology organized within the legal discourse constitutes the focal point for the issues discussed in the French *linguistique juridique*. This paradigm for the legal-linguistic research is well grounded in G. Cornu's lexicographic work *Vocabulaire juridique* available currently in its eighth edition at PUF (2000) and in the sixth edition at Quadrige. Further works that have shaped the silhouette of the modern French *linguistique juridique* had been the classics such as Fr. Gény, *Science et technique en droit privé positif* (1921) and M. Foucault's studies dealing with *épistémologie* of science and with the concept of discourse, especially his *Les mots et les choses* (1966) and *L'archéologie du savoir* (1969) as well as G. Kalinowski's *Introduction à la logique juridique* (1965). Last but not least, Ch. Perelman's epoch-making *Logique juridique, nouvelle rhétorique* (1979) has been incorporated into the general paradigm of the French *linguistique juridique* due to its fundamental importance for the legal argumentation. G. Cornu (2005: 40–51) provides a general bibliography for the francophone legal-linguistic research that has developed more or less closely around the main paradigm. Today, legal-semiotic research is eminently represented in works by Anne Wagner (2006, 2008, 2009). Recently, F. Martineau (2008) characterized the argumentative skills necessary in professional work in French courts. He mostly uses the concepts of the traditional rhetoric to describe skills that are foremost demanded from attorneys. His approach is therefore practical, as the conception proposed by him is explicitly forensic (FR *judiciaire*). It makes part of the broader view that is presented in this book in form of a legal argumentation that would have to be rendered by (FR *juridique*). Furthermore, Josiane Boutet (2008) described pragmatic mechanisms that steer language use in conditions determined by labor contracts. Historically, the legislation concerning speaking at the working place included such pragmatically relevant constellations as the strict prohibition to speak while working, limiting the use of language and using formatted language. These restrictions, in turn, engendered linguistic mechanisms of compensation for the prohibition to speak such as jokes, chat, laughing etc. The work shows the anthropological consequences of restrictions aiming at prescribing the use of language in labor processes and especially their limits.

2.1.3.3 Polish legal theory and legal linguistics

In Poland, the legal-linguistic research developed on the basis of the legal theory (Petzel 2006: 153). The Polish legal theoretician Eugeniusz Bautro (1891–1961) developed and published already in 1935 a linguistically founded theory of law that originates in the philosophy of law initiated by I. Kant and later expanded by G. del Vecchio. His monograph is also mentioned by A. Schaff (1962: 367) as an important contribution to semantics. As far as the language of law is concerned Bautro (1935: 12) writes:

> *...we need the description of the relationship between jurisprudence and linguistics as well as the idea of legal linguistics, and especially its main part, namely legal semantics. We accept not only a possibility, but also a necessity to form and to conduct them. We think that in this way the research on law will be deepened, and the understanding and the formulation of its structure and functioning as well as its logics and action will be facilitated. What is more, we expect that then we will gain the proper foundation, examination and material for the legal theory and practice. Semantics (and linguistics in general) and logistics while interacting, will manage to elucidate all legal processes, all legal views, and in general logical structure of the world of human thoughts and acts in law.*

In the precedent quote, translated into English by A. Matulewska, the term (PL) *lingwistyka prawnicza* has been used at a very early stage of the development of our discipline.

Since the first modern theoretical work on the language of law by B. Wróblewski, *Język prawny i prawniczy* (1948), the research has been dominated by approaches rooted in the philosophy of language and in logic (Kotarbiński 1955). T. Gizbert-

Studnicki (1979) published the first research perceived as truly linguistic (Petzel 2006: 153). The linguistic trend was continued by J. Pieńkos (1999) and by K. Brodziak (2004) as well as by W. Kwarciński (2004) who introduced pragmalinguistic concepts into the debate. A position less dependent on legal theory is represented by B. Z. Kielar (1979) who rather favored terminology-oriented approaches to the legal language. She also published a renowned book on legal translation (Kielar 1977). The Polish legal-linguistic debate has been dominated by the question whether the language of law that has been identified by legal theoreticians can be construed as language in terms of linguistics (Petzel 2006: 163). Today, pragmalinguistically oriented researchers (cf. Brodziak 2004: 123–124) stress the *pragmatic competence* as a characteristic feature in the functioning of the legal language as language while other scholars rather tend toward a formalized and strict view upon language as a system of signs or rules that opposes the perception of the language used in law as language (Petzel 2006: 163). The recent monograph on the Polish legal language by A. Malinowski (2006) takes an intermediate standing and combines quantitative research with pragmatic concepts. A. Matulewska (2007, 2013) and L. Biel (2014) wrote about legal translation, A. Jopek-Bosiacka (2006, 2011) researched aspects of legal translation and legal communication. Language use in courtrooms was researched by M. Rzeszutko (2003). Legal-linguistic issues were studied systematically during decades of meticulous research by Maria Teresa Lizisowa (2006, 2012, 2013a, 2013b), mainly from the neostructuralist point of view that also integrates textological and pragmatic aspects of language use. Her research culminated in *Komunikacyjna teoria języka prawnego* (2017, in print), a magnum opus that sums up and expands the achievements of Polish legilinguistics and Polish legal theory. M. T. Lizisowa proceeds in B. Wróblewski's footsteps and uses as a point of departure his theory of legal language construed as statutory language (cf. Wróblewski 1948). This theory is still accepted by many researchers in Poland as a legilinguistic benchmark, yet it has been also further developed by T. Gizbert-Studnicki (1986, 2004, 2009) and some others. M. T. Lizisowa's communicational theory of the legal language focuses on statutory language as a text composed of sentences that communicate law. She argues that the normative language of law is characterized by performative, modal and axiological elements that are adjusted to the text type of legal communication. With the help of the semiotic framework of reference, Lizisowa synchronized the legal signs and the legal notions to which they relate within their context of use. While so doing, she was able to explain the sender-dominated composition and the recipient-oriented functioning of legal texts. In this changing research perspective between the sender of the legal text and its recipient she identified the structural device responsible for the emergence of directives in law and their understanding. At this point, the pragmatic coherence in text interpretation guarantees the normative, performative and coercive force of an act of communication in law. M.T. Lizisowa's monograph is unique in the sense that it uses the totality of the descriptive framework of linguistics to characterize legal communication. Overall, Polish contributions to legal linguistics make plain that the determination of the concept of language is an essential precondition of every legal-linguistic research. An overview of the research into legal Polish is included in the monograph by J. Nowak-Michalska (2012: 15–20).

2.1.3.4 Approaches to legal Russian in Russia and abroad

Traditionally, research approaches to the legal Russian language were dominated by the methodological divide into spoken and standard literary language. This research tradition was adopted in the Russian linguistics relatively early, at the beginning of structuralist and formalist movements in social sciences that can be traced back to the twentieth of the 20th century. The approach to standard language seen as divided into spoken and literary standards dominated the research in the Soviet times and is also preponderant in contemporary Russian legal-linguistics studies (cf. Lehmann 2013). Before the Soviet revolution, positivist, historical and etymological interests as well as editorial philology of elderly Russian legal texts marked the academic research into the formation and development of legal Russian (cf. Ewers 1826, Jagić 1910: 148–149, Stang 1935, 1939). This research focused mainly on the editing of documents perceived as sources of legal history; linguistic analysis in them is therefore often rather rudimentary (Koshkin 2008: 5, Kaiser 1965, cf. also Sowinski 1983: 13). Works by Russian and foreign authors such as Napierski (1868) and Shahmatov (1886) are construed in this vein. They are therefore interesting as sources for legal-linguistic research that deals with diachronic aspects of the legal language rather than as results of such research. Later structuralist and formalist approaches have their roots in the research paradigms that focused on diachronic aspects of law and its language. In Soviet Russia, semiotic and formalized approaches to the legal language shaped the researchers' level of problem awareness. They led to the increased interest in formal aspects of the legal language. Today, also structuralist and post-structuralist approaches as well as semiotic studies that include philosophical and linguistic pragmatics of Anglo-American origin are present in the Russian legal linguistics (cf. Kusov 2004, Korolev 2010, Dubrovskaya 2010, 2014). Meanwhile, corpus-oriented historical and terminological investigations continue the tradition initiated already in Imperial Russia.

Above mentioned approaches to the Russian legal language resulted in the determination of its linguistic status as a sub-genre of the standard literary language (Bartoszewicz 1979: 80). This legal sub-genre of the standard literary language is characterized by a specific style. In the research committed to the textological perspective, oral samples were contrasted with the language of written documents. The main result of the traditional research relevant to the development of modern approaches to legal language was the finding that in legally relevant linguistic surroundings functional linguistic change dominates over structural change (Bartoszewicz 1979: 16). The reason for this regularity is that function is determined by the sphere of language use. This result paved the way to a research perspective that focuses on language use in legally relevant communicative situations. Interestingly, and unlike in the Polish legal linguistics, neither in the Soviet times nor in post-Soviet Russia the very existence of the legal language was ever questioned in the debate about the characteristic features of the legal language (Pigolkin 1990: 16–17).

The term *juridicheskaja lingvistika* (*юридическая лингвистика*) for *legal linguistics* is largely used in contemporary research in the field (cf. Goletiani 2011: 242). Previous, Soviet time research referred rather to statutory language (*jazyk zakona* / *язык закона*) (cf. Pigolkin 1990). Among main achievements of this period that was dominated by semiotic perspectives and attempts at formalization of the legal language are the elucidation of explicit aspects of statutory language and the prevalence of meaning-related studies over form-centered textological analyses. In this research the concealed, implicit element of meaning was identified as the main problem in interpretation and application of legal texts (Pigolkin 1990: 180–188). Latent or implicit information in normative texts was perceived as acceptable solely under conditions of text economy where meaning can be easily inferred from the totality of legal acts. This is rather a rare case and therefore researchers claimed that it would be necessary to increase the explicit component in normative acts. Russian scholars focused, like the majority of researchers in the area of legal terminology especially on unification and standardization of legal language toward the background of the automatic data processing (Pigolkin 1990: 21). Rationalization of legal terminology and standardization of its use are understandable goals for legal linguistics. However, standardization is an offshoot rather than a process in the development of the legal language. The framework for the emergence of legal terminology is the conceptualization of legal subject matters and their parallel lexicalization. Their products are concepts and terms which the authors of (RU) *Язык закона* (*Iazyk zakona*) also frequently stress in their collective work (Pigolkin 1990: 15). Yet, they do not make this distinction operative in their conception of the legal language. The specific approach in Pigolkin (1990) is therefore useful within the data processing models for legal terminology. At any rate, legal terminology goes its own ways and it would be challenging to press it into standardized patterns. The tendency to dominate law by means of informatics is perceptible especially in the social practice. Nevertheless, the assumption that some day law will dominate informatics is more probable due to historical experience made with legal mechanisms. Therefore, it would be more important to develop data processing patterns which would correspond to legal terminology rather than to try to adapt the legal language to requirements of data processing as it is done in *Iazyk zakona*.

L. Goletiani (2011) perceives the Russian legal linguistics as a multifaceted field where areas such as legal stylistics, forensic phonetics, legal translation, legal terminology, understanding the language of legislation, the history of legal language, speech in the courtroom etc. are represented in publications and methodological approaches. Broad paradigmatic research programs were developed by A.S. Aleksandrov (2003) and by N.S. Plotnikova (2010) who combined history of language and discourse analysis. Forensic linguistics is actually the most visible part of the Russian legal linguistics within Russian judicial institutions (cf. Mushchinina

2009: 23–24). In the area of forensic linguistics, co-operation between legal linguists and courts is increasing, mainly regarding defamation cases – libel and slander – as well as hate crimes (cf. Kusov 2004, Baranov 2011). Currently, pragmatically oriented research is gaining momentum in Russia. Researchers such as N.D. Arutiunova, N.K. Rjabceva (1995), N. D. Golev (2004) and T. Dubrovskaya (2010, 2014) make use of pragmalinguistic methods and discourse analysis. Discourse analysis and speech act theory are fundamental to Russian legal linguistics developed abroad by G. Freidhof (1995, 1996). Also Vlasenko (1997) developed in his (RU) *Язык права* (*Iazyk prava*) a semiotically oriented approach to legal-linguistic issues which is mostly grounded in research available in Russia (Mattila 2006: 9). The on-line research project *Jurislingvistika*, (RU) *Юрислингвистика*, based at the Altai State University, provides in the Russian language information about legal-linguistic research in Russia and abroad.

2.1.3.5 Greek legal linguistics

A review of the legal-linguistic research accomplished in Greece in the recent decades has been prepared by Karolina Gortych-Michalak (2013). In the review, around thirty monographs have been used to distill the results of research efforts that include works by G. Angelidis, D. Mexis, A. Stavrakis, G. Rallis, D. Evrygenis, E. Panaretou, H. Paparizos, as well as G. Brousalis and G. Mikros. The monograph also includes an overview of the relevant legilinguistic research concerning the Cypriot law in the Greek language. Likewise, the author mentions the particular situation in Greece that has been the controversial debate about the use of *dimotiki* in the legislation. These aspects have been previously scrutinized in the legal-linguistic research by Heikki E.S. Mattila (2012) as well as Jaakko Husa (2007). For Gortych-Michalak, these aspects constitute a particularity in the development of the legal language in Greece. They are also responsible for some delays in treatment of other legal-linguistic characteristics that were canvassed more fully in other countries. The approach to the Greek language in the monographs is decidedly neohellenistic and it particularly stresses the development determined by the use of dimotiki in the Greek legislation. Furthermore, when taking into account the Cypriot legislation in the Greek language, Gortych-Michalak discovers the correlation between the structure of texts and their belonging to different legal traditions of common law and civil law. At this point, it would be also important to contrast the development of the textual structure of the Greek law with German texts that have influenced the modern Greek law, as done e.g. by J. Husa in his quoted work on the Greek legal language (pp. 133–134). J. Husa also stressed that Greek texts are not particularly difficult to translate into Finnish due to the conceptual affinity provided by the Continental law. Eleni Panaretou (2005, 2009) proposed an analysis of the contemporary Greek legal language that she approached as a type of discourse. Her work concentrates upon the language of Greek statutes and stresses the synchronic perspective in the analysis of the legal language. It might be also perceived as introducing the paradigmatic change into the Greek legal-linguistic research. In the more traditional research, historical aspects of the development of the Greek legal language as well as the shift from the more classical form known as *katharevousa* to the demotic form absorbed the researchers. Due to the historically founded specifics in the legal-linguistic debate in Greece the synchronic approach was much less present. E. Panaretou's work contributed therefore to the modernization of the Greek legal-linguistic research. Furthermore, classical Greek law and language were studied by Gernet (1964), Biscardi (1982), Avotins (1986) and Laffi (2013).

2.1.3.6 Legal theory and legal language in Scandinavia

Furthermore, it would be important to stress particularly the development in Scandinavia and the Scandinavian legal realism where scholars such as Karl Olivekrona attempted to implement the linguistic turn in law (Olivekrona 1969: 10; cf. also Peczenik 1986: 168–175). The Scandinavian legal-linguistic tradition is far-reaching and particularly important for the development of the legal argumentation (Peczenik 1995). Serpe (2006) demonstrates on the example of human rights that the linguistic analysis in the Scandinavian legal realism was since the forties of the past century embedded in conceptual clarifications. Yet, in difference to any other variety of conceptual analysis the Scandinavian scholars attempted also an ontological determination of concepts used in law and in the legal language in general. In his overview A. Serpe stresses the contributions by T. Eckhoff, P.O. Ekelöf (cf. also Peczenik 1986: 261–263), I. Strahl, A. Hägerström, K. Olivecrona, V. Lundstedt, A. Wedberg, N.K. Sundby, T. Opsahl and F. Castberg. Unsurprisingly, Alf Ross' investigations of concepts in law as hollow words without independent semantic reference (cf. Ross 1957) take a particular place in the Scandinavian legal-linguistic research. Some aspects of the Scandinavian approaches to legal language are mentioned in Galdia (1995); the research by N. Jareborg (1972) into fraudulent acts committed through the abuse of language is mentioned in Galdia (2008). Meanwhile, also in Scandinavian countries interest in law and language issues emerged chronologically in historical and philological studies. In Sweden researchers such as A. Ahlström (1912), N. Jörgensen (1987), T. Wennström (1946), P.A. Wiktorsson (1981), H. Landqvist (2008) dealt with the emergence of the legal terminology and the style in historical legal documents. B. Wedberg (1928) and B. Wennström (1996) dealt with the legal style, E. Wessén (1965) authored a monograph on the Swedish legal language. C. I. Ståhle (1958) and B. Ruthström (2003) dealt with structural, syntactic and philological aspects of Old Norse legal language, B.M. Löfstedt dealt with Medieval Latin in the law of the Langobards. In Denmark, S. Benson (1994) researched into elderly Danish legal language in maritime legislation. In Norway, M. Sørlie (1965) dealt with elderly Faeroese legal terminology. Nordic law and its language were researched also by scholars abroad: K. von Amira (1882/85), K. von See (1964), H. Beck (1983), and U. Ebel (1994). Today, in Danmark J. Engberg (1997, 2001, 2013b) developed a theoretical approach to legal language anchored in applied linguistics; he published widely on general aspects of the use of legal language, frequently in contrastive research that includes also Danish. A.L. Kjær (1990) dealt with legal phraseology in a contrastive perspective. In Norway, I. Simonnaes (2012) dealt with legal communication and legal translation. The second trend typical of most other regions is the plain language debate (Nilsson 1976: 49–54) that starts with Geers (1853). In Sweden, P.E. Nilsson (1976) dealt with legal language as specialized register. M. Hadryan (2015) published in Poland a monograph on the development of plain language drafting strategies in Poland and in Sweden. Heikki E.S. Mattila (2005: 44) underlines the use of national languages in Scandinavia; Galdia (2003: 124–125) mentions the emergence of the Finnish legal vocabulary based on Swedish lexemes; Landqvist (2008: 157–171) characterized the influence that D. Ehrenståle Nehrman exercised in the process of formation of legal Swedish, he also researched the formation of the Swedish legal terminology (Landqvist 2003). Also the Finnish legal linguistics is rooted in the legal theory. The collection of articles offered Heikki E.S. Mattila *Kielen ja oikeuden kohtaamisia* (Foley et al. 2008) shows the diversity of approaches to the legal language there. It focuses on Heikki E.S. Mattila's approach that could be seen as complementing the existing Finnish legal theory in which scholars such as Aulis Aarnio addressed questions of the interpretation of legal texts and legal argumentation (Galdia 2008: 18). Its roots may be found in works by Osvi Lahtinen and Kaarle Makkonen who researched the linguistic and logical basis of the law (Galdia 1995: 33–34). Additionally, Pajula (1960) provided an overview over the history of the legal Finnish; Bonsdorf (1984) sketched the development of the Swedish legal language in Finland. Recently, Mattila described the development of legal dictionaries and stressed the necessity of terminological research into legal Finnish (2009). A. Aarnio (2014) published a summary of his theory of legal interpretation and legal argumentation (cf. also Aarnio 1989), T. Kinnunen (2006) dealt with the relation of legal translation and legal interpretation, T. Fonsén (2011) wrote about the influence of legal German upon legal Finnish, J. Niemi-Kiesiläinen (2006, 2007), P. Honkatukia, H. Karma and M. Ruuskanen dealt with discursive aspects of law, E. Lindroos (2015) compared phraseologisms in German and Finnish court decisions in the area of criminal law. Overall, Finnish scholars have primarily tied their work in with the hermeneutic, pragmatic and general semiotic facets of the legal language and published their findings in occasional volumes (Hirvonen, Tuori (eds.) 1990; Jyränki (ed.) 1999; Salmi-Tolonen (ed.) 2001). Heikki E.S. Mattila synthesized most of these views in his conception of the comparative legal linguistics. His work is the most advanced and systematic attempt to cope with the legal-linguistic diversity in the world. Therefore, due to the multidirectional and interdisciplinary vision his conception remains open to its further development toward comparative law or toward legal theory as well as toward a merger of both. The particular strength of the legal-linguistic research in Finland is its usefulness for lexicological or forensic-linguistic projects (cf. Mattila 2004; Working Group 2001). In Mattila et al. (2010b) a step forwards has been undertaken in order to show more comprehensively the development of the Finnish legal language as well as the situation of the Swedish language used as another official language in legal contexts in Finland.

2.1.3.6.1 Heikki E.S. Mattila's comparative legal linguistics

Particularly productive for the development of the legal-linguistic research has been the approach developed by Heikki E.S. Mattila in Finland that he termed *comparative legal linguistic.* Mattila developed his conception of *comparative legal linguistics* in close relation to comparative law. The initial matrix of comparative legal linguistics can be found in R. David's *comparative law* (cf. David 1978, translated by Mattila into Finnish and published between 1982–1986) and G. Cornu's conception of *legal linguistics* (Cornu 2005, first edition 1990). These two conceptions merged in Mattila's thinking into *comparative legal linguistics.* Yet, unlike most legal comparatists, he did not concentrate on the functional or structural elements of different legal systems. Instead, he focused rather on the linguistic form of law and predominantly on the legal terminology. He finally combined the analysis of legal terminology with communicative aspects of law. By so doing, he made an important step toward the consolidation of the disparate data that legal-linguistic research engendered when he started his systematizing work in legal linguistics. In his research published mainly in the Finnish language Mattila pondered over the systematic frame of reference for the comparative-linguistic approach that he now follows with admirable consequence (cf. Mattila 2008, 2010c). Mattila started with general features of the legal language that he had distilled through the analysis of particular legal languages. He focuses particularly on problems of legal terminology that he also synthesized in his chapter *Legal Vocabulary* (cf. Mattila 2012b) in the otherwise rather unsystematic *The Oxford Handbook of Language and Law.* Legal-linguistic comparison emerged in his conception of legal linguistics between rivalry and complementarity of legal languages. Consequently, Mattila can justly claim that some languages play a formatting role in this process while others mostly follow paths beaten by the dominating legal languages. This result justifies the choice of languages that are analyzed in his works. His survey of languages starts with legal Latin, continues over German, French, and Spanish up to the English legal language. For Mattila, legal Latin has always been fundamental to the development and the understanding of legal language. Mattila insisted therefore in many of his publications upon the importance of legal Latin for the legal-linguistic research (cf. Mattila 2004, 2010a). Unlike many other legal writers, he did not limit his involvement in this area to erudite statements, but became engaged in a series of research projects into legal Latin and its contemporary use that led to surprising results. They are accounted for in his book's chapter on legal Latin (Mattila 2013a). Recently, also scholars such as J.-L. Halpérin, J. Husa, and M. Zabłocka stressed the fundamental role of Latin as a basis for the understanding of the legal language. J. Husa (2011) perceived legal Latin as a linguistic context or grammar of law. M. Zabłocka (2010) spoke about the Roman roots of the contemporary legal language. For J.-L. Halpérin (2009: 59) it is evident that legal Latin and Roman law are eminently present in the process of legal globalization. Therefore, it is very convincing that Mattila discusses in his books the heritage of legal Latin exhaustively. Other main languages that are treated in his works combine diachronic and synchronic aspects and stress the linguistic interrelations in the process of emergence of singular legal languages.

2.1.3.7 Diversity of legal Chinese and understandability of legal Japanese

Likewise, a group of Chinese researchers attempted to determine the scope of legal linguistics (Zhou 2003). They dealt with the linguistic legislation and with different private law traditions in mainland China and in Hong Kong which has been strongly influenced by common law. They had also to cope with the unusually long history of development of legal terminology from the Tang to the Qing dynasty and within the Occidentalization process in the Chinese law. They also underscored the importance of linguistic legislation in China that in their view results from the power exercised by language. Later, Hongying Liu (2007) published an introduction into legal linguistics. Modern voice analyzing methods as well as quantitative analyses are explored as well (Zhou 2003). Forensic linguistics seems to dominate practically oriented research, e.g. in Zhang Cuiling's *An Acoustic Study on Disguised Voices*, published 2005 as a PhD-thesis by the Department of Forensic Science of the Nankai University (Salmi-Tolonen 2008a: 380). Also Du Jinbang (2004) published a work dedicated to the construction of forensic linguistics and stressed its systematic structure as well as its theoretical research basis. Explicitly pragmalinguistic research on illocutionary and perlocutionary acts in legal discourses has been undertaken by Weiming Liu (2005). Suqing Yu (2010) analyzed the legal language. In Hong Kong, Ho Yan Chan (2012, 2014) developed an innovative approach to legal lexicography. Kwai Hang Ng (2009) wrote about legal bilingualism in Hong Kong. Central to modern systematic research into the Chinese language of law has been the semiotic approach developed by Deborah Cao (2004). Cao focuses upon the contemporary language of law toward the background of cultural and social values coined and inherited by the Chinese during their particularly long period of uninterrupted and traceable development of their state and society. The first innovation introduced by Cao is the interest in meaning and interpretation as dominating features of law. Classical interest in the philosophical analysis of Chinese legal concepts, although not really abandoned appears in Cao's approach in another light. Second, Cao makes regularly use of the comparative perspective when investigating the Chinese legal language. She found out that the legal Chinese when compared with legal English appears ordinary and plain (Cao 2004: vii). She stressed however that the lack of complexity in linguistic utterances does not necessarily make them easy to apply. This finding is also in accordance with pragmatic approaches to the legal language where legal-linguistic operations such as interpretation are perceived as structural constants of law that cannot be overcome with linguistic plainness (Galdia 2014: 246). Cao discovered in this context the imprecision of the Chinese legal language that causes more interpretive problems than many complex formulations in English legalese. D. Cao (2008) also discussed ambiguity and vagueness issues in the legal Chinese in a cross-linguistic perspective. Third, Cao stressed communicative and discursive aspects of the use of language in law, also in the diachronic perspective that looks at the classics (Cao 2004: 20–34). Cao's research into the Chinese legal language is the first serious step toward the establishing of legal Sinology postulated already by J. Escarra (1936). Abroad, next to J. Escarra (1936), R. May (1980), V. Pasternak (1996), S. Gu (2006), J. Grzybek (2013) and G. Mannoni (2015) dealt with legal Chinese. In Hong Kong, the *International Journal of Legal Discourse* informs about developments in this broad area of research.

In Japan, researchers such as T. Okubo, S. Hayashi, E. Iwabuchi and T. Nakano dealt with the Japanese legal register mostly from the perspective of its understandability (Okawara 1998: 73–80). Hayashi pointed already 1959 to the fact that lengthy sentences in legal Japanese texts result from embedded modifiers, conjunction clauses and distant placement of subject and object (Okawara 1989: 74). This initiated the modern discussion about the relation between the length of a sentence and its understandability that is mentioned later in this book (cf. 2.3.2.3). Y. Horie and P. Trzaskawka (2015) analyzed and compiled characteristic features of the Japanese legal language and contrasted it with legal Polish (cf. also Horie 2010a). Y. Horie (2010b) dealt also with translation problems, especially in Japanese-Polish translation. Also S. Hotta (2009, 2010) dealt with legal Japanese. Furthermore, Y.J. Youn (2016) wrote about the Korean and the German legal languages.

2.1.3.8 Tendency toward rationalization of language use in the USA

American authors stressed in the beginning of the research into Law and Language issues such as the emergence of the English legal terminology. They then developed a tendency toward forming a modernized legal language in that they responded to the claims in the plain language movement for a legal language directly accessible to citizens (cf. Tiersma 1999: 211). This particular interest is anchored in the American tradition initiated by D. Mellinkoff (1963) to deal with legal language from the most striking perspective for its users. Mellinkoff assumed that this language use is mostly linked to specific legal concepts which draw the attention of the users because they differ from the ordinary language. He tried then to explain the etymology of those concepts with the intention to make the legal terminology understandable. Yet he also stressed the necessity of rationalization of legal English (Mellinkoff 1963: VII). P. Tiersma drew from it the conclusion that the understandability of the legal language can be achieved through its modernization rather than through etymological and historically oriented research, although he also allotted a considerable part of his work to the historical development of legal English. Another research topic in the U.S. is the analysis of the speech in the courtroom where sometimes methods of the conversational analysis or methods neighboring this specific pragmalinguistic approach are used in relation to narratives, pleadings, cross-examination, why-questions or code switching (Solan 1993; Tiersma 1999: 147–198). P. Tiersma also stressed the importance of the speech act theory in the analysis of the legal language (1999: vii) and applied it in the discussion of some characteristic constructions of the legal language. Another American legal-linguistic specialty is forensic linguistics (Shuy 2006, 2012, 2014) and a research field called artificial intelligence and law that includes aspects of formalization in the legal language, esp. the open-texture concepts (Berman and Hafner 1987). This interest is reflected in the general-linguistic modeling-approach to language that initiates with the generative grammar by N. Chomsky and continues to more contemporary works by Mark C. Baker (2002) and Ray Jackendorff (2002). Last but not least, the American legal theory includes voluminous contributions to issues that are fundamental to legal linguistics such as argumentation and interpretation in law (cf. Atiyah/Summers 1987). Andrei Marmor (2014) proposed an overview of pragmatic issues relevant to legal linguistics that also form the conceptual basis of this book (cf. also Marmor/Soames 2011). Issues of linguistic indeterminacy in its relation to law have been explored by B. Bix (1993, 2012). Brian G. Slocum (2016) continued his exploration of legal interpretation, especially the use of the argument of ordinary meaning as an interpretive standard (cf. also Slocum 2012).

2.1.3.9 A note on Latin America

Latin-American legal linguistics has its roots in the legal theory that was traditionally based upon European legal theory and legal philosophy (cf. Alchourrón/Bulygin 1971, Bulygin 1983). More recently the influence of investigations by Manuel Atienza related to legal argumentation has been pointed out as central to the legal-theoretical discussion there (cf. Matias Camargo 2012). The legal-semiotic perspective has been represented already at an early stage by R. Carrión Wam (1982). Recently also the analytic philosophy of Anglo-American origin and the discourse analysis gave rise to legal-linguistic works that correspond to the approach adopted in this book such as F. Constantino Martínez's and M.A. Rivera León's *Elementos de lingüistica jurídica* (2010) or A.A. de Souza's *Linguagem jurídica e poder* (2005). Legal language has been also scrutinized by T.S. Ferraz Júnior (1997) and Eduardo C.B. Bittar (2009). Legal translation is a recurrent topic in many research papers on the American continent (cf. Mittmann 2003). Particularly strong is the interest in and support for the use of indigenous languages as legal languages (Oliveira 2004, Morello 2012). Some research abroad concerns Latin American legal languages and their specific features, for instance the Argentinian slang *Lunfardo* that includes lexical units related to law (cf. Nowak 2010).

2.1.3.10 A glimpse of Africa

Legal-linguistic research in Sub-Saharan Africa is difficult to be stated in its entirety due to problems with the access to publications. However, some tendencies can be identified. Sub-Saharan African legal linguistics develops toward the background of research into former colonial legal languages such as English or French that dominate the juridical reality in many African countries (cf. Opeibi 2012: 282). The research perspective that focuses upon local languages mainly developed around the topics of linguistic legislation, language planning, and linguistic policy (Ikobwa

2008, Ayub 2010, Mukhwana 2010 and 2013, Opeibi 2012, Becker 2013, Oduor et al. 2016). Gender issues in the legal language are reflected by L.N. Omondi (1989). Also issues related to legal translation became more relevant in African countries under conditions of increasing access to courts of citizens who do not speak any former colonial language used in judicial institutions (Moeketsi 1999, Onsongo 2010, Wangui 2015). In this context also research into legal literacy developed to mark the necessity to communicate legal regulation to citizens in a more accessible way (cf. Ngugi 1994). Equally, linguistic pragmatics (cf. Mwangi 2003) and the general theory of terminology (Mohammed 1987) are present in the African research. This book also provides a brief overview of some terminological issues in legal Swahili (cf. 5.1.4.1).

2.1.3.11 Particular and international research

H.E.S. Mattila (2006) quotes recent studies into particular issues of the legal language. This sort of detailed research into particular aspects of the legal language is and will remain for some time fundamental to the development of legal linguistics. This detailed research concerns for instance the use of the conjunction *hvis* (NO for *if*) in the Norwegian legal language (Mattila 2006: 73), verbal substantives in the legal Swedish (ib.), use of verbs in the legislative language (ib.), use of tenses and modes, especially the conditional (Nowak-Michalska 2012), use of passive mode (ib.), prison slang (Mattila 2006: 6), professional jargon used among jurists (Mattila 2006: 5), legislative drafting (Mattila 2006: 10), forensic linguistics (Mattila 2006: 11), pronunciation of Latin in the common law countries (Mattila 2006: 12), legal symbols in Finland (Mattila 2006: 13) and in Russia (ib.), legal Latin (Mattila 2006: 125–158). A group of Finnish lexicologists prepared an innovative dictionary of legal abbreviations (Mattila 2004) which continues lexicographic efforts undertaken there in the publication of Finnish court terminology (Working Group: 2001). Also in Japan a Standard Bilingual English-Japanese Dictionary of Legal Terms has been completed by a working group of the Cabinet Secretariat in 2006 (Anderson/Okuda 2007: 139). J. Husa (2007: 52, 53) dealt within his broader research into the Greek legal language with prepositions and prefixes in Greek legal texts. Markhardt (2006) prepared a dictionary of Austrian legal, business and administrative terminology in which the specific Austrian-German lexical units were collected. Warda-Radys (2006) scrutinized Polish language administrative documents in medieval German-language Dantzig. Znamenáčková (2007) researched nominal, verbal and prepositional word clusters in different text types of the German civil law in the perspective of their stability and variability. In Vilar Sánches (2007) microfunctional linguistic analysis has been applied by different researchers upon German and Spanish language employment contracts. Microfunctions such as conditions or obligations and many others were analyzed there in a comparative perspective. In Heller/Ehlich (2007) terminological, contrastive and communicational aspects of the legal language are discussed. Legal Arabic was researched by S. Gu (2006), Š. Ramić (2003), and L. Edzard (1998). Next to these works, international legal-linguistic research is present in collections of articles prepared by scholars from diverse continents. For instance, Kredens and al. (2007) insisted upon the international perspective in the legal-linguistic research. Wagner and Cacciaguidi-Fahy (2008) edited a volume on the understandability of the legal language in different legal cultures. A group of legal lexicologists (Mac Aodha 2014) prepared a collection of articles about history, theory and practice of legal lexicography. A. Durant and J.H.C. Leung (2016) authored a modern introduction into legal linguistics. Also my book fits better into the international rather than into the national or geographically determined research perspective.

Overall, the increasing number of detailed research centered on legal linguistics is encouraging. Nevertheless, no generalization of the research data is possible at this stage, partly due to the methodological pluralism in the research and partly because the general theory of legal linguistics is still underdeveloped. However, two main fundamental tendencies seem to dominate the research. The first is grounded in the legal theory and the other is rather independent of the legal science, and develops an autonomous view upon the legal language from the perspective of the general linguistic theory. In terms of methodology, I rather favor a synthesis of both because the purely legal-theoretical research stresses mostly the procedural aspects of language use and avoids any involvement in material issues of legal argumentation. The purely linguistic research, in turn, risks drifting into the conception of a legal linguistics without law that is less productive than the synthetic or interdisciplinary legal linguistics.

2.1.4 Conceptions of Legal Linguistics

In the above description I concentrated on topics discussed in the legal-linguistic research according to their geographic distribution. However, also a conceptual characterization of the research is worthwhile considering. This characterization helps overcome geographic boundaries and it also helps develop a unified legal linguistics. This is a task for the future legal linguistics as nowadays the interaction between the different tendencies and schools all over the world is not particularly close (Mattila 2006: 9). Therefore, paradoxically, it is easier to characterize tendencies in the development of legal linguistics in terms of geography than in terms of its conceptions and approaches.

It may also be premature to write a history of the subject legal linguistics. Yet, a sketch of an outline appears possible at this stage. It seems that the discussion of the style used by jurists in their speaking and writing about law initiated further going exploration of the subject as a first step toward establishing a new branch of knowledge. Scholars pretended that jurist were using a specific, legal style that they tended to characterize (Dölle 1949; Bartoszewicz 1979; Pigolkin 1990). Attention then turned to legal concepts that for a long time constituted the main point of interest for legal positivists. Later on, with increasing internationalization of legal contacts the incompatibility of these concepts in legal translation has been discovered as a particular problem. These problems, so the research of these times, were not caused by insufficient language knowledge of translators but by the lack of a common reference system for legal concepts. It has been found out that all these concepts were embedded in broader textual units that form the legal discourse. In parallel to these developments, in the U.S. the interest in the problem of understandability of legal language came up. As a result of these efforts, legal linguistics became institutionalized as a research object and as a teaching subject. It took several decades to achieve the results mentioned above with a couple of words. While keeping in mind these particular historical developments we can now engage in the discussion of some particular issues that concern the object of all attempts at understanding law from the linguistic perspective, i.e. the legal language.

2.1.4.1 Legal linguistics as semiotics of law

The most fundamental approach to legal language is the one based explicitly on the conceptual framework of general semiotics. As a matter of fact, the general semiotic analysis seems to be the most appropriate tool for the analysis of language simply because language is a sign system (Pigolkin 1990: 4, Galdia 2014: 113–164). No other approach can therefore compete with the semiotic one in the attempt to display the legal language in all its complexity. Explicitly semiotic works aim therefore at describing law as a sign system. Sometimes they reveal ambitions to lay foundations for a semiotically sensitive theory of law (Jackson 1985: ix). Sometimes they may attempt at clarifying semiotic presuppositions and perspectives of other theoretical works in which the inherent semiotic foundations have to be uncovered (Jackson 1985: 147–225, Ahonen 1988, Kevelson 1990). Roque Carrión Wam (1982) described the background and the development of the legal-semiotic research until 1980. In his report the origins of legal-semiotic investigations are seen in Félix E. Oppenheim's *Outline of a logical analysis of law* (published in Philosophy of Science 11, 1944) and later in works by George Kalinowski, especially in his already mentioned *Introduction à la logique juridique* (1965). However, only rare are studies which deal with legally relevant material against the background of the semiotic conceptual apparatus. For instance, A. Greimas (1976) undertook an analysis of the French Company Law Statute from 1966, (FR) Loi n. 66–537, but his work remained in every term an exception (cf. Jackson 1985: 33). Also A. Wagner and S. Cacciaguidi-Fahy contribute regularly to the development of legal semiotics. Nowadays, especially the *International Journal for the Semiotics of Law* publishes contributions to this field of interdisciplinary studies.

2.1.4.1.1 E. Bülow's semiotic conception of legal linguistics

A semiotically founded pragmalinguistic conception of legal linguistics has been developed in Germany by Edeltraud Bülow, mostly in her teaching on the theoretical fundamentals of the subject in the 80s of the past century. The semiotic basis of law has been seen there in non-verbal signs inventories covering both the spatial and the temporal dimensions of the phenomenon (proxemy and chronomy) as well as in its complementary features such as gestures, mimics or kinetics. According to Bülow, legal signs emerge in this broad spectrum and constitute more specific units such as statutes, commentaries or contracts which can be analyzed as text types. Moreover, many of these text types, mostly specimens of legislation and judicial decisions, come about in institutionalized processes. These text types which reflect narration, exposition, description, argumentation, instruction and so on can be further specified with the help of the speech act theory. There, propositions can be qualified, for instance, as threat or promise. In addition to it, temporal and spatial aspects of the legal language became manifest in the specific use of deixis and anaphora in legal texts. Furthermore, the signs of law are used in discourses dominated by ethical or political issues (Bülow 1986: 105). Therefore, next to the broad context of their spatial and temporal emergence also their particular use in these contexts must be taken into consideration. Only then are the signs of law construed in their entirety as parts of the life form in which humans interact toward the background of their complex culture in which societies are formed as results of historical processes. Bülow's approach (1985: 36) is grounded in general semiotics and anthropology which provide an orientation for pragmalinguistics that in some other approaches occasionally hangs in a vacuum. E. Bülow herself characterized her approach as follows:

> *Rechtslinguistik untersucht die besonderen Beziehungen zwischen Sprache und Recht bzw. der Rechtsgemeinschaft, zwischen den sprachlichen und nichtsprachlichen Zeichensystemen, die nicht nur in den Institutionen von Rechtsprechung und Rechtspflege verwendet werden, sondern auch im Rechtsbewusstsein des Laien eine zentrale Orientierungsfunktion haben für die Organisation sozialen Handelns.*

E. Bülow also provided examples of particular areas of legal-linguistic research:

> *Das Kommunikationsverhältnis von Angeklagten vor Gericht und die dazugehörigen Rituale sowie die institutionsspezifischen Textsorten (Gutachten, Urteil, Anklageschrift, Plädoyer) werden dabei genauso untersucht wie die Gestaltung von Räumlichkeiten, in denen Gerichtsverhandlungen stattfinden (z.B. Sitzordnung und Anordnung der Sitze, Kleidung, Utensilien verschiedenster Art). Ein weiterer wichtiger Forschungsschwerpunkt ist der Bedeutungswandel juristischer und ethischer Grundbegriffe, wie z.B. „Leben" und „Tod", „Arbeit", „Gewalt" u.a.*

In many respects, Bülow's fundamentals of legal linguistics come close to B. Jackson's conception of legal semiotics and to the broad epistemologically founded view that dominates the work of Maria Teresa Lizisowa in her *Komunikacyjna teoria języka prawnego* (2017), (cf. 2.1.3.3). In above conceptions the spatial and temporal spectrum in which legal signs emerge reaches the outer limits of the space where legal signs are constituted in the societal communication. Bülow adds to it the social-pragmatic perspective in which legal signs are used in society whereas Jackson concentrates mostly on the process in which the legal signs emerge. E. Bülow's semiotic conception of legal linguistics underlies these lectures and my conception of legal linguistics as a discursive practice.

2.1.4.2 Legal linguistics as hermeneutics of law

Traditional hermeneutic methods that aimed at determining the objective meaning of texts were broadly used in the legal theory and in the legal sciences (Đorđević 2002: 6). Since H.G. Gadamer's (D) *Wahrheit und Methode* (1965), (UK) *Truth and Method* (1975), hermeneutic standards have significantly changed. The understanding of texts is based there on a hermeneutic circle which means in essence that the understanding of the whole text depends on the understanding of its parts and vice versa (Juhl 1986: 7). The text is no longer construed in an objective isolation from its reader; its understanding presupposes the fusion of the textual horizon and that of the reader (Juhl 1986: 7). This conclusion is crucial to the interpretation of legal texts in legal linguistics (Gizbert-Studnicki 1987: 478). Finally, authors using contemporary hermeneutic approaches to law such as Jürgen Habermas (1988) stressed the ideological facets of law which they perceive as enclosed in social mechanisms legitimizing judicial decisions. Critical views upon language use in law dominate also in F. Müller (1999), H. Rottleuthner (1981), and H. Rodingen (1977). Other hermeneutic approaches stress the interpretive nature of activities connected to law (Đorđević 2002: 6). Hermeneutic research includes also numerous works about hermeneutics of the judicial decision making process (cf. Forsthoff 1940/54; Rottleuthner 1973; Wróblewski 1988). Judicial decisions are discussed there usually in a broader perspective than ours. Therefore, many of them belong to the general legal theory rather than to legal linguistics.

2.1.4.3 Legal linguistics as introduction into law

For Gérard Cornu (2005) legal linguistics could function as an introduction to legal studies and especially to the legal terminology. In the consequence of this approach law would be perceived as a linguistic phenomenon stated in texts where aspects of the specific legal terminology and the structure of the legal discourse dominate the overall view. Cornu's approach differs from ours in that it is based on semantics; we however, focus on pragmatic aspects of law. Like Cornu, I posit that legal linguistics can be instrumental as an introduction to law and additionally I stress that it can even function as its theory. Legal linguistics would be thinkable and useful even if the role that language plays in law would be much more constrained than it seems to be now. Cornu (2005: 1) notes in a context different from ours the existence of law as a language: *Dans de plus vastes perspectives, on aurait à se demander si le droit même n'est pas, en soi, un language.* Later on, the same author refuses however to consider the existence of the grammar of legal language: *L'étude grammaticale d'un énoncé de droit est un exercice utile; une grammaire juridique une absurdité* (Cornu 2005: 29). Let me remark at this stage that the destiny of a legal grammar depends very much upon the notion of grammar one is inclined to adopt. For instance,

B. Jackson (1985: 111) devoted a whole chapter to the conception of 'Legal Grammar' in his work on semiotics and legal theory. Notwithstanding some conceptual divergencies, the overall approach to legal linguistics as an introduction into law is a step worth considering, especially in the legal education.

2.1.4.4 Legal linguistics as part of comparative law

Heikki E.S. Mattila anchored his conception of legal linguistics in comparative law (Galdia 2006: 271, cf. also Lundmark 2012, pp. 51 sqq.). In his fundamental work *Vertaileva oikeuslingvistiikka* (2002b) as well as in the English (Mattila 2006, 2013a) and the French editions (2012a) of the Finnish original he provided first of all an overview of existing issues within legal linguistics perceived as a product of crossing legal and linguistic systems. His comparative approach is distinct from the monolingual perspective adapted by other researchers, such as G. Cornu or P. Tiersma, who usually focused on the relation between the ordinary language and the legal language perceived as special register. Mattila prepared the ground, both in terms of diachronic and synchronic research, for the mapping of the conceptual landscape in legal linguistics. He identified the method for comparative research into legal terminology and legal translation. Additionally, he also selected the relevant languages for the legal-linguistic research. Mattila stressed, unlike many other writers dealing with Law and Language, the shaping role that Latin language has had for the emergence of the legal language and engaged in detailed, also quantitative analyses in this largely abandoned area (Mattila 2002c). In his approach he revigorated the research into legal Latin which may have consequences for the processes in which the language of the global law is coming into being. Finally, his research facilitates the broadening of the perspective in legal linguistics, particularly concerning speech acts in law, toward pragmatic issues which are stressed in this book. Mattila's approach is not only developed along the lines of comparative law, it can be made operative in comparative law as well. Also non-linguistically construed conceptions of comparative law like R. Kraakman's comparative and functional approach toward corporate law stress the necessity to develop an appropriate language in which issues of comparative corporate law could be addressed without confusion and misinterpretation. Kraakman (2004: 4) writes about this goal: "Of equal importance, we wish to offer a common language and a general analytic framework with which to understand the purposes that can potentially be served by corporate law, and with which to compare and evaluate the efficacy of different legal regimes in serving those purposes." Innovative concept creation like *corporate constituencies, non-shareholder constituencies* or the modified concepts of *legal personality* of *company* or of *agency* (Kraakman 2004: 7) are examples of the efficiency of this approach. Mattila's work is suitable to function as a background source for this sort of detailed legal-linguistic constructions. Also B. Grossfeld (1990: 103) argued from the perspective of comparative law that legal language is its essential concomitant which in his view does not make it any easier. We will see later that the emerging global law will also need a new language. Works such as Mattila's are fundamental to its development. Meanwhile, comparative law is closest to legal linguistics in the research directed toward contrasting or comparing legal-linguistic operations such as legal argumentation and legal justification. On the other side, legal comparative research that focuses upon legal regulation is rather remote from the objectives pursued by legal linguists as is the research into foreign law, i.e. a law of a foreign country (cf. Husa 2015a: 32).

2.1.4.5 Legal linguistics as forensic linguistics

Forensic linguistics focuses upon the use of language within judicial institutions of different sorts (Mattila 2006: 11). For this part of the research not the specific legal register is decisive but the institutional framework in which different varieties of language can be used. Even if legal professionals and laypersons use different varieties of language in different discourses within legal institutions, they nevertheless used to speak differently there than outside institutional legal settings. This approach is particularly valuable because it makes plain that the language used in law is necessarily bound to institutions and apparently would not survive long without or beyond them. For many, especially in the English speaking countries, forensic linguistics is an applied branch of linguistic studies which concentrates on the identification of speakers through voice analysis. This part of forensic linguistics is dominated by technological processes which use phonetic research for investigative or evidential purposes within legal proceedings (Salmi-Tolonen 2008a: 375), especially when authorship issues are at stake (Olsson 2007: 28–29). Alderman (2005) characterized the methods of forensic speaker identification and described the *Bayesian Likelihood Ratio* that is instrumental in discriminating same-speaker pairs of speech samples from different speaker pairs. Forensic linguistics is sometimes limited to courtroom discourse, sometimes even to the communication between legal professionals and witnesses, as is the case in Olanrewaju (2009). Olanrewaju analyzed various forms of questions, the wh-questions, alternative questions, yes/no questions and declarative questions as samples of the legal discourse. In the light of this research, lawyers as specialists in formulating questions typical of the legal procedure maintain tight control of the courtroom discourse.

An example that illustrates legal-forensic interests is the research into *prosopagnosia* and *phonagnosia.* Prosopagnosia and phonagnosia both play a role in the procedurality of law. Prosopagnosia or faulty identification of offenders by eyewitnesses due to their mistakes in distinguishing faces is a challenge to the procedure of testifying that relies on this ability. Testifying in courts leads regularly to wrong convictions for crimes because witnesses have falsely identified them and they rely on their imaginary recollections. Meantime, some people have also problems with recognizing familiar faces or familiar voices on telephone (phonagnosia). Both prosopagnosia and phonagnosia defined by the research as dissociation between familiar and unfamiliar voices may therefore deform the court procedure that blindly trusts in human capacities which as a rule are not tested in courts. Common law experience with forensic linguistics is reflected in Shuy (2006). Last but not least, forensic linguistics is perceived as combining aspects of voice analysis (forensic phonetics) and semantic or pragmatic studies which relate to language use in courts as underlined by Salmi-Tolonen (2008a: 393). Both Coulthard and Johnson (2007: 5–7) as well as Olsson (2007: 4–8) sketched the history of the subject in their introductory books. Oxburgh et al. (2015) combined forensic psychology, linguistics and law enforcement. In this book forensic linguistics is understood in the broader sense described by Salmi-Tolonen. The *International Journal of Speech, Language and the Law*, published by the International Association of Forensic Linguists and the International Association for Forensic Phonetics and Acoustics informs about particular research in this area.

2.1.4.6 Legal linguistics as interlingual comparison

The interlingual perspective upon the language use in law comes close to philological research. The researcher concentrates there upon one national language, for instance on Finnish or English. She may elucidate the emergence of the legal language toward the background of the ordinary language or describe the processes which underlie the evolution of conceptual meaning in the legal texts. Works such as Risto Hiltunen's *Chapters on Legal English* (1990) are deliberately situated within philology or linguistics and do not expose any ambitions to contribute to legal sciences or to the legal theory in particular. In this sort of research documents, mostly historical sources are used as a basis for the description of the development of the scrutinized language. Thus, they limit their scope to their proper discipline, in the case to English philology. They make clear how legal language changes with time and illustrate problems which non-jurists unaware of the legal language encounter when they try to understand legal texts. Also the author of these lines while working on (FIN) *Lakisaksa* (German legal language) used linguistic research on special registers to cope with linguistic terminology. Legal linguistics emerged in my *Lakisaksa* (Galdia 1999) as a matrix of legal systems expressed within one natural language (namely German). This type of legal linguistics provides insights that are important for general linguistics. It is equally interesting for jurists because it influences their daily practice, especially the way how they draft statutes or other legal documents.

As I have already mentioned, it is cumbersome if not impossible to characterize the state of the art in contemporary legal linguistics. The reason for this calamity is first of all the vast spectrum of approaches – a characteristic feature which legal linguistics shares with other disciplines. However, there is also another reason which seems to be particular, unique to legal linguistics. Observations relevant to legal linguistics appear regularly in works of legal doctrine, e.g. on contracts or on property that at least by their main topics are not explicitly related to our domain (Galdia 2008: 20). They risk therefore to be – and in most cases also are – overlooked by legal linguists. In this book I tried to incorporate some examples of this sort of legal-linguistically relevant research that belongs predominantly to other branches of the legal science. On the other side, many publications that concern practicalities of language use in the area of law such as guidelines aiming at improving jurists' linguistic or argumentative skills or their knowledge of foreign legal terminology are not central to legal-linguistic explorations. Notwithstanding their practical value in particular situations, such works are rarely mentioned in this book.

2.1.5 What is legal linguistics and what it is not?

In all above approaches one legal-linguistic feature seems to re-emerge regularly, namely that language is constitutive of law (cf. Bülow 1985: 25). Indeed, as we have noticed here regularly and are tempted to repeat at this place – law in its theoretical form is predominantly legal linguistics. The reason for this is that legal linguistics which focuses on two central issues of creation of law with linguistic means and on its application, i.e. interpretation and argumentation, is its theory. It is *a* theory of law. Other conceptions of legal theory are thinkable and even practiced with more success than legal linguistics. This notwithstanding, I will concentrate on approaches and achievements of the philosophical and linguistics pragmatics which I perceive as the most advanced theoretical approaches to law and language. I will not try to draw any distinctive lines between the philosophical and the linguistic pragmatics as both are closely related, the linguistic current following the philosophical in time and method. The distinction between both is for me a matter of courtesy toward researchers who used to stress this distinction rather than a theoretical necessity. I address this issue here simply by anticipating possible questions. Despite the mentioned problems with the current state of the art in legal linguistics, which I perceive as a practical rather than a theoretical problem, it seems to me to be possible to attempt a description of the role that philosophical and linguistic pragmatics play in this domain. And, I will do it by asking what legal linguistics is and what it is not. This procedure is part of our quest for legal linguistics that was initiated in the introductory part of this book.

2.1.5.1 Legal linguistics is not philology

Philology concentrates upon the reconstruction and the protection of written texts as cultural achievements of mankind (cf. Lepper 2012: 17). One of its major tasks is to reconstitute the original written text and to determine the time of its appearance and the meaning of words in it at the time of its creation. For instance, a paper by G. Falcone (1991) *Per una datazione del "De verborum quae ad ius pertinent significatione" di Elio Gallo* belongs to this group of works. Philology has therefore a role to play in all attempts to reconstruct historical legal texts and to determine linguistically appropriate interpretation of historical sources like those of the classical Roman law. Its task is mainly directed toward the preservation of the initial meaning of texts that may be later interpreted differently due to the multitude of approaches toward texts and their interpretation (cf. 3.6.1.2). Furthermore, its methods are crucial to the editing of historical as well as contemporaneous legal texts. The editorial philological methods comprise the preparation of the authentic text for print and the ways of its presentation including a critical commentary. They are used for editing statutes and case collections, both historical and contemporary. Unlike legal linguistics, philology concentrates on purely linguistic aspects of legal texts. It does not look at them through the prism of legal sciences. Therefore, the philological research does not replace legal linguistics; it has an auxiliary role to play there. Works such as Risto Hiltunen's (1990) which provide a substantial contribution to legal linguistics but perceive themselves rather as parts of general linguistics or national language-philology must be properly transformed within the conceptual framework of legal linguistics to become truly operative there (cf. 2.1.4.6).

2.1.5.2 Legal linguistics is not philosophy of law

Legal linguistics deals with many philosophical issues. One may even have the impression that it deals exclusively with philosophical issues. How should we otherwise understand the signification processes in which legal concepts emerge, the procedures of interpretation and argumentation or the shift of signification when incompatible legal concepts must be translated between two or more networks of legal rules expressed in different national languages? These issues are deeply philosophical in their core and I try to approach them here from the perspective of pragmatics which is not only linguistics, for many it is philosophy. However, the legal philosopher deals with philosophical issues in law differently than I am doing it. Her interest is directed toward the subject matter of the legal provisions which she scrutinizes from the philosophical perspective. For instance, in the constitutional law she would ask the fundamental question what is good governance, in criminal law, what is free will and what is causation, in contracts she would ask how parties of different economic standing can be perceived as equal in law. Additionally, she could ask why the legislator actually prefers to protect family and treats it differently from many other social groups or why does he protect the environment or deals with issues pertaining to bioethics? Finally, she could ask why the legislator uses rights and not other conceptual forms in which political positions can be termed as an instrument of their expression and protection. Our answer to all these questions would be monotonous and not interesting for the legal philosopher. We would always repeat that all this is a matter of linguistic creation and appropriate legal argumentation. The legal philosopher would certainly be bored by our lack of imagination. What fascinates the legal philosopher is the subject matter of law reflected or evaluated from the philosophical point of view. We, instead, take law in the sense it interests the legal philosopher for granted.

2.1.5.3 Legal linguistics is not sociology of law (and not legal anthropology)

Sociology of law deals with the social reality in which law is created and applied. Works of classics such as Eugene Ehrlich and Roscoe Pound show the fundamental differences between the sociological and legal-doctrinal views upon law. For them, the question how the doctrine imagines the law to be is of secondary importance. In its approach sociology of law is close to legal linguistics which also focuses upon reality in creation and application of law. The main distinction in the object of studies is that legal linguistics focuses exclusively on linguistic aspects of law, whereas in the sociology of law issues concerning the use of power in society through law dominate the perspective (cf. also Milgram 1983 approaching obedience from the psychological perspective, Nerhot 1992, Supiot 2005, Souza 2005, Stein et al 2008, Wee 2011). Similarly, legal anthropology supplies narratives used in law which enable us to understand the legal culture. While referring to C. Geertz, M. A. Glendon et al. (1999: 13) speak about stories which not only influence the way "how legal norms are invented and applied within (that) system, but on how facts are perceived and translated into the language and the concepts of law." Again, legal linguistics takes most of these fundamental culture creating processes for granted. It definitely also creates and analyzes the legal culture but it proceeds within a much more limited scope of application. It therefore cannot explain what is law in terms of cultural creation of mankind, but it can explain how we create and use language within our complex legal institutions. And this is already quite a progress. Therefore, legal linguistics is not legal anthropology which is in a sense broader because it includes the use of language in law as part of the human culture. Legal anthropology insists upon the primacy of man and his needs over law (Lampe 1970: 17). It differs from legal linguistics in terms of methodology (cf. Lampe 1970). As far as legal anthropology deals with social principles and rules governing indigenous societies where legal rules are not reflected in the way adapted in the tradition of the Roman law it differs significantly from the goal of legal linguistics that is to contribute practically to the emergence of the global law. This emerging law will definitely be based on the tradition of creation and application of law grounded in the Roman tradition. However, both sociology of law and legal anthropology are in many respects very close to legal linguistics.

2.1.5.4 Legal linguistics is not law

Legal linguistics cannot replace the law. Law has next to its linguistic form also another material component which is its subject matter. Law includes rules which provide regulation concerning specific socially relevant issues. A substantial part of the legal training consists of learning which legal provisions concern which subject matters, and how subject matters in question are regulated in law. For the legal linguist all these subject matters are an *x*, a *quantité negligeable*. This, however, does not mean that legal linguistics tries to reduce the importance of law or restructure its position among social sciences. As an example, reductive theoretical processes concerning the law are dealt with in the theories of Law and Economics. There, attempts had been undertaken to reduce the role of law as an autonomous social institution. R. Posner and many others were of the opinion that law should have an auxiliary function in the social reality which is determined by economic processes (Posner 1987). According to this view, law would provide legal instruments (i.e. regulation) which fit best these processes. I might have provoked the same impression when talking about law and legal linguistics. As there is quite a lot of language in law one might be tempted to pretend that also legal linguistics can replace the law or at least replace the legal science. In my view upon law, in which legal linguistics definitely plays a preponderant role, such a shift in ontology and methodology remains impossible. For the legal linguist, law is a construction made with and driven by words. She is not interested in knowing what exactly the legislator regulates in an act relating to the operations of hedge funds in a country. Neither is she interested in the question whether these regulations are justified by the reality that dominates financial markets. She will exclusively focus on the way in which the legislator uses language while creating such regulatory legal acts. Therefore, legal linguistics cannot replace the law. It cannot replace its teaching and learning either. But it can contribute to that both would be done differently in future.

2.1.5.5 Legal linguistics is not legal doctrine

I stress the distinction between legal linguistics and legal doctrine also called *legal dogmatics* in the civil law because of the fundamental difference between both. Legal doctrine dominates academic studies and the professional methodology of jurists notwithstanding the criticism concerning its theoretical weaknesses. This criticism, which is expressed also by jurists, stresses the point that an area of science cannot be dogmatic as a matter of principle (cf. Kirchhof et al. 2012). Criticism on legal doctrine in legal theory is abundant. We are said that the legal doctrine proceeds in areas interesting us in a way that presupposes the right solution to a legal problem within the so-called legal system. It establishes a fictitious formal procedure of inferring this solution from relevant legal provisions. I do not believe in this procedure and I exposed reasons for this view in this book extensively. Legal doctrine tends toward the *reification* of the legal language. Therefore, not only language but also law and legal linguistics constitute an insurmountable obstacle for the legal doctrine as it is practised in the civil law countries. Let us illustrate the problem on a few small examples. A typical doctrinal problem is represented in the distinction between *relative* and *absolute rights. Absolute rights* are generally defined as the sum of the applicable legal provisions in a society that take effect against everyone, whereas *subjective rights* concern the legal position of an individual. Usually, in the civil law tradition, rights which emerge under contracts have been perceived as *subjective* because they are binding only the parties involved. Property rights, instead, have been construed as *absolute* because they are effective against everybody. Needless to say that the quality of a party to a contract and an offender of a property right are only conventional. It means that they are a matter of perspective. One could argue that *subjective* and *absolute* rights provide the same protection for those exposed to the breach of contract or to the violation of a property right. They do not concern persons who are not involved in the matter. To assume that the property right protects the home owner against all inhabitants of his country is a metaphysical construct. The protection right becomes effective only against those who intend or actively attempt to violate this right. Another doubtful conceptual pair is the one of *public law* and *private law* (Guimezanes 1995: 27–28, Husa 2015a: 12–15). Law, as we have seen, is effective only within the public sphere. It cannot function on the basis of private arrangements that are otherwise welcome in society (cf. Berman 1993: 4) but they are not law when they cannot be enforced in the public sphere. D. Kennedy (1982) spoke therefore of the *arbitrariness of the public-private distinction*. Finally, we have referred already to the doctrinal tendency to split events relevant to law in a *substantive* and a *procedural* part (cf. 1.1.4.1). Such a method would contradict the legal-linguistic efforts because it imposes metaphysics upon the understanding of law. Moreover, the Continental *doctrine of legal sources* usually excludes *precedents*. It is difficult to accept in legal linguistics this artificial and unjustified selection. In the common law the *doctrine of consideration* is equally problematic because it does not respect the daily social (i.e. also linguistic) practice. Cooter/Ulen (2004: 192) characterized the American court decisions that deal with *consideration* as *Humpty-Dumpty jurisprudence*. In sum, the legal-linguistic methodology does not coincide with the methods of legal doctrine. The legal doctrine seems to be based on an implicit theory of language; occasionally it appears to legal linguists as a legal linguistics without linguistic theory. Although the legal doctrine provides legal-linguistic materials and is therefore a legal linguist's daily bread, it is at the same time remote from the methodical realm of legal linguistics. Therefore, legal linguistics will rather critically follow this sort of doctrinal thinking in law.

2.1.5.6 Legal linguistics is not logic for lawyers

The linguistic approach to law is complementary to or sometimes even identical with the logical approach. Logic, however, uses a different language when it characterizes reality. Therefore, the parallels between linguistic and logical approaches are not always immediately visible. Through the attempts to formalize legal rules logic goes behind their lexicalization and asks specifically for the form of rules behind the rules in words. It develops forms of legal rules such as p→q which suit its epistemological interests best. More specifically, *deontic logics* developed by G. H. von Wright (1951) disclosed the most abstract and formal structure of legal norms. To date, no valid argumentation has been provided to fundamentally question this approach (Atienza 2006: 125). Our approach to law seems to be, however, more practical as it is grounded in problems of interpreting concrete legal provisions and in applying concrete rules in concrete cases. In contrast, the strength of legal logic could be seen in its attempts to generalize our knowledge about the legal language on a very high level of abstraction. Moreover, logic comprises rules for *descriptive* language as well as rules for *prescriptive* language, like the language of law (Weinberger/Weinberger 1979). In its scrutiny of *prescriptive* language it deals with deontic modalities: *prohibited, permitted* and *required* (Frändberg 2001:13). It establishes *validity* as the mode of existence of legal norms. These deontic modalities can incite the legal linguist to look closer to how they manifest themselves in the legal-linguistic praxis. One could for instance ask how Chinese modal verbs 得/*děi* (must), 该/*gāi* (shall), 应当/*yīngdāng* (shall), 不得 /*bùdé* (shall not) or 可以/*kěyǐ* and 可/*kě* (may) function in Chinese legal texts (cf. also Cao 2004: 56–70). The function of normative language and especially of verbs in it seems to be an area of a possible close cooperation between logic and legal linguistics. However, legal linguistics goes beyond deontic operators (cf. Jackson 1985: 47) and comprises the entire linguistically relevant vocabulary of a language or an area which we call legal thesaurus. Another common domain for logic and legal linguistics is legal argumentation. The relation between law and logic has not been free of paradoxes there. Non-valid argumentation in law had been identified by logicians in legal contexts. These specific argumentative structures may appear to logicians as fallacies, (FR) *paralogismes.* Yet, they are frequently justified by jurists as a specific way of how jurists speak and write. They were also termed as specific legal rationality. Some researchers therefore maintain that formal logic cannot be perceived as an exclusive or the most appropriate analytical instrument for the appraisal of legal argumentation (Verschueren/Östman 1995: 60). Rational argumentation as well as the interest in an argumentative discourse (cf. Aarnio 1987) remain however central to logic and legal linguistics. Regarding other traditional issues in logic, such as truth and meaning, the contrastive approach seems more appropriate. Can we distinguish between truth and interpretation in law? What is the truth in law? We may use Tarski's formulation of a truth condition: It is true that it was raining in New York at 11.50 today if it was raining there at this time. This statement of a truth condition is not banal at all. Tarski asks what is the criterion of a material – not purely formal – truth of an utterance and he provides the simplest and the formally and materially most pervasive test for an utterance about facts. In setting up the test, he provides the most convincing criterion, not an argument, because in the case in which someone would still question the result of the test we simply cannot talk with him in a reasonable way as a rational criterion does not appeal to him. Tarski's most simple criterion is not the end of the search for tests determining material truth in utterances; it is only the beginning of it. Providing tests for more sophisticated utterances is more difficult and providing criteria of that sort for propositions about law is impossible. This is the effect of Ronald Dworkin's theory of law as an interpretive concept. There, validity of the best argument counts for truth in law. Indeed, law is about interpretation and argumentation, not about truth criteria. Social facts cannot be verified according to Tarski's test. There is no truth in such utterances other than the one being subject to legal interpretation. Law is dominated by linguistic conventions. However, there, where conventions are missing, logic is particularly welcome. Notwithstanding theoretical limits, the specific truth in legal utterances and W. Hohfeld's (1913) fundamental logical relations in law (*rights, duties, powers* and *liabilities*) form still a conceptual basis for attempts to formalize the law (cf. Ashley 1990; Bench-Capon/Coenen 1992; Berman/Hafner 1987 and 1993; Branting 1991). Problems connected to *open-texture concepts*, reasoning with cases to interpret open-texture concepts or conflicting legal rules and concepts as well as adversarial reasoning, i.e. the ability to create persuasive arguments for both sides of an issue seem to be unsolvable in all attempts to formalize law (cf. Galdia/Liaci 2016). Developments in this area are described in the periodical *Artificial Intelligence and Law.*

The least problematic in our context is the traditional legal logic. It consists mostly of analyses of legal reasoning and legal argumentation including its specific cases, legal interpretation and legal justification. We have already identified these topics as belonging to legal linguistics and can accommodate them in our pragmatic conception because we basically deal with the same issues. Moreover, traditional logic and the question of a systemic character of law came up in the civil law tradition and were discussed with less interest in the common law countries. Some authors were seeking the reason for this disparity in different approaches to law in both dominant legal traditions (Mattila 2006: 224). The civil law developed as university doctrine based on *substantive law* whereas the common law has been developed by courts which turn their attention to *procedure.* It may therefore be understandable that civil law lawyers were always interested in the systemic character of law which dominates the substantive law and which was determined to provide a solid basis for civil codes. In turn, procedure has been rather neglected in academic teaching and research. In the common law countries procedure has been central; its teaching technique is case analysis as no case exists beyond the procedure. In both legal traditions cognitive interests developed differently, and the consequences are perceptible today in the research. This is also one of the reasons why I insist upon the linguistic turn in legal sciences.

2.1.5.7 Unification or specialization in legal linguistics

The discussion about the most appropriate approach to legal-linguistic studies and about the name of the discipline have been recently discussed by J. Engberg and A.L. Kjaer (2011) in their note where the point was made toward a legal linguistics with a stronger methodological profile. There, also criticism was brought against an all-embracing legal linguistics. Whether this suggestion will be followed by researchers who identify themselves with Law and Language studies or legal linguistics remains open for the time being. Especially, the general Law and Language studies and forensic linguistics seem to be less interested in dealing with fundamental methodological questions. Meanwhile, Engberg and Kjaer make clear in their common position that methodological discussions are central to the further development of research developed under the label *legal linguistics* or *Law and Language studies.* Another decisive point is the paradigmatic approach to legal-linguistic issues. Many researchers perceive the area as belonging to applied linguistics and structure their research accordingly. Others, also the author of these lines, focus on aspects particularly important for general linguistics, legal theory and the philosophy of language. These areas seem to be better suited for the fundamental research that deals with the solution of the most basic conceptual issues in legal linguistics. Issues such as the nature of legal language, the notion of legal discourse, and the emergence of meaning in law cannot be fully grasped within a research paradigm that is based solely upon the methodological apparatus of applied linguistics. Therefore, the future of legal linguistics depends also on the choice of the epistemological perspective in the legal-linguistic research.

2.1.6 What is legal linguistics, then?

I have somewhat categorically cut off the links between legal linguistics and all other kindred disciplines. Nevertheless all these disciplines remain parts of one big family, i.e. the legal science. They approach and characterize law from different perspectives, but law remains law exactly as all these related disciplines remain kindred parts of the legal science. As members of the same family they have some resemblance. Still, every family member is a distinct creature. This holds true also for legal linguistics. It deals with the most essential linguistic phenomena and linguistic operations in law. It approaches and describes law as a linguistic phenomenon based on the conviction that language is constitutive of law. In this sense, legal linguistics is its theory. As stressed above, problems of law are not always problems of language. However, the problems of the legal theory are essentially linguistic problems; this is why we may call our legal linguistics also a theory of law. It is not *the* theory of law, because law can be approached from different perspectives; for us however the linguistic perspective is the decisive one for the description of theoretical problems in law. All other problems are for us practical problems. But also they may give rise to legal theories.

2.1.6.1 Legal-linguistic conceptual network

Currently, legal linguistics is best positioned on the intersection of semantics and pragmatics, at least as long as the debate about the conceptual borders of both semantics and pragmatics is going on (cf. Notes and Commented Materials no. 1 and Pohl 2008, Börjesson 2014). Its background is the theory of syntax that could prove particularly prolific when applied to legal texts and the morphophonology that would also have a role to play in legal linguistics, although a limited one. In addition, the two traditional levels of description of linguistic phenomena, the synchronic and the diachronic are also taken into consideration. To date, legal linguistics operates with conceptual instruments of different value. Several central notions such as *discourse, text type, speech acts, narrative, style, prototype-stereotype, form of life, equivalence in legal translation* dominate texts belonging to legal linguistics. Moreover, a substantial part of texts oscillates around *concept* and *term.* In addition, the conceptual frame of reference of general semiotics is often applied in such texts. In a more advanced conception of this new branch of knowledge which would belong to legal sciences or linguistics, or to both, this conceptual apparatus would have to be redefined in order to function as a coherent conceptual set for *legal* linguistics. Therefore, the notions of *legal* discourse, *legal* text type, *legal* style and *legal* narrative, *legal* term and *legal* concept must become operational. The current problem of legal linguistics is furthermore that its main concepts are distributed asymmetrically and somewhat capriciously. All concepts identified as central to legal linguistics should operate in a network which provides for their balanced distribution. The pragmatic frame of reference proposed here can integrate these partly heterogeneous concepts. As long as it is materially related to *legal* texts it is also reliable in the sense that it guarantees the appropriate level of *'legalness'* within the conceptual network. It is suitable to describe some of the linguistic operations in law such as interpretation, argumentation, translation and many others. It is also elastic enough as it does not put any artificial limits to the identification and the description of further linguistic operations in law.

2.1.7 Is legal linguistics really more than legal linguistics?

From the above follows that legal linguistics deals with legally relevant aspects of language use. Occasionally, the attempt to determine whether a specific legal-linguistic operation is relevant in law may become problematic (cf. Mannoni 2016: 106). As a test for such cases the *juridicity* of the text has been used here. Nevertheless, some general semiotic aspects of textual constitution and application go beyond the pure juridicity, i.e. the role a linguistic unit plays for the legal decision taken in a specific case or the choice of a formulation. Therefore, next to the juridicity of language use, also the role that a linguistic or para-linguistic unit (such as a gesture) plays in the legal culture must be taken into consideration. Doubtless, therefore, legal linguistics makes also part of general legal semiotics which provides for the most exhaustive scientific description of the phenomenon 'law' (cf. Bülow 1986: 93). Furthermore, the results reached in this book until now show that legal linguistics could be equally well perceived as a theory of law. Reasons for this are multiple. First of all, legal linguistics includes the most relevant legal-linguistic operations such as legal argumentation, legal interpretation and legal translation which have been traditionally also dealt with in legal theory. In legal theory as in legal linguistics those operations are treated as parts of the legal discourse as an overarching linguistic entity. In addition, in some approaches legal linguistics emerged in the theoretical context of the legal theory or has been supported by the legal theory (Galdia 2008: 16). This is the case also as far as this book is concerned as it is unthinkable without its roots in the legal-theoretical discussion.

2.1.7.1 Family resemblances

The affinity between legal theory and legal linguistics may also be perceived as challenging. If namely legal linguistics deals with the issues identified as relevant in the legal language by the legal theory it could simply be perceived as belonging to the established legal theory. No need would therefore exist for the emergence of a new discipline which doubles the efforts undertaken in the field of legal theory. However, the partition of tasks among disciplines is not always undertaken with surgical exactness. Academic disciplines, like the tools described by L. Wittgenstein (1984: 243) in his famous metaphor, can resemble each other as family members do. Some features are equal, while others constitute differences upon which personality can be based. The relation between legal theory and legal linguistics can be therefore characterized within the argumentative framework of family resemblances. Legal linguistics seen from the perspective of legal theory is a linguistic view upon law and legal theory. This is one more reason why legal linguistics can be – at least as far as the pragmatic perspective adopted in this book is concerned – also perceived as a specific theory of law.

2.1.7.2 Analytical philosophy and legal linguistics

Occasionally we have referred here to concepts and conceptions having their origins in the analytical philosophy. Issues such as *meaning*, *truth* and *reference* have been its central notions and also the most relevant areas of scientific analysis (cf. Scarpelli 1953, Putnam 1975, Quine 1983, Recanati 2008). The same holds true for law, although with slightly modified emphasis. Meaning remains central to both. Jurists had established, and since R. Dworkin's works they also understand the way in which they interpret legal rules. This will say that they now know how they conceive and create the meaning of legal concepts and rules. At this specific point they may be even more advanced than many philosophers who still inquire into the presuppositions of meaning in texts engendered in their field. Truth, in turn, is a delicate subject for jurists (cf. 2.1.5.6). Legal rules are rather valid or void; propositions about their content rather acceptable or unacceptable, more or less appropriate in a given social context. Truth may concern facts to which law is applied. It is relevant in briefs provided by attorneys in litigation or in witness testimony. Yet, in general, jurists have their institutional and procedural truth that they define in terms of validity which is a social and linguistic construct. This juridical truth is equally constructed as is the world of referents at which the law is pointing. Therefore, jurists have no problems with reference because law refers to a constructed world of concepts and argumentative methods. All this is gratifying as it shows that law is a relatively easy subject, at least when compared with philosophy. But, unlike philosophy, law exists in application and makes sense only in processes confronting socially relevant action and legal rules. At this point it is much more complicated than is philosophy even in its analytical form. Jurists cannot hide behind general or generalized rules. They have to apply them to concrete cases and they have to document this process which ends with a written and signed legal decision. In recent years, the linguistic wing of the analytical and post-analytical philosophy came close to cognitive sciences and the philosophy of mind. Toward this background, Recanati (2008: 9) advocates the unity of the linguistic philosophy and the philosophy of mind. The main reason for his claim seems to be the necessity to overcome the split between reasoning and language as signalled in the cognitive sciences (Aroui 1993: 127; cf. also Bülow 1985: 29). Indeed, mental phenomena analyzed in the philosophy of mind and notions of the philosophy of language such as *reference, denotation, connotation* or *intentionality* are at least interrelated. Thus, the problems of reference of legal notions, their denotation and connotation may be reappraised in the philosophy of mind and in the cognitive sciences. Within the philosophy of mind three approaches to *interpretation* have been developed (Engel 1994: 93). First, the indeterminacy of meaning thesis defended by W. Quine (Engel

2001: 75); second, the theory of popular meaning that tried to reconstruct the mental background of interpretive processes (Engel 2001: 76), and third, the projectivist conception that warned against overemphasizing rationality in interpretation (Engel 2001: 78). Aspects of the indeterminacy theory are discussed here under 3.7.8. Other findings are equally relevant in the legal-linguistic contexts because spontaneous emergence of meaning in law is limited. Therefore, its intentionality is more explicit than the intentionality in the ordinary discourse. Finally, *legal discourses* convey *meaning* that is anchored in the validity of their underlying norms and not in logically verifiable procedures. Discourses about validity of norms are by necessity discourses about rationality. Such discourses cannot be reduced to mental representations; again, the necessity to unify grammar and discourse becomes pertinent (Du Bois 2002: 47). Forensic linguistics may offer a research pattern for this type of innovative legal-linguistic analyses.

2.1.7.3 Legal linguistics as legal pragmatics

A conception relatively close to ours is the one of legal pragmatics. Legal pragmatics could be construed as a vision of law, i.e. its theory which stresses its aspects of application. Legal linguistics is in many respects also legal pragmatics and the theoretical exposition of problems in both is roughly the same only that legal linguistics reflects upon legal issues from the perspective of language use. The broader conceptual frameworks of both do not collide nor are research results known which would show basic differences between both perspectives issued from the same tendency within social sciences. Thus, the theoretical difference between both is purely distributional in that both occasionally stress different aspects within the same approach. This result cannot take by surprise as both linguistics and pragmatics are unthinkable outside the social context. For the language already the classic of the analytical philosophy, L. Wittgenstein, claimed that a private language could not exist (cf. Ayer 1966: 251–266; Rhees 1966: 267–285). In social sciences no developed conception of a human being living outside society and being independent of it has been seriously considered. Moreover, within pragmatic approaches *praxiology* developed by Tadeusz Kotarbiński (1886–1981) has an impact on legal linguistics and legal pragmatics. Kotarbiński's approach to legal language (1955: 16) enables to integrate issues which jurists used to discuss as terminological, especially legal concepts, into a pragmatically founded legal linguistics. It has equally further going implications because it mainly concerns effective action (id.: 6). In law, it would be fundamental to the justification of legal decisions or to the effective use of arguments in legal contexts.

2.1.7.4 Legal linguistics for linguists

The perspective adopted in this book stresses the importance of linguistic analysis in legal contexts. The most general sense of it is to characterize linguistic operations in law and to accomplish the linguistic turn in the legal science. It may seem that these results are interesting for jurists rather than for linguists. The sense of legal linguistics for linguists is not only to show that the linguistic analysis, for instance the application of the speech act theory and of the discourse theory is possible in law, as no other result could realistically be expected by linguists. However, the analysis of legal-linguistic operations shows the linguistic means and the linguistic prerequisites of the language use in law. It illustrates in this way what legal language is actually about, at least when seen from the pragmatic perspective. Until now, at least the research related to main aspects of legal language as language for special purposes, equivalence in legal translation and institutional aspects of legal interpretation and legal argumentation brought some new insights into linguistics as a result of the methodological and empirical exchange between legal sciences and linguistics. This notwithstanding, the interdisciplinarity in legal linguistics is somehow unidirectional: lawyers constantly benefit from linguistic theories while linguists only apply their methods and concepts to existing linguistic materials. As far as I can see no fundamental linguistic finding has been questioned by results obtained through the application of linguistic methods upon legal samples. This observation is revealing in terms of our initial problem setting and it also helps determine the nature and the scope of legal linguistics. Meanwhile, research into the possible and the actual use of language in the area of law might indicate that linguists all too hastily assumed that the language of law is by its nature inextricably linked to special registers. By so doing, they underestimated the potential of the ordinary language to function as a means of legal communication. In legal semantics, some linguists have also overestimated the importance of decoding of meaning in legal texts that are dominated by creative interpretation. Likewise, legal linguistics warns linguists against involvement in terminological studies based on the scrutiny of isolated terms as terms become meaningful solely within legal discourses.

2.1.8 Legal-linguistic education

Legal linguistics should be integrated into regular curricula for all law students. The reason for this claim is that legal linguistics deals with the most fundamental issues in law, i.e. legal-linguistic operations such as legal argumentation, legal interpretation, legal translation and others, for instance defining. Introducing legal-linguistic courses at a later stage of legal education supports the view which is hostile to legal-linguistic interests as it posits that legal linguistics is a random discipline in law that deals with quixotic and academic questions that may interest only some enthusiasts. Also in the educational perspective I perceive legal linguistics as a specific theory of law. Therefore, in my view, all law students should be exposed to legal-linguistic education from the very beginning of their studies. All of them use legal language daily. They must therefore understand how language is used in most relevant legal-linguistic operations such as legal argumentation, legal interpretation, or legal translation.

Practical benefits of legal-linguistic education are manifold. When legal linguistics is perceived as a theory of law, the benefits for lawyers are obvious. First of all, a lawyer who reflects upon legal-linguistic issues begins to understand the essence of the activities he/she performs, i.e. using language efficiently in legally relevant social contexts. Basically, all activities exercised by lawyers are covered by this broad description. Therefore, a lawyer who deals with legal linguistics understands the rules that govern his/her profession. Also legal translators profit from legal-linguistic education. Legal translation without legal linguistics is blind. It is unsystematic and nebulous. Legal linguistics is able to describe the problems of legal translation and it shows why this profession is and will remain challenging. It prevents mechanistic approaches to legal translation and prepares the translator for creative work. Legal translators become professionals through legal linguistic education. Neither language courses alone, nor separate legal education, nor both tracks completed one after the other can replace legal-linguistic education. Legal linguistics allows linguists, sociologists, philosophers and other representatives of arts and social sciences to approach law from a perspective that is understandable for them. It makes plain for them how law is created and how it is applied. When described in terms of legal linguistics law as a social phenomenon can be integrated into methodological approaches that dominate these branches of knowledge. This is a great progress because the methodology of the traditional subject 'law' is much too particular and hermetical to become accessible to other professions. Therefore, legal linguistics functions also as a bridge between law as an academic discipline and other social disciplines (Galdia 2014: 65, 165). This shows again how central this branch of knowledge actually is. Also Christopher Goddard (2010a, 2010b) concentrated upon the relation between the emerging academic discipline termed by him 'legal linguistics' and the professional status of legal linguists beyond the academic sphere of activities. As a matter of fact, the question whether a practical profession of a legal linguist actually exists is relevant to the future development of the field. As long as legal linguists are perceived as scholars researching legal-linguistic issues the legal-linguistic activity will remain confined by the habits of the academic world and will have only little impact upon society. Goddard's research shows at least that a need exists among professionals dealing with legal translation and legal drafting for a professional profiling that would enable them to be perceived by society as specialists in a specific area of socially relevant activity (cf. Goddard 2010a: 209).

2.1.8.1 Core and peripheral legal-linguistic skills

Ch. Goddard distinguishes between core and peripheral legal-linguistic skills (Goddard 2010b). In fact, to master legal linguistics means being able to use language efficiently in all social contexts relevant to law. These social contexts (situations in which language is used) are mostly institutional (language use in courts, in administrative proceedings, attorney's advice etc). Legal-linguistic skills are therefore closely linked to institutions because legal language does not exist outside contexts that are defined by social institutions such as courts of law. Incidentally, institutions also define these skills; there is no private legal language. Therefore, at least theoretically, the most salient legal-linguistic skill is to use language efficiently under conditions defined by others, i.e. by institutions that impose the rules for its use. Practically, when the improvement of such skills should be reached, some methodical steps must be taken. First, the circumstances of language use must be identified; second, the relevant legal-linguistic skills must be defined and trained. For instance, (1.) cross-examination is identified as a relevant linguistic operation in law, (2.) language use strategies that are most appropriate and efficient in such a context of use are identified and trained with students. Legal-linguistic skills are acquired in numerous such language games. As a matter of fact, in common law countries some of these skills are already trained, yet at random and unsystematically, e.g. in moot courts or in case briefings. In the civil law countries this practical training is even more reduced or does not exist at all. Disappointingly, today, this professional training in legal-linguistic skills takes place only in practical life, haphazardly and superficially. Academic institutions that should provide legal education offer sterile legal doctrine instead of professional training in legal-linguistic skills. Consequently, law as a teaching subject is deficient because it does not teach the most essential skills for the practice of law, i.e. the efficient use of the legal language. Legal linguistics addresses this deficiency and provides remedies for these shortcomings that are viewed by many law students rather critically. Central legal-linguistic skills are regularly overlooked because academic institutions still focus on legal doctrine. Meanwhile, efficient use of language in all legally relevant communicative situations can be identified and subsequently also evaluated by experienced users of the legal language. These users, in turn, would have to be convinced that problematic issues concerning language use in the legal practice can be addressed systematically in educational institutions. It seems that this is a precondition for any further development of legal linguistics as an academic discipline. Other legal-linguistic skills may be called peripheral. These skills mainly include qualities cherished by administrative bodies: 'good' grammar, correct spelling, using language that sounds formally and is perceived as presentable, editing skills and quick drafting. In all, they evoke the image of a legal linguist who is a perfect secretary. Legal linguistics includes also these skills as an incidental part of all legal-linguistic operations. Meanwhile, educational institutions seem to spend time and efforts on strengthening these skills (that can also be acquired implicitly) in explicitly designed courses.

2.2 Do Lawyers Have Their Own Language?

2.2.1 Paradoxical answers

In their practical argumentation lawyers developed an efficient answer to embarrassing questions. Whenever a controversy about abstract issues threatens to destroy the coherence of their reflections they used to answer: *'yes and no'*. And indeed, this rhetorical trick, which at the first glance may appear somewhat infantile, may bear in itself a very specific justification. In fact, legal linguistics begins for many with the question whether the legal language really exists. Doubtless, lawyers did not develop any genuine language in the sense of natural languages such as English or Chinese, and researchers regularly refer to this fact when talking about the legal language (Mattila 2006: 3). In this sense the infantile 'no' from our elusive answer seems to be justified. However, also a 'yes' would be a convincing answer due to the particular way in which lawyers communicate. These 'nos' and 'yes' are in fact too elusive to satisfy our curiosity about the subject. Nevertheless, they constitute a first, although paradoxical, answer. In general, paradoxical answers emerge in our language when our world view is troubled by a logical inconsistency of which we are unaware. Indeed, to answer our question by a simultaneous 'yes' and 'no' cannot be sufficient. Reasons for this dilemma are not only purely logical. They have their roots in the subject matter. Therefore, we will work on our perspective upon the legal language in order to determine the answer. As a matter of fact, initially, the legal language has been perceived as a question of style (Dölle 1949). Also in Pigolkin (1990: 4, 16) the legal language is characterized as a specific functional style of the literary language. The issues of style have been related to the rhetoric of legal texts and it was stressed that the legislative language is characterized by rhetoric neutrality (Pigolkin 1990: 8). Yet, in this view the concept of style is undetermined. We could define it as a specific way to see the world with linguistic means (Goodman 1978: 3, cf. also Henderson 2015). However, in this perspective the legislative language appears profoundly rhetorical, abounding with rhetorical figures, emotions and understatements and definitely not as neutral. I prefer, therefore, to integrate the debate relating to style and rhetoric into legal argumentation where it can be understood in a broader context. Furthermore, other scholars emphasized the specific professional terminology as a characteristic feature of the legal language. Some scholars, however, questioned the existence of a particular legal language and pointed to a specific register rather than to language (Gizbert-Studnicki 1979: 49–60). By contrast, in some already classical works on this issue such as D. Mellinkoff's *The Language of the Law* (1963) the term *legal language* is used in an equivalent transformation. Therefore, a conclusive answer to the question whether lawyers have their own language depends – as always – on the definition of language adopted in the research. Nevertheless, in general, one can retain from the classical discussion that language used in legal contexts is somehow specific, although in elderly research this specificity remained rather nebulous. For example, the mentioned questions of style or specific professional register refer to aspects of language use rather than to a language typology. These and many other linguistic aspects of law are the area of legal linguistics. They comprise the whole arsenal of the legal discourse, an organized set of legal-linguistic signs. Nowadays, the legal language can be therefore adequately characterized as language used within a specific type of discourse, i.e. in the legal discourse. This is why lawyers have their own language, although they actually do not have any.

2.2.2 How language used in law became special?

As noted, the legal language is mostly perceived as a professional register, i.e. a specific language use based on ordinary language in communicative situations which take place within social (judicial) institutions. Now, this specific use must at a stage be discernible to the language users, speakers and listeners alike. When do language users realize that the appropriate register to use is the legal-linguistic one? We could easily imagine a layperson entering a court of law and speaking the ordinary language. Besides, this happens regularly in the legal practice if not for want of any better linguistic skill as laypersons usually master the legal language only rudimentarily, if at all. Yet, the user of the ordinary language in a court procedure will soon realize that the linguistic situation in which he is expected to act requires a different language use to perform in it in an optimal way, i.e. to produce and understand legal speech acts correctly. Otherwise, his language use which entails producing and understanding legal speech acts will lead to infelicitous performance, i.e. to legal speech acts which only partly engender the intended consequences and sometimes may produce even the opposite of the intended. The stress upon action in institutionalized settings such as courts of law is necessary in legal linguistics. Otherwise, misunderstandings could come up as to the quality of the legal language that legal linguistics is expected to analyze. One of such misunderstandings would be to focus exclusively upon legal terminology as a source for legal-linguistic research. This misunderstanding would be particularly deplorable as the linguistic situation that is analyzed by a legal linguist is dynamic, it is an action. Definitely, words are used in it, yet they are used in specific actions and in specific institutions. Complex transformations of these words take place when speech dominates in legal institutions. Due to this specificity, legal linguistics deals with legal-linguistic operations as the most salient aspects of language use in law. They will be scrutinized more fully in the third part of this book.

2.2.3 Text types in law

Speakers and hearers notice the different circumstances in which language is used and they realize that they have to make use of various registers in order to cope with the linguistic situation in which they are acting. Linguistically, this difference can be observed on different text types that emerge as a result of this differentiation of language use. In fact, language use in legal texts differs considerably. Until now, these differences have been scrutinized rather intuitively and formal juridical criteria were applied in order to set up a broader matrix of text types in law (Galdia 1998: 551). However, it would be expedient to work out other than juridical criteria for the typology of texts used in law. This typology should be based on linguistic rather than juridical characteristics. It would show whether intuitively identified text types correspond to a matrix which would be developed by linguists. At this stage of development, one can assume that some of the text types would coincide with the linguistic criteria while others might overlap and form broader or narrower text types. The typology used today mostly comprises:

- Language of statutes (language of legislation)
- Language of legal decisions including fact description
- Language of the legal doctrine
- Language used by lawyers in professional discussions and pleadings
- Language used by laypersons in legal contexts (testimony, comments on legal decisions)
- Language used by administrative clerks

In turn, the traditional linguistic text typology includes e.g. *narration, description, exposition, argumentation, instruction.* More advanced typologies include *informative, appellative* or *declarative* texts. One of such traditional text types is the *memorandum*, also called *memo.* The first reference to this text type dates apparently from England's Rolls of Parliament of 1433. Also, in a written communication from 1465 there is reference to a "*memorandum to Thomas Moore because ye myzt foryete myne errand to Maister Bernay, I pray you rede hym my bille.*" This text type like the court opinion is particularly resistant to change. Court opinions and statutes are typical legal text types upon which the legal-linguistic research has been focusing since its very inception. With time, more and more text types that are characteristic of law have been identified and analyzed. They will be mentioned cursorily as we will advance with our scrutiny. Meanwhile, one can classify one legal text as belonging to several types, for instance: *All rights reserved. No part of this book may be reprinted or reproduced or utilized in any form or by any electronic, mechanical or other means, now known or hereafter invented, including photocopying and recording, or in any information storage or retrieval system, without permission in writing from the publishers* may be perceived as *informative* or *appellative* in the sense that it appeals to the user not to violate its terms. The classification method applied above is analogous to the identification of speech acts. Both ways of classification prove the context dependent quality of text types used in law. The text type may convey messages with different pragmatic load that change with time; the samples from different versions of Japan's constitutions illustrate this phenomenon (cf. Notes and Commented Materials no. 17). Finally, narratives are often identifiable as fiction only due to an introductory note that sometimes is used as a disclaimer: *This book is a work of fiction. Names, characters, places, and incidents are either the product of the author's imagination or are used fictitiously, and any resemblance to actual persons, living or dead, business establishments, events, or locales is entirely coincidental.* Such disclaimers are used as a rule when the impression imposes itself that the work actually refers to all those subjects and objects that it excludes in the disclaimer. The disclaimer denies the relation of the work to reality and creates fiction out of reality.

A general matrix for work on texts is proposed by Beaugrande and Dressler (1981). It comprises following constitutive features of *text*: cohesion, coherence, intentionality, acceptability, informativity, situationality and intertextuality. These features have been regularly used also in the legal-linguistic research. It is important to keep in mind that they also constitute a methodological link to discourse analysis. B. Sowinski (1983) proposed a classification of texts (also legal texts) that is based upon the philological dichotomy of *primary* and *secondary texts* (cf. Sowinski 1983: 11, 14). In the area of law, Sowinski differentiates between *primary legal texts* such as statutes or contracts and *secondary legal texts* such as commentaries (i.e. basically all texts that refer to primary texts). From the pragmalinguistic perspective such a differentiation is problematic because the status of a text as primary or secondary is determined in the communicative situation in which a text is used. The same text may appear to be primary or secondary due to specific interests of speakers in a particular communicative situation. In fact, structuralist and neo-structuralist approaches to legal texts are therefore frequently deficient because they propose a static concept of a legal text or a legal text type. Pragmatic legal linguistics seems to be more advanced in considering communicative interests and it is also more aware of the needs of jurists and other users of legal texts than other linguistic approaches to this question. Epistemological interests and different attitudes of speakers in speech situations are better suited as criteria that allow to distinguish legal text types that emerge in the actual use of these texts. Therefore, legal linguistics is not interested in the development of a final and immovable classification of legal texts.

Also F. Rabelais listed, ironically if not sarcastically, in chapter 39 of the third book of his *Gargantua and Pantagruel* (1533–1552) the legal-linguistic text types of his time:

> *For having well and exactly seen, surveyed, overlooked, reviewed, recognized, read, and read over again, turned and tossed over, seriously perused and examined the bills of complaint, accusations, impeachments, indictments, warnings, citations, summonings, comparitions, appearances, mandates, commissions, delegations, instructions, informations, inquests, preparatories, productions, evidences, proofs, allegations, depositions, cross speeches, contradictions, supplications, requests, petitions, inquires, instruments of the deposition of witnesses, rejoinders, replies, confirmations of former assertions, duplies, triplies, answers to rejoinders, writings, deeds, reproaches, disabling of exceptions taken, grievances, salvation-bills, re-examination of witnesses, confronting of them together, declarations, denunciations, libels, certificates, royal missives, letters of appeal, letters of attorney, instruments of compulsion, declinatories, anticipatories, evocations, messages, dimissions, issues, exceptions, dilatory pleas, demurs, compositions, injunctions, reliefs, reports, returns, confessions, acknowledgements, exploits, executions, and other such like confects, and spiceries, both at the one and the other side, as a good judge ought to do, conform to what hath been noted thereupon.* (English translation by Sir Thomas Urquhart).

This typology might prove quite inspirational.

2.2.3.1 Text type dependent transformations of legal language

Basic to any conception of legal text types is the transformational theory of legal language. Its hard core is the contention that all lexical units of a legislative act, i.e. those explicitly belonging to the legal terminology and those taken from the ordinary language become in the transformation which produces a legal act (a law, a decree or others) part of normative language (Pigolkin 1990: 151). The normative character of the act unifies the terminology used in it and transforms it into a normative text without distinguishing the lexical classification of terms. Only lexical units with purely auxiliary character may be excluded from this process. All terms in a legal act should be therefore perceived as having an equal status (Pigolkin, ibid.). This is understandable when scientific terminology (e.g. *multiculturalism, gender, race*) is introduced into the legal language (Galdia 2004: 172). Otherwise, the exclusion of auxiliary lexical units, and the authors of *Iazyk zakona* (cf. Pigolkin 1990) apparently mean prepositions etc., is not convincing as they may gain specific importance in legal acts and contracts. This has regularly been the case with expressions involving time and calculating deadlines (*until, not before, in three weeks* etc.). The preposition *before* caused problems at least in the U.S. Supreme Court decision University of Texas Southwestern Medical Center v. N. Nassar (133 S.Ct. 2517, 2013). The court discussed the proper interpretation of *because of* in its relation to causation, especially in contrast to *but-for* acts, in contradistinction to *because* understood as *based on* (cf. Holmes v. Securities Investor Protection Corp., 503 U.S. 258, 1992). In Holmes, the court noted that *because of* meant *based on* and *based on* indicated a *but-for* causal relationship. In Nassar, the court stressed that according to dictionaries, which in its view state the ordinary meaning, *because of* meant *by reason of* or *on account of.* Yet this reference seems not to be particularly helpful as it does not solve the main question in Nassar. Contrastively, the use of prepositions is particularly problematic in translations, cf. (FR) *Le contrat sera signé avant deux mois* and (ENG) *The contract will be signed within two months.* It would be therefore more persuasive to perceive the normative language as fully unified through its normative text type, as proposed in Galdia (1989: 330). The normative text type forms also the basis for further linguistic differentiation of text types used in legal contexts.

2.2.3.2 Legal language transgresses law

Legal linguistics goes beyond law in that it includes also legal usage which is not acceptable as a proposition of law or as valid legal-linguistic use. For instance, an Incoterm clause such as *FOB Mexico City* is for us part of the legal-linguistic use because it has been applied in a legal-linguistic context. It does not matter that the contractual clause which includes this Incoterm as such does not make sense in law. Similarly, a clause in an English-language contract providing for a *guarantee of good standing* in a case where the application of the German law is agreed upon by the parties does not make sense in terms of law because the German law, unlike the common law, does not know any such guarantee. Legally, the clause does not make sense but as an utterance in a legal context it is a valid object of legal-linguistic interest. In addition, manifestly erroneous court opinions and propositions of law presented there are interesting for us although they may be perceived by the legal profession as useless. Dissenting or concurring opinions are no less interesting for us than the majority opinions. Language in overruled precedents is for legal linguistics equally important as the language in the overruling decision. Practicing lawyers have to distinguish carefully between them as some of them state the law while others do not. Alleged linguistic mistakes and fallacies also fall within the spectrum of legal linguistics. Equally, incorrect translations are a source of information for the legal linguist (cf. Notes and Commented Materials no. 19). Meanwhile, legal language enters other special registers, also the academic language: "After reviewing more than two hundred papers on the issue, D.G. criticized the supraorganismal perspectives then in vogue in ecosystem ecology and concluded that Elton's diversity-stability hypothesis was not supported by a preponderance of evidence" (cf. Daedalus 2012, vol. 141). For legal linguists, such texts represent language used in discourses about law in equal degree. In this sense legal linguistics goes beyond the law.

2.2.4 Legal language as ordinary language

Apparently, legal language is less perfect and less complete than our ordinary language is. Generally, no particular semantic problems come up in our daily communication. Troubles in understanding in the ordinary language use can be easily solved in a communicative situation. Equally, idiosyncratic linguistic use can be explained or is perceptible in the communicative situation by the participants. Should a semantically ambiguous sentence be pronounced in a conversation, e.g. *I like my secretary better than my wife,* a simple question will suffice to disambiguate it (Juhl 1986: 52). Law does not provide us with such comfort. Yet still, would it not be enough to have a look at the use to determine the meaning of a legal concept? In some situations it may even be the case, while in others the interpreter of a legal rule risks to fall into a trap prepared by the users of ordinary language. The repetitive requests for precision in the legal language (cf. Schmidt 1972, Schwintowski 2003, Mattila 2006: 65) are the best illustration of this dilemma. The request for precision links the debate to the possible use of ordinary language in law. The idea is not particularly popular among lawyers, partly due to the corporatist view based upon the assumption that lawyers are responsible for guarding and passing further their professional terminology (Galdia 2003: 12, cf. also Pozzo 2005, Slocum 2016). Furthermore, legal language and especially legal terminology guarantee for many the correct functioning of the judicial apparatus. However, legal terminology and legal language developed and function as an elaborate form of the ordinary language (Gémar 2004: 738). Put in pragmatic terms, the difference between the ordinary language and the special register of law is that the legal language attempts to draw precise semantic borders among words and the users of the ordinary language are less worried about this task. However, in law the distinction should be made between the postulate of a conceptually clear legal language and the existing legal language. Speakers, even lawyers – with possible exception of some legal scholars – rarely perceive legal language as particularly clear. The constant use of interpretive and argumentative techniques in the application of law proves that the legal language is all but clear, i.e. univocal.

Theoretically, a specialized language such as the legal language presupposes the existence of the ordinary language of which it is the extension. Were it not so, one would not be able to learn it because all knowledge about the specialized language is acquired through the ordinary language (Savigny 1981: 323). Some additional basic assumptions about the relation between the specialized language S and the ordinary language O were stated by Savigny (1981: 348). According to him, any utterance in S can be expressed in O; no utterance in S would make sense would in not at least in some contexts be translatable into O; every utterance in S is meaningful due to rules formulated in O; S develops historically among speakers of O; O must be learned before S is learned; the speaker has to master O in order to master S but not vice versa; some convictions of O are valuable in S; in order to understand S one must share some convictions formulated in O. The main distinction between the specialized language and the ordinary language is that some knowledge is not available in the ordinary language; instead it is proposed in the specialized language. Yet, this does not mean that this knowledge could not be expressed in the ordinary language. It is not available there simply because some results of science are achieved in specialized communities of experts who speak and write the specialized language. Yet, it could at any moment be translated into the ordinary language. Through this translation the knowledge would not become more or less true or more or less false. The mere circumstance that an utterance containing knowledge is expressed in the specialized language is not a guarantee that the utterance is true. And vice versa, the use of ordinary language in the transfer of knowledge does not make this knowledge less true or less false. The result of the translation from the specialized language into the ordinary language is a quality mark of a branch of science. Wherever this linguistic transfer does not function justified mistrust against scientific theories may come up (Savigny 1981: 322). Therefore, regular and thorough transformation of knowledge available in a branch of science into the ordinary language seems to be in its well understood self-interest. Equally, the concepts used in the transfer of knowledge do not say anything about the existence of objects to which their lexicalization might refer. That the word *unicorn* exists does not mean that the unicorn exists in reality (cf. Recanati 2008: 39). This result does not change even if the sublime tapestry in the Museum of Cluny known as *La Licorne* shows a unicorn in all detail. Even cross-culturally, the statuettes of 'Chinese' unicorns, (CN) *dú jiǎoshòu,* can prove the ubiquity of the image, but not the real existence of this sublime, yet virtual animal. Within natural sciences this issue of possible existence or non-existence of postulated concepts may lead to additional methodological problems of justification (Bülow 1985: 24). In law, the situation is less complicated. The legal language is special in the sense that its concepts generally do not exist in the physical reality; they are pure linguistic creations.

In some semantic theories this sort of concepts used in law is perceived as shorthand script. Thus, *adverse possession* or *unjust enrichment* do not exist in reality. Instead, they refer to specific existing social situations in which sets of facts previously characterized as decisive in law are conceptualized and labelled with terms. This procedure simplifies their use in law. The fate of such concepts is unequal either. Some, mostly vivid concepts which can be easily simplified in the ordinary language like *unjust enrichment* find easily their way into it, others like *adverse possession* or *promissory estoppel* may attract the speakers of the ordinary language only in very specific situations, if at all. This selection may even decide their destiny in law; concepts disappear from law not only through changes in law but also through preferential changes which speakers impose upon the legal language. Therefore, the two concepts, specialized language and ordinary language are not constant. It is occasionally difficult to draw the line between them because they are not only interdependent, they are also in contact. Concepts of scientific language such as *electron* or *unjust enrichment* enter the ordinary language and it is often only a question of time until a concept from the specialized register of a branch of science is perceived by speakers as belonging to the ordinary language albeit with a simplified meaning. Intralingual polysemy like the use of *instrument* in whatever daily context, for instance music instrument and the use of *instrument* in the international law to describe a legal act, usually an international convention, are typical situations of the use of the same word in two registers. Both registers are also less homogeneous as one would wish in a research partly based upon their mutual distinction. Needless to add that in contemporary law they have also a multilingual dimension (Mattila 2006: 32). Furthermore, the language of statutes differs from the language of court decisions or administrative correspondence although we used to treat this usage as characteristic of one legal language. Equally, ordinary language used by persons with different levels of formal education usually differs, provided their education has not been a mere formality. The same speakers may use their ordinary language differently in emotionally loaded situations and speak another variety of ordinary language in circumstances which they perceive as emotionally neutral. In addition, there exist specialized languages which are more specialized than others (also within one branch of science) as there exist ordinary languages less ordinary than others (Savigny 1981: 347). In sum, no convincing theoretical reasons exist for not using ordinary language to express law. Legal concepts can be expressed in ordinary language as well in that they are described in it. Furthermore, the legal language is not constituted of concepts alone. For the forming of the modern law, it would be more appropriate to concentrate on description of actions and characterization of legal speech acts rather than on developing new legal concepts. Significant progress would be reached in this way and law would become at least more rational and easier accepted. Moreover, in relation to the global law it is important to keep in mind that also national legal languages are sometimes more and sometimes less close to ordinary language (Galdia 2003: 21). A global law expressed in a language which is not adapted to this linguistic usage will not be understood, nor will it be applied properly.

2.2.4.1 *Fictions in legal language*

Law expressed with linguistic means appears in the semiotic perspective as a fiction. It is a secondary sign system (Jackson 1985: 13, cf. also Wegmann 2016) which refers to a primary system of signs, such as society or state. While referring to the primary sign system law provides rules for this system. These rules say how the primary system should be. Therefore, one must assume that law would not exist were the primary sign systems generally reflecting and applying these rules. The ontological difference between *is* and *ought to be* is the precondition for the existence of law. The tension between the two sign systems is focused upon by legal sociologists. The sense of their activity is to research the relation between the secondary and the primary sign systems. The discrepancy between both systems which legal sociologists could succinctly express as *state and society are often not what they should be in terms of law* demonstrate materially the genuine condition of the existence of law. Therefore, again, were rules which we perceive as legal generally known, generally accepted and generally applied in state and society no law would be needed. Almost certainly, under these circumstances, law as a collection of explicit rules would not even come up. Regularly, legal rules are linguistically expressed in forms which may suggest that they simply state facts (cf. Minda 1995: 239). They appear then in the cloth of a primary sign system while being by their nature secondary, although no less important. The ontological difference that has been mentioned helps distinguish legal rules as engendered by a secondary sign system from rules of primary sign systems. This is not a distinction without difference because it makes plain what legal interpretation is about. It does not describe the law as it is. Instead, it tries to set up propositions of law which would fit the requirements of the secondary sign system aiming to provide guidelines for the primary sign systems. Signs in law have therefore a constitutive, not a descriptive function. They engender meaning, instead of only representing it. Generally, the fictitious character of law manifests itself also linguistically. Statutory provisions include numerous formulations, such as (D) *gilt als (is perceived as)* or (FIN) *on katsottava, että*, which are instrumentalized in order to provide equal legal consequences to unequal factual constellations (cf. Lachmeyer 1979). The most basic example of such fictions is the sign *No dogs!* Placed at the entrance of an institution it is regularly interpreted in the sense of the message to animals' owners meaning that animals are – to put it mildly – not welcome there. Other linguistic fictions are eventually more complex. These linguistic fictions were construed by F. Lachmeyer (id.) as a particular boldness of jurists to create equality between evidently unequal things or events. This is definitely the case when, for instance, in the contract law a late acceptance of an offer to enter into a contract is perceived as a new offer (cf. § 150 I BGB or Sec. 40 of the (U.S.) Restatement (Second) of Contracts). Without the understanding of the fictitious character of legal signs the creation and the application of law cannot succeed.

2.3 Characteristic Features of Language Used in Law

2.3.1 Descriptive models and their sense

The linguistic characterization of language used in legal contexts can be accomplished within the notional framework provided by general linguistics for the description of natural languages. It may reflect their textual structure and start with *text* or *text types* and go over to their *semantic* and *syntactic constituents* (van Dijk 1980: 41). It may equally well follow a descriptive model that is divided into *linguistic levels* and comprise *phonology* and *phonetics, morphology, syntax* and *semantics* (van Dijk 1980: 19; Akmajian 2001: xi, Sowinski 1983: 64–123). As an annex to this model, one may mention the communicative levels of language use understood there as *pragmatics* (Akmajian 2001: 3). The mainstream legal-linguistic research favors the last model that is based on structural aspects of language to which communicative or functional aspects are added. This model splits the language in discrete units that are easier to handle at the beginning than complex structures where phonological issues are combined with morphological or semantic issues are combined with syntactic. Nevertheless, the description of language is achieved only when these levels are linked, in other words when the structural components of language are combined with its functional properties (Akmajian 2001: 5). As a result, the descriptive model based on the scrutiny of discrete units on different and separated levels is easy to start with but it complicates the descriptive task on a more advanced stage. However, the integrative goal of linguistic description that focuses on more complex units such as *text* (Mattila 2006: 65) or *discourse* (Galdia 2014) is central to the task of legal linguistics. Therefore, in this paragraph the two-fold descriptive model will be used to make plain what linguists and lawyers found out about the legal language while applying it. At the same time, it will make clear, at least implicitly, why in this book rather the pragmatic approach is stressed and why results achieved within the two-fold descriptive model must be reinterpreted in legal linguistics that is based on the pragmatic model.

2.3.2 Linguistic levels

2.3.2.1 Phonology and phonetics

Phonology of the legal language provides a set of issues with a legal background, like e.g. the pronunciation of Latin legal terms, especially the traditional English pronunciation of Latin and the upcoming Italianized or classical pronunciation in the U.S. (Tiersma 1999: 53–55; Mattila 2006: 151). Spelling *domicile* as *domicil* reflects different pronunciation varieties; *judgment* and *judgement*, while spelt differently are however pronounced in the same way. Pragmatically interesting is, for instance, the voice tone that rules in some courts, the hypercorrectness in the pronunciation or notaries' routine reading of legal documents. Research into phonetical and phonological issues in law is concentrated rather around their practical application within the forensic linguistics where also the term *forensic phonetics* is used (Olsson

2007: 156–187). Also the tendency toward gemination of pronunciation of (FR) *illégal* is caused by its spelling (Pollack 1983: 143). Prosody plays a role in the composition of legal texts. For instance, rhyme is an underlying compositional structure of the French constitutional devise in Art. 2 of the Constitution: *La devise de la République est: Liberté, Egalité, Fraternité.* It has been mentioned in some sarcastic comments that the third term in the devise was added in order to establish a full rhyme. The constitutionalist G. Carcassone in *La Constitution* (2005: 46) described the embarrassment about the third term: *Quant à la devise, ses deux premiers termes figurent explicitement dans les règles et principes de valeur constitutionelle, tandis que le troisième a plus de difficultés à se frayer une place. Mais, gravée au fronton de tous les monuments publics, la devise s'en est trouvée pétrifiée.* Furthermore, in Art. 2 also the fundamental principle of the republic is rendered in rhythmic language: *Son principe est: gouvernement du peuple, par le peuple et pour le peuple.* The formula has been borrowed from Abraham Lincoln's famous *Gettysburg Address.* G. Carcassone (2005: 46) remarked about the legal value of the formula*: La formule a plus de sonorité que de sens...Ce qui est pompeux, en étant de surcroît inexact, est assez ridicule.* Also the headline of the subtitle 3 of the third book of the German Civil Code (BGB) *Verbindung, Vermischung, Verarbeitung* is based on euphony. In fact, prosody has its limits in legal texts that are written to steer society rather than to entertain it. Moreover, sound patterns are constitutive of many memorization rules and juridical adages: *He who comes to equity must come with clean hands* or (D) *Aus zweier Zeugen Mund wird die Wahrheit kund.* Also in Art. 17 (1) of OECD Model Convention on International Taxation the morphonological differentiation between (ENG) *artist* and (ENG) *artiste* is semantically decisive: *...income derived by a resident of a Contracting State as an entertainer, such as theatre, motion picture, radio, or television* ***artiste****, or a musician, or as a sportsman, from his personal activities as such exercised in the other Contracting State, may be taxed in that other State.* This difference is rendered in the German language by *Künstler* and *darstellender Künstler* that are formed beyond the morphonological connotations of the English pair of terms.

2.3.2.2 Morphology

Morphological implications in the legal terminology concern primarily the meaning of complex words. For instance, the word *payable* used by a banker who says that a bill is *payable* on October 1 does not mean that this bill *can* be paid on that date but that it *should* be paid (Akmajian 2001: 49). This word does not follow the pattern represented by e.g. *fixable* – able to be fixed or *mendable* – able to be mended. Furthermore, in the court jargon an offence is *jailable* in difference to a *fine-only offence* (Atwater v. Lago Vista U.S. Supreme Court 195 F. 3d 242, 2001) in the sense that it may lead to detention. Hałas (1995: 53) referred for the Polish legal language to a parallel process concerning the formant (PL) *–lny*, e.g. in (PL) *karalny* able to be punished/that should be punished or (PL) *zaskarżalny* able to be charged/that should be charged. The example concerning the word *payable* demonstrates that the meaning of some complex words is not composed of the meanings of their parts (Akmajian 2001: 49). The suffix *–able* differentiates between the forms *void* and *voidable* (e.g. contracts) where a *voidable* contract can be declared *void* at the option of one of the parties. Nominalizations such as *merchantability, habitability, assignability* of rights, *non-delegability* of personal duties belong in the same context of emergence. These rather abstract nominalizations are however not typical of the legal language; they are perfectly functional in literary texts as well: *Now, of course, the quality and the seasonability of these winter dreams varied, but the stuff of them remained.* (in: F. Scott Fitzgerald, *Winter Dreams*). We are able to grasp the meaning of such words only in the context of their use. Here, once again, our pragmatic approach facilitates also the understanding of morphological implications in the legal terminology and prevents cumbersome analyses of isolated lexical units. Influence of English terminology upon legal French has been received critically in France; use of adjectival forms ending with *–el*, e.g. (FR) *constitutionnel*, has been perceived as acceptable as soon as their use is not overwhelming in the text, direct borrowings such as (FR) *instances internationals* have been rejected (cf. Dubois 1983: 164–165). Occasionally, words such as (FR) *un claim* that only partly corresponds to the English *claim* in its meaning of *mining claim*, the French term covering only gold mining, were discovered (cf. Harmer 1983: 254). Morphonological problems can also emerge in situations where two terms such as *insistence* and *insistency* are perceived as synonymous in a language, but could have been used to mark conceptual differences in the legal language. Traditional legal terminology of Germanic or Romance languages is rather strict in this respect, whereas the Finnish terminology is much more flexible (Galdia 2003: 13). Furthermore, in the morphology of the legal language one can mention the general absence of verb forms in the second person plural or singular (Hałas 1995: 42). The verb *to plead* is used in the past tense mostly in the form *pleaded* in British English; in the U.S. and in Scotland the form *pled*, e.g. *he pled guilty* prevails. Statutory texts are increasingly gender-neutral. However, gender-neutral language is not always preferred: *No person accused of any offence shall be compelled to be witness against himself* (Art. 21 (3) of the Constitution of India in the version modified until December 1, 2007). Additionally, Tiersma (1999: 87) points out the antiquated morphological formations in legal English, e.g. *This policy witnesseth that…*

2.3.2.3 Syntax

in sentences composed by lawyers is specific (Gustafsson 1975; Hiltunen 2001). Simple sentences are rare in law. A typical sentence is a composed one, it is often build up in accordance with complicated syntactic patterns (Hiltunen 1990: 70–74). It seems that the syntax of the legal English became more transparent with time; e.g. a phrase in the English Act of Settlement from 1700 clarifying the succession to the throne consists of 182 words, taking 13 lines in modern print (cf. Barnett 1999: 25):

> *And it was thereby further enacted that all and every person and persons that then were or afterwards should be reconciled to or shall hold communion with the see or church of Rome or should professe the popish religion or marry a papist should be excluded and are*

by that Act made for ever incapable to inherit possess or enjoy the crown and government of this realm and Ireland and the dominions thereunto belonging or any part of the same or to have use or exercise any regall power authority or jurisdiction within the same and in all and every such case and cases the people of this realm shall be and are thereby absolved of their allegiance and that the said crown and government shall from time to time descend to and be enjoyed the same in case the said person so reconciled holding communion professing or marrying as aforesaid were naturally dead.

However, some text types such as the Italian *massime di giurisprudenza* remain amazingly resistant as to their syntactic patterns (cf. Notes and Commented Materials no. 21).

Overall, long sentences do not necessarily impede understandability of texts. In legal texts, layers of embedding make legal sentences appear longer and more difficult to parce (Okawara 2006). This can be demonstrated on the mentioned (IT) *massime di giurisprudenza* that can be easily reformulated in simple sentences. Following this rule, an Italian legal writer develops his argument as follows:

L'ultimo esempio è quello relativo alla direttiva sulla vendita dei beni di consumo, la cui attuazione, lungi dall'uniformare i diritti nazionali, ha sortito l'effetto di esaltarne le differenze, come fra il diritto spagnolo da un lato e quelli tedesco e italiano dall'altro, per ciò che attiene all'azione in garanzia del consumatore, che è azione diretta verso il produttore in Spagna, ed è all'opposto azione verso l'ultimo rivenditore in Germania e in Italia, salve le interne rivalse lungo l'intera catena distributiva. (in: F. Galgano 2005: 56).

Notwithstanding the obvious syntactic complexity of the text sample, the message is clearly readable and it is also expressed in a way that appeals to the reader. Long phrases emerge in textual surroundings of mostly shorter phrases. From this circumstance their intentional use can be inferred:

It is of course possible that all or any of our beliefs may be mistaken, and therefore all ought to be held with at least some slight element of doubt. But we cannot have reason to reject a belief except on the ground of some other belief. Hence, by organizing our instinctive beliefs and their consequences, by considering which among them is most possible, if necessary, to modify and abandon, we can arrive, on the basis of accepting as our sole data what we instinctively believe, at an orderly systematic organization of our knowledge, in which, though the possibility of error remains, its likelihood is diminished by the interrelation of the parts and by the critical scrutiny which has preceded acquiescence. (in: B. Russell, The Problems of Philosophy, London/New York: Oxford University Press 1912; here 1962: 25).

In Russell's third phrase the syntactic structure is particularly elaborate; it is definitely not a matter of coincidence as only a few people may be able to speak this sort of syntactically complex language spontaneously. Moreover, in an attempt to facilitate reader's orientation Russell sets the words *possible, reason,* and *possibility* in italics; he is apparently aware of the circumstance that he demands a particular effort from his readers.

Many texts that do not belong to the area of law have been composed since the ancient Greeks in syntactic patterns that are far from simple. A long phrase borrowed from English literature is illustrative in this respect:

> *Now if nature should intermit her course and leave altogether, though it were but for a while, the observation of her own laws; if those principal and mother elements of the world, whereof all things in this lower world are made, should lose the qualities which now they have; if the frame of that heavenly arch erected over our heads should loosen and dissolve itself; if celestial spheres should forget their wonted motions, and by irregular volubility turn themselves any way as it might happen; if the prince of the lights of heaven, which now as a giant doth run his unwearied course, should, as it were through a languishing faintness, begin to stand and to rest himself; if the moon should wander from her beaten way, the times and seasons of the year blend themselves by disordered and confused mixture, the winds breathe out their last gasp, the clouds yield no rain, the earth be defeated of heavenly influence, the fruits of the earth pine away as children at the withered breasts of their mother no longer able to yield them relief – what would become of man himself, whom these things now do all serve?* (in: Thomas Hooker, Of the Laws of Ecclesiastical Polity, 1594).

The phrase contains eighteen subordinate clauses, seventeen of them leading up to the single main clause and the eighteenth bringing up the end. It may no longer appeal to most modern ears, but its clauses fit together neatly and even after four hundred years they are understandable to everyone who is interested in the subject.

The aesthetic value of long and well composed phrases is a cultural achievement of the human mind. In 1870, Walt Whitman closed his essay on American Literature in his *Democratic Vistas* with an uncorrupted phrase:

> *While, current and novel, the grandest events and revolutions, and stormiest passions of history, are crossing to-day with unparallel'd rapidity and magnificence over the stages of our own and all the continents, offering new materials, opening new vistas, with largest needs, inviting the daring launching forth of conceptions in literature, inspired by them, soaring in highest regions, serving art in its highest, (which is only the other name for serving God, and serving humanity), where is the man of letters, where is the book, with any nobler aim than to follow in the old track, repeat what has been said before – and, as its utmost triumph, sell well, and be erudite or elegant?*

Were this phrase not existing, would the American literature 'to-day' still be the same? It took centuries for the human mind to develop capacities that enable the composition of composed phrases. This achievement should not be put in peril by well-intentioned attempts to simplify the language used in legal settings that come up mostly within the plain language movement. Instead, educational efforts in society must be strengthened in order to allow all citizens to read and write language of some complexity.

Preference for long phrases is not particularly typical of law. A technical patent description for waffle fries (Lamb Weston, Inc., v. McCain Foods, Ltd. 78 F.3d 540, 1996) reads as follows:

A parfried potato product, suitable for reconstitution by cooking, comprising: a frozen, sliced potato section having a substantially ellipsoidal shape and a variable thickness, including a peak to peak thickness within the range of about 4/16 to 10/16 inch; the section including opposed first and second sides, each side having longitudinal ridges and grooves there-between, the ridges and grooves of the first side extending angularly to the ridges and grooves of the second side; the grooves of the first and second sides having a depth sufficient to intersect one another to form a grid of openings in the potato section; the section, before reconstitution, having an oil content of about 6–20 percent, by weight, and a solids content of about 32–40 percent by weight; whereby the product, upon reconstitution by cooking, is characterized by very thin, crisp portions of locally increased oil flavor adjacent the openings, relatively thick portions defined by intersecting ridges having an internal mealy texture and strong potato flavor similar to thick-cut french fried potato strips, and portions of intermediate thickness whose characteristics are similar to french fried shoe string potato strips.

Meanwhile, less usual English syntactic structures such as *His barons and members of clergy in revolt over costly, unsuccessful military ventures, England's king John finally agreed to grant them certain rights*...caused interpretive problems in cases related to the Amendment II of the U.S. Constitution: *A well regulated Militia, being necessary to the security of a free State, the right of people to keep and bear Arms, shall not be infringed* (cf. Galdia 2014: 140–141). However, the English translation of the French *Declaration of the Rights of Man and of Citizen* (1789) suggests a syntactic construction that reduces ambiguity in constructions such as those mentioned above: *Art. 12: A public force being necessary to give security to the rights of men and of citizens, that force is instituted for the benefit of the community and not for the particular benefit of the persons to whom it is entrusted.*

Moreover, in written legal language forms typical of the spoken language such as unfinished sentences, false starts, self-corrections, and changes of syntactical direction in mid-sentence are rare. Syntactically striking is further the omission of the definite article before the terms *plaintiff* or *defendant* in judicial decisions, e.g. *...it is clear, defendant believed it could comply with the contract by delivering stewing chickens. Plaintiff asserts that it is equally plain that plaintiff's own subjective intent was to obtain broilers and fryers.* (Frigaliment Importing Co. v. B.N.S. International Sales Corp. 190 F. Supp. 116, S.D.N.Y. 1960). Syntactic particularities include structures common to openings in pleadings, e.g. *Comes now plaintiff* for *Here comes the plaintiff* (Tiersma 1999: 88). Word order in legal English follows occasionally the French pattern of the adjective set behind the noun, e.g.: *attorney general, court martial* or *fee simple absolute.* Reversed word order occurs also in Italian court decisions: *Ritiene questa Corte che non ...* (cf. Notes and Commented Materials no. 36).

Syntactic complexity may cause peculiar formulations that might have been easily avoided. For instance, Art. 919 of the German Civil Code (BGB) stipulates in a way that caused hilarity in imaginative minds: (D) *Der Eigentümer eines Grundstücks kann von dem Eigentümer eines Nachbargrundstücks verlangen, dass dieser zur*

Errichtung fester Grenzzeichen und, wenn ein Grenzzeichen ***verrückt*** *oder unkenntlich geworden ist, bis zur Wiederherstellung mitwirkt.* (emphasis added) The contrast between the wooden earnestness of the sentence and the syntactic ambiguity is definitely not intended by the legislator.

2.3.2.4 Semantics

in law has been dominated by definitional questions. We can refer to the definition of *house* in an English bill (cf. 2.3.3.2.1). The ambition of jurists dealing with semantic questions has been to define the legal-linguistic use. Semantic processes in law usually broaden or streamline the ordinary language notions. They may include additional semantic components, e.g. (D) *Wilderei* (poaching) according to the Sec. 296 of the German Penal Code includes trafficking of parts of animal bodies such as horns which are not covered by the German ordinary language use of poaching. Under the (US) UCITA an ATM is a *computer*, while a calculator is not. A ferry boat is not a *vehicle* in a context of taxing *carriages and other vehicles used for passengers for hire* (Duckwall v. City of New Albany, 25 Ind. 283, cf. also Hutton 2014: 183). Moreover, *crabs* are covered by the Polish statute on fishery although they clearly are not fishes (Hałas 1995: 25). However, purely semantic analyses based on isolated terms may lead to unjustified distinctions in the terminology. When for instance Pigolkin (1990: 118) points out that the lexical unit (RU) *брак/brak* may mean in the Russian language *marriage* or *defect* so is this perfectly right. The lexical unit (RU) *brak* is used in appropriate contexts in the Russian legislation, e.g. in the legislation on marriage and in provisions on the sale of goods with the respective meaning. Pigolkin does not show that this homonymy might lead to confusion or other problems in the understanding or in the application of laws which comprise the term (RU) *brak.*

A semantic field may be structured around a leading term, such as *remand. To remand* can mean to send someone accused of a crime away from court until his trial begins: *She was remanded on theft charges. The accused was remanded in custody for a week* meaning that he was kept in prison. *The accused may also be remanded on bail* that means that he may return home provided he deposits a sum of money as a guarantee that he will appear in court for his trial. The semantic field allows for more familiar speech: *He was held on remand in the Boston prison for 16 month.* In the UK, juvenile offenders are sent to *remand centers* until their trail begins. In the US legal parlance a decision is *remanded,* which means that it is sent back to the previous court with an order to issue another decision. Also the term *asylum-seeker* presupposes syntagmas such as to *seek/to apply for asylum.* In fact, legal terminology clearly sets patterns, cf. (D) *Überhang* (cf. Art. 910 BGB), *Überfall* (cf. Art. 911 BGB), and *Überbau* (cf. Art. 912 BGB) that are formed rather rigidly and (CAT) *pena de mort* and (CAT) *sota pena de vida* that allow more imaginative creation.

2.3.3 Lexicology

Legal lexicology comprises issues of general nature such as the choice of lexical units, lexical borrowings, synonyms and phraseology as well as etymology. The choice of vocabulary used in law from the vast number of words that are at our disposal has been rarely researched (Bülow 1986: 33). Mattila (2006: 4–6) dealt with the legal jargon and the counter-language of the criminal fraternity (cf. also Nowak 2010). Overall, the lexicological research shows that lexical units undergo a process of selection and change in which they acquire a more precise meaning within the special register of law. We can illustrate this process on the example of the verb *pre-empt* and the noun *preemption.* The modified use of preempt (pre-empt) in the American legal terminology can be illustrated with reference to its specific usage in the constitutional law. For instance, the Secretary of Administration and Finance of Massachusetts was sued by a trade association in a case concerning the constitutionality of the Myanmar-statute, enacted 1996. In the litigation the plaintiff argued that the Massachusetts "anti-Myanmar" statute was pre-empted by the Supremacy Clause of the Constitution... The Supreme Court held that it was just this plenitude of executive authority that controls the issue of preemption here (Crosby v. National Foreign Trade Council 530 U.S. 363, 120 S.Ct. 2288, 2000 U.S. Lexis 4153). Under preemption as a U.S. judicial doctrine we understand the supremacy of federal legislation over state legislation. The U.S. Congress may, when it legislates in an area of federal concern, specifically pre-empt all state legislation. State legislatures may also pre-empt local governments in the same manner: *Neither Avena nor the President's Memorandum constitutes directly enforceable federal law that pre-empts state limitations on the filing of successive habeas petitions* (Medellín v. Texas, U.S. 06–984, 2007). Originally, preemption in the common law expressed the right of the king to buy provisions in preference of others. In the American usage it concerned the right to purchase publicly owned land on which someone is settling before others have the chance to do so. In international law, it expressed the right to detain goods of a foreigner in transit so as to afford its subjects a preference of purchase. Moreover, pre-emptive rights specified in a charter of a corporation grant to shareholders the first opportunity to buy a new issue of stock: *Most states allow the existence of pre-emptive rights to be determined by the articles of incorporation.* In fact, the original meaning of *preempt* is connected to purchasing by preemption, i.e. before others have a chance or rather the right to buy. The meaning of preempt as causing something to have no influence or force any more is based on the original meaning. Also the use in the ordinary language, e.g. *We were looking forward to watching our favorite television show, but it had been preempted by a political talk* or *The political movement had been preempted by a group of evil men* or in the military parlance: *Several preemptive attacks on the enemy's airforce bases,* further: *But Republicans rammed Trumpcare through key committees, literally in the dead of night, without waiting for the C.B.O. score – and they have been pre-emptively denouncing the budget office, which is likely to find that the bill would cause millions to lose health coverage* (Krugman 2017) ground in the legal-linguistic usage. The origin of the lexical unit is linguistically not reflected by speakers any more; the Latin *emptio*, i.e. purchase, is not present in the meaning of the last three examples. The legal usage still refers to it, at least partly. In our entry example ordinary linguistic usage apparently imposed itself upon the legal usage and established itself as a new concurring meaning of this concept in law. This additional semantization of the legal term is based on its ordinary linguistic meaning.

2.3.3.1 Synonyms

The systemic synonymy of *proxy* is an example. The person authorized to vote for someone is known as *proxy*, apparently an abbreviation of *proxy holder*. The same term refers to the grant of voting authority and finally, also to the document which grants the shareholder the right to vote. *Equity* as a term used in accounting is not intelligible in the context of *equitable remedies* or *equity powers* of courts or securities in form of *equities*. In accounting, the term *equity* refers to the ownership interest in the company (ordinary share) and derives from the equity court's recognition of the *equity of redemption*. Questions of synonymy are sometimes difficult to solve. Language use concerning for instance *obligated* and *obliged* differs considerably and native English speakers have different views about the meaning of both lexical units. They differ for some speakers as far as the intensity of the obligation is concerned or simply in respect of the solemnity of expression while others perceive them as purely synonymous. The same concerns the terms *bankruptcy* and *insolvency*. The later term seems to reflect for some speakers and also for legal professionals popular usage. For some others exactly the contrary is the case in English. Problematic are partial synonyms such as *merchandises* and *goods* that refer to objects of rights. *Expropriation* and *nationalization* are semantically equivalent, yet the legal operation is described in them from different perspectives. The function of such diverse formulations in law is unclear. Some terminological problems may have time limits: Calling long life or UHT milk *fresh milk* or innovatively *freshmilk*, (D) *frische Milch* or *Frischmilch* depends on generation specific views upon the question what actually is fresh milk. Furthermore, Art 1 (2) of the Warsaw Convention for the unification of certain rules relating to international carriage by air distinguishes in its French original between *souveraineté* and *suzeraineté*. Also the English version of the Warsaw Convention differentiates between *sovereignty* and *suzerainty*. However, some of such examples illustrate linguistic distinction without difference.

2.3.3.2 Definitions

Functionally closely related to concepts, definitions interested jurists, also those dealing with legal linguistics, much less than terminological issues *sensu stricto*, i.e. analyses and comparison of concepts. This lack of particular interest occurs not without reasons. Since the Roman times jurists cherished mistrust toward definitions, but strangely enough relied heavily on concepts. Meanwhile, the book L (50) of the *Corpus Iuris Civilis* known as *De verborum significatione* is almost entirely devoted to definitions. The adage *Omnis definitio in jure civili periculosa est* – known in many versions which aim at conveying the same message, namely that the definition finally does not matter much in law – was traditionally quoted in the legal doctrine, especially in works on the theory of private law. Jurists create definitions with the same idea in mind as when they create concepts in legal texts; they try to minimize the risk of polysemy (cf. Mattila 2006: 66). Definition in the strict sense of the term has been characterized as a description which allows for replacement of the concept through the definiens in any context (Savigny 1981: 326). For instance, the U.S. Court of Appeals for the District of Columbia defined the hedge fund as *any pooled investment vehicle that is privately organized, administered by professional investment managers, and not widely available to the public* (Goldstein v. SEC , No. 04–1434, 2006). This type of explicit definition does not work in law because it is too general. Likewise, knowing the definition of *negligence* as tort where the violation of a statute or ordinance constitutes the breach of the duty of care, we are still unable to solve the legal question exposed, for instance in Palsgraf v. The Long Island Railroad Company, i.e. whether the company acted negligently toward Ms. Palsgraf (248 N.Y. 339, 161 N.E. 99, 1928 N.Y. Lexis 1269 N.Y., cf. Notes and Commented Materials no. 53). The definition provides a first orientation about the concept used in law and can be used as a framework for the development of the legal argument relevant in the case. Yet, it cannot replace it. Therefore, jurists deem it to be of limited importance for their work. With this finding in mind, Judge Randolph resumed in the above case Goldstein v. SEC (p. 8 of the decision): "The lack of a statutory definition of a word does not necessarily render the meaning of a word ambiguous, just as the presence of a definition does not necessarily make the meaning clearer. A definition only pushes the problem back to the defining terms." Also in terms of textuality, legal texts accord best with *general principles* or *legal standards* where strict definitions can be avoided.

2.3.3.2.1 Examples of legal definitions

Definitions are in terms of text analysis akin to generalization and conceptualization (cf. Rimmon-Kenan 1989: 60). They may occasionally illustrate the process of gradual emergence of a concept rather than provide the final result. Classically, Aristotle in his *Politics* (1256a40) wrote therefore: Animals that are viviparous have food for their offspring in themselves, for a certain time, of the nature of what is called *milk*. The static impression which the authoritative legal definitions usually provide is alleviated by the process of defining which is shown in the definition. The definition below is illustrative of such a procedure. It is also quoted and commented by Mattila (2006: 68). The legal definition of *house* in the (UK) Leasehold Reform Act (1967):

2. Meaning of "House" and "House and Premises", and Adjustment of Boundary.-

(1) For purposes of this Part of this Act, "house" includes any building designated or adapted for living and reasonably so called, notwithstanding that the building is not

structurally detached, or was or is not solely designed or adapted for living in, or is divided horizontally into flats or maisonettes; and –

(a) where a building is divided horizontally, the flats or other units into which it is so divided are not separate "houses", though the building as a whole may be; and

(b) where a building is divided vertically the building as a whole is not a "house" though any of the units into which it is divided may be.

(2) References in this Part of this Act to a house do not apply to a house which is not structurally detached and of which a material part lays above or below a part of the structure not comprised in the house.

(3) Subject to the following provisions of this section, where in relation to a house let to and occupied by a tenant reference is made in this Part of this Act to the house and premises, the reference to premises is to be taken as referring to any garage, outhouse, garden, yard and appurtenances which at the relevant time are let to him with the house and are occupied with and used for the purposes of the house or any part of it by him or by another occupant.

(4) In relation to the exercise by a tenant of any right conferred by this Part of this Act there shall be treated as included in the house and premises any other premises let with the house and premises but not (...)

The Italian legislator, in turn, deals specifically with the definition of *window* in Art. 900 sqq of the Codice civile. The linguistic operation in question is classical defining through creation *per genus et differentiam*:

Art 900. Specie di finestre. – Le finestre o altre apperture sul fondo del vicino sono di due specie. Luci, quando danno passaggio alla luce e all'aria, ma non permettono di affacciarsi sul fondo del vicino; vedute o prospetti, quando permettono di affacciarsi e di guardare di fronte, obliquamente o lateralmente.

Art. 901. Luci. – Le luci che si aprono sul fondo del vicino devono: (1) essere munite di un'inferriata idonea a garantire la sicurezza del vicino e di una grata fissa in metallo le cui maglie non siano maggiori di tre centimetri quadrati; (2) avere un lato inferiore a un'altezza non minore di due metri e mezzo dal pavimento o dal suole del luogo al quale si vuole dare luce e aria, se esse sono al piano terreno, e non minore di due metri se sono ai piani superiori; (3) avere il lato inferiore a un'altezza non minore di due metri e mezzo dal suolo del fondo vicino, a meno che se tratti di locale che sia in tutto o in parte a livello inferiore al suolo del vicino e la condizione dei luoghi non consenta di osservare l'altezza stessa.

The classical definition such as the one below does not illustrate the way in which it came about. Defining as such is a semiotic process which took place before the final text was put on paper. It provides, therefore, a rational and authoritative impression of a final and supra-temporal generalization. In order to facilitate the interpretation of the general concept of *security* the definition below proceeds by presentation of examples. It comes close to indirect presentation of *security* rather than to an abstract description *per genus et differentiam*. In its attempt to create an abstract and general concept it stops halfway:

Any note, stock or similar security, certificate of interest or participation in any profit sharing agreement, pre-organization certificate or subscription, transferable share, voting trust certificate or certificate of deposit for an equity security, limited partnership interest, interest in a joint venture, or certificate of interest in a business trust; or any security convertible, with or without consideration into such a security, or carrying any warrant or right to subscribe to or purchase such a security; or any such warrant or right; or any put, call, straddle, or other option or privilege of buying such a security from or selling such a security to another without being bound to do so. (cf. Sec. 2 (1) of the (U.S.) Securities Act of 1933)

Moreover, also the *enterprise*, (IT) *azienda* is defined by the Italian legislator in the classical sense: *Art. 2555. Nozione. – L'azienda è il complesso dei beni organizzati dall'imprenditore per l'esercizio dell'impresa.*

Examples in definitions may occasionally impede readability of texts, cf. the definition of *discrimination* under ADA § 12182(b)(2)(A)(ii):

A failure to make reasonable modifications in policies, practices, or procedures, when such modifications are necessary to afford such goods, services, facilities, privileges, advantages, or accommodations to individuals with disabilities, unless the entity can demonstrate that making such modifications would fundamentally alter the nature of such goods, services, facilities, privileges, advantages, or accommodations.

UCITA Art 1030 (e) defines the term 'computer' in a similar way: *an electronic, magnetic, optical, electrochemical, or other high speed processing...or storage functions, and includes any data storage facility or communications facility operating in conjunction with such device, but such term does not include an auto... portable hand held calculator, or any similar device.* This statutory definition includes automated teller machines.

Today, working definitions gain momentum. For instance, NASA uses a working definition of *life* as *a self-sustaining chemical system capable of Darwinian evolution.* A dictionary of the Catalan language defines in the same string *leg* (CAT *cama*) as *extremitat inferior del cos humá que uneix el tronc amb el peu.* Philosophical definitions are of different kind. I. Kant defined *life* in the first sentence of his *General Introduction to the Metaphysics of Morals* as *the capacity of a being to act in conformity with his own representations.* Fundamental to the understanding of such definitions is their context-dependence. In sciences, this context-dependence coincides with their intertextuality. Kant's definition of *life* is not understandable without the knowledge of Kantian philosophy. Equally, the working definition proposed by NASA remains mysterious to persons ignorant of natural sciences.

Legal definitions were also ridiculed in literature. The German writer Ludwig Reiners includes in his style primer *Der sichere Weg zum guten Deutsch* (C.H. Beck, München 1951, p. 73) a parody definition of the former German Supreme Court (D *Reichsgericht*) as a reaction to the definition of *railway* proposed by this court (cf. also definition of *railway* in Mattila 2013a: 91–92):

(D) *Ein Reichsgericht ist eine Einrichtung, welche dem allgemeinen Verständnis entgegenkommen sollende, aber bisweilen durch sich nicht ganz vermeiden lassende, nicht ganz unbedeutende bzw. verhältnismäßig gewaltige Fehler im Satzbau auf der schiefen Ebene des durch verschnörkelte und ineinandergeschachtelte Perioden ungenießbar gemachten Kanzleistils herabgerollte Definition, welche eine das menschliche Sprachgefühl verletzende Wirkung zu erzeugen fähig ist, liefert.*

2.3.3.3 Phraseology in law

Phraseology is connected to terminological research, e.g. to analyses of adages, maxims etc. (cf. Pigolkin 1990: 162). For the French usage I may refer to (FR) *Ce jugement fera jurisprudence.* Also Cato's *Ceterum censeo Carthaginem esse delendam* is a classical example of a phraseologism with legal implications. Again, American phraseology may differ from the British usage, cf. (UK) *called to the bar,* (US) *admitted to practice* (Mellinkoff 1963: 7). Furthermore, Mellinkoff (1963: 122) provides a list of binomials in legal English including: *save and except, final and conclusive, fit and proper, free and clear, goods and chattels, keep and maintain, peace and quiet.* Binomials may be perceived as typical of the English legal language: e.g. the terms *leakage and breakage* have been inserted in bills of lading or charterparties, e.g. *not accountable for leakage and breakage.* Historically, they were also used in the legal French, e.g. (FR) *né et natif, sûr et certain, les us et les coutumes,* or *certificat de bonne vie et moeurs.*

Legal phraseologisms are conservative; they may transfer the imagery of things long past: (FR) *la réduction sera faite au marc le franc* meaning *pro rata* (cf. Art. 926 French Civil Code). Pragmatic aspects of phraseologisms in law attract more and more the interest of researchers (cf. Kjaer 1990, Lindroos 2015). Some problems of contemporary legal phraseology are discussed in Forget (2014: 223–264). Also in literature, some speech acts referring to the arrest of thieves are rendered as phraseologisms: (ENG) *Stop the thief!* (SWAHILI) *Mshike mwizi!* (CAT) *És el lladre, atrapin-lo*! or (LAT) *Ķeriet zagli, turiet viņu ! Zaglis, zaglis! Iesēdiniet viņu uz pāris gadiem! Lai nezog, bet dzīvo godīgi*! or (D) *Haltet den Dieb!* It is clear that speech acts that demand from others to take hold of and arrest thieves exist in ordinary language and that occasionally also comments are made with reference to the arrest of criminals. It remains however open as to what extent literature renders the reality of the use of such speech acts.

Formulaic language is related to textual patterns: *Plaintiff appeals from an order entered August 19, 1996. We review de novo the grant of the dismissive motion. The district court raised sua sponte the issue of the court's subject matter jurisdiction. We affirm the district court. The Justice Department, as amicus, argues that...* Form is also explicitly reflected in *cease and desist* letters. Pure terminological invention such as *'subject matter jurisdiction'* and *'alienage jurisdiction'* may engender full textual patterns around them. Originality, however, should not be confused with the patent law requirements of novelty or merit; it is linguistic, c.f. (FR) *Il génère des nuisances sonores.* Syntactic modifications also occur, mostly in order to avoid reformulation of textual patterns, e.g. *X Act, as amended 1956.* In the common law the formula *I sentence you to be hanged by the neck until death* has been frequently discussed by legal historians due to its nebulous motivation and its surprising exactness. The entire formula goes as follows: (full name of the prisoner) *you are sentenced to be taken hence to the prison in which you were confined and from there to a place of execution where you will be hanged by the neck until death and thereafter your body buried within the precincts of the prison and may the Lord have mercy with your soul.* It seems that the detailed language of the formula has been perceived as particularly morally devastating to the convict with whom only 'the Lord' yet not society may have mercy.

2.3.3.4 Etymology

Etymological issues play traditionally a role in the legal doctrine, especially in the research into legal terminology. They were even the origin of the research related to legal terminology. The reason for this research pattern might have been the vain hope that the original meaning of a legal term might guarantee its appropriate use and function as a guideline for its application. Nowadays, we are aware of the circumstance that etymological information is interesting in terms of language change in law. It is also clear that it is perfectly neutral in the area of the application of legal provisions. An example from a text that does not concern law may make it clearer: in the sentence *As long as such ideas prowl about in this theory, its future cannot be fully extricated from its past.* The etymology of *extricate* is known, the etymology of *prowl*, however, is still undetermined in the English philology. The understanding of the sentence is not hampered by this circumstance; the etymologically undetermined *prowl* is easier accessible to an average English speaker than the philologically perfectly characterized *extricate*. The etymological knowledge is irrelevant to everyday understanding of the phrase. Etymology in law may be however crucial because it enables to discover law's fundamental linguistic features. It explains why we use words that we use in law. Nevertheless, we must understand that we could also use totally different words for legal concepts and that this would in no way change the material basis of our law. Also B. Grossfeld (1990: 94) stressed that etymology attracts lawyers in comparative legal studies. In this context H. Mattila (2002: 178) observed however that in comparative legal studies it is more substantial to fix terms in their conceptual interrelation rather than in their time perspective.

Meanwhile, etymology is without doubt valuable to the understanding of the legal culture: our *law* comes from Old English *lagu*, and this comes from Old Norse *lag* that means something laid down or fixed. It is a word of Germanic origin, related to *lay*. I.M. Tronskij (2001:458) revealed an etymologically relevant parallelism between (GR) δίκη (law, justice) and Old Indian *diçā* that means direction. This parallelism is visible in a morphological context of the Indo-european language that interested the mentioned researcher. E. Auerbach (1992: 63) referred to the meaning of (LAT) *auctor* and (LAT) *auctoritas* in the ancient Roman Law of Twelve Tables that primarily referred to the establishing of property rights. The contemporary reading of such terms is therefore well informed by etymological findings. Further, (LAT) *ore tenus* stands for verbally, orally. In legal English the expression goes back to former pleadings that were exclusively oral; here etymology and legal history provide the necessary information. The German word *Musteil,* used for instance in the medieval law book *Sachsenspiegel* in the form *musteile* means (D) *Witwenteil,* i.e. legal part due to a widow, and is composed of *muos* (food) and *teile* (partition). Historians of law definitely need this sort of information to be able to cope with legal terms no longer in use. Occasionally, awareness of historical aspects of legal terminology may be relevant in the process of determining the range of property rights. This is especially the case with newly formulated rights of indigenous peoples (cf. for property rights of Saami population in Finland: Enbuske 2008: 17). Furthermore, the French word *échevin* comes from (FRQ) *skapi,* i.e. judge and (D) *Schöffe* may have the same etymology that is typical of the European legal culture. A medieval French manuscript *Queste del Saint Graal* includes a reference to the etymology of 'attorney' in a context rather different from law: *Bien estes enfantosmés par cele qui ne vous aime se petit non. Elle vous a si atornés que vous en avés perdue la joye des cieulz et la compaignie des anges et toute honneur terrienne, et estes venuz a toutes hontes recevoir.* (cf. MS. B.N. fr. 120, f. 540 v°, col. 2). The (UK) *Sterling* that refers to silver sterling and to a more or less legendary background of minting coins in ancient times with a star pattern. The (US) *posse* meaning a group of men assembled to assist in law enforcement goes back to Latin *posse comitatus.* The name of *America* goes back to Amerigo Vespucci. The heuristic value of this etymological knowledge is limited. It is cultural than rather epistemological. Equally, back in 1781, *Los Angeles* was called in Spanish *El Pueblo de Nuestra Señora de Los Angeles de Porciuncula*; the reference to the New Testament remains historically interesting, although it is irrelevant to the contemporary secular nature of that town. When, however, in the language of the Maya, the same word signifies *prophecy* and *law,* than significant conclusions can be drawn by anthropologists and legal historians from this linguistic parallelism (cf. Todorov 1992: 66).

2.3.3.5 Spelling and writing

Writing is essential to human language that however remains dominated by speech (cf. Bülow 2013: 7). For the development of the legal language writing has been of utmost importance (Galdia 2014: 266–269). Anecdotic is the American spelling of *judgment* in U.S. judicial institutions, although *judgement,* a spelling form predominant in the U.K. usage, is also in occasional use. In English courts an old style of handwriting called *court-hand,* a modification of the Norman style, had been in use from the 16th century until it was abolished by King George II in the 18th century. Abbreviations play a special role in legal texts. Their characteristic feature is the institutionally regulated form of their existence (cf. Mattila/Jussila/Kaltio (2004), Mattila (2013: 114–121), also in Notes and Commented Materials no. 20 and 2.3.5.h). Numbers in legal settings are frequently also rendered in verbal communication, mainly due to the human propensity to commit errors when writing coded messages in numerical form. In the Chinese language, particular signs exist to render numerical magnitudes, (cf. 壹、貳、參、肆、伍、陸、柒、捌、玖、拾、佰、仟).

Furthermore, a legal term, for instance 法治 (*fazhi* /the rule *of* law) may be easily confused in spoken Chinese with the rule *by* law also called *fazhi*, yet written slightly differently, i.e. 法制. Other signs, e.g. musical notation are rare in legal texts (cf. Notes and Commented Materials nos. 29 and 30).

2.3.4 Textual aspects

Textual aspects dominate the jurist's work with legal provisions. Legal analysis concerns mostly linguistic units that surpass the sentence or even a sequence of sentences. It mostly concerns texts constituted around coherent information in sequences of sentences (cf. van Dijk 1980: 41). For instance, Art. 68 of the French Constitution that provides for the responsibility of the President of the Republic in case of *high treason* says:

> *Le Président de la République n'est responsable des actes accomplis dans l'exercice de ses fonctions qu'en cas de haute trahison. Il ne peut être mis en accusation que par les deux assemblées statuant par un vote identique au scrutin public et à la majorité absolue des membres les composant; il est jugé par la Haute Cour de Justice.*

Both sentences in the provision are linked by their meaning. This link is however not visible in the lexical structure of the provision. Therefore, its textuality is open and allows for different – at least two – readings of the provision (Carcassonne 2005: 314). Were the sentences linked by e.g. (FR) *Dans ce cas* the textual structure would be limited and it would disambiguate the meaning of the whole provision. Similarly, sec. 11 of the (US) Securities Act gives the right of action to *any person acquiring such security*. However, in the text of the Act there is no direct antecedent for *such;* therefore courts had to construe it as meaning *any security registered by the registration statement.* Generally, the readability, i.e. the understandability of texts depends on their textual structure. The more explicitly the coherence among phrases is marked, the less is the reader's margin of appreciation and the risk of misunderstandings. Textual ambiguity in constitutional provisions is rather common, although one could expect more care in avoiding it. Art. 1 of the French Constitution says: *La France est une République indivisible, laïque, démocratique et sociale. Elle assure l'égalité devant la loi de tous les citoyens, sans distinction d'origine, de race ou de religion. Elle respecte toutes les croyances. Son organisation est décentralisée.* Here, as both *France* and *République* are of feminine gender in French, it is unclear to which of them the personal pronoun *elle* actually refers. This formulation has been disambiguated by the amendment of March 28, 2003 that introduced an additional phrase into the text of the Art. 1: *Son organization est décentralisée* (Carcassonne 2005: 44). The provision is now unequivocal as *elle* refers to *République* and not to *France* in the supplied sentence. Occasionally, the textual structure of codified statutory provisions may give rise to interpretive problems due to their incoherent order. For instance, Art. 1353 of the German Civil Code (BGB) stipulates that marriage is concluded for life, (D) *Die Ehe wird auf Lebenszeit geschlossen.* Meanwhile, the subsequent Art. 1564 deals with the dissolution of marriage, (D) *Scheidung der*

Ehe. The formal order of the provisions indicates an apparent contradiction in the legal code that seems unintended. Also Art. 1 of the German Constitution saying: *Die Würde des Menschen ist unantastbar. Sie zu achten und zu schützen ist Verpflichtung aller staatlichen Gewalt...Die nachfolgenden Grundrechte binden Gesetzgebung, vollziehende Gewalt und Rechtsprechung als unmittelbar geltendes Recht,* is ambiguous. The provision declares human dignity inalienable and states in the final phrase that the *following provisions* (D *nachfolgende Grundrechte*) are binding on all public authorities. The question arose then as to whether the Art. 1 is also binding in the light of this formulation. For me, the structure of the constitutional text and the character of the Constitution as a legal text suggest the normativity of all formulations, also of Art. 1 (Galdia 1989: 330). Hence, problems of textual structure reflect themselves in the legal argumentation as a natural cause of its being. They call arguments into their legal existence.

The mentioned textual ambiguity is not regulated in law; it follows from the general structure of texts in relation to the problem of their understandability. Some textual forms in law such as the juridical decisions follow a specific pattern. For the German judicial decision the (D) *Urteilsstil*, a method of legal argumentation opposite to (D) *Gutachtenstil* which is used by law students, is perceived as the basic structure of this legal text type. In Notes and Commented Materials no. 38 I propose an example of this style. In some common law decisions this style is used as well: "Because a debt arising from a medical malpractice judgment attributable to negligent or reckless conduct does not fall within the § 523 (a)(6) exception, the debt is dischargeable in bankruptcy. Section (a)(6)'s words strongly support the Eighth Circuit's reading that only acts done with the actual intent to cause injury fall within the exception's scope." Furthermore, according to the French tradition of drafting court decisions, the syllogism should dominate the outfit of the decision. In the Notes and Commented Materials nos. 33, 34 and 35 I provide an (FR) *arrêt en forme de syllogisme* constituted of three parts: (FR) 1. *règle générale applicable (majeure)*, 2. *cas particulier de l'espèce (mineure),* and 3. *application du général au particulier (décision prise, conclusion).* Also considerations of courtesy are displayed in legal texts. For instance, the German orders issued to convicted criminals who are awaiting the beginning of their prison term do not include the otherwise usual honorific address (D) *Sehr geehrter Herr* (i.e. Dear Sir) at the beginning of the letter nor the final formula (D) *Mit freundlichen Grüßen* (i.e. Yours sincerely). Instead, the more formal (D) *Hochachtungsvoll* is used by the authorities in accordance with internal drafting rules.

2.3.5 Particular descriptive features

Next to the above descriptive pattern based on linguistic levels and research areas, specific descriptive features of the legal language have been determined. Research concentrated upon establishing a catalogue of characteristic features of the language used in law (Mattila 2006: 65–103). These features are best distinguished within the framework of postulated and established features. In fact, the discussion about language use in law has a long tradition. Therefore, often different authors mixed opinions about what language they would wish to be used in law with the language really used. On the other side, non-postulatory, i.e. descriptive research into legal language is still quite limited and it is difficult to characterize the legal language on the basis of the research already done. Most criteria are still verified intuitively. Research into legal Latin shows that results of quantitative analyses may differ considerably from intuitive opinions lawyers hold about the use of legal Latin in different countries (Mattila 2002c). It may be assumed that the situation is very much the same when whatever other language than Latin is at stake. The characteristic features which dominate the discussion are: precision (tautology, definitions and enumerations), information (over)load, universality and aloofness, systemic character (references and consistent use of terms), structure and formalism (form of judgments, contracts, and legislative acts), sentence complexity, archaism and solemnity, obscurity (Mattila 2006: 65–92). Some textual examples may illustrate them:

a. Precision: *Plaintiff asserts that it is equally plain that plaintiff's own subjective intent was to obtain broilers and fryers* (Frigaliment Importing Co. v. B.N.S. International Sales Corp. 190 F. Supp, S.D.N.Y. 1960). This intensity of information is also typical of newspapers headlines reporting*: Beef prices have risen sharply after cattle failed to fatten up during the harsh US winter and ranchers culled herds to cope with the slump.*

Another example comes from the legal French: *Il est donné notification par le Ministre d'Etat par lettre recommandée avec demande d'avis de réception, cinq jours ouvrables à compter du dépôt du dossier tendant à l'obtention de l'autorisation d' exercer une des activités visées à l'article premier, soit de la recevabilité de la demande d'autorisation, soit de l'irrecevabilité de la demande lorsque le dossier est incomplet* (From an administrative instruction of the Principality of Monaco).

b. Information load: *Texas law makes it a misdemeanour, punishable only by a fine, either for a front-seat passenger in a car equipped with safety belts not to wear one or for the driver to fail to secure any small child riding in front.* (Atwater v. Lago Alto, U.S. Supreme Court 195 F. 3d 242)

Exceptions to this exemption for after-acquired property include previously non-assignable real property rights that become assignable within 6 months after bankruptcy, and property rights vesting in the bankrupt within 6 months of the bankruptcy.

(FR) Quand les fournisseurs d'accès à Internet et les opérateurs télécom, qui bénéficient depuis près de 10 ans d'un enrichissement sans cause par le transport et les échanges majoritairement non autorisés d'œuvres protégés, seront-ils vraiment appelés à participer à la rémunération d'une création sans laquelle ils ne connaîtraient pas un tel développement ?

c. Obscurity: *The distribution of the distributable residue of the movables of the deceased is (in general) governed by the law of the deceased's domicile (lex domicilii) at the time of his death* (Dicey's Conflict of Laws, 6th ed. p. 814). Furthermore, Art 31 B of the Constitution of India that concerns the "validation of certain Acts and Regulations" provides:

Without prejudice to the generality of the provisions contained in article 31 A, none of the Acts and Regulations specified in the Ninth Schedule nor any of the provisions thereof shall be deemed to be void, or ever to have become void, on the ground that such Act, Regulation or provision is inconsistent with, or takes away or abridges any of the rights conferred by any provisions of this Part, and notwithstanding any judgment, decree or order of any court or Tribunal to the contrary, each of the said Acts and Regulations shall, subject to the power of any competent Legislature to repeal or amend it, continue in force.

The indictment is endorsed by the foreman as a true bill.

(FR) *Une loi organique porte statut des magistrats.* (cf. French Constitution, Art. 64).

(FR) *Jugé que le droit de concession funéraire est un droit complexe empruntant à la fois au droit de propriété et au droit d'usufruit* (Court of Bordeaux, 4 mars 1991).

Obscurity characterizes also the professional jargon: *Can you plead collateral estoppel?*

d. Schematized language: *The ECPA* ***makes it a crime*** *to intercept an electronic formulation at the point of transmission, while in transit, when stored by a router or server, or after receipt by the intended recipient.* (emphasis added)

Texas law ***makes it a misdemeanour...*** (emphasis added)

In reviewing legal insufficiency points or no evidence points, we must consider only the evidence tending to support the finding, viewing it ***in the light most favorable*** *to the finding, giving effect to all reasonable inferences that may properly be drawn from the evidence...(Texaco, Inc. v. Pennzoil, Co. 729 S.W. 2d 768, 1987).*

e. Formal vocabulary is preferred in law, e.g. *timepiece* is used instead of *watch* (Bulova Watch Company, Inc. v. K. Hattori & Co., Ltd., 508 F. Supp. 1322, 1981). Verbs are transformed into complex structures, e.g. (D) *vorwerfen* into *zum Vorwurf machen, anklagen* into *Anklage erheben, aufrechnen* into *Aufrechnung erklären* (Dölle 1949: 71), (FIN) *maksaa* in (FIN) *suorittaa maksu* (Mattila 2008: 1150), *to accomplish an apportionment of losses* (Cooter-Ulen 2004: 6) is used instead of *to divide losses.* In their attempt to engender sterile language administrative agencies may also produce forms perceived as inappropriate, by using e.g. (FR) *intervenir* instead of (FR) *se produire: l'administration... ne dit pas qu'un événement est arrivé ou s'est passé, mais qu'il est intervenu, qu'un vote a eu lieu, mais qu'il est intervenue* (cf. Harmer 1983: 248). Jurists avoid whimsically sounding terms typical of modern physics such as *big bang* theory, *quarks, neutrinos, selectrons, sleptons* (i.e. hypothetical supersymmetric partners of electrons), *bosons* and many others.

f. Enumeration increases the complexity of syntactically simple sentences: *Any right, power, capacity, disability or legal relationship which has been created by the law of any civilized country applicable according to the English rules of the conflict of laws is recognized and, in general, enforced by the English courts, and no right, power, capacity, disability or legal relationship which has not been so created is enforced or, in general,* *recognized by the English courts.* (J.H.C. Morris (ed.), Dicey's Conflict of Laws, 7th ed. 1958, Stevens & Sons, London).

g. ***Archaism and solemnity:*** British legal acts enacted by the Parliament begin with the formula: *Be it enacted by the Queen's most Excellent Majesty, by and with the advice and consent of the Lords Spiritual and Temporal, and Commons, in this present Parliament assembled, and by the authority of the same, as follows* – (An Act to Amend the Theft Act 1968 and the Theft Act 1978, dated 18 December 1996). An example of a British act is rendered under no. 62 in Notes and Commented Materials).

Senior officials formulate their declarations in a way that engenders solemnity through archaic language use: *Now, therefore, I, Sir William Joseph Slim, the Governor General in and over the Commonwealth of Australia acting with the advice of the Federal Executive Council and in the exercise of all powers me thereunto enabling do by the presents accede in the name and on behalf of Her Majesty in respect of the Commonwealth of Australia and the Territories of Papua and Norfolk Island and the Trust Territories of New Guinea and Nauru to the convention aforesaid subject to the following reservations,...* (from Australia's Reservations and Declarations relative to the International Convention for the Unification of Certain Rules of Law Relating to Bills of Lading, 1924).

The Monegasque formula for proclaiming laws reads as follows :

Loi n° 1.351 du 28 octobre 2008 relative à la détention de chiens.

Albert II par la grace de Dieu Prince Souverain de Monaco

Avons sanctionné et sanctionnons la loi dont la teneur suit, que le Conseil National a adoptée dans sa séance du 21 octobre 2008.

...(here appears the text of the statute)

Fait en Notre Palais à Monaco, le vingt-huit octobre...

Also the expression *avons sanctionné et sanctionnons* manifests pragmatic connotations.

In UK, *yea* and *nay* are used by parliamentarians: *The House of Commons can say yea or nay to the executive judgment*; *yeah, yep* or *nop* are not used in the context of parliamentary debates.

Dates may be expressed in a solemn way: (IT) *L'anno duemilaotto, il giorno ventisette del mese di febbraio* for February 27, 2010 (in a notary document, (IT) *atto costitutivo associazione denominata*). This legalistic pedantry, which turns exactness into its contrary, has been often parodied, so by Miguel de Cervantes in *The History of Don Quixote de la Mancha*: *Done in the heart of the Sierra Morena, the twenty-seventh of August of this present year.*

Oath is sworn frequently with the use of preformulated utterances that include solemn expressions: *I swear to tell the truth, so help me God.*

Solemn language use may also be mysterious, in that the intention inherent in the formulation remains undisclosed: Art. 1 Constitution of India: *India, that is Bharat, shall be a Union of States.*

Some countries have solemn, less known official names: *República Bolivariana de Venezuela* (Bolivarian Republic of Venezuela) according to the Constitution of 1999. *Greece* is called in the English translation *Hellas* or *Greece*, for instance in book titles: Spyropoulos, P.C. *Constitutional law in Hellas*, Stathopoulos, M. *Contract law in Hellas*, but Karakostas, I. *Environmental law in Greece*. The author of this book contributes regularly to the *Hellenic Review of European Law – Revue hellénique de droit européen.*

This use of ceremonious language is common in elderly documents. For instance, the (ESP) *Capitulaciones de Santa Fe* (1492) that clarified the privileges of Christopher Columbus provide in their version preserved in the Archive of the Crown of Aragon as follows (spelling is original): *Las cosas suplicadas e que vuestras altezas* ***dan e otorgan*** *a don Christoual de colon en alguna satisfacion de lo que ha descubierto en las mares oçeanas y del viage que agora con el ayuda de dios ha de fazer por ellas en seruicio de vuestras altezas son las que se siguen…* (emphasis added)

h. Abbreviations: Formulations such as *Br. Of Pet'r at 17* for *Brief of Petitioner at 17* do not seem unavoidable and increase the understanding problems rather than contribute to a more economical language use. Still more, in a newspaper report about a police intervention: (FR) *Les policiers, grâce à une collaboration exemplaire inter-service signée BRAB-CAC-BAC, sont allés de surprise en aveux* (Nice Matin, June 25, 2008) the administrative jargon is quoted. The phrase is understandable when the initialisms of the multiple police services are deciphered : BRAB – *Brigade de la répression des atteintes aux biens*, CAC – *Cellule anticambriolage de la sûreté départementale*, BAC – *Brigade anticriminalité*. The administration has the tendency to produce abbreviations, possibly also due to its professional tradition, e.g.: (FR) *D.G.R.C.S.T. – Direction générale des relations culturelles, scientifiques et techniques*, a unit of the French Ministry of Foreign Affairs in charge of promotion of the French language abroad (Baylon 1991 : 193). Abbreviations, mostly in form of acronyms, may shape also the ordinary language: (D) *Bafög* for *Bundesausbildungsförderungsgesetz* is used not only among German students as a synonym of a grant, (FR) *PACS* for *Pacte civil de solidarité* led to the coinage (FR) *se pacser* largely used in informal spoken French. Since 2011 the term (FR) *tigiste* that refers to (FR) *TIG* (*Travail d'intérêt général*) is in use. In some countries, there exist publications that list the abbreviations in legal texts, e.g. Kirchner/Pannier (2008) in Germany or Mattila, Jussila, Kaltio (2004) in Finland. Abbreviations like all other linguistic means may support or hinder communication (Mattila 2006: 89).

Juridical abbreviations have been parodied in literature, e.g. in F. Rabelais' *Gargantua and Pantagruel* (1545–1552): *That the imperfections of nature should never be imputed unto any for crimes and transgressions; as appareth, ff. de re milit. l. qui cum uno. ff de reg. Jur. l. fere. ff. de aedil. edict. per totum. ff. de term. mod. l. Divus Adrianus, resolved by Lud. Rom. in l. si vero. ff. Sol. Mat.* or: *And it is mentioned l favorabiliores ff. de reg. jur. et in cap. cum sunt eod. tit. lib. 6…* (cf. Book Three, Chapter 39). This sarcastic reference to sources of the Roman law, frequently used by Rabelais all over the book as a satirical device, makes clear the limits of the technique of abbreviations that may prove disruptive rather than helpful at attempts to understand texts.

Functionally close to abbreviations are references. The technique of internal referencing may have an effect of systematization within a codification, e.g. Art. 1158 of the Italian Civil Code (IT *Codice Civile*): *Usucapione dei beni immobili e dei diritti reali immobiliari – La proprietà dei beni immobili e gli altri diritti reali di godimento (952, 957, 978, 1021, 1022, 1031) sui beni medesimi si acquistano (922, 948, 1041 n.1, 1042, 1061, 1073, 1164, 1422) in virtù del possesso (1140, 1163) continuato per venti anni (66, 71, 73, 533, 714, 1159, 1166, 2651).* Thus, a new text is produced that can be understood only when the statutory provisions referred to in Art. 1158 are read together with the main text and in the order indicated in the main text.

i. Arcane language: i.e. specific formulations which are understandable to lawyers due to socialization processes to which they have been exposed can be perceived as an accidental element in the legal language. They are shortcomings rather than linguistic phenomena justified by the necessity of professional linguistic practices. Elderly usage such as *plaintiff in error* or *defendant in error* in cases concerning the *writ of error* are a good example of such use. Neither the plaintiff nor the defendant need to err, they take part in a litigation concerning the writ of error (cf. for instance *Plessy v. Ferguson, 163 U.S. 537, 1896* in Notes and Commented Materials no. 40). Furthermore, a specific type of arcane language represent in the English legal language French appendices which are in fact either redundant or manieristic: *A child born anywhere in a lawful wedlock is* ***(semble)*** *legitimate* (emphasis supplied), (in: A.W. Scott, Private International Law, 2nd ed. MacDonalds and Evans, Plymouth, p. 183). Such expressions have of course their hidden sense in that they signal that the assumption is conditioned and can be challenged with legal means. Nevertheless, they provide in this arcane language a piece of information which is known to the expert anyhow and which for the non-expert will not be understandable and remain hidden. They are therefore not helpful in the legal language, although they clearly have a function in it. They namely stress the erudition of their authors. Still further, decisions of the U.S. Supreme Court can be rendered a.o. as *majority* or *plurality decisions* depending upon the number of justices voting. The terminological difference is distinctive because the *plurality decision* which settles the case does not become precedent for future cases unlike the *majority decision.* This distinction is not marked in the terms, it is arcane. When courts refer to facts and persons unrelated to the case, the reference may not be intelligible to laypersons. For instance: *When Cardozo enunciated the standard for doing business in New York, there would have been little need to consider how, or whether, a foreign-based multinational enterprise would be found to be doing business in New York* (cf. Bulova v. Hattori (508 F. Supp. 1322, 1981). Only a professional reader will realize that the person mentioned in the decision is Justice Benjamin Cardozo, one of the most influential judges in the history of U.S. law. However, many laypersons may not be aware of his achievements.

j. ***Redundant terms:*** Terminological redundancies in law have their roots in the historical development of the legal language which unlike many other scientific thesauruses has a tradition of at least two thousand years. Therefore, the legal terminology incorporates traditional terms and expressions which had their role to play in the past legal practice but sometimes lost it in the course of times. Additionally, specific features in the development of national legal languages such as binomials in the legal English (e.g. *null and void* or *last will and testament*) may lead to problems when applied in contemporary legal texts, for instance in court decisions or contracts. All these linguistic creations are deeply rooted in the history of the English legal language (Beveridge 2002: 62). Today, nevertheless, they might and sometimes are perceived as redundant in the English legal language (Adams 2005: 3). To illustrate, in numerous agreements under the common law, assertions of facts are referred to as *representations and warranties*. The use of two different terms in one expression signals a possible conceptual difference. This difference is usually difficult to identify in contracts. In the U.S. law, only in the *Model Stock Purchase Agreement* (1995) and in the *Model Asset Purchase Agreement* (2001), both documents prepared by the American Bar Association, a distinction between both terms is established. The agreements read as far as *representations and warranties* are concerned: ***representations*** *are statements of past or existing facts and* ***warranties*** *are promises that the existing or future facts are or will be true* (emphasis added). Only one case had been identified in which this distinction plays a role, namely Krys v. Hendersen (69 S.E. 2d 635, 637) and it has been argued that the distinction is much more subtle than assumed (Adams 2005: 1). This leads to the conclusion that courts frequently use both terms as synonyms (Adams 2005: 2) and that therefore the terms *representation* and *represent* would be fully sufficient to convey the proper legal meaning of the concept (Adams 2005: 3). Moreover, the common law distinguishes between *conditions precedent* and *conditions subsequent. Conditions precedent* means that a specified event must occur before a party is obliged to perform contractual duties while *conditions subsequent* relates to a situation where an event excuses the performance of an existing contractual duty to perform. This terminological difference is applied in numerous common law and international contracts (Beveridge 2002: 74). For the U.S., the Restatement (Second) of Contracts eliminates in its Sec. 224 the distinction between *conditions precedent* and *conditions subsequent*. The UCC mentions in § 2–615 *presupposed* conditions. In international contracts, especially when common law is not applicable, the use of these terms or the strict distinction between them does not make much sense (Beveridge 2002: 74). Under the U.S. law, to distinguish between both terms in sale contracts would be redundant. Redundancy may also be assumed in the heading of Art. 71 of the Constitution of India: *Matters relating to, or connected with, the election of a President or Vice-President*. Next to these conceptual redundancies, especially in the legal treatises, internal reference is used to fill the empty space in texts, e.g. (ESP) *como ya emos visto, comprobaremos más adelante, ha sido ya considerado* (Lasarte 2006: 24). Also in this book expressions such as *Needless to say* or *As already mentioned* are frequently used in order to form a more coherent exposition of thoughts and to facilitate the orientation in the text. Strictly speaking, all of them are of course logically redundant.

Furthermore, Art. 599 French Civil Code: (FR) *Le propriétaire ne peut,* ***par son fait, ni de quelque manière que se soit****, nuire aux droits de l'usufruitier* demonstrates by the aspect of apparent redundancy (marked by me in the text) the pragmatic element in the legal language. Its role in the above formulation is to stress the prohibited action, not to mention it. The same role play formulations such as *Strictly prohibited* or *Smoking absolutely prohibited* that state more than a purely logical act of prohibition.

Legal tricks that represent fallacies and are based on the structure of syllogism make part of jokes: (FR) *Le peuple est souverain, le Parlement représente le peuple, le Parlement est souverain* (cf. Carcassonne 2005: 19). Further, the sarcastic quote from Billy Bragg's song *Rotting on Remand* became part of the popular English legal discourse: *I said 'There is no justice' and they led me out the door/ And the judge said, 'This isn't a court of justice son, this is a court of law'*. Textually, the judge's answer apparently goes back to an ironical remark made by Oliver Wendell Holmes: *This is a court of law, young man, not a court of justice.*

2.3.6 Monolingual and multilingual linguistic corpus

Legal language has been analyzed either in the monolingual perspective as a special register of a given natural language (cf. Korte 1974, Schwyter 1996, Williams 2005, Goźdź-Roszkowski 2011) or as special register contrasted with other special registers belonging to other natural languages. Many languages have been already scrutinized in this perspective. To illustrate, Mattila (2013: 273–304) as well as Villa-Real/Arco Torres (1999) and Gandasegui (1998) characterized the evolution of the legal culture in Spain from the Roman conquest and the introduction of the Roman law in the peninsula, over the West Goths influence and *ius commune* around 1100. In 13th century Castilia introduces *Las Siete Partidas* that remain particularly valuable in terms of legal linguistics as they are written in the local language and not in Latin although they are deeply rooted in the spirit of the Roman law. In parts of the peninsula that were governed by Arabs the situation was more complex. After the reunification of the country, especially in 19th century the influence of the French Code civil remains particularly strong. This concerns also Spanish-speaking countries of Latin America that eagerly received this new legal code. Legal French even influenced the syntax of legal Spanish, for instance (ES) *Orden disponiendo la creación...*for (ES) *Orden que dispone la creación...*Legal English has been analyzed as a part of common English (Hiltunen 1990), legal English used in the UK was compared with legal English used in the USA or India (Mattila 2006: 246–249). S. Goźdź-Roszkowski (2011) stressed in his corpus-based study the variation of recurrent linguistic patterns while concentrating upon legal English in the U.S. Furthermore, legal English has been compared with legal French (Mattila 2006: 231). This research perspective has been adapted to numerous languages and valuable results have been obtained thus far. Both, the monolingual and the multilingual perspectives have their *raisons d'être*. The monolingual perspective explores one natural language and makes clear its complexity. The multilingual perspective shows languages in contrast and in contact and is complementary to the monolingual point of view.

2.3.6.1 Multilinguality of the legal language

Multilinguality in the legal language is rare. In court opinions, especially those rendered within the common law, Latin and occasionally French expressions may occur. In some jurisdictions, e.g. in Germany, however, foreign or Latin vocabulary is strictly avoided mostly with reference to procedural rules providing for the use of the State language in legal acts. A German court would never use the term (LAT) *culpa in contrahendo*. Instead, the German equivalent (D) *Verschulden bei Vertragsschluss* will be invoked, although the deciding judges might have used exclusively the popular Latin term when discussing the case before rendering the decision. Use of foreign vocabulary in the legislation is even more seldom. Nowadays, the number of direct quotes from legal English is increasing. For instance, in the Italian Civil Code, art. 2427bis the English term *fair value* is rendered in Italian in the headline of the provision as (IT) *valore equo*; later on it is used in the Italian text of the statutory provision without any translation into Italian. The term *joint venture* is rendered in English only and is not marked particularly in the text, unlike *fair value*:

> *2427bis. Informazioni relative al valore equo* ***"fair value"*** *degli strumenti finanziari.*
> *(1) – 1. Nella nota integrativa sono indicati: 1) per ciascuna categoria di strumenti finanziari derivati: a) il loro* ***fair value****; b) informazioni sulla loro entità e sulla loro natura; 2) per le immobilizzazioni finanziarie iscritte a un valore superiore al loro* ***fair value****, con esclusione delle partecipazioni in società controllate e collegate ai sensi dell'articolo 2359 e delle partecipazioni in joint venture...*

Furthermore, a German statutory provision (Art. 112 Investmentgesetz) provides for a regulation of *hedge funds* which it calls (D) *Sondervermögen mit zusätzlichen Risiken*. However, it supplies the English term in brackets in the headline of the provision (D) *Vermögen mit zusätzlichen Risiken (Hedgefunds)*. Furthermore, it uses the term *leverage* for (D) *unbeschränkte Aufnahme von Krediten für gemeinschaftliche Rechnung der Anleger oder über Einsatz von Derivaten*. However, it does not use the term *short sales*, and speaks instead of (D) *Leerverkauf* (cf. Art. 112 I 2 Investmentgesetz).

In the English version of the *Constitution of India* (Art. 31A) specific property rights are mentioned in their original linguistic form: (2) In this article, (a) the expression "estate" shall, in relation to any local area, have the same meaning as that expression or its local equivalent has in the existing law relating to land tenures in force in that area and shall also include (i) any *jagir*, *inam* or *muafi* or other similar grant in the states of (Tamil Nadu) and Kerala, any *janman* right; (ii) any land held under *ryotwari* settlement...(b) the expression "rights", in relation to an estate, shall include any rights vesting in a proprietor, sub-proprietor, under-proprietor, tenure-holder, (*raiyat*, *under-raiyat*) or other intermediary and any rights or privileges in respect of land revenue (emphasis added). Additionally, the Constitution of India stipulates in its Art. 23 (1): Traffic in human beings and *begar* and other similar forms of forced labour are prohibited and any contravention of this provision shall be an offence punishable by the law. Also in the Explanation I to Art. 25 the same phenomenon can be traced: The wearing and carrying of *kirpans* shall be deemed to be included in the profession of the Sikh religion.

Incorporating foreign terminology is not a rare drafting procedure. The English *Magna Carta* (1215) displays some English terms in their Latin surroundings, for instance in its Art. 25: *Omnes comitatus, hundredi, wapentakii, et trethingi sint ad antiquas firmas absque ullo incremento, exceptis dominicis maneriis nostris.*

2.3.6.2 Influence of legal Russian upon other legal languages

In an excursus, some remarks upon the influence of legal Russian may be worthwhile considering. The legal Russian language was mainly productive on the territory of the Russian Empire and later in the Soviet Union. Its most poignant influence can be seen in the formation of legal terminology of many minority languages spoken on Russia's territory (cf. Wydra/Galdia 2010). Many of these languages borrowed the Russian terminology directly, some used it to form linguistic calques. For instance, terms such as *arbitrazh* (*арбитраж*), *gosudarstvennyi* (*государственный*) or *Soviet* (*Совет*) have been incorporated directly into Mari (Galdia/Höpp 1993: 189). In the Chuvash language, terms such as *atkas* (*aткас*), *āshtraf* (*aштраф*), *vakkat* (ваккат from Russian *advokat*), *vinavat* (*винават*), *vulăs* (*вулас* from Russian *volost'*) are borrowings from Russian (cf. Fedotov, 1996). In smaller Caucasian languages (cf. Klimov/Halilov 2003) lexical units such as Abkhazian *āsud* (*āсуд*), Chechen and Ingushetian *sud* (*суд*), Chamalinian and Tindinian sud (*суд*) for *court of law* are obvious borrowings from Russian. The same transfer process concerns the Russian word *sud'ja* (*судья*) (judge) in Abazinian *sudja* (*судя*), Kabardinian *sudja* (*судя*), in Lak *sudja* (*судя*), in Darginian *sudja* (*судя*). Also Russian *shtraf* (*штраф* for sanction or fine) was borrowed in Abkhazian *āshtraf* (*āштраф*), in Kabardinian *shtraf* (*штраф*) and some other smaller languages. However, not only terminology but also textual patterns were borrowed from Russian, especially in smaller languages. Although detailed research into this issue is missing, it seems that Uralic languages spoken on the Russian territory were the most exposed to the influence of legal Russian. In previous times, in the Soviet Union, Russian legal language functioned as an instrument that formed the legal language in all republics of the Union and in other languages spoken on the territory of the Soviet Union.

2.3.7 Legal language changes

A considerable part of the reflection upon law has been devoted to the issue of changes in law (cf. Mattila 2008: 1151). The fact that legal regulation changes is a practical problem with which every lawyer must cope and he also has to find out the appropriate method for the up-date of his own legal knowledge. Therefore, it cannot surprise that changes in law are often also changes in the use of language in law. Interesting is the sort of changes which take place within the legal language. The competition between *counsellor* and *counsel* in law ended with the victory of *counsel*, a form predominantly used today in British English. An old ceremonious formula for '*calling new silks to the bar*', i.e. appointing new king's counsels retains the term *counsellor*: *Mr X, His Majesty having been pleased to appoint you one of His Majesty's Counsellors at law, will you please take your place within the Bar!* The additional tendency in the development of the legal language is its relative dependence upon the ordinary language and changes which occur there. For the English legal language Risto Hiltunen showed the most significant transformation from Old (legal) English to legal English rooted in legal Latin and Norman-French heritage (Hiltunen 1990: 21–48). I include an excerpt in my Notes to illustrate this radical transformation (cf. Notes and Commented Materials no. 13). Both, Hiltunen (1990: 55–62) and Mattila (2006: 226–228) also showed the relative independence in the development of ordinary English and of Law French in England as well as the process of approximation of ordinary and legal English in contemporary times toward the background of relative interdependence of both linguistic varieties. The development of the most significant legal languages for the Western tradition has been aptly characterized in the research. Mattila (2006) describes linguistic changes in legal Latin, French, English and German as well as the development within the EU. Heller (1992) focused on the reform of the legal German in 18th century. For the emergence of legal Russian the absence of Old Church Slavonic terminology in *Russkaya pravda* has been stressed (Unbegaun 1969: 53); in turn, the Serbian legal language previously grounded in the Old Church Slavonic terminology (Bartoszewicz 1979: 50). The main discernible tendency in this development is the one of increasing specialization of language use. This tendency may be in a sense counteracted by the plain language use in the English-language legislation in the U.S. However, it may be premature to assert that this tendency – whose efficiency has not been proven yet – would dominate language use in legislative bodies and in the judicature of the future. Meanwhile, new structuring legal concepts such as (FR) *droit privatif* in the cyberlaw emerge constantly: *C'est vainement que les défendeurs font valoir que la réservation d'un nom de domaine ne serait génératrice d'aucun « droit privatif » et permettrait seulement de revendiquer une antériorité, alors qu'en réservant le nom de domaine « boistropicaux.com », l'association s'est vue reconnaître un droit d'occupation sur ce terme, en vertu duquel elle est en droit de s'opposer à toute réservation d'un nom de domaine quasi-identique destinée à profiter indûment de sa notoriété et à générer une confusion* (TGI Lille 10 July 2001). Now, in a short case study we may look at legal Spanish.

2.3.7.1 Evolution of legal Spanish

The development of legal Spanish is well covered in the research. R. Menéndez Pidal studied numerous ancient documents (ESP *diplomas*) and tried to trace the development of Castilian from Medieval Latin. His *Documentos lingüísticos de Es-*

paña. I. Reino de Castilla, Madrid, 1919 and *Orígines del español. Estado lingüístico de la Peninsula Ibérica hasta el siglo XI,* Madrid, 1929, include textual examples of this linguistic evolution, also in respect of the legal language. A document (ESP *declaración de derechos*) issued circa 1030 reads as follows:

> *Ipsos infanciones de Spelia abuerunt fuero per anutba tenere in Gormaz et in Oxima et in Sancti Stefani; quando prenderunt ipsas casas mauros, mandavit domno Sancio comite que tenuissent ipsas anutbas in Karazo et in Penna fidele, quomodo totos infantiones faciebant, et non quesierunt infantiones de Spelia su mandato facere. Proinde presot ille comite tota Spelia, et non eis laxabit nisi mas hereditatelias.*

Another document issued circa 1090 reads:

> *De illa particigon que feci senigor Sango Garcese. Ad Galino Acenarece era lorika, ero kabalo, era mulla, era espata. Ad Sango Scemenones ero kabalo, era mulla, era espata, era ellemo. Ad Scemeno Fertungones, si tene illa onore, tienga ero kabalo per meno de Cornelga; e si lesca era onore, ero kabalo segat suo engenobo; e dos elmos.*

The language of both documents is basically still Latin, with some modified forms such as *infanciones* (spelled also *infantiones* in the text), *anutba,* or *hereditatelias* that manifest already characteristic features of a Romance language. Meanwhile, *anutba,* in modern form *anúteba,* from the Arabic word whose meaning was 'war tribute' and *gualardón* from Germanic *widarlón* mark two most prolific sources which, next to the dominating legal Latin, contributed to the development of the Spanish legal terminology. Menéndez Pidal resumed the results illustrated above in his *El idioma español en sus primeros tiempos,* Colec. Austral, nr. 250, Buenos Aires, 1942 and in *Carácter originario de Castilla* and in *La Unidad del idioma,* both published in: *Castilla, La tradición. El idioma.,* Colec. Austral, nr. 501, Buenos Aires, 1945, pp. 9–40 and pp. 171–218 respectively. Unlike in other Romance languages, Latin-based yet already Spanish legal terminology emerges rather early in the Castilian language. Latin is not used in *Las Siete Partidas* that is perceived as fundamental to the development of the Spanish legal language (Mattila 2002b: 307). The volume originally called *Libro de las leyes* or *Fuero de las leyes* has been apparently prepared in Sevilla, between 1251 and 1256. The author or authors of *Las Siete Partidas* have not been determined with convincing arguments; researchers point to the influence of King Alfonso X, called El Sabio, upon the work. Furthermore, the fascination for the number seven, typical of medieval mysticism, is expressed also in a textual detail: *Las leyes han de ser en siete maneras: creer, ordenar las cosas, mandar, ayuntar, galardonar, vedar y escarmentar*; King Alfonso's name is composed of seven letters that also correspond to the initial letters of every of the seven parts of the work (cf. E. Diez-Echarri, J.M. Roca Franquesa, *Historia de la literatura española e hispano-americana,* 2. ed., Madrid: Aguilar, 1966, p. 74–75). Some Spanish legal terminology is of Arabic origin, e.g. *albacea* (last will administrator) comes from Arabic *sahb alwasiyya.* Legal Spanish is an example of a very well research language in terms of its development.

2.4 Legal Terminology and Legal Language

2.4.1 First contact with legal terminology

The first contact with law often concerns its terminology. As already mentioned, the terminology is in our view not the most salient aspect of the legal language, nor does it dominate our conception of legal linguistics. Nevertheless, it is the beginning of the reflection about law for many persons, especially for those who approach the law from the non-professional perspective. Therefore, some introductory remarks about legal terminology are well founded at this place of our work. For many researchers the distinction between legal concepts and legal terms is fundamental to the analysis of the legal terminology in monolingual as in bi- or multilingual contexts. Paradoxically, the comparative approach to legal concepts and terms seems to be more prolific than its monolingual complement. I will therefore base my introductory remarks upon a compromise, and begin with a bilingual example. In private law, while analyzing contracts from the comparative perspective, we encounter a contract type in the common law that is called there *unilateral contract.* The French *Code civil* provided in its Art. 1103 (before 2016) a legal definition of a contract type called there *contrat unilatéral.* However, it would be premature and even negligent to assume that both terms cover the same contract type. The common law *unilateral contract* is a one-sided agreement whereby one party makes a promise to do or to refrain from doing something in return for a performance, not a promise. Traditionally, the common law *bilateral contract* was reduced to the formula that it concerned a promise for a promise, whereas the *unilateral contract* concerned a promise for an act. The civil law developed the concept of a unilateral contract as opposed to the synallagmatic contract in order to distinguish contracts obliging both parties to perform and those which bind only one party (cf. *contrat synallagmatique* or *bilatéral* in Art. 1102 French *Code civil* in its version before amendments of 2016). This aim is visible from the wording and the systematics of the Articles 1102 and 1103 in the French Code civil (in application before October 1, 2016):

> *Art. 1102 Le contrat est* ***synallagmatique*** *ou* ***bilatéral*** *lorsque les contractants s'obligent réciproquement les uns envers les autres.*
>
> *Art. 1103 Il est* ***unilatéral*** *lorsqu'une ou plusieurs personnes sont obligées envers une ou plusieurs autres, sans que de la part de ces dernières il y ait d'engagement.* (emphasis added)

Contrat unilatéral of the French Code civil is in terms of the common law contract doctrine not a contract at all as it lacks *consideration.* In the common law, something of value must correspond to a promise given and this corresponding element is called there *consideration.* In the civil law, there is no need for the *consideration* as a contract can bind only one party. This result follows not only from the Articles 1102 and 1103 of the French Code civil but also from other codes and contract doctrines on the European continent and not only there. Therefore, *unilateral contract* and *contrat unilatéral* are two different concepts as they are two different terms in

English and French respectively. Needless to say that *consideration* cannot be translated into French as (FR) *considération* because it would not refer to any concept of the French or Continental private law. (FR) *considération* as a purported equivalent of the common law *consideration* would be an empty, misleading and therefore also redundant term in the translation. Assumed the existence of a bilingual French and English uniform legal system which is grounded in the common law concepts of the *unilateral contract* and *consideration* and which uses these terms, both French terms *contrat unilatéral* and *considération* could be used in the French linguistic version of this legal system within their common law conceptual field. They would be misleading for a French user who is not familiar with this constructed legal system and who perceives the French legal terms through the French legal concepts. The risk of misconception that was described above corresponds to the nature of the legal terminology. Monolingual or multilingual legal terminology cannot be learned or understood when separated from the law in which it functions. The price to be paid for the insistence on the contrary view is the misconception of the meaning of legal rules or legal texts in general or, at least, the increased risk of such misconceptions.

The amendment to the above provisions that entered into force on October 1, 2016 reads as follows:

> Art. 1104: *Le contrat est synallagmatique lorsque les contractants s'obligent réciproquement les uns envers les autres. Il est unilatéral lorsqu'une ou plusieurs personnes s'obligent envers une ou plusieurs autres sans qu'il y ait d'engagement réciproque de celles-ci.*

The proposed amendment is interesting for legal linguists because it reformulates Art. 1102 and Art. 1103 and forms a new Art. 1104 without changing the doctrinal content of law (cf. Leveneur 2016). Thus, the stability of the legal doctrine prevails over linguistic change.

Traditionally, legal linguistics devoted much time and space to the analysis of legal notions. There are good reasons for this and we will also engage in conceptual analyses especially toward a comparative background. But before we make this step we should ask why actually this sort of analyses attracts the attention of researchers in law. In fact, law has been perceived by many as an ongoing debate about the content of concepts. This type of debates emerges, according to P. F Strawson (1992: 4), when the pragmatic perspective is neglected. Strawson writes: "...disorders never arise when our concepts ideas are actually at work, but only when they are idle." Strawson's observation concerning metaphysical concepts used in philosophy seems to fit perfectly the embarrassing situation we are confronted with in law. As long as the legal notions are idle, i.e. are named in statutes or precedents, they seem to be at least relatively clear. Problems emerge when these notions are to be applied in new cases. There, suddenly, the notions used in statutes or defined in the doctrine give rise to debates about their content. When used in precedents they lead to questions about their possible applicability in new cases. In law, we operate with posited concepts whose content was apparently only partially defined by the legislator or the judge. As soon as these concepts should become operative in a new context we are confronted with the problems of application which cannot be as easily solved as misunderstandings in the daily use of language. Misunderstandings about the content of concepts that are used in ordinary language come up rarely and when they come up, they can be easily clarified in discourses through disambiguation (cf. 2.2.4).

2.4.2 Legal concepts and legal terms

Fundamental to the analysis of legal terminology has been the distinction between legal concepts and legal terms (Mattila 2006: 108). This distinction is of logical origin. It enables to access the legal language, especially its legal terms in respect of their content and in respect of their form. More fundamentally, general linguistics has been interested in terms in opposition to non-terms (Hałas 1995: 4). It furthermore maintained that a *term* is ontologically grounded in a contrast to another term without which it would not emerge. In general linguistics, the definition of *term* is not finally clarified (Kesola 2007: 14). In law, however, the fascination for terms has been nourished by the vain hope that they would convey unequivocal meaning which would be independent from the context (Kesola 2007: 21). Moreover, certain researchers stressed that legal terminology is numerically rather limited when compared with other areas of science (Pigolkin 1990: 15). Therefore, it may surprise that it gained a central role in the legal-linguistic research. The traditional distinction between concept and term can be shown on the following examples. We can distinguish between two legal terms from business law, (US) *sole proprietor* and (UK) *sole trader.* Both terms are functional equivalents and stand for a person running business alone with unlimited liability. Thus, the common law concept represented in these two terms is the same. In addition, UK business law terms *articles of association* and *memorandum* correspond conceptually to US terms *articles of incorporation* and *bylaws* respectively. Still more, terms describing branches of law differ linguistically, e.g. (US) *corporate* law, (UK) *company* law; both however correspond conceptually. Within the UK, private wrongdoings are termed *torts* for the use in the English law and *delicts* for the Scottish law in the same legal act (cf. (UK) Private International Law (Miscellaneous Provisions) Act 1995 (c.42) Part III, 9). Moreover, in the international law the term *convention* is used in connection with multilateral agreements, as opposed to bilateral *agreements.* For instance, the Vienna Convention on the Law of Treaties defines a *treaty* as an international agreement between states that is governed by international law. Terms in law, seen in relation to concepts, appear to be fairly colorless. Conceptually, it does not matter whether a person who initiates a lawsuit is called *plaintiff* or *claimant.* Neither do other terms such as *appellant* or *petitioner* influence the conceptual setting within the legal procedure. In terms of concepts, seen from the pragmatic perspective, we used to deal in an adversary judicial process with a proponent and an opponent. Even a linguistic error in a legal translation such as (D) **Verklagter* instead of (D) *Beklagter* for defendant cannot distort the conceptual framework of the legal procedure (cf. Notes and Commented Materials no. 19). Moreover, the conceptual framework and the user's knowledge about it reconstruct the appropriate legal-linguistic usage. In our last example, the professional hearer dealing with the error in the translation will without problems reconstruct the correct linguistic form of the legal term used in the text. Therefore, it may seem that terms finally do not matter in law. Later on, we will demonstrate that they have a role to play in the argumentative legal discourse and in its environment, i.e. in the legal (doctrinal) systematics.

Equally, concepts created in economics prefigure the argumentative structures of the economic discourse (cf. Cooter/Ulen 2004: ix). The fundamental economic discourse oscillates in a perspective limited by linguistic constructs such as: *incentive effects, opportunity costs, risk aversion, transaction costs, free-riding, prisoner's dilemma, Nash equilibrium, dominant strategy, asymmetric information, collective choice, open-access resource, median rule, regulatory capture, rent-seeking, credible commitments, moral hazard, adverse selection, market failure, monopoly power, price discrimination, Pareto efficiency, dynamic pricing,* and *cost-benefit analysis.* The universality of this fundamental economic discourse can be proved through reference to textbooks on economics all over the world that are centered on these concepts used there in their respective linguistic versions. Also legal terms such as *judgment-proof injurers* enter into the language of economics so that some expect a further convergence of both areas due to the infusion of legal language into the conceptual realm of economics (cf. Cuter/Ulen 2004: 11). R. Khurana (2007: 480) refers to Sumantra Ghoshal's work where a link has been posited between language and managerial education. According to Ghoshal, language plays a role in the sense that it shapes MBA students' ideas about managerial organization and the role of management in organizations. Ghoshal argued that the managerial theory was a mechanism to persuade students of the legitimate role of management. Therefore, it cannot be perceived as a discursively neutral construct.

The discursively marked difference between concept and term requires a thorough scrutiny from the pragmalinguistic perspective. In daily life, we can imagine a dog without saying: *dog*. Meanwhile, already more complex ideas like *liberty* cause problems in this respect. Doubtless, however, we cannot imagine the *promissory estoppel* without using its linguistic expression in one way or another. Basically, in the area of law there is no legal concept without a corresponding legal term. Apparently, it would be impossible to think about a legal concept were a term not at speaker's disposal. The linguistic expression of a concept is the term, which means that both are linked like the two sides of a coin. One could therefore ask why legal theory still operates with the split of one thing in two. The reason may be practical, as shown on the example of the coin. *Adverse possession* in the American law and *Ersitzung* in the German law refer to the same concept, yet express it with different linguistic means. Certain linguists and comparative lawyers perceive this superficial difference of term formation as substantial. They will say that two terms correspond to one concept. The divide between concept and term is used to mark this difference. From the pragmalinguistic perspective the propositional content of the terms is the same, no split in term and concept is necessary. In daily life, speech acts such as (FIN) *Kiitos käynnistä* and (S) *Välkommen igen* may again look differently yet they are functionally equivalent. This understanding of concepts in speech acts might help legal linguists and legal comparatists to come to terms with the challenge represented in the distinction between terms and concepts.

2.4.3 How do terms and concepts work in law?

The interrelation between term and concept is complex in law, especially when also the diachronic perspective is incorporated into it. Therefore, it is appropriate to ask how legal concepts expressed in terms function in law. Let us have a look at one of them, for instance the common law notion of *adverse possession.* It refers to a situation in which someone without being owner acquires under specific circumstances full title to land against all others including the record owner. To benefit from this unusually generous proposal made by the legislator certain acts over an uninterrupted period of time, which is prescribed by statute, are necessary. As a rule, it is prescribed additionally that such possession must be *actual, visible, open, notorious, hostile, under claim of right, definite, continuous,* and *exclusive.* This is quite a lot for one concept. Therefore, some call the adverse possession a 'method' to obtain the title to land, and not that much a concept (cf. Barron's Law Dictionary).

In addition, some constellations like possession by a mortgageor are generally not considered as leading to adverse possession because mortgage is neither notorious nor hostile. The above description includes several situations. The first set relates to different factual constellations in which persons occupy land that does not belong to them. The other one comprises a set of related situations which all together create the circumstances of the acquisition of property by a non-owner in an exceptional situation. To determine this exceptional situation certain requirements are set up. All of them are expressed with the help of legal concepts. The last set of situations comprises those legal constellations, which like mortgage, are perceived as typically not leading to adverse possession. The concept so composed enables a regular argumentation in a case related to acquisition of property under exceptional circumstances. This argumentation must take place within the indicated sets of situations to be complete. It must furthermore test these situations toward the background of concepts provided by the doctrine in order to exclude abuse because *adverse possession* is an exception to the general rule that protects the rightful owner. Furthermore, the concepts used in the test must be interpreted because they, in their generality, say everything and nothing. The interpretation of those concepts follows the guidelines of the doctrine, occasionally expressed in form of definitions. For instance, the possession is *notorious* when it is open, undisguised, and conspicuous to the point where such a possession is known or recognized. Moreover, the possession is *hostile* when it takes place without the permission of anyone claiming paramount title and is coupled with the claim of ownership, express or implied, against all others including the record owner. For instance, a holding like a lease is not a case of hostile possession. One could counter that all this is not a big help and that it jeopardizes the test rather than promotes the efforts toward a rational solution of a case related to *adverse possession.* But, we are dealing here with requirements for professional argumentation which may not be accessible to non-jurists. It nevertheless must pass the test of rationality within the legal community. And this challenge seems to matter to jurists most.

The argumentative structure based on legal notions is universal. In Spanish property law following conceptual requirements are set up for the (ESP) *usucapión* according to Art. 1941 of the Código civil: *en concepto de dueño, pública, pacífica, ininterrumpida.* The argumentation concerning a possible *usucapión* based on possession, (ESP) *posesión hábil,* is developed around these concepts (Lasarte 2006: 239). Both situational and conceptual requirements of completeness are necessary to make the conceptual structure work in the argumentation. It seems that the conceptual requirements of test completeness are more difficult to fulfill than the situational ones. Their final test is the test of rationality passed within the legal community.

2.4.4 Legal notions are shorthand script

Legal notions have an ontology that is determined by the way they come about. When we analyze the use of (FR) *prescription* we will easily find out that it precludes claims to be effectively enforced in French courts due to a certain time limit which must pass. These claims are in the terminology of the common law *statute barred* because there is a statute which sets a time limit for the enforcement of claims of whatever sort. This is also the rationale of the term *prescription* in the French law. The fact that it is used in the legal practice does not mean that it has the same ontological status as *gravitation* or *bicycle.* Its existence is a result of a deliberate and institutionalized setting which facilitates legal operations by making them more efficient. Definitely, (FR) *prescription* does not exist in the same way as *gravitation* or *bicycle* do. What exists in a case is a claim which is statute barred, not the statutory limitation as such. This specific statutory limitation, (FR) *prescription* is shorthand for the situation in which there exists a statute limiting the time in which claims can be enforced by courts and the claim which is allegedly barred by the statute of limitations. The legal term can be traced back to an utterance that does not include any abstract terms (Kotarbiński 1986: 20). The rest is the application of the statute upon the claim. In the application process the shorthand *statute barred claim* or (FR) *prescription* can be used to facilitate the legal operation in question, i.e. the test providing the answer to the question whether a claim is actually statute barred or not. Kotarbiński's approach helps overcome metaphysical fallacies in dealing with legal concepts that have been characterized by others as *ghosts,* i.e. purely psychical phenomena (Petrażycki 1955: 123 sqq) or *hollow words* (Ross 1957: 818). The existence of a legal notion depends upon the wish of the legislator. Thus, the question whether (FR) *contract d'adhesion* exists in the French law or not depends on the legislator's intention to introduce into the legal system a notion known by legal scholars from the history of law and the comparative law. Should the French legislator not wish to introduce the notion into the French legal system, the term will exist only as a social fact or a notion used in the scientific discourse. Its legal existence depends upon the decision of the legislator to make a legal notion of it.

In law, there is no such thing as a *contract d'adhesion* as such without the legislator introducing it. It may, of course, be postulated *de lege ferenda* and would have a place in the discussion about the future of law – but only there. Nevertheless, it will exist in the legal language. This problem setting is not new for the comparative lawyer. When the comparative lawyer is dealing with the common law procedure of *discovery* in a case involving a court in a civil law country he certainly will not simply introduce the notion of *discovery* into his systemic knowledge of this particular civil law but perceive it as a part of the other, foreign law system. He is doing this because the legislator of the civil law country in case did not introduce the notion *discovery* into this civil law system. For the comparatist, the relative existence of legal notions is his daily bread. In the hypothetical case sketched above he simply will not apply the procedures of discovery, because they do not exist for him as long as they are not anchored in the legal system by the legislator. For the comparatist, it goes without saying that this anchorage in his legal system may look differently. It may be constituted by the decision to introduce the procedure of discovery into this particular civil law system, it may also be a result of a provision related to the conflict of laws or a simple result of legislation concerning recognition of foreign judgments or other court decisions. In all three cases the existence of the common law *discovery* procedure in the particular civil law system is of different nature. Yet, without the legislative decision it simply does not exist there at all. This shorthand and relative existence of legal notions has consequences for the daily work of lawyers and for the public debate about law. It makes clear what it means that law is posited, i.e. that it is set. It allows for the most vigorous sort of freedom in the discussion about law and in its creation as the limits of legal notions are the limits of our societal goals and no other boundaries exist. Simultaneously, it excludes from the debate about the creation of new laws and interpreting precedents arguments pertaining to the existence of legal notions which allegedly could not be modified. Existing legal notions can always be modified, replaced by other notions or simply abolished. In the legal science, and especially in legal linguistics, the prerequisites of such evolution are problematic but not the issue as such. Finally, we may note that in terms of pragmatics, the interdependence between legal concepts and legal terms is unclear. It may at the end of the day be a misunderstanding, a wrongly put hypothesis with a strong metaphysical background. The linguistic principle of arbitrariness of linguistic signs may serve as a response to the problem (cf. 3.6.2 regarding the use of (RU) *brak*). The connections between term and concept are arbitrary; they cannot be further elaborated nor justified. Terms have their etymology and their inner-systemic motivation, but they do not emerge in linguistic dependence upon concepts.

2.4.4.1 Implied terms and concepts

Terminology used in the transfer of legal concepts and terms leads to theoretical problems which are a challenge within the known approaches to legal linguistics. One could ask what actually happens when a common law term such as *punitive damages* is translated as (FR) *condamnation à dommages et intérêts punitifs* (Carval 1995) or (D) *Strafschadensersatz*. One could boldly counter that nothing happens because no *punitive damages* are known in the German or the French legal systems and therefore (D) *Strafschadensersatz* does not belong to the German legal language and does not mean anything there. The same could be valid for the French equivalent. This courageous and possibly even acceptable answer – at least in the perspective of some approaches to legal linguistics – does not fully satisfy. Similar to this case is a situation where a term from another language, e.g. (D) *Verhältnissmässigkeitsgrundsatz* is introduced as (FR) *principe de proportionnalité* into French-language legal acts within the EU although it does not exist as a term in the French terminology. The case is even more complicated when it is considered that the French *Conseil d'État* in the decision Benjamin from 19 May 1933 clearly applied the principle of proportionality, but did not mention it in a form of a term. Berteloot (2002: 94) posits therefore: *So we can say that the concept surely existed, but without being uttered in a short and expressive way*. Yet, can we say this? We could risk an analogous remark in regard to two terms of the EU law which are rendered in (FR) with *légitimation active* and *légitimation passive* and which do not exist in the French legal system (Berteloot 2002: 94). They were coined in approximation to the (D) *Aktivlegitimation* and (D) *Passivlegitimation*. As said, they may not exist as such in the French legal system. Nevertheless, they are thinkable and would make sense in it. Yet, what sort of existence would it be? In terms of terminological research it would probably be the existence as a term because a concept – even implied – must exist in the relevant legal system should a borrowed term make sense in it. The initial example quoted by Berteloot proves this assumption; (FR) *principe de proportionnalité* even if not explicitly used in the French law is nevertheless understandable in it because it could explicitly be used there. Even (D) *Strafschadensersatz* as a postulated equivalence for *punitive damages* means something in the German legal system as it can be explained through the reference to the German system of monetary damages (cf. Schwintowski 2003: 633). In this perspective, neither the concept nor the term (D) *Strafschadensersatz* would exist as concept and term of the German system of monetary damages. Nevertheless both are comprehensible toward the background of the German legal system. The difference is that (FR) *principe de proportionnalité* is understandable also in the French legal system whereas (D) *Strafschadensersatz* is understandable only toward the background of the German legal system. Equally, while discussing the structure of the contract under CISG Moens and Gillies (2006: 17) admit that it does not include the requisite of *consideration* that is typical of common law contracts. Yet, they maintain that the *consideration* is de facto included also in the CISG-type of contracts because sale contracts that are embraced by the convention always will have to include a form of *consideration* by logical necessity. In this view, and it would be difficult to claim the opposite, a sale contract is a result of a bargain between the parties who will provide each other something; otherwise it would not make much sense to get involved in this sort of transactions. Here, we witness another form of potential existence in law.

Professional speakers who witness the emergence of new legal-linguistic units have the rare privilege to distinguish them automatically from the classical legal vocabulary. For instance, a new tort termed *intentional infliction of emotional distress* has been added to the established list of common law torts such as *trespass, assault* or *battery*. The doctrinal aspect which means that a new tort type has been added to the classical list and that it has been accepted by the common law courts is less interesting in our context. The decisive issue is the emergence of a concept termed in this way and the choice that is exercised in its lexicalization. As an example we may mention that the Japanese law distinguishes between *injury to honor* and *injury to reputation* (Anderson/Okuda 2007: 150). Authors of legal-linguistic neologisms can be sometimes identified by their names. For instance, the term *common heritage of mankind* has been launched by the Maltese Ambassador Arvid Pardo in 1967 (Cassese 2005: 92). Does this circumstance have an impact upon our understanding of legal terminology? It certainly does. The understanding of legal terminology, be it monolingual or multilingual, is based upon institutionalized creation and interpretation of legal concepts and terms, preponderantly by the legislator and by courts. Spontaneous and anonymous creation is limited under such circumstances.

2.4.5 Classification of terms

Terms can be classified in several ways. They can be purely technical, i.e. be used only in law, e.g. *promissory estoppel, renvoi, certiorari* or *replevin*. Furthermore, (FR) *emphytéose, préciput, prôtet,* and *sursurestarie* are counted among ca. 250–400 lexical units that are perceived as belonging to the French legal language exclusively (Cornu 2005: 62–65). Some terms in law may have a meaning that differs from the ordinary language, e.g. *consideration, characterization, equity*. Legal terms may differ within one natural language, e.g. *domicile* in the US or the UK usage where one lexical unit covers different, only partly overlapping concepts. They may display preferences in use within one natural language, e.g. *warranty* preferred in the US, and *guarantee* rather used in the UK. The same concerns (US) *antitrust legislation* and (UK) *competition legislation* or (US) *corporation* and (UK) *company*. Also specific is the use of (US) *affirm* or *reverse* and the (UK) usage of *allow* or *dismiss* in connection with judgments. *Terms* appear to be polysemic within one legal language, e.g. *civil law* meaning 1. private law or 2. Continental legal tradition in legal English. Finally, terms may be seen in a diachronic dimension, e.g. *university* or (LAT) *universitas* that had been a form of economic or territorial organization or (FR) *Parlement de Paris, Parlement de Bretagne* which had been *courts of law* and not *Parliaments*. In the diachronic dimension they may display some stylistic features of the legal language as is the case with the English binomials, e.g. *terms and conditions* or *null and void*. Terms as those mentioned can be compared in a multilingual perspective, e.g. (US) *promissory estoppel* and (FR) *principe de cohérance contractuelle*, (LAT) *culpa in contrahendo* and (US) *infringment of the rules of good faith*, (US) *piercing the corporate veil* – (D) *Durchgriffshaftung* or *unjust enrichment* and (FR) *enrichissement sans cause*. The problem connected to this comparison is the systemic incompatibility of legal concepts. Nevertheless, this problem does not always appear, e.g. (US) *voidable transfer* and (D) *Konkursanfechtung* are largely equivalent. Functional differences can be easily overcome even if a lexical unit may belong to the *faux amis*-expressions due to its polysemy in language contact, e.g. (S) *proposition* versus (UK) *government bill* or (FR) *proposition de loi* and (FR) *projet de loi* (Carcassonne 2005: 376) or (CAT) *avantprojecte de llei* as provisional proposals for another, more definitive legislative project. Functionally corresponding administrative institutions may be called differently, (US) *Internal Revenue* and (UK) *Inland Revenue.*

Also G. Cornu concentrated in his work on legal language (Cornu 2005) largely on terminological issues. He showed that terms in legal texts can belong to the legal parlance exclusively and that they can stand in a relation of internal and external polysemy (Cornu 2005: 89–111). Furthermore, he dealt with the issue of synonymy in law. According to Pigolkin (1990: 15, 73) legal terms are not particularly numerous in the legal language. Cornu however estimates that circa ten thousand legal terms are used in legal French (Cornu 2005: 53). The divergence in estimation is not a question of differences among legal cultures, as legal Russian is definitely not less developed than legal French. It is a result of different approaches to the definition of '*legal term* '.

2.4.6 Diachrony and synchrony in legal terminology

I will illustrate the interplay of diachrony and synchrony in the legal terminology on few examples. Terms like *university, international, antitrust*, and *cartel* reflect this complex relation even if approached from a purely positivist perspective. For instance, *university* in the legal context concerns also the diachronic use of the term. In the Roman law *university* (LAT *universitas*) was close to corporations; even in the Middle Ages it resembled a unity of assets rather than an educational institution (cf. Savigny 1840: 378, 384 about *universitas iuris* and *adquisitio per universitatem*). In the public law, *university* was a long time an organizational form of towns as opposed to municipalities. So had been the Principality of Monaco in which this book was mainly written organized in the Middle Ages as a *university*, in Latin *universitas.* The general meaning of *universitas* in the Latin language is preserved e.g. in Lucius Ampelius' *Liber Memorialis* (I.1 De Mundo): *Mundus est universitas rerum, in quo omnia sunt et extra quem nihil; qui Graece dicitur cosmos.* Furthermore, the use of the term *international* is very specific in the legal context. It may be understood as concerning relations between states, as is the case in the public international law or to concern international cases, e.g. in the private international law. In fact, all states have their own private international laws and their provisions regularly differ in a way that only cases which these laws concern are international because they include an international element. The law as such remains national in essence, although it refers in its structure to the rules developed in the *ius commune* for dealing with cases that contain a foreign element. In the International Business Law *international* refers to the type of cases rather than to the applicable law. In these *international* cases, frequently also *international instruments* such as the CISG must be applied.

They are enforced by national courts and this process of enforcement is also part of International Business Law while constituting a national element in it. Its treatment in the legislation is also different. Moreover, according to the German company law an enterprise cannot include the adjective *international* in its name when it does not develop any substantial international activities; no such restriction exists in the U.S. legislation concerning the names of American enterprises. *International* sounds like a Latin word. However, it did not belong to the lexicon of the ancient Romans; there terms such as (LAT) *mundanus* or paraphrases, e.g. (LAT) *qui/quod ad nonnullas/omnes gentes pertinet* were in use (Mattila 2002d: 273). Some specialists are therefore reluctant to use the word (LAT) *internationalis* that is a late coinage in contemporaneous Latin texts. Nowadays, also the term *cosmopoliticum* is in use in the translation of the emerging term *global law* as *ius cosmopoliticum*, apparently in order to contrast it with *international law* (Cassese 2005: 21). *Cartel* that in the legal language means an association of business persons with the purpose of maintaining prices at a high level and restricting competition comes as a term from political language. It seems that it had been first used in relation to the coalition of the Conservative and the National Liberal parties in Germany in 1887 and meant later any such political agreement. Subsequently, it has been used to denote trade agreements. *Anti-trust* which in the U.S. legal terminology designs legislation aiming at the prevention of measures impeding free competition has its origins in trade agreements which were called *trusts*. The legislation has been designed to counteract the trusts which were deemed as detrimental to the development of economy. The terminological diachrony did not lead to problems in the understanding of legal texts. The reason for this seems to be that terminology adapts to synchronized legal texts in that it follows the legal knowledge of our times. Therefore, no speaker or hearer will be confused by hearing the term *university* or *cartel* even if they have been semantically profoundly modified in time.

2.4.7 Scientific terms introduced into law

Increasingly, terms from other sciences are introduced into legal texts, especially into statutes. Can these terms retain their own meaning or will they have a new meaning due to their new lexical status as parts of the legal language? One could spontaneously imagine that terms representing concepts belonging to other sciences than law must necessarily retain their initial meaning, and that every thought to the contrary would be absurd. The situation is however more complicated. A scientific term which is incorporated into a bill passes a procedure in the Parliament where not only the vote takes place. The term is also discussed starting from the very first draft. In the materials which accompany the preparatory work in the Parliament, interpretive guidelines, definitions and other information is contained which enables the interpretation of the concept when it becomes part of a statute. Interpretive materials may introduce a specific meaning, broader or narrower than the scientific one. Furthermore, terms developed in other sciences may not be univocal there as usually several theoretical approaches compete in the particular branch of sciences for the correct understanding of their methods and their conceptual basis. For instance, when the Canadian legislator passed the Multilingualism Act *multilingualism* became a legal term in the Canadian legislation. Do we understand this term properly while applying the concept of multilingualism developed in linguistics and used in anthropology or both? Which understanding of *multilingualism* used in these particular social sciences is the right one? It would be difficult to use more than one meaning when implementing the act. The same concerns medical terms like *alcoholic* or *drug addict* which may be understood in law differently. The scientific term becoming a legal term lives its own life and may acquire a different meaning from the one used in the particular branch of science where it emerged. In this context, Pigolkin (1990: 70) differentiates between technical terms and legal terms. Technical terms are for him those introduced into law from other scientific disciplines and which remain unchanged there. In the light of the above argument it is difficult to maintain this distinction. Technical terms become legal terms and also legal notions once they were introduced into law. The possibility that in many singular cases they may also keep their initial meaning is not excluded. It is however not possible to generally maintain the conceptual contents of a scientific notion in law as required by Pigolkin (1990: 74). The distinction introduced by Pigolkin shows a particularity in the development of legal terminology. Yet, finally, it proves the coherence of the category rather than the supposed distinctiveness of terms.

2.4.8 Verbs in law

Legal-linguistic analyses of legal terms and concepts usually focused upon nouns and adjectives. Even adverbs attracted jurists more than verbs. In the past, attempts to determine the relation between *obliged* and *obligated* were not particularly successful. R. Dworkin (1977: 19) refers to H.L.A. Hart who in his *Concept of Law* tried to define the distinction in the usage of both participles. Hart's analysis (1961: 89) is a reference to J. Austin's theoretical arguments and seems a scholarly founded convention rather than a research into the use of the two participles. Surprisingly, verbs, the very residue of action, were not as appealing to jurists as were concepts expressed by terms in the form of nouns. Instead, mainly pragmatists such as J.L. Austin or J. Searle turned with passionate subtlety to them in the hope to arrive at the heart of our language. Fortunately, the *West's Encyclopedia of American Law* (Lehman/Phelps 2005) treats verbs on equal footing with other parts of speech; under A it lists e.g.: *adduce, adequate, accrue, accredit, abut, abet* and many others. In addition, deontic modality (cf. Coates 1983) in the language of law has been systematically researched, mainly by Polish scholars (Matulewska 2009, 2010, Nowak-Michalska 2012). Analogous research is available for legal Chinese (cf. 2.1.5.6), legal Finnish and legal Polish (Rydzewska-Siemiątkowska 2016), legal Russian and legal Ukrainian (Goletiani 2016). This research clearly indicates that deontic modality is not only expressed by modal verbs and associated syntagmas. Multiple legal speech acts can transmit deontic modality; as a rule the context of an utterance signals its deontic modality (cf. Nowak-Michalska 2012: 55). Within the linguistic context, the choice of verbs from the list of existing modal verbs in a language is largely arbitrary; some verbs that transfer modality, for instance (PL) *pozwala się*, are traditionally not used in Polish legal texts (Nowak-Michalska 2012: 56).

2.4.8.1 Verbs in Article 2 UCC and in CISG

As said, terminological research has been traditionally noun-oriented and dominated by questions concerning the interpretation of legal concepts. Meanwhile, verbs in law offer a perspective which stresses the dynamic aspect of language in law, i.e. the aspect directed toward and based upon action. Moreover, verbs may be even more suitable than nouns to display pragmatic aspects in the legal language. I will illustrate it on examples from the UCC and the CISG. The UCC's Article 2 *Sales* as well as the CISG are dominated by verbs describing action related to sale contracts (relevant provisions of the UCC are quoted in Notes and Commented Materials no. 25). § 2–201 UCC introduces the Article 2 which *shall be known and may be cited* accordingly. This ceremonious formulation refers to a specific quality of verbs to convey fictitious and prospective action without marking it additionally. Furthermore, verbs may convey interpretive guidelines of different degree of intensity, e.g. § 2–207(2) UCC where additional terms in acceptance or confirmation of sale contracts *are to be construed* as proposals. In § 2–208 UCC the express terms of the agreement...*shall be construed* whenever reasonable as consistent with each other, in § 2–210 (4) UCC a prohibition of assignment *is to be construed as* barring a specific declaration, in § 2–720 UCC specific expressions *shall not be construed as* a renunciation or discharge and in § 2–317 warranties *shall be construed as* consistent with each other if reasonable. The expressions *are/is to be construed* and *shall (not) be construed* function as synonyms. Other fictitious expressions are used in § 2–207 (1) UCC where a definite and seasonable expression *operates as* an acceptance, in § 2–305 (2) UCC a price *means* a price to be fixed in good faith. In § 2–206 (2) UCC an offeror *may treat the offer as having lapsed* under the stated circumstances, in § 2–205 (3) UCC the party *may* at his option *treat the contract as cancelled.* In § 2–204 (2) UCC an agreement *sufficient to constitute* a contract for sale *may be found.* This fictitious use is contrasted with declaratory verbs such as *is* in § 2–308 (a) UCC where the place of delivery *is* the seller's place of business, in § 2–323 (3) where a shipment by water *is overseas* insofar as it is subject to practices characteristic of international deep water commerce and in § 2–328 (2) where the sale by auction *is complete* when the auctioneer so announces. However, from the pragmatic perspective the difference made by the drafters of the UCC between the fictitious and the declaratory use is not convincing. In § 2–308 (a) UCC no change in the meaning would occur through the replacement of *is* by *shall be construed as* which would mean that the place of delivery *shall be construed* as the seller's place of business. In legal norms the fictitious element is an inherent characteristic of all speech acts, declarations are therefore performative even if possibly not so intended by the drafters of the UCC. Shortcut expressions as in § 2–301 UCC where the obligation of the seller *is to transfer and deliver* and that of the buyer *is to accept and pay* omit the otherwise obligatory object while subscribing to the professional parlance where the goods and the price are implied. By so doing, it modifies the rection of verbs used. This is not the case with the CISG where according to Article 30 the seller *must deliver the goods...and transfer the property in the goods* and further according to Article 53 the buyer *must pay the price for the goods.* The UCC follows the figurative professional language while allowing the buyer in § 2–711 (1a) UCC to "*cover*" and have damages, i.e. to be able to *recover damages* as stated in (1b) of the same provision. The linguistic balance between "*cover*" and *recover* is intended in the UCC and used frequently. Nevertheless, the drafters were apparently aware of this non-juridic, merchant-like use of "cover" in the legal language and decided to put it between quotation marks. Although "cover" is defined according to § 2–103 (2) UCC in § 2–712 (1) UCC and may therefore be also perceived as a legal notion, only the expression *to effect cover* is used without quotation marks. Other merchant-like expressions are incorporated into the UCC, yet they are put between quotation marks, e.g. implied warranties expressed by *as is* or *with all faults* in § 2–316 UCC.

It goes without saying that the CISG cannot make any use of such professional expressions because it is based on a universal legal language which is only vaguely based on the language spoken in a specific legal or commercial practice and does not reflect any particular professional usage or any particular national legal language. Instead, it enables the emergence of an international neutral language use which may prove in future more effective than the reference to particular local linguistic usage and practices in the UCC. However, the different goals and territorial spheres of application of the UCC and the CISG make this difference understandable. For instance, explicitly fictitious formulations are rare in the CISG (relevant provisions of the CISG are quoted in Notes and Commented Materials no. 24). Article 81 CISG is representative of factual statements used in the convention. The convention creates the fictitious legal reality of international sale contracts by using the factual language. It would be redundant to stress constantly in the text that all provisions of the convention should be construed as fictions created by law and therefore binding certain parties under specified circumstances. According to its Article 1 the convention *applies* under specified conditions, according to its Articles 2 or 3 (2) CISG it *does not apply* to certain contracts. In Article 4 CISG the regulation *governs* certain aspects of the contract and in Article 18 CISG a statement indicating an offer *is* an acceptance. In the parlance of the UCC the Article 18 CISG would probably read: a statement *should be construed as acceptance.* In some provisions the CISG falls back into the UCC wording and becomes then less transparent. In Article 1 (2) CISG a specific fact *has to be disregarded,* in Article 1 (3) CISG it *is to be taken into consideration.* In Article 7 CISG regard *is to be had* to the international character of the contract and in Article 8 (1) and (2) CISG statements *are to be interpreted.* In Article 8 (2) CISG statements are to be interpreted according to the understanding that a reasonable person *would have had,* the formulation being reiterated in Article 8 (3) CISG. Furthermore, in Article 38 (3) CISG the seller *knew or ought to have known* of a possibility of redirection or of a redispatch of the goods. The fictionality of formulations becomes however doubtful when it does not correspond any more to the context of use of certain words. It is the case in Article 43 (2) where the seller *is not entitled to rely* upon the provisions of the Article 43 (1) if he knew of certain circumstances. In fact, we rely rightfully or not on certain circumstances or features and this reliance is not further conditioned in our language. The formulation of Article 43 (2) introduces an understandable legal limitation to reliance used as a defense but it is doing it in a way contrary to the language use. This impedes its understanding. In Article 80 this legal position is expressed more convincingly by saying that a party *may not rely* on the failure of the other party to perform under the stated circumstances although here too the limitation of reliance that is understandable to the jurist may surprise the layperson. Legal positions can be expressed, and are in fact expressed, convincingly in the CISG in most other cases. In Article 85 CISG the seller *is entitled to retain* goods until he has been reimbursed, an expression reiterated in Article 86 (1) CISG. Being *entitled to retain* pertains to a right while being *not entitled to rely* pertains to the facts of one's inner forum which unlike the legal consequences of this reliance cannot be limited by a legal regulation.

When the CISG engages in a dialogue with the UCC and the common law its English wording marks this systematic challenge. In Article 24 CISG the acceptance becomes effective when it "*reaches*" the addressee. The provision aims at the clarification that the common law *mailbox rule* is not applicable under the convention. In the English text, the verb has been put between quotation marks in order to stress this linguistic difference. All above verbs help determine speech acts expressed in the statutory provisions. However, a simple classification of verbs to determine speech acts is not sufficient (Baylon 1991: 276). The verb can determine the speech act solely when taken in its context. For instance, the first sentence of Art. 41 CISG reads in its English and French linguistic versions (emphasis added):

> *The seller must deliver goods which are free from any right or claim of a third party, unless the buyer* ***agreed*** *to take the goods subject to that right or claim.*

> *Le vendeur doit livrer les marchandises libres de tout droit ou prétention d'un tiers, à moins que l'acheteur* ***n'accepte*** *de prendre les marchandises dans ces conditions.*

The verbs *agreed* and (FR) *n'accepter* (*de prendre*) are definitely not equivalent when isolated. In the text of Art. 41 they should be construed as having a meaning that covers also tacit declarations made by the parties (Loewe 1989: 62). Hence, interpretation is unavoidable in such cases. The legal speech act in which law is expressed linguistically has some specifics. To begin with, it must be identifiable as such. Here, usually either the context or the text type signal to the speaker that he is operating within the sphere of law. Furthermore, the legal speech act must be expressed in a form which enables its operationalization in law. It must mark linguistically its characteristic feature as a legal speech act, for instance, with a verb signalling that the speech act is a legal one, i.e. that it introduces a binding and enforceable legal rule. The speech act operates in the legal sphere and will therefore fail when certain legal requirements are not fulfilled when it is uttered. As mentioned, the legal speech act fails especially when it cannot be institutionally enforced. Generalizing, we can say that verbs in law represent the essence of the legal language. For the aims of our deliberations we construe law as linguistically formulated social rules of binding nature. The binding nature of legal rules grounds in their institutional enforceability which constitutes their main difference in comparison with other social rules. Also the institutional enforceability is specific because it unlike other social rules includes the legitimate use of forceful measures.

2.4.8.2 Legal 'shall' and legal 'may'

In law it is expected that the binding force of a rule be specifically expressed (cf. Engberg 2001, Witczak-Plisiecka 2004, Udvari 2013). Parties of a contract may, for instance, formulate a binding rule in the following way: *Any person bidding at the auction* ***shall*** *stand surety as for his own debt until full payment is made for purchased merchandise.* Constitutive of the speech act is the verb *shall* which institutes the binding character of the contractual clause. Its enforceability depends on many factors provided by the contract law which is applicable upon the contract in question. Among them can be: legality of the contractual aim, admissibility of the modifications the parties made in the applicable contract law, etc. Without taking these requirements into consideration the distinctively constituted legal speech act will fail, i.e. it will not be enforceable. Constitutive force of an utterance must be properly identified. In the above example the meaning of *shall* cannot be properly understood when qualified as introducing future tense. In legal texts it institutes the legal speech act and introduces the binding force of the utterance, i.e. it establishes its enforceability. Therefore, the speakers must identify properly the context of the utterance to be able to grasp the message in the legal speech act. First of all, they must distance themselves from the school grammarian's perspective upon language and the possibly memorized rule that *shall* introduces future tense in the English language. Thus, the translation from English into French of such utterances will have to transform this legal-linguistic property of *shall* accordingly. In examples such a transformation may look as follows: *This Act shall apply...*(FR) *La présente loi s'applique* or *There shall be a legal committee...* (FR) *Un comité juridique est institué...* (Gémar 2004: 740). When the context of the utterance is incorrectly identified, misunderstandings will occur. The Canadian Supreme Court has perceived in a legal document the English formulation *shall operate notwithstanding* as ambiguously expressed in French with *a effect indépendemment* insisting on the meaning of *shall* as including also the element of future (Gémar 2004: 740). The court, apparently blinded by school grammarians' teaching, did not recognize the constitutive force that *shall* has introduced into the interpreted utterance. In legal-linguistic contexts also *may* is used specifically, especially in utterances concerning authority or permission. In those utterances it has the meaning of *having right to,* e.g. *In certain circumstances a police officer* ***may*** *ask the driver to take a breath test* (the breath test is definitely not optional for the driver) or *If convicted, an accused person* ***may*** *appeal* (meaning that the accused has the right to appeal). Meanwhile, Art. 14 of the *Constitution of India* defines the right to equality in negative terms: The state *shall* *not deny* to any person equality before the law or the equal protection of laws within the territory of India. By contrast, the right to freedom of speech is formulated positively in Art. 19 (1) of the Constitution: *All citizens shall have the right- (a) to freedom of speech and expression;...* In the French constitutional law the use of the present indicative in its Art. 49 (*Le Premier Ministre...engage ...la responsabilité du Gouvernement...*) has been discussed as possibly indicating an obligation to act (cf. Carcassonne 2005: 235). Surprisingly, therefore, it seems to be possible to overlook the momentum of constitution of an utterance as part of the legal text. Such situations come about when speakers are misled by other interpretive rules than those at work in the legal language. It is not particularly probable to assume that judges who acted in the above Canadian case would have problems with interpreting the meaning of *shall* in ordinary utterances in their daily life. Should they – against my assumption – have such practical problems so would the explanation for their confusion have to be sought in misleading interpretive rules they were provided from outside of the immediate factual and linguistic contexts. Such rules could, for instance, have their origin in wrongly transmitted or construed formalized information about the meaning of words in utterances. I therefore insist here upon the process of the constitution of legal speech acts and perceive the constitution of legal rules with the help of language as one of the main linguistic operations in law because it seems not always to be evident to all participants in the legal discourse. The role of pragmatic legal linguistics is at this point to make this process of the constitution of legal rules with words transparent to the participants.

2.4.9 Toward modernized legal terminology

Another recurrent topic concerns the modernization of legal terminology through replacing outmoded lexical units by more contemporary ones, creation of neologisms and semantic change, modernization of the legal language through plain language rules based on principles of readability or understandability. Legal linguistics has to follow these tendencies and comment upon them as it is also competent to provide advice on language use. The tendency toward the development of a modernized legal terminology reflects a broader problem of modernized language use in law. Earlier I have reflected upon the use of ordinary language in shaping legal terminology (Galdia 2003: 12). This approach is not particularly popular among jurists. For instance, G. Cornu (2005: 87) opposed this idea pointing to the necessity of technical legal terminology and H.E.S. Mattila stressed the omnipresent argumentation among jurists to preserve their special register (Mattila 2006: 52). Moreover, jurists automatically ask themselves about the legal status of provisions concerning language use in law. This status can be at least twofold, imperative or recommendatory (Pigolkin 1990: 134). These provisions are different from bills regulating the interpretation of statutes such as the New York Law on Statute Interpretation which are by their nature peremptory (cf. 3.6.6.1). Specifically, the Private Securities Litigation Reform Act of 1995 (15 U.S.C. § 77a et seq) regulated the presentation of information in investment prospectuses. Along the lines of the act, vague information does not engender any liability; assertions lacking a reasonable basis may result in damage claims when taken on faith by investors. In legal decisions concerning stock offerings American courts insisted upon the use of plain English, i.e. a non-technical language which would enable an untrained investor to make an investment decision on the basis of mostly written information provided to him (Lemmer v. Nu-Kote Holding, Inc., 2001 U.S. Dist. LEXIS 13987; Zeid v. Kimberley, 2001 U.S. App. LEXIS 7266). However, the courts imposed on the plaintiffs the burden of proof related to misleading language or false information. Semantic change or historical semantization like *consideration* (i.e. something of value that is given in exchange for a promise) are actually phenomena of the traditional legal language. While developing the modern terminology one nevertheless should bear in mind that they regularly give rise to misunderstandings among non-lawyers who do not expect such broadly used concepts to have totally different meaning in law and in ordinary language. In their reception by the speakers they can be contrasted with explicitly legal concepts such as *promissory estoppel* which cannot be confused by laypersons because they are used in the legal language only. This warranty has nevertheless a price, namely this of unintelligibility of specialized concepts like *promissory estoppel* to laypersons. This example also reflects the traditional dilemma of legal language perceived by some as specialized language and by others as plain language that should be understandable to everyone. The solution to the problem would be apparently to abandon specialized language and especially expressions introduced through semantic change as well as historical coinages and to use an explicit and descriptive language based on or identical with the ordinary language. For instance, the replacement of the term *writ of certiorari* by *certification* in some U.S. jurisdictions does not increase the understanding of the legal text although it modernizes the language use. The phrase: *His conviction and sentence were affirmed on direct appeal and certification was denied* in a decision of the Superior Court of New Jersey in the matter State of New Jersey v. Marshall Roundtree (A-2043-02T1) from September 21, 2006 is not per se better understandable than the phrase: *His conviction and sentence were affirmed and certiorari was denied* because *certiorari* and *certification* are used in both phrases as technical terms, the second being a linguistically modernised version of the first. They are understandable to laypersons only when an explanation of procedural details, for instance of the writ of certiorari or the certification is provided as additional information. Also the tendency toward establishing neologisms in the legal language is becoming stronger. In business promotion opportunities it is represented by *mentor/ mentee* or by *tipper/ tippee* in the insider trading cases. This tendency is well established and productive in the legal English: *acquitee, arrestee, lessee* or *patentee,* furthermore *asylee, condemnee, abortee* were identified in English legal texts (Tiersma 1999: 98). In the following, I will discuss problems regarding the modernization of legal terminology and of the legal language in general.

2.4.9.1 Updating legal terminology

Criticism upon the legal language in the broader public concerns mostly legal vocabulary which is often perceived as antiquated and arcane. Regularly, governments and legal scholars provide instructions and expert advice and parliaments order changes in the legal vocabulary with the help of different legislative measures. Attempts toward this goal like the Plain Language Movement in the U.S. and results accomplished in the application of such approaches are encouraging (Hiltunen 1990: 106–108). This tendency has long reaching roots. Many historical examples could be brought to show the process of linguistic adjustment of legal terms, for instance (UK) *The Habitual Drunkards Act* from 1879 was already 1889 renamed *Inebriates Act.* Modern examples may be more appealing. For instance, on December 13, 2010 U.S. President Barack Obama signed into law the *Healthy, Hunger-Free Kids Act* which reauthorized child nutrition programs in the U.S. Thus, the term *kid* previously perceived as belonging to the familiar repertoire of the American parlance became part of the American legal English. It corresponds to the replacement of *infant* by *child* in the British legal language. Furthermore, the *USA Patriot Act* and the *USA Freedom Act* are typical specimens of this method of terminological coinage. In the UK, terminological changes have been introduced 1999 as a result of the Woolf report in the course of the reform of civil procedure. Some typical old terms have been replaced by words taken from the ordinary language or neologisms. These changes concern foremost following old and new term pairs: *writ – claim form, pleading – statement of case, plaintiff – claimant, minor/infant – child, in camera – in private, ex parte – without notice, guardian ad litem – litigation friend, Mareva injunction – freezing injunction, Anton Piller order – search order.* The terminology of older Acts of Parliament, for instance the *Minors' Contract Act* (1987), was not changed in the course of the reform which has been limited to the civil procedure rules and *minors* survive in the earlier acts of the substantive law but they are *children* in the civil procedure. Still further, since 1952 the term *alien* makes part of the codified American administrative law in its varieties such as *non-permanent resident aliens, alien entrepreneurs* and *aliens of extraordinary ability.* Some speakers perceive such terms as dehumanizing and disparaging and would prefer the terms *foreigner* or *immigrant.* The same speakers often also perceive terms such as *spinster* as odd in contemporary legislative texts. In August 2015 the term *alien* was removed from the labor legislation in California. Meanwhile, terminology reflects speakers' attitudes; the term *alien* is better suited in a discourse hostile to immigration as *foreigner* may suit better a discourse that reflects the openness of the world where migration of people according to their needs and preferences is perceived as natural. Therefore, in all attempts to modernize legal terminology the discursive background of its use should be reflected. Finally, through linguistic transformation not the language is modernized but the worldview of speakers who use this language.

In France, the *Commission de modernisation de la langue judiciaire* introduced 1977 substantial changes into the legal vocabulary. Among numerous changes following pairs of old and new terms were concerned: *intérêts de droit – intérêts au taux légal, es qualité de tuteur – en qualité de tuteur, exploit – acte, il échet – il échoit, emender – réformer* (Gazette du Palais 1977, 2e sem.). Other French governmental directives simplified the language use in legal acts. Some new coinage (Cornu 2005: 110), e.g. (FR) *juge aux affaires familiales*, (FR) *divorce sur demande conjointe* or (FR) *autorité parentale* follow the tendency toward the convergence of legal and ordinary language. However others, like (FR) *action à fins de subsides, régime de participation aux acquêts, administration légale pure et simple* contradict this principle. Apparently, the changes introduced in the UK and in France modernize the legal vocabulary in the sense that new terms sound to laypersons as if they were parts of the contemporary colloquial or literary language. However, the question whether they are also better understood by laypersons remains open, as no research into this problem is known. The problem of understanding concerns the legal concept rather than the legal term. The legal term may appeal to laypersons in its contemporary form as more up-to-date but it is not per se easier to grasp in its application as a legal concept. The fact that a judicial decision is not issued any more *ex parte* but *without notice* does not necessarily guarantee better understanding of the notion as long as there is no additional explanation about whom or what this omitted notice might actually concern. Similarly, the (FR) *intérêts de droit* and the modernized (FR) *intérêts au taux légal* remain a mystery to someone who does not know the notion of interest due in litigation and the rules governing it.

2.4.9.2 Dissolution of terms or concepts?

Legal terminology is steadily developing and until recently it usually followed the conceptual framework of the Roman law that it modified. This was, for instance, the case with the introduction of (LAT) *culpa in contrahendo* into the modern theory of private law in civil law countries. This tendency is stable in both continental and common law. For instance, the approach by the authors of *The Anatomy of Corporate Law* generally follows this type of conceptualization (Kraakman 2004). Some concepts are used there in a modified conceptual setting; others are added to the traditional terminology. Yet, all of them function and reflect the Roman heritage in the terminology. This tendency in the development of legal terminology is very strong. Mattila provides an example for a generally known legal maxim, that of (LAT) *lex retro non agit* which seems to be constructed upon recourse to the Roman law yet appears to be of recent origin (Mattila 2006: 154). However, a tendency toward conceptualization of a new type is nevertheless there. In it, the term does not rigidly correspond to a concept any more. Instead, different terms in different linguistic forms reflect the content of a legal concept. In the legal-linguistic perspective, rules correspond to terms as norms correspond to concepts. The consequences for law are far reaching. For instance, metaphorical concept creation like *piercing the corporate veil* is of different lexicological type than its terminological counterpart in the German legal language (D) *Durchgriffshaftung*. In the English terminology of the (UK) Companies Act also the term *lifting the corporate veil* is used. It corresponds in terms of terminology to (ESP) *levantamiento de velo,* whereas the German term

(D) *Durchgriffshaftung* is composed in a closer relation to *piercing* that is typical of the American usage. The concept *piercing the corporate veil* is not used in a petrified sense. It may vary in its linguistic form due to its syntactic surroundings of use, e.g.: "A rule permitting **veil-piercing** in undercapitalized firms, for example, can be seen as a penalty default that creates an incentive for firms with low net capital to disclose that fact when contracting with potential creditors, so that the creditors will be estopped from **piercing**" (Kraakman 2004: 30). Still further, the notion of *reasonable man* has been used in the common law as a standard to determine the appropriate interpretation of party intent in the contract law or the appropriate, especially non-negligent, action in the tort law. This concept creation was not unexpectedly supported by the most eminent representative of Law and Economics, Richard Posner, who characterized the *reasonable man* as average person (Posner 1973: 183). The concept gave rise to terminological modifications in the tort law of professional negligence, especially in medical malpractice. There, the notion of the *reasonable doctor* functions as an equivalent to the *reasonable man* of the general contract and tort doctrines. A related notion of the *reasonable bystander* emerged in the common law contract law as an element of the objective theory of contract formation. The notion of *reasonable bystander* is frequently used there as synonymous with the *reasonable third party.* Recently, the term *reasonable person* deemed as neutral in terms of gender relations gained some importance. It replaces occasionally the *reasonable man* in the legal writings. *Reasonable* is further developed and differentiated. For instance, in the *Principles of Corporate Governance: Analysis and Recommendation*, a set of legal guidelines on managerial duties assembled 1992 by the American Law Institute, ordinary language differences are functionalized:

> *§ 4.01 Duty of Care of Directors and Officers; the Business Judgment Rule (...)*
> (c) *A director or officer who makes a business judgement in good faith fulfills the duty under this section if the director or officer: (...)*
> (2) *is informed with respect to the subject of the business judgment to the extent the director or officer* ***reasonably*** *believes to be appropriate under these circumstances; and*
> (3) ***rationally*** *believes that the business judgment is in the best interest of the corporation*

This standard intended to provide directors and officers a wide ambit of discretion. *Rational* has a close semantic tie to *reasonable* and, at times, the two words are used almost interchangeably. In the above standard a distinction has been made between *rationally believes* which permits a significantly wider range of discretion than *reasonable*; it might fall outside the term *reasonable* but is not so remote from the realm of reason that liability should be incurred. In this context, the (U.S.) Restatement (Second) of Contracts provides in its § 19 comment b for a distinction between *reason to know* and *should know.* The *reason to know* refers to a situation where a person has access to a piece of information from which someone of similar intelligence would infer that the fact in question does or does not exist. In turn, *should know* imports the duty to ascertain facts, and is relatively unconcerned with actual knowledge. The new terms *piercing the corporate veil* and *reasonable man* are dynamic; their linguistic status varies and depends upon the structural (mostly textual) circumstances of use. They adapt themselves to requirements of ordinary syntax rather than force the syntax to follow the rules of the legal language (cf. example from Kraakman 2004 cited above). Also euphemisms are used in the statutory language as placeholders for more precise concepts, for instance in addressing poverty. Regularly, poor people or poor families are characterized as *destitute* or *needy*, for instance in the U.S. bill called *Temporary Assistance for Needy Families* (TANF) from 1996. Poor unwed mothers become *disconnected single mothers* with *no visible means of cash income from any source*. Persons suffering under severe poverty are *truly destitute* like the *virtually cashless poor*. Euphemisms are connected to the linguistic subculture of political correctness that replaces the discourse about the subject matter with the discourse about the appropriate language use.

From the theoretical perspective it would be particularly interesting to determine whether the tendency to develop a more dynamic terminology is related to changes in the structure of law itself. A theoretically interesting question would be whether the linguistic turn in law that I propose would lead to a paradigmatic change in the legal sciences. Ambitious attempts to characterize a language-related paradigmatic change in law, such as Broekman's (1984: 156) insist upon *the dissolution of a syllogism-based understanding of text and reality*. Surprisingly, a new creation such as *soft law* does not necessarily introduce a different type of language into law. *Soft law*'s main distinctive feature seems to be that it gains momentum as a legal text type although certain formal requirements for its entry into force as a legal act are not fulfilled. Its legality may therefore be based on customary use in certain situations. However, *soft law* represents an innovation in the catalogue of the sources of law. As an innovative instrument it may also tend toward innovative language use in future. We may therefore courageously assume that future language used in law will be more descriptive and explicit than the contemporary conceptual language of the legal doctrine. It will be possibly also closer to the ordinary language, its vocabulary and syntax. One can also expect that due to the increase in awareness about language use in law, authorities would issue more guidelines and other legal acts with reference to linguistic aspects of creation and application of law.

2.4.9.3 Modernized legal terminology is not unproblematic

Understanding legal texts has been addressed from the point of view of their readability and in the light of methodological problems concerning the assessment of official texts' readability (Piehl 2002: 101). The corresponding pragmatic notion to the readability is the writeability that includes principles of drafting legal provisions in a way which increases their comprehension. For instance, problems of (US) *unconscionability* of contract terms and their UK equivalents *unfair terms* have been also mentioned in this context. However, the issue of unconscionable or unfair terms in a contract is not always linked to language use. Usually, terms are deemed unconscionable or unfair because of their content which is not in line with principles or public policy in a legal system. Modernized legal terminology has the tendency to refer to the ordinary language. However, this tendency is not unproblematic in terms of understandability of such new legal-linguistic creations. It concerns foremost the introduction of terms based on colloquial or inoffensive ordinary language. I call inoffensive terms technically advanced legal vocabulary that appears in casual dress of colloquial language. Terms such as *administrator, opinion* or *information* are representative of this type of terms. In the translation theory they are commonly referred to as *faux amis.* Conceptual differences can be introduced into the inoffensive – ordinary language – usage in groups of corresponding, mutually related terms. Thus, the U.S. corporate law distinguishes between *domestic, foreign* and *alien corporations.* A corporation is *domestic* in the U.S. state in which it is incorporated. It is a *foreign* corporation in U.S. states other than the one in which it is incorporated. Finally, it is an *alien* corporation in the U.S. if it is incorporated outside the U.S. All three terms which form one conceptual field are mutually related and provide a specific legal meaning which is restrictive of their broad semantic and pragmatic usage in the ordinary language. Next to this terminology, less formal terms are used as well, e.g. *a foreign-based multinational enterprise* (Bulova Watch Company, Inc. v. K. Hattori & Co. Ltd, 508 F. Supp. 1322, 1981). We may mention that a new term *globally integrated enterprise* has emerged and may join this semantic field in future. *Series LLC* is another new term that was coined within the semantic field of *LLC.*

Concept creation with the help of metaphors has also its limits as far as understanding by laypersons is concerned. In the U.S. constitutional law, plaintiffs frequently *challenge facially* a legal provision. For instance, *Anheuser-Busch, Inc., filed suit in federal court,* ***facially challenging*** *the constitutionality of the ordinance under the First Amendment (Anheuser-Busch Inc., v. Schmoke 63 F.3d 1305, 1995).* For a non-lawyer it is difficult to recognize that the *facial challenge* of the constitutionality of the provision is a specific procedure in the U.S. constitutional law that is different from procedures concerning the ambit of the challenged provision. Furthermore, expressions like *issue of first impression* are usually not perceived as legal concepts from the point of view of a non-lawyer. For instance, *The precise issue before us in the case sub judice is one of* ***first impression,*** means that there is no precedent to which the court could refer (Schalk v. Texas, 823 S.W. 2d 633 1991). Another group of concepts is represented by forms composed of terms of ordinary language like *summary judgment, statute of limitations* or *default judgment.* Nevertheless, they are not understandable to non-lawyers due to their fragmentary form. The default in the *default judgment* is the default of a party to participate in the lawsuit (cf. (FR) *jugement par default*), the limitation in the *statute of limitations* concerns the time period for filing suits and summary in *summary judgment* concerns the judgment without the participation of the jury when the litigation concerns only the controversy about law and not about facts. Thus, legal concepts expressed in terms used also in the ordinary language may still be unintelligible to laypersons due to missing knowledge about the motivation that underlies the process of their coinage. This prerequisite of understandability can be illustrated with the following example. In the U.S., state securities laws are referred to as *blue sky* laws. The term sounds appealing but it is as all such terms only understandable under the circumstances of its professional use. It derives from a formulation in a court decision which described the purpose of securities legislation as aiming to prevent *speculative schemes which have no more basis than so many feet of blue sky* (Hall v. Geiger-Jones Co., 242 U.S. 539, 550, 1917). Next to the *blue sky laws,* also *lemon laws* exist. In the U.S., most states enacted statutes providing for procedures for consumers who are confronted with mechanical problems concerning their vehicles. *Lemon laws* establish a simplified administrative procedure which can be applied in cases where the car dealer does not correct a recurring defect in a vehicle within a specified period of time and a specified number of attempted repairs. In such cases the purchaser can rescind the sale contract and recover a full refund of the vehicle's purchase price. Furthermore, *long-arm statutes* extend under certain circumstances a U.S. federal state's jurisdiction to non-residents. In the agency law, an independent contractor who is a professional, such as a lawyer, is called a *professional agent.* The more traditional usage of terms with colloquial connotation such as *winding up* in the sense of closing down the business had been generally accepted although they are perceived by some speakers as odd. Furthermore, the (U.S.) Restatement (Third) of Agency brought terminological changes. It proposed *nonemployee agent* instead of *independent contractor* and *unidentified principal* for *partial disclosed principal.* Furthermore, the U.S. *Protection of Lawful Commerce in Arms Act* (2005) linguistically promotes and justifies such transactions. For the French legal language, the (FR) Commission générale de terminologie et de néologie has approved the term '*cybersquatting*' as a French term in the cyberlaw, also including '*cybersquat*' and '*cybersquatteur*' in the list of accepted French legal neologisms (cf. Journal Officiel April 17, 2008). Additionally, (FR) *action de groupe* was created 2012 to render the English term *class action.*

Other socially relevant domains such as informatics and computer programming boldly introduced even colloquial expressions such as *cookies* into their technical vocabulary. Despite its banal reference the technical term *cookie* is understandable only to someone who masters the programming technique or has been explained its technical implications. After having received the explanation, this person will also be able to understand the motivation behind the new term. Nevertheless, the banalization of the vocabulary formation does not lead to increased understanding or operationability of the new technical concept. It may, at best, increase its acceptability in some groups of computer programs users. Therefore, it seems to be an issue of fashion or taste rather than of modern technical language which might advance progress in sciences. The programmer language, e.g. *Abort: cannot find alternate!* as a message which may appear on the computer screen is comprehensible only to some users. It, therefore, does not matter that a technical phenomenon is called *cookie* and not e.g. **claumisius ephemeridae,* as both are equally unintelligible to the uninitiated user. Likewise, terms understandable due to the reference to the ordinary language such as *trade secret* obtain legal meaning in their judicial application. They are misleading rather than helpful, and finally join the group of polysemic expressions. An inoffensive legal term such as *trade secret* is understandable in ordinary language without further explication. Its application in law is much more complicated. In Schalk v. Texas (823 S.W. 2d 633, 1991) the Court of Criminal Appeals had to determine whether an act constituted a violation of a trade secret under Texas law. Both appellants in this case, specialists in speech processing programs, before leaving their employer TI copied the entire contents of the directories assigned to them and transferred them to computers at their new working place. They were charged with breaking the trade secret of their prior employer and sentenced accordingly. Texas Penal Code defines in § 31.05:

> *Theft of trade secrets: (a) For purposes of this section (4) "Trade secret" means the whole or any part of any scientific or technical information, design, process, procedure, formula or improvement that has value and that the owner has taken measures to prevent from becoming available to persons other than those selected by the owner to have access for limited purposes.*

The court had to deal with the question of what detailed measures constitute the protection required by the statute, as the Penal Code does not define them further. In addition, the court had to determine whether the information disclosed by the appellants has fallen within the ambit of the provision. In the opinion of the court:

> *...it is axiomatic that the core element of a trade secret must be that it remains a secret. However,* ***absolute secrecy*** *is not required. A trade secret can exist in a combination of characteristics and components, each of which, in unique combination, affords a competitive advantage and is a protectable secret. We find based on the record in this case that the limited disclosure made by TI in regard to speech research lab activities merely described the application and configuration of certain elements of the software but did not reveal the actual composition of the programs. The measures used by TI to secure its premises to prevent unauthorized personnel from admission to or exposure to its proprietary research data were reasonable under the circumstances. We need not decide today their trade secret status. We do find that the combination of employment agreements, strict plant security, restricted computer access, the nonauthorization of disclosure of the subject programs and the general nondisclosure of those programs by TI and its employees served to support the trade secret status of the computer programs that are the subject of the instant indictments. Appellants* ***neither requested nor received permission*** *to copy the files containing the programs.* (emphasis added)

Legal-linguistic innovations such as *shrink-wrap contract*, *click-wrap licence* or *browse-wrap licence* are no more comprehensible than *promissory estoppel* or *replevin* only because they refer to a banalized form of colloquial English. The language of IT-programmers is injected into the legal terminology without any attempts to provide an alternative notion which would be closer to ordinary language. Judges seem to perceive the *shrink-wrap licence* as a legal term sui generis because they use it sometimes between quotation marks, like in M.A. Mortenson, Inc. v. Timberline Software Corp. (140 Wn. 2d 568; 998 P.2d 305; 2000 Wash. LEXIS 287). In the decision of the Supreme Court of Washington the new term spelled as one word is constantly used without any further description; however the distance is marked in the beginning of the decision through the constant use of quotation marks or the provisional 'so-called': e.g. "Timberline further argues that so-called 'shrinkwrap' software licenses have been found enforceable by other courts, and that both trade usage and course of dealing support enforcement in the present case" (id.). Later on, in the text of the decision the quotation marks are dropped off. Surprisingly, the dissenting opinion that follows the decision of the majority includes a descriptive definition of a *'shrinkwrap' licence agreement* included in a note. This note says: "Vendors of computer software use plastic shrink-wrapping as a mechanism of attaching terms under which they purport to make their product available. In the mass market/consumer context, the shrink-wrap license provides an efficient way for the software vendor to dictate the terms of each sale. When a business purchases a specialized software program, it typically negotiates, with the vendor, its rights of use in the software. In the mass market setting, however, the negotiation of terms for each sale is clearly impractical." The note in the dissenting opinion refers to Robert J. Morrill, Contract Formation and the Shrink Wrap Licence: A Case Comment on ProCD, Inc. v. Zeidenberg (in: 32 New Eng. L. Rev. 513, 516, 1998). To clarify the legal problem discussed in the court opinion we may add that UCITA embraces the theory of *layered contracting*, which acknowledges that while some contracts are formed and their terms are fully defined at a single point in time, many transactions involve a rolling or layered process. Under the theory of layered contracting, an agreement exists, but its terms are clarified or created over time (cf. UCITA sec. 208 cmt. 3 of the Approved Official Draft).

Overall, it seems that some efforts directed toward the modernization of legal terms may not lead to an increase in understandability or operationability of the legal language. This disenchanting assumption concerns especially the tendency toward banalization of the language used in law that finally conceals problems instead of facilitating understanding. It simply produces facile language. On the other hand, legal vocabulary is rarely used and understood in an isolated linguistic unit. It is used rather in legal texts. Therefore, attempts undertaken to increase the understability of legal texts should primarily focus on the structure of legal texts and avoid their pseudo-democratization. Use of everyday words does not guarantee readable and unequivocal legal texts because in law precision matters particularly (Okawara 1998: 204). With all this in mind, the modernization of legal vocabulary remains a task for the legislator and should be regularly undertaken. However, its impact upon the understanding of legal texts should not be overestimated.

2.4.10 Legal Thesaurus

Our analysis of the legal language and the legal terminology leads not only to theoretical results. It enables also to establish an exhaustive databasis of the legal language and to set up modalities of its use in various legal-linguistic operations. The preliminary question is, of course, what vocabulary to include. The solution to the question requires a choice based on the conception of legal language that is one of the foremost issues of legal linguistics. The question is somehow circular as only legal terminology should be represented in a lexicon of legal language. We have realized that what is legal terminology and what it is not is in terms of pragmatics an issue of context, i.e. of the circumstances of language use. For instance, Husa (2007: 311–370) identified in his list of Greek legal vocabulary lexical units equivalent to English words such as *sister, brother, opinion, direct, relative, equal, general, to wait* or *to end* as belonging to the legal vocabulary due to specifics of their use in the legal Greek. Gémar (2004: 738) relies upon the pragmatic criterion of language use for distinguishing legal and non-legal terminology. He quotes (FR) *accord, acte, demande, terme* as examples of terms primarily used in ordinary language. However, when these lexical units become characterized, as in (FR) *accord synallagmatique, acte exécutoire, demande incidante, terme extinctif,* they become part of the legal terminology. The use provides first information about the semantic value of a lexical unit; the real meaning of a lexical unit is provided in the discourse in which it is used. Gémar continues: *Si l'usage confère sa valeur sémantique première à un mot, c'est le contexte de son emploi, le mot mis en discours, qui en détermine toutefois sa signification réelle.* In our approach to language we did not stress the primary and the secondary use of lexical units as the borderline between them is sometimes relatively difficult to determine. The procedure as it was proposed by Gémar is nevertheless convincing and can be implemented in lexicographic work. The criterion of use as criterion demonstrates again that in legal linguistics we have to deal with legally relevant language use rather than with legal language (Galdia 2008: 15). The criterion of use is also the most efficient tool in identifying legal terminology which should be included in a legal dictionary. Nowadays, electronic data processing allows a broad, if not practically unlimited lexical corpus to be included in a dictionary (Galdia 2003b: 130). Formerly forwarded arguments of impracticability of broad vocabulary and the necessity to save space are not relevant any more in technologically advanced lexicographic projects. New technical possibilities make therefore the idea of a Legal Thesaurus, a lexicographic work that is broader than a dictionary, feasible. Such a work would include not only the legally relevant lexical material but also samples of context, examples of use in form of phraseological units, texts and doctrinal commentaries. It could even include language used by laypersons in legal contexts with all its intricacies. Thus, the phenomenon which I for practical purposes call here *legal language* would become perceptible in all its communicative implications. In some contemporary works such as *Encyclopaedia Iuridica Fennica* (EIF) legal concepts form the structure of the whole work. The EIF – although not primarily construed to be a dictionary of legal terminology – can occasionally function as such. Some contemporary lexicographers tend toward the adoption of concept-based lexicographic works. Therefore, Mattila (2002a: 183, 188) distinguishes between traditional lexicographic approaches based on terms (appearances of concepts) and approaches based on concepts (mental abstractions). Lexicographic works based on legal concepts may have the advantage of mapping the whole conceptual field which includes typical terms used in it. However, they neglect structural (inner) aspects of the legal language for which the use of various terms outweigh their conceptual background. Needless to add that practical needs of legal translators speak for the conception of a legal dictionary based on terms. This, in turn, leads back to problems reflected in this chapter.

2.4.10.1 Practical consequences for legal dictionaries

The results that follow from lexicological and lexicographic analyses in the area of legal language are rather discouraging. First, it seems that the Thesaurus of the legal language would be a particularly time consuming enterprise. Second, a bi- or multilingual legal dictionary seen toward the background of the contemporary research seems to be a task which cannot be accomplished in a way which would satisfy scientific requirements (cf. Lundmark 1999, 2006). Nevertheless, legal translators need in their daily work dictionaries which would facilitate their efforts. In fact, the professional translator does not necessarily need the ambitious Thesaurus of the legal language as she usually will master the particular language and at least the basic legal terminology. She will therefore not need the corresponding terms of the words *claim* or *brother-in-law* which both may appear in a legally relevant context. She will rather need help in situations where also legal comparatists have their problems, e.g. with finding equivalents to (US/UK) *promissory estoppel,* (FR) *acte sous seing privé,* (D) *negative Drittzwischenfeststellungswiderklage,* (D) *Drittschadensliquidation,* (D) *gefahrgeneigte Arbeit,* (D) *positive Forderungsverletzung,* (S) *skuldebrev* or (FIN) *liitännäisvanhentuminen.* She needs suggestions for practically oriented solutions in dealing with terminology. The translator may well understand that differences between legal systems and conceptual networks which are transported there make a static solution to lexicological problems impossible. She will nevertheless have to advance with her work. In such situations it would be helpful to provide in special problem-words oriented dictionaries some context-determined suggestions, e.g. (FR) *préciput* for *overhead,* (FR) *affacturage* for *factoring,* (PL) *fundusz hedgingowy* for *hedge fund* or (D) *gemeinschaftlicher Besitzstand* for (EU/F) *acquis communautaire* or (D) *gute Unternehmensführung* for *corporate governance.* The same holds true for the vocabulary close to legal contexts, e.g. (D) *nachhaltige Entwicklung* for *sustainable development* or (PL) *firma headhunterska* for *headhunter firm* which may be unknown even to translators who master their working languages very well. Some terms, e.g. (FR) *réserve légale,* (S) *laglott* are notoriously difficult to deal with due to differences between legal systems but constantly needed in English texts where they can be rendered by *legal portion* or *statutory share.* Thus, comparative lawyers can provide effective help in such situations. Practical requirements of professionals whose tasks are connected to law in multilingual settings can be accommodated in legal-lexicographic works without exposing their authors to the criticism of engaging in obscure lexicographic undertakings.

2.4.11 What does terminology mean in terms of pragmatics?

Our conclusion on legal terminology and linguistic pragmatics may seem paradoxical. As a matter of fact, the study of legal terminology does not alter our view upon special registers in the language. Problems in the legal terminology are centered on the notion of polysemy. Polysemy is largely known in linguistics and research into legal terminology provides only some details to this knowledge. They concern especially the polysemy within one national language with different legal systems such as English within the UK and the US or German in Germany and in Austria. Nevertheless, some detailed observations may also be of some importance for linguists. For instance, anaphora can function in order to avoid misunderstandings, e.g. *Plaintiff asserts that it is equally plain that plaintiff's own subjective intent was to obtain broilers and fryers.* (Frigaliment Importing Co. v. B.N.S. International Sales Corp. 190 F. Supp. 116, S.D.N.Y., 1960). This exaggerated intention to avoid misunderstandings may be counterproductive, as the use of *its* or *his* in the quoted example would most probably not lead to confusion. Instead, the sentence is formulated in a way which captures reader's attention and impedes smooth reading of the text. It reaches therefore the opposite of the expected legal clarity. Pragmatic legal linguistics makes also clear that there is a difference between the claim to produce a precise and clear legal language and the achieved result. Thus, it makes necessary a shift in the perception of the legal language. Finally and more generally, our overview makes clear that we can use the term *legal language* as shorthand for legally relevant aspects of language use. In fact, pragmatic legal linguistics shows that any attempt to freeze the relation between the word and its object in law must fail. It counteracts the tendency in law to label social facts with linguistic data for good and prevents reification of language (Jackson 1985: 11) as well as its ossification (Mattila 2006: 58) which customarily jeopardize legal reasoning. It furthermore depicts how legal concepts are used as a structural background for legal argumentation. It also opposes the banalization in modernizing legal terminology. Finally, it makes clear that legal language is much more than terminology. In fact, legal language becomes operative in larger linguistic units such as speech acts. Their study is more beneficial but also more complicated. However, terminology in a legal text may signal a concrete speech act. J.L. Austin himself worked on lists of verbs which were typically used in specific speech acts. We can assume that in the legal usage the speech acts have the same property. Therefore, in the following chapter we will modify our perspective upon the legal language.

Part 3: Linguistic Operations in Law

While characterizing the language use in the preceding chapter we found out that legal terminology, although as such interesting and of practical importance, is nevertheless not the essential topic in pragmatically oriented legal linguistics. Therefore, in the following chapter I will introduce another, more relevant concept of a linguistic operation in law. Subsequently, I will analyze some legal-linguistic operations such as argumentation, interpretation, and translation, mostly from the perspective of the speech act theory and the discourse theory. Finally, I will clarify why legal-linguistic operations are essential to legal discourses. After having studied this chapter the reader will master the legal-linguistic method and she will be able to work as a legal linguist. In order to work professionally on legal-linguistic problems some experience is needed. This experience can be acquired from Notes and Commented Materials that form the last part of this book. In any case, studying cases should be taken seriously because purely theoretical knowledge that is acquired from the scrutiny of legal-linguistic methodology remains sterile. I may recall at this point that legal linguistics aims at the transformation of the legal science in accordance with the legal-linguistic method that is called here briefly 'linguistic turn'. The linguistic turn in law cannot be achieved solely through reflection upon the problems of contemporary legal science. Practical work on cases and materials is therefore a methodological necessity in legal linguistics.

3.1 Overcoming Terminological Boundaries

In the foregoing chapter we have invested substantial amounts of time and intellectual efforts in the analysis of legal terminology. On the other side, we regularly maintained that analyzing isolated lexical units cannot be the central task of a pragmatically oriented legal linguistics. Yet, there is no contradiction between our interest in the legal terminology (and in the legal 'conceptology') and our attention to more dynamic aspects of language use in law. However, it would be insufficient to argue that we are interested in the legal terms and concepts because others – professional and non-professional users of the legal language – are predominantly interested in them. These groups of users – even if they represent an impressive number of participants in legal discourses – might have determined wrongly the significant and the non-significant problems in law. We, however, think that these groups of legal language users did not err. Rather, to the contrary, we would posit that they stopped halfway. For us, the legal language does not consist of legal terms or legal concepts alone. It is grounded in complex rules of use of legal arguments in speech acts where terms or concepts have an auxiliary role to play. They provide anchors for legal arguments within the legal discourse and help determine the legal speech acts. Without legal terms the legal discourse would be much less clearly structured and finally also less predictable in its social consequences and also less rational. Therefore, we are here also interested in legal terms and in legal concepts. Nevertheless, our enthusiasm for them is limited as is limited the role they have to play in legal discourses. We will therefore turn now to issues which seem for us essential in legal linguistics. First of all, we used to approach different material manifestations of law – the signs of law – from the perspective of language use. We discovered that all these manifestations of law – judicial decisions, legislative acts, witness testimonies in courts and many others – have one feature in common. They cannot exist without the use of language and at the same time they are not intelligible when language is not used in them in a very specific way. This specific way of language use in law we called *aspects of legal language* because in all these communicative situations language use varies from case to case being more or less legal or more or less ordinary. In the legal language our interest was directed toward cases in which aspects of legal language manifested themselves rather strongly. The reason for this interest is that these cases lead to problems in law; they represent the most complicated issues in the creation and the application of law with linguistic means. Here again, I was not able to deal with all phenomena which one may observe in such situations. I therefore admit to cover only some aspects of the legal language use. Furthermore, I identified some linguistic operations in law which seem to us more urgent than others to be treated in legal linguistics at this stage of its development. In this chapter we will have a closer look at the question what linguistic operations in law are actually about.

3.1.1 Linguistic operations in law

We will perceive the law as a set of prescriptive texts (mostly statutes and judicial decisions) created and implemented in a given social context, i.e. under specific social circumstances. We will furthermore posit that we are able with the help of this approach to clarify the most striking features of law, such as:

- creation of law with the help of language
- legal argumentation
- legal interpretation
- legal translation

We will hopefully arrive at the conclusion that while using pragmatic instruments we can reach the necessary and sufficient certainty in terms of legal application about the contents of legal provisions under specific social circumstances and apply them in a way which satisfies social needs and professional requirements. Many other linguistic operations, such as justification of legal decisions, providing legal advice or negotiations of private contracts, stating and commenting the law, interrogatories, and witness testimony could be included in this list. All these operations are actions performed with linguistic means. Also ethically less edifying practices such as intentional linguistic manipulation, lies, and utterances expressed under duress make part of these operations. The task of legal linguistics is to make these operations discernible. Certainly, while dealing with the selected legal-linguistic operations we will also cover some additional aspects of systematization and understanding of law which have been the object of jurisprudence from its start as a particular scientific discipline. I will do it again in a pragmatic perspective in which they slightly change their shape. The professional reader will be confronted with things he already knows but I will color these things differently. Moreover, in a more restricted pragmatic theory of legal creation, legal argumentation, legal interpretation and legal translation I will ask whether:

Legal creation consists of establishing specific speech acts;
Legal interpretation deals with the identifying of speech acts;
Legal argumentation is the implementation of the interpretive speech acts;
Legal translation is a systemic transformation or qualification of speech acts between conceptual networks perceived as different.

This approach will clarify some characteristic features of speech acts used in law. It is a necessary step toward developing a more generalized conception of a legal speech act. This conception will emerge gradually toward the background of efforts undertaken in legal-linguistic and other theoretical research into law. At this point we will also have to reiterate and to reformulate one of our basic questions, i.e. could we master legal-linguistic operations without knowing the law? This question may take the reader by surprise, especially after all that was said here about legal language. We construe the legal language as spoken mainly by specialists, by persons who were provided legal education. It would then seem that speaking this language would not be possible without the knowledge of the subject matter. This holds true especially in the case where the legal language is perceived as a part of the ordinary language which features particular aspects. The situation is however different when linguistic operations begin to dominate. It seems that there this specific knowledge is decisive and more valuable than subject matter related data knowledge that I call legal regulation. This assumption may seem paradoxical but it may also show the strength of the legal-linguistic method.

3.1.2 Is systematization a legal-linguistic operation?

We use here a fairly broad concept of *legal-linguistic operation*. It enables the incorporation of simple speech acts such as *promise* or of a complex speech act such as *legal text*. It can be easily adapted to include all relevant aspect of the *form of life* necessary for the determination of the speech act as well as the further development of its contents in an argumentative interpretation. Previously, we have determined several legal-linguistic operations such as interpretation or translation. Additionally, in the introductory chapter we also dealt with legal systematization. We return now to the problems of legal systematization that we will approach from the legal-linguistic perspective. We do it because systematization is one of central tasks of the legal science. Yet, from the legal-linguistic point of view we have to inquire whether legal systematization can be perceived as a legal-linguistic operation. In order to find out the answer to this fundamental question an analysis of material samples will be necessary.

For instance, in the commentary to the French Code Civil (ed. Dalloz) comments to the articles are centered on the text of the provision, e.g.:

Art. 1131 *L'obligation sans cause, ou sur une fausse cause, ou sur une cause illicite, ne peut avoir aucun effet.*

References to court opinions and comments are centered on following key notions: (FR) *détermination de la cause, absence de cause, cause illicite ou immorale.*

Art. 1133 *La cause est illicite, quand elle est prohibée par la loi, quand elle est contraire aux bonnes moeurs ou à l'ordre public.*

Topics around which the commentary is organized are: (FR) *déontologie, fiançailles, clauses de célibat, courtage matrimonial, courtage d'adoption, liberalités entre concubins, clause de non-concurrence.*

Interestingly, also in legal commentaries such as Palandt's Commentary to the German Civil Code, (D) Bürgerliches Gesetzbuch (BGB), arguments from judicial decisions and scholarly writings are included as notes referring to salient concepts or terms of legal provisions commented there. Thus, a commentary of this sort reflects the structure of a possible and even of the successful legal argumentation. It provides arguments which can or should be used in it, should the whole argumentation in regard of a legal problem be successful. It also lists arguments which were used in lawsuits but which proved unsuccessful there. Here, once again, we realize that legal linguistics is in a way a new creation, but it is simultaneously also rooted in traditional legal-linguistic operations such as argumentation. These operations were (and still are) its characteristic features in the course of its emergence along the development of legal sciences that the contemporary legal linguistics critically accompanies and shapes. Legal systematization is based on concepts (cf. Mattila 2006: 14). It prepares argumentation and presupposes interpretation. In our view, this result should be used for preparing the linguistic turn in law in that the focus of systematization would shift from concepts to arguments. Similarly, A. Peczenik (2005: 1) perceived the legal science as a general legal doctrine that describes and systematizes legal sources and legal arguments. For him, the legal doctrine combines descriptive and normative elements in the legal language and in argumentation; systematization aims at reformulation of legal norms in an abstract manner, in relation to certain basic concepts (Peczenik 2005: 3). Such a systematization would be definitely a linguistic operation and could be perceived even as one of the central tasks of the legal science.

3.2 Legal Speech Acts and Legal Discourse

3.2.1 How speech acts matter to law (from the pragmatic point of view)

One of the central elements of the pragmatic analysis was the approach to language developed by J. L. Austin who focused on the speech act as the basic unit of language and of linguistic analysis. J. L. Austin concentrated in his *How to Do Things with Words* upon the distinction between performative and other utterances, mainly statements. This distinction became classical and Austin's input will in no way be diminished by occasional reference made to Hume's *Enquires* in which the later also mentioned some specific utterances subsequently named by Austin – although in a different context – *performatives* in analogy to *imperatives.* Progressively, the distinction between performatives and statements had been abandoned by Austin to the benefit of a more general notion of an *illocutionary force* of utterances. The illocutionary force enabled to lay foundations not only for Austin's classification of speech acts but also for the later work by John Searle on the issue of their classification. Not surprisingly for jurists, J. L. Austin had stressed that jurists should be best aware of "the true state of affairs" (Austin 1962: 4) as they were regularly confronted with performatives of the sort quoted by him (e.g. marriage formulae, promise, betting). Yet, they "succumb to their timorous fiction that a statement of the 'law' is a statement of fact" (Austin 1962: 4). This remark, which includes some central issues of contemporary legal theory makes of J. L. Austin a successor of J. Austin, the classic of English jurisprudence, with whom his writing is so often confounded. Let us reiterate the simple thought that J. L. Austin had expressed. He argued that utterances of our ordinary language are not always statements of facts, a simple but in his times rarely understood idea which R. Dworkin (1975) had to elaborate upon with full strength. Indeed, jurists are regularly confronted with performatives like those quoted by J.L. Austin and with others, which are contractual in origin like *I bet* or declaratives, e.g. *I declare war.* J. L. Austin aptly demonstrated that these numerous speech acts are fundamental to law in that they do not simply describe legal propositions but have a constitutive role to play in them. Without the conventional linguistic formulae expressed, for instance, during the wedding ceremony by legally authorized participants no legally binding marriage would exist. As a matter of fact, utterances like the above are numerous in law. Our question is whether they are typical in the sense that they would characterize the relation between law and language. Were it so, then language would be constitutive of legal acts and consequently it would be also the fundament of law. The application of law at its different stages of the legal decision making process manifests itself in a linguistic form that imposes an answer to our question which might prove premature. Language, however, may play different roles in the process of creation and application of law at different stages of the communicational process of which the legal decision making is a variety among many others. J. L. Austin has been aware of this specific variety of communicational processes. Following an observation by H. L. A. Hart, J. L. Austin compared his performatives with operative clauses used by lawyers, e.g. in acts of property conveyance which give effect to a transaction and he contrasted them with other clauses which only "recite the circumstances in which the transaction is to be effected" (Austin 1962: 7). Furthermore, Austin qualified direct testimony in a court of law as performative in contrast to a statement of hear-say which is not admitted as evidence and is perceived by him as a mere statement of facts. Still further, it is worthwhile mentioning that H. L. A. Hart (1961: ch. 5) spoke about *operative utterances* in the sense of Austinian *performative utterances.* In the end, both names describe slightly different facets of one and the same phenomenon. The first focuses upon the process of emergence of a speech act and the other upon its results which enable further qualification of the speech act, e.g. as acceptance of a contractual offer.

John L. Austin's tentative thoughts about the theory of legal language can be reconstructed from his article *A Plea for Excuses* (1956). Austin assumes there that the ordinary language has to be the starting point for any philosophical enquiry, also into legal language. As most linguistic data that is relevant to law is available in the ordinary language, the deadlock that the multifarious ordinary language engenders when law is applied has to be solved. This deadlock is overcome by the creation of a type of specialized language that reduces the contourless variability of ordinary language. This specialized language, that could be called legal language, enables law to function as a social mechanism. The above sketch of the Austinian argument is based on following remarks about ordinary language in his mentioned article: First, when introducing the ordinary language as a focus of philosophical enquiry Austin does not wish to overestimate its importance. He solely posits that the enquiry starts with the ordinary language, yet not necessarily ends with it. Austin says:

> *...ordinary language has no claim to be the last word, if there is such a thing. It embodies, indeed, something better than the metaphysics of the Stone Age, namely, as was said, the inherited experience and acumen of many generations of men. But then, that acumen has been concentrated primarily upon the practical business of life...Certainly, then, ordinary language is not the last word: in principle it can everywhere be supplemented and improved upon and superseded. Only remember, it is the first word.*

With this statement Austin opens up the linguistic perspective that can meaningfully include other than ordinary registers. Second, when reflecting upon the multitude of juridical matters he applies this statement as a device to describe law:

> *In the law a constant stream of actual cases, more novel and more tortuous than the mere imagination could contrive, are brought up for decision – that is, formulae for docketing them must somehow be found. Hence it is necessary first to be careful with, but also to be brutal with, to torture, to fake and to override, ordinary language...*

On a simple example he marks the shift from the ordinary to a more specific language in terms of law. A statement referring to a fact may be worded as: '*He took her money*', yet also '*He robbed her*'. Also '*He said Done*! as compared with '*He ac-*

cepted the offer' is illustrative of the same principle. The second statement in both pairs is clearly more explicit in terms of applied legal reasoning than is the first. The second statement is also more expedient in linguistic mechanisms where law is applied. Were the first statement and other such factual utterances dominant in the legal language, law would almost certainly become ineffective as a means of societal regulation. Some such ordinary language with reference to law is illustrative of this process. A speech act (not cited by Austin), such as '*You'll be hearing from my attorney!*', which may express threat, is in its ordinary language dress much too vague to function as the element of an efficient regulative social mechanism. Such language may be efficient under given circumstances, yet it is not sufficiently explicit to steer society in more general contexts. Hence, in the light of Austin's argument, legal language is a more appropriate choice because it represents a specialized register that has to become effective to fulfill the task of steering state and society. Interestingly, also L. Bloomfield (1914: 76, 91) observed analogous transformations that involved jurists' linguistic considerations. He referred to a situation of language use where a lawyer "after some consideration of the technical validity of a paper says: Forgery." The use of specialized linguistic register functions here like shorthand script that also constitutes the context of the speech act as belonging to the legal discourse. This circumstance was however less relevant to Austin. Third, Austin sees that in law the question of diversity of interests is argumentatively omnipresent and law therefore cannot be reduced to a purely rational discourse, at least in the practice of judicial institutions: "Law has a biased interest in life." This biased interest structures speech: "there is the overriding requirement that a decision be reached, and a relatively black or white decision – guilty or not guilty – for the plaintiff or for the defendant." Such a requirement, which is a rule, creates language. Fourth, "there is the general requirement that the charge or action and the pleadings be brought under...procedures that have come in the course of history to be accepted by the Courts." Speaking in procedures does not discourage Austin "as these though fairly numerous, are few and stereotyped in comparison with the accusations and defences of daily life." Speaking in procedures is therefore typical of language, the ordinary and the specialized. Speaking in legal procedures is specific because it depends on institutions. Austin (1975: 28) says in *How to Do Things with Words*:

> *...on a desert island you may say to me 'Go and pick up wood'; and I may say 'I don't take orders from you' or 'you're not entitled to give me orders' – I do not take orders from you when you try to 'assert your authority' (which I might fall in with but may not) on a desert island, as opposed to the case when you are captain on a ship and therefore genuinely have authority.*

In sum, institutionally guaranteed values, beliefs, commitments of all sorts make part of the law and its language as does the ordinary language with all its primary imprecision and vagueness. Legal language emerges in order to cope with the linguistic and factual complexity of life that is primarily expressed in ordinary language. Practically speaking, jurists invent legal terminology to cope with this challenge (Austin 1975: 24). Law that is expressed in this way considers life from the perspective of values, beliefs, and commitments that it also conveys. This consideration of life is expressed in performatives such as those described by Austin in *How to Do Things with Words* (1975). Performatives function in procedures that determine the validity of their use (cf. v. Dijk 1978: 16). A speech act of sentencing *I sentence you to ten years in prison* is valid in law when the context is a trial, the speaker is a judge and the recipient is an accused. Furthermore, it requires regulation (statute or precedent) that would justify the range of the sentence. For Austin, regulation makes part of linguistic procedures. Austin dealt in *How to Do Things with Words* with numerous legal problems, such as mistakes, mainly from the perspective of the legal doctrine. He might have been influenced at this point by H.L.A. Hart, with whom he also taught a course at Oxford. This specific interest led Austin to deal with conceptual analysis from the point of view of the legal doctrine that impeded progress in the development of his theory. For him, law remained rooted in logic and not in social discourse. One does definitely not exclude the other, yet the results obtained in Austin's analysis show rather the legal doctrine in the light of the speech act theory and logic. 'Discourse' is however also present in Austin's theoretical pondering. J.O. Urmson (1992: 233) referred to *areas* in Austin's writings that are in his view "areas of discourse." As could be seen, Austin's approach is only implicitly discursive, as it on its face favors terminological analysis in limited contexts. Also in ideological terms, it is rather affirmative of power structures where people have 'genuine authority' to rule over others. This is how language functions in law according to J.L. Austin. This theory of legal language has been later expanded by John Searle (2011) to a more comprehensive description of legal language as a mechanism of legal discourse. This broad theory of legal language made this book possible.

3.2.1.1 Following Austin

For a jurist, the paradoxical part of J. L. Austin's theory resides in his attempt to introduce new aspects into philosophy while using among others numerous examples from law. Austin's philosophical ambition was clearly stated by him in his writings; he wished to show that philosophically relevant language use is not necessarily limited to statements. In this he succeeded fully. Much more problematic is however the input of his approach to law – a matter Austin did not think about nor did he explicitly wish to contribute to. Nevertheless, J. L. Austin's *How to Do Things with Words* can be taken for the first, although limited in scope, modern treatise on legal linguistics. His reception in the legal theory is complicated because Austin's lectures had followed a different goal – namely a philosophical or a linguistic one. Meanwhile, as a result of J.L. Austin's efforts, we are able to distinguish linguistically expressed norms which are not only descriptive but seem to be non-constitutive of the legal norm like rules prescribing driving on the right-hand side of the road. We used to call such rules *regulative* following the distinction introduced by John Searle (Searle 1999: 123). We underline their difference from *constitutive* rules because they do not engender any legal acts but limit themselves to their prescription. They are constitutive of the emergence of the legal speech acts. Typologically, they are different from purely constitutive rules although they also in a certain way constitute driving on the right-hand side of the road as legal only in contrast to all other directions of driving, especially on the left-hand side of the road. Technically possible and efficient driving on the left-hand side of the road violates the provisions of the road code (as stated in most countries) and makes this driving illegal in the light of this norm. Constitutiveness of institutional speech acts in law is best understood when based on formal examples which concern extreme situations. Imagine that the U.S. Congress acting in accordance with the Constitutional provisions and procedures would declare war to a state or to a group of states. Legally, the U.S. would be engaged in the state of war with this state or the group of states even if no military actions would go on or take place until the formal termination of the Congressional declaration. In this sense we can say that purely constitutive rules differ from regulative ones although the latter may also display a constitutive legal aspect. They are linguistically constitutive by being descriptive; they are constitutive in that they are necessary for the existence of the speech act while being essentially descriptive. Moreover, no one can pretend to be legally married without exchanging the traditional formulae in the presence of the authorized clerk while the driver in our example could successfully (although illegally) drive on the left-hand side of the road. He could even drive on the right-hand side of the road by liking and not by obedience to legal rules and the traffic rules in particular or declare not to respect the law in general as a matter of principle. These paradoxical statements are possible because the rules in question are linguistically regulative and not strictly constitutive. We are now convinced about the existence of different linguistically relevant constitutive and regulative rules in law. Legal speech acts follow this distinction but they are more differentiated and go beyond the realm defined by the dichotomy of *regulative* and *constitutive* rules. The number of speech acts is of course enormous and classification patterns engender even manifold characterizations for one and the same utterance and this procedure increases the number of speech acts and makes limitations impossible. Such limitations would also be unnecessary in the sense of the speech act theory. The amount of possible characterizations of speech acts is dependent upon illocutionary points which function as focal points for the classification of speech acts. Also they are numerous. John Searle distinguishes five particular types of illocutionary force according to which speech acts are identified and characterized (Searle 1999: 149–150):

- *assertives* are propositions representing a state of affairs in the world which can be tested and identified as being true or false
- *directives* are propositions which influence the behavior like orders, commands, and requests. They cannot be true or false but can be obeyed, complied with or violated.
- *commissives* are propositions embracing commitments to undertake something like promises, pledges, contracts, guarantees. They cannot be true or false but are instead respected or not.

- *expressives* convey sincerity conditions of the speech act, e.g. apologies, thanks; truth in them is taken for granted.
- *declarations* are mostly performatives which make changes in the world when uttered like the marriage formula declaring candidates 'man and wife'. They depend usually on extralinguistic institutions.

I will not engage here in the discussion and the retrospection upon the process in which various types of speech acts have been classified, initially by J. L. Austin, later by J. Searle and many others. The multitude of descriptions and types of speech acts is indicative of the creative potential residing in our utterances and is per se neither embarrassing nor is it discouraging. It is one of the characteristic features of our language, its multiple functions and facets. The reason why I will not engage in the debate is primarily that I need only some of these types because not all of them are productive in the legal-linguistic usage.

3.2.2 Classification of legal speech acts

For our classification certain linguistic criteria will be more decisive than others. The most popular and the most reliable criterion that determines the classification is the verb present in an utterance. When we trace a verb like *state, warn, command, contract, guarantee* or *complain* in an utterance we will at first be able to almost automatically characterize the speech act as a statement, warning, command, contract, guarantee or complaint. However, as the context of such utterances may be more complex or untypical, a revision of the characterization may become necessary. In such a situation we will be compelled to redress the initial characterization of an utterance when it has been made much too automatically in close accordance with its explicit wording alone. This – in parenthesis – is also a problem typical of legal interpretation and the daily work of every practicing lawyer. Like lawyers in their practice we will have to rely on the purpose inherent in the utterance to be able to finally classify a speech act. The number of purposes can differ. John Searle proposed the five quoted above and this is acceptable for us in a research limited to language use in the legal context.

The existence of *assertives* in law is questionable. As a rule, a legal text, predominantly a statute (e.g. an Act, a Bill, a Law on..., a Decree etc.) is of prescriptive nature, statements being rare in statutes. Statutes prescribe, injunctions order etc. Legal texts may include parts of assertives that might undergo the test determining truth or falsity like a witness testimony reported in a court decision. However, their role may be more important in *soft law* texts which take the form of legally binding prescriptive texts while lacking this propriety in terms of law. *Directives*, embracing orders, commands or requests are the realm of the state administration. A part of them constitute legal texts such as ordinances or decrees. Others are linked to explicitly legal texts by some elements, like e.g. official correspondence. As said, statutes (and legal texts on different hierarchical levels such as ordinances or decrees) are typical directives. *Commissives* which include commitments of the speaker are first of all found in the private law, especially in contracts. There, guarantees, pledges and promises of all sorts abound. They too, like laws, cannot be true or false, but only kept or broken. They have their own characteristics. They are framed in a language of condition with *if, subject to, on condition, provided that* or in a language of promise with *I promise, I will* etc. *Expressions* manifesting the sincerity conditions of a speech act are rare in legal texts due to the emotional element inherent in sincerity. One may assume that some texts of constitutional preambles may include expressive elements (cf. 4.3.2, cf. also Malinowska 2012). Also the lack of sincerity in signing a check with the name *William Shakespeare* may become relevant in law. Therefore, for instance, in assignments of rights under the common law the linguistic expression must be precise. It is important to use the present or future tense, e.g. *I assign, I will assign* or *I promise to assign*. Otherwise, the validity of an assignment could be challenged.

3.2.2.1 Some examples

Performative utterances that were central in J. L. Austin's reasoning may easily create institutional facts. A well known example (Searle 1999: 115) is the text on the 100 U.S. dollar note saying: *This note is a public tender for all debts, public and private* that on the note is accompanied by a facsimile of the signature of the U.S. Federal Treasurer and of the seal of the U.S. Federal Reserve. The phrase in its institutional surroundings does not or not only describe the creation of valid money. It creates this means of payment by saying in a way authorized by the Constitution that the note in question is a means of payment, a legal tender. Adequately, it creates the fact it describes. That said, one could now ask whether it is necessary to produce this effect. The answer may be yes and no. It will generally be necessary because a declaration of acceptability of money as money by the authorized institution is a prerequisite of its existence. Of course, when the means of payment in form of banknotes became general, the public also became aware of the fact that they are issued by a competent authority and can therefore be legally used as means of payment. Nowadays no one – exception made for very scrupulous debtors and intrigued researchers – studies the text on the hundred dollar note any more. The initial performative act produced its effects; it created a medium which became part of our legal culture in such effective way that no further interpretation in a particular case concerning payment is necessary any more. This is also the reason why on the rather sterile 100 euro note we will not find any such constructive utterance any more. It has simply been replaced by the symbolic use of banknotes in our society and is therefore redundant to its constitution. The legal institution, i.e. payment of debts with banknotes had been successfully established in society and their use had been internalized by the public. Likewise, their symbolic form is generally recognized and functionalized. Using the quoted phrase of the 100 dollars note on the recently designed 100 euro note would constitute not only a formal but a formalistic act because no additional performative effect could be reached today with this antiquated formula.

Overall, the legal speech act – like any other speech act – cannot be separated from its physical appearance, i.e. its locution. In law, locution that appears in its different text types that I call narration or legal narrative enables the speakers to identify the speech act as legal. The text type signals to the speakers that they have to deal with a specific speech act that can function efficiently solely under special conditions of use. At this early stage, the difference is made by the speakers between e.g. *accusation* of daily practice (for instance in a dispute between spouses) and *accusation* by the public prosecutor in a legal procedure. Only the institutionalized narrative or legal text type enables the speakers to grasp the difference, as the structure of the linguistic act of accusing someone remains otherwise the same in both cases. The proposition that emerges in this process can be called *regulation*, e.g. acquittal of an accused person or the understanding that driving in towns is allowed at the speed up to fifty kilometres per hour. The most problematic part of the legal speech act is its illocution. It determines the efficiency of the legal speech act as judgement or accusation. Its felicity conditions are different from those of general speech acts. While the general speech acts can be tested along the logical distinction between true and false, the legal speech acts function in the spectrum determined by institutional legal parameters such as valid or void. The perlocutionary element that in general speech acts concerns the impact of the speech act appears in the legal speech act as legal action. In short, one could say that the legal speech act is efficient when the action that it constitutes can be perceived as legal.

3.2.2.2 Legal speech acts in comparison

The performative character of legal speech acts is quite intricate. They exist in many variations. H. Mattila (2006: 32) quoting D. Kurzon provides an example of promise in three forms: 1. *I hereby promise...*; 2. *I do promise*; 3. *I promise by these presents...* The qualification of promise as legal speech act must also reflect these varieties. Understanding the aspects of speech act use is important. The archaic use of *do* in the above *I do promise* or in *I do appoint* may falsely suggest emphasis to speakers unaware of the intricacies of the legal English (Tiersma 1999: 207). Performativity, instead, is clearly stressed in the first example by the use of *hereby*. Comparative studies available to date show that legal speech acts largely correspond. In French, they are centered on some verbs with legal connotations, for instance (FR) *je promets, j'offre, j'autorise, je reconnais, je jure, ordonnons, condamnons* (Cornu 2005: 38). Likewise, (IT) *L'inchiesta fu archiviata* and (FR) *L'affaire a été classée* prove the pragmatic nature of legal language. Certain legal-linguistic speech acts are cross-culturally stable, for instance policemen's requests for checking personal documents: (FR) *Papiers, s'il vous plaît!*, (ESP) *¡Documentación, por favor!*; others are stable as to their form, but not as to their content like statements referring to terminating an investigation is the above Italian and French examples. All have in common the existence of an institutional pattern that is constitutive of the relevant legal-linguistic speech act that lexically may vary quite considerably. In an exchange with a custom officer who may be asking *Have you anything to declare* or *Have you* *anything liable to duty?* the standard answers may be *Nothing* or *Not that I know of* or *Only things for my own use.* Usually, the answers are rather ambiguous *Not that I know of* will be almost certainly perceived as a negative answer. However, as long as no profound comparative effort in the analysis of legal speech acts has been undertaken, it might be premature to say that this resemblance is due to the specifics of the legal culture which in all its diversity leads back to its Roman-Greek roots and thus provides patterns for the formation of legal speech acts.

3.2.2.3 Mode of existence of legal speech acts

The evolution in the use of speech acts is evident in the above case contrasting the dollar and the euro banknotes. It also shows another characteristic feature of speech acts which might be more productive in legal linguistics than the problem of their formal classification. It shows the conditions of fit for the speech acts, which are their conditions of being true or false, valid or void. Already J. L. Austin realized that the conditions of functioning are essential to speech acts. Performatives such as *promise* cannot be true or false, but only implemented; they can be broken or void, etc. The mode of their existence is different from factual statements which can be true or false. Legal speech acts function under specific conditions of which three are essential. They are: appropriate procedure, authorized actors and no abuse of procedure of use (e.g. not believing what one is saying or not meaning seriously what one is saying). Therefore, identifying speech acts in law might be perceived as a sterile exercise. And indeed, what matters is the speech act in its context. In law, speech acts are often encountered in a narrativized context (Jackson 1988: 227). For Jackson, the fact of giving evidence is less interesting than the story of the giving of evidence (Jackson 1988: 227). Again, in law, a speech act cannot become operational as long as it cannot be used in the interpretation of a precedent or a legal act. Legal interpretation has in this sense two prongs, it makes the identification of a speech act possible as a speech act and it ensures its further operativeness in the legal argumentation. Because of this implication the whole potential of a speech act must be exploited in order to make it operational in law. Procedural aspects of *telling, asserting, claiming* as well as *questioning*, e.g. in cross-examination or acts of *naming* or *adoption* are complex and should not be reduced to their structural skeleton. The same concerns the central speech act of law – the *judge's decision* which constitutes an entirely new legal speech act. The reaction of law to the complexity of the subject matter has been the increase in the complexity of legal speech acts. Legal speech acts such as *promise* or *warranty* have a different degree of complexity than *argumentation* or *interpretation.* Frequently, our highly complex law is therefore simplified by using gestures and other forms of non-lexical communication. Transactions of daily life, purchasing newspapers at a newsstand or tickets in an automat as well as withdrawing cash from a teller are reduced to gestures which replace complex transactional communication. The silent law, (IT *diritto muto*) (Benedetti 1999: 138–139; Mattila 2006: 33; Sacco 2010), dominates standard legal transactions. Therefore, laypersons involved in such procedures are often not even aware of their entering the domain of law.

3.2.3 Implementing speech acts in law

As already mentioned, the biggest influence on pragmatically oriented legal theory and legal linguistics have had the speech acts, initially identified as substantial to any natural language by J. L. Austin and further elaborated by J. Searle. Meanwhile, the speech act theory established itself in the legal theory as its uncontested element. Its domain of application, i.e. its scope and its bearing for the legal theory, however, remains somehow unclear. Some researchers concentrate on tracing speech acts in the legal language in order to prove the universal character of speech acts which are not limited to ordinary language. Others use this theoretical approach as a vantage point of legal theories. Especially, the interrelation of social institutions and speech acts has been underlined and made prolific in the legal theory. Attempts to implement the speech act theory in law show that the number of legal speech acts which is finally dependent upon linguistic acts performed in law allows many different, yet complementary descriptive theories of law. J. Searle distinguished *constitutive* and *regulative* rules. H. L. A. Hart developed an influential theory which grounds basically in the distinction between *primary* and *secondary* rules. Also A. M. Honoré attempted a description of legal rules which comes close to the Austinian model (MacCormick & Bańkowski 1986: 133). He also characterized the academic atmosphere of his time in a passage which I quote in my notes because it explains in an original way the beginnings of the thinking which dominates also my work (cf. Notes and Commented Materials no. 4). N. MacCormick added a typology of legal rules based on three different types called *institutive, consequential* and *terminative* rules (cf. 3.2.3.2). Also M. Atienza and J. Ruiz Manero (1996) identified utterances as constitutive parts of the law. They differentiated between (ESP) *enunciados permisivos, enunciados normativos* and *enunciados valorativos*. For the two authors values proclaimed in law serve as interpretive guidelines; the fact that values are present in legislative acts explains why legal norms actually can guide human actions. Other typologies of speech acts and their underlying rules are thinkable as well (cf. Helin 1990: 153). This multitude represents the strength of a legal theory which resorts to speech acts.

3.2.3.1 Institutionalized language use

In fact, speaking a language is engaging in a rule-governed form of behavior, i.e. performing speech acts, e.g. making statements, giving commands, asking questions or making promises (Searle 1969: 16). In the light of this theoretical approach the speech act is the most fundamental unit of linguistic communication. Fundamental in this sense is not a symbol, a word or a sentence but rather the production/issuance of symbols, words or sentences in the performance of a speech act (Searle 1969: 19). Wherever two illocutionary acts contain the same reference and predication – providing that the meaning of the sentence is the same – one could pretend that the same proposition has been expressed. A proposition must be distinguished from the assertion or statement in which it is expressed. Especially, the institutional character of legal language and legal action became clarified in examples in which they were presented by the two classics of the speech act theory. Hence, the utterance *I sentence you to ten years in prison* is appropriate in a legal setting only when the situation is a trial and the speaker is a judge (Levinson 1983: 229). Would this not be the case, the utterance like the cited would be 'infelicitous' and might occur in a joke or in a film or be another metaphor not interesting in a legal context. Furthermore, it was noted in the consequence of this observation that the entire legal language is constituted in a specific legal procedure and cannot exist independently of it (cf. Levinson 1983: 230). At this moment the concept of institutionalized language use in law became anchored in the speech act theory. This conceptual development of the legal-linguistic theory itself had a profound impact upon the view of law adopted also in the modern legal theory. This impact must, in turn, be reflected in legal linguistics.

3.2.3.2 Communication in hostile landscapes

Another specific feature of legal speech acts is the circumstance that law is applied in situations where antagonistic interests dominate. In antagonistic and hostile communication landscapes speech is used as a means of confrontation. Many professionals of law tend to use confrontational language that displays hostility toward the opponent. Their clients are frequently impressed by such language. Meanwhile, no evidence is there that would support this sort of language use as being particularly efficient. Language use includes elements of irrationality, and hostile language that is perceived as a particularly impressive achievement by professionals is one of such examples of irrationality in the legal discourse. Nonconfrontational attitudes of certain judges may be equally deceiving. Judges have an interest in smooth proceedings and they are aware that confrontational language may amplify conflict. Therefore, their attitudes toward the parties should not be misunderstood as signs of solidarity or complacency with one party. They represent the use of argumentative strategies in action.

3.2.3.3 Legal speech acts and institutions

The speech act theory led to the application of its fundamental notions in jurisprudence, primarily in Neil MacCormick's and Ota Weinbergers's (1986) institutional theory of law. Following John Searle, both authors maintain that legal facts are institutional facts. Our knowledge about them is grounded in interpretation along constitutive rules which construct these facts. They could be in the view of the authors reduced to utterances which could be tested for their truth or falsity, but the test seems to be complicated as it involves our total knowledge about the world. Moreover, the legal doctrine appears to the authors to be possible because of the alleged testability of rules as true or false. The authors stress that legal speech acts such as marriage formulae tend to come organized in sets or institutions like marriage (cf. Jackson 1988: 243). Therefore, rules exist to determine which speech acts are necessary to create a legally valid marriage (*institutive rules*). Other rules tell us which speech acts are permitted or required once the marriage has been created (*consequential rules*). Finally, some rules refer to the termination of a marriage (*terminative rules*). The authors also distinguish between formal and informal speech acts in law. An informal speech act is an assertion that *x might be guilty of a murder* whereas the speech act: *guilty* done by the foreman of the jury in a court of law is a formal act. The theory of legal speech acts deals with formal speech acts. They are structured like the following one: A jury foreman having the right qualification to perform the act and having the intention to perform it within the right procedure along the lines of felicity conditions for speech acts developed by J. L. Austin performs the act. Normative consequences follow from a valid legal speech act, e.g. a person declared guilty of a murder is sentenced to lifelong imprisonment. Operations which I have in mind are kindred with 'acts in the law', a notion defined as *acts which often (indeed usually) are carried out by means of the utterance of words* (MacCormick & Bańkowski 1986: 122). However, the operations which interest us are explicitly linguistic and in this way they differ from all other acts in law. They are not undertaken in the vacuum and therefore all other acts in law stand very close to them. In this circumstance we can see their resemblance with all possible acts in law, the linguistic and the non-linguistic or not predominantly linguistic acts. The last group would, for instance, include legally relevant linguistic operations such as making an offer or accepting it in contract negotiations which are accompanied by threat or open use of violence. An expression of intention under duress remains for us a speech act. It fails, however, under Austinian criteria for the felicity of speech acts and therefore we would argue that finally the linguistic element is not decisive in such an act although it is undeniably present there. We have also to assume that some acts in law are not linguistic acts as not all rules can be created by rule-creating linguistic acts (MacCormick & Bańkowski 1986: 123). With MacCormick and Bańkowski (ib.) we have therefore to state that normative utterances cannot all be explicable in terms of performative utterances or in terms of acts in the law. We move here in a territory which H. Kelsen (1967) tried to apprehend with his *basic norm*, or F. Lachmayer (1979) with his (D) *präkonstitutionelles Gewohnheitsrecht*. This is the realm of power where law is constituted in terms other than the linguistic ones. This statement makes plain why a theory of norms is crucial to the theory of legal speech acts. The opposite view to this one would be to assume that there can exist speech acts which are not rule-defined or derivative from norms and which are therefore called informal acts (MacCormick & Bańkowski 1986: 125). Generally, however a linguistic argument can be used against the 'imperative fallacy'; one cannot derive an *ought* from an imperative *shall* nor can one derive it from the indicative *is* (MacCormick and Bańkowski 1986: 128). Yet again, we can imagine such acts in law only where pure political will is at stake, where no established rules matter. I promised in the beginning of my work to demonstrate the realm of law without language and here it is.

As indicated, N. MacCormic developed an original analysis of legal norms while distinguishing *institutive*, *consequential* and *terminative* rules. Critics argued however that his distinctions were less convincing than Searle's *constitutive* and *regulative* rules. Furthermore, some critics maintained that in the terminative rules expressing prerequisites for termination of legal facts a constitutive rule has been used finally in its specific role. Thus, they questioned the necessity of this concept. The institutional theory of law found some interested researchers and successors. But, generally, it did not develop to a leading trend in the legal science. There may exist several reasons for this. Critics mentioned that the two authors – who represent slightly different philosophical positions – did not bring about any coherent theory but rather published in the work quoted above a series of articles with a programmatic introduction (Helin 1990: 150). Some critics suggested that the reliance on the legal doctrine and the verification methods might have been perceived as uncritical by readers and potential successors. And indeed, the approach results in a structural theory of law which its authors rightly also call legal positivism. R. Dworkin (1977 and 1991) showed the limits of such theories. Efforts undertaken by N. MacCormick and O. Weinberger resulted however in the rise of awareness about the specific felicity conditions for legal speech acts. MacCormick and Weinberger made explicit the institutional boundaries of any action undertaken in law (cf. Salas 2001: 226). This part of their theory is essential to pragmalinguistically oriented models of legal interpretation (cf. Kwarciński 2005) and basically also to all attempts to understand and describe the legal discourse. Finally, this is also the reason why today we can maintain that in terms of the speech act theory to work effectively with legal norms means to set up requirements for felicitous legal speech acts which would justify their normative consequences. However, as the legal speech acts do not exist in a vacuum, but are part of larger linguistic units, also their felicity conditions must be searched for there. Therefore, the conditions of an effective legal discourse and linguistic operations undertaken there, especially in the legal interpretation and in the legal argumentation, determine the whole set of felicity requirements for the effective use of language in law.

3.2.3.1 Linguistic operations in law and legal speech acts

I will distinguish here between linguistic operations in law as general concepts and legal speech acts as particular acts which represent law in a linguistic form. I felt obliged to introduce this distinction because both phenomena refer to different levels on which legal signs are constituted and interpreted. Legal speech acts concern the material aspect of language use in law while the linguistic operations in law include also theoretical prerequisites and professional interpretive aspects relative to these acts. For instance, a legal speech act can represent an interpretation of a legal provision or its translation into another legal language. Legal speech acts are of different quality; some are simple, others particularly complex. They do not exist in a vacuum; instead, they are elements of legal discourses. There, they function according to the rules of discourse composition. In turn, linguistic operations in law such as legal interpretation or legal translation include the meta-level of the speech acts involved, i.e. the theory of their use. They include namely the theory of legal interpretation or the theory of legal translation. In sum, the linguistic operation in law is a speech act evaluated from the perspective of legal theory. Legal speech acts are institutionally embedded and they are rarely efficient beyond their institutionalized contexts. The institutional moment in the application of laws was stressed already in *The Federalist* (no. 22): "Laws are a dead letter without courts to expound and define their true meaning and operation." It may also be assumed that the imposed or self-imposed limits to the freedom of argumentation in these courts may be finally responsible for the crisis of the legal discourse.

3.2.3.5 Language games

Already H. L. A. Hart repeated regularly that language and the rules based on it contain both a core of settled meaning and a penumbra of uncertainty (Schauer 1993: xiv). The subsequent discussion concerned the question of how far the settled area actually extends and whether the notion of core is coherent at all. Serious criticism addressed this challenging issue and it was stressed that solely a wide range of varying contextual factors enables the speaker to grasp the meaning of any item of language. We have seen that J. L. Austin had found a solution to this dilemma with his speech acts. In a parallel approach to J. L. Austin, Ludwig Wittgenstein (1984: 250) developed his notion of language games which were in his view constitutive of any understanding of language and were necessarily bound to vast contexts named *forms of life*. This notion has been until now not as successfully used in the area of legal studies as Austin's speech acts. Nevertheless, its bearing for the understanding of the legal language as for any other variety of language remains uncontested. Law is in terms of this approach a normative language game (Minda 1995: 239). Following Wittgenstein's conception of language games, Th. Morawetz (1992) characterizes law as a deliberative practice in *Epistemology of Judging. Wittgenstein and Deliberative Practices*. He developed a theory of law as a radical deliberative practice. For Morawetz, the deliberative legal practice embraces participants with different commitments to different argumentative strategies and goals. They are not bound together by shared rules but by mutual recognition of relevant rules of proceedings. Deliberation proceeds as an activity in which each participant reaches and justifies arguments and deploys his justificatory strategy in part to persuade others to adopt it but also to claim his own way of making sense of experience. The players play different plays but aim at one result (cf. Galdia 1995: 69). A. Aarnio recognized this situation and proposed to split the players into at least two auditoria in order to better distinguish between more and less convincing arguments in the legal deliberation (Galdia 1995: 34). For jurists it is interesting to notice that Wittgenstein abandoned in his approach definitions and took *family resemblances* between different uses of a word for the basis of meaning. We identify one use as a paradigm and examine others in terms of degree and nature of divergence from a paradigm. Hilary Putnam coined therefore the term *cluster concept*. Other approaches, such as Georges Kleiber's introduced the *prototype* as a framework for the determination of meaning (Kleiber 1990: 49). All of these conceptions insist on the broad, if not broadest, context of language use. A theory of legal interpretation or of legal argumentation would not be possible would the conceptual context be defined more narrowly. The mentioned approaches based on language games are decisive for legal linguistics. The normative language games established and seen in the broad context of forms of life could justify the thesis that law is actually and exclusively about language. Within Wittgensteinian hermeneutics human understanding occurs in language games (Minda 1995: 239). These linguistic operations are anchored in broad social practices which also are linguistic. Therefore, from the Wittgensteinian perspective we deal exclusively with language when we analyze law.

3.2.3.6 'Différance' in law

One of the consequences of the reflected divide into legal norms and other norms may be, as said, a newly structured discourse that attempts at integrating the formalistically split levels of speech and action into a broader unit. The legal discourse of '*différance*' used by Jacques Derrida and François Lyotard makes clear the difference between the positivist discourse about law as a discourse about facts and a reflection that focuses on the interplay between facts and norms that constantly change shape in the legal discourse. The constitution of meaning in legal discourses of this type shows the dynamic of law in application, i.e. its social existence. It includes one more fundamental element, i.e. the attitudes to forms and contents in law. These concepts were largely neglected in the traditional legal theory. Meanwhile, our approach to law, the angle from which we view it, is decisive for whatever discussion about the emergence of meaning in law. This angle or perspective controls the emergence of relevant arguments in the legal discourse. It is therefore one of the most salient elements of the legal context. It includes such fundamental, yet rarely mentioned attitudes to law as *'taking law seriously'* or *'neglecting law'* in one's biographical project. Often the *'reliance upon law'* as social mechanism has been quoted as one more attitudinal example. Finally, 'différance' shows law's real face. For legal texts the approach of 'différance' has one more consequence in that it annihilates the alleged unity of text and discourse in law. Jurists, especially the positivists, tend to perceive legal texts and legal discourses as a harmonious form that resembles sacred texts commented by theologists. Splits, inconsequences, breaches, chasms, tilts and some other figures typical of legal argumentation are perceived there as intrusions into the harmonious sphere of law as it ought to be. Meanwhile, law as the discourse of 'différance' manifests itself in breaches, fragments, splits and tilts. It may be an unpleasant experience for all citizens who participate in acts of application of law of this kind. Meanwhile, it is worthwhile remembering that legal discourses are not religious ceremonies or artistic events. They are not philosophical symposions, neither are they exercises in legal rhetoric. They take place toward the background of numerous discursive forms that influence them without making part of them. Legal discourses cannot influence the emergence of such surrounding discourses, yet the 'différance' helps trace the borderline between legal and other discursive practices.

3.2.3.7 *Discursiveness and meaning determination*

Discursiveness has at least one serious adversary that is the idea of determinate meaning in language (and also in law). 'Determinate' means in the sense of analytical philosophy that the meaning can be unequivocally proven. Meanwhile, language engenders meaning in that it shapes our view upon the world, it clearly does not simply mirror the world (Fischer/Forester 1993: 1). Language is never neutral; language in law manifests itself as a discursive conception of power. As meaning emerges according to R. Brandom (2000) in an interaction, so do also opinions about law. Meaning alternatives attributed in them are successively understood; they are gathered into a whole by the process called 'discourse' (Innis 1985: 102). The meaning of law is constituted in a discourse. This discourse can be situated between polemic and dialogue, where the interaction takes place with changing majorities in analogy with the rule of a minority government. According to Searle (1999: 4) L. Wittgenstein had shown that our discourse consists of series of mutually translatable and incommensurable language games. We are not engaged in one big language game, in which there are universal standards of rationality and where everything is intelligible to everybody. The discourses are formed of series of smaller language games, each with its own inner standards of intelligibility. Also, W. Quine is supposed by many – so Searle (1999: 11) – to have refuted the view that the words of our language have determinate meaning. All these views constitute a challenge to the legal doctrine because there the language of law is perceived as determined or mechanically determinable. Legal-linguistic operations are misconstrued in the traditional approaches to law as devices that decode this pre-determined meaning. No procedure could be more misleading than the deterministic approach to legal language.

3.2.3.8 *Externalism, inferentialism, LOTH and analytical philosophy*

For legal linguistics the development of some particular semantic theories in the analytical philosophy is of utmost importance. All of them concern the processes in which meaning is constituted in linguistic utterances. *Externalism* pretends that meaning is identified by the language user in social practices in which he is living (cf. Burge 1979 and 1986), so to say in the background of speech acts in terms of J. Searle's linguistic theory. Meaning according to externalists is not in our heads, but in social institutions and in the physical environment that constitutes our minds (cf. Putnam 1975, Brueckner 2003, Burge 2010). *Inferentialism* (cf. 1.2.7, 3.5.3.2, and 3.6.3.3, cf. also Canale 2015) pretends that the language user is able to infer this meaning from texts due to the involvement of speakers in complex social interactions that enable them to understand language, i.e. to shape meaning in these interactions (cf. Boghossian 1992). In legal linguistics, these approaches oppose the positivist views of law and of the legal language. They make clear that meaning in legal discourses is not encoded or deducted from texts according to semantic rules the speaker might have in his mind. Instead it is constructed in complex social discourses in which the speaker participates together with others. As can be seen, the two approaches are close to M. Bakhtin's *dialogism* and J. Searle's *social constructivism.* They shift however the processes in which meaning is constituted more toward the external environment of the speaker, away from his intentional mental states that form only the matrix for broader semantic and pragmatic operations where the speaker develops meaning in interaction with other speakers. They help clarify the external conditions of meaning constitutions that until now have been only sketched by some theoreticians, for instance by J. Searle in his work on the background of speech acts. They do not eliminate meaning from the linguistic theory nor do they exclude meaningful introspection (cf. Burge 2013). Introspection is the speaker's privileged access to his mental states and it enables him to identify his preferences. Introspection is important in legal linguistics because it supports efforts of jurists and especially of judges to determine their ethical and other value-laden personal preferences when they issue judgments or interpret them. Jurists cannot pretend any more that introspection is not their task as they only apply law in the form in which it is linguistically stated. Meanwhile, it seems that another semantically relevant theory that emerged within the philosophy of mind, called *LOTH*, i.e. *language of thought hypothesis* (cf. Fodor 1975, Fodor 2008) might have less impact upon the development of the legal-linguistic research. LOTH proposes a description of the language of our mind, which is the representational substrate of a natural language. This substrate is called *mentalese* and is the requisite for learning and speaking a natural language. J. Fodor and some other researchers try to discover its grammar. The main reason for this assumption that LOTH is more relevant to the ordinary language than to special registers is the finding that legal language like all professional language is primarily a social construct. Volitive elements in it are definitely connected to innate capacities of our brain. Yet, the constructive procedure in language formation dominates the whole process of meaning emergence and therefore it is difficult to reduce it to purely biological interaction between the world and the brain of the speaker. For instance, our judgments about perceptions and judgments about the understanding of language might be well integrated under the common capture of psychological nativism in the sense of LOTH (cf. Ferretti 2001). One might however doubt whether the judicial judgment is related to these two concepts in terms of LOTH, which is dominated by the preponderance of primitive and undefinable concept of daily life (cf. Fodor 1990). It seems more probable that the judicial judgment represents another level of concept formation and, at least textologically, it is close to a metaphor rather than to a primary representation of a mental state. Logical operations that underlie a judicial judgment might very well be perceived as primary mental states, yet the judicial judgment as a legal-linguistic operation seems remote from the realm of LOTH. LOTH might however contribute to a better understanding of the way in which concepts, also the professional legal concepts are formed linguistically. The above assumption is valid under the proviso that attempts to naturalize linguistics may bring results that would question fundamentally our hypothesis (Galdia 2014: 228–229). Doubtless, all the named newer semantic approaches to language and social reality allow the legal linguist to argue that meaning is constructed in the language of law and that this view cannot be eliminated from legal linguistics. They also facilitate the approach to the legal language from the point of view of cognitive science for legal linguists who might be particularly interested in this challenging and innovative area.

3.3 Legal Argumentation

Our utmost interest in legal linguistics is directed toward two of the main linguistic operations in law, the legal argumentation and the legal interpretation. They are particularly challenging because they represent highly complex legal speech acts in discourses. Therefore, it seems to be appropriate to have a closer look at both at this stage. Argumentation as a linguistic phenomenon aims at the explanation of facts and situations or at the justification of actions. As a linguistic act argumentation is particularly complex. This is the reason why its analysis is burdensome and until now not really satisfactory although considerable research into its foundations is available. Traditionally, the *syllogism* based on premises and leading to a conclusion has been perceived as its ideal conceptual structure. Nevertheless, already the classical rhetoric recognized problems in application of syllogisms in the ordinary language. The specific rhetorical syllogism – *enthymeme* (lat. *argumentum*) – is mentioned already by Quintilian (Curtius 1996: 320). Therefore, the pervasive force of enthymemes had been stressed even there. Enthymemes cannot lead to unquestionable results like syllogisms. Their conclusions are always exposed to criticism and debates. Their argumentative force has been seen in their potential to convince the audience about the just result reached in the argumentation. The criterion for their correct application is the coherence of the proposition made. Likewise, in the traditional research, scholars dealt with linguistic and logical instruments which controlled argumentation. They were the modalities of logical reasoning, consistence of utterances, coherence and lack of contradictions as well as topoi. Logicians dealt with issues which excluded context and socially relevant action from the analyses of argumentation. They developed an abstract form of argumentation that only under specific circumstances can be productive in law. Especially, research concerning *topoi* which manifest themselves in maxims or Latin proverbs provided remarkable results in law. It showed how specific fixed argumentative structures can dominate the argumentation and even replace the search for rationality in it. Speech acts regularly show this implication especially in statements, recommendations, motivations, and justifications. After all, argumentation is always part of a social situation; it is bound to speech acts like those named and many others. When argumentation is not convincing, the speech act which transports its purpose fails.

3.3.1 Legal rhetoric

Argumentation has been perceived by many researchers in the past as central to law (Viehweg 1954: 29). Nevertheless, I must also admit that studies concerning this issue played rather a peripheral role in the teaching and the application of law. Not only in Cicero's *Topics*, but also in various other learned works on legal rhetoric questions related to the use of arguments in law have been canvassed.

Meanwhile, Mack (2011) indicated that between 1460 and 1700 more than 3,500 works on rhetoric were published. Most of them were not explicitly related to law, yet the Renaissance rhetoric and the renaissance of rhetoric did not remain without influence upon the practice of law. In the beginning of the Middle Ages it has lost importance as a basis for legal decision making due to the decrease in quality of legal procedures. Its knowledge, nevertheless, had been upheld (Curtius 1996: 117). Numerous *modi arguendi* have been developed in the Middle Ages around Boethius' *De differentiis topicis*, written ca. 522, mostly for the use of law students (Hohmann 1998: 40). Equally, serious efforts were undertaken in the past to understand and make operative the argumentative practices in law but also to explain law in terms of argumentation. Jurists frequently construed this topic as belonging to *legal logic*. Next to the mentioned *Topica* by Aristotle and Cicero's *Topica* in the Middle Ages and later profound literature was developed to provide jurists with handy arguments and a canon for the interpretation of laws. Particularly well-known are works such as: *Topicorum seu locorum legalium opus de inventione et argumentatione* (1516) by N. Everardus, later printed as *Loci argumentorum legales, Legalis dialectica in qua de modo argumentandi et locis argumentorum legaliter disputatur* (1507) by P.A. Grammarus, *Topica regalia* by C. Cantiuncula (1520) and later on *Dialecticae legalis libri quinque* (1531) by Ch. Hegendorf, *De dialectica ex iure libri tres* (1546) by B. Walther, *De logica iureconsultorum libri duo* (1582) by J. Freigius, *Dialectica iuris* (1610) by M. Stephani, *Logica iuridica, hoc est regulae, precepta et modus argumentandi per inductiones et interpretationes legum* (1615) by M. Schickhard. I have quoted the above works to show how far reaching in time the discussion about legal argumentation in fact is. Today, our view on legal arguments has changed due to the development of the philosophy of language. We do not believe any more that argumentation in law consists of the application of a selected set of argumentative forms and formulations. Neither do we believe that the argumentative interpretation consists of the application of a limited set of interpretive canons which automatically lead to the identification of the right content of words in law. Finally, we do not believe that jurists follow or have to develop a logic of its own, a legal logic which would be characteristic of their profession. Nevertheless, we have to admit that knowledge about most issues concerning argumentation in law we have today is a result of an ongoing scientific discussion about the legal argumentation which lasts already more than two thousand years. Definitely, there is much discontinuity in this continuity but it is fascinating to see how the paradigms of legal argumentation change while their topics remain stable since the ancient Greeks. Rare are scientific disciplines which today can still use some of their past achievements or at least read five hundred-year-old works without bursting into life endangering laughter.

3.3.1.1 Argumentation and rhetoric

As mentioned, argumentation has been for a long time perceived as a rhetorical operation, i.e. the application of specific arguments in discourses. The classification of arguments caused problems as no convincing matrix for all of them could be proposed. Denominations for arguments often covered different functions. Arguments have been divided into rational, e.g. *ad rem* and irrational, e.g. *ad hominem*; universal, i.e. directed to whatever audience and contextual, i.e. related to selected audience, e.g. legal experts; correct and incorrect; argumentation as regards the number of participating persons, e.g. some, many, one person (Krasilnikova 2006: 180). In her research Krasilnikova provides a classification based on traditional methods and retains the Latin names which are traditionally provided for arguments in rhetoric. Krasilnikova (2006: 182) distinguishes: arguments (*a.*, i.e. LAT *argumentum*) with connection to logic: *a. primarium, a. ad absurdum, a. ab exemplo, a. a contrario, a. ex silentio, a. a simili, a. minimum probant, a. a fortiori* as well as some general groups of arguments called *a. ad rem* or *a. ad oratorem.* Some arguments seem to be close to methods: *a. ad auditorem, a. ad populum, a. ad ignorantiam, a. ad socordiam, retorsio argumenti.* Another type may concern the authority of the addressed person: *a. ad hominem, a. ad personam, a. tu quoque, a. ad verecundiam, a. ad reverentiam, a. ad vanitatem, a. ad fidem, a. ad iudicium, a. ad superstitionem, a. ex concessis, a. ex consensu gentium, a. ad vertiginem, a. ad invidiam, a. ad misericordiam, a. ad passiones, a. ad ridiculum, a. ad superbiam, vexatio, a. ad amicitiam, a. ad antiquitatem.* Close to this type are: *a. ad baculum, a. ad carotam, a. ad consequentiam, a. ad crumenam, a. ab utili, a. ad quietatem, a. ad metum.* Means of persuasion are not necessarily only arguments. Also pseudoarguments, i.e. illogical arguments (fallacies) and eristic tricks are used in rhetoric. Eristic writings began apparently with the Greek rhetorician Maximos (cf. Kotarbiński 1955: 6, 184), who described rhetoric tricks that may be used to win lawsuits to the detriment of truth and equity in his (GR) Περί τών άλυτων άντιθέσεων (*Peri ton alyton antitheseon*). A. Schopenhauer concentrated on this issue in his *Eristische Dialektik oder die Kunst Recht zu behalten* (ca. 1830/31). The problems with the classification of arguments and other means of persuasion show the limits of traditional rhetoric (cf. also Zgółka/Zieliński 2003). Schopenhauer attempted to represent argumentation in action and came already close to modern argumentation theories which focus on procedures in argumentation rather than on the classification of traditional arguments (Wohlrapp 1995: 27). The existing classification of arguments exhibits a resemblance to speech acts. Yet, unlike the speech act classification, it remains static and even rigid. Therefore, the contemporary general theory of argumentation unites pragmatic and dialectic aspects (cf. van Eemeren/Grootendorst 2004). It treats them explicitly as communicational aspects of law.

Communicational aspects of law were placed in the center of interest of jurists since the beginning of the legal practice. Ancient Greeks paid attention to rhetorical aspects of law, ancient Romans developed a stringent legal vocabulary. Chinese and Indian classics addressed analogous issues. All of them concentrated on a function of law that is today best characterized as 'communication'. Nowadays, communicational approaches to law dominate the work of many legal linguists such as Heikki E.S. Mattila (2012, 2013) and Jan Engberg (1997, 2007, 2013b). In Mattila's work the interest in the historical processes of emergence of the legal language is particularly stressed. In his approach, the emergence of legal vocabulary is integrated into the aspects of communicational theory. Thus, the scrutiny of legal vocabulary gains finality and can be analyzed from a broader perspective and in context. Notwithstanding the specifics of individual research perspectives, linguistic communication concerns mainly the functionality of discourses. In other words, the discourse functions when it communicates messages. For this, it needs an advanced variety of language because simple language or pre-linguistic imagery cannot provide information that interests others (cf. Searle 2006). In the ordinary discourse this function is unproblematic because there is usually enough language at speaker's disposal. If not, the speaker may create some language that he can propose to other speakers. In legal discourses this task is more complex, because the language that transfers messages must be created as the use of ordinary language is not perceived as sufficient in these discourses that are closely related to the exercise of power. In the pragmatically oriented legal linguistics, the question whether communication is a speech act or the condition of speech is theoretically interesting. In our context, the question would sound: is legal communication a legal-linguistic operation such as legal interpretation or legal argumentation? It would apparently be possible to construe legal communication as an overarching linguistic speech act (cf. Grabowski 1999). Yet, one could also construe it as an operative device in law that enables the emergence of legal speech acts. Communication's function would be to guarantee intersubjectivity in the process of emergence of meaning. This is essential to legal linguistics because according to the view presented in these lectures there cannot be any 'private' law. Creating legal language, shaping legal information and establishing structures in which this information is communicated are the main concerns of legal communication.

3.3.1.2 Argumentation in East Asian tradition

Argumentation is not a Western invention. It seems to accompany language wherever it develops to an advanced tool of social interaction. In the traditional Chinese culture argumentation followed the dialectical principle of Yin and Yang (Zhang 2004: 5) and oscillated among pairs of opposite concepts. This argumentative scheme included especially contradictory conceptual pairs based on the idea of relativity. Among those most frequently used were: inter-promotion and inter-restraint, restriction of destruction and support to construction, safety and danger, dynamic and static, left and right, up and down, complete and incomplete, noble and ignoble, superior and inferior, sense and sensibility, as well as knowledge and practice (Zhang 2004: 5). Some other opposites were immediately relevant to the legal argumentation. Let us mention some of them such as: false and true, real and unreal, life and death, sudden enlightenment and gradual enlightenment, relative and absolute, finite and infinite, whole and part, temporary and eternal (Zhang 2004: 127). Speech formed toward the background of such dialectical mechanisms animated the development of the two traditions of legal thought in China, Confucianism and Legalism. Finally, it led to their merger by the time of the Western Han (206 BC to 24 AD). At any rate, also the Chinese thinkers tended toward the absorption of rational factors structuring speech and toward remoulding them as time went by (Zhang 2004: 127).

Nothing points to any practice of argumentation in which these opposites would have been applied as a strict canon. The classical Chinese argumentation is as flexible as the European argumentation and definitively not less efficient. This dialectic argumentation did not concern legal texts in the sense exposed by the Romans. It concerned general ethical principles and cases which sometimes would be perceived as legal in the Western sense and sometimes not. However, already in the ancient time ritual forms and the rule of law were emphasized in order to maintain social stability. Thus, rules that from the traditional Western perspective may be perceived as belonging to ethics might have been perceived by the ancient Chinese as strictly legal. The tradition of legal thinking has apparently a much longer tradition in China than sometimes presumed. The mere existence of legalistic reasoning contradicts the occasionally expressed assumption that the traditional Chinese philosophical reasoning did not distinguish between moral and legal rules and that it construed them as one ideal entity (Upham 1990: 83). In the legalistic writings they were apparently clearly apprehended as different. Another thing is the reaction which the Chinese thinkers of the past developed toward purely legal arguments and rules. These arguments and rules had been in the past not particularly cherished and may even today not be popular among parts of the population. They have nevertheless, like other rites and rules, accompanied the development of the Chinese society and shaped the structure of the social discourse there. As far as the classical Chinese language is concerned, M. Granet (1934: 203) argued that it was less appropriate to conceptual analysis: "Le language vise, avant tout, à agir. Il prétend moins à informer clairement qu'à diriger la conduite." Instead, he stressed its pragmatic dimension in which conveing feelings in order to convince and to influence behavior are fundamental (id. 1934: 82): "La langue chinoise n'apparaît point organisée pour noter des concepts, analyser des idées, exposer discursivement des doctrines. Elle est tout entière façonnée pour communiquer des attitudes sentimentales, pour suggérer des conduites, pour convaincre, pour convertir." Therefore, classical Chinese legal reasoning can be understood solely within the pragmatic dimension (May 1980: 196). This means that it makes sense to analyze it toward the background of argumentation which aims at directing behavior and regulating action. It would not be particularly fruitful, however, to engage in complex conceptual analyses of legal and semi-legal, i.e. ethical terms, where they not have been perceived as crucial. Moreover, attention should be paid to *topoi* used in such texts (May ibid.). This reasoning has also another pragmatic connotation in that it tends to avoid the idea of subjective rights which presupposes an antagonistic conception of law (May 1980: 05). The Occidentalization of China, of its legal language and of its legal culture, has also introduced changes at this point. Nowadays, Chinese legal treatises are being developed in narrow contact with the Western legal tradition (cf. Zhang 2002). Their authors follow generally the methods known there and apply doctrinal, especially conceptual analytic legal reasoning in their works. This reasoning includes subjective rights with all their consequences. Today, the countries of East Asia all joined the family of the Western European law and even the classics of the ancient Roman law had been translated into Chinese. Not many traditional East

Asian elements remain in the laws of that region. However, the legislation is only one element of the legal culture (Munday 1983: 191). The legislation must be applied and when applied it must be justified. This holds true also for East Asia. One can assume, as research into these topics is unknown (at least to me) that some specific argumentation would be discernible even today in the written legal texts of East Asia, for instance in Japanese, Chinese, Korean or Vietnamese court decisions (cf. Notes and Commented Materials no. 17 and 18). Sometimes, however, this type of argumentation may be less visible because it developed, in the East and in the West, along the lines of the same logic and it is based here and there on identical dialectic distinctions which are, however, termed differently in both argumentative traditions. Any pragmatic organization of texts is subject to cross-linguistic variation (Levinson 1983: xi), therefore the assumption of similarities but also of differences is theoretically well founded. Interestingly, Krasilnikova (2006: 178) argues in her research that argumentation can differ as to the type of arguments used even between close cultures and related languages such as Polish and Russian. The same may be true for argumentation in East Asia.

3.3.1.2.1 Chinese discourse about maintenance of power

Traditional Chinese argumentation may be reconstructed with recourse to the historical discourse that was fixed in the ancient writings. For instance, Chinese historical writings as well as the contemporary reference to historical events in China oscillate around and refer to the dynasty timeline. As a matter of fact, China has been ruled by a succession of dynasties that has been regularly interrupted by civil wars or territorial fragmentation. Therefore, in formal terms, the dynasty timeline as a frame of reference makes sense in historical and cultural research. When properly understood as a chronological system of orientation the traditional dynasty timeline does not blur the retrospective upon historically relevant events that might have been dominated or determined by other than dynastic considerations. Meanwhile, the breaks in the dynasty timeline are particularly interesting for the argumentation research. Regularly, new rulers were aware of the necessity to establish legitimacy for their taking power and establishing a new dynasty or rather for terminating the rule of the previous dynasty. A structural constant in this argumentation that pertains to justification of the change of rule is the mandate of heaven (天命 – *tian ming*). The mandate of heaven is the notional basis for the exercise of power in China (Kalinowski 2011: LXXVII, Perry 2002). It is acquired by divine grace and not by people's choice. Therefore, new rulers claimed that the previous dynasty has displeased the gods and lost the mandate of heaven (Loewe 2004: 421–456). This, so the argument goes, became manifest in the very fact that the gods allowed this loss of power and its transfer to the new ruler. The transfer – the argument continues – would not be possible, would it not please the gods under the mandate of heaven. In terms of law, the mandate of heaven has been withdrawn from the disgraced ruler and attributed to the new ruler and founder of the new dynasty. Reference to and analysis of the argument in the classical Chinese literature, for instance in Ban

Biao's *On Kings' Destiny* (王命论 – *Wang Ming Lun*) manifests conscious use of the argumentative structure beyond essentialist or religious contexts that are definitely also present in the classical Chinese discussion about the mandate of heaven. Another salient point in the structure of justifying and legitimizing argumentation is the unlimited power of the Chinese Emperor. Only the mandate of heaven as an argumentative narrative can provide such a type of power. Without the backing of the divine grace, the Emperor would be reduced to a citizen who would have to convince others about the range of his prerogatives and privileges that he claims in state and society. The mandate of heaven corresponds poorly to the rule of law. It seems to be the most classical argument that protects the exercise of power in China.

A corresponding argumentative structure pertaining to order and social stability can be traced back to Confucian writings. Today, public perception of the Confucian teaching is largely limited to the concept of obedience to authorities that also clearly favors these authorities, yet not the social doctrine later named Confucianism in the Occident. In the modern Chinese society its detailed knowledge should not be overestimated (cf. Cao 2004: 3), yet it survives in parallel and simplified narratives that underlie the daily action of people. Confucian social doctrine is based on the dialectic of giving and taking, in casu, of the obedience that is recompensed with care. As a doctrine or theory it is also 'Aristotelian' in that it establishes a model that may or may not be evaluated with sociological parameters, as it in principle remains theoretical or more exactly doctrinal. For Confucius, a citizen has to obey the State as the State has to take care about him. That the State may not act according to his doctrine does not appeal to him as a theoretical argument. The wrong action is for Confucius purely practical. This fundamental prerequisite to the understanding of Confucian thinking is frequently neglected nowadays and the doctrine is reduced to slogans that propagate law and order ideology. Preservation of social stability (维稳 – *weiwen*) is the major argument in governmental argumentation. The frequently used phrase about 'constructing a harmonious society' and 'a new social management system' are the main rhetorical features in the public discourse. Language that oscillates around 'instability' and measures to counter 'social instability' abounds in Mainland China (Liebman 2014: 97). Meanwhile, already the classical Chinese social doctrine, to which *Xiao Jing* (孝经 – *Treaty on Filial Piety*) dating from 480 BC is fundamental, includes thoughts about remonstances to authorities in cases when they commit errors which distort the harmony between the ruled and the rulers. Therefore, doctrinally anchored forms of social criticism such as remonstrances and representations mentioned in *Xiao Jing* prove that criticism has not been perceived generally as a social action that would destroy social stability, at least within theoretical approaches to forming the Chinese society and its state. Therefore, social stability that the doctrine is expected to engender does not produce a deadly quiet society, as is frequently suggested in the argumentation relating to Confucianism. Also the filial argument is not missing in contemporary argumentation. The argument as such is one of the most persistent remnants of Confucianism in the Chinese society. It is based on the somehow surprising idea that obedience to government, which at Confucius' time equalled the person of the ruler, is based on the initial relation between parents and their children as a source of moral inspiration for further socially relevant action such as government or obedience to it (cf. Maspero 1950).

Constitutive of such arguments is their reference to the idea of *justice*, which is linguistically expressed with the help of different concepts such as *equity* or *fairness* or more recently with the concept of the *rule of law*. For China, the last concept emerged in contradistinction to the *rule of men* (Husa 2015a: 162, Galdia/Liaci 2016). The process of its emergence is analogous to the shaping of the idea of the *rule of law* in ancient Greece (Galdia 2014: 54). In this sense, the meta-arguments of law appear to be common for the East Asian and the European legal traditions. Other arguments, mainly those pertaining to constitutionalism might be of more recent origin. These recent legal arguments and social mechanism witness also to the process of the emergence of cross-cultural legal-linguistic rationality. Arguments of Occidental origin, especially those referring to constitutionalism, were incorporated into the Chinese culture under the slogan *Chinese learning for the essentials and Western learning for the practicalities* (中学为体，西学为用 – *zhong xue wei ti, xi xue wei yong*). Hybridity of legal argumentation is therefore a well reflected process in the Chinese culture (Husa 2015a: 47). The *rule of law* as an Occidental concept that relates to democracy and not to law-and-order ideologies may be perceived as a relatively new argumentative structure in the Chinese law. Yet, as in the Occidental legal cultures the rule of law takes in East Asia frequently the shape of a bureaucratic principle that impedes rather than expands the framework of the legal argumentation.

3.3.1.2.2 Argumentation in India

The argumentative tradition in India has a long history. Indian classical epics *Ramayana* and *Mahabharata* are explicitly argumentative. Amartya Sen (2005: 3) who stresses the link between dialogue and meaning characterizes them as procedures composed of arguments and counterarguments spread over incessant debates and disputations full of dialogues, dilemmas and alternative perspectives. In a section of *Mahabharata* known as *Bhagavad Gita* two moral portions with legal bearing compete for recognition. These are Krishna's emphasis on doing one's duty and Arjuna's attempt to anticipate consequences of fullfilling one's duties and stressing the good aims and avoidance of negative consequences rather than obedience to formalistic rules. Sen (2005: 5) argues that Krishna got away with an incomplete and unconvincing argument of fighting for a just cause as opposed to Arjuna's objection of how can good come from killing so many people. The interpretation of this debate in Hindu philosophy attempted to dilute Arjuna's objections and strengthen Krishna's position that has been perceived as religiously correct. The use of dialectic is equally manifest in *Rigveda* and in *Ramayana* a bold and sceptical opinion is expressed about the nature of rules: *"the injunctions about the worship of gods, sacrifice, gifts and penance have been laid down in the ancient sastras by clever people, just to rule over (other) clever people"* (quoted in Sen 2005: xii). The Buddhist emperor of India, Ashoka set up in the third century BCE rules for conducting debates where opponents should be duly honored in every way on all occasions. The argumentative rule based on the principle that the state must remain equidistant to all religions came from the Muslim Indian emperor Akbar. Sen (2005: xiii) perceives it as the most powerful defense of toleration in the Indian history. Sen's understanding of the dialectics of argumentation goes further and reflects a situation where a defeated argument that refuses to be obliterated can remain very alive (Sen 2005: 6).

Dialectic reasoning was reflected upon in the treatise *Sarva Darsana Damgraha*. It states that extension based on direct observation (e.g. smoke implies fire) remains problematic as inference requires justification; while inferring we finally have to rely on a proposition that connects one object to another: "Nor can inference be the means of knowledge of the universal proposition, since in the case of this inference we should also require another inference to establish it, and so on, and hence would arise the fallacy of an ad infinitum retrogression" (quoted after Sen 2005: 27). In fact, the discipline of arguments and dispute seems to dominate the classical Indian thinking about the material world, at least in the Loka yata tradition (cf. Sen 2005: 27). Indian classical speaking and writing is therefore deeply rooted in a practice that John Rawls called the exercise of public reason and that was for him a central feature of democracy (Rawls 1971). Sen sees the role of argumentative speaking in reaching beyond its structural priorities. It may, if used with deliberation and commitment in the social debate, be instrumental in removing poverty and deprivation (Sen 2005: xiii). Therefore also Sen perceives democracy as public reasoning (Sen 2005: 12). In this context, N. Mandela (1994: 21) writes about the practice of local African meetings:

> *Everyone who wanted to speak did so. It was democracy in its purest form. There may have been a hierarchy of importance among the speakers, but everyone was heard, chief and subject, warrior and medicine man, shopkeeper and farmer, landowner and laborer... The foundation of self-government was that all men were free to voice their opinions and equal in their value as citizens.*

As said, tolerance in India was expressly invoked by the Buddhist emperor Ashoka (Sen 2005: xii). The acceptance of heterodoxy of opinions was stresses in the formula adopted by the Muslim ruler of India, Emperor Akbar. A. Sen (2005: 35) stresses the Sanskrit term *swikriti* (acceptance) as a principle of traditional Hindu thinking that enabled the construction of a tolerant society where heterodox views can be expressed without fear and that 'enable to lead an own life'. This acceptance comes close to tolerance that Sen positions within the modern debate about multiculturalism (Sen 2005: 35). The acceptance of other views and religious beliefs enables to lay down a concept of Indianness (cf. Sen 2005: 51) as an overarching concept that integrates all inhabitants of India. Sen (2005: 69) writes:

> *Despite the veritable flood of religious practices in India, there is also a resilient undercurrent of conviction across the country that religious beliefs, while personally significant, are socially unimportant and should be politically inconsequential.*

Indian philosophy includes a fully-fledged system of argumentation that is applied in numerous legal and ethical works with a consequence that proves the deep anchorage of this type of reasoning in the culture of the subcontinent.

3.3.2 Are legal arguments sophisms?

While attempting to use arguments we have first of all to determine the field in which we can safely move, i.e. who can bring arguments and what sort of arguments can be used. The answer of dominant legal cultures to these questions has been different. Ancient Greece defined the quality of participants rather broadly and allowed arguments which left room for inventiveness and creation. Ancient Rome restricted with its scientific law the spectrum of possible arguments; it also limited the number of participants and clearly determined their status. The epistemological analysis of both ancient laws makes this distinction clear. The Romans were first to delimit which opinion could be duly pronounced in a court of law and which was inappropriate. This formalization of the procedure began with the setting up of formal – if not formalistic – procedural formulae and ended with the full-fledged institutionalized framework of reference, the *Corpus Iuris Civilis,* in which the players and their text were clearly defined. Between these two stages there is a wide field of argumentative and epistemological work performed by the Romans. Its reconstruction is the legal theory of both ancient laws. Occasionally, it had been claimed that the status of jurisprudence is limited to sophisms developed in the tradition of ancient Greek protagonists of this art. We know them as Socrates' adversaries in the Platonic dialogues. Here again, the conceptual field has to be clarified. We have to ask ourselves whether the alleged difference in epistemology and argumentation in these dialogues between the Sophists and the Socratic tradition prolonged by Plato and Aristotle until Kant really exists. The contribution of sophists such as Protagoras, Gorgias, Lykophron, Antiphon, Hippias, Prodikos, Thrasymachos, Kritias, and Alkidamas has been analyzed by Schirren and Zinsmaier (2003). The other question is whether the procedure developed by the Greek sophists – when cleared from Plato's tarnishing attempts – was really that irrational and non-scientific as argued by many. As far as the development of argumentative techniques is concerned the Sophists' contribution has been increasingly acknowledged in the research (Plantin 1996: 5).

The two above fundamental questions may help reconstruct the epistemological background of modern law and clarify the importance of argumentation in it from the historically proven beginning of this institution. To reach this aim we favor the method of epistemological interpretation based on the works by M. Foucault. The epistemological interpretation focuses on the process of emergence and structure of interpreted notions. It shows the conceptual background and the way in which they had been constructed and further developed in use. It therefore concerns the most fundamental process in which signification emerges in law. I will apply it later in the chapter dealing with the global law and its conceptual background (Part 5 of this book).

3.3.3 Argumentation in legal discourse

Legal arguments do not exist in a vacuum. They are interrelated as parts of a general discourse about law. The general legal discourse may be divided into discourses and counter-discourses along the linguistic and extra-linguistic interactions in which its participants used to act. Interest in the structure of the spoken type of discourse in law has long historical roots and reaches until the legendary Greek orators Corax and Tisias (Sloane 2001: 418) and their argumentative strategy of litigation (Plantin 1996: 4). Later on, the interest shifted to the analysis of written court decisions and their interpretation and the spoken legal arguments were less analyzed. Only recently spoken word in the legal context, especially in witness testimony, gained momentum in the research. The discourse type which interests the legal linguist most is one comprised in institutional boundaries (Plantin 1996: 8) because law is above all an institutional phenomenon. It consists of a series of argumentative utterances organized and planned in advance which aim at obtaining a specified goal within the audience toward which they are directed. Needless to stress that the free discourse about law which is not limited by professional and institutional argumentative boundaries has basically the same structure with the difference that the acceptability of the arguments used in it is not determined by a legal institution such as a court or a professional corporation of jurists (cf. Galdia 2014). The discourse about law outside its institutional boundaries is definitely also interesting but it relates less to the main topic of these lectures and it can be easily analyzed in relative independence from the professional institutionalized discourse about law. The structure of the institutionalized legal discourse interests us more because this type of complex linguistic activity constitutes a challenge for the legal theory and the legal practice. From a theoretical perspective, the extra-institutional discourse about law as a free discourse relates mainly to issues concerning the acceptability of legal norms and reactions to court decisions among the broader public. Its analysis helps develop argumentative means for the legislative work and court decisions which would increase the level of their emotional and/or rational acceptability among the broader public. On the other hand, the institutional legal discourse aims at achieving acceptance within the professional audience with professional legal arguments which multiply its complexity. Also M. Atienza made clear in his early research into legal argumentation that it is vain to expect one single form of it in the legal discourse. The understanding of what actually is legal argumentation depends upon the theoretical position taken toward the law (Atienza 1999: 37). Relevant arguments and valid argumentation are determined by the perspective upon the argumentation that can be based on legal normativism, legal realism or natural law. He furthermore stresses that the multiplicity of arguments that is engendered by this variety of approaches to law does not mean that the results of such argumentative discourses would be incompatible; he perceives them rather as complementary (Atienza 1999: 44). In our view this assumption is strengthened also by the structure of the legal discourse in which legal arguments of different paradigmatic origin usually intertwine. Sterile legal discourses, i.e. those based on one conception of law are rare both in lawsuits and in legislative debates.

Contemporary legal linguistics concentrates upon the elements of the general legal discourse and presupposes rather than convincingly proves the existence of such a general linguistic structure which would roof over the singular and often also contradictory legal arguments. However, the principles of textual coherence which can be identified in whatever rational legal argument as well as their provable interrelation, without which the singular arguments would not make much sense, allow introducing a general concept of a linguistic entity such as the legal discourse into legal linguistics. The characteristic feature of the argumentative language is its deliberative aspect, the way in which lawyers legitimize their decisions by reference to reasons for them. They aim at convincing the recipients and other readers about the fact that their decisions were correct – just or justified – and consequently also legal. The traditional theoretical question to ask at this point would be: could they not try to achieve their means with purely logical instruments? Could not these lawyers simply demonstrate that through induction and deduction results had been achieved in their decisions which guarantee that a rational legal decision had been taken? Such a procedure would ensure the logical character of the decision and convince through its logical character alone. Apparently this is not possible and in the parts of this book devoted to interpretive aspects of law I have appraised these problems. There, I have underlined the necessity to activate other than purely logical mechanisms in order to understand the process of application of laws or understanding contracts. Moreover, criticism toward the use of normative syllogism as a basis for the legal argumentation led to the rejection of this model (Jackson 1988: 239). According to the basic structure of the normative syllogism in all cases *p* consequences *q* ought to follow. The minor premise there is a categorization of the facts of the particular case being adjudicated: this is a case of *p*. The conclusion which should follow would be: *q* ought to be applied. Even if one would assume that it is a workable tool in some cases, the so-called hard cases definitely cannot be solved with the application of normative syllogisms alone. Jackson posits that the inter-discursiveness between the general rule and the particular case is the result of an intentional model of discourse. For him, a looser logical model of subsumption, a sort of "narrative comparison" would be more appropriate for legal argumentation (Jackson 1988: 242). Unsurprisingly, therefore, specific argumentation such as the legal one emerges when pure logical induction cannot help. This is especially the case when transformations take place which enable propositions of different linguistic quality. When a relation $p \longrightarrow q$ is not operational than pTq is worthwhile considering (Aarnio/Peczenik 1983: 14) When *p* is indicated as a reason for *q* and *p* does not follow logically from *q*, i.e. when deductively the relation $p \longrightarrow q$ cannot be justified through an additional proposition then we have to deal with such a specific construction. The transformation which took place must therefore be justified (Aarnio/Peczenik 1983: 36) and this is for some authors the basis of the rational legal argumentation.

3.3.4 Procedural aspects of legal argumentation

Some authors prefer procedural aspects in argumentation while leaving material elements of argumentation to the participants of the argumentative discourse. For them, practical rationality is grounded in the discursive practice. Robert Alexy (1983) underlined the limitation of the professional legal argumentation through precedents and doctrine. He concentrated upon the development of rules for the rational linguistic argumentation in law. He distinguished between procedural and universal rationality. These were grounded in two different sets of rules: those pertaining to the structure of arguments (e.g. lack of inconsistency) called also monological applications and others pertaining to the procedure of the discourse, e.g. every speaker can participate in the discourse. In his view, first of all the rules of rational linguistic argumentation known from the general discourse have to be accepted by the participants. They are: lack of contradictions, coherence, sincerity of arguments, readiness to apply concepts in changing contexts and speaking the same language (Aarnio/Peczenik 1988: 43). Other rules concerning participants are: everyone is able to speak and use all possible approaches, wishes and needs and present his own views, no one should be impeded to participate. However, the rules have to assure the reasonability of the discussion (Alexy 1983: 36). Arguments used are termed in form of the burden of proof and expressed in the procedure by general maxims, e.g. *we have always done it this way* and particular arguments, e.g. *argumentum ad hominem.* The argumentation takes place toward the background of limitations to which the legal discourse is exposed. Alexy reflected in his approach J. Habermas' general discourse theory (Habermas 1988) which he transposed upon legal discourses. While doing so, he also discovered the limitations of the professional legal discourse as compared with the general discourse that has been described by Habermas (1988) and Aarnio (1989). O. Weinberger opposed this model of rational argumentation arguing that the discourse cannot replace or guarantee truth in or correctness of a judicial decision. Other formal approaches such as A. Aarnio's stress consensus, acceptability of results and interpretation through a specialized auditorium as formal requirements of convincing legal argumentation. Their aim is equally the rationality of decisions: the higher is the justified level of rationality the higher is the readiness to accept the result. The Wittgensteinian *life form* provides the basis for the acceptability of decisions. The life form is at the same time also the natural limit to any form of rationality in the general and in the particular discourse (Aarnio/Peczenik 1983: 81). All these theories claim to be able to determine appropriate conditions for making convincing and justified utterances about law.

3.3.4.1 Façade-argumentation

When a decision does not correspond to its own heuristic or justification requirements, it is perceived as a *façade*-argumentation (Aarnio 1989: 25). Alf Ross (1966: 57, 183) aptly characterized this specific type of argumentation. An illustrative example of this type of argumentation is the court opinion Kinney Shoe Corp.

v. Polan (939 F. 2d 209, 4th Cir., 1991). The defendant Polan formed two corporations, let us call them A and B. He concluded a lease agreement for office premises on behalf of A that remained passive as he apparently run his business activities exclusively with B. When sued for unpaid rent he admitted the contractual duties of A, the assetless company. The landlord Kinney sued Polan personally claiming that the corporate veil that Polan created around himself as an owner of A corporation must be pierced. The court applied in this case the doctrine of piercing the corporate veil and found that Polan was personally liable for the debts of A. The test applied included: 1) the unity of interest requirement between the company and the owner and 2) the undercapitalization of the company. Both requirements are here clearly fulfilled. However, a problem remains. The landlord is a renowned and experienced company that did not pay any attention to the financial situation of A that existed only 'on paper' when the lease contract was signed. Did he merit protection under such circumstances? One might tend to the verdict that the landlord would have to assume the risk of insolvability of a contract partner whom he carelessly accepted. The court decided differently. It admitted that the test used is in fact three-prong and not two-prong as initially indicated and that it additionally requires that the creditor must be unaware of the potential risk. Yet, it held restrictively that this requirement is only permissive and not mandatory and that it primarily concerns financial institutions and the like, e.g. insurance companies. The landlord, a nationwide shoe dealer did not belong to this group of creditors that must be particularly vigilant while entering into contracts. However, the impression remains that the court established Polan's liability mainly to sanction his apparent business plan and prevent him from keeping the profits engendered by B. This intention is however not mentioned in the decision, because it represents an extra-legal motivation. Occasionally, dissenting opinions reveal the strategy of the majority opinion as *façade*. Thus, in Atwater v. Lago Vista (532 U.S. 318, 2001; 195 F. 3d 242) the U.S. Supreme Court had to decide whether the Fourth Amendment of the U.S. Constitution prohibits a warrantless arrest for a minor criminal offence. In the case the plaintiff, a lady who drove a car with her two small children has been stopped by a policeman and subsequently taken into custody for not having put her seatbelt on while driving. The U.S. Supreme Court rejected her complaint. Not unexpectedly, a dissenting opinion followed. In it, the four dissenting justices held that the Fourth Amendment guaranteed the right to be free from *unreasonable searches and seizures.* They saw a contradiction between the holding of the majority that the arrest of Ms. Atwater under the circumstances of the case had been a *pointless indignity* but nevertheless constitutionally permissible. The dissenting judges referred to the language of the Fourth Amendment while establishing their argumentation: "A full custodial arrest, such as the one to which Ms. Atwater was subjected, is the quintessential seizure...When a full custodial arrest is effected without a warrant, the plain language of the Fourth Amendment requires that the arrest be reasonable." Certainly, the issue of reasonability had not been taken by the majority for full value. Rather, formal and historical elements dominated its finding which ended in the contradiction challenged in the dissenting opinion. One can assume that the court intended to avoid problems for policemen who sometimes under unclear circumstances and in haste have to take decisions that lead to the arrest of suspected persons. Again, these apparent motives are not spelled out in the majority decision. Furthermore, one could perceive as complementary to a *façade*-decision all judicial reasoning aiming at distinguishing undistinguishable cases and introducing counter-intuitive interpretations about the propositions of law into judgments. Reasons for this particular phenomenon can be manifold. One of them could be the pretence to discover new legal arguments and to gain respect in the professional community. The other could be characterological inclinations to prove to others that things are different than others assume them to be. Both are equally terrifying in law.

3.3.5 More and less sophisticated argumentation models in law

Legal argumentation is by its very nature a complex linguistic operation. Were it simple, no reasons for complicated and often even controversial court decisions would exist. The first theoretical problem of the argumentation in law is therefore how to structure it and how to structure the reflection about it on a professional level. Models for structuring argumentation in law can themselves be more or less complex and a preference for one model among many is always difficult because it necessarily leads to the loss in our understanding of the phenomenon. In short, is the model of argumentation too simple, it does not provide any valuable insights into this complex and decisive linguistic operation in law. Is it too complex, it threatens to choke the arguments to death and it will not be reflected by lawyers in their work. To be useful in law, a model of legal argumentation must be sufficiently descriptive but it must also be based on material research which shows its application in law, both in the interpretation of statutes and in its use in the precedents. I will therefore concentrate here less on purely theoretical models of legal argumentation and their discussion in the legal theory when they are not based on material (i.e. also linguistic) application of their theoretical basis. Also M. Atienza (2006: 247–279) stressed the pragmatic aspects in the legal argumentation that are for him anchored in linguistic interaction (cf. also Atienza 1999: 44). In the context relevant here he insists upon the use of arguments as a linguistic activity (Atienza 1999: 40). The linguistic activity involves a set of utterances that leads to the conclusion as its final point; utterances have premises as points of departure and are linked with the conclusion by specific relations (Atienza ibid.). I have adopted here a very broad definition of argumentation which is for me the process of identifying utterances and the requirements for their acceptability in speech acts. The arguments represented in speech acts may be of different nature and here too I am very tolerant and do not exclude any. Some would say that it is necessary to distinguish argumentation which must be based on reasonable grounds, simple quarrelling of the parties as well as statements based on emotions. I will not do it, mainly because in practice the distinction between reasonable and emotional arguments is blurred.

3.3.5.1 *Argumentation in law can be very simple*

The simplest model of an argumentative action would consist of a beginning, a main part, and an end. At the first glance, this model may seem simplistic. However, it explains a lot about argumentative communication. To begin with, a situation has to emerge in which argumentation is necessary. Our daily communication does not consist predominantly of argumentative acts because we simply do not need them in many routine situations. There, rather simple reference to facts and objects is sufficient because daily practice is grounded in internalized socio-linguistic procedures, like language games or discourses. In law, the argumentation comes up mainly when a disaccord emerges between at least two parties about a proposition of law. In such a situation, the parties may engage in a discourse about valid and void in the propositions of law. They may also not do so and prefer to use other methods of persuasion such as violence, threat with use of force etc. These means are extra-legal and are therefore not interesting here. When the parties engage in a discourse about the validity of a proposition of law they have to use arguments which count in law, i.e. legal arguments (Alexy 1983: 41). As a rule, they will also use many other types of arguments but the persuasive force of such arguments is rather low. Should they not be able to reach a conclusive result they will turn to a court of law for decision. There, the process which we boldly called main part of argumentation continues until it is terminated by a judicial decision which ends formally the disaccord between the parties about the validity of certain propositions in law. That the disaccord is formally terminated means that it ends in terms of law, even if one of the parties or both of them are still convinced about their own views that were not accepted by the court. When the court procedure allows an appeal, the parties can choose this solution and the main part of argumentation will recommence until it will find an end in a formally final judicial decision. Does this model still seem simplistic? One could answer yes and no. It is not simplistic at all because it shows the structurally fundamental stages in the use of argumentative speech which is for us decisive from the point of view of pragmatic theory. It also shows the communicative prerequisites of argumentative speech acts, i.e. the situation of a disaccord or controversy without which no significant argumentation in law comes about. I will not treat here situations such as legal training or doctrinary comments where controversies may be assumed or constructed to enable a professional discourse about the validity of propositions about law for educational purposes. The simple model shows us not only the disaccord between the parties as an entry stage into the legal argumentation. It also makes plain that one party alone cannot simply abandon the discourse at whatever stage once it engaged in it. Participation in the legal discourse can be imposed by the means of law; it is therefore a very specific institutionalized participation in the discourse. Finally, it proves the necessity of a disaccord in law for the emergence of legal argumentation rather than the contrary. This notwithstanding, the descriptive model presented above is simplistic because it does not show how arguments are used in order to reach the final and binding decision. This part must be explored when legal argumentation is perceived as a linguistic operation, i.e. as rooted in rules about language use. Furthermore, procedural aspects are only mentioned there; yet they are not characterized. It is said that the court will apply procedural rules when examining the propositions presented by the parties. However, it is not said what this procedure looks like and especially what is its status as a legal-linguistic procedure. This procedure, be it civil, penal or administrative, has been described by generations of jurists in innumerable volumes, but it has been described from the legal – and not from the legal-linguistic – point of view. A legal-linguistic theory must show what is linguistic in the procedures used when courts decide controversies about law. Controversies may also concern facts and they are also solved with linguistic means. Basically, the same legal procedures are applicable there, their legal-linguistic status may however differ (cf. MacCormick 1984: 53).

Another simple model, called by Plantin (1996: 22) *schéma argumentative minimal* has been proposed to describe the essentials of the argumentative act. It refers to the model developed by S. Toulmin (1958) and consists of data input (FR *donnée)* and of the conclusion in the most simple case. This scheme is widened by an operation where the conclusion is characterized as drawn from the data input with the help of a warrant (FR *loi de passage)* in the more advanced form of the model (Plantin ib.). At this stage it becomes plain that in the argumentation not a linear sequence of linguistic acts is decisive, but the linguistic operation which allows for the conclusion to be drawn from them. Therefore, the minimal models can provide some insight into the structure of argumentation. Simultaneously, they also show that it is necessary to shift attention from the sequence of argumentative utterances to linguistic processes or operations which make argumentation of them, i.e. provide conclusions apt at terminating a disaccord.

3.3.5.2 A more complicated model of legal argumentation

This model would include the analyses of procedures in which legal arguments are used. It would concentrate upon formal aspects such as procedural beginning, procedural main part and procedural termination of situations in which the validity of legal arguments is tested. It would include participative rules which determine, for instance, the burden of proof in evidence that is provided by the parties. In addition, it would examine the tests determining the material validity of propositions in law. As a pragmatic model, it would also reflect upon the persuasive aspect of the final legal decision, i.e. whether it has convinced the parties and materially – not only formally – terminated the disaccord between them. Legal argumentation is also institutionalized in the sense that the participants have no choice of argumentative models. They do not need to agree on an argumentative model either. Most ordinary discourses are also based on specific rules, yet the parties may modify or abandon them. As indicated, the named three particularities of arguments used in law may not be distinctive, i.e. limited in their application to law. They are, nevertheless, frequent in legal contexts and should therefore be taken into consideration while characterizing the legal argumentation.

3.3.5.3 Advanced models of legal argumentation

Advanced models of legal argumentation free themselves from situational boundaries upon which I initially relied, while developing simple and less simple descriptive models. They try to describe legal arguments and the argumentative discourse in terms of logical analysis. For general argumentation, Toulmin (1958: 100, 106) showed the necessity of the already mentioned warrants, grounds and qualifiers in a model of argumentation. In the reading of this model by Plantin (1996: 23) such an argumentative discourse provides the justification of the proposition in question and considers also its modality. Through the introduction of reserves and guaranties as basic concepts into the model Toulmin developed a scheme which can be used also for the analysis of legal argumentation. Different from this type of reasoning is the justification *sensu stricto*. It is perceived by many as an argumentative operation in which the decision taken within an institution is rationalized *post hoc*. This means that a decision may be taken irrationally or within the limits of daily rationality, and is afterwards reformulated in order to match up to the requirements of professional rationality and other constitutional and procedural standards. It will be mentioned later more specifically. Toulmin's model has been used in law for the analysis of statute interpretation by Dominicy (1993: 246–249). Dominicy also stressed that the speech act theory and especially the Austinian notion of illocutionary force play an important role in Toulmin's model (Dominicy 1993: 243). This has the advantage that an argumentative speech act in order to be identified and understood has to be perceived as an integral part of the context of the utterance. This procedure makes argumentation and the understanding of arguments much easier as it prevents the dissociations of notions (cf. Perelman/Olbrechts-Tyteca 1983: 550–609). It has been perceived as one of the most significant challenges in the model of argumentation since it is used as a tool for manipulating arguments in the argumentative practice. Dominicy also applied strategies preventing the dissociations of notions in the interpretation of a statutory provision. In my reading, he came very close to the Dworkinian model of creative interpretation applied in so-called hard cases.

Furthermore, legal argumentation has some particular features which make it interesting for pragmatics. Yet, these characteristic features do not make it necessarily distinctive. For instance, specific reasoning that omits the precise *premissa major* is typical of the judicial decisions. In Jones v. Free Flight Sport Aviation, Inc. (623 P.2d 370, 1981 Colo. Lexis 571) the Supreme Court of Colorado had to deal with the time period within which a minor who became major had to disaffirm a voidable contract made during his minority. In the case, the minor who signed a contract for the use of recreational sky-diving facilities that included a covenant not to sue and an exculpatory clause, has been injured during a flight, ten months after his 18th birthday. The court decided that the plaintiff had ratified the contract made during his minority through accepting its benefits during his majority and could not disaffirm it after the time period of ten months. The court did not determine what is the reasonable time period for the disaffirmation of voidable contracts for minors who become majors. Instead, it posited that the disaffirmation must take place *within a reasonable time*. This implies that the time period of ten months was not *reasonable* in the opinion of the court. However, no rigorous logical reasoning is possible in this case because a clearly stated *premissa major* is missing. Nevertheless, the minimal consistency requirements for a rational decision are fulfilled and the decision as such is understandable to jurists as well as to laypersons. It follows reasoning patterns in the ordinary language, and, although it is doubtful from the point of view of formal logic, it is neither inconsistent nor is it irrational.

3.4 Argumentation in Legal Practice

Argumentation in the legal practice raised unusual interest in the 20th century. Nowadays, argumentative approaches even dominate the debate about the nature of law. Argumentative approaches to law replaced the centuries-old paradigm in which law has been viewed as a system of rules based on legal concepts. However, it is also useful to ask whether the shift of attention in the area of law from the legal system based on concepts to legal argumentation is a real change in the paradigm of the legal research. Due to the sluggish reception of argumentative approaches in the legal doctrine we might also have to do with co-existing contradictory approaches. It could also be that only a new layer has been added to the traditional systematic (doctrinal) legal reasoning. The relatively weak position of legal linguistics within legal sciences might suggest such a conclusion. However, answers to the above questions, both practical as well as theoretical are complex. It is not debatable that in critical modern societies the necessity to understand, i.e. to be able to follow the reasoning in a legal decision or in a statute are more important than in previous forms of societies that were based on the affirmation of the ruling social groups and their decisions (Mattila 2008: 1151). The attempt at understanding also dominates the debate about law which concerns broader spheres of the public and is not limited any more to a group of legal experts discussing some abstract questions of systematic coherence in law. Therefore, nowadays, a judicial decision is rarely accepted on the reason alone that it had been rendered by a competent authority that followed the views expressed in the legal doctrine. Also the doctrinal structure of law and the doctrinal understanding appear less decisive in the discourse about law. It is therefore understandable that the attention turned to points identified as central to the understanding of law. They reflect mostly the way how lawyers used to speak and write. Meanwhile, traditional positivist approaches to law still exist. Legal linguistics must therefore reflect this dichotomy in its research into the legal language.

3.4.1 Argumentation in U.S. court decisions

In order to understand the prerequisites of the theory of legal argumentation material analysis is necessary. In the following paragraphs I will therefore deal with some selected U.S. court opinions. They will be scrutinized in thematic blocks because the factual interdependence among them may illustrate or even reveal some argumentative interdependence. Such a scrutiny has to start with the question of how courts react to interpretive differences and how they reflect upon problems of argumentation in their opinions. It also includes the vision of non-judges, e.g. attorneys-at-law and laypersons on the way in which institutions act in argumentative situations. It makes plain the results of these institutional reflections, i.e. mostly established procedures for dealing with argumentative problems, the lexicalization based on such procedures in the material argumentative structures, nature of arguments used and remedies that improve the quality of argumentation and the rationality of the decisions taken. The essence of all such efforts is developing tests in which arguments are used in order to prove the validity of a proposition of law. They are not easy to formalize. This characteristic feature will be shown on the following examples.

3.4.1.1 Constitutional issues

Legal argumentation in constitutional matters may be perceived as very advanced because in the rare cases in which the U. S. Supreme Court accepts to hear a case considerable efforts on all sides are undertaken to make the best of the arguments used. Still, these efforts also have limits. For instance, in 1996, the U.S. Congress enacted the Child Pornography Prevention Act (CPPA). Section 2256 (8) (B) of the act prohibits "any visual depiction, including any photograph, film, video, picture, or computer-generated image or picture" that "is, or appears to be, of a minor engaging in sexually explicit conduct." The section has been generally understood to include also computer-generated images known as virtual child pornography. The U.S. Supreme Court had to deal with the question whether Section 2256 (8) (B) violates the Free Speech Clause of the First Amendment of the U.S. Constitution in that it criminalizes virtual child pornography. In its decision Ashcroft, Attorney General v. The Free Speech Coalition (U.S. Lexis 2789, 2002) the court scrutinized the rationale provided by the Attorney General who supported the regulation. Its first argument had been that virtual child pornography encourages the paedophiles to engage in illegal conduct. This rationale did not convince the court as it would lead to the control of thought. The court stated that "the government may not prohibit speech because it increases the chance an unlawful act will be committed at some indefinite future time." The second argument provided by the Attorney General to support the regulation had been that even experts have problems to distinguish virtual child pornography from the imaging which features real children due to high technological standards of computer imaging, and that it therefore must be prohibited like real child pornography. This argument did not convince the court either. The court stated: "The argument, in essence, is that protected speech may be banned as a means to ban unprotected speech. This analysis turns the First Amendment upside down. The Government may not suppress lawful speech as the means to suppress unlawful speech." The court limited its scrutiny to the arguments provided by the government. The arguments were rather weak and not difficult to turn down. It remains the impression that something like a third argument was missing which would make the regulation more plausible. Meanwhile, in U.S. v. Williams (128 S.Ct. 1830, 2008), the U. S. Supreme Court referred to the Congressional amendment that is a reaction to the Ashcroft-decision. This decision may be perceived as a reaction to the missing third argument.

In general, controversies about the meaning of statutes and precedents manifest themselves in constitutional law as matters relating to the constitutionality of legal provisions. In order to overcome these controversies about the propositions of constitutional law *tests* of constitutionality had been established (Tribe 2000: 6 sqq). These tests apply *doctrines*, e.g. the doctrine of substantial overbreadth or the doctrine of vagueness when dealing with the semantic intricacies in the propositions expressing the content of law. U.S. Supreme Court opinions deal with these doctrines especially in cases concerning the First Amendment of the U.S. constitution that guarantees the freedom of speech. In Broadrick v. Oklahoma (1973), Board of Airport Commissoners v. Jews for Jesus (1987) and Virginia v. Hicks (2003) the court developed and specified the doctrine of substantial overbreadth. The U.S. Supreme Court distinguished within its constitutionality test *protected* and *unprotected speech* under the First Amendment. The unprotected speech that may be totally prohibited by the Government comprises: dangerous speech, provocative speech (Chaplinski v. New Hampshire 315 U.S. 568, 62 S.Ct. 766, 1942 U.S. Lexis 851), speech inciting to violent overthrow of the government (Brandenburg v. Ohio 395 U.S. 444, 89 S. Ct. 1827, 1969 U.S. Lexis 1367), defamatory language (Beauharnais v. Illinois 343 U.S. 250, 72 S.Ct. 725, 1952 U.S. Lexis 2799), child pornography (New York v. Ferber 458 U.S. 747, 102 S. Ct. 3348, 1982 U.S. Lexis 12), obscene speech (Miller v. California, Jacobellis v. Ohio 378 U.S. 184, 84 S.Ct. 1676, 1964 U.S. Lexis 822). Hence, the developed test distinguishes different types of speech, and provides a first help for dealing with such cases. The overall argumentation in such cases remains however still complex and less transparent. Therefore, more sophisticated tests were developed in other cases. For instance, in equal protection cases two major standards are used for the review of their constitutionality. The 'strict scrutiny' which allows differential treatment only if 1) drawn as narrowly as possible, and 2) necessary to achieve a compelling governmental interest. This standard is used in cases involving adverse impact on racial, religious, and national minorities. The 'rationality basis' deems differential treatment constitutional when it is reasonable and related to a permissible governmental goal. It is used in cases involving business regulation or 'nonsuspect' classes. Finally, we can retain at this stage that social values underlie all such controversial decisions. This holds true also for cases that may appear rather technical. For instance, Art. 1 § 8 of the U.S. Constitution defines the legislative competence of the Congress. As a rule, matters that are not delegated to the Congress remain within the competence of federal states as reiterated in Amendment X. In particular, two general clauses in sec. 8 of Art. 1 gained predominant importance in determining the scope of Congressional competence, the *interstate commerce clause* and the *necessary and proper clause*. However, as nowadays almost all daily events are linked to interstate relations and are at least to some extent related to economic activities the semantic boundaries of both clauses have become increasingly flawed. Here one should, of course, keep in mind that both clauses had been drafted in a general manner which from the very beginning deliberately left a considerable margin for interpretive appreciation. This is understandable, because I already mentioned that values play in such decisions a preponderant role. That said, the U.S. Supreme Court in 2000 rejected the view that the U.S. Congress be authorized to regulate gender-motivated violence under the commercial clause qualifying the relation to interstate commerce as too tenuous (U.S. v. Morrison, 529 U.S. 598, 120 S.Ct. 170, 146 L. Ed. 2d 658, 2000). The power of the Congress to regulate interstate commerce has been traditionally perceived as an issue involving advanced argumentation. Congress has passed statutes that bar discrimination and regulate business activities which are very limited in scope and which are clearly of local character. In almost all cases the courts have upheld this legislation under the affectation doctrine which states that as long as an activity which is regulated by the Congress affects interstate commerce, it is within Congressional regulatory authority. The term *affects* is quite broadly interpreted by the courts. Even in a situation where the business is explicitly local like a small restaurant in which out-of-state purchases are minimal a federal ban of racial discrimination has been successfully imposed by the Congress due to the affectation doctrine. The provision of the Civil Rights Act (42 U.S.C. § 2000 a et sq.) which was quoted in U.S. v. Morrison had dealt with the abolition of racial discrimination, and was not based on the equal protection clause of Amendment XIV. Presumably, the legislator reflected upon the interpretation of this clause in Plessy v. Fergusson and later in Brown (1965) concerning the doctrine of 'separate but equal' (cf. Notes and Commented Materials no. 40 and no. 41). The Supreme Court provided in Brown a 15 year period for the implementation of the guaranteed rights. Previously, the clause had been used to justify federal legislation aiming at the abolition of racial discrimination and established the right of black citizens to occupy the same type of seats in busses in interstate traffic as white citizens. Both decisions may not be particularly pervasive in terms of argumentation, especially the Brown-decision is perceived sometimes as wanting (Tribe 2000: 3). This becomes evident when the majority decision in Brown is compared with the dissenting opinion. They reveal however the argumentative procedure in which the Constitution and its values are tied together.

3.4.1.2 Criminal matters

Convictions about the being of the world underlie decisions as do ethical values. In the case People v. Ralph J. Tortorici (92 N.Y. 2d 757, 709 N.E. 2d 87, 686 N.Y.S. 2d 346, 1999) the New York Court of Appeals rejected the appeal by a defendant who waived his right to participation in the trial of his case. According to Art. 730 of the Criminal Procedure Law the criminal trial of a defendant *"who as a result of mental disease or defect lacks capacity to understand the proceedings against him or to assist in his own defense"* must be prevented. In the trial the defendant clearly expressed his wish not to participate, and added a remark about alleged implants of chips in his brain undertaken by the Government in order to spy out his most intimate thoughts. Psychiatrists deemed the defendant therefore mentally ill. The court, however, after having ordered to x-ray the defendant deemed him sane as far as his allegations concerned the right to participation in his trial and affirmed the initial order in this case. It differentiated between the defendant's both allegations as if they were disconnected. Overall, problems associated with the insanity defense in the American penal law led to the formulation of necessary standards of proof which seem to invoke the evident fact of insanity. Thus, the federal criminal legislation provides for *clear and convincing evidence* which must be proven by the defendant (cf. 18 U.S.C.A. § 17 (16)). Some U.S. states require a proof *by a preponderance of evidence*, while others shift the burden of proof *beyond the reasonable doubt.* These formulations cover an ongoing debate about the necessary degree of proof in the American criminal law and signal rather the contrary of what the existing standards seem to invoke, i.e. the certainty about the mental state of a person. Cases such as Tortorici make plain the necessity to improve the evaluation of argumentative standards in criminal cases. Moreover, criminal cases such as the above one or many *hate speech* cases show better than others the interrelation of professional and laypersons discourse in law. Professional interpretive standards seem to be better adapted to professional discourses within which they function. Communicative frictions emerge at the contact point of both. An argumentation that does not reflect professional standards usually fails. Laypersons' speech is paradoxically not understood properly because it does not fit into the discursive structure established for processing it. In such cases, the risk of language reification is eminent.

3.4.1.3 Business Law

Business law cases may be perceived as less spectacular and the argumentation in them may seem rather formalistic because of their routine nature and limited efforts that are invested in their solution by courts and other participating lawyers. Nonetheless, they reveal important characteristic features of legal argumentation.

In Rollerblade Inc. v. U.S. (282 F. 3d 1349, Fed. Cir. 2002) the classification of roller skating protective gear under Harmonized Tariffs Schedules (HTSUS) became an issue for litigation because the different classification of goods under the HTSUS led to the application of different duty rates upon the imports (cf. Notes and Commented Materials no. 48). Rollerblade Inc. had brought to U.S. roller skating protective gear which it classified under the HTSUS as *accessory* to roller skaters. This classification would lead to freedom of custom duties on these imports. Meanwhile, the U.S. Custom Services classified the goods as *other sport equipment* which carries a duty rate of 4% ad valorem. Rollerblade Inc. perceived its roller skating protective gear as *accessory* because they were manufactured and marketed solely for the use with in-line roller skates. Moreover, Rollerblade Inc. argued that the gear is part of the roller skates because it contributes to the safe and effective operation of the skates and is designed solely with them. Under the HTSUS when a good is subject to more than one section or heading number the General Rule of Interpretation should be applied to determine the appropriate classification number. The primary rule is the rule of specificity: the rule providing a more specific characterization of the product should be applied. Is there no specific rule or is more than one rule specific then the essential character of the goods is used as criterion for the characterization whereby their function, materials or components should be reflected upon. Terms used in HTSUS should be given a common and popular meaning unless the commercial meaning was clearly intended. HTSUS do not define *accessory.* Undefined terms in the HTSUS should in such cases be given their "common, popular meaning as set forth in dictionaries, scientific authorities and other reliable information sources." The court held in this case that accessories and parts must have a direct relationship to the primary article rather than to the general activity (in casu skating) in which the primary article is used. It perceived the gear as related to the activity of skating and not to the primary article as such. Rollerblade Inc. lost its case.

What interpretive strategy has been adopted by the court to reach its result? The court did not set up any specific definitions of *accessory* and of *part.* Instead, it adopted a particular approach to the goods in question by introducing a notion of a *primary article.* Subsequently, it stated that the relation of *accessory* to the *primary article* must be direct which means for the court that it concerns the primary article and not its use. The court did not follow dictionary definitions of *accessory.* In the Longman's dictionary it would read under *accessory*: "something which is not a necessary part of something larger but which makes it more beautiful, useful, effective etc. a black dress with matching accessories (e.g. hat, shoes)." In the Oxford's dictionary it could read: "a thing which can be added to something else in order to make it more useful, versatile, or attractive." As can be seen from the above definitions, the lexical analysis alone cannot lead to the interpretation adopted by the court. The application of lexicological definitions to this case leads to the result that protective gear could be perceived as *accessory* in the English language usage or could not be perceived as such with equally good reason. The only interpretive method which can be of use in such a situation is the creative interpretation. The creative interpretation cannot function in a vacuum. A specific interpretive strategy was necessary to make the decision in this case. It was based on public interest in the interpretation of the HTSUS. In controversial cases, taxation should prevail over a possible no-tax result because this solution is more beneficial to the public interest, at least from the governmental point of view. The interpretive strategy adopted by the court is to defer to the Custom's definition. It does not take one by surprise, as the public policy rule applied in such controversial cases is as follows: tax rather than let enter tax free. Rollerblade's interpretive strategy is of course contrary to it, on reasons well understandable. Overall, our pragmatic approach to language pays here once again because it shows that we should speak about linguistic aspects of law rather than about legal language. In this case it would be difficult to draw a line between the legal and the non-legal definition of *accessory.* In contrast with the general lexicological definition, the interpretation undertaken by the court is a pragmatic approach in this situation rather than a binding legal definition of *accessory.* To put it short, words may under specific circumstances have a specific meaning in law; in other situations they may not have it.

Analogous interpretive strategies became apparent in U.S. v. Haggar Apparel Company (526 US 380, 1999), rendered here in Notes and Commented Materials no. 47. In this case, the appeal court defers to the interpretive guidelines to HTSUS set up by the Customs Service and perceives these regulations as binding for the otherwise independent court. The court says: "Deference to any agency's expertise in construing a statutory command is not inconsistent with reaching the correct decision. If the agency's statutory interpretation fills a gap or defines a term in a way that is reasonable in the light of the legislator's revealed design, we give that judgement controlling weight." In this case the parties conflicted over customs classification of reimported garments which were permapressed in Mexico. Permapressing is a procedure which involves oven-baking that causes chemical changes in the fabric and is designed to maintain a garment's crease and avoid wrinkles. Re-importing goods assembled abroad is custom free according to HTSUS. Sec. 9802 HTSUS allows importers to deduct the value of assembly from duty assessment. The exemption is given for "articles assembled abroad in whole or in part of fabricated components that are products of the US." It also extends to any advancement or improvement of goods which are a result of "operations incidental to the assembly process." Haggar claimed that permapressing which goes beyond pure assembling is *an operation incidental to the assembly process* and as such duty free. In turn, Customs Service contended that permapressing is an additional operation which reaches beyond *assembly* and, which because of this, involves custom duties. It referred to own regulation which a.o. says: "The following are examples of operations not incidental to assembly: Chemical treatment of components or assembled articles to impart new characteristics such as...permapressing." Haggar claimed that the court is not bound by this regulation as it is charged "to reach the correct decision" in determining the proper classification of goods. Haggar Co. lost its case because the court deferred to the view of the specialized agency.

Likewise, in Samsonite Corp. v. U.S. (889 F.2d 1074 Fed. Cir., 1989) the parties conflicted over sec. 9802 HTSUS relating to re-imported metal strips which were exported in straight form and re-imported as bent and incorporated into travel bag frames. To obtain the mentioned tax deduction the goods assembled abroad must according to the HTSUS: 1) be exported from the U.S. in a condition ready for assembly without further fabrication, 2) not have lost their physical identity by change of form, shape etc., 3) not have been changed except by being assembled, and 4) except by operations being incidental to the assembly process such as cleaning, lubricating and painting. The court held that the strips were not exported in condition ready for *assembly* and that the bending process to which the strips were subjected did more than adjust the article. The essence of the process has been the configuration, without the resultant shape it would not be possible to insert the frames into the bottom of the luggage. Thus, in the view of the court the process that the strips underwent constituted fabrication and not mere *assembly.* Here again, language use in the legal context is controlled by the text of the provision which provides examples of *operations incidental to assembly* in the interpretive guidelines. The distinction between *fabrication* and *assembly* is nevertheless made by the court due to its institutional privilege. The court did not provide any examples of assembly which would approach fabrication. Yet, exactly this would be a persuasive test for determining the appropriate language use. Such a reaction signals that the court was making use of its interpretive privilege rather than interpreting the provision in its linguistic and legal context. Interpretive strategies are set up to control the ordinary language use and no reference is made in them to the subject matter. Language use is institutionalized in them and a state agency is given authority to determine whether e.g. permapressing is in fact an operation *incidental to the assembly process.* The court stated that if "the agency provides a reasonable interpretation and implementation of unambiguous statutory provision, it must be given judicial deference."

By contrast, in Lamb-Weston, Inc. v. McCain Foods, Ltd. (78 F.3rd 540, 1996) the United States Court of Appeals for the Federal Circuit had to decide a patent case and to determine whether a patent delivered by the Patent Board to the plaintiff had been properly provided for an invention which must be novel, useful, and non-obvious to be patented. The question whether the patent provided for plaintiff's process of making frozen, partially fried, lattice-shaped French fries concerned a non-obvious invention was controversial between the parties – competitors on the market. The court decided for the obviousness of the invention previously patented by the Patent Board and affirmed the decision of the court of appeals which had been challenged by the plaintiff. The court ruled that the process of making waffle fries was too obvious to be patentable. It held: "The ultimate determination of obviousness is a legal conclusion, resting on factual determinations. ...The evidence of prior use and sale of waffle fries and parfried potato products provides sufficient motivation to combine the known waffle-cut shape and the parfry cooking method. This combination renders the '084 patent obvious." Unlike in the previous decisions concerning the customs regulations, the court did not defer to the view of the specialized state agency, in casu the Patent Board. Instead, it decided the question of the obviousness of the patented invention in its own responsibility and according to its own knowledge. The argument used in the previous cases of a better professional knowledge about the subject matter in specialized state agencies was not used here. Still further, in J.E.M. Ag Supply, Inc., v. Pioneer Hi-Bred International, Inc. (534 U.S. 124, 122 S.Ct. 593, 2001 U.S Lexis 10949, 2001) the U.S. Supreme Court dealt with the question whether sexually reproducing hybrid plants are a patentable subject matter. The court answered this question affirmatively. In its decision it expressly referred to the practice of the specialized state agency in this matter, the Patent and Trade Office (PTO). It held that "It has been the unbroken practice of the PTO since that time to confer utility patents for plants. To obtain utility patent protection, a plant breeder must show that the plant he has developed is new, useful and non-obvious." Here, the court not only used but also deferred to the view and practice of the specialized state agency. Generally, in the U.S. law, an administrative agency is afforded judicial deference when it interprets the statutes that enable it to act (cf. CNG Transmission Corp. v. New York State Public Service Comm'n A.D. 2d 671, 585 N.Y.S. 2d 916). This is especially the case in situations where specialized knowledge is involved (Dworman v. New York State Division of Housing, 94 N.Y. 2d 359, 70 N.Y.S. 2d 192, 1999). Courts are usually deferential to administrative agencies in cases where the interpretation is based on "knowledge and understanding of underlying operational practices or entails an evaluation of...data and inferences to be drawn there from" (New York Telephone Company v. PSC 95 N.Y. 2d. 40, 710 N.Y.S. 2d 305, 2000). However, this deference is by no means absolute (National Merchandising Corp. v. New York Public Service Comm'n, 5 N.Y. 2d 485, 186 N.Y. s. 2d 47, 1959 and Consolidated Edison Co. of New York, Inc. v. New York Public Service Comm'n, 417 N.Y.S. 2d 30, 1979). Thus, balancing between deference to the knowledge of the administrative agency and the relative nature of this interpretive rule is needed. However, a rule stating general deference which nevertheless should not be perceived in absolute terms does not help. Striking the right balance is again a question of creative interpretation. Apparently, legal arguments are of a volatile nature; they do not change their structure, but are largely undetermined as to their contexts of application. In a specific context the same argument appears almost by tradition while in some cases positioned in the same or at least analogous context the expected argument is missing. This is the lesson learned from above cases.

Legal argumentation reaches beyond technicalities of the concept-oriented legal science. Legal and purely imaginative language may also cross in the court argumentation. Descriptive language which refers to facts is contrasted with interpretive language which refers to statutes or rules developed from precedents. In Two Pesos, Inc. v. Taco Cabana, Inc. (505 U.S. 763, 112 S.Ct. 2753, 1992 U.S. Lexis 4533) the court had to decide whether a trade dress had been distinctive and thus protected under the Lanham Act. This would be definitely the case had the trade dress in question acquired *secondary meaning*. The court had to ask whether the trade dress in casu had been so distinctive that it could have acquired protection even without the proof of secondary meaning. Finally, the court affirmed this view stating that: "We see no basis for requiring secondary meaning for inherently distinctive trade dress protection. Adding a secondary meaning requirement could have anticompetitive effects, creating particular burdens on the start-up of small companies." Rule interpretation is here dominated by the non-linguistic imaginary which the court has acquired from witness and photographic testimony during the litigation. The description of the necessary grade of distinctiveness yields the way to the impression which is decisive and which underlies the language used in the justification of the result. The two areas of linguistic argumentation based on imaginative, non-linguistic impressions may, however, be transformed into a purely linguistic argumentation. In Ty, Inc. v. GMA Accessories, Inc. (132 F. 3d 1167, 1997) the judge had to compare two toys, small stuffed pigs, to determine whether one was a copy of another. The court held its observations in the decision which affirmed the copyright infringement claim:

> *The two pigs are so nearly identical that if the second is a copy of the first, the second clearly infringes Ty's copyright. But identity is not infringement. The Copyright Act forbids only copying; if independent creation results in an identical work, the creator of that work is free to sell it...But identity can be a powerful evidence of copying. The more a work is both like an already copyrighted work and – for this is equally important – unlike anything that is in the public domain, the less likely it is to be an independent creation...GMA's pig*

is strikingly similar to Ty's pig but not to anything in the public domain – a real pig for example...Preston resembles only Squealer, and resembles him so closely as to warrant an inference that GMA copied Squealer.

The pig case was decided in the U.S. Court of Appeals for the Seventh Circuit by Chief Justice R. Posner. The language used in the decision lexicalizes the impression which the court acquired by viewing the two stuffed pigs. There is no reference to the objectively invisible realm of imaginary but a clear description of intertwined visual impression within the interpretive language. The lexicalization of the visualized material clearly increases the persuasiveness of the decision. Unlike in Two Pesos v. Taco Cabana, this sort of language warrants the justification test in that in makes the decision plausible in its entirety. It does not force the reader to imagine what sort of visual evidence must have been presented to the court to achieve the impression that underlies the decision. The higher is the degree of lexicalization in a decision, the higher is also the effectiveness of the rationality test in it. As a result, the increased level of acceptability is reached by the improved quality of argumentation.

Legal argumentation which stresses emotions increases the interest in the case. In Barnett v. Merck & Co., Inc. (MDL no. 1657) the judge of the U.S. District Court of Louisiana criticized in one of the so-called Vioxx cases the jury verdict awarding the plaintiff USD 50 million compensatory damages as "excessive under any conceivable substantive standard of excessiveness...No reasonable jury could have found that the plaintiff was entitled to USD 50 million in compensatory damages." The judge ordered upon the motion for judgment notwithstanding the verdict that a new trial should take place. In casu, the plaintiff suffered a heart attack after being treated with a drug manufactured by the defendant. Evidence was presented in the case showing both the causal relation between the product and the heart attack and defendant's liability for the product. The formulation criticizing the amount awarded by the jury became famous as media quoted it regularly while reporting about this case in 2006. However, public interest which increased due to the emotional formulation chosen by the judge does not necessarily increase the effectiveness of the rationality test. The judgment would have been more persuasive if the judge would have explained the reasons why he perceived the amount in question as outrageous toward the background of other jury verdicts in U.S. in cases concerning product liability. The judge reflected in the case only upon the relation between the illness suffered by the plaintiff and the amount of compensatory damages. The judge did not criticize the jury verdict concerning the punitive damages, although also this part might be perceived as problematic. Therefore, an argumentative gap is perceptible between the judge's opinion that the jury has issued the right verdict concerning all matters of law and especially the three theories of product liability which were central to the legal debate in this case. At the same time, the judge referred to precedents in South Carolina according to which a damage award is grossly excessive if it appears "to be the result of passion, caprice, prejudice, or some other influence outside the evidence." The role of the judge would be to show that the jury acted under influence of at least one of the named motives. Unsurprisingly, in this case he limited himself to quote the amount awarded which should apparently speak for itself. However, the impressive amounts of money which attract magnetically the attention of readers are per se not a proof of unreasonable jury verdicts. The lexicalization of the essential problem in this case did not take place. Therefore, the decision taken by the judge is not particularly convincing. All in all, the emotional argument seems to draw attention to the case rather than to pave the way to the appropriate solution of that case.

3.4.2 Argumentation in concurring and dissenting opinions

In some jurisdictions, and especially in the common law, concurring and dissenting opinions make part of the legal tradition. Their very existence proves the argumentative nature of law, i.e. its dependence upon argumentation. Their role in legal science and in legal linguistics is different because they are not perceived as sources of law. Meanwhile, as pointed out by M.I. Urofsky (2015), several dissenting opinions issued by U.S. Supreme Court Judges, for instance Justice J. Harlan's dissent in Plessy v. Ferguson from 1896 (cf. Notes and Commented Materials no. 40) or the dissent in Dred Scott v. Sanford became after decades the position of the court majority. The time needed for evolution is sometimes long, as is visible from the dissent in Plessy v. Ferguson that materialized only 1954 in Brown v. Board of Education. For the legal linguist, however, dissents are perfect sources of the legal language. I will illustrate their usefulness with few examples:

In State of Spain v. Treasury Solicitor (All LR 1953 vol. 2 p. 1579) the House of Lords dealt with the question of characterization in a case concerning the conflict of laws. The State of Spain applied for the letter of administration to intestate succession of a Spanish citizen deceased in England while the English Crown claimed the estate for itself perceiving it as bona vacantia. The legal question grounded in the problem from which legal point of view, i.e. the one of the Spanish or the English substantive law the characterization of the claim to intestate succession should be undertaken in cases where there is no other heir but the State. The House of Lords opted for the law of citizenship of the decedent. The Master of the Rolls, Sir Raymond Evershed, wrote:

> *If by the law of Spain it is possible to limit or to define the individuals who can claim to be successors, that is, individuals having some connection by blood or marriage with the deceased, I can see no reason why the law of Spain should not nominate or constitute as heir, in default of such individual, any person or corporation, including the State itself... There is before us no evidence of what the law of Spain would be in the converse case of an English national dying domiciled in England intestate without next of kin under the English law and leaving movables in Spain. I am, however, not able to reject the argument of counsel for the State of Spain on the ground that this question has not been subject of any direct decision but the distinction might not be reciprocal in Spain. I think the appeal fails and must be dismissed.*

In the concurring opinion the second judge stated: *Accordingly, for the reasons stated by Sir Raymond Evershed, M.R., and for such additional reasons that I have been able to offer, I agree that this appeal fails and should be dismissed.* The third judge continued in his concurring opinion: *It is, I think, well settled that where a person dies domiciled in a foreign country our courts will follow and apply the law of that country when dealing with the succession...The substance of the matter, as it seems to me, is that by the law to which reference is made, the property in England is not left ownerless, but is to pass to an heir, that heir being the State of Spain. I think that this appeal fails.* The preceding case belongs to the group of leading English cases in the area of conflict of laws. The House of Lords has taken in it a sound position which can be easily justified. The judgment is written technically as a seriatim opinion in the tradition of the British courts. In a seriatim opinion the views of the judges follow one upon another, unlike in the Continental tradition where one judge drafts the opinion and develops a coherent legal argument in the name of the participating judges who may have voted differently in the internal vote. J. Rosen (2013: 26) discouraged the use of the technique of issuing separate opinions because "a court should act as a court." Indeed, the mere fact that the three judges who decided the case delivered three different justifications impedes the readability of the decision and limits its persuasiveness. It would look differently when the arguments would be collected in a synthesized opinion. Such a decision would be easier to analyze under the requirements of rationality tests. Otherwise, one could have the impression that the judges who agree in principle follow different conceptions of legal rationality. At this point, this decision is particularly interesting because it shows that different arguments, sometimes even arguments grounded in different conceptions of legal rationality, can be successfully integrated in one legal decision as long as no disagreement about the result comes up.

In Grupo Mexicano de Desarrollo S.A. v. Alliance Bond Fund, Inc. (No. 98–231, 1999) the U.S. Supreme Court had to decide whether a preliminary injunction preventing the transfer of assets situated abroad can be obtained under federal law. The court denied this possibility. Its main argument has been that preliminary injunctions in federal law are possible under the limits set by the Judiciary Act of 1789 and that they must be based on equity measures acknowledged at that time. The court argued that no preliminary injunctions in equity were in use in the common law of England by 1789 and therefore cannot be issued today by U.S. federal courts. It referred furthermore to the English *Mareva-injunction* established around 1975 as an additional proof for the absence of such an equitable remedy before that date in the common law. In the dissenting opinion this view, which may be perceived as mechanical jurisprudence has been challenged. It may be, so the dissenting judges, that the English common law before 1789 did not know and did not consider any equitable remedies like the preliminary injunction to freeze assets abroad. Yet, it included principles enabling the issuance of such an injunction which is proven by the subsequent development leading to the issuance of the Mareva-injunction. Here, the rule in the interpretation is not mechanical. It is constructive and it aims to find the best interpretation which would fit the situation we have to deal with today.

The text type *dissenting opinion* (LAT *votum separatum*) has become more productive in the recent years; already (D) *abweichende Meinungen*, (PL) *zdania odrębne do wyroku*) and (ESP) *votos particulares* are in use and this not only in the terminology but also in legal procedures. P. Joxe (2009) advocates introducing this text type into French constitutional decisions as (FR) *opinion différente*. Textually, the American dissenting opinions include usually the final formula of the dissenting judge *I respectfully dissent*, sometimes *respectfully* is ambiguously omitted, e.g. *I dissent* in the dissenting opinion by Sanders, J. in M.A. Mortenson Company, Inc. v. Timberline Software (2000 Wash. LEXIS 287). Sometimes the dissent remains ambiguously respectful while simultaneously providing reasons for professional disrespect, as in J. Breyer's dissenting opinion in Medellín v. Texas (552 U.S. 06–984, 2008):

> *In sum, a strong line of precedent, likely reflecting the views of the Founders, indicates that the treaty provisions before us and the judgment of the International Court of Justice address themselves to the Judicial Branch and consequently are self-executing. In reaching a contrary conclusion, the Court has failed to take proper account of that precedent and, as a result, the Nation may well break its word even though the President seeks to live up to that word and Congress has done nothing to suggest the contrary. For the reasons set forth, I respectfully dissent.*

Justice Harlan in Plessy v. Ferguson (in Notes and Commented Materials no. 40) terminated his dissenting opinion by saying: *For the reason stated, I am constrained to withhold my assent from the opinion and judgment of the majority.* Sometimes, however, a neutral modification such as *For the foregoing reasons, I must respectfully dissent* is supplied. Hence, the final formula is at times employed as an argumentative tool, at times it remains a pure formality. This is one more example of the volatility of legal arguments. Meanwhile, the combination of majority, concurring and dissenting opinions may structurally overburden the judgment, as in Citizens United v. Federal Election Commission (558 U.S. 08–205, 2010) were the U.S. Supreme Court minutiously listed the ways in which the judges participated in the decision making:

> *Kennedy, J. delivered the opinion of the Court, in which Roberts, C.J. and Scalia and Alito, JJ., joined, in which Thomas, J. joined as to all but part IV, and in which Stevens, Ginsburg, Breyer, and Sotomayor, JJ., joined as to Part IV. Scalia, J., filed a concurring opinion, in which Alito, J., joined, and in which Thomas, J. joined in part. Stevens, J., filed an opinion concurring in part and dissenting in part, in which Ginsburg, Breyer, and Sotomayor, JJ., joined. Thomas, J., filed an opinion concurring in part and dissenting in part.*

Concurring and dissenting opinions are innovative judicial text types. Their main role can be seen in narrowing the gap between the ideology represented in judicial institutions and in particular opinions that underlie particular judgments. Through the expression of the personal yet also professional view the concurring and the dissenting judges contribute to the clarification and transparency in the legal discourse. Dissenting opinions may also become sources of inspiration for future law and for argumentation aiming at overruling the adjudicative practice of courts (Urofsky 2015). They may however also become a source of personal polemics among judges. This is the case when a U.S. Supreme Court judge in a decision concerning the federal tax subsidies under the *Affordable Care Act* calls the majority opinion *pure applesauce*. An expression like *pure applesauce* is much too indeterminate to function as an argument in doctrinal debates. In legal texts this sort of language is counterproductive. It is worthwhile to maintain that in terms of pragmatics the textual form as such never engenders any relevant results. Instead it is used in argumentative action that it supports, yet it does not replace it. Therefore, there is no perfect form of a judicial text type. We can speak only about the perfect use of a judicial text type by a court or a judge.

3.4.3 Argumentation in International Law

Rules of international law are created and applied slightly differently than legal rules of domestic law. Also legal argumentation in the international law displays some characteristic features. The first of them seems to be that the existence of a routine case in the international law is denied. The argumentation around an international case is usually developed as a unique event toward which all political influence and legal skills have to contribute. Second, an international case is like a constitutional case prominent in the sense that particular care is involved in dealing with it. In this sense it is furthermore perceived as rhetorical and as analogical (Reus-Smit 2005: 356). It is like all legal argumentation rhetorically strategic in the sense that it grounds in an interpretation developed by an interested party and does not provide any purely logically deducted arguments which subsequently might be applied automatically to the case. In this context, Reus-Smit quotes F. Kratochwil who emphasized that argumentation in the international legal turns on the issues whether the interpretation is acceptable rather than true (Reus-Smit 2005: 356). The framework for this argumentation has been characterized as pending between apology of the established order and the utopian view that international law could civilize nations (Koskenniemi 1989). Moreover, argumentation in international law is also analogical in the sense that it seeks to establish similarities and dissimilarities among rules, actions and cases (Kratochwil as quoted by Reus-Smit 2005: 356). All in all, argumentation in international law restricts the argumentative framework and it limits its own methodological spectrum. Therefore, it constitutes a special type of legal argumentation.

3.4.4 Argumentation in negotiations

Legal language or at least some of its characteristic features are also used in commercial and diplomatic negotiations. Both domains of its application are a mixture of different registers, but elements of the legal language play definitely a role in it. Both are related toward the making of a final decision which would be perceived by involved parties as binding, i.e. as law set by them. In commercial negotiations the parties will frequently use commercial language as an addition to legal formulations or as dominating register. A. Koskensalo (2002) dealt with business correspondence in respect of functionality in the globalizing world. She argued that modern communication techniques such as e-mail strengthen dialogue-like communication (Koskensalo 2002: 57). She contrasted them with the monologue-like traditional business letters and posited a more contemplative element in them. She also stressed that the legislator reacted to changes in communicative habits in business life and introduced provisions such as § 126a BGB. Also in the U.S., new legal provisions addressed issues related to the electronic signature in the Electronic Signatures in Global and National Commerce Act (E-Signature-Act) from October 2000. Language used in business activities is also connected to the legal language. There is some research concerning this issue (e.g. Ohlin 1976, Hartig 1997, Clancy 1998, Clegg 2010). The language used in business communication displays some particularities that are worth mentioning. Debt collection as a business practice is actually a legal activity. Its language in business practice is close to legal. Business communication tends toward the development of polyvalent speech. Polyvalent language consists of phrases that can be used at many occasions. Instructions are passed in an equally flawed language: *We are being asked to process derivatives orders in short order, but are being told 'if you skrew it up, it's your risk'.* Language used in enterprises includes self-defined ranks and description of organisational structure. Departments previously called *Personnel* are today stylistically upgraded to *Human Resources* following the linguistic modification of terminology used in economical science. Cryptic language is typical of the financial industry: *The long-only guys are moving into the space mainly through 130/30 funds* meaning that they use 30 percent of the fund to bet on shares' fall. Flawed semantics flourishes: *The risk of the redemption in the marketplace causes you to position your portfolio accordingly* implies the simple truth that clients may withdraw their deposits from money market funds at whatever moment. Slang and familiar expressions are mixed with more advanced style and vocabulary: *Nominating committees are all too often a scam, pure and simple* or *After the collapse of the X merger, they had to do another deal to refill reserves because the cookie jar was running low.* Linguistic strategies that support ethically doubtful action are framed in principle-like sophisticated form: strategic silence is different from outright lying. The language used in business activities may include 'humorous' expressions that banalize violations of law in the professional sphere such as *cooking the books* for falsification of entries in accounting records.

Furthermore, in diplomatic negotiations the final decision is found in an amalgam of linguistic registers reaching from political to legal (cf. Kovačević 2004: 26). The use of arguments there is close to the procedure in international law, with the modification that political arguments may play a stronger role than the legal ones. Interests, attitudes and strategies structure the process of negotiating like any other linguistic operation. Positional bargaining, trade-offs and linkage of disconnected issues are typical strategies in diplomatic negotiations (Kovačević 2004: 113). Other general strategies aim at ensuring the maintenance of the negotiating process. The preformulated diplomatic notes and other samples of diplomatic correspondence (Feltham 1998: 31) reduce the risk of tensions because they limit the risk for interpretive discrepancies. Abundant courtesy is their most salient element. The obligatory use of titles, e.g. *Your Excellency* (Feltham 1998: 15) and the use of final formulas in diplomatic notes: *The Embassy avails itself of this opportunity of assuring the Ministry of its highest consideration* may reduce the negative impact of disadvantageous messages. However, some countries such as the U.S. omit the final courtesy formula in their notes (Feltham 1998: 31). Formal politeness of the diplomatic note (*official note* or *note verbale*) is emphasized by the lack of any identifiable signature as the notes are solely initialled and sealed. Formulations perceived as particularly polite, especially understatements such as *I'm afraid that the continuation of such practices might reflect negatively on relations between our two countries* or intentional emotional graduation, e.g. *I view with concern...* as compared with *I view with grave concern...* enable to express negative attitudes without exposing the other party to the risk of losing its face and being forced to terminate the negotiation. Understatements in fact dominate the language of diplomacy. The Chinese defense minister Chang Wanquan was quoted as mentioning to his U.S. counterpart, defense secretary Ashton Carter, in a matter concerning U.S. naval missions in the South China Sea: *We need to do things that help us defend our territory, and I need to be very clear to you that there is a bottom line to this.* In the context of this remark, Ashton Carter is reported to have reaffirmed that the US will continue to fly, sail and operate wherever international law allows and that the South China Sea will not be an exception (in: Financial Times Nov 4, 2015). In 2008, a dispute between Canada and the U.S. concerned the possibility of importing oil from Canada's oil sand deposits. The sec. 526 of the U.S. Energy Independence and Security Act of 2007, when interpreted accordingly, might have limited such possibilities. Canada then warned the U.S. government that import restrictions due to the narrow interpretation of this legislative act might have "*unintended consequences for both countries*." Equally, the Chinese diplomats used at least 130 times since 1959 the phrase *hurting the feelings of the Chinese people* in statements that react to foreign action and to statements that they perceive as criticism of the Chinese state and its politics (cf. The Economist, February 6, 2016: Diplomatic insults – A world of hurt). More conflictual language is found in reporting: On March 21st the chargé d'affaires at China's embassy in Jakarta was *hauled in to receive a stiff protest* (in: The Economist, March 26th 2016, p. 49). Efficiency of such language use might however be questioned. For instance, the U.S. State Department commented the military coup in Burkina Faso of September 2015 by stating through its spokesman: "The United States strongly condemns any attempt to seize power through extraconstitutional means or resolve internal political agreements using force." Some other formulas such as *different factors are at play* are even more inexplicit. Catch-all formulas are easy to use but they are also bleak and often pass unmarked. Fixing results or interim results in protocols or memoranda, esp. in a memorandum of understanding reduces uncertainties as to the binding force of negotiated results. Including a *road map* helps maintain the dialogue despite political changes. Global diplomatic discourse focuses on conceptual creations such as: *new world order, foreign affairs, equilibrium, Realpolitik, containment, geopolitics, international system, national state, balance of power, collective security, détente or peaceful coexistence, quiet diplomacy* (cf. Kissinger 1994). Hence, content wins over form.

3.5 Successful Legal Argumentation

In this chapter I will return to theoretical issues whose exposition has been interrupted by our case studies. I will introduce the results obtained in the case analysis into theoretical remarks upon legal argumentation. I will deal with elements of argumentation and with the quality of arguments as preconditions for successful argumentation. Finally, I will sketch further possible developments in this field.

3.5.1 Theoretical problems

The first structural element in legal argumentation is the development of tests within interpretive standards as a reaction of courts to interpretive differences. In these tests the validity of arguments is tested. As the initial tests mostly prove to be too general, additional test criteria are included in them. Finally, however, social values as interpreted by the court and the view it takes upon the facts in its institutionally privileged way determine the decision taken. Not only legal linguists but also citizens at large may have problems with this sort of argumentation. Furthermore, it remains open whether the courts are satisfied with the results they reach because judges usually do not mark in their decisions any doubts about the argumentative strategies they have used. What is more, the right to argumentative interpretation is by its very nature not particularly well adapted to be exercised in an authoritative way. Still, a valid legal norm is one identified as such by the authorized institution on the basis of the sources of law enforced by a legal system or a legal culture. The validity of the norm is tested according to constitutive rules applied in a given society. The law in force is not pure rationality but is linked to society, its culture and last but not least to the constitutive rule which states which rule in a society is perceived as a valid rule of law and which is not. Here, one could have the impression that the process is circular. Yet, society is a living, which means a dynamic organism. Values in legal cultures change. Hence, also constitutive rules provide changing answers to like questions. Therefore, an authoritarian argumentation, i.e. one which is based on the institutional privilege alone cannot be perceived as particularly appealing in modern societies. Apparently, a better argumentation is needed and should be nowadays also prescribed by laws in order to ensure that argumentation exercised in courts reaches convincing standards of rational argumentation. Overall, our case material demonstrates that this improved argumentation will also include emotions (cf. Frijda/Mesquita 2000). There is no linguistic communication without rhetoric and this finding is equally valid in the area of law. Rhetorical means evolve and correspond to the culture in which they are used. Practising lawyers have always been aware of this challenge. Also the legislator became slowly but steadily aware of the fact that legislation must be linguistically appealing to citizens should it be more readily accepted. Captions from the U.S. American legislation like the Oregon

Death with Dignity Act, the *Government in the Sunshine Act* or the *Americans with Disabilities Act*, the *Defence of Marriage Act*, and finally the *Patriot Act*, abound nowadays in emotions and are in blatant contrast with the style of most European legislators who still prefer bureaucratically bleak formulations. Some of them, however, like the *Prosecutorial Remedies and Other Tools to end the Exploitation of Children Today Act* of 2003 are less convincing as linguistic creation. Overall, the improved argumentation must convince through its quality and not through the deference to authoritative bodies. Its core is the rationality in the application of legal rules. This rationality is not technical. Instead, it is grounded in ethical values and convictions shared in society at a given moment. Law is therefore more than social engineering; it develops still more complex mechanisms for legal argumentation. These mechanisms are linguistic in essence. Therefore, legal argumentation is one of the most important if not the central legal-linguistic operation.

3.5.2 Elements of legal argumentation

In the analyzed cases some central structural features such as: arguments, selection rules for application (validity) of arguments, participants and forum, rationality test, argumentative gaps and argumentative volatility, chains of arguments as a part of legal reasoning became apparent. Their legal-linguistic status is different as is different their weight in the legal theory. However, they allow the first tentative description of legal argumentation toward the background of the analyzed materials. Generally, arguments are the fundamental elements of argumentation. This holds true even if the procedural rules concerning the selection of arguments and participants in an argumentative practice, e.g. the court proceedings, may occasionally impose themselves upon the subject matter of the argumentative act. Arguments are embodied in legal speech acts which transfer them into legal arguments and ensure their operationability within the institutionalized process of the application of law. They are employed to increase the rationality of legal argumentation. In the modern legal argumentation the pure victory does not matter. Decisive is the victory of best arguments, i.e. those which advance socially relevant goals. However, even modern argumentation is provided in traditional forms, for instance in majority or dissenting opinions. This process is visible in decisions such as Martin v. PDA (case VI of our Introduction, cf. 1.3.2) where the majority opinion was anchored in the public policy that empowers disabled citizens. There, the remnants of argumentative positions which reflect traditional views are traceable in the dissenting opinion. Arguments are provided in a procedure, and are tested and retested in appeals where different judges participate in the review of arguments. Rules concerning participation are central; the right to participate is debated as an issue independent of the main subject matter, as in the already mentioned case the People v. Tortorici (cf. 3.4.1.2). Arguments are furthermore advanced in chains; a court opinion is rarely based on one sole argument. To solve the argumentative challenge the court applies a rationality test and uses, as in Martin v. PDA, expert opinions to clarify facts viewed in the perspective of the legislative intent. Thus, the circle of participants is broadened by the participation of non-legal experts in the decision making. Arguments are not always used in a perfect way, sometimes an argumentative gap is perceptible in a court decision or in the views expressed by the parties, e.g. in the mentioned decision Ashcroft v. Free Speech Coalition (cf. 3.4.1 and Notes and Commented Materials no. 50). Qualitative differences and the volatility of arguments are characteristic of legal argumentation that is part of discursive practices, i.e. that it is not a monologue.

3.5.3 Toward a more convincing argumentation

3.5.3.1 Quality of arguments

The cases analyzed above enable us to argue that the quality of professional argumentation in them differs. We were able to identify texts in which argumentation was more adapted to the solution of the case and therefore more convincing than in other cases. In other words, argumentation in some cases has been more successful than in others in the sense that it better suited the goals of professional justification than in some other cases. We have also reflected the recipient level and found out that some arguments of decisional justification may promote the decision within the non-professional audience, whereas others may be perceived as less persuasive. Indeed, the formal legal obligation imposed upon judges to justify their decisions in writing can be fulfilled in different ways. Some types of justification are of a formal type, while others are material in the sense that the judge tries not only to document the way in which he has reached his decision but also to convince his professional surroundings that his decision has been right. The judge may furthermore try to convince the broader public that the legal solution embedded in his decision is the most appropriate one. Meanwhile, the quality of arguments used cannot depend on the result achieved with them, for instance in a lawsuit. This has been the case in the area of traditional rhetoric that provided argumentative schemes that would lead to success in litigations. The question who has won or how to win in litigation is not central to modern legal linguistics. In modern legal linguistics, it is more interesting to know which arguments are rational and which are not because legal argumentation should primarily advance the level of rationality in law. Nevertheless, victories achieved with better, i.e. rational arguments, are welcome also in legal linguistics.

3.5.3.2 Inferential model of linguistic communication

Argumentation takes place within broader frameworks of communicational practices. Meanwhile, one might ask what sort of communication is characteristic of legal argumentation. The above case analyses demonstrate that legal argumentation cannot be integrated into a communicational model based on sending encoded messages by a speaker that are received by a hearer who simply decodes them. The message model of communication must be broadened and encompass strategies which at least enable it to cope with the disambiguation of complex messages. The inferential model of linguistic communication widens the conceptual framework of the message model (Akmajian 2001: 370). It is directed toward the identification of speaker's intentions and is therefore suitable for the analysis of communication in legal contexts. Strategies of successful communication which are based on this model stress that communication is to be perceived as successful when the hearer recognizes speaker's intention. They are grounded in the conviction that successful communication is possible only when the speaker and the hearer share a system of inferential strategies leading from the utterance of an expression to the recognition of the communicative intent (Akmajian, ibid.). These strategies enable us to distinguish between expressions communicated directly and indirectly and include strategies for differentiation between literal and nonliteral meaning. However, such strategies would not work were they not grounded in common presumptions about linguistic communication (Brandom 2000). Thus, in legal argumentation their foundation must be searched for in the institutional nature of the use of arguments. The analyzed cases showed that without taking this particular feature into consideration the specific rationality of the judicial decisions cannot be successfully construed. Neither is it possible to successfully apply arguments in law without taking into account this major structural feature of legal argumentation.

3.6 Legal Interpretation

3.6.1 Why we interpret?

After having extensively treated legal argumentation let us now turn to legal interpretation. In the above chapter I was not inclined to artificially distinguish argumentative and interpretative language use where both coincide or come very close to each other. In fact, interpretive and argumentative language is often used in related speech acts. Since antiquity, interpretation has been treated in the context of logic, argument and dialectic, e.g. in Aristotle's Περί Ἑρμηνείας, known better under its Latin title *De Interpretatione*. However, in the legal disciplines traditionally a distinction has been made between argumentation and interpretation. Here, I maintain the traditional distinction between argumentative and interpretive speech acts, although doubts might come up about such necessity. These doubts are caused by the complexity and the lack of transparency in argumentation and interpretation. In legal linguistics it would be important to ask whether this distinction can be proved in the language use. In fact, interpreting linguistic utterances is part of our daily experience. This daily experience may also be the reason why we do not know much about interpreting (Baylon 1991: 208). Furthermore, some knowledge we have is frequently rather confusing and inconsistent. Apparently, we are inclined to underestimate the daily experience and turn, rather, to lofty ideas to understand interpretive action. We seem to conceive such ideas, doctrines or theories as more promising because they are not directly anchored in our daily experience which for many equals banality or trivia. Also the modern analytical philosophy showed how deeply we had erred and still occasionally err while neglecting the most fundamental daily experience in our individual and in our social practice (Engel 2000: 63). A part of it consists of, as mentioned above, interpreting speech with which we are confronted. It could also be that we have reached perfection in interpreting and this is why we scarcely realize this activity in everyday life. Argumentation seems to be different, at least in this respect. Argumentation is namely easier identified and better understood in daily discourse by non-specialists. The result is that speakers tend to use arguments intentionally and at the same time they may underestimate the interpretive task that is inherent in such argumentative speech. Nevertheless, no one would argue that we are not constantly involved in the interpretation of linguistic utterances, both spoken and written.

Occasionally, however, when confronted with issues or notions which are explicitly equivocal for us we consciously engage in interpreting, i.e. in asking for their meaning. In these situations, we are also usually less perfect than in the daily life. Why does this happen? In controversial situations, in which one proposed meaning of an utterance is contested we are shaken up in our life form which regularly provides us the right guidance for the daily, regular interpretation of utterances. This last situation interests us particularly. Its fundamentals are the lack of knowledge – which sometimes manifests itself in the form of contradictory propositions – about the meaning of a concept in a given context. Semantics and pragmatics deliver a host of examples for such situations. The question whether the Buckingham Palace is also a *house* is a typical example of such a situation in daily life. This presupposes, of course, a conversational context in which such a proposition could be expressed meaningfully or be contested. The solution to such questions through definitions is difficult. Legal definitions may sometimes provide a remedy, but they also cause new interpretive problems because they either make plain the meaning in a language or determine it (Savigny 1973: 30). The controversial cases are very special but still they do not mean that interpretation concerns exclusively controversial or *hard cases* in the legal parlance and that it excludes daily routine. Sometimes we wish to discover the initial meaning of things in texts or in other artifacts with a long history and ask ourselves what that original meaning had been. This happens regularly when we interpret a literary work, especially one which was written in times remote from ours or which belongs to a different cultural tradition (Juhl 1986: 3). In such cases we used to interpret because we do not know the meaning or we have the impression that the meaning we intuitively grasp cannot be the historically or culturally right one. This necessity to interpret which is embedded in our cultural context led however in law to the conviction that a search for objective meaning – the only right one – would be possible in the legal science. This assumption had some formal prerequisites, the first being that things are as they are (which is definitely true as a tautology) and that this being so is a fact which can be known in an uncontroversial way (and this is, of course, a problem). Another extreme situation is the deference to purely subjective meaning which dominated the notion of meaning adopted by some theorists. Lawyers had been aware of these problems and they were also piecemeal and increasingly becoming aware of their own ignorance in this matter (Atria/MacCormick 2003). We could describe this shift in attitudes from the conviction that lawyers simply knew the law as their profession to the conviction that lawyers were ignorant about law – but this in a very professional way (Galdia 1995: 62). What the lawyers knew was the method of how to acquire knowledge about law needed in the case, how to use argumentatively statutes and precedents, as well as the legal doctrine including general principles upon which the law was based, in the deliberation about the appropriate solution of a legal case. Their arguments were specific and sometimes they were not understandable to the bigger community of laypersons, simply because they were part of a professional argumentation. We realize already at this stage that the community of interpreters was split in at least two organisms composed of professionals and non-professionals of law.

3.6.1.1 Interpreting statutes and precedents

Attempts at interpreting statutes, and foremost their terminology, concentrated methodologically on a canon composed of: *grammatical* interpretation, *logical* interpretation, *systematic* interpretation and *teleological* interpretation (cf. Wank 2015). These interpretive methods do not lead to convincing results in controversial cases (Alexy 1983: 19; Wróblewski 1988: 128–148). They may at best characterize features of interpretation in a daily language game, i.e. in a given context of a life form. Therefore, from the 'use' as it is, it is not possible to infer the 'use' as it ought to be. This paradox of traditional doctrine of interpretation is valid in this form both in the civil law and in the common law and it constitutes the most salient point of criticism against the doctrinal theory of interpretation. Apparently, more was necessary to deal with interpretation, a further step had to be taken and the prerequisites of a language game of legal interpretation had to be revisited if not discovered. Legal interpretation emerged as a challenging language game played by skillful players, professionals who master complex interpretive rules. Lawyers fully realized that they had to adopt their interpretive rules to the *text type* they interpreted. Legal professionals approach statutes differently than contracts and witness testimonies or other factual declarations. Research projects such as *Interpreting statutes. A comparative study* by Neil McCormick and Robert Summers (eds.) from 1991 as well as *Interpreting precedents. A comparative study* prepared in 1997 by the mentioned editors, make plain this difference. Interpreting statutes and interpreting precedents or contracts are close but finally distinct activities. They are methodologically connected by the factor of intention which is decisive in all of them. In the interpretation of statutes, the legislative intention plays traditionally a major role. In the interpretation of contracts, the intention of the parties should prevail when legally possible. Otherwise, concluding private contracts would not make much sense. In precedents, the intention of the deciding court is the focal point of every professional interpretation. There, however, most problems emerge because courts often do not provide any detailed explanations for their motives.

As already noted, while interpreting we identify the institutionally determined speech act (cf. 3.1.1). Determination of meaning concerning ordinary language can be undertaken by courts or by the legislator. In Frigaliment v. B.N.S. (Notes and Commented Materials no. 45) a court decided the meaning of *chicken* in a contract between the parties. It used the procedure of the burden of proof for this. The plaintiff argued that with *chicken* the parties meant only young birds, whereas the defendant contested it and argued that all types of birds such as fowls, broilers and the like were meant in the contract among the parties. The plaintiff had to meet the requirements of the burden of proof but the witness testimony provided by him did not convince the court. He therefore lost his case. This means that *chicken* retained its meaning in the contract between the parties as suggested by the defendant. The determination of the meaning of a term belonging to the ordinary language has been procedural. Also the legislator may determine the meaning of concepts of ordinary language which he introduces into the legal language. This has been done by the British legislator concerning the notion of *house* (cf. 2.3.3.2.1). This determination differs from the previous one as it takes the form of a definition. *House* is defined in terms of the legal act in which it is used. The determination here is institutional. Like the courts in our previous cases analyzed under 3.4.1, the legislator determines his own position due to his institutional powers. Clearly, legal interpretation is more than decoding a meaning of a particular concept. It is also more than disambiguation of concepts (Juhl 1986: 93). Therefore, the creative interpretation in Dworkinian sense is a rule in interpretation rather than an exceptional or metaphorical use of the concept (Dworkin 1991: 51). In law, the limit of this interpretation is problematic. Its limit seems to be an arbitrary decision about meaning. Legal paradigms cannot be easily challenged without the blame of unprofessionalism or adventurism: "Every community has paradigms of law, propositions that in practice cannot be challenged without suggesting either corruption or ignorance" (Dworkin 1991: 88). Already H. Kelsen (1960: 353) pointed to the structural limits of interpretation in his *Reine Rechtslehre* by saying: „Rechtswissenschaftliche Interpretation kann nichts anderes als mögliche Bedeutungen einer Rechtsnorm herausstellen." The difference between interpretation in legal sciences mentioned by Kelsen, and interpretation undertaken by the judge resides in the character of their work (Carcassonne 2005: 294). The legal scholar may limit her work to mentioning different possible semantic varieties whereas the judge must decide the question which party wins in litigation. The judge is therefore obliged to draw conclusions from interpretive analyses. In Frigaliment v. B.N.S. we have seen that the judge interprets the law within the boundaries of procedural rules. He may therefore use the rule of the burden of proof in litigation as a specific semantic limit.

Interpretation requires the necessity to understand. Argumentation, in turn, requires the need to convince that the knowledge advanced in case is the right one. Interpretation as a linguistic mechanism is uniform in character. It does not differ due to changes in its object, e.g. natural phenomena, arts or social issues. It does not change as the character of the sale contract does not change when we purchase cars, bread, airplanes or computer programs. It adapts to the situational circumstances like the sale contract adapts to its different objects without changing its nature. It differs doubtlessly as its validity criteria change. Different criteria reign among literary critics or general public. Similarly, legal criteria applied among laypersons differ as well. In law, interpretation is problematic exclusively because of its acceptability by a community (validity in this community), not because of the character of the operation itself. These criteria exclude eccentric or radical interpretations. Institutional justifications of propositional statements differ as well. The increasing number of forums competent to interpret the law, especially in the international setting, may lead to an increase in quality of argumentation in the legal decisions rendered by them because it stimulates courts and tribunals to hand down better-reasoned judgments and to provide explicit and convincing arguments (Cassese 2005: 286). Furthermore, the court hierarchy warrants a more effective use of arguments in the interpretation that makes it more rational (cf. Medellín v. U.S. commented here under 3.8.2).

3.6.1.2 Exegesis, philology and hermeneutics

The method of textual exegesis is rarely used as an exclusive instrument for the identification of meaning in a legal text. In literary criticism however it is used frequently. Exegesis aims at clarifying the initial, i.e. original meaning of the text, mostly based upon the author's intention (subjective approach) or the general understanding in times of the composition of the text (objective approach). The use of the term is restricted to historical texts (Sowinski 1983: 12, Đorđević 2002: 16). Nevertheless, the exegesis of religious texts – especially in its modernized dress – often transgresses these boundaries and approaches general interpretation. The theologian A. Tanquerey (1909: 688) describes the exegesis as a hermeneutical procedure:

> *Omnis legitima interpretatio eo tendit, ut, legibus grammaticae, historicisque adjunctis sedulo inspectis, lector recte intelligat ideas quas auctor scribendo in mente habuit; ad quod obtinendum non parum prosunt textus, contextus, paralleli loci variaque commentaria.*

The scholastic method was used by medieval theologians in their dogmatic debates. Adolphe Tanquerey (1909: 7) writes about this procedure:

> *Scholastica vero dicitur ea quae dogmata fidei methodice et philosophice scrutatur, eorum sensum magis accurate definiendo; fidei dogmata cum rationis principiis, in quantum fieri licet, conciliando; conclusiones in dogmatibus contentas dilucide aperiendo; nexum, qui inter veritates revelatas existit, ostendendo; easdem in unum doctrinae corpus coadunando; uno verbo, dogmata fidei scientifice illustrando.*

Later, Wilhelm von Humboldt (*Researches into the Early Inhabitants of Spain by the Help of the Basque Language*, 1821), Ulrich von Wilamowitz-Moellendorff and Friedrich Nietzsche, especially in *On Truth and Lying in the Extra-Moral Sense* (1873) turned away from (D) *Wortphilologie* and interpreted texts in their broader cultural contexts. Their ideal was the (D) *Totalitätsanspruch* introduced by Friedrich Gottlieb

Welker, i.e. understanding texts in their entirety. Modern hermeneutical procedures in philology are even more advanced. Matthew S. Santirocco (2016: 10) remarked about the methodological progress in dealing with classical written texts:

> *Just as the "meaning" of a text or material artifact is now understood to be a function not only of the historical and social contexts in which it was produced and used, but also of how other and later communities have interpreted it, so too the study of the Greco-Roman world in all its aspects is no longer just the study of the past.*

Brooke Holmes (2016: 20) mentioned another methodological facet: "*...determining the meaning of any ancient text requires that we embed it within a larger network of power and a broader field of signs (Athenian democracy, for example...).*" Additionally, Emily Greenwood (2016: 44) remarks:

> *The idea that a text is inert without readers to give it meaning is a given in reception studies, specifically the reader-response theory exemplified by the work of Wolfgang Iser, who argued that "the convergence of text and reader brings the literary work into existence."*

Legal linguistics can benefit from the above views upon interpretation of texts that refer to extra-textual contexts for the understanding of semantic potentialities of written artifacts. Meanwhile, the exegetical method, which is typical of philological, historical and theological work on written texts covers only one aspect of legal interpretation. Legal interpretation, especially when it is understood as creative interpretation is a vast semiotic enterprise.

3.6.1.2.1 Jewish hermeneutics

Interpretive methods related to religious written artifacts, especially the Hebrew Bible and the biblical law led to the development of interpretive rules in the rabbinic tradition of the tannaim. These rules are primarily connected with the name of rabbi Hillel (70 BCE–10 CE). According to Hyam Maccoby (1989: 76) the classical set of hermeneutic rules ascribed to Hillel included following seven methods, called *middot* (HEB *mida* means measure): 1. argumentum a fortiori (*qal wahomer*) i.e. 'all the more so', 2. verbal similarity (*gezerah shawah*), 3. introduction (*binyan ab*) or induction in terms of classical logic, 4. two verses (*sheney ketubim*) as a method of reconciliation of textual contradictions, 5. the general and the particular (*kelal uperat*) stating that the general proposition prevails over the particular, 6. the particular and the general (*perat ukelal*) stating that the opposite of rule 5 applies when a particular rule is stated first, and 7. something that is understood through its contexts (*dabar halamed me'inyano*), a rule of textual disambiguation. These rules were later expanded by rabbi Ishmael ben Elisha (90–135) to thirteen. The classical rules had apparently been known previously, under rabbis Shemaiah and Autalyon; yet they had not been codified at their time. Rabbi Eliezer ben Yosse ha Gelili expanded the rules stated by Hillel under influence of Greek philosophy, using especially Plato's and Aristotle's writings; although the influence of the Greeks has been judged as limited (cf. Wigoder 1996: 470, 478). Additionally, H. Maccoby

(1989:79) stressed particular achievements of the rabbinic hermeneutical school in its expansion of the Greek syllogism, which

> *suits the purposes of scientific classification, but not of law, which requires a logic of analogy, enabling us to decide which cases are similar to other cases, or dissimilar from them. This the Greeks never developed, and the achievement of the rabbis in developing a logic of analogy suitable for legal argument and the comparing of cases has not been sufficiently recognized.*

Also classical rhetoric figures are less visible in the rabbinic writings, which abound in parables, than in the Greek philosophical classics. As can be seen, some of the classical rules are of logical origin (rules 1, 3, 5 and 6) whereas others are purely hermeneutical. Problematic in terms of their application upon biblical law that is perceived as revealed are rules that require creative interpretation. These rules are a challenge to all interpretive systems that are in their nature doctrinaire as they cause problems in the process of determination of limits in the interpretation of texts perceived as revealed or at least semantically predetermined. Therefore, the method of interpretation known today as purposive was the dominating hermeneutical approach to such interpretive problems (cf. about purposive interpretation Barak 2005). In the rabbinic tradition rabbi Akiba opposed innovative interpretation of biblical texts that in his view were written not in the divine but in the human language where meaning manifests itself more directly. This view gained popularity in the rabbinic tradition and led to the emergence of the interpretation close to the letter of the text (*peshat*). *Peshat* has been opposed to *derash*, the homiletic meaning. Meanwhile, law in the rabbinic conception "*was regarded not so much as something to be learnt, but as something to be created. The ideal was that the law was a continuous legislative process in which all Jews played an active role*" (Maccoby 1989: 80). Therefore also more popular forms of interpretations developed. The dialectic method of *pilpul* is one of examples of popular interpretation that often uses the *argumentum ad absurdum* and engenders over-interpretation. Pilpul, which had flourished in Eastern Europe's Jewish schools was also regularly criticized in the rabbinic tradition for being excessive (cf. Wigoder 1996: 796). In the Middle Ages the interpretive methods were formed around: 1. *peshat* – literal meaning, 2. *remez* – allusive meaning, 3. *derash* – homiletic meaning, and 4. *sod* – esoteric or mystical meaning. An interesting feature of the rabbinic hermeneutics is the fact that it is not consolidated in a treatise but spread around in particular writings of *Midrash* and *Talmud* such as *Tosefta, Sanhedrin, Sifra, Niddah, Zevahim, Pesahim, Menahot, Shabbat,* etc., with no explicit treatise devoted to interpretation of texts being known.

3.6.1.2.2 Interpretation in Islamic law

Interpretation in Islamic law (AR *sharia*) developed in schools of Islamic jurisprudence (AR *ijtihād*). All of them use the Quran and the Hadith, which is related to Quran as their sources of reference; however, they approach these sources differently. Most scholars are of the opinion that the Quran does not state the Islamic law (*fiqh*), instead it contains the law (Weiss 1978: 199, cf. also Ramić 2003). Thus, the Islamic law has to be derived from its textual, sacred source. As this textual source is linguistically ambiguous, interpretation is not only necessary, it is unavoidable. In the Islamic tradition it is generally accepted that Islamic law has been fully developed until the 10th century CE (David 1978: 482). After that date only its study for purposes of application is possible; therefore Islamic law is perceived in its doctrine as static (David 1978: 470–471). R. David (1978: 471) writes about these self-imposed limits:

> *La loi divine est élaborée. Le devoir qui s'impose au musulman est d'observer le taqlid : il doit "reconnaître l'autorité" des docteurs des générations passées ; une interprétation originale des sources lui est interdite. Aussi bien depuis des siècles les mêmes ouvrages servent-ils à l'enseignement du droit musulman...Toute l'œuvre de la doctrine consiste à faire l'exégèse des œuvres considérées comme classiques, la seul chose permise étant de rassembler, comparer, éclairer et expliquer les solutions proposées par les grands jurisconsultes du passé...*

The Islamic ideology underscores the uniqueness of provisions in Islamic law; the Islamic doctrine discourages abstraction as well as generalization, systematization, codification and legal definitions (David 1978: 472). Instead, the doctrine relies on casuistry. Although Islamic law perceives *analogy* (AR *qiyās*) as its main interpretive device, it is as other legal systems dominated by the principle of authority (David 1978: 472). Therefore, it does not represent a discourse disconnected from power structures. Overall, laws of contemporary Islamic countries rarely display an orthodox reliance upon Islamic sources and practically represent rather mixed legal systems.There exists a multitude of jurisprudential schools in the Islamic tradition. These numerous intellectual tendencies can be condensed to several dominating currants such as: Sunni schools (Hanafi, Shafi'i, Hanbali), Shia schools (Ja'fari, Zaidi), as well as the Ibadi and the Zahiri school. C. Mallat (2007) stressed that Islamic law differs from other legal traditions due to its style; yet Islamic law also stresses as its characteristic feature that 'law conforms with reason' (Mallat 2007: 1). This basic theoretical assumption unites it with other legal traditions (Mallat 2007: 11). Islamic law developed in exchange with other legal traditions (cf. David 1978: 474, Ladjili-Mouchette 1990). As a result, it applies legal-linguistic interpretive devices as whatever law. Some specific features that are however not dominant are mentioned in Galdia (2014: 372–373). An example of a court opinion based upon Islamic law is provided in Cases and Commented Materials no. 51.

3.6.2 Do utterances which need not to be interpreted exist in law?

In law, traditionally, utterances are divided into those which are unequivocal per se and others which must be interpreted. In this context the classical devise (LAT) *interpretatio cessat in claris* is regularly invoked by the legal theorists. While speaking about the distinction of hard and routine cases I already expressed doubts about the possibility of such a structural divide. Pragmatics and legal theory provide further arguments against this classical but still less and less convincing view of interpretation which is needed only when a text is unclear. This presupposes logically that texts can be divided into clear and unclear. J. Searle is quoted by Levinson (1983: 8) with following words:

> *There is no such thing as the zero or null context for the interpretation of sentences...We understand the meaning of such sentences only against a set of background assumptions about the context in which the sentence could be appropriately uttered.*

This concerns also utterances in law. In many cases the interpretation of legal rules or precedents may not be particularly challenging. Nevertheless, it must take place. Jerzy Wróblewski (1988: 117) posits that doubts concerning the content of legal provisions can always come up; also clear texts are interpreted. The question whether a text is clear or unclear depends upon its evaluation by the user (Wróblewski 1988: 117). According to Wróblewski the interpretation is not a part of the process of application of a legal norm. This could mean that is should be perceived as purely linguistic. He however accepts views expressed by N. Bobbio and many others who described the interpretation as an inherent part of the application process. The conceptual separation upon which Wróblewski seems to insist is neutral in our context where the unavoidable interpretation is perceived as a linguistic operation in law. However, it may have consequences for the mainstream legal theory.

3.6.3 Limits of legal interpretation

Interpretation is a linguistic operation. Thus, its limits are the limits of our language. They are first of all formal, i.e. syntactic (Davidson 2001: 270). What cannot be formulated in line with syntactic rules cannot be said. This at least holds true for the language of law which is shaped along syntactic rules. In daily life, these rules are of course frequently violated, for instance by children or by foreigners who master only the rudiments of the language in which they try to communicate. They are regularly modified by poets as well (Juhl 1986: 108). These groups of speakers are not particularly relevant in our context. Beyond syntactic boundaries no other limit of interpretation is imposed upon us as our brain can provide us with an unlimited number of syntactically correct utterances with arbitrary contents (Searle 2004: 19). They may include paradoxes, lies, or other consciously manipulative language use. Legal interpretation, however, has its particular intrinsic limits. It is determined with reference to the use of specific arguments. These arguments are: first, those generally perceived by professional lawyers as legal arguments (received opinion of lawyers), second, some arguments with uncertain or controversial status like the arguments of professional minorities (e.g. dissenting opinions), and third, arguments which are generally not perceived as professional but which at the end of the day lead to changes in the adjudication, especially in supreme courts. All other arguments regarding law are usually perceived as lay arguments. They are not considered in the legal decision making process. Legal interpretation has also other limits. These are the limits of our inventiveness as jurists. Jurists learn in their professional training a number of specified arguments, and some of them learn also arguments used in the remote past, for instance in the classical Roman law. Later on, in their professional life jurists tend to rely on this knowledge and are not particularly inventive.

On the other side, most cases jurists deal with are routine cases where particular inventiveness is limited by the structure of the subject matter and the minimal chance that the practice concerning a routine case could engender innovative legal decisions. Legal arguments ground in our social values. Legal theorists such as R. Dworkin have demonstrated it with sufficient persuasiveness. R. Dworkin also showed the way how the best argumentation should be formed in order to achieve the best available legal decision. Finally, the seemingly unlimited freedom of jurists to interpret appears as determined by so many minor burdens and more substantial constraints that one could have the impression that a free interpretive legal decision can only be an arbitrary one. After all, this is not necessarily an unwelcome result. Work done on the establishing of requirements for legal arguments has been accomplished with the aim in mind to exclude arbitrary and irrational legal decisions (Alexy 1983: 36). The constraints imposed upon legal interpretation shall guarantee that arbitrariness becomes evident in the decision and that such a decision will be corrected on appeal. As far as these constraints are linguistic, they are of pragmatic nature.

3.6.3.1 The implicit in law

A further limit to legal interpretation is a warning against dealing with legal provisions in their literal sense that are legion in all legal traditions. This holds true for the past as well as for the contemporary legal methodology. For jurists the legal text, be it a statute or a contract between private parties, had always a meaning situated somewhere else, i.e. not in itself. Therefore, nowhere law had been studied as an amalgam of provisions which, when read through, could function as a basis for solving legal cases. In the civil law tradition, French, Italian and German civil codes underline both for legal provisions and for contractual stipulations that their literal meaning is often immaterial, that judges have to look into the intentions of parties and the intention of the legislator rather than to the written lines of a legal document (cf. Notes and Commented Materials no. 27). It is surprising, but also illuminating, that totalitarian regimes like, for instance, the Soviet system also stressed this aspect of law. In the Soviet legal methodology not the text of the law but the understanding of its meaning, issue, idea or problem had been central (Pigolkin 1990: 187). For us, the written legal text is constituted of material text elements and also the immaterial ones which are parts of its context. Therefore, we have fewer problems with the theoretical part of the question. It is perfectly understandable for us that a written legal text, like all other types of texts, cannot be interpreted exclusively on the basis of its material elements. But, this does not solve the practical question that jurists, especially judges are exposed to texts which can be understood only in their appropriate context and this is practically a challenge for them. This experience could justify the thesis of the implicit law in the legal provisions (Pigolkin 1990: 180). The implicit or hidden, non-public element of law is for Pigolkin inherent in whatever text. It is for him a means of economy in a linguistic utterance. The text includes information which is not explicitly formulated in it but understandable to the professionals or to the parties concerned. An example would be a formulation in a contractual clause such as *This contract is governed by the laws of France* where it is not mentioned that the contract in question is a lease contract. That the contract in question is in fact a lease contract may become apparent either from its headline, from another clause in the same contract, or from its aim. Pigolkin distinguishes between implicit and *latent* elements which he would like to have banned from laws. The latent information is according to this view not inherent in the text, it is connected to it. An example for it is a reference in a legal act to other legal provisions not included in it. Basically, all provisions or circumstances not expressed in the legal text and not inherent in it could be perceived as latent (Pigolkin 1990: 183).

However, blanket norms are deemed by Pigolkin as bearing an implicit and not a latent element because they refer to the general context of legislation and cannot be interpreted by using univocal terms from other sources of information (Pigolkin 1990: 184). This argumentation is less convincing and it seems to qualify the blanket norms as a borderline case between implicit and latent rather than clearly assigning them to one of the named categories. The latent information can be a source of problems for the application of law because for its identification the broad systemic legal and factual contexts have to be analyzed. This is the reason why Pigolkin supports in his theoretical approach the implicit information but opposes the latent one (Pigolkin 1990: 183). In terms of semantics, the distinguishing between implicit and latent may be of some interest for the development of the legal language. However, an approach based on pragmatic parameters focuses on the material law as it is. Law, in statutes and in contracts includes elements which Pigolkin calls 'latent'. They will not disappear from legal texts because they are parts of the pragmatics of language use in law. Theoretically, it would be possible to prohibit the legislator or parties of a private contract from referring to latent elements or to omit them in contracts. This procedure has been used by several legislators, for instance in Art. 12 of the Chinese Unified Contract Law where detailed information is required for the contract to be valid. However, this sort of legislation would never be able to identify all possible sources of latent information in a statute or in a contract. Its result may be the increase of the informational load of a legal text but not a solution to the problem of latent elements in law. The speech act theory integrates successfully both the implicit and the latent aspects of law in that it identifies legal speech acts in their contextual surroundings. Its advantage over the approach proposed by Pigolkin et al. is that it does not exclude any data from law. It is therefore realistic and applicable unlike the interesting approach presented by Pigolkin et al. which remains prescriptive and therefore idealistic. Such models simply never work in law. Whatever position we would take toward the assumption that law consists also of implicit and latent elements, one issue remains uncontested. Law, when expressed in legal provisions cannot be studied or applied under the impression reached from the reading experience of legal texts. The methodology of the legal science is grounded in this principle. Because law is definitely not only what is written on a piece of paper but much more than that, interpretation and argumentation will be always crucial to its studies and its application.

3.6.3.2 Aporetic character of law

Another potentially discouraging aspect of legal interpretation is the aporetic character of law which manifests itself in the circularity of right and wrong law among judicial instances in the legal process. Inferior courts are bound by precedents of higher courts and especially the Supreme Court until they are overruled or at least substantially expanded. They provide wrong law when their decisions are overruled by the Supreme Court when the court changes its standing practice, e.g. in Brown v. Board of Education (347 U.S. 483, 74 S.Ct. 686, 1954). In fact, while saying the law in conformity with the legal practice of the moment the lower courts are wrong, although they were right in following precedents acknowledged by higher courts of their time (Dworkin 1991: 6). When right is wrong and wrong is right, ancient Greeks used to speak about απορία (aporia). We will do the same but we will not fear this notion as it is symptomatic of laws made with words. The situation may be described differently, for instance with a paradox introduced by Dworkin (1991: 453) about law which seems to be different for the higher courts and for the lower courts. Dworkin asks himself how to cope with this linguistic and legal complexity. As an interpretive practice it can be generally right or wrong, its propositions valid or void, sound or unsound. In its institutional setting, which imposes constraints on its argumentation it is aporetic. Aporia is one of the characteristic features of law, not its paradox. Therefore no evasive theory is needed to drive it away. Meanwhile, does this circumstance not mean otherwise that law was what it was in the first instance but then the judges in the higher instance simply changed it? The decision of the lower court becomes invalid due to the ruling of the higher court. Nevertheless, the fact that two different laws – 'propositions of law' – existed simultaneously in a legal system remains a challenge for the theoretical reasoning about law. Having this challenge in mind, Th. Viehweg referred in his *Topik und Jurisprudenz* (1954) to the classical rhetoric sources of legal argumentation that go back to Aristotle and Cicero. He stressed the development of legal rhetoric in the Middle Ages and later on in Gian Battista Vico's *De nostri temporis studiorum ratione* (1708). In making this part of argumentative legal thinking discernible Viehweg has successfully shaken up traditional system-oriented approaches. A. Siitonen (1989: 130) remarks that according to Vieweg's conception legal argumentation cannot be based on an axiomatic-deductive system but rather on a problem-oriented discussion method. He puts nevertheless Viehweg's approach and the results of his analysis in the right light. In his view, Viehweg's thesis should be perceived as complementary to systemic approaches (Siitonen 1989: 131). The cognitive technique of problem thinking and problem solving in law cannot be perceived as totally system-free.

Problem thinking can be the basis for systematization which proceeds along logical rules and principles (Siitonen 1989: 132). There exist however distinctions between both approaches in that in the logical systems arguments are demonstrated and the topical structures are used to invent arguments. Their focal point could be seen in the division of labor as the logical reasoning proceeds from premises to conclusions, whereas the topical reasoning is a method of searching for premises. Therefore, for Siitonen, in jurisprudence not a system but a vague plurality of systems is at work. To avoid conflicts among these systems interpretation is needed (Siitonen 1989: 131).

3.6.3.3 Inferentialist explanation of meaning

The necessity of interpretation and the concept of meaning can be further explained with the help of the inferentialist model. This model has been used here already to characterize aspects of advanced legal argumentation (cf. 3.5.3.2). The inferentialist model is based on certain preconditions which hearers and speakers must share in order to understand each other. It is based on context sensibility, process sensitivity (interaction of speakers, lawyers, judges) as well as the account of contextual constraints and correctness conditions (Canale and Tuzet 2007: 40). The model is therefore in its essence pragmatic. Any assertion in it can be seen as a speech act that commits the speaker to a determinate set of inferences which are in turn considered by hearers who keep track of them and use them when they become involved in communicative situations (Brandom 2000). In order to characterize meaning within this model Canale and Tuzet (2007: 36) referred to Wilfrid Sellars for whom the meaning of a concept is determined by a set of material inferences; conceptual contents are understood in inferential roles. For instance, to grasp the concept of *contract* we must analyze the inferences speakers and hearers take to be correct when they engage in communication regarding a contract. W. Kwarciński (2005) argued that procedures and principles of the multi-level model of legal interpretation that were developed in the Polish jurisprudence were in many respects homologous to central concepts of the inferential version of the speech act theory. The multi-level model comprises descriptive, prescriptive, and presuppositional levels on which three different worlds are reconstructed by the interpreter respectively; they are independent and hierarchically structured (cf. Kwarciński ib.). The legal text both describes and creates a possible legal world. At the descriptive level, legal provisions can be interpreted by anyone with sufficient linguistic competence, at the directive level legal training is necessary in order to engage in the interpretation (cf. Kwarciński ib.). The multi-level model – when limited to the elements described here – makes plain that legal interpretation is an institutionalized type of utterance understanding.

3.6.3.4 Parties' intent

Courts customarily use pragmatic strategies to determine the intent of the parties. Interestingly, parties' intent is apt to set limits to professional legal interpretation. Three classical English cases are illustrative of this procedure. All three cases date from the 19th century, i.e. from times where scholars could only dream of linguistic pragmatics or inferential model of meaning. First, in Dashwood v. Magniac (1891) one party devised to the other party an estate with *a power to cut timber for the repair of the estate.* Subsequently, the parties conflicted about the meaning of the term *timber* used in their locality. Evidence was therefore admitted in this case to find out the local meaning of *timber.* As a result, the court held that *timber* in the locality in question included beech in addition to the usual meaning which comprises oak, ash, and elm. Second, in Grant v. Maddox (1846) the parties interpreted differently the provision in an employment contract for an actor which stated that it was concluded *for a year.* The theater representative pretended that *year* in theatrical usage means those parts of the year during which the theater is open. This interpretation has been endorsed in court by evidence. Third, in Smith v. Wilson (1832) evidence was admitted to prove that in a lease of a rabbit warren the words *thousand rabbits* meant in that particular locality twelve hundred. Also in the classical English case Raffles v. Wichelhaus (59 Eng. Rep. 375, 1864) the intent of the parties finally determined the outcome of the lawsuit. In the case, the parties agreed on the delivery of cotton from Bombay by a ship named Peerless. As has been found out subsequently, two ships bare this name and no party was ready to accept the sailing time of any of the Peerless ships in case it would be detrimental to its interests. The English court that decided this case held that no binding contract had been concluded between the parties because each party apparently had a different ship in mind while making the contract. The approach which takes into consideration the parties' intent rather than objective semantics is general in the legal methodology and is in no way limited to the common law. In the opinion of the German *Reichsgericht* (RGZ 99, 148) the Norwegian word (NO) *haakjöringsköd* which means objectively in English *shark meat* was interpreted as *whale meat* due to the common (objectively wrong) understanding of the parties which had in mind *whale meat* while agreeing on the delivery in a sale contract drafted in German where only the product as such had been named in the Norwegian language. The subjective meaning that the parties attached to the Norwegian word has been decisive for the (D) *Reichsgericht.* Thus, the parties' intent determined in an objectively unacceptable way the meaning of a Norwegian word. However, the linguistic reflex of the contract law is to establish the intent of the parties and not to reconstruct the semantics of the English or the Norwegian languages at a particular moment. The decisive point is the meaning which the parties provided to terms they had used (cf. Guimezanes 1995: 204). The courts follow this intent even if the choice of the parties is not particularly convincing or might even be perceived as incorrect from the point of view of standard English or Norwegian language speakers. Only the use established among the parties matters for the judge. Pragmatically important for the understanding of contractual contents is the requirement that parties share the common interpretive background that consists of factual knowledge and interpretive skills. For instance, in a contract for rent of a private garden around a manor house for purposes of filming the clause providing for participation of *ca. twenty mainly juvenile actors* may include or not the presence of around seventy-five people in the private garden during the film production. This depends on the knowledge that the number of people behind the camera is regularly much higher than the number of actors in front of the camera. It might be questionable whether this sort of knowledge is general or obvious. Common background knowledge of this sort is therefore a source of controversies in courts. In addition, mastering interpretive techniques also has limits. One could expect from persons involved in the contract to make an effort in understanding it and not to take it literally, i.e. understanding that the indication of the number of actors participating in the film would equal the number of people who would be present on the ground. Limits of this interpretive skill are determined at least by our mastery of the ordinary language that includes the interpretive skills within the limits of the use of the ordinary language. Overall, the language used in private contracts which are not always or not entirely drafted by legal professionals represents a hybrid form and is a challenge to every conception of legal linguistics, but especially to the one based on linguistic pragmatics. It is necessary to maintain that its analysis in law has been regularly pragmatic, i.e. context-sensitive.

3.6.4 Interpretation and linguistic manipulation

Persons confronted with the deliberative character of law frequently construe this characteristic feature of creation and application of law as linguistic manipulation. They, and many of them are law students, argue that this characteristic feature in academic or other public language usage is called interpretation in order to make it sound more objectively. This is definitely not my intention. I distinguish between legal interpretation and linguistic manipulation. Legal interpretation is a linguistic operation which necessarily has to be applied in linguistically ambiguous contexts when a univocal meaning is required. Manipulation is an abuse of this procedure. While manipulating arguments linguistic strategies are used in order to confuse the recipient of the message and impose on him a solution which may be detrimental to him. Let's have an example. When the X Corn flakes corporation established a subsidy in a country formerly belonging to the Soviet Union its manager criticized in an interview the consumers for not buying the products in sufficiently high rates. He pretended that the local consumers would "not understand that they had to eat the X Corn flakes for breakfast". Additionally, he argued that it took his company 20 years to make it clear to Brazilians that they had to buy the flakes and renounce their traditional breakfast habits. The corporate official pretended in the formulations he used that buying his products was a necessity, a mere automatism due to the fact that it was produced for being used as breakfast food. Not explicitly addressed but subliminal is also the message that the product developed by a Western food company is of better quality and more appropriate for being taken at breakfast than the traditional food. This linguistic manipulation is grounded in the strategy to disorient the recipients of the message and conceal from them the possibility of choice and of manifesting personal preferences. In his argumentation the corporate officer suggested that the consumers had no choice. Manipulating meaning is also accounted for in courts. For instance, in Goldstein v. SEC (discussed under 3.9.5) the court states explicitly: "That the Commission wanted a hook on which to hang more comprehensive regulation of hedge funds may be understandable. But the Commission may not accomplish its objective by a manipulation of meaning." This means that manipulative linguistic practices are identified in legal procedures with the help of tests in which the correspondence of arguments with underlying values of legislative acts is verified.

3.6.4.1 Interpretation and misinterpretation

How to distinguish an interpretation from a misinterpretation? In times dominated by approaches like the famous *everything goes* formula the very participation in interpretive practices may seem vain. Conventions for interpretation are mostly of social nature. Methods and regulative standards are set up through numerous educational and sanctioning processes in which the legal community produces *"agreements about certain interpretive conventions"* (Glass 1988: 454). Legal interpretation is, therefore, an institutional legal practice (Glass 1988: 454). Standards, criteria of evidence, procedures and awareness of what is reasonable are provided by the interpretive community (Glass 1988: 451). Dworkin argues that the notion of interpretive community cannot operate as a check upon the indeterminacy of interpretation, for it just makes a good interpretation one which is accepted by this community and he cannot imagine a weaker constraint (cf. Glass ibid.). Interpretation requires, like all language use, fairness and openness to its message. When the interpreter is ill intentioned and manipulative or blinded or incapable to understand the complexity of a text, then the interpretation procedure is simply misused, it is a misinterpretation. With this in mind, Perelman and others established the connection between interpretation and argumentation by referring to rationality (Plantin 1996: 10). Exactly because there is no interpretive method which would provide incontestable interpretive results, argumentation is necessary. This is also why we usually do not treat judicial disagreement as irrational (Glass 1988: 453). In fact, legal rationality is multiple, it is also complex.

3.6.4.2 Over-interpretation

Close to linguistic manipulation is over-interpretation. One could perceive as *over-interpretation* an attempt to interpret into the text what is semantically not included there. It is a bold statement as criticism may come up as to the right to control what is and what is not semantically included in an utterance. Meanwhile, we can assume that the interpretation of the provision of the European road codes that in Continental Europe cars have to drive on the right-hand side of the road because of the right-wing political sympathies of the Continental Europeans would be perceived as over-interpretation of the context of emergence of the provision. Contexts of language use are broad and difficult to limit, therefore it is impossible to exclude in pragmatics an utterance as incorrect or meaningless without inquiring into the context of its use. However, it is necessary to insist on meaning as a conventional feature of language

(Searle 1999: 140). Whatever other transformations an utterance may experience in its use, it is primarily understood through the reference to linguistic conventions. The speaker meaning must be and usually also is explicated because conventionality is inherent in language. When a speaker claims *It is raining now* and means with it *A car accident took place* she will have to explain her specific use of language (that may be justified) and she will do it with reference to the conventional meaning. Otherwise her explanation would not be understood. When both, speaker meaning and utterance meaning are made plain, no communicational problems exist any more. Understanding legal-linguistic utterances follows the same track. For instance, Art. 1, 1st sentence of the French Declaration of Human Rights says: (FR) *Les hommes naissent et demeurent libres et égaux en droits* (Men are born and remain free having equal rights.) Some interpreters wished to see in the phrase that men are *born* (FR *naissent*) the foundation of the principle of equality between men and women (Carcassonne 2005: 398). They claimed that when men are born they are necessarily born of men and women who jointly form the basis for humanity. One would nevertheless claim that the conventional meaning of the sentence does not include such semantic alternatives. We would be ready to acknowledge the interpretive variety were we provided further contexts of use that would indicate such possibility. This is however not the case here. The interpretation remains a contention in law, and such unproven contentions are over-interpretations. Over-interpretation concerns the textuality of law; it comes close to linguistic manipulation because it pretends that the text includes a meaning that for most speakers is not recognizable there. Creative interpretation, in turn, admits the shortcomings of the text and develops it further. It is therefore one thing to pretend that Art. 1 of the French Declaration of Human Rights provided for parity between men and women, and another to say that nowadays such a text that did not provide for this right should be interpreted in terms of law as including the principle that men and women are equal. Such an interpretive strategy is perfectly acceptable because it reveals the linguistic mechanism in which it has emerged. Additionally, interpretation may also concern the conceptual rather than the textual basis. The above fundamental provision has been perceived as logically deficient in that it seems to set freedom over equality. For many, equality is the basis and source of freedom and other rights (Carcassonne 2005: 397). Some would therefore wish to reformulate the text that should say *equal and free* instead of *free and equal*. They refer to Art 1., 2nd sentence of the current French Constitution that mentions equality, yet not freedom: *Elle* (la République – suppl. author's) *assure l´égalité devant la loi des tous les citoyens, sans distinction d'origine, de race ou de religion*. Such a conceptual interpretation is free from textual constraints and comes close to creative interpretation. It is not an over-interpretation but an interpretation of a different sort.

3.6.4.3 Professional errors

One of the most problematic issues within the discussion of legal interpretation is the possibility of a professional mistake in the application of law by courts. Generally, we have adopted the point of view that the only one right interpretation in law does not exist. We have therefore to accept divergent judicial decisions of one and the same case rendered in the hierarchy of courts as well as divergent decisions made by different judges concerning similar cases. All these decisions are rooted in the mechanisms of the professional application of law. They differ as far as choices done by judges in the application of interpretive rules and goals may differ. Does this view, however, exclude the possibility of a professional error in law? In other words, are divergent judicial opinions results of the differences in the legal interpretation or the professional use of this interpretation? For instance, in Filanto S.P.A. v. Chilewich International Corp. (789 F. Supp. 1229) the issue of the validity of an arbitral clause incorporated into the sale contract between the parties has been decided according to the CISG and especially its Article 8 (2). However, the CISG provides for its own application according to the Article 4 (1) upon issues concerning the formation of the international sale contract. The validity of the arbitration clause which is an autonomous part incorporated into the sale contract document would have to be decided according to the substantive law identified with the help of the conflict of law rules. Several courts, among them OLG Frankfurt, stressed this view after the Filanto-decision has been rendered in 1992 by a Court in New York (cf. OLG Frankfurt NJW 1992: 633). The Filanto-decision is therefore perceived by many as wrong due to a professional error and not as an interesting or innovative court opinion. Furthermore, in international contracts which are frequently drafted in the English language the unreflected use of common law terminology leads to serious interpretation problems (Beveridge 2002: 55–79). In such a case, use of foreign, e.g. Italian legal terminology, by an attorney-at-law in a contract drafted in English where constantly common law terms are used may be perceived as a professional error. Overall, the result of an act of legal interpretation is deemed as being professional when it is accepted as such by at least one part of the professional legal auditorium. This legal auditorium can be construed as composed of judges, attorneys-at-law or legal scholars. Is a judicial decision wrong in the sense of the law in force when the result of legal interpretation is not approved by any of the corporative legal bodies? Or is this a very original, innovative interpretive proposition about the law in force?

3.6.5 Creative interpretation in legal linguistics

Unlike in many other areas of life, people – lawyers and laypersons alike – used to argue what the right law is about. This fact demonstrates again that law is at its core an interpretive (creative and argumentative) social practice. People argue about the propositions of law in different ways. Laypersons argue unprofessionally, they often mix arguments *de lege lata* and *de lege ferenda*, natural law postulates and positive law. The social dimension of these arguments cannot be underestimated. Political majorities in democracies are constituted of laypersons who, in turn, influence legislative mechanisms and contents. They shape the law. We retain from this circumstance that in law also the unprofessional argumentation matters. Legal argumentation used by professionals in their work shows how it matters and we will concentrate on this specific question. According to R. Dworkin professional legal argumentation consists in the best justification of our legal practice (Dworkin 1991: preface). It engenders competing narrative stories with different levels of persuasiveness. This mechanism shows best in complicated borderline cases (*hard cases*) but is equally operational although less perceptible in *routine cases* as well. Legal argumentation is limited by the constraints of the legal profession. However, it is the indeterminacy of law that enables judges to be more creative (Minda 1995: 33). The evaluation of different legal narratives, competing stories and the search for valid legal propositions in them are the real challenge for the judge because they are rooted in the social and political reality which is sometimes vague and elusive. Meanwhile, this difficulty proves that argumentation about law is necessary and unavoidable and that it is not a result of a simple lack of knowledge about law. All lawyers must be perceived as unknowledgeable in this sense. Their lack of knowledge is part of their profession; it is the unknowlegeability *lege artis* (i.e. according to the state of their art). In legal linguistics, we do not artificially limit the scope of linguistic mechanisms in law but rather intervene where they manifest themselves most profoundly. This is also why I will treat legal interpretation as an explicitly linguistic process while keeping in mind its social and ethical implications. Conceptions about law, about what it is and what it is not are all linguistic. However, I cannot follow a conception which is purely semantic, i.e. which seems to decode the language of law in the process of its application. This form of positivism is dangerous because it encourages obedience to immoral law (Minda 1995: 51) that is not the intention behind legal linguistics. Also Dworkin clearly demonstrated that the positivist approach does not work, at least in hard cases. Dworkin's theory of interpretation in law and its concept of integrity are central to any general conception of linguistic aspects of law, which aim at describing legal argumentation as a merely linguistic mechanism. Therefore, I will have to dwell longer upon it and trace its linguistic foundations which make part of the approach adopted here. Some evolutionary steps in these theoretical conceptions – even if not Dworkinian in their core – will be taken as well.

3.6.5.1 Law as integrity

Based on some legal materials, mostly court decisions under common law in borderline cases and criticism of dominating conceptions of the 20th century known as conventionalism and pragmatism as well as the earlier conception of legal positivism treated in *Taking Rights Seriously* (1977), R. Dworkin arrives at a conception of law called *law as integrity*. In his conception of law he unites aspects related to the past and the necessary prospects of modern application of law that is adapted to the requirements of contemporary society. He views integrity as a coherent set of legal rules which enable the law to function in its historical settings as well as in its tendency to shape future developments and provide acceptable solutions to contemporary legal problems. The mechanism which ensures this application of law is the *constructive* interpretation. At least in hard cases this interpretive approach is based on an inevitable interpretive attitude which the interpreter (in Dworkin's cases the judge) takes when trying to find a solution to legal intricacies. Its goal is to adopt an attitude which would guarantee the best proposition of law in a case. The integrity of the legal system functions as a background correlative element in the interplay of views about the best proposition of law. I may again expose myself to the suspicion of nihilism while advocating the preponderant role of linguistic mechanisms in law to the apparent detriment of material socio-political implications. Here, it might again look like that law is not only about words but, even more so, that it is exclusively words. The hypothesis which I used to mention here regularly that there is nothing more in law than words must be scrutinized. It is much less destructive than supposed. In fact, our ordinary language reflects perfectly our form of life – the conditions under which we live in society – it incorporates its social practices and does not exist beyond these practices. When we follow linguistic practices in society we almost certainly also subscribe to the most substantial values which shape these linguistic practices. Even when creating legal terminology we do not create extralinguistic reality. Terms like *causality*, *constitutionality*, or *mailbox rule* do not change the order of the real world. They help us – due to their reistic background as metaphors or hypostases (Kotarbiński 1955: 16) – to cope with the linguistic complexity in law. They create law with words and not with objects. These words, in turn, fit perfectly into the legal language as they function in linguistic mechanisms (e.g. language games, speech acts) of the general linguistic practice.

A linguistic conception of law is therefore not unrealistic. Dworkin insists in his jurisprudential theory of law as a creative social practice on integrity as a basic concept of this theory. With 'integrity' he means that a system of rights must be interpreted as a coherent vision of justice in a country (Dworkin 1991: 368). He stresses integrity rather than the systemic character of law and this with good reason. For the interpretation of law, which is for him the test for the best available proposition of law, its formal and material elements are more pertinent than a purely logical systemic approach based on formal logical mechanisms. With the same idea in mind, I insist here on a linguistic rather than systemic approach to law, its interpretation, i.e. creation of propositions of law by means of legal argumentation. I am doing this because I do not believe that formal systemic argumentation would produce convincing, i.e. best eligible propositions about the law in a given social context at a particular moment. Formal and material arguments about the valid – right – sound propositions of law must merge in a legal narrative if it is aimed at persuading the legal community or the public at large. I do not exclude the aspects of material justice in a society or in a legal culture as accidental but rather integrate them into the larger spectrum of legal decision making, both in the legislation and in the adjudication. Otherwise, our debate about the propositions of law would remain sterile and purely academic. I try to avoid this result and strive to elaborate a general conception of law toward a pragmatic philosophical background which means for me an unconditioned anchorage in the legal practice. I can imagine law thought as a pure and coherent system of principles and rules beyond the social practice. At the same time, I am opposed to this reasoning as I deem it counterproductive in the society exposed to concrete problems hindering its progress.

3.6.5.2 Hard and routine cases

Dworkin is specifically interested in situations where law books are silent, where law is ambiguous or unclear. This makes plausible his interest in *hard cases.* I have nevertheless tried to show that law even when applied in line with presumed clear statutes or precedents is not less fascinating than hard cases where alleged gaps in law must be filled by courts with legal substance. Issues like gaps in law and judicial discretion (a positivist term according to Dworkin in the preface to his *Law's Empire*) merge in the interpretive approach and seem to be metaphors in legal argumentation rather than legal problems or necessary legal doctrines. In my view, the linguistic potential of a case blurs the distinction between hard cases and routine cases and even more, it shows that this distinction is only temporary. It is based on a problem finding procedure – an analysis undertaken by a lawyer – which might in any case lead to the discovery of a legal problem in it (cf. Saarenpää 1980: 25). The legal problem will be one of interpretation. Dworkin describes a situation in which a single argument might be decisive to solve a case and addresses the situation where it might not have struck the judge in the right moment. This situation is regularly the source of the emergence of hard cases out of daily routine in the courts. The process is largely accidental as it is based on invention, professional creativity of judges and attorneys. To understand better the temporary character of the distinction between routine and hard cases let us have a look at the rules of the German Traffic Act. Art. 2 of the statute provides, like in most countries, for driving on the right-hand side of the road. At a first glance there is nothing clearer than that. However, precedents concerning road accidents show that the rule of the traffic code may be violated when the driver comes closer to the right edge of the road than 60 cm. Sometimes, the driver on a narrow road at the countryside may be more on the left-hand than on the right-hand side or in the middle of the road and not violate the rule. Traffic rules were popular as examples among legal theorists because they were held by many as being unequivocal. Historically, a debate engaged H. L. A. Hart (1958) and L. Fuller (1958) about the indeterminate meaning of an inoffensive phrase *No vehicles are permitted in the park.* As a result, the semantic and the pragmatic intricacy of this banal formulation became plain. What makes our traffic cases and all analogous cases to hard cases is not that much the inherent semantic indeterminacy as such but the discovery of it, i.e. their pragmatic aspect, the result of an inevitable interpretive attitude we have to adopt when applying law in a professional way.

Thus, interpretation remains dependent upon the lawyer's aptitude to discover legal problems in cases while he is applying law. In this sense, every case is potentially a hard case and its qualification as a routine, simple case is temporary. While insisting upon the temporary distinction between routine and hard cases I support a more general strategic goal. Would I advocate the contrary view, i.e. would I argue that routine cases are ontologically different from hard cases, I would also have to answer the question how legal-linguistic theory, which should comprise all creation and application of law, should match up to these requirements when it focuses upon hard cases which undeniably represent the absolute minority of cases decided by courts all over the world. Routine interpretation is not possible in law because it would presuppose the determination of all contexts of application of legal rules in advance which is clearly impossible (cf. Glass 1986: 458). Yet, my choice spares me this sort of puzzle solutions. Add to this that it would be difficult to defend the thesis accepted by most legal theorists that law is an argumentative social practice. What role would legal argumentation have to play were law comprised in terms of routine which does not accord much place to reasoning? In a world governed by such a law there is neither a place for legal theory, nor is there a place for legal linguistics. In fact, the obstinacy about the distinction between hard and routine cases is typical of defendants of an idea of law as a system based on concepts. For those opponents of an argumentative approach to law the system guarantees the right judicial decisions; for them problems with the application of law are due to the lack of legal knowledge. Dworkin and many others showed that the positivist and the systemic approach to law which is close to it are untenable both of them. Definitely, law and also the legal science need order to remain operative, yet this order is not necessarily a formalized system. I occasionally use here the term *network* and speak nevertheless about *systematization efforts* in law which I support with some reservation. This reservation concerns not that much the activity as such as the role it plays in law. For me, systematization concerns first of all the realm of arguments, not of concepts. I have therefore no problems with backing it in this form.

3.6.5.3 Why follow Dworkin?

In countries dominated by the common law the questions of interpretation are dealt with toward the background of the court, esp. appellate decisions. Statutes play in this reasoning a less decisive role (Munday 1983: 192). In civil law countries interpretation is associated mostly with statutes and meaning attributed to them by jurists. Judiciary decisions are in their entirety rarely analyzed in this context (Glass 1988: 460). Glass observes that for Dworkin the necessity to interpret a text is strictly differentiated from the transformation of the text into a different one. The criteria which Dworkin set up for the interpretation follow from this fundamental distinction (Glass 1988: 444). An acceptable legal interpretation in line with Dworkin's assumptions is one which satisfies the two dimensions of fit. They are formal features of coherence and correspondence with the existing legal rules and the dimension of value involving substantive considerations of policy and morality that make one ruling preferable to another. According to Glass, both Fish and Dworkin tried to describe interpretation in ways which avoid presenting it as being either determined or undetermined, objective or subjective, rule-bound or free. In doing this, both consider useful analogies which can be drawn between literary criticism and legal interpretation. Moreover, Glass criticized Dworkin for not looking closely to the legal practice and the rules according to which judges interpret statutes and precedents (Glass 1988: 455). He argued that Dworkin would set up a normative-prescriptive theory of legal interpretation. Glass also pointed to the fact that Dworkin does not analyze the traditional method of interpretation in common law or the doctrine of stare decisis. Why is this so? We can scarcely assume that Dworkin had not been aware of those aspects of the legal practice. Why then is he not interested in them? For Dworkin, legal interpretation concerns controlling the context of interpretation. The controlling institution is the court authorized to render decisions on the subject matter in question. As we have seen from above examples, courts do not hesitate to exercise their power to interpret precedents and statutes. The result of their work is the institutional interpretation which becomes law. This is its characteristic feature and the distinction from all other types of interpretation including other traditional forms of legal interpretation. Lawyers not vested with the authority to decide a subjudicial case like attorneys-at-law, legal scholars or judges not involved in the case may also be able to interpret statutes and precedents and they may do it in a convincing way. However, their professional interpretation will not obtain any legal force even if it were more persuasive than decisions rendered by the authorized court. Dissenting opinions in common law countries are the best example of the institutionalized character of legal interpretation. They are often appealing, yet they are not law. Also laypersons may interpret the law in their unprofessional way. Their interpretation, although sometimes highly convincing, cannot become part of the law either, due to the institutionalized nature of the phenomenon itself. A legal decision rendered by a competent court grounds in the normative character of this type of texts. Also in this way it strictly differs from all other types of interpretation.

I tried to incorporate R. Dworkin's views into my preliminary thoughts about the theory of legal interpretation. The concepts of *constructive interpretation* and *law as integrity* correspond to main ideas of interpretation perceived here as a legal-linguistic operation. I do not forget that R. Dworkin did not wish to establish a legal-linguistic theory. His approach to law in terms of theory is different from mine. It developed in contrast to H. L. A. Hart's theory of legitimacy in law. R. Dworkin contributed to it a theory of justification. I, in turn, deal with all the issues mentioned by those and other legal theorists from the linguistic point of view. My linguistic approach is based on language use and therefore it cannot be applied to projections of law because future language use is undetermined yet. Here, again, formal and material arguments merge in my conception. Likewise, in a typical case analysis such as the following one legal and legal-linguistic issues merge (cf. 3.6.5.4). Legal linguistics is particularly interested in linguistic operations in such an analysis. Lawyers and legal theoreticians may prefer other aspects of systematization in law that are equally helpful because they may display other unexpected aspects of language use in law.

3.6.5.4 Controversies about law or language?

I will illustrate the interrelation of legal and linguistic aspects with short case studies. The American securities market regulations have been previously interpreted as providing for the private right of action in cases of aiding and abetting in securities transactions. Since the Supreme Court decision Central Bank of Denver v. First Interstate Bank of Denver from 1994 this is not the case any more. Moreover, the Supreme Court reiterated its view 2008 in Stoneridge v. Scientific Atlanta. The case involved a cable company which inflated its revenues by using bogus transactions with two suppliers. Investors sued the suppliers claiming that they participated in a scheme to defraud them. The U.S. Supreme Court had to decide the question whether the securities laws allow shareholders to sue third parties who, knowingly or unwittingly, participate in a scheme to defraud – even if they did not directly mislead investors. The court stated that under the Securities Exchange Act Sec. 10 (b) and Rule 10b-5 there is no private right to sue the *secondary participants* as the provision establishes the right against *primary participants* only. Shareholders can therefore be successful in this type of securities litigation only if they prove that the involved party (e.g. an accountant or an attorney-at-law) should be perceived as *primary* and not as a *secondary participant* due to his particular involvement in the securities transaction. Also the SEC can sue in such cases. According to Sec. 20 (f) Private Securities Litigation Reform Act (PSLRA) it can sue "any person that knowingly provides to another person substantial assistance" in committing a securities violation. The Sec. 20 (f) PSLRA covers therefore the constellation of aiding and abetting and clearly encompasses *secondary participants.* As a result, it could happen that shareholders would be able to convince the court that their defendant is a *primary participant,* and the SEC would enforce a claim running parallel to it that would be based on aiding and abetting in a securities transaction against a participant whom it qualifies as *secondary participant* (Cox 2006: 764). The same defendant could theoretically and simultaneously appear in terms of securities regulations as *primary* and as *secondary participant.* Shareholders as plaintiffs would have a problem in their litigations to refer to the SEC enforcement actions in which their prospective defendants have been perceived as *secondary participants.* Here, legal and linguistic problems intertwine. An involved person cannot be perceived linguistically as *primary* and *secondary participant* in the same event, as it cannot be perceived in law as both at the same time. Concededly, the perception of participation as *primary* or *secondary,* both linguistically and legally, is a question of perspective. And, legal argumentation can support only one view taken from a perspective that offers several options. Otherwise, it would become meaningless. Hence, the above basic contradiction is a limit to legal argumentation. However, it remains open what is a contradiction in law. Logic and pragmatics may have different views upon this question because they relate to it from different perspectives. This constellation is therefore a challenge for legal argumentation and for legal interpretation. Meanwhile, in Reves v. Ernst and Young (494 U.S. 56, 1990) the U.S. Supreme Court while interpreting the notion of *security* under the U.S. financial market regulation provisions recognized that interpretive issues in law are well settled within the concept of *family resemblance*. J. Marshall who wrote the court opinion quoted the concept of family resemblance probably without any specific thoughts for L. Wittgenstein's innovative concept. However, he made plain that legal interpretation does not consist of analyzing isolated legal concepts. In recognizing this he comes close to B. Cardozo who in *Hynes* (in Notes and Commented Materials no. 54) referred to argumentative forms such as *concentric spheres* in facts and doctrine which led to the emergence of more complex interpretive methods than it had been frequently assumed in approaches dominated by legal positivism. The judge uses the notion of *family resemblance* as a test in order to determine whether promissory notes payable on demand by the holder can be perceived as *securities*. He says:

> *he "family resemblance" and "investment versus commercial" tests are really two ways of formulating the same general approach. Because we think the "family resemblance" test provides a more promising framework for analysis, however, we adopt it. The test begins with the language of the statute; because the Securities Act defines "security" to include "any note," we begin with the presumption that every note is a security. We nonetheless recognize that this presumption cannot be irrebuttable...Congress was concerned with regulating the investment market, not with creating a general federal cause of action for fraud. In an attempt to give more content to this dividing line, the Second Circuit has identified a list of instruments commonly denominated "notes" that nonetheless fall without the "security" category. See Exchange National Bank, supra, at 1138 (types of notes that are not "securities" include "the note delivered in consumer financing, the note secured by a mortgage on a home, the short-term note secured by a lien on a small business or some of its assets, the note evidencing a 'character' loan to a bank customer, short-term notes secured by an assignment of accounts receivable, or a note which simply formalizes an open-account debt of the customer of the broker, it is collateralized)"; Chemical Bank, supra, at 939 (adding to the list "notes evidencing loans by commercial banks for current operations").*

The judge then applies the test in several steps: "First, we examine the transaction to assess the motivations that would prompt a reasonable seller and buyer to enter into it...Second, we examine the plan for the distribution of the instrument...Finally, we examine whether some factor such as the existence of another regulatory scheme significantly reduces the risk of the instrument, thereby rendering application of the Securities Acts unnecessary." Based on the four above factors, the judge draws his conclusions:

> *We conclude, then, that in determining whether an instrument denominated a "note" is a "security", courts are to apply the version of "family resemblance" test that we have articulated here: a note is presumed to be a "security," and the presumption may be rebutted only by a showing that the note bears a strong resemblance (in terms of the factors we have identified) to one of the enumerated categories of instrument. If the instrument is not sufficiently similar to an item on the list, the decision whether another category should be added is to be made by examining the same factors. Applying the family resemblance*

approach to this case, we have little difficulty in concluding that the notes at issue here are "securities." Ernst & Young admits that "a demand note does not closely resemble any of the Second Circuit's family resemblance examples." Nor does an examination of the four factors we have identified as being relevant to our inquiry suggest that the demand notes here are not "securities" despite their lack of similarity to any of the enumerated categories.

The above U.S. Supreme Court decision from 1990 manifests an advanced degree of legal argumentation and legal interpretation. First of all, it interprets legal concepts within their context of use and not in a splendid isolation of doctrinal debates. Moreover, it makes its approach also plain to those who – like the four partly dissenting justices in this case – may for whatever reasons prefer other interpretive strategies. One may observe on the margin that the notion of family resemblance as used here comes close to *prototype* analyzed by G. Kleiber (1990) and others (cf. 3.2.3.4).

3.6.6 Particular problems in interpreting statutes and contracts

Problems regarding the interpretation of statutes and other related legal documents such as governmental decrees appear in at least three-fold constellation of language use. First, courts competent to decide complaints in which such issues arise are institutionally competent to provide a binding interpretation of an open statutory issue. The courts determine the meaning in an interpretive speech act (Savigny 1973: 30). Second, all persons dealing in a professional way with legal statutes have to interpret them in order to grasp their meaning. Such persons elaborate the meaning or meaning alternatives for an open legal issue (Savigny 1973: 30). This is, for instance, the case when a legal scholar engages in the systematization of legal provisions and discovers interpretive problems in a statute that have not been decided in courts. Systematization and interpretation were therefore perceived as interrelated operations (Aarnio 1989: 301). Third, legal statutes can be read in an unprofessional way, e.g. by writers or other interested persons for the use in essays, novels or parodies. In the following, the two first varieties will be dealt with and the third will be mentioned in the chapter on Literature and Law.

3.6.6.1 Statutes on interpretation

The legislative answer to the problem of statute interpretation could be the legislation on the interpretation of statutes. Why should the legislator not regulate the issue of statutory interpretation when all other essential aspects of social reality are regulated by norms? The first problem connected to this issue is of logical sort. The statute would necessarily include legal concepts in a form which requires interpretation. Should these concepts be interpreted according to the interpretive guidelines provided by the statute in question or would a new statute on interpretation of the Statute on Interpretation become indispensable? Even if the concepts of the Statute on Interpretation would be interpretable according to the statutory provisions of the named statute, would this increase legal certainty or guarantee the appropriate interpretation of statutes by the authorized institutions? It seems that such legislation would not substantially contribute to the question of statute interpretation because the theoretical issue of interpretation remains unchanged notwithstanding whatever statutory regulation. Sporadically existing legislation on interpretation is illustrative of theoretical implications of interpretive operations that are explicitly regulated by the legislator. The New York Statute's § 94 provides an explanation on how to construe conceptual meaning in statutes in that it states that "legislative intent is to be ascertained from the words and language used, and the statutory language is generally construed according to its natural and obvious sense, without resorting to an artificial and forced construction." The general approach of the legislator is understandable in this formulation. The legislator intends to increase the awareness of interpreting institutions of the text of a statute they deal with. But, the instrument which it provides to achieve this goal is disappointing. It does not explain how to distinguish between the natural and obvious sense and to protect interpretive attempts against artificial and forced constructions. It is not surprising that § 94 had been subjected to numerous decisions of New York courts which had to determine what is the appropriate interpretation of the legislative intent. In Debevoise & Plimpton v. New York State Department of Finance (N.Y. 2d 657, 593 N.Y.S. 2d 974, 1993) the Court of Appeals stressed that "words of ordinary import in a statute are to be given their natural and commonly understood meaning, unless it is clear from the statutory language that a different meaning was intended." In the course of application of the interpretive rule the court then rejected the Tax Departments' interpretation of New York Tax Law § 1105. The Tax Department had to interpret the term *refrigeration and steam service* which according to the court did not include rent paid by the plaintiff to its landlord for overtime heating and air conditioning. The methodological gap which has to be bridged between the interpretive rule and the application in casu is evident. The result could be achieved also without resorting to the interpretive rule. Furthermore, in Manhattan Pizza Hut, Inc. v. New York State Human Rights Appeal Bd., (51 N.Y. 2d 506, 434 N.Y. S. 2d 96, 1980) the Court of Appeals dealt with the interpretation of the term *marital status* in New York Executive Law § 269. It held that the term *marital status* did not include questions concerning the identity of occupation of a spouse but only the characterization as single, married or divorced. Here again, the court quoted the interpretive rule stating that "words of common usage are to be given their ordinary meaning." Subsequently, it interpreted the legal notion *marital status* in terms of the legal language and did not reflect upon the ordinary usage which might, as a matter of fact, not include identity or occupation of a spouse but might include the category of widow/widower or even bigamist. In addition, the New York Statute's § 93 regulates the temporary aspect of interpretation by stating that "a statute speaks, not from the time...when the courts are called on to interpret it, but as of the time it took effect." It prevents the adaptation of statutes to changing circumstances and by so doing it also reflects the approach to legislative acts in the Anglo-American legal tradition where statutes should be interpreted narrowly (Mattila 2006: 36). Moreover, in a situation of changed circumstances a change of the statute by the legislator is preferred to the adjustment of the statutory provision by the authorized institution to the changes occurred as it is frequently practiced in the civil law countries. Although the New York Statute on the interpretation of legislative intent has been perceived as an interesting approach to the challenge of statutory interpretation and had been even admiringly mentioned in the then Soviet legal literature (Pigolkin 1990: 130), it clearly shows the limits of a legislative measure directed toward structuring statutory interpretation.

Other countries have also introduced provisions to the same aim. The (UK) Interpretation Act from 1978 is a statute which includes provisions regarding the construction of statutes and provides definitions and rules for their understanding. It states among other things that words importing the masculine gender include females, words in the singular include the plural and words in plural include the singular, the expression *person* includes a body corporate etc. Some U.K. statutes include sections expressly incorporating the Interpretation Act. Some statutes include interpretation sections, such as the (UK) Theft Act of 1968 where in sec. 34 the definition of *goods* is provided. Courts also use preambles of statutes as an aid to interpretation. As already stated, these interpretive instruments do not replace interpretation; they may however render it less opaque. Additionally, in Notes and Commented Materials no. 27 some French, Italian and German provisions concerning interpretation are quoted. Particularly relevant to the French law is Art. 1156 French Civil Code as contrasted with Art. 111–4 French Penal Code that provides for strict interpretation in criminal law, (FR): *La loi pénale est d'interprétation stricte* (cf. also Slocum 2015: 9).

With all that being said, it seems to be preferable to develop guidelines for interpretation of legislative acts wherever needed. Their positive impact can be seen in raising jurists' awareness about the problem of statutory interpretation. Nevertheless, problems concerning creative interpretation as characterized by Dworkin will remain in the center of interpretive activities. Those activities cannot be reduced to applicational schemes which in a situation where statutory interpretation is needed would automatically lead to an acceptable solution. They are complex legal-linguistic operations. Some effort and professional skills must always be invested in the legal interpretive activities.

3.6.6.2 Interpreting statutes

Interpretive strategies used by courts are centered on the notion of *creative interpretation* introduced into the legal theory by R. Dworkin. They are less visible than the traditional interpretive canons (Alexy 1983: 19) because courts usually do not mark explicitly in their decisions the creative moments in their interpretation. These strategies are centered on the notion of *creative interpretation* rather loosely because the dose of creativity in them differs. Structurally, they ground in the idea of the probability of meaning (cf. Slocum 2012, 2015: 10). For instance, in Goldstein v. SEC (p. 13) the court observed that "it may be that the strict dichotomy between clarity and ambiguity is artificial, that what we have is a continuum, a probability of meaning." Legal theory structures statute interpretation more systematically. In MacCormic and Summers (1991: 512 sqq) following types of arguments were held characteristic of statutory interpretation: argument from *ordinary meaning*, argument from *technical meaning*, argument from *contextual harmonization*, argument from *precedent*, argument from *analogy*, argument from relevant *principles of law*, argument from *history*, argument from *purpose*, argument from *substantive reasons* and argument from *intention*. The interpretive strategy to determine the meaning of a statutory provision may be based on existing precedents and interpretive standards. In such a case, it is based on professional argumentative skills rather than on particularly creative linguistic innovations. The pertaining interpretive strategy used to be based on the legislative intent. It is equally centered on the *creative interpretation* because the legislative intent itself is a creative argument. For instance, in Water, Waste & Land Inc. dba Westec v. Lanham (955 P.2d 997, 1998) the Supreme Court of Colorado had to interpret the section 7–80-208 of the Colorado Limited Liability Company Act (1997). The section states: "The fact that the articles of organization are on file in the office of the secretary of state is notice that the limited liability company is a limited liability company and is notice of all other facts set forth therein which are required to be set forth in the articles of organization." In the case, managers of an LLC acted without revealing that they represent the LLC and were therefore sued personally. At trial, they admitted the liability of the LLC. The court had therefore to decide whether the fact that the managers failed to disclose the existence as well as the identity of the LLC led to their personal liability under the rules of agency. The court had to consider the above section which places third parties on constructive notice regarding the character of the company and especially its limited liability. The court decided that the personal liability of the managers was established by their acting without a clear reference to the LLC. Otherwise, so the court, third parties which relied on the personal liability of their interlocutors could easily become victims of deceit and outright fraud. Thus, the court asked first of all for the rationale of the provision which – when literally interpreted – could also justify the opposite result. Finally, the court grounded its interpretation in the authority of the General Assembly which as the court presumed "*did not intend to create a safe harbor for deceit*". Apparently, the court expected that its interpretation may not be sufficiently persuasive and needed a stronger argument which it also found in the form of reference to an authority vested with broad powers. In sum, it is typical of statutory interpretation that arguments of different origin are used in it. Their choice depends on the selected interpretive strategy.

Frequently, statutes are interpreted by jurists without reference to an authoritative interpretation in situations where no precedents exist for an issue. To illustrate, the Act to Ensure Truth in Music Advertising enacted by the U.S. State of Maine and effective September 2007 (rendered in Notes and Commented Materials no. 26) has not been subject to judicial scrutiny. The act strategically anticipates interpretive issues in its § 1157 and provides definitions for notions which may lead to interpretive problems, e.g. *performing group, person, recording group* or *sound recording*. However, definitional guidelines regarding nouns used in a text

their context and in the light of its object and purpose. The convention embraces the traditional interpretive canon termed in three components: *literal, systematic* and *teleological* (Cassese 2005: 179). Art. 32 mentions *preparatory materials* that can be used to elucidate obscure formulations in treaties when the literal, systematic and teleological methods did not lead to satisfying results. Art. 33 presumes the same meaning in treaties drafted in different linguistic versions; in doubtful cases the meaning that best supports the text of the treaty as regards its object and purpose is preferred. The convention recommends a guiding interpretive principle of effectiveness of the treaty – (LAT) *ut res magis valeat quam pereat* – to the detriment of the mentioned maxim *in dubio mitius* that emphasized the sovereign right and the least unfavorable content of a controversial provision for the state as an addressee of legal duties under a treaty (Cassese ibid.). Next to the Articles 31–33 of the Vienna Convention also some interpretive standards developed under national law were incorporated into the interpretive strategies in the international law. The *implied powers doctrine* that had been developed by the U.S. Supreme Court in the case McCulloch v. the State of Maryland in 1819 has been applied to problems related to determining tasks and prerogatives of international organizations. Hence, a doctrine of domestic law that aimed at elaborating the ambit of state law in the confrontation with federal provisions has been applied analogously upon relations between international organizations and their member states. This interpretive strategy called *federal analogy* has been sometimes criticized as providing excessive powers to international organizations (Cassese 2005: 180). Recently, J. Smolka and B. Pirker (2016) addressed methodological issues related to interpretation in international law from the pragmatic perspective.

3.6.6.5 Finalist interpretation

Some interpretive strategies are frequently followed, yet rarely referred to in the legal practice. One of them is the finalist interpretation. The finalist interpretation is an interpretive strategy that consists in proving with the help of a text an already existing assumption. This strategy is largely applied also outside legal texts, and one may actually ask whether it is interpretation at all. In his anthropological and literary study *The Conquest of America* Tzvetan Todorov (1992) analyzed Columbus's letters about the discovery of West Indies and he identified a prevalent interpretive strategy in Columbus's writings that he calls finalist. He realized that Columbus had seen the discovered lands through the prism of his anterior knowledge about remote countries and the terrestrial paradise that the antique and later literature provided to sometimes rather naïve readers. Todorov writes:

> *Columbus performs a "finalist" strategy of interpretation, in the same manner in which the Church Fathers interpreted the Bible: the ultimate meaning is given from the start (this is Christian doctrine); what is sought is the path linking the initial meaning (the apparent signification of the words of the biblical text) with the ultimate meaning. There is nothing of the modern empiricist about Columbus: the decisive argument is an argu-*

> *ment of authority, not of experience. He knows in advance what he will find; the concrete experience is there to illustrate a truth already possessed, not to be interrogated according to pre-established rules in order to seek the truth* (Todorov 1992: 17).

Todorov calls this interpretive choice a hermeneutic behavior; it changes only when Columbus reflects on the beauty of surrounding nature (Todorov 1992: 17). The finalist strategy prevails however in Columbus's thinking; he is not seeking the truth, he is only interested in finding confirmation of a truth known in advance. The fate of the finalist interpretive strategy in law is largely unexplored. For the one, an anecdote mentions the medieval jurists Bartolus and Baldus describing Baldus to seek Bartolus's advice for the justification of a preconceived solution to a legal problem. For the other, many legal interpretive acts seem to be based on preconceived views about the appropriate meaning of the law. Legal linguistics would have to develop a suitable methodology to trace such decisions.

In my *Legal Discourses* I also discussed a paradigmatic interpretive situation called there Martian interpretation (cf. Galdia 2014: 126). Although a pure construct, the Martian interpretation is worthwhile considering together with the constructive interpretation and the finalist interpretation. The finalist interpretation is the logically contrary operation to the constructive interpretation that has been introduced here in its Dworkinian version. All of them seem to me prototypical in terms of legal interpretation that really takes place in the legal practice. The sociological interpretation that will be discussed last constitutes a factual background within the interpretive practice and is close to anthropological constants of action that is undertaken within juridical institutions and also in society at large.

3.6.6.6 Sociological interpretation

This type of interpretation goes beyond the traditional canon of legal interpretive techniques. Nevertheless, it is also a sort of interpretation present in law and applied by lawyers. For instance, the penal law is permeated by the principle of *presumption of innocence*. Yet, from quantitative research it is known that most accused – the exact number differs from jurisdiction to jurisdiction – are actually convicted. Therefore, it cannot be readily expected that jurists would treat indicted suspects as innocent; they know that most of them will be held guilty. Among those acquitted will be many acquitted for formal reasons; cases where accused persons get free because they are simply innocent are rare. This fact constitutes the essence of the sociological interpretation. It is legal like all others mentioned here. Meanwhile, it transgresses the traditional interpretive canon. Its future in the legal theory is therefore uncertain. It has, and it has always had a place in legal linguistics.

In a modern society, professional and non-professional communicational strategies merge and engender a dynamic law. R.C. Berring (2000: 1704) dealt with the problem of interpretation of court decisions that regularly appear to professional readers as cryptic. He proposed a possible solution for the future: "Scholarship on the meaning of the case lies elsewhere. Indeed, we do not even require that the judges clearly set out the point of law that they decide. Think how much easier the law would be to understand if each opinion had to begin with an official judicially authored summary of the case. We could even ask judges to write these in a controlled vocabulary. We could ask them to tell us precisely how the decision is intended to affect the law. Rather than major decisions being followed by fractious debate as to what the Court intended, we could simply ask the Court to tell us." Berring is aware of chances to have his proposal implemented: "I cannot imagine that the scenario of the previous paragraph will come to pass in my lifetime, but it serves to indicate how much change is needed. Judicial opinions do not have to be cryptic. There is a great deal of ritual associated with the courts..." Likewise, the picture of a jurist could be adjusted. Th. Jefferson is remembered for advocating the notion of a lawyer as a 'public citizen'. According to D.M. Douglas (2001: 197) this 'public citizen' can be defined as "someone who would place public interest ahead of private interest and exercise leadership in preserving republicanism." In this conception, the picture of a lawyer who arbitrarily represents private interests for money is a distortion of the profession that is connected to law. Law construed as a paid battle for private interests is practically thinkable and it is also regularly practiced as such, yet it appears in the hindsight as a failure or a parody of law. Lawyers as a learned profession are well suited to become public citizens because they unlike practical people, for instance merchants or landowners, do not form any distinct interest in society, as mentioned by A. Hamilton in *The Federalist*, no. 35. Hamilton insisted that the learned professions "will be indiscriminately the objects of confidence and of choice of each other and of other parts of the community." Hamilton concluded the argument:

> *Will not the man of the learned profession, who will feel a neutrality to the rivalships between the different branches of industry, be likely to prove an impartial arbiter between them, ready to promote either, so far as it shall appear to him conducive to the general interest of the society?*

This conception of jurists as public citizens requires commitment to law, while the attitude that is preponderant nowadays stresses knowledge of law rather than commitment to law as the main feature of professionalism. This knowledge of law without commitment puts in question the very fundamentals of a learned and liberal profession. It is also one of the main causes of the crisis of law.

3.6.7 Is law based on interpretive or argumentative practices?

The relation between interpretation and argumentation remains unclear in the academic discussion (cf. Atienza 1999: 45). In research works and in specialized encyclopaedias both topics are usually treated separately. This occurs because apparently no logically necessary link is perceived between both operations. One can therefore try to discuss issues related to interpretation without explicitly engaging in the debate about argumentation. In such a debate, argumentation would provide the tacit background to the discussion about preference given to one or another interpretive variety of a text. Argumentation might be in this context perceived as the formal part of interpretation, an issue concerning the structure of arguments used in the interpretation and specifically in a situation where preference must be given to one of different available varieties. Conversely, interpretation may be described as practical argumentation (Eriksson 1997: 14). This interrelation is particularly interesting in law. Some scholars tried to link interpretation and argumentation while using the structural model of emission and reception of messages. For A. Greimas (1976), interpretation is the linguistic activity (FR *faire interpretative*) of the receiver of the message, argumentation (FR *faire persuasive*), in turn, concerns the emitter of the message (Jackson 1985: 57). For Greimas, this distinction did not play any particular role because he was primarily interested in the signification act itself, where it does not matter whether it is interpretation or argumentation. Both distinctive notions belong to the pragmatics of discourse (Jackson 1985: 57) and might play a significant role there. Is the interpretation understood in a narrow, philological sense as a search for the initial meaning of the text, then law can be meaningfully construed as an argumentative and not as an interpretive praxis (Grasnich 2001: 33). Some argumentative features may require interpretive preparation; analogical arguments in law rely on interpretive acts as their essential preliminary (Nerhot 1992: 23). When different approaches to signification, argumentation and interpretation are taken into consideration, the indistinctive model relating to signification as such might be useful. It would integrate both the interpretive results and its argumentative form and elucidate conditions for signification processes in them. This is particularly persuasive in the model developed by Greimas. Apparently, it would not be necessary to distinguish between creation and translation in law either and it would be possible to view these processes through the unifying concept of signification. Nevertheless, I am here more interested in the pragmatic aspects of language use and will therefore use and distinguish both notions for practical reasons. Furthermore, I will also use the notions *creation* and *translation of law*. While doing so, I am aware of the finding that the underlying processes in which signification comes about are constitutive of whatever form of language use, i.e. of every speech act. I believe that through the procedure of distinguishing between different speech acts I remain closer to my material which is the language as it is used in legal contexts. The other procedure, advocated by A. Greimas, has the advantage that it allows to construct a coherent semiotic model of signification processes while including legal contexts. By proceeding in this way, it proves that it is universally applicable as a semiotic theory. Yet, it benefits more the semiotic theory than it benefits law. My ambition is different. While being impressed by several semiotic and pragmatic models I try to make them operational in the area of law. As a result of these efforts, linguistic operations in law should become more transparent and also controllable in a more rational way. Unsurprisingly, the case analyses, even those not particularly numerous which I undertook here, show the interdependence of argumentative and interpretive issues. Law is a discursive practice and cannot be created nor applied without recourse to arguments. Interpretive contexts which are also argumentative in its character will remain the central problem of the application of law.

3.6.8 Interpretation in natural sciences

It may be worthwhile to compare legal interpretation to interpretation in natural sciences. In terms of methodology, interpretation in natural sciences follows experimentation and concerns primarily data which emerge as a result of an experiment. Interpretation is perceived as explication, i.e. attributing sense to data gathered in experiments and in particular theories set up subsequently (cf. Rosenberg 2000: 23, 37). One and the same fact (data) can be interpreted differently in the light of the theory shared by the interpreting scientists (Searle1999: 6, cf. also Uus 1994: 11, 267–279). A new theory causes new interpretation of data. Social and cultural factors definitely play a role in the evolution of theories in natural sciences as well as in their internal paradigmatic developments. Theoretical and empirical levels are interrelated there. However, data may also give rise to different theories. The problem does not concern the access to data, but the inherited categories used for their interpretation (Searle 1999: 69). In natural sciences the dependence of interpretation and facts has never been questioned as had been that of interpretation and theorems on which it is based. J.J. Kaag (2009: 68) while referring to C.S. Peirce and his metaphor *nature is a book which science interprets* also stressed the intersubjective interpretation that dominates the work of scientists and that is not limited to *"matters of objective facts."* By contrast, legal sciences had been dominated by the view that a written legal rule could be interpreted univocally and that it could lead to the only right legal decision in a case. The classical idea of justice makes it understandably difficult to accept that a legal provision can be interpreted differently in the light of different approaches or interpretive strategies. Nevertheless, the legal science cannot guarantee more than the best possible decision which is reached in the recourse to legal-argumentative mechanisms and the specific creative potentiality in interpretive techniques which only increase their legitimacy. The main difference between the legal science and the natural sciences is therefore not of qualitative art. It is grounded in different attitudes toward interpretation of data within the respective professional communities.

3.7 Legal Translation

3.7.1 Linguistic transformations of law

Legal translation is for me one of the central linguistic operations in law, especially in all its international contexts. While identifying the most fundamental linguistic operations in law I insisted upon creation of legally binding rules through legal speech acts. Subsequently, I have identified one more central process in law, i.e. the application of legal rules expressed through language. However, this process is too complex to be incorporated into legal linguistics with all its implications. I focused therefore upon the two main and inevitable legal-linguistic operations in the application of law; i.e. argumentation and interpretation. In the international context another central legal-linguistic operation must be added to those already discussed dominant varieties of legal-linguistic operations. Frequently, law in the international context cannot be applied directly in a case. Instead it must be linguistically transformed in order to become operative. This additional indirect variety of a linguistic operation in law is the legal translation. In pragmatic terms, this linguistic transformation regards legal speech acts responsible for the creation of legal rules. Our main concern will therefore be the procedure in which legal speech acts of the source language are transformed into meaningful and equivalent legal speech acts in the target language. This operation, seen also beyond the legal context, has been perceived as one of typical language games (Wittgenstein 1984: 250). Therefore, researchers pondered intensively how to preserve the speech act's original meaning in the specific context as defined by the law to which it refers and which it also shapes with linguistic means. The starting point for an analysis of this type is the identification of the legal speech act which must be transformed. In the case when this seems to be evident, its classification within the two respective legal-linguistic contexts has to take place. This activity has a long background that is worth mentioning in the following paragraph.

3.7.2 A retrospective upon legal translation

Translation of legal texts is a practice boasting a long history. The best known artifacts in this field include the peace treaty between Egypt and the Hittite Empire concluded 1271 BC as well as the translation of the *Corpus Iuris Civilis* into numerous languages after its initial translation into Greek (cf. Husa 2013: 83–84). We are also told that the Assyrian king Kargon let the laws of his kingdom be translated into the languages of his subjects around 3000 BC; 2100 BC a group of translators worked on the preparation of the linguistic varieties of the Babylonian Hammurabi code (Arsova-Nikolić 1999: 13). Some artifacts that played a preponderant role for other disciplines such as the Rosetta Stone that enabled the deciphering of the Egyptian hieroglyphs included text types that would be classified today as legal texts (cf. Spiegelberg 1922: 11). The Rosetta Stone bears a decree issued by the pharaoh Ptolemeus V in 196 BC in two variants of the Egyptian script and in Greek. The translators of these and other legal texts from past centuries – most of whom remain unknown to us – must certainly have reflected upon methodological problems associated with their complex and demanding task. Unfortunately, these reflections have not been handed down in history. Systematic study has only recently begun in the field of legal translation, but most significant problems have already been identified and the research has certainly shown its practical application with the help of comparative law, legal linguistics and legal data processing (Stolze 2005: 9). It would be tempting to assume that translation of texts actually began with legal translations as even today some specialists mention legal translation as the beginning of studies about the general translation of texts (Arsova-Nikolić 1999: 13). This assumption is very realistic because the need for legal translation emerges with transgressing the borders of one's own culture that in the past were also frequently borders of one's own state. Nowadays, a parallel process that is based on transgressing national borders emerges within the European Union (Mattila 2006: 25). Although the development of the European Union law has undeniably stimulated the discussion about legal translation, officially bilingual or multilingual countries (for instance Canada, Switzerland and Finland) have been familiar with the problem for some time. In these countries, the subject makes up one of the standard topics for legal research and education.

3.7.3 Terminological equivalence

To date, legal translation has primarily been researched through the perspective of terminology. In this regard, the emphasis has fallen largely on the question of how terms indigenous to one legal system can be conveyed in the equivalent terms of another legal system. Research aimed at demarcating areas of semantic correspondence among legal terms, e.g. (IT) *beni*, (FR) *biens* or (UK/US) *goods*. Moreover, legal linguistics has shown that the transfer of information not only takes place within the context of legal systems, but also concerns two predominantly technical language systems. This poses two significant problems. First, there is the question of the conditions under which the target legal text corresponds to the source legal text, whereby the requirements of equivalence must be ascertained in the context of a technical language. Second, specific problems must be resolved, depending on which source language is being translated into which target language. After all, a legal system with numerous institutions that have developed over time represents only one of the challenges for the translator. The language system itself with its syntactic and semantic implications places certain demands on the translator and even creates limits for the translation. The theory of translation has to solve this intricacy. It is based on an understanding of two texts: a source text which is to be translated and a target text which is the result of the actual translation process. The task of the translator is to establish a relationship of equivalence between the source and the target texts, i.e. a substantive homogeneity.

The term *equivalence* has been discussed in numerous linguistic works (cf. Galdia 2013). In this regard, the spectrum of opinions ranges from an 'everything goes' approach to the assertion of the fundamental impossibility inherent in the act of translation – in other words, the factually contingent and unavoidable failure through intermediary approaches presenting requirements for approximate equivalence, or suggesting the redefinition of the concept of equivalence (Torop 1998: 137). Occasionally, equivalence has been described as an illusion (Snell-Hornby 1986: 13). For all intents and purposes, this diversity of opinion is neither surprising nor accidental. It is the natural result of different linguistic approaches which have proposed various solutions to the problem of equivalence on the basis of conflicting theorems (Mounin 1963: 9). However, once the term *equivalence* has been clearly defined, as for instance in Reiss-Vermeer (1984: 140), it performs an important function in the science of translation. Reiss and Vermeer frame *equivalence* in terms of the *skopos*-theory. This theory focuses upon the aim under which the translation is effectuated (cf. also Madsen 2007). For instance, a Japanese poem may be translated primarily as regards its form or its content, dependent upon the aim of the translation. The problems relating to legal translation – especially in the field of terminology – can be more easily presented with the help of the definition proposed by Reiss and Vermeer that can be perceived as introducing functional translation into terminological work. It is largely operative in law when e.g. (FR) *acte sous seing privé* is translated as (D) *mit Unterschrift versehene Privaturkunde* or (FR) *dépeçage* is translated as (D) *gespaltene Anknüpfung*. As there are no German legal terms corresponding to the French ones an innovative translation that renders the meaning of the French concepts can be used in accordance with the *skopos*-theory. *Skopos*-theoretical choices must be exercised for instance in translating names of institutions, courts etc. The name of a Swedish court (S) *hovrätt* can be transformed 1) literally, 2) while taking into consideration its historical background, 3) in a descriptive way and 4) functionally (cf. Mattila 2002d: 277). Mostly, the functional translation will be needed; therefore (S) *hovrätt* will be translated as (FR) *cour d'appel* or (FIN) *hovioikeus*. While translating (S) *Svea hovrätt* a descriptive or a mixed functional/descriptive translation (with a description in brackets or in footnotes) may be better suited. The needs of the translation determine the choice. Nevertheless, functional equivalence depends not only on the terminology but also on the legal text, with all its syntactic, semantic and pragmatic implications; e.g. (S) *talan om äktenskapsskillnad väcktes* corresponds to (D) *die Scheidungsklage wurde eingereicht*. Thus, the claim that has been filed is rendered with (D) *eingereicht* or (S) *väcktes*. In this case, there is no need for *skopos*-theoretical choices because both legal languages, German and Swedish, dispose of exact context-bound syntagmas used in respective speech acts.

Many such background notions have been extensively discussed in the research. Weisgerber (1961) launched the debate on translation problems as an analysis of errors, working from the premise of the fundamental impossibility of textual translation. Weisgerber's perception is paradoxical insofar as the editorial suggestions he makes in his critique of an international treaty text actually manifest the possibility of translation rather than the impossibility that he maintains. Barbara Kielar (1977) makes an insightful link between the problem areas from the analytical point of view. She perceives the technical legal language as interconnected with the systematic structure of the law and the language. This specialized and technical legal language can be separated from the general language by means of contrastive analysis. This formal approach may initially satisfy the requirements of a descriptive model. However, our remarks about legal terminology show that formal boundaries are difficult to draw. *Promissory estoppel* is definitely a legal concept; *mother-in-law* may become a legal concept depending on the context of its use. When a court decision is taken in a French court (FR) *en chambre du conseil* is this formulation legal-linguistic or simply linguistic in its essence? The translation *behind closed doors* or (FIN) *suljetuin ovin* (Mattila 2002b: 505) may indicate the possibility of a non-professional translation. Yet, this sample of translation of the French sophisticated phrase requires legal knowledge. Also Vogel (1988) made an attempt at describing legal translation. His analysis of the translation process differentiates between general language terms and legal terminology. The choice of non-technical words such as (D) *Verbindung* or (D) *Bindung* – made with reference to a text concerning the relationship between West Germany and the then West Berlin – can contain as much legal relevance as legal concepts, e.g. a trading company or partnership (*Handelsgesellschaft* in German) or public limited company (*Aktiengesellschaft* in German) (Vogel 1988: 43). For instance, (D) *Verbindung* or (D) *Bindung* both mean 'ties', but they were understood by negotiators of the Berlin Agreement as conveying varying degrees of intensity. (D) *Verbindung* suggests 'ties' such as 'connections', e.g. train connections while (D) *Bindung* – literally a 'knot' – denotes a stronger bond. Some other conceptions of legal translation also focus on the area of legal terminology. In these views, legal terms refer to the relevant areas of a legal system; a technical translation therefore requires a descriptive language that can render the incompatible legal terms without any material losses in terms of content. De Groot (1987) follows a similar track. He discusses the problems of legal translation in terms of comparative law, which in his view comprises the key element in legal translation. In his view, the level of difficulty of a legal translation does not primarily depend on linguistically determined differences, but rather on structural differences between legal systems (de Groot in Balkema/de Groot 1987: 18). In this respect, the relationship between the languages is only of secondary importance in comparison with the relationship between the legal systems. As an example, de Groot cites the largely unproblematic case of translations from Danish into Norwegian, and in the case of multilingual states with a single legal system – such as Finland – where the problem falls anyway entirely, despite linguistic differences between Finnish and Swedish, the two national languages of the country. Making legal language uniform at the international level is of utmost importance for de Groot. He therefore advocates the development of a legal metalanguage in order to convey legal terms that are defined by national laws (de Groot in de Groot/Schulze 1999). A complete equivalence between the terms of two legal systems can only be attained if both legal languages refer to the same legal system, positing an acceptable equivalence between two legal systems and not two languages. If no equivalence can be established, de Groot suggests several alternatives: citation of the non-translated term, paraphrasing, and the creation of neologisms or a combination of these.

Finally, structural similarity between translation of legal terms and the process of *qualification* – (US) *characterization* – in the private international law is obvious for jurists specialized in comparative law. It can be exemplified on the Maldonado case rendered in Notes and Commented Materials no. 61. The qualification of a legal concept transforms it into an equivalent concept of the other law in order to make it understandable to foreign lawyers. Initial discussions of this problem in the conflict of laws doctrine pointed to the fundamental impossibility of qualification (Bartin 1897) due to incompatibility of legal systems. The mere fact that qualification of legal concepts regularly takes place outside of static classification processes already runs counter to the idea of the fundamental impossibility of qualification (Rabel 1956: 13). Thus, the problem of qualification can basically be resolved. This presupposes, however, the application of methodologically sound techniques. Ernst Rabel (1956: 23) defined it as a comparison of conflict of laws' concepts with those belonging to other jurisdictions. For the translator, this means having to rely on a methodical resource in answering questions of qualification which may arise in individual cases. Nevertheless, the significance of the act of qualification in private international law in the descriptive model of legal translation has not been conclusively defined. It must be therefore determined whether qualification is the method of legal translation or whether it is only an aid in the translation process. Finally, it is not sure that the legal transformation of concepts also necessitates their linguistic transformation as the conditio sine qua non of translation. Should this not be the case, both qualification and legal translation would be interrelated but essentially independent operations. Meanwhile, from the perspective of a linguist, J. Engberg (2013a) stressed that comparative law matters to legal translation notwithstanding the different epistemological and practical interests of legal comparatists and legal translators.

3.7.4 Descriptive model of legal translation

While describing legal translation it is helpful to distinguish the subject matter oriented research and research about the discipline proper on a meta-level of reflection; this is rather a demanding task as the translation theory is not a consolidated field (Borja Albi 2004: 1–2). New linguistic approaches – of which the analysis by S. Šarčević may be paradigmatic – concentrate rather on pragmatic aspects of legal texts and underscore the need for the development of general translation strategies. In contrast, examinations undertaken from the legal perspective by authors such as Heikki E.S. Mattila place the emphasis on comparative law elements, although textual aspects are increasingly included in these comparative legal analyses (Mattila 2002b). Increasingly also interpretive strategies are mentioned in prefaces to translations and terminological problems are discussed in footnotes to translations (cf. Anderson/Okuda 2007). However, both of these trends are characterized by increased tendency toward approximation and efforts to discuss legal translation problems within a broader context, more in keeping with the complexity of legal and linguistic problems (Galdia 2003a: 21). Recently, M. Mannoni (2016: 103) stressed the necessity of a more comprehensive approach to translations in the area of law while challenging the concept of the legal text. Approaches such as Mannoni's may correspond to the perspective upon legal language as language used in social situations that are related to the creation and the application of law. In the light of such approaches, which are supported in this book, legal text becomes less important and legal discourse is established as dominating and most productive legal-linguistic structure.

The discussion of terminological problems of legal translation revolves around the term 'denotation'. A legal concept under legal system A, understood as a systemic concept, is transformed into another concept under legal system B, by finding a term that corresponds with the function of the legal concept under legal system A. This allows, for example, the English legal term *trust* to be translated into German as *Treuhand* in certain instances. In the translation of legal terms, one often resorts to pairs of terms which appear somehow connected by a relationship of equivalence. The legal denoters which have to date been applied in the descriptive model – e.g. (D) *Versäumnisurteil* for *default judgment* and (FIN) *yksipuolinen tuomio* have the same legal meaning, but the question is what do they denote? The difficulty of answering this question may provide more fertile ground for further analysis than the eventual answer itself. At the very last, the difficulty may illustrate that the two designated terms might lack a common denoter. They function differently than synonyms; the terms 'mean' the same things to jurists, even though they are not identical. They are also not really similar because they exist in the context of different legal and language systems, but still they remain comparable. It can be safely said that the functional method of comparative law has proven the comparability of such legal terms. The aforementioned concepts can also be compared by reference to their connotations. In respect of the first term, it would be sufficient to provide a linguistic basis for the functional comparative law term in order to determine the connotations of the legal terms.

How could one characterize the elements of the descriptive model for legal translation? It follows from the various above mentioned studies that legal translation is primarily characterized by the denotative components of the technical language, whereas the legal system itself guarantees the basis of translation. Denotation forms only a part of the entire process of translation, although its importance cannot be denied. In fact, an entire text – and not just terms – is the subject of translation, even though many translators predominantly concentrate on terms as such. Every text also has a connotative level, which is semantically as important as the denotative level. Furthermore, the text is defined by tense, mood and other linguistic categories (van Dijk 1980: 24). It is constituted by but also limited to the specific linguistic system. The descriptive model which up to now has been based on denoters is weighed down by one problem. As mentioned, it is unclear how the denotation referred to by the denoters is to be understood. The denoters depicted as the pillars of the descriptive model – i.e. the relevant legal terms – must refer to a common subject matter in order for the descriptive model to function. Since this fact has generally been acknowledged, a call emerged for a metalanguage as the descriptive 'instrument' for the individual legal languages. References were made in this regard to civil law theory, comparative law and the exemplary description of all legal systems in order to produce a usable object for denotation. Naturally, connotative aspects of a legal language are incorporated into the translation. Thus, the denotation and connotation of legal terms enable the determination of the feasibility of functional equivalence. The relevant legal term in the source text denotes and connotes a position or an area within its own legal and language system. Furthermore, this term forms a part of a complex technical language structure, which in turn also defines it. In practice, existing conceptions point to a translation which is of a technical nature. The relevant technical legal language is marked by lexical, semantic and often intercultural facets which must be taken into consideration in the translation process. The syntactic implications for translation – a much neglected area in the study of translation theory – will most certainly gain importance as research in this field continues. Toward this complex structural background the legal speech act can be properly identified and linguistically transformed.

3.7.5 Legal metalanguage

Another model for technical translation is the translation into a metalanguage as the universal descriptive language for the propositional content of legal texts. The framework for developing this language is found in comparative law, which examines basic terms and legal structures in an international context (cf. Rabel 1956: 66). By taking into account the legal-linguistic components of legal languages – in particular, the syntactic structure and the pragmatic meaning of legal texts, a metalanguage will emerge that not only contains a few succinct legal words, but also represents a thesaurus of the legal language. A metalanguage already exists with regard to legal terminology for fundamental problems of contemporary continental civil law: the Latin of the Roman law. At most, however, the Latin legal language allows only an understanding of certain basic problems relating to traditional legal doctrine which are seldom the topic of legal translations. For instance, a quasi-contractual obligation such as (FR) *gestion d'affaire,* (D) *Geschäftsführung ohne Auftrag,* (JAP) *jimu kanri* can be referred to as (LAT) *negotiorum gestio* where a description, e.g. *management of affairs without mandate* or a comparative explication, e.g. *it is roughly similar to liability for agency by necessity* seem less helpful or cumbersome (cf. Anderson/Okuda 2007: 148). This problem has lent increasing support to arguments for a metalanguage based on comparative law as the best medium for legal translation. An antithetical concept of technical legal translation could be based on the fundamental structure of the ordinary language. I mentioned this possibility also in the context of the emergence of the legal language as a thinkable alternative to the special register favored by most jurists (cf. 2.2.4). Here I may therefore ask again one of the central legal-linguistic questions: if the ordinary language offers an adequate guarantee for the meaning of words, then why should it not qualify as the universal descriptive language of law? This especially holds true for areas such as international legal relations that are still wrestling with their own language. However, this concept has not been given much consideration in research to date (Galdia 2003a: 11–12). As mentioned already in the chapters on legal argumentation and legal interpretation, the ordinary language is an alternative tool for building all legal speech acts, i.e. argumentative, interpretive, translative and so on. The future will show what role it will play in the legal communication, especially in the global law.

3.7.6 Interdisciplinary aspects

The question arises as to the extent that the discussion to date has helped to solve problems relating to the translation of legal texts. In essence, it concerns the question of whether the problem of legal translation can be solved by means of the application of linguistic theorems or only through an interdisciplinary approach.

Although a clear answer to this question might seem obvious, it should be nevertheless explicitly formulated. The current discussion of legal translation could create the impression that the discussion concerning the substance of foreign law and its comparability, which was originally the foreground, has become less important, given the slew of description models with a purely linguistic orientation and debates on argumentation. However, this initial impression is deceptive, since legal translation is and remains at its core linked to the contents of the respective legal institutions. Therefore, the legal-linguistic studies which highlight the comparative law method seem to point in the right direction. These include for instance research on *unjust enrichment* (Mattila 2002b: 515), a private law institution in numerous legal systems, which was aimed at establishing the relevant contents of the term for translation purposes before translation into the applicable legal terms (NL) *onrechtvaardige verrijking* or (FR) *enrichissement sans cause* is possible. These decisions, which form an integral part of the translation process, are made by taking into account the structural differences between the relevant legal systems and the functional embodiment of the respective terms in the national law framework, which contextually either allow or preclude the relevant systemic concepts. However, such an analysis can only be applied broadly, since structural and functional differences do not become obvious otherwise, thereby prompting the translator to use terms that are lexically related, but inappropriate from a comparative law perspective. This problem is also illustrated by reference to criminal law terminology. For example, based on the former system of differentiation prevailing in French law, the general term (FR) *infraction* (German: *Straftat*, Italian: *reato*, English: *crime*) has three subcategories, represented by the terms *crime, délit* and *contravention* (English: *felony, misdemeanour, petty offence*), which in turn correspond with historical legal terms in Italian (*crimine, delitto, contravvenzione*) and German (*Verbrechen, Vergehen, Übertretung*). However, in both Italian and German criminal law, the terminological structure has changed to the extent that (D) *Straftat* in German law is now classified as either (D) *Verbrechen* or *Vergehen* and the general category of (IT) *reato* in Italian law is subdivided into *delitto* or *contravvenzione*, although the subcategories in Italian and German no more overlap in terms of their content. Comparative research on terminology in German and Finnish criminal law yields similar results (Galdia 2003a: 17), which goes back to the fact that the Finnish system has only one standard term that can be rendered in legal German as *Straftat*, as Finnish criminal law no longer distinguishes between concepts comparable with (D) *Verbrechen* and (D) *Vergehen*. Overall, the approximation of law that was illustrated in the above example often takes place via indirect avenues, and comparative legal research has shown that the historical *ius commune* sometimes better reflected the current perceptions of harmonized law than its modern counterpart. Of course, the complexity of legal relations was of different nature then, which in turn makes some of the more ambitious developments in national legal systems understandable. Nowadays, the structural feature common to legal translation that focuses on terminological analyses – the absence of universally operative terms of reference in the sense of Beaudoin (2002: 119) – can be overcome only through the comparison of legal institutions on a case-by-case basis, as illustrated above.

3.7.6.1 A new approach to legal translation

Among newer approaches to legal translation Aleksandra Matulewska's *Legilinguistic Translatology* (2013) is the most systematic, if not the most advanced. The author's approach is rooted in axiomatic linguistics developed in Poland by Jerzy Bańczerowski (1982, 1996). This approach allows a parametric perspective upon translations. The work also resumes the contemporary knowledge about legal translation in a systematized way according to the parameters that allow the generalization of ideas and beliefs about legal translation. The parametric approach makes also possible another step, i.e. the setting of an algorithm for legal translation. The available knowledge is formalized on a very high level of abstraction. This result is particularly valuable as it enables to evaluate the existing and often contradictory methodological approaches to legal translation and the translatorial strategies used by professionals. Matulewska's approach is normative; it does not exclusively reflect what are translators doing but establishes criteria for proper or sufficient translative equivalents (Matulewska 2013: 253). Thus, translation becomes accessible to investigation. Its matrix is based on dimensions of translative reality seen as a set of translative objects and relations. Therefore, Matulewska's approach allows for "conscious choices" to be made in legal translation (Matulewska 2013: 253).

3.7.7 Translating legal speech acts

The focus upon legal terminology in many works that belong to legal linguistics and to the theory of legal translation may lead to the false conclusion that while translating we replace some words by some others. In fact, translating is not based on words or lexicology as language does not consist solely of words. The bricks of the translation are speech acts which must be rendered in the target language. This is equally evident in literature and in law. Examples borrowed from the CISG may illustrate this procedure. The Art. 25 of the convention deals with the breach of contract. Its wording in English, French and German reads in the official translation as follows:

> *Art. 25 A breach of contract committed by one of the parties is* ***fundamental*** *if it results in such detriment to the other party as* ***substantially*** *to deprive him of what he is entitled to expect under the contract, unless the party in breach did not foresee and a reasonable person of the same kind in the same circumstances would not have foreseen such a result.*

> *Art. 25 Une contravention au contrat commise par l'une des parties est* ***essentielle*** *lorsqu'elle cause à l'autre partie un préjudice tel qu'elle la prive* ***substantiellement*** *de ce que celle-ci était en droit d'attendre du contrat, à moins que la partie en défaut n'ait pas prévu un tel résultat et qu'une personne raisonnable de même qualité placée dans la même situation ne l'aurait pas prévu non plus.*

Art. 25 Eine von einer Partei begangene Vertragsverletzung ist ***wesentlich****, wenn sie für die andere Partei solchen Nachteil zur Folge hat, dass ihr im* ***wesentlichen*** *entgeht, was sie nach dem Vertrag hätte erwarten dürfen, es sei denn, dass die vertragsbrüchige Partei diese Folge nicht vorausgesehen hat und eine vernünftige Person der gleichen Art diese Folge unter den gleichen Umständen auch nicht vorausgesehen hätte.*

In the above text, lexical units corresponding to the terms *fundamental* and *substantial* have been emphasized. It would be however vain to discuss here the possible differences among *fundamental, substantial* and eventually also *essential,* and favor one to the detriment of others. Loewe (1989: 11) argues that the choice of the terminological equivalents in Art. 25 does not influence its meaning, especially when compared with the German variety that uses one and the same word to render *fundamental* and *substantial,* namely (D) *wesentlich* and the Spanish translation that follows the French dichotomy of *essentielle* and *substantielle* by using accordingly (ESP) *esencial* and *substancialmente.* The sense of the translator's work is to render the meaning of the speech act concerning some circumstances of the breach of the contract. An intersection between sentence and utterance must be reflected, but the utterance remains the dominating force in the determination of the speech act (Stolze 2005: 125). Moreover, an isolated lexicological analysis would not help the translator, because the application of general terms upon a contract is a matter of interpretation. There, the difference may or may not matter, as the breach of the contract depends upon the circumstances of the case and not upon the preformulated meaning of a word in a specific language. The translator's task is to focus on the difference that may matter. As an example, it can be assumed that the difference between the English and the German versions where the party is perceived as being of male gender (*he* in the English text) or of female gender (D) *sie* in the German text) would not matter for the meaning of the legal speech act that constitutes the Art. 25 of the CISG. Legal speech acts manifest themselves in the application of linguistically determined legal norms. Only in the dynamic of the application process that – dependent on the legal-theoretical view may or may not include interpretation (cf. 3.6.2) – words acquire their proper meaning. Therefore, the possible differences among *fundamental, substantial* and *essential* become interesting when the terms are used. In the translation, when the terms are not confronted with facts that may constitute a breach of contract, i.e. while being idle, their use may be well founded. An idle speech act adopts its meaning according to the circumstances of the use that mark the limits of the legal translation and of the work the translator is able to achieve.

3.7.8 Intentionality in translation

In terms of pragmatics, legal translation can be therefore best characterized as a translation of a legal norm, a legal decision or a legal act with subsequent volitive consequences (Herbots 1987: 814). These legal constructs with volitive features are linguistically reflected in legal speech acts. And exactly these volitive features must be transferred from the legal source language into the legal target language. The volitive element is connected to intention, and intentionality in language is the essence of every speech act. The appropriate transformation of the source speech act into the target speech act is the pragmatic goal of the legal translation. Therefore, the principle of expressionability as developed in the speech act theory by J. Searle (Searle 1969: 68; 87 sq) is fundamental to the pragmatic view upon the translation of legal texts. Searle also posits that whatever can be mentally construed can be expressed with linguistic means. Extreme views mentioned above about the principal impossibility of translation are therefore inconsistent at least with pragmatic mechanisms. The same concerns philosophical experiments where a language intranslatable into English is imagined as well as 'translations' from Saturnian into Plutonian that cause problems to some eminent scholars in contexts different from ours (Davidson 2001: 186). In terms of the philosophy of language and linguistic pragmatics the problem of translatability appears as dominant (cf. Bartsch 2016, also Apter 2013). In this context, Clifford Ando (2005: 43) mentions that the legal idiom (LAT) *dari spondes? spondeo* was said to be untranslatable by Gaius in his *Institutiones* (3.93): *adeo propria civium Romanorum est, ut ne quidem in Graecum sermonem per interpretationem proprie transferri possit.* The ancient Romans had problems with the understanding of translation as an act of interpretation, although their own language includes the interrelated terms *interpretari, vertere,* and *transferre* (cf. Most 2003). Meanwhile, Gaius was also the first jurist to stress the pragmatic nature of 'obligatio' (cf. Texts and Commented Materials no. 10). In less sophisticated circumstances, when (FR) *je promets* can be translated into English with *I promise* it is possible only due to the existing common performance rules in both languages (cf. Searle 2004: 66–74).

Therefore, different languages can be perceived as realizations of linguistic conventions which in their diversity refer to one rule system, it is one of conventions (Searle 1969: 39–40). Forms of life in which rules of ordinary speech acts are rooted are no more diverse than are different legal systems expressed in legal speech acts. At the first sight, the above view could be perceived as contrary to the views expressed by W. Quine (1983) and R. Davidson (2001) about the indeterminacy of translation. However, it seems that the indeterminacy as developed by Quine in his *gavagai* example concerns rather the semantic and not the pragmatic perspective in language. Quine discussed in his almost anecdotal example the situation where a linguist tries to understand an indigenous pronouncing the word (*) *gavagai* and pointing in the direction of a running rabbit. Indeed, it is at first undetermined what this *gavagai* may mean. It could mean, *rabbit* or *rabbit is passing* or *let us hunt this rabbit* or whatever. As such, in this situation, it is undetermined and cannot be translated. However, the context which will be explored by the linguist and his observations of use of the word *gavagai* will sooner or later clear up the meaning of the expression which at first may seem hazy. Here again our broader concept of pragmatics helps overcome some theoretical problems which have been perceived by many as principal objections to translatability of texts, and especially legal texts. Legal texts may seem untranslatable in the sense of the *gavagai*-example provided by Quine but they become meaningful and translatable in the process of the identification of legal speech acts in them. These identified legal speech acts are subsequently translatable, and this is guaranteed by the principle of expressionability that is rooted in the functionability of speech acts in the cultural context that includes law. Equally, when Saturnian is translatable into English and Plutonian while Plutonian is not translatable into English (as supposed by Davidson 2001: 186) the Plutonian-English translation will become gradually possible in the process of the identification of speech acts in these languages. Were it not so, neither English nor Saturnian nor Plutonian could qualify for being counted among languages in equal degree.

3.7.8.1 Complexity of legal translation processes as networks of skills, strategies and tools

Despite all mentioned improvements, legal translation remains a professionally demanding task because it includes the necessity of strategic choices in an area where professional language is used. All too often it is still perceived as demanding mainly because it would require excellent knowledge of the translation languages that clearly is also the case. Uncompromisingly, therefore, also the legal translation theory requires from translators the most advanced level of proficiency in both translation languages. This requirement comes close to bilingual competence. Yet, bilingual competence is regularly of functional type; it is limited to certain circumstances of language use. Some models of legal translation rely therefore more realistically on continuous improvement and monitoring of translator's linguistic skills (Gortych 2009: 192). What is more, the skopos-theory enabled the first fundamental insight into every practical translation process: the (bilingual) translator is not simply changing words. Translating means making strategical choices about language use that are goal-oriented; translation is not a downright "derivative of language competence" (Prieto Ramos 2011: 18). Evidently, proficiency in at least two languages is a tacit prerequisite for becoming a translator. Yet, translation is a profession that goes beyond this formal and undeniably also fundamental practical condition. Translatorial competences include the language proficiency as main logical requirement, as well as other pragmatic and technical skills. Essential in terms of linguistic pragmatics are intercultural competence, thematic competence, and last but not least, translation service provision competence (Prieto Ramos 2011: 10) that enable the translator to cope with her task practically. Practically essential is also the awareness of auxiliary sources called sometimes "instrumental competence" or "information mining competence" (Prieto Ramos 2011: 13). It enables the translator to choose the appropriate sort of documents or tools that will facilitate the translation process. Translatorial practice is therefore best characterized as a process in which strategical decisions based on professional competences are made toward the background of solid yet always vulnerable translator's linguistic proficiency. In addition to the linguistic requirement, legal knowledge is indispensable in order to exercise this profession in a responsible manner. To cope with this problem some researchers proposed to introduce the element of systematic legal training into the model of legal-linguistic translation (Prieto Ramos 2011: 12). Structural complexity of legal texts, especially of international conventions and longer statutory texts such as codes, excludes the possibility of translation that would be based solely on translator's linguistic proficiency and basic legal knowledge. What remains to be developed nowadays in the general translation theory and in the theory of legal translation is the explicit model of hitherto implicitly followed particular translatorial strategies in relation to all types of translation tools. Translation strategies that have to be construed as singular yet intertwined steps in the translation process are grounded in the main skopos-relevant translatorial choice.

3.7.8.2 Newer translatorial strategies

Also translator's commitment to interpreted message may be counted among newer translatorial strategies. Interestingly and increasingly, especially in business interpretation cases, parties require interpreters' personal commitment to the message that is interpreted (Clegg, 2010). Traditionally, the interpreter has been a foreigner to the transaction negotiated by the parties as he was expected to preserve distance to both parties and the message. This distance is also stressed by working conditions, where interpreters sit in booths and may be even invisible to the parties that use their services. This may for some have the advantage to prevent that parties look at the interpreter instead of facing each other. Yet, distance and commitment to grammatical exactness of the target language text may not always be appreciated. Occasionally, interpreters' aloofness is made responsible for failures in contract negotiations (Clegg, 2010). Garbled communication is caused by the situation where "*there is none of the give and the take of chatting freely in your own language*" (Clegg, ib.). Increasingly, therefore, it is required that the interpreter joins the parties and works with them on the negotiation; of course, this technique is feasible only when the interpreter belongs to the entity where he interprets. This is the case when the interpreter's services are used in discussions among different subsidies of an international corporation, where the common language does not exist. Therefore, it seems important to brief the interpreter before a meeting about its essentials and goals. It is, however, also important to prepare parties to use the services of an interpreter and describe for them the intricacies of translated communication to which they would have to adapt. Historically, it has been perceived as an achievement by translators and interpreters that they are not responsible for the content of messages they interpret. These messages may include perjuries, slander, or offence of whatever sort. It may be that in changing communicative contexts the question of responsibility would have to be addressed again, although from a different point of view. In the context of sociology of translation one may also mention pragmatically relevant tasks that are performed by 'escort interpreters' or 'contact translators' (S *kontakttolkar*) who act as intermediaries on labor market, in hospitals and in social institutions and accompany their clients while fulfilling also other than purely linguistic tasks defined by client's interests (cf. also Nordbäck-Lindner 1972: 41–43).

3.7.9 Avoiding translation

Legal translation is a specific text type within translating and it can be compared with the literary translation; yet it remains independent of other text types in its essence (cf. Arsova-Nikolić 1999: 291). Therefore, it can also use techniques that are unusual for other types of translating. An innovative approach to the translation of legislative acts is the bilingual drafting, (FR) *corédaction bilingue* (Gémar 2004: 744) where the text is drafted in a parallel way in the respective language versions rather than translated from one version into another. The process of parallel drafting includes at least a reflection upon the linguistic versions in question which is close to that of a translator. Here, the transformation of the speech acts takes place earlier than in the ordinary speech acts of translation. The illocutionary act in the drafted texts must be identified properly in order to enable the bilingual legislative text to emerge in this process. The classical translator is doing exactly the same thing; she identifies the legal speech act of the source language and transforms it into a legal speech act in the target language. We can assume, as no precise research into this question is known, that the bilingual translator in reality identifies and qualifies speech acts more or less simultaneously with the process of their transformation. Otherwise, simultaneous interpretation would not work. The action undertaken by the interpreter is therefore identical; the time factor makes the difference. In the classical translation the professional steps are better discernible, but they are not qualitatively different. Therefore, the pragmatic approach to legal language is well adapted to cover these specific linguistic operations which may induce some translation studies specialists to ask the question whether the type of operation such as parallel drafting can be perceived as translation at all. Yet, it seems to be an efficient answer to the problem of legal translating. Therefore, an approach which integrates drafting and translating appears in the light of recent experience in legislative or administrative bodies concerned by this activity to be the best practice to follow. Also ZhaoYuhong (2008: 3, 24) stressed the necessity of bilingual drafting of the Chinese language versions of laws enacted in Hong Kong, mostly in order to avoid Anglicized Chinese and a Europeanized syntax in modern written Chinese.

Moreover, some formalized international terms such as the *Incoterms,* e.g. *FOB* or *CIF,* are usually not translated in the legal acts and documents (Mattila 2002b: 492). Likewise, names of institutions are frequently left in their original linguistic form and their origin is marked by an abbreviation, e.g. *The Korkein hallinto-oikeus (FIN) referred the following question to the Court of Justice for a preliminary ruling* or *The Överklagandenämnden för högskolan (S) referred...,* or *The Tribunale di Larino (IT) decided to stay proceedings ...*or *The Tribunal de grande instance de Nancy (FR) granted all of Céline SA applications....* These samples are also examples of a translating strategy that avoids the translating process or the translation of cumbersome terms. Doubtless, the informativity of the target text suffers under this innovative technique. Therefore, it might be preferable to engage in legal comparative studies instead of avoiding translation in such cases (cf. Mattila 2006: 264). Close to the above technique is the *constructive translation* (Stolze 2005: 238) in which the translator renders the meaning with her own words. This method is best suited for professional recipients because the knowledge of the constructive principles is necessary to understand correctly the product of the constructive translation. Otherwise, the risk of misunderstandings persists as to the shape of the original. I did not identify any constructive translation of statutes or court decisions. In turn, scholarly writings that pertain to the law are frequently translated with the help of this technique.

3.7.10 Prospects for legal translation

The existing findings of mostly terminology-oriented studies on the translation of legal texts have defined the essential problems in the legal translation as the linguistic equivalence and the legal qualification of legal notions. The linguistic equivalence can be achieved under the *skopos*-theory. The problem of the legal qualification (characterization) understood as the reinterpretation of mostly incompatible legal notions can be solved only by comparative law methods. More generally, however, legal translation grounds in legal interpretation and legal argumentation. Legal speech acts that form the legal discourse in one legal language are transformed there into equivalent legal speech acts of the target legal language. Difficulties in rendering legal speech acts in other legal languages lead to strategies of avoidance of translation or modified methods such as constructive translating. Likewise, the scope of debates surrounding the legal translation is characterized by an increasing amount of questions which relate to the technical language and its pragmatic aspects, especially the translation strategies. These are, in turn, elements of legal linguistics – which is indeed an evolving field of study for which the conditions and methods I try to clarify in these lectures. The conceptual convergence of two parent disciplines of legal linguistics may result in procedures that will facilitate the methodically sound translation of legal texts. Still, the classical legal translation remains a reliable legal-linguistic operation provided that its pragmatic prerequisites and its limits are taken into consideration.

In fact, recent developments in legal linguistics enable the repositioning of legal-linguistic research items within the spectrum of legal-linguistic concepts, operations and methods. The reassessment of legal translation is partly also a disillusionment. Translation is a transformation. Yet, unlike in its mathematical prototype, meaning is transferred in accordance with the interpretor's understanding and not absolutely because – at least in the light of pragmatic theories of translation – meaning cannot be transferred automatically without interference of a semiotic level of transfer that restructures the translated signs around the axis prefigured by the theoretical approach adapted by the translator.

Meanwhile, the emergence of global English diminishes the scope of applications of the theory of legal translation as speakers increasingly use global English in international commercial and other contacts. They use and develop this language spontaneously and their former English teachers would have been scared by the results that come about in these creative and uncontrolled transformative processes. Whatever the opinions of specialists of English might be, this group of speakers, and middle size enterprises are leading there, will not be interested in the services of professional legal translators and rather cope on their own as long as no particular problems emerge. Small or middle size enterprises will in negotiating and drafting commercial contracts between them tend to avoid linguistic intermediaries and come to terms without foreign help, mostly because of costs. It seems that the decline in numbers of legal translations corresponds to the advancement in theoretical knowledge about translation. Knowledge about legal translation nowadays is firm. Theoretically, we are not lost in translation any more. Meanwhile, in certain parts of the world possibilities to apply this knowledge practically diminish.

3.8 Other Legal-Linguistic Operations

Other legal-linguistic operations such as *justification*, *fact description* and *legal research* will be noted here in passing. The main reason for this spatial restriction is that there exist numerous other legal-linguistic operations in pure form or as mixtures of some others so that an exhaustive description of them is equally difficult as the description of all possible speech acts in a natural language. The focus on two selected samples should primarily enhance further research into this topic.

3.8.1 Justifying argumentation

Justification as a specific type of legal argumentation is used mostly in situations where professional views compete directly. There, status questions become relevant, especially in decisions where the professional quality of the opinion can be explicitly challenged. This is for instance the case in concurring and dissenting opinions in relation to the majority opinion. In the U.S. Supreme Court opinion *Medellín v. Texas* (552 U.S. 06–984, 2008) a concurring and a dissenting opinion were delivered. The concurring opinion begins with the words complimenting the dissent: *There is a great deal of wisdom in Justice Breyer's dissent* which places the whole following text in a close relationship to the dissent. This argumentative strategy stresses the intertextuality of the concurring opinion and builds up the distance to the majority opinion that it, nevertheless, finally endorses. Initially, the concurring judge signals support for the dissent with additional assertions constructed around *I agree, I also endorse, I think this case presents a closer question than the Court's opinion allows.* The following phrase *In the end, however, I am persuaded that...* reverses the argumentation to the detriment of the initially admiringly treated dissent. The dissent itself is even more pronounced in its respect or disrespect of the majority opinion and uses language that directly questions the professionalism in the criticized decision: "At best the Court is hunting the snark. At worst it erects legalistic hurdles that can threaten the application of provisions in many existing commercial and other treaties and make it more difficult to negotiate new ones." The majority opinion is more independent from the concurring opinion and the dissent in its argumentation that is primarily structured as a dialogue with arguments provided by the petitioner, a Mexican citizen sentenced to death for murder, e.g. *Medellín argues that..., Medellín first contends..., He argues that..., Medellín and his amici nonetheless contend that..., Further, Medellín frames his argument as though.., Rather, Medellín argues that..., What is more, on Medellín's view....* While developing a fictitious dialogue with the petitioner whom it also linguistically treats as the author of highly complex legal arguments due to the textual convention of drafting court opinions, the majority decision remains in a relation of explicit intertextuality to the concurring and the dissenting opinions through direct and frequent reference to them. It devotes a whole chapter (B) to the dissent and starts the justification of its own decision by quoting a convincing critical phrase from the dissent: "The dissent faults our analysis because it "looks for the wrong thing (explicit textual expression about self-execution) using the wrong standard (clarity) in the wrong place (the treaty language)." This strategy is surprising as it does not reflect the experience made in the classical rhetoric that discouraged the mentioning of critical quotes which may be perceived as particularly convincing by the reader. The *justification* is built around the most salient arguments provided in all three opinions which form one text that is understandable only when all three opinions are taken into consideration due to internal references in them. This textual feature makes of the *justification* a specific legal-linguistic operation. I should also mention that there exists a *justification sensu stricto* that has a slightly different background from the main type depicted here (cf. 3.3.5.3).

3.8.2 Describing facts

Fact description, which will be treated later on in the part of this book devoted to Literature and Law, is equally specific as it provides more than facts for the reader. In the above majority opinion the judges feel obliged to report the circumstances that led to petitioner's conviction to death. The description reads as follows:

> *Petitioner José Ernesto Medellín, a Mexican national, has lived in the United States since preschool. A member of the "Blacks and Whites" gang, Medellín was convicted of capital murder and sentenced to death in Texas for the gang rape and brutal murders on two Houston teenagers. On June 24, 1993, 14-year-old Jennifer Ertman and 16-year-old Elizabeth Pena were walking home when they encountered Medellín and several fellow gang members. Medellín attempted to engage Elizabeth in conversation. When she tried to run, petitioner threw her to the ground. Jennifer was grabbed by other gang members when she, in response to her friend's cries, ran back to help. The gang members raped both girls for over an hour. Then, to prevent their victims from identifying them, Medellín and his fellow gang members murdered the girls and discarded their bodies in a wooded area. Medellín was personally responsible for strangling at least one of the girls with her own shoelace. Medellín was arrested at approximately 4 a.m. on June 29, 1993. A few hours later, between 5:54 and 7:23 a.m., Medellín was given Miranda warnings; he then signed a written waver and gave a detailed written confession.*

The subjudicial case concerned the question whether a decision issued by the International Court of Justice in The Hague can be applied in the U.S. directly, i.e. whether it is self-executing in the U.S. as the supreme law of the land. This is rather a formal issue and, it is definitely not related to the crime committed by the petitioner that lies outside the purview of the court. The court is free in such a case to relate the background of the matter that concerns the petitioner without being obliged to quote all details. The majority chose a detailed referral to Medellín's crime in the opinion. By reference to particularities such as the time frame of Medellín's first interrogation that is irrelevant to the decision as such the Supreme Court marks its apparent distance and exactness in an effort to prove an unbiased, professional approach to the petitioner's case. The descriptive strategy adapted in the majority opinion tends toward creating an emotional atmosphere of repugnance toward Medellín whatever the legal question of his case may be. It is introduced into the majority opinion with the intention to show that the petitioner is a particularly abominable murderer and that his guilt was proven beyond doubt. Sympathy with the victims is expressed a.o. by reference to their age. In turn, Medellín's age is not indicated in the court decision on any of its 37 pages. (It is known from press reports that he was born in 1975; hence, while perpetrating the murder he was 18; he was executed on August 5, 2008 in Texas). After the description of the crime committed by the petitioner the court has most readers on its side. The readers wish the petitioner's request to be turned down whatever its content might be. Finally, the petitioner's request is indeed turned down by the court, unsurprisingly based on rather technical reasons. In the light of the above short analysis, the specific facts quoted by the court appear therefore as representing more than facts. Their nature will be elucidated later on.

3.8.3 Legal research

It goes without saying that the activity like the one exercised in this book is also a linguistic operation in law. All academic research, e.g. analyses of court opinions or legal provisions belong to it. Paradigms of this research change as changes the language used in them. These epistemic legal-linguistic transformations are best researched within the legal theory and the theory of legal sciences that focus on paradigmatic changes in legal sciences. Legal linguistics reflects linguistic attitudes in the paradigmatic change. It signals the change in language use that may be perceived as a beginning of a tendency toward paradigmatic change.

3.9 Legal-Linguistic Operations in Legal Discourse

3.9.1 Centrality of legal discourse

It has been mentioned already that legal-linguistic operations such as legal argumentation or legal translation do not exist in a vacuum. They form bigger textual units and can be adequately understood within the boundaries of these superimposed units, such as the *legal discourse.* The legal discourse is fundamental to legal linguistics because all legal-linguistic operations can be construed as contributions to it like bricks that are used for the construction of a house. Undeniably, most time and space has been spent here on the analysis of singular legal-linguistic operations. Their contribution to a higher organizational linguistic level has been until now only assumed. Finally, the legal discourse consists of different legal-linguistic operations as a house consists of bricks. Arguably, though, the higher unit of textual organization has its own ontology and also own rules which govern it. The legal discourse is not a simple amalgam of legal-linguistic operations as a house is not a heap of bricks. We used to live in houses and not in heaps of bricks piled upon another as we create and apply the law in legal discourses, and not in one or more particular legal-linguistic operations. Therefore, when talking about legal-linguistic operations in law we implicitly also kept in mind the legal discourse (cf. Galdia 2014: 395–460). All analyzed samples of legal-linguistic operations in this book are parts of such a discourse.

3.9.2 Notion of legal discourse

Etymologically, (LAT) *discursus* comes from *discurro*, i.e. to run or to running apart, e.g. *Nilus manu canalibus factis per totam discurrit Aegyptum* or *discursus militum.* Academic definitions of discourse are numerous (cf. Notes and Commented Materials no. 2). Definitions that can be found in the legal-linguistic scholarship are rather general. G. Cornu (2005: 207) develops the notion of the legal discourse in contrast with the legal vocabulary. For him, the legal discourse is the legal language in action – *Le discours juridique est, par opposition au vocabulaire juridique, l'autre versant du language du droit: c'est le language du droit en action* (Cornu, ibid.). He insists also on two different aspects of the legal discourse, the linguistic and the juridical and undertakes a first attempt to categorize it by identifying the legislative (FR *discours législatif*), the juridical (FR *discours juridictionnel*), the customary (FR *discours coutumier*) discourses as well as the corporeal expression in the discourse (Cornu 2005: 211). It is understandable that his research is based on a rather general concept of the juridical discourse because all judicial activity makes in one way or another part of it. This seems also to be the reason for the absence of the general notion of discourse in a standard legal-linguistic work such as H.E.S. Mattila's *Comparative Legal Linguistics* where it is mentioned solely in the cover text. This generality allows for different forms of classification of legal discourses as undertaken by G. Cornu (2005: 213–419). One may also adapt a more abstract notion of the legal discourse that would comprise the totality of the linguistic activity in law which seems to be compatible with Cornu's preliminary general definition (cf. Galdia 2014: 34). The flexibility of the notion of the general, not necessarily only legal discourse that has been construed in this way by Michel Foucault (1966: 102) and others has a further advantage. It allows a more specific conceptualization of the context to which frequent reference has been made here. Foucault employed it to characterize the transformation of primary texts into discourses which necessitate interpretation (Foucault 1966: 93). It is worth mentioning that also historically the discourse has been defined rather broadly, e.g. by Dionysius of Halicarnassus as an arrangement of words such disposed that they form a more complete meaning.

The general definition of discourse says at least that utterances must follow in an arrangement and cannot stand freely in the speech and that the discourse constitutes a larger unit of meaning called already by Dionysius, not unproblematically, complete meaning. Moreover, discourse provides information of different origin and quality. Therefore, it can be understood as a structured context (Baylon 1991: 222) that constitutes a part of the reality such that it creates the context or represents what the participants know already (Baylon 1991: 278; 280). It has also a practical component because it links closer what is said with what is done (Baylon 1991: 253). This specific feature is important within the modern conception of legal argumentation which should promote the rationality of discourse and avoid empty or intentionally false arguments that are employed solely in order to win and without any attention paid to the socially relevant subject matter within a legal question. Furthermore, discourse provides contextual rather than syntactic information (Baylon 1991: 276). This, in turn, favors the general concept rather than the classification of varieties because the discourse provides an unlimited number of vantage points that could be used for its classification. Cornu's analysis of the numerous possibilities to classify the legal discourses on two hundred pages illustrates best this problem.

3.9.3 Structure of legal discourse

Analyzing discourse has been described as a banal activity (Baylon 1991: 235). And, as a matter of fact, this unusual characterization holds true because we analyze discourses every day when reading our morning newspaper, listening to the radio or reading documents in the office. We need this ongoing analysis because the meaning of messages – especially those addressed to an undetermined circle of recipients – is not always immediately clear. Due to our linguistic competence we are able to identify communicative situations where we must hold on and think about the content of messages that we received. We do it in order to avoid misunderstandings. The whole process may be called interpretation of the discourse (cf. Baylon 1991: 235). This discourse can be understood and ambiguities in it can be clarified because it is structured. We distinguish *cohesion*, *coherence* and *relevance* as the most characteristic features of its internal organization (Baylon 1991: 236). These elements have a specific meaning in the legal discourse that is based on an institutional and professionally restricted argumentation. Hence, the legal discourse displays at least the following internal elements: *legal cohesion*, *legal coherence* and *legal relevance*. Legal cohesion concerns its textual form that is usually prescribed either by statutes or by the legal culture generally. For instance, legal discourses must take place in a specific form as trials or court decisions must be drafted in a professional manner and in accordance with pre-established textual patterns. Legal coherence concerns the way arguments are presented in the discourse. Sometimes, in legal texts, it is represented rather formalistically, as in D. O'Byrne v. Sanofi Pasteur (Notes and Commented Materials no. 64). Legal argumentation is efficient only because arguments are presented in a coherent way, i.e. that they are interrelated. Legal relevance refers to suppositions and implications that the interpreter of a legal discourse needs in order to be able to understand it. It means that arguments will be effective when they affect the subject matter as closely as possible and when they also take into consideration the knowledge of their recipients (Baylon 1991: 238). Meanwhile, the language of legal speech acts and legal discourses is definitely not neutral. Public space is filled with assertions that are part of the struggle for meaning. Without this prerequisite no legal discourse would ever be formed, as no need would be there to confront the public with issues without any relevance for citizenry at large. Not only that this language is not neutral, it is not rooted in essentially true convictions, as all convictions about ethical questions are discursive and constructive; there is no room for essentialism in law although its language all too often indicates the contrary.

3.9.4 Legal discourse and creativity

Legal discourse does not only represent or form the context in which legally relevant utterances are made (cf. Notes and Commented Materials no. 3). It is also the framework in which linguistic creativity takes place (Baylon 1991: 237). Next to its mentioned constitutive elements it has further conditions of being. It is limited by linguistic constraints, i.e. only issues that can be lexicalized in a grammatically correct way can be uttered in it and by the conditions of its resurgence in broader social and political contexts. They were analyzed from different perspectives by scholars such as M. Bakhtin, J. Habermas, R. Dworkin and other researchers mostly representing political sciences or sociology. These fundamental constraints have linguistically relevant consequences. First, the exigency of linguistic exactness and extreme correctness in drafting statutes or court opinions may lead to the reification of language. Reification is the most dangerous consequence for the users of language (Jackson 1985: 11) because language ceases to function as a means of effective and creative communication and becomes a rigid cast where pre-formulated utterances are repeated over and over without precise reference to their context (cf. Lindroos 2015). Second, the legal discourse is not simply formed on the street but in complex political and other professional structures that provide interpretive ingredients to its context. If this constraint is ignored, then law is not understood or applied properly because creativity in it is limited by the conditions of its constitution. The broader context of the resurgence of discursive practices is however not our main topic. While dealing with the legal discourse it is nevertheless necessary to remember that it is equally pre-conditioned and does not exist in a vacuum like the legal-linguistic operations that are our recurrent issue.

3.9.5 How does the legal discourse work?

It is easier to show the legal discourse as a linguistic action than to propose an exhaustive definition of it. Such an enterprise may help disambiguate and also possibly demystify the notion. To this aim one may use a court decision as a starting point, e.g. Goldstein v. SEC issued 2006 by the U.S. Court of Appeals for the District of Columbia Circuit (451 F.3d 873). In it, the D.C. Circuit invalidated the so-called Hedge Fund Rule and described it as an example of arbitrary rulemaking by the SEC. The main legal question in this litigation has been the notion of *client* of a hedge fund under the Investment Adviser Act of 1940. The petitioner Goldstein and the SEC have interpreted the notion differently. The background of the interpretive disagreement has been the section 3 of the mentioned act, which has been construed by many as allowing most hedge fund advisers to avoid registration with the SEC because in practice they had fewer than fifteen clients when *client* means limited partnership that invests money in a fund. The SEC's hedge fund rule of 2004 reinterpreted the notion of *client* in that it equated it with *investor*. This would have the consequence that most hedge fund advisers would have to register with the SEC before starting their activities. However, the court held that *client* for purposes of the fifteen-client rule of § 203(b) (3) means the investing limited partnership and not the individual partners. The decision has been commented in Harvard Law Review, vol. 120, pp. 1394–1401. The rationale of such a comment is the systematization of the decision within the structure of the American public law under its principles and precedents. The decision has been criticized in the comment as contrary to the American doctrine of administrative law that tends toward obliging courts to pay deference to administrative agencies' reasonable views (cf. 3.9.1). This follows, as mentioned here in the chapter on legal argumentation, from case law represented mainly by Chevron U.S.A., Inc. v. Natural Res. Def. Council, Inc. (467 U.S. 837, 844, 1984) of which the argumentatively crucial topic is characterized with the words: "We accord deference...because of a presumption that Congress, when it left ambiguity in a statute meant for the implementation by an agency,...desired the agency (rather than the courts) to possess whatever degree of discretion the ambiguity allows." The comment criticized the decision as being *improper under Chevron* (p. 1398), i.e. it systematized it under a particular classification of relevant precedents. These specific aspects of the internal structure of the American law are not reflected upon in the broader discourse about the decision, be it among professional fund advisers or in the broader public. Next to the internal perspective, the comment includes also a reflection of ethical consequences the decision might have: "More importantly, the court missed an opportunity to adapt its jurisprudence to a rulemaking context that may be unique to the financial sector, in which systemic risk is high and regulated parties face strong incentives – and have substantial power – to avoid regulation" (p. 1397) and, additionally: "The Amaranth debacle, occurring less than three months after the court handed down its opinion, illustrates the dangers that motivated the rule in the first place, and the need for a doctrine of administrative law that recognizes the importance of agency flexibility in meeting the goals that Congress has set" (p. 1401). In the comment, ethical arguments are never articulated in isolation from the systemic recurrences of the American law. Instead, they are tied to arguments related to the internal structure of the law, e.g. *deference, longstanding administrative law doctrine, Congress intent, eliminate abuse, permissible construction of a statute, fundamental purpose, policy standpoint,* etc., in order to stress that not only an emotional opinion about the court decision has been expressed. This strategy makes clear the attempt at gaining acceptance within the community of legal experts (judges, scholars, attorneys-at-law etc.) where a purely ethical evaluation of the decision might be perceived as non-professional. The decision has been also commented by the interested financial institutions and an emotive discussion on this issue can be easily traced in the internet. The professional discourse led to the proposal of a new rule 206(4)-8 that would lead to the initially envisaged aim. In turn, the emotive discourse within the professional community of investment advisers seems to have ended rather inconclusively. For instance, the rhetoric question *Goldstein: a hero or a fool?* has been raised there toward the background of a possible *'revenge'* the SEC would take on the whole branch of hedge funds managers for the lost litigation.

The above short case study illustrates the complexity of the legal discourse. The legal discourse takes place within the legal procedure in a court of law and the decision rendered by the court is binding. It includes smaller discourses concerning the interpretation of *client* where the parties bring arguments that may back their views. It includes furthermore the systematizing discourse within the academic community which must find a place for the court decision within the complex structure of the law and cope with a decision that is legally binding although it does not find any support from the professional commentator of the Harvard Law Review. The discourse outside the community of legal experts is egotistic rather than focused on the legal issue. It mainly concerns possible steps which could be and actually were taken by the SEC after the unfavorable court opinion has been rendered. This discourse did not address the general legal problems in the opinion because it is exclusively concerned about the outcome. As is so often the case, the discourse about law is divided between the professional legal community interested in the inner perspective of the law and the non-professional community interested in the results of litigation. It is unclear in how far the particular discourses are interrelated. Special research would be necessary to find out this circumstance. I tried to describe some of its parameters in my *Legal Discourses* (2014). In line with my findings in *Legal Discourses,* a socially productive legal discourse would be one that integrates both perspectives into a discourse that comprises the internal view on the law where only professional legal arguments matter and the external discourse that focuses on the repercussions that the legal decision may have in society. The legal discourse in Western societies seems to be still characterized by the mentioned dichotomy and argumentative selectivity.

3.9.5.1 Courtroom discourse analysis

Particularly complex are legal discourses held in courtrooms. Research on this subject is abundant. It shows the complexity of legal discourses in courtrooms where laypersons and especially jury's linguistic habits are confronted with professional legal language, in its oral and in its written form. Consequences that may be drawn from this research concern understandability and readability of law as well as law's efficiency as a mechanism of democratic society in general. Linguists' interest in the investigation of oral legal discourses seems to have been caused by the observation that language use in these discourses differs significantly from the daily language use. This fundamental finding concerns mostly courtroom discourses (cf. Hoffmann 1983, Ilie 1995, Xu 1998). Therefore, legal-linguistic discourse analysis comprises foremost courtroom discourse analysis yet also the analysis of other less formally structured legal discourses. It is clearly dominated by courtroom speech analysis, especially in the area of penal law. Law, however, is much more than a repressive mechanism of criminal prosecution. The struggle for law in society concerns, as a rule, other than criminal cases. Other areas of public and private law may be more significant to the development of discursive practices in societies. However, it could also be that in terms of their main structural features the non-criminal courtroom discourses do not differ particularly from the criminal courtroom discourses. At least, it seems that the most significant structural feature of language use is ubiquitous in all courtroom settings. Speakers, both professional and non-professional users of language in the legal context, do not speak in courts of law as they used to speak in daily non-professional life. This observation is based on the finding made by Gail Stygall (2012: 370) that *ordinary conversational turn-taking...disappears in a courtroom.* This means that speakers cannot simply converse during court proceedings; the accused and his judges cannot just speak with each other whenever they wish and express whatever desires or beliefs. Research stresses conversational turns that are characteristic of this type of discourse. Typical turns from trials that are familiar to most speakers are: *How does your client plead? – Not guilty, your honor* or *Objection, your honor. Calls for a conclusion. – Objection is overruled.* Such formulations as *Your Honor, if it please the court...* or *There will be order in this court or I'll have the gallery cleared* fascinate the public mainly due to their institutional anchorage that represents power in action. The order of speaking in courtrooms is strictly predetermined and the roles are hierarchical. These roles are played within discursive genres that are predefined in the court procedure. Stygall (2012: 371–380) identified following genres as prefigured in the American legislation: *pleas, pleadings, voir dire, opening statements, testimony,* and *closing arguments.* One interesting feature of the courtroom discourse is its interdependence relation with the written part of the legal discourse that is expressed in documents. All participants regularly refer in their speeches to written elements of the discourse. Classical courtroom speech analysis focused primarily on understandability in the courtroom discourse. In the course of more nuanced research, the issue of exercise of power through language use became increasingly important (Stygall 2012: 370). It seems furthermore that the most obtrusive element is not the legal vocabulary but the unusual turns that the oral courtroom discourse imposes upon lay participants. As a remedy for this discursive friction, Stygall (2012: 380) proposed to prepare laypersons better for the participation in courtroom discourses. One could, however, also think about the change of courtroom speech rules that could be more closely aligned with the general discourse of ordinary language. General aspects of participation in legal discourses have been also elucidated with sociological means. Greenhouse (2012: 69) asked whether American public opinion has an impact upon the decisions of the U.S. Supreme Court. Research that is available about this issue provides somehow ambiguous results. It is generally assumed that there is an influence from the public in particularly spectacular cases such as Roe v. Wade (410 U.S. 113, 1973). Mechanisms of incorporation of public opinion into Supreme Court's decision making processes remain however unclear. Interestingly, Justice William H. Rehnquist mentioned 1986 that "family and friends" rather than "the public at large" would influence judges' views (Greenhouse 2012: 71). Meanwhile, it seems also that the U.S. Supreme Court tries to align itself with the public moral (cf. Rosen 2013). Research available today allows the statement that public opinion has a role to play in the development of the legal discourse about U.S. Supreme Court's decisions.

3.10 Some Tentative Results of Retrospective View upon Law and its Language

3.10.1 What means creation in the legal language?

Generally, legal language emerges in legal discourses marked by different degrees of speciality depending on their participants. Discourses of lawyers differ in quality from discourses about law between lawyers and laypersons and from discourses about the law among laypersons. Professional skills of participants do not determine the complexity of the discourse. Laypersons may develop complicated argumentative structures as lawyers may remain tied to insipid *topoi* that are perceived in their community as particularly professional. Interpretive and argumentative legal speech acts are formed in these discourses. They focus on terminology of different kind; some terms are professional, others innovative or spontaneous. The process of emergence of these phenomena is the formation of the legal language. Legal-linguistic practices are value-laden, therefore the legal language changes. The main features of this transformation are *semantic change* and *lexical innovation.* More complex legal speech acts such as legal argumentation or legal interpretation undergo fewer changes as they are in their use less exposed to the evolution of social values. Creating legal language is therefore not creation of words. It is a discursive practice in which among other things also words emerge (cf. Galdia 2014).

3.10.2 Creation and interpretation in law

Creation of legal provisions and processes in which lawsuits are decided were less frequently analyzed in the research than were the interpretation of existing legal provisions and the impact legal decisions (precedents) have had on their actual interpretation. The idea that law should be written by trained legal scholars is not new and, in fact, many civil codes in Europe were construed and drafted by famous legal scholars (Gaudemet 2001: 369). To date, scholarly law (D *wissenschaftliches Recht*) which would provide statutes or rules for the legislator as competing projects that might convince him or not is not existent, although it is thinkable and even recommendable. Apart from these facts, in most countries guidelines for ministerial and parliamentary administrative bodies dealing with the drafting of legal provisions have been developed.

3.10.2.1 Legislative drafting and understandability

Creation of legislation is the most challenging task among legal activities mainly because jurists usually have only a limited role to play in the whole process which remains in its nature political. Democratic processes within the legislative follow their own rules that are remote from our subject that is related to language and law. The auxiliary role jurists play is much more demanding than the adjudication in which they can follow and apply professional rules which they master. Within the legislative process they play the role which other professions rarely accept. They are reduced to the role of advisers and secretaries who transform the wishes of their clients in words but they are also limited by these wishes. They are like physicians who observe their patients indulge in self-medication and in non-indicated treatment, but are unable to stop them. This state of affairs may surprise even more, because jurists will in future apply laws that were passed with, at best, their partial participation. What is more, statutes are regularly results of political compromises. Were jurists participating more actively in these processes, statutes could be formulated in a more professional way. The lack of professional standards about statute drafting, especially in the form of a generally studied and developed legal discipline, are visible in the problems of legislation. Statutes drafted according to administrative guidelines for ministries along the line of political instructions cannot fit harmoniously into the legal world occupied by jurists. Instead, they will constantly lead to problems in interpretation and application. Already in ancient Rome the opinion that jurists as professionals of law have a particular role to play in the development of law has been recognized. Attempts to relativize this view are not particularly convincing (cf. Gaudemet 2001: 11). Nothing prevents jurists to present to the interested or to the broad public drafts of legislation which may compete with others. Views on what is the best law *de lege ferenda* often prevailed in ancient Rome due to the high quality of the work done and not necessarily due to the position of the drafter in the hierarchy of governmental administration.

The linguistic aspect of the legislation is another problem. Nowadays drafts are regularly controlled with respect to their linguistic correctness. The legislator apparently understands this correctness in terms of grammatical and orthographic rules and, at best, in terms of readability. The form of judicial decisions has been perceived, especially within the judicial body, as particularly important. Legal decisions in many countries follow rigid, sometimes formalistic patterns (cf. Arntz 2002: 37). Sometimes even the use of a specific tense is regulated by internal guidelines of courts or through professional usage. Pragmatic aspects of legislation concern its acceptability among the persons concerned. Therefore, a scientifically founded practice of legislation should include mechanisms enabling it to increase acceptability of legislative acts among citizens. Thornton (1996: 47) characterizes the aims of legislative drafting as delimiting the law and communicating the law to society and in particular to persons affected by it. The communicative aspect in the legislative process has been an issue for the legal theory. Some legal theorists pretended that law is communicated to jurists, i.e. primarily to judges who are charged with its application. For instance, H. Kelsen (1991) differentiated between *direct* and *indirect addressees* of legal acts; J. Sager (1990: 102) argued in the context of understanding legal terminology that the knowledge base of producers and receivers in the specialized communication is presumed to be the same. Others insisted upon the rights of citizens to be communicated the law and added also recently the right to an understandable legislation (cf. Mattila 2006: 18). Meanwhile, both in the legal-theoretical and in the legal-linguistic literature the question has been raised as to the addressee of the legislative message. Answers to this question have been multiple: no one, every one, i.e. all citizens or all readers, judges etc (cf. Lizisowa 2017). Needless to stress that problems connected to *understandability of law* depend on the *recipient issue*. Jurists, judges or attorneys-at-law alike, will obviously have less problems with the understanding of legislative acts than citizens without legal training. Jurists will doubtless have other problems with the understanding of law; yet these problems are anchored in the specifics of their profession and not in the understandability of the text as a linguistic entity produced in a natural language. In a modern democratic society the idea of law that is written in specialists' language and directed to specialists is not appealing any more. Jurists are among the addressees of legislative acts and may have a special role to play in their application; they are however not the exclusive target group of the legislative intent any more. The acceptability of law among the citizenry would be jeopardized would this citizenry be excluded from the circle of addressees, i.e. potential readers of legislative acts. Over long, the idea of expressing law in ordinary language that has been occasionally mentioned in this book (c.f. 2.2.4) may be perceived as a practicable solution to problems discussed today under the topics of *understandability* or *readability* of legislative acts (cf. Galdia 2014).

Meanwhile, inexplicitness is a preferred tool of the legislator in forming politically delicate provisions. Art. 49 of the French Constitution from 1958 stipulates: (FR) *Le Premier Ministre, après délibération du Conseil des Ministres, engage devant l'Assemblée Nationale la responsabilité du Gouvernement sur son programme ou éven-*

tuellement sur une déclaration de politique générale. The enigmatic (FR) *engage...la responsabilité du Gouvernement* means that the Prime Minister seeks the vote of confidence that may cause the dissolution of the government and that is as such not mentioned in the text (cf. Carcassonne 2005: 235). The same formulation is repeated in Art. 49 (3) with equal dose of inexplicitness: *Le Premier Ministre peut, après délibération du Conseil des Ministres, engager la responsabilité du Gouvernement devant l'Assemblée Nationale sur le vote d'un texte.* Here, the 'vote of a text' means the vote of a bill that otherwise would not be approved by the Parliament. Thus, the more intricate the situation is in political terms, the more mysterious becomes the wording of Art. 49. This state of affairs seems to be a regularity in processes of drafting statutory provisions. Toward the background of such experience with legal textuality the calls for the use of the plain language in legislation, which frequently come from governments, may wear thin.

3.10.2.2 Recipients' reliance and textual reception

Problems concerning the reception of legal texts have been traditionally avoided in the research as emotionally loaded. Instead, most researchers concentrated on the creation of legislative acts. Lawyers developed theories about legislation and linguists contributed to them their observations on readability and understandability of statutory texts and materials related to them. Jurists concentrated on the sender's perspective of the traditional communicative model, i.e. the perspective of the legislator, linguists partly shared this approach, yet they broadened it by the recipient's perspective. The issues of acceptability of legislative texts by their readers have been added, probably under influence of sociological and linguistic theories of communication. Pragmatically, one would have to assume that the legislative text has at least one addressee, namely the judge. Next to the approaches based on the traditional model of linguistic communication that oscillates around the speaker, the hearer and the message transferred as well as the conditions of the physical act of transmission, a broader model, that might include textological facets of legal texts might be instrumental. In such an approach, the reliance of the person concerned upon the message transferred in the legal text (statutory regulation or judgment) would be central. For instance, it is known that generally citizens' reliance upon the constitutional texts is limited (Galdia 2014: 306). This attitude displays the theoretical distinction between the constitutional textuality and the constitutional reality, stressed in traditional constitutional law. The crisis of constitutionalism and constitutions (cf. Galdia 2014: 308) has its roots in this dichotomy. It means that future law would have to overcome this dichotomy or abandon the constitution as a text genre in law altogether.

Reliance upon court decisions is connected to credibility. Judgments can be read toward the background of their textual credibility. The Canadian decision Regina v. Jackson (2007) (Notes and Commented Materials no. 63) is an example of a decision that at least on its face may not convince readers. Credibility does not primarily concern the knowledge of law but the way in which the majority decision is linguistically justified in the court opinion. The decision whether the accused has been guilty or not is based on cumulative evidence: "the accused's conviction does not rest merely on his presence at the scene...(but) on the cumulative effect of his apprehension at the scene, the rejection of his explanation for being there, the particular nature of his offence, the context in which it was committed, and other circumstantial evidence of his guilt." The court dresses its opinion in legal phrasemes (*cumulative effect of his apprehension at the scene*) and generalizations (*particular nature of his offence*) that facilitate writing. Meanwhile, they also weaken the persuasive effect of the decision as far as evidence is concerned. Further, the court uses metaphoric language: "the accused's prolonged and unexplained presence on the marijuana plantation was a cornerstone of the Crown's case against him, but not its entire evidentiary edifice." The metaphor is problematic in the context of fact finding because the accused explained his prolonged presence, yet the court found his explanation incredible. Finally, the majority decision fails the test of credibility because it does not engage in linguistically founded description of facts and their linguistic evaluation. This result does not mean that the accused must have been necessarily innocent, yet the evidence of his guilt is linguistically poorly rendered in the decision.

3.10.3 Discursive parameters

This general retrospection allows us also to sketch parts of the development of the legal language. It concerns legal concepts in legal arguments, i.e. the legal terminology that is discourse-dependent. Concepts facilitate the argumentation and are more visible than complex speech acts. Therefore, they also draw most attention to themselves. This circumstance led in the past to excessive focusing on concepts in legal sciences and in emerging legal-linguistic deliberations. The Roman law provides the best source of materials for researching the emergence of concepts. Let us return to some of them and deal with their discursive parameters. For instance, the creation of the concept of *person* has been fundamental to the development of law. It enabled to create and to center subjective rights and duties around the bearer of these rights and duties. These *rights* are a creation that makes legal operations in law necessary; as *rights* have an abstract content and can be construed differently only the legal discourse can provide a solution that, however, will not satisfy everyone (cf. Koskenniemi 1999: 99). The concept of *person* had been specified through the creation of *legal* or *juridical persons* and distinguished from *natural persons.* The creation of an artificial *person,* i.e. the *legal* person, has been admired by lawyers and by non-specialists as an impressive conceptual construction which enabled to maintain legal systems operational in complex societies. Ladjili-Mouchette (1990: 454) refers to J. Gaudemet who argued that the term *legal person* had been coined upon *universtitas.* It seems, however, that the creation of the general concept of *person* which had been provided subjectivity had been the most challenging step in the creation of the original legal language and its structure, i.e. the network of legal concepts. In the legal language *person* means that it can be a bearer of rights and duties independently of the community (social group, corporation) to which it more or less voluntarily belongs. The creation of the concept of *legal person* as a separate legal entity depends – as always in law – upon its acceptance by the legislator. He is the formal creator of legal concepts in law, even if the concept as such is created by a specified author who might under more favorable circumstances claim an intellectual property right for his creation. The creation of the corresponding *object* of rights and duties which subsequently materialized in multiple forms had been its rather evident follow-up. The object can be a contract, a property right or forbearance. The *object* is therefore a corresponding, secondary creation in the conceptual network. *Contractual* legal language oscillates between the formation of the promise and its enforcement. The problem of contract enforcement emerges mostly when one party entirely or partly denies the relevant circumstances described by the other party. For this, the general linguistic scheme of a contract composed of *offer* and *acceptance* provides a first remedy. When one party offered something to the other party and the other party accepted it, it is already very probable that the parties have concluded a contract. Other elements of a valid contract such as *consideration* in common law countries, the capacity of the parties and the legality of the contractual transaction follow suit. Jurists used to say that in order to have an agreement the minds of the parties must meet. With this formulation the jurists achieve a description of an agreement which could not be better expressed even by most prominent pragmatists. Also, as a matter of fact, in order to agree both parties must mean exactly the same. First of all, the parties must have the intention to create legal relations. This is a fundamental pragmatic requirement for a contract which is a legal institute. The interlocutors cannot simply chat just about whatever subject or make situational jokes; both must know that they engaged in contract negotiations which may result in reciprocal rights and obligations. They must be aware of the fact that they negotiate in a situation in which customarily binding agreements come about. The validity requirement however would not be realistic would it concern all circumstances of offer and acceptance. It is not particularly probable that two interlocutors agree about absolutely everything in a discourse even if they manifest agreement and are subjectively convinced to agree with each other. The legally relevant part of these circumstances is therefore limited in law to the *essentialia negotii*, i.e. to those topics without which a contract cannot be identified as such.

The linguistic formulation of basic concepts in the law of contracts serves this goal. It goes even further and provides tests and remedies for the situation when the minds of the parties did not meet or did not meet entirely. A mistake can happen, and can under certain circumstances be invoked by one of the parties. Some terms of the contract are express, they are explicitly mentioned by the parties while others are implied and must be reconstructed when judicial enforcement is required by one of the parties. Formalities imposed upon the parties by the legislator and the precedents facilitate the enforcement of the contract. They make the contract visible to others and make testing parties' intentions more reliable. Furthermore, *torts* are a linguistic creation connected to compensation for losses. Only an action which is perceived as a tort can lead to monetary compensation. In the common law a set of intentional torts like *battery, assault, trespass* or *infliction of mental distress* were created to characterize the wrongful action. In the civil law a unified type of (FR) *délit* fulfills this function. This type refers to certain typical situations for which monetary compensation has been provided. Later on, *negligence* and *unintentional torts* were added to the existing types. They covered situations in which a duty of care has been violated so that a damage occurred which was caused involuntarily. A particular problem here is the causation. It is important for us because it could be that this is not a linguistic problem. This would be the case when causation would not be primarily determined by linguistic means but by other extra-linguistic methods. It seems however that negligence like causation is – at least in law – a linguistic construct (cf. Palsgraf v. Long Island Railroad in Notes and Commented Materials no. 53). It is based on certain formulations and texts which – when compared – allow the judge to say that a party *acted negligently* or that it *caused damage*. *Strict liability* goes even a step further and imposes liability with the help of a linguistic formulation without any intent to harm because it creates liability without fault. Still further, *property* law attributes and protects property. It establishes with linguistic means the protected objects, such as the *intellectual property rights*. Property is equally defined in rights, not in goods (cf. Koskenniemi 1999: 91). It is conceptually more stable than other branches of private law due to conservative relations of ownership that rule in the Western society.

The multitude of rights and duties related to *objects* and focused in a *person* has been formalized in *procedural rules*. Procedural rules are linguistic programs in which rights of legal subjects (persons) toward objects are exercised. They include organizational rules as well as *claims* and *defenses* with which the parties act within the procedure. Procedure in law is based upon the rule that equal situations should be processed in an equal way in courts of law. In legal discourses, procedure links concepts with argumentation. The legal doctrine established *sources of law* which it perceives as indicators of legal validity of rules grounded in them. It means that a rule established upon reference to a source of law has a bigger chance to be approved in a court of law as a rule stating the law than one which cannot be based on an acknowledged source of law. For the U.S., the sources of law are: the U.S. Constitution, state constitutions, federal and state statutes, ordinances, administrative agency rules and regulations, executive orders, and judicial decisions by federal and state courts. In France, international treaties, the constitution, laws, and (FR) *règlements* are generally accepted by the doctrine as sources of French law. Other possible sources, such as usages or general principles of law or legal decisions are subject to controversies as to their status as sources of French law. Overall, through establishing a source of law the legal doctrine endorses it as a text with legal force. It creates a specific category of texts which are 'more legal' than others because they are sanctioned by the doctrine with specific functions which are, first of all, to state the law of the country better than other possible sources. In terms of legal linguistics this operation of the doctrine means that certain texts are declared as belonging doubtlessly to the type of legal texts while others are subjected to discussion. The process in which this determination takes place is institutionalized (Galdia 2014). At any rate, it would be difficult to postulate that a text perceived by the doctrine as a source of law is not a legal text. However, the scientific dispute about the quality of court decisions as sources of law in various non-common law countries shows that the institutionalized procedure for determining what is a legal text has its limits and may be challenged. Wherever language use is not analyzed in its entirety and selective procedures are preferred instead, conflicts about the quality and acceptability of results will emerge. – When the legislator or the doctrine call a cat "a dog" there will emerge problems with the acceptability of the result and additional argumentation will be needed to balance the lack of credibility caused by such a procedure. – The dispute about the quality of legal decisions as the source of law in several countries is an illustrative example of a shortcoming described in terms of linguistic pragmatics. From this perspective it appears advisable to adopt as sources of law all linguistic sources used for the formulation of a legal rule. It is possible and even beneficial to introduce a hierarchy of legal sources which prevents conflicts in case when conflicting results would emerge from different legal sources. However, the selective process of artificially terming some documents legal sources and denying this quality to others is at least from the perspective of pragmatic legal linguistics not justified (cf. 2.3.5).

I have canvassed above some characteristic discursive parameters used in law and the prerequisites of their use. A fully-fledged legal linguistics would comprise a broad catalogue of such elements as part of the general grammar of law.

Part 4: Textuality of Law or Literature and Law

In the preceding analysis of the linguistic operations in law we found out that textuality is one of the most specific features of law. It is also the conditio sine qua non of literature. In both, stories and narratives about concrete and abstract issues are composed and developed. In the following chapter I will therefore ask whether legal linguistics can learn from literary criticism and literature that is rooted in fictitious worlds. The most challenging question in this respect could be therefore reduced to the formulation: are novel writers pursuing a creative activity unlike judges who apply law and nothing more than that? When namely both the writer and the judge are equally creative, then legal linguistics is of primordial importance for the legal sciences. Are only writers creative? If so, then the legal linguist would have to satisfy his ambitions with being occasionally mentioned in footnotes. Furthermore, the question as to which types of texts function best in law appears essential to legal linguistics. Legal linguists must be aware of the textual potentiality of law in order to be able to advise jurists on best possible ways to compose legal texts such as constitutions, legal codes and legal commentaries. Narrativity in law is therefore primarily not centered upon the regulation, i.e. the question of what is allowed or what is prohibited. Instead, it concerns mainly the narrative form that regulation obtains in legal-linguistic operations and especially in the creation of law with linguistic means. While studying the following paragraphs it is therefore worthwhile to keep in mind the main objective of the legal-linguistic interest in the narrativity of law.

4.1 Writing and Reading in Law and Elsewhere

4.1.1 Resemblances and differences

In this chapter of our study we will be dealing with aspects common to law and to literature as well as with issues which clearly distinguish the one from the other. This initial statement is made here without further proof for the fundamental resemblances and differences between both phenomena because indices are there which strengthen the impression that law is not only literature as literature cannot be approached like law. On the other side, amazing analogies were discovered between fictitious literary texts and legal non-fictitious texts (cf. Ward 1995: 3). With literature I mean here mainly *fiction* but I am ready to accept other *narrative forms* like reports or news, which refer to social reality. They use a specific form for the purposes of narration which is not a simple reference to the discourse of ordinary language. Partly, we could even perceive scholarly legal research as narrative as well. I have also reversed the traditional order of topics in the heading of this chapter. And there are good reasons for this. We will namely be looking for forms in legal texts which resemble fiction and we will have to do it from the point of view of literary theory. At this stage we would not be able to proceed differently because no classification of legal texts due to their literary aspects exists to-date. My approach differs slightly from the widespread tendency in Law and Literature to look into how certain novelists, e.g. Franz Kafka or Fyodor Dostoyevsky, dealt with legal issues in their works. Within this approach, even literature for children has been analyzed in terms of its legal-ideological anchorage (cf. Ward 1995: 90–118) I do not oppose this tendency as such. Substantial knowledge about law can be reached with the help of such comparative analyses. However, for the specific reasons of my approach I have to adopt a different perspective. I will look mainly at legal texts and ask whether they could be read as literary texts. The answer seems to be obvious. One could pretend that we can read whatever texts as literary and abstain from reflecting upon their foundations in their subject matters. Yet, our experience shows also that we do not read legal texts in the way we used to read literary texts. The reader adopts a specific perspective upon legal texts and distinguishes literary/fictitious texts from non-fiction in legal texts. The reader seems to know or even to have internalized the appropriate approach to every type of text. He is able to identify a text as literary, i.e. fictitious and construe it accordingly. Similarly, he reads a court decision in a way which does not resemble his reception of fictitious texts. And indeed, *facts* claim to be true and not merely credible, *events* in novels do not (cf. Jackson 1988: 246) and the reader seems to identify this distinction almost automatically. Sincerity is not assumed in literature (Baylon 1991: 238), while in law it is. In this extra-textual criterion may lay the reason for the different perspectives readers adopt toward literary and legal texts. The distinction between facts and events makes sense for me and in the following paragraphs I will not try to establish that facts are as fictitious as events might be and pretend that no borderline between both could be proven convincingly. With John Searle (1999: 32) I believe that facts exist in reality and I will therefore reflect upon the specific nature of social facts which jurists mostly used to deal with. However, language use in dealing with facts will dominate our deliberations because I try to find out in what relation facts or events stand to the final narrative product and how language contributes to it. I mentioned already the fundamental role that language plays in shaping our view upon reality, i.e. mainly upon our view of natural and social facts. Both sorts of facts could not be expressed without language, be it only the formal language of mathematics. Our perception of facts clearly depends upon the language used in their *description*. This description is in a very specific way also their *creation*, at least in many cases. And exactly these cases are the most interesting for jurists. Yet, in the paragraphs which will follow I cannot reflect upon all the approaches and ideas which emerged in the past debate about Law and Literature. I may remind that I have committed myself to a specific perspective upon language and law, i.e. to the pragmatic approach. I will try to show that language and law seen in the pragmatic perspective not only reflect past debates, but also serve to pave the way toward an understanding of the subject which reflects the textuality of both. In spite of or rather due to my linguistic perspective I will show that law even when viewed from the linguistic perspective remains a social phenomenon and that it therefore cannot be separated from the society in which it is growing.

4.1.2 Rules in texts

Indeed, the unique feature of law is its *textuality*. Laws nowadays rarely exist in a non-written form. In the Western legal tradition the written judicial decisions usually must be provided a written justification. And, this textual requirement determines our perspective upon law. Legal texts must be created along specified rules, otherwise they would not be perceived as legal. For us it is crucial to observe that both law and language are rule-oriented. A speaker can understand a sentence he has never heard before only due to the linguistic rules he masters. Likewise, we understand the law only because we master rules which enable us to identify and to apply it. We insist here on textuality as characteristic of the modern law, although social sciences may add to it many other features pertaining mostly to power structures in state and society. Nevertheless, wherever law is applied, it is also invoked and determined in its textual form. If the textual form is missing, then we usually have to do with the enforcement of the legal decision that belongs to the context of law or an action with relation to law that itself is not part of it, such as the non-verbal perpetration of a crime. What is more, law may create with texts linguistic and political entities as well as legal notions. For instance, the (English) Treaty of Union from 1706 states in its Art. I: *That the two kingdoms of England and Scotland shall be united in the kingdom by the name Great Britain.* Occasionally, additional criteria are needed to figure out whether a textual sample is creative in terms of law. For instance, in the absence of a written constitution in England it may sometimes be difficult to determine whether a particular text belongs to the constitutional law, i.e. whether it forms the corpus of legal constitutional acts of England (cf. Barnett 1999: 19 and Notes and Commented Materials no. 31 for the Act abolishing the State of Prussia). Doubtless, also the legal argumentation grounds in textuality. Prefigurations such as procedural concepts, e.g. *summary judgment, default judgment, demurrer* or *judgment notwithstanding the verdict* determine the argumentation which is applied in them. Interestingly, *summary judgment* may be used beyond legal contexts, as in Todorov (1992): "Thus, by gradual stages, Columbus will shift from assimilationism, which implied an equality of principle, to an ideology of enslavement, and hence to the assertion of the Indian's inferiority. We could already guess this from several **summary judgments** appearing in the first contacts. "They would make good and industrious servants" (11/10/1492). "They are fit to be ruled" (16/12/1492)." The summary judgment is construed in Todorov's text (emphasis is mine) as a very general judgment, unlike the legal term that concerns decisions where there is no open issue concerning material facts and only the applicable law matters. Legal argumentation develops around the inherent structural elements of those concepts. This seems to be an appendix to Toulmin's model of argumentation that concentrates upon other aspects of the argumentative speech act. Meanwhile, all these conceptual prefigurations of argumentation are texts that are operative in law.

4.1.3 Reading texts and applying rules

As said, textuality is the largest common denominator which can be found for literature and law. There exist of course numerous logical or semiotical common features of both areas such as signification processes (Jackson 1985: 13), but they also manifest themselves primarily or secondarily in written or oral texts. Textuality is an extremely reliable criterion for both law and literature. Meanwhile, although law frequently functions through the spoken word and literature is sometimes read aloud, their only uncontested form is the written one. All other forms of their existence including meaning varieties can be questioned and regularly oral texts, which C. Geertz (1983) called 'acted documents' pass unnoticed in the processes of the application of law. This does not mean that the written textual form would be dominant in the signification processes or in the application of law. Rather the contrary seems to be the case. Nevertheless, the written textual form is useful as a point of departure for all comparative approaches to literature and to law due to its unconcealed materiality. The written text is immediately traceable, although meaning is distilled from it after time-consuming analyzing and testing. The textuality as a fundamental feature is also an intermediate phenomenon. In law, our main problem with textuality is that it seems to be pragmatically uninteresting. Lawyers do not apply *texts* on cases; they apply legal *rules* which are developed on the basis of legal texts. These rules have doubtlessly also a written textual form, but they are applied as rules and according to the structure of rules and not of texts. Textuality lacks the dynamic force which drives pragmatics and all other operations undertaken under its auspices. It is pragmatically mostly perceptible in intertextual contexts which will be demonstrated later on examples. However, the textuality of rules has a pragmatic component that is the text of the rule stated as a part of a speech act which constitutes it. This may appear not to be much, because it comprises only the material formulation of the legal speech act, the locutionary act. Yet, the material formulation is not without importance due to the limitations to which legal texts are exposed and to the institutional limits of their application.

4.1.4 Complexity of literary texts

Complexity, which for us comprises the information load of a text, is definitely not a characteristic feature of legal texts. Generally, also all scientific texts are perceived as complex. The problem is to find the right example for simple texts. This task is difficult to achieve as daily spoken or written texts beginning with conversations and news reporting manifest intricacies which were rather late discovered by the researchers. It seems that no simple-structured text type exists, but that texts under specific circumstances can be simpler or more complex. Thus, the legal text is not by definition complex and the daily conversational text by definition simple. Generally, there are simple and complex legal texts as there are simple and complex conversational texts. The same can be posited in relation to literary texts. In fact, the material formulation of the legal texts, the thoughts expressed in them can be formally determined (Laurén 2002: 18). For instance, two texts of which one belonged to the area of electrical engineering and the other to legal writings were transformed into lines of x-signes and compared in Laurén's mentioned research. The design of the legal text, its long paragraphs, complicated syntax and advanced layering were easily discernible in this form. The contrastive approach showed that thoughts expressed in them are formulated differently in the process of lexicalization. In the legal texts the form reflects the specific legal argumentation (Laurén 2002: 19). This argumentation and its form are not accidental. Therefore, Laurén reflects upon the Roman law and Latin's specific influence upon the syntax of the contemporary legal language. The specific form of the legal text allows Laurén to talk about its *iconism*, i.e. that signs used resemble the represented object, the law (Laurén 2002: 16). However, also this specific form may be dynamic and vary according to the circumstances of language use. It can also be expressed with other terms according to linguistic strategies adopted for the creation of legal texts. In the literary fiction the situation is analogous. There too, the form can be represented as a model and is due to the specifics of the epoch or the writer's personal style that is also discernible from his other texts. For instance, Raskolnikov in *Crime and Punishment* makes a final statement definite in terms of law while declaring: "I then robbed and murdered the old lady and her sister Lizaveta with an axe." The urge toward legal explicitness may have been caused by the fact that Raskolnikov studied law. It may also be illustrative of a linguistic practice that binds him on its legal-textual standards in a situation as extreme as the above. Dostoyevsky formulated Raskolnikov's statement explicitly as he apparently connected it to the idea of repentance that might have subliminally developed in Raskolnikov's conscience. It is striking that he seems to have been compelled to use legal language to mark this nuance.

4.1.5 Written legal texts

The particular iconic form demonstrates the interrelation between the object and the signs representing it. And we can assume that texts generally display this feature. However, the mere belonging to one of customarily established technical or legal categories does not establish their pragmatic difference, i.e. the different circumstances of their use. Technical texts like legal texts can and certainly also do establish rules for the application of specific procedures. And, both texts are used as a source of information. Novels as well are used in this sense; the information provided in them is applicable in the socially relevant practice. The influence that literary fiction has had on social life proves this specific features of texts.

I have adopted a rather broad working definition of a legal text which for me, at least at this stage, includes all utterances oral or written which are relevant in the legal context. As far as narrative forms are concerned, especially the written form is interesting in a contrastive approach because it is characteristic of advanced literary texts. The question how oral narrative forms may be contrasted or made instrumental in law would also be interesting. I assume that their complex structure would substantially differ from the written structure of contemporary legal texts (cf. Galdia 2014: 266–268). Additional research would be needed to clarify this question. I will illustrate the problem with the help of an example. A written legal text, for instance a court decision, may read:

> *Petitioner Edmondson sued respondent Leesville Concrete Co. in the District Court, alleging that Leesville's negligence had caused him personal injury. During* ***voir dire,*** *Leesville used two of its three* ***peremptory*** *challenges authorized by statute to remove black persons from the prospective jury. Citing Batson v. Kentucky, 476 U.S. 79, Edmondson, who is black, requested that the court require Leesville to* ***articulate a race-neutral explanation for the peremptory strikes****. The court refused on the ground that Batson does not apply in civil proceedings, and the empanelled jury which consisted of 11 white persons and 1 black, rendered a verdict unfavourable to Edmondson. The Court of Appeals affirmed, holding that a private litigant in a civil case can exercise* ***peremptory*** *challenges without accountability for alleged racial classification.* (cf. Edmondson v. Leesville Concret Co. 500 U.S. 614, 1991)

Emphasis has been supplied to the text to mark parts of it which a layperson may not understand. A layperson should be able to infer from the above fragment of the case syllabus that the respondent attempted at eliminating black persons from the jury and that the petitioner ultimately lost his case. Probably, the layperson will not understand the procedural questions related to the peremptory challenges, which make it clear for the lawyer why exactly the court refused petitioner's request during the voir dire. The layperson should be furthermore capable to understand that Batson is a precedent decided by the U.S. Supreme Court and that in the view of the deciding court it does not apply to civil proceedings like the one in question. Furthermore, we may assume that not only legal notions such as *voir dire* or *peremptory challenges* may not be understandable to a non-lawyer but also formulations like *to articulate a race-neutral explanation for the peremptory strikes* or the holding of the Court of Appeals. The layperson will furthermore not know what has exactly happened to the petitioner as the syllabus informs only that he suffered personal injury. What does this understanding mean in terms of literature? First of all, it shows a parallel because literary texts are 'incomplete' in the sense that they do not include the information some readers would like to obtain. They are, however, complete in the sense of the authorial intention. They are as they are, hermetically delimited and fenced off against intruding questions. For such texts no extra-contextual information can exist. The same concerns in our example the inquiry into the injuries suffered by the petitioner. They are not part of the information provided in the case neither are they a part of the legally relevant context of the case. It does not matter what really happened to petitioner because this is not the issue in question. The issue of the case are the peremptory challenges. Of course, the interested reader could inquire into the factual background of the case and find out the sort of injuries allegedly caused by the respondent and by so doing fill the alleged gaps in the text (cf. regarding the so-called gaps in literary texts Juhl 1986: 198; Rimmon-Kenan 1989: 128). Beginning law students sometimes act in this way and attempt to fill the alleged informational gaps and by overstretching their inquisitorial skills unwillingly manifest that they do not understand the legal issue of the case, here notably the peremptory challenges.

In terms of a literary narrative one could say that those inquisitive readers do not understand what the text is about. No difference exists between the syllabus formulation regarding the injuries and a literary text in which the information about the profession of a protagonist is missing. In both cases, the text does not deal with this sort of information and it does not matter that in the legal text the information could be discovered and in the literary text it is not the case. One could however imagine a situation in which the author of a literary text would be asked about the profession of his protagonist, which was not indicated in the text and which he nevertheless imagined while writing his text and about which he would wilfully inform the enquiring reader. But, this information would be extra-contextual as well. Would the author not be alive any more or be unwilling to provide the answer, the situation would be comparable to the practical impossibility to find out factual information, for instance in the internet. It remains the situation in which the writer did not imagine any profession for his protagonist and willingly informs the reader about it, but this case is quintessentially extra-contextual. Insofar, we did not discover any difference between the legal and the literary text in terms of their structure, although we might have caused the impression to have traced at least one.

4.1.6 How are good legal texts written?

As said, legal texts are – like good literary texts – written according to established criteria for exemplary legal texts. They have to follow their constitutive linguistic rules. In law, these rules are less transparent than in literature because criticism of legal texts is less developed than is literary criticism. Yet, professionals dealing daily with legal texts could easily establish a set of criteria based on textuality and intertextuality as well as compositional standards developed for legal texts, such as statutes or judgments. For instance, in the U.S. jurisprudence the texts written by Benjamin Cardozo are perceived as qualitatively better than average production delivered by judges (cf. Weisberg 1992: 12). There must exist reasons for this interpretation. Legislators and their staff, judges, attorneys-at-law, legal translators constantly compose texts. They also use spoken word, and, as long as research into the proportions of spoken and written word in law is missing, we can assume that the written word is as important as is the spoken word in all legal activities. All jurists follow professional rules while writing, and while so doing, they behave like their colleagues, the writers of belles-lettres. In law as in literature we distinguish between well and poorly written texts. However, the criteria for their distinction are clearer in literature than in law due to shortcomings in the legal-linguistic research.

4.1.7 Intertextuality in law

Texts follow specific formal and substantial patterns that can give rise to other texts. Novels look as they look like because their authors read certain novels before and during the time they wrote them. Literary criticism has devoted impressive energy upon the discovery of textual links between different literary texts. For instance, parts of F. Scott Fitzgerald's *Great Gatsby* were influenced by Petronius' *Satyricon.* Wherever there is literature, intertextual links emerge. Intertextuality is also common in law, but sometimes it is less obvious. It concerns first of all the textual form of legal texts. Like the *sonnet* or the *short story* the *code* and the *statute* spread around the world from the culture of their origin. The content of legal texts is equally subject to intertextual relations. For instance, the Bill of Rights from 1689 that is perceived as a document of constitutional importance in England (Barnett 1999: 24) states in its Art. X: *...excessive bail ought not to be required, nor excessive fines imposed, nor cruel or unusual punishment inflicted.* The formulation *cruel and unusual punishment* is currently used in the U.S. Constitution's VIII Amendment that states: *Excessive bail shall not be required, nor excessive fines imposed, nor cruel and unusual punishment inflicted.* The above quotation can be perceived as the most obvious example of legal intertextuality, as the quotation of the English bill is almost literally reiterated in the VIII Amendment of the U.S. Constitution. Also in literature reference to the eighth Amendment of the U.S. Constitution is evident in book titles such as *Cruel and Unusual* by Patricia D. Cornwell (1993?) or text samples such as: "Though it truly had been Glitsky's intention to 'sweat' the young man in the interrogation room, this might be cruel but it wasn't unusual – homicide inspectors did it frequently" (in: John Lescroart, *The Hearing*, 2001). Also Billy Bragg's popular song *Rotting on Remand* recalls "judges quick to sentence more down from above/It's cruel unusual punishment that society demands/Innocent till proven guilty..."

Moreover, intertextuality does not concern exclusively one legal system or one language in which different systems may be expressed linguistically. It appears regularly in legal acts which are created with open or concealed reference to legal provisions contrived in other legal systems and in other languages. The existing international cooperation in the area of legislative development favors this type of text creation. The copyright does not protect legal provisions from being copied or translated by others, and rightly so. For instance, some provisions of the Italian and of the French civil codes concerning interpretation are almost identical (cf. Notes and Commented Materials no. 27). Art. 1156 French Code civil saying: *On doit dans les conventions rechercher quelle a été la commune intention des parties contractantes, plutôt que de s'arrêter au sens litteral des termes* and Art. 1362 Italian Codice civile: *Nell'interpretare il contratto si deve indagare quale sia stata la comuna intenzione delle parti e non limitarsi al senso letterale delle parole* are that close as to their content and linguistic form that one may assume that the one is the translation of the other. Furthermore, the formulation of the Art. 1161 French Code civil: *Toutes les clauses des conventions* ***s'interprètent les unes par les autres****, en donnant à chacune le sens qui résulte de l'act entier* corresponds to Art. 1363 Italian

Codice civile : *Le clausole del contratto* ***si interpretano le une per mezzo delle altre****, attribuendo a ciascuna il senso che risulta dal complesso dell'atto* (emphasis added). As this resemblance cannot be coincidental because it even comprises set phrases, it can be posited that they stand to each other in a relation of intertextuality, i.e. that the one has been developed because the other existed already. As the French Civil code dates from 1804 and the Italian Codice civile entered into force only 1942 one can claim that the Italian provision is the translation of the French one. Analogous formulations can be found also in Art. 1.285 of the Spanish civil code and Art. 1.289 and Art. 1.370 of the Italian civil code. In the way of another example one may quote the legislation on animal protection. In recent decades, many countries modified in their private laws the legal status of animals that were previously perceived as chattel. The legislators in these countries follow largely the same textual pattern when drafting the clauses referring to the animal status in their respective codes. The Civil Code of Catalonia – Codi Civil de Catalunya (CCC) stipulates in its Art. 511–1 (3) *Els animals, que no es consideren coses, estan sota la protecció especial de les lleis. Només se'ls apliquen les regles dels béns en allò que permet llur naturalesa.* Art. 515–14 of the French Civil Code stipulates: *Les animaux sont des êtres vivants doués de sensibilité. Sous réserve des lois qui les protègent, les animaux sont soumis au régime des biens.* Art. 90a of the German Civil Code says: *Tiere sind keine Sachen. Auf sie sind die für Sachen geltenden Vorschriften entsprechend anzuwenden, soweit nicht etwas anderes bestimmt ist.* All above examples reflect the same legal-linguistic textual pattern. Also contractual clauses manifest close links: "(IT) Tutti i diritti sono riservati. Nessuna parte di questa pubblicazione può essere fotocopiata, riprodotta, archiviata, memorizzata o trasmessa in qualsiasi forma o mezzo – elettronico, meccanico, reprografico, digitale – se non nei termini previsti dalla legge che tutela il Diritto d'Autore." Their wording that consists of exemplary word cascades points to their origin in common law clause drafting; the distinction between (IT) *forma o mezzo* is the best evidence for this otherwise unusual fascination with largely negligible details. Examples of intertextuality such as the preceding ones are very frequent in the legislation of countries belonging to the civil or to the common law traditions respectively due to their common legal heritage and regular borrowings from legislative acts which are perceived by legal comparatists as particularly well formulated. They prove again a close structural link between legal and literary texts.

4.2 Textuality and Interpretation

4.2.1 Is there only language in literature?

I asked already an analogous question regarding the law. As an intermediary result, I may invoke that literature is grounded in textual rules for its creation. There, also the plot is identifiable as a creation in language with specific means. These means are called literary techniques. Plots and literary techniques (rules of composition) produce literary genres. It seems therefore that there is quite a lot in literature, but all this may be a very specific use of complex language. In law, I may recall, language is also used as being anchored in language games as a part of life forms. We found out that in this sense law is about language and nothing more. In literature the situation is analogous. The decisive hinge is the view upon language and not upon the subject matter that we discuss here. Yet, literature as well as law may have other limits.

4.2.2 Limits of legal and literary texts

Legal texts are not constructed freely under the impression of a given moment of time and in a contextual vacuum. Legislative techniques provide forms for their creation. They keep ready textual patterns for laws, decrees, ordinances etc. They also determine their textual composition and partition in chapters, sections, subsections until the determination of the use of Arabic or Roman numbers in them (cf. the French administrative instruction on these issues in Notes and Commented Materials no. 28). Moreover, their formulation depends upon the legal language of the specific legal culture. They are formulated in a way which is usually predictable for any professional involved in text creating activities specific to the given legal culture. When applied, the rules embodied in written texts are incorporated in forms of judicial decisions, injunctions and judgments, which are petrified in the most productive legal cultures. Not much room for textual inventiveness or creativity for drafters or judges is left there. Similarly, literature develops under the constraints of literary techniques. Good literature is good only if it matches up to the requirements established for good literature that are grounded in the existing patterns for writing novels or poetry in a specific period of time. Inventiveness and creativity operate within these boundaries. These boundaries are not only textual; they are also institutional because they are set by experienced professional public, like literary critics, scholars or editors. A writer may not accept these boundaries and write as he desires but then the result of his efforts will not be perceived as good literature within the institutionally constituted audience. Exactly the same happens to a judge who does not accept textual forms of legal texts or other institutional boundaries in his activity. His judgment will still remain a judgment in the opinion of his peers, only a bad one. In fact, such a court decision displays also the juridical intertextuality in action. This aspect did not interest jurists until now and was not discussed in the legal theory either.

Legal intertextuality is manifest in the reference to statutory provisions in court opinions, mostly through use of numbers, rarely by direct quotations. Court opinions are parts of a textual succession on the hierarchical ladder of instances. More often than not, they are understandable only toward the background of foregoing decisions of lower courts. This is another aspect of their legal intertextuality that is illustrated by the case Northeast Iowa Ethanol, LLC v. Drizin in Cases and Commented Materials under no. 57). Also the length of court decisions has a selective effect as it may allow access to a decision for everyone ready to make the effort to understand it or limit the reception to professionals due to its (excessive) length.

Meanwhile, hypocrisy with reference to law is frequent in literary texts. For instance a waiver such as: *This book is a work of fiction. Names, characters, places, and incidents are either the product of the author's imagination or are used fictitiously, and any resemblance to actual persons, living or dead, business establishments, events, or locales is entirely coincidental* usually accompanies texts that follow closely real events, places and persons. A French writer aptly put this ambiguity into words: *Les personnages de ce roman sont imaginaires. Rien cependant ne les empêche d'extister.*

4.2.3 Legal and literary interpretation

A judge interprets a case or a statute in order to apply the results of the interpretation on another case while a literary critic interprets the literary work for itself, although not out of context. He is like the judge bound by the rules of interpretation specific to his profession. No reader or writer is free or independent of the interpretive context. The magic triangle of literary reception *writer – text – reader* provides the necessary framework for the discussion of all issues concerning the meaning of a literary work. It includes, but is not limited to, and this confession will not surprise here, the creation, the interpretation, the argumentation and the translation of and in literary texts. We have realized that in a text that is a linguistic product no inherent mechanism is apt to prevent whatever interpretation. The text usually bears whatever interpretation provided that persuasive argumentation has been prepared. The acceptability of an interpretation depends upon criteria in the professional community which under specific circumstances may favor some interpretations to the detriment of others. This process is especially striking in law where the professional community (foremost in the supreme courts) sets up institutional mechanisms that determine which interpretive rules can be applied and which results be accepted. The community of laypersons uses different mechanisms in interpreting legal texts which lead to divergences in the social discourse about right and wrong in judicial decisions (cf. 3.9.5). These mechanisms are less visible in literature because the literary criticism is less formally structured. The mechanisms that allow certain interpretations while excluding others are analogous in literature. Interpretive constraints are therefore not in the text, but in the context.

In literary criticism, the ambit of inquires into the context is disputed (Juhl 1986: 90). In law, the creative interpretation that we favor is also disputed. Moreover, it is limited by the institutional mechanisms that set requirements for what is acceptable interpretation and what is not. This is especially the case in the so-called *hard cases* where the interpretation method applied is the one of pure creativity in law perceived according to R. Dworkin as integrity. Therefore, for R. Dworkin interpretation is not reconstruction of meaning. Instead, the necessity to understand determines the meaning in its social context and it undermines interpretation there. Similarly, for H.G. Gadamer, a forestructure of understanding, (D) *Vorverständnis*, determines this process (Gadamer 1965). In literature, it merely makes sense to find out the writer's initial idea whereas in law, especially in cases of explicit creative interpretation, it would be redundant to search for the initial meaning. Nevertheless, such interpretive practice would be legitimate in any case. Only that it would be finally irrelevant to the decision taken. Therefore, the necessity to interpret creatively in law should not be understood as an impediment but as a precondition of understanding. Here again, law and literature meet.

4.2.4 Aren't we able to cope with narrative or textual ambiguity?

Traditionally, avoiding polysemy, homonymy and lexical, textual or narrative ambiguity makes part of the claims for the development of a model legal language or at least its terminology (Mattila 2006: 111). These claims have been rarely challenged, but when questioned they lead to results contrary to the received opinion. Indeed, it may surprise that lawyers – usually skillful users of language – should not be able to overcome the ambiguity of language used in legal contexts and make a step toward a more univocal and precise language use. Is this a coincidence? Or is it a strategy of language use and legal argumentation? As far as lexical vagueness or ambiguity is concerned some researchers claimed that this is an intentional strategy of language use that aims at reaching the optimal application range of the propositions about law (cf. Monica Den Boer, in an unpublished paper). Nevertheless, until now, the lack of linguistic univocality is perceived as a negative feature and as a shortcoming of language use in legal contexts rather than a characteristic feature of their textuality (Luzzati 1990, Mattila 2008: 1150, Gizbert-Studnicki 2009, Raffman 2014). Also the transparency in legal texts is perceived by many as problematic. Transparency, however, is a feature of the textuality in which the text is created. Its degree therefore differs and also this has reasons. In literary texts, some question the need of transparency, e.g. in poems (Baylon 1991: 251). Yet, even the most individualistic poet usually wishes to be understood by her readers; at least it seems improbable that she ignores the problem of transparency in texts. Therefore, transparency and ambiguity in different degrees of their manifestation seem to be structurally tied to the legal textuality. Hence, every criticism on their degree must be formulated with care. Similarly, yet in another context, Schauer (1993: xi) remarks that researchers are preoccupied with linguistic breakdown rather than with linguistic success in law. Doubtless, much would be won through the change in perspective upon ambiguity or transparency in legal text. Law, in fact, has never been simple and it apparently never will be perceived as such whatever efforts would be undertaken to simplify it (Mattila 2006: 99). Law addresses complex issues in complex societies. It cannot be simpler than society that it reflects. However, legal linguistics can contribute to the process of reducing the complexity to a level which makes law operational and effective as well as clearly structured.

4.3 Creating Laws and Creating Fiction

One distinctive feature of law and literature could be seen in the supposed free creation of a novel writer limited only by his fantasy and the work of a judge who applies the law without interfering into it. The first activity would be creative, the other purely mechanical. Our analysis of the linguistic operations in law brought about results which clearly contradict such an assumption. A comparison with literature, i.e. with the creation of belles-lettres makes plain why the assumption that until today is shared by many cannot hold place. In fact, we persistently claim that legal texts are created through linguistic rules. Yet, what are the results of such creation? As to their form they are mostly statutes and related legislative acts as well as court opinions (i.e. precedents). These forms are very rare in literary fiction. Occasionally, writers invent legal provisions or create court decisions but such text types have a marginal role to play in the complexity of a literary work. The legal texts may however come closer to literature as far as their contents are considered. In such cases, law and literature would again come closer to each other than often assumed.

4.3.1 Narrativity of legal texts

Narrativity is not a concept which traditionally would be associated with technical or scientific texts. Recipients are used to categorizing texts along the difference of telling stories from life or about life and those relating facts. However, all texts have a specific narration (cf. Broekman 2011: 3); all have a story to tell. These stories are alike. To jurists legal texts tell many legal stories. Recipients of literary fiction are sometimes not used to reading other scientific or technical texts and they identify them therefore as different because the subject treated in them is different, or because for them they lack a story, a plot. All texts have a narration and this narration can be read and analyzed (Jackson 1985: 13, 57). We can assume that the narration of the text allows us to keep it in mind (Laurén 2002: 12). The more concrete a text is, the more material becomes the law. Therefore we usually understand and easier keep in mind cases than abstract legal provisions. The less abstract a legal provision is, the easier it is read and understood. Abstract provisions are not less narrative than others; their story is generalized and is readable only with the help of complex analytical instruments that comprise legal methodology. Like complex literary fiction the generalized legal texts cannot be read by whomever. A substantial part of the population is not able to read Joyce or Proust. For those readers, these texts when technically decoded through pronouncing the printed letters of the written texts do not say much even if they master the respective languages of both works. Yet, it is possible to learn the appropriate methodology and then these texts become accessible like all other texts. It is like through learning a foreign language we obtain gradually access to texts in this language, beginning with simple door inscriptions, when our efforts start, until the arcane historical layers of classical texts in this language, when we reach excellence in mastering it.

4.3.2 Literality of legal texts

Narrativity of legal texts concerns primarily the legal element in them. Meanwhile in the research, language use concerning the description of facts in witness testimonies, at trials, in police protocols and in court opinions has been focused upon with most attention. The result of this type of research can be reduced to the conclusion that language skills and language use largely influence the application of law in situations where its factual background has to be rendered linguistically. Yet this type of analyzed texts is not primarily legal. We can call 'primarily legal' texts that render law. This type of texts has been less researched although it is decisive to our understanding of the role that language plays in law. In the historical perspective, it seems that the ancient Romans have initiated this sort of understanding of law as text. Paulus (D. 50, 17, 1) says about the legal rule and its emergence: "Regula est, quae rem quae est breviter enarrat, non ex regula ius sumatur, sed ex iure quod est regula fiat. Per regulam igitur brevis rerum narratio traditur, et, ut ait Sabinus, quasi causae coniectio est, quae simul cum in aliquo vitiata est, perdit officium suum." Law is thus rendered in the language and the result of the process is called by Paulus *regula.* The rule renders and clarifies law; an unclear rule is useless for the purposes of administration of law. A medieval gloss to Paulus's comment, called *glossa 'regula est'* remarks that the mode of emergence of the rule is to be found in the logical procedure of generalization (*universali signo denotante universalem affirmationem vel negationem*). The rule aims at describing and consolidating law (*intendit narrare et coniungere iura*). Exceptions are therefore not the domain of law, although they also have to be stated in it. Therefore, language is constitutive of law in the sense that it renders law linguistically. Law that is not stated in words is unreliable and difficult to apply. For instance, the rules of driving could be learned from practice and be inferred from the observation of the way how other people drive. Yet such knowledge of law would be fragmentary and often also contradictory. The written Code of the Road is a better alternative to our learning and applying law. Law deprived of narratives would be an impoverished and hazardous social practice. It follows from the legal-linguistic experience that all law of the country should be explicitly stated in linguistic form. The explicit statement of law is also the most fundamental legal-linguistic postulate that is constitutive of the structure of the modern law. This statement can be imagined in the form of the Roman rule or described as regulation that is the term preferred in this book. Paradigmatically, it might also be construed in line with traditional textual patterns of the Spanish *Las Siete Partidas* or the Ethiopian *Fetha Nagast* that use explicitness as a procedure of text constitution. Meanwhile, the explicitness and the linguistic procedure of narration cannot be excluded from the structure of modern law.

Legal regulation renders a content. This content is not necessarily the domain of lawyers, as they are obliged to know it yet they do not need to endorse it. Content of legal regulation comes about (at least in Western-type democracies) in democratic procedures where legal knowledge is not essential. Some contents, however, transfer textually elements of fundamental normativity of state and society and are therefore worth studying in the legal-linguistic research. As texts they are all but independent creations. They are rooted in interdependent philosophical or literary traditions of legal landscapes where they came about. Intertextuality is therefore another structural feature of legal texts.

What legal texts are also about? Legal texts, e.g. judicial decisions or statutes, include enunciations which in every culture are perceived as essential, ethically fundamental and therefore representing specific truths, values basic for society. Let us have a look at some examples:

Generally know are Roman legal maxims that teach us that:

> *Salus rei publicae suprema lex.*
>
> *Ubi societas, ibi ius.*

Ulpian's maxims in the first volume of the *Corpus Iuris Civilis* are even more specific:

> *Iustitia est constans et perpetua voluntas ius suum cuique tribuendi.*
>
> *Iuris praecepta sunt haec: honeste vivere, alterum non laedere, suum cuique tribuere.*
>
> *Iuris prudentia est divinarum atque humanarum rerum notitia, iusti atque injusti scientia.*

Constitutional preambles create texts that are perceived as visionary and are frequently invoked by citizens, cf. the U.S. Constitution:

> *We the People of the United States, in Order to form a more perfect Union, establish Justice, insure domestic Tranquility, provide for the common defence, promote the general Welfare, and secure the Blessings of Liberty to ourselves and our Posterity, do ordain and establish this Constitution for the United States of America.*

The same concerns the Preamble of the Constitution of India with amendments:

> *We, the People of India, having solemnly resolved to constitute India into a (sovereign socialist secular democratic republic) and to secure to all its citizens: Justice, social, economic and political; Liberty of thought, expression, belief, faith and worship; Equality of status and of opportunity; and to promote among them all Fraternity assuring the dignity of the individual and the (unity and integrity of the Nation), in our Constituent Assembly this twenty-sixth day of November, 1949, do hereby adopt, enact and give to ourselves this Constitution.*

The Italian Constitution from 1947 stipulates in its Art. 1: *L'Italia è una Repubblica democratica, fondata sul lavoro.*

The preamble of the French Declaration of Human and Citizen's Rights is not less visionary:

> *Les représentants du Peuple Français, constitués en Assemblée Nationale, considérant que l'ignorance, l'oubli ou le mépris des droits de l'homme sont les seules causes des malheurs publics et de la corruption des Gouvernements, ont résolu d'exposer, dans une Déclaration solennelle, les droits naturels, inaliénables et sacrés de l'Homme, afin que cette Déclaration,*

constamment présente à tous les Membres du corps social, leur rappelle sans cesse leurs droits et leurs devoirs ; afin que les actes du pouvoir législatif et ceux du pouvoir exécutif, pouvant être à chaque instant comparés avec le but de toute institution politique, en soient plus respectés ; afin que les réclamations des Citoyens, fondées désormais sur des principes simples et incontestable, tournent toujours au maintien de la Constitution, et au bonheur de tous. En conséquence, l'Assemblée Nationale reconnaît et déclare, en présence et sous les auspices de l'Être suprême, les droits suivants de l'Homme et du Citoyen.

And finally, statutes are equally fundamental in their formulations:

§ 1621 Perjury generally (U.S. Code Title 18 Part I Chapter 79 § 1621):
Whoever –

(1) *having taken an oath before a competent tribunal, officer, or person, in any case in which a law of the United States authorizes an oath to be administered, that he will testify, declare, depose, or certify truly, or that any written testimony, declaration, deposition, or certificate by him subscribed, is true, willfully and contrary to such oath states or subscribes any material matter which he does not believe to be true; or*
(2) *in any declaration, certificate, verification or statement under penalty of perjury as permitted under section 1746 of title 28, United States Code, willfully subscribes as true any material matter which he does not believe to be true; is guilty of perjury and shall, except as otherwise expressly provided by law, be fined under this title or imprisoned not more than five years, or both. This section is applicable whether the statement or subscription is made within or without the United States.*

The quoted texts are not less fundamental, ethical, or true for society than other texts traditionally perceived as literary or philosophical. Benjamin Cardozo's decisions such as Hynes (in Notes and Commented Materials no. 54) or Palsgraf (in Notes and Commented Materials no. 53) – both already mentioned here – are examples of this sort of fundamental texts. And, they do not lack certain dramatics either. To illustrate this dramatics or literality we will now turn to precedents.

4.3.3 Literality of precedents

Court opinions may include or even mainly consist of texts with substantial dramatic input. The following is an excerpt from Hynes v. New York Central Railroad Co. (231 N.Y. 229, 131 N.E. 898, 17 A.L.R 803) decided by Benjamin Cardozo in 1921:

On this day Hynes and his companions climbed on the top of the bulkhead, intending to leap into the water. One of them made the plunge in safety. Hynes followed to the front of the springboard, and stood poised for his dive. At that moment a cross-arm with electric wires fell from the ***defendant's*** *pole. The wires struck the diver, flung him from the shattered board, and plunged him to his death below.*

No linguistic element in this fragment of the court decision, except for *defendant*, indicates that it does not make part of a novel. Yet, can occasional use of legal terminology qualify a text as a legal one? Literary parodies, which use legalese in order to caricature language used by jurists would rarely be qualified as making part of legal texts, mainly because the intention of their authors has not been seriously directed toward the creation of a legal text. Is therefore Cardozo's opinion or the quoted paragraph of it a legal text because it has been created by a judge intending to establish a legal text? What do we know about Judge Cardozo's intention? We know quite a lot about his ambitions and his specific style. Can we assume that he had no intention to create a text which would be acceptable as being (also) a literary text? Can we assume that he excluded the idea that his opinion might be perceived as a literary text? Can we exclude that Cardozo has seen no particular borderline or contradiction between legal and literary texts? In fact, also some samples from Cardozo's academic writings taken from *The Nature of the Judicial Process* (1928) show that the author was not primarily concerned with fitting into stylistic criteria of the genre but with pragmatic aspects of his writing, namely that it should convince the reader about the rightness of the proposition of law made there:

Back of precedents are the basic juridical conceptions which are the postulates of judicial reasoning, and further back are the habits of life, the institutions of society, in which those conceptions had their origin, and which, by a process of interaction, they have modified in turn.

All this may be true, but we must not press the truth too far. Logical consistency does not cease to be a good because it is not the supreme good. Holmes has told us in a sentence which is now classic that "the life of the law has not been logic; it has been experience." But Holmes did not tell us that logic has to be ignored when experience is silent.

Property, like liberty, though immune under the Constitution from destruction, is not immune from regulation essential for the common good. What that regulation shall be, every generation must work out for itself.

The case of Benjamin Cardozo, who was a judge and a legal writer, shows that not all jurists experience the necessity to distinguish strictly between legal and extra-legal literary genres. Even if this approach was unreflected it would still be most illustrative of inherent structural potentialities of texts, legal and non-legal ones.

Let us return now to Hynes. The Hynes-case can be easily reformulated and re-edited in the sense of a literary text through the omission of the specific legal terminology. It looks then like this:

Harvey Hynes, a lad of 16, swam with two companions from Manhattan to the Bronx side of the Harlem River. Along the Bronx side of the river the New York Central Railroad operated its trains by high-tension wires, strung on poles and cross-arms. Projecting from a bulk-head above the waters of the river was a plank or springboard, from which boys of the neighborhood used to dive. For more than five years swimmers had used it as a diving board without protest or obstruction. On this day Hynes and his companions climbed on the top of the bulkhead, intending to leap into the water. One of them made the plunge in safety. Hynes followed to the front of the springboard, and stood poised for his dive. At that moment a cross-arm with electric wires fell from the pole. The wires struck the diver, flung him from the shattered board, and plunged him to his death.

We may contrast the above text sample with a citation from F. Scott Fitzgerald's *Great Gatsby,* written 1926, a few years after Cardozo's *Hynes*:

> *The wind had blown off, leaving a loud, bright night, with wings beating in the trees and a persistent organ sound as the full bellows of the earth blew the frogs full of life. The silhouette of a moving cat wavered across the moonlight, and, turning my head to watch it, I saw that I was not alone – fifty feet away a figure had emerged from the shadow of my neighbour's mansion and was standing with his hands in his pockets regarding the silver pepper of the stars. Something in his leisurely movements and the secure position of his feet upon the lawn suggested that it was Mr Gatsby himself, come out to determine what share was his of our local heavens.*

The reformulated part of the original Cardozo text concerns facts. Legal issues were not paraphrased there. This is however possible. Let us look at the continuation of the court opinion:

> *His mother, suing as administratrix, brings this action for her damages. Thus far the courts have held that Hynes at the end of the springboard above public waters was a trespasser on the defendant's land. They have thought it immaterial that the board itself was a trespass, an encroachment to the public waters. They have thought it of no significance that Hynes would have met the same fate if he had been below the board and not above it.*

Here, too, the transformation into ordinary language is not particularly complicated:

> *His mother sued the Railway Company in a court, but lost. Judges there thought that Hynes entered the land without permission and therefore was himself responsible for his fate. They did not care about that the board itself was not fixed by the Railroad and was actually illegal because it reached over the river where everybody has the right to swim. They did not realize either that Hynes would have died were he swimming in the river below the plank.*

And, also here we may continue with Scott Fitzgerald's *Gatsby*:

> *The little dog was sitting on the table looking with blind eyes through the smoke, and from time to time groaning faintly. People disappeared, reappeared, made plans to go somewhere, and then lost each other, searched for each other, found each other a few feet away. Some time towards midnight Tom Buchanan and Mrs Wilson stood face to face discussing, in impassioned voices, whether Mrs Wilson had any right to mention Daisy's name.*

I could again expose myself to criticism because I have chosen as an example a text largely known among American jurists as a masterpiece of judicial opinion. Moreover, my transformation may not live up to the expectations of some readers used to read English classics, either. Yet, its sense is only to show the possibility of a transformation of a judicial opinion into literary or ordinary language. And this task is surprisingly easy. What is more, I quoted *Gatsby* here as a sample of a literary text that is doubtlessly fictitious. The narration in it does not differ from *Hynes*. Both tell us a story. And, we discovered that readers' perspectives in both are interchangeable. Legal texts can be read as fiction as well as novels can be read as factual reports. The difference is again, as in interpretation, not in the text but in the context. The interpretive context includes choices of attitudes which readers exercise in order to be able to cope with texts. As they are part of social practices, readers' choices are well settled within daily conventions. This means that the readers more or less automatically adopt the socially adequate interpretive attitude to texts. They read legal texts as reports about social facts and novels as social fiction. Nevertheless, the problem is one of choice, not of structure.

4.3.4 Reading cases as if they were stories

Samples from routine cases prove the regularity we insist upon. We engage in them to show that the choice of interpretive attitudes is not limited to cases written by prominent and particularly talented judges. In Walker v. Quillen (622 A. 2d 1097, 1993) the imagery is steering the decision making process in the case. The Supreme Court of Delaware had to decide whether the plaintiffs could claim an implied easement or an easement by necessity to pass defendant's land which was their only means of access to the public road. The plaintiffs owned a tract of land, the Bluff Point, which previously belonged also to the defendant's dominant estate. The tract of land owned by the plaintiffs was surrounded on three sides by a bay and on the fourth side by the defendant's estate. It could not be reached from the bay due to the shallowness of the water there. Thus, it was completely landlocked. The defendant did not allow any access through the dirt road leading through his estate to the tract of land owned by the plaintiffs. It is not surprising in the light of the description of facts in this case that the court finally granted the implied easement. The facts seemed to speak for themselves and the court relied on them as if they would be programing the decision. Descriptive imagery dominates some decisions to a point that the decision making seems more or less automatic. In Nollan v. California Coastal Commission (483 U.S. 825) the U.S. Supreme Court dealt with the question whether the easement upon the estate of the plaintiffs ordered by the authorities amounted to taking which is illegal when imposed without compensation. The plaintiffs owned a beachfront lot in the neighborhood of an Oceanside public park. They tried to obtain a costal development permit in order to demolish a bungalow on their lot and replace it by a new one. The defendant granted them the permit subject to the condition that they allow the public an easement to pass across their lot to get to the public park and the neighboring beaches. The plaintiffs objected this decision. The U.S. Supreme Court reacted in an emotionally loaded language to the facts: "The building restriction is not a valid regulation of land use, but an out-and-out plan of extortion. We therefore find that the Commission's imposition of the permit condition cannot be treated as an exercise of its land-use power. To obtain easements of access to private property the state must proceed through its eminent power domain." Clearly, the court did not oppose the idea that an easement could be imposed upon the plaintiffs when there is sufficient public interest to be served. But it excluded the procedure that links an administrative decision to acts amounting to taking.

However, the imagery is not always the best predictability test for the court decision. In Michigan Mutual Insurance Co. v. Marriott Corporation (1992 WL 82498 N.D.III.) the court dealt with an insurance case. The owner of the insured Probe Prevost customized coach attempted unsuccessfully to park the coach in the hotel's valet parking area. At the request of the hotel's personnel he moved the coach to the hotel's general parking lot across the street, in front of the hotel. There, the coach had been stolen at night. The owner's insurance company claimed compensation from the hotel under the doctrine of bailment. However, the claim failed because the plaintiff could not prove that the defendant had accepted delivery and possession of the coach which are the prerequisites of bailment claims under Illinois law. As the coach owner kept the keys to the coach, he and not the hotel had the control over it so that no bailment existed. The imagery without the 'key' element is thus deceptive.

4.3.5 Facts in law

Controversies about raw facts dominate daily juridical procedures. F. Schauer (2014: 107) asked whether courts are actually well prepared to deal with issues concerning verification of facts. He also criticized the rules of legal evidence as restrictive and insufficient as they all too often exclude conclusions that are made in daily linguistic practice and proved efficient there. Meanwhile, questions of fact and issues of law are regularly distinguished in the legal argumentation and rightly so. They are different in nature and pertain to different aspects of adjudication. Another issue is whether they are as strictly isolated as the judicial practice would like us to believe. For us, they are rather interrelated (cf. Brooks 1996). Furthermore, we would have to ask what sort of interrelation determines their symbolic appearance which is at least textually contingent because issues of law emerge where also facts are in question. In the adjudication, abstract legal issues are rarely discussed, and should this happen, so they are related to the legal questions of the case. Moreover, under the common law, precedents map the way in which facts are stated in the decision and they constitute the focus of the decision when the judge distinguishes between precedents in the case at bar. The skill of a legal writer, such as a judge or an attorney-at law, in describing facts depends upon the identification of relevant events and chains of events in terms of the legal discourse. The legal discourse determines what is a relevant fact in terms of law and what is irrelevant (Broekman 1984: 159). The skillful legal writer distills from social reality these relevant facts of the story. This is the reason why sometimes a layperson may have the impression that something is missing in a legal narrative. What is 'missing' is simply irrelevant and therefore not a fact in terms of law. It remains a piece of information, but a redundant one. I already dealt with the situation that a novel reader has an impression that some information is missing there. This feeling is equally misleading, and I have explained the reasons for it. Like the novel writer who sees only the fictitious world of his narration, the legal writer sees only the legally relevant facts. This is so because both master the institutionalized rules of their profession.

Fact reporting often occurs in explicit language: *Captain S. was accused of wrecking the ship, by bringing it too close to shore, where a rocky ledge tore a gash in its side and made it keel over and become submerged.* Meanwhile, many legal texts may read as follows: (US) Federal Rules of Bankruptcy, Rule 9021 Entry of Judgment: "Except as otherwise provided herein, Rule 58 F.R. Civ. P. applies in cases under the Code. Every judgment entered in an adversary proceeding or contested matter shall be set forth on a separate document. A judgment is effected when entered as provided in Rule 5003. The reference in Rule 58 F.R.Civ. P. to Rule 79 (a) F.R. Civ.P. shall be read as a reference to Rule 5003 of these rules." The comment to the Rule 9021 reads as follows: "Former subdivision (a) was derived from Rule 58 F.R.Civ.P. As amended, Rule 9021 adopts Rule 58. The reference in Rule 58 to Rule 79(a) F.R.Civ.P. is to be read as a reference to Rule 5003." The avoidance of explicit speech may have many reasons. For some speakers explicit speech may be too complex to articulate (Tannen 2013). Others may assume that communicative value of speech is best preserved when implicit and explicit elements as well as known and unknown information are mixed in it as hearers or readers may have their problems with following exclusively explicit speech. However, for legal linguistics institutional and corporatist habits of language use seem to be the decisive motive for the choice of the variety of language to communicate the law and the facts relevant to its application.

4.3.5.1 A case study

In Torres v. Reardon (3 Cal. App. 4th 831, 5 Cal. Rptr. 2nd 52, 1992 Cal.App. Lexis 198, in Notes and Commented Materials no. 55) the parties disagreed about the liability for consequences of an accident that occurred to the plaintiff when he worked on the defendant's plot. The plaintiff was a self-employed gardener and was contracted by the defendant to take care of his garden in weekly turns. Some day, he had to trim a tree in their garden. While at work, the plaintiff fell from the tree due to a misfortune caused by a person who assisted him. This accident rendered him a paraplegic. He sued the defendant for damages pretending to have acted as his employee and being without the necessary workers' compensation insurance which the plaintiff allegedly was obliged to provide but did not. The defendant however contended that Torres had acted as an independent contractor to whom he had not been liable. In fact, the case as such is not particularly complicated in terms of law and it will not surprise any jurist that the plaintiff lost in all instances. It is nevertheless typical of language use in judicial decisions, and for this reason we will dwell a while upon it. The narrative provided by the court in its decision refers to aptly visualized scenery. Torres arrives as every week at the estate of the Reardons to take care of their garden. The Reardons are not at home but their neighbor instructs Torres what is to be done. A branch that overhung the neighbor's house should be cut. Torres climbs on the tree and the neighbor holds a rope tied to the branch in order to pull it out of his house when it would fall. The neighbor pulls on the rope when Torres does not expect it; Torres falls down and is made invalided for life. As a legal question, the court had to establish whether Torres worked as employee or as independent contractor. It examined evidence and held that Torres was self-employed and was doing business under the name of Jose Torres Gardening Services and was working for the plaintiff as well as for numerous other clients. He provided tools and equipment for the work and owned a truck which he used for his business. He himself had employees who assisted him in his business. Thus, the court denied Reardons' liability for the injuries Torres suffered because he was not an employee, but rather an independent contractor in the light of established facts. However, we have here two sorts of facts. First, the scenery of the accident and second, the facts establishing the background of Torres' business and his relation to the Reardons. The first group of facts is not controversial. These facts are easy to find out and to relate in the judicial decision. The second group of facts establishing the legal relation between Torres and the Reardons are of different nature. They are based on the distinguishing of employees and independent contractors under the doctrine of agency. Therefore, it is the doctrine of agency which dictates the way in which the court examines the background facts and it provides criteria for inclusion or exclusion of facts from the description (Brooks 1996: 19). Moreover, fact finding is law finding. The court of appeals put it unsurprisingly short: "The evidence establishes *as a matter of law* that Torres was not an employee of the Reardons, but was an independent contractor at the time he was injured" (emphasis added). With the help of this formulation the court establishes the difference between legal and other facts. The other facts could, in turn, become legal facts would the court ask whether a tort had been committed here. However, it did not as it did not establish any sufficient ground for defendant's liability toward the plaintiff. Some facts remained a pure narrative while others were decisive for the judgment rendered by the court. The metamorphosis of facts makes plain the narrative potentiality of the judicial decision. It does not matter in terms of law that the accident occurred on June 20, 1988. Yet it could, had data relevant in the light of the statute of limitations for torts been the issue. It does not matter that the accident happened at 11.00 AM, it furthermore does not matter whether June 20, 1988 had been a Wednesday or not. The interplay between legal rules and facts with all their potentiality for transformations is constitutive of the structure of judicial decisions as narratives. This interests us here. Words create law not only for Cardozo (Weisberg 1992: 6). They are not a mere translation of a holding into words (Weisberg ib.). While writing a court opinion the judge makes choices and determines facts interesting for the decision. The facts like the law are not simply there, they are created. Judges create them as they create the law on the basis of their professional knowledge. In this they resemble writers who create novels based on their professional knowledge of literature, its techniques, its history and the literary criticism. It appears that the legal linguist can learn from literature one essential thing about law: legal writing is a creative process. This discovery also explains why the description of the work that judges undertake with linguistic means is so complicated. Were it a simple, mechanical application of law and nothing more than that, no reason would exist for legal-linguistic activities. In this hypothetical case, the jurist interested in the legal language would have to limit her inquisitive mood to etymological issues. Therefore, legal conclusions in court decisions are always a mixture between law and facts. And court decisions also prove this mechanism: "*The failure of the defendant to respond to the intestate's outcries is immaterial*" stated the judge in Osterlind v. Hill (231 N.Y. 229, 131, N.E. 898, 17) after having distinguished between precedents pertaining to assistance under private law (contracts and torts) to persons not incapacitated and thus responsible for their own fate. Here, a non-incapacitated person had fallen into the lake from a canoe and was in vain crying for help from the renting agent Hill. According to the judge, no duty to rescue the drowning person could have been established on the basis of the facts that were provided by others, as the interested '*intestate*' could not contribute to the litigation by reasons well understandable. Undoubtedly, facts and law can easily be separated in Osterlind v. Hill but in the judicial decision they nevertheless constitute an interwoven entity.

4.3.6 Judges apply law and more than that

Every court opinion documents the way in which judges create the law. Creative narration emerges when rhetoric in the act of adjudication does not assist the argument but is the argument (Weisberg 1992: 16). In the world of growing multimedia communication the importance of law in the media should not be overestimated, because possibilities of visualisation of law are limited. Nevertheless, legal cases and lawyers as protagonists and characters fascinated many writers and led to the emergence of the lawyer as a literary type (Weisberg 1992: 54). What might be the reason for this rather one-sided fascination? Is it that lawyers use language more carefully than do novelists? Or are rather the social implications law makes clear in society the reason for novelists to deal with the law and the lawyers? Novelists approach the law from the outside perspective; they are less interested in doctrinal intricacies of the legal practice. There, they provide reflections upon the interpretive background of law, especially its ethical underpinnings. But still, is this a convincing explanation of the relation between law and literature? Weisberg insists on the textual parallelism grounded in a structure-oriented interpretation of both literary and legal texts. Indeed, as he posits, some formulations in ambiguous contracts or statutes may force the interpreter to refer to the structure of the text in order to identify its meaning (Weisberg 1992: 11). This structure is a broad term. When analyzing Melville's *Billy Budd, Sailor* Weisberg refers to the naval law and uses the Articles of War in order to provide an interpretation about sound or unsound, humane or legalistic legality of the plot. Finally, he joins Dworkin who also provides a broad concept of interpretation within his conception of law as integrity where a simple look into a statute would not enable to solve the Billy Budd case. In fact, deconstructive terminology is helpful in determining certain traits of interpretation in law. First of all, the specific limitations judges adopt when reading and composing legal texts can be characterized as a professional strategy of dealing with texts (Weisberg 1992: xiii). It follows from it that the plain textual meaning and the indeterminacy of meaning always enjoyed a hidden life in law and had finally to be addressed in order to end the myth of a professional judge strictly applying the law and nothing more than that. Postmodernist theory had at least an impact on jurisprudence in that it substantiated the occasionally expressed suspicion against the positivist ideal of an honest judge applying the law and nothing more than that. They established the conceptual instruments which make it possible to prove the anti-positivist claim. One of the foregoers of this attitude had been the Danish legal theorist Alf Ross who described the legal decision as a *façade*. He came close to the perspective of the American legal realists while pointing at the social and personal background of the judicial decision (cf. 3.3.4.1).

4.3.7 Literality and the institutional character of judicial opinions

Judicial opinions differ from other literary texts in that they are bound to judicial institutions. The texts produced by judges materially link judicial decisions to judicial institutions. Procedural rules assure the legality of this relation. Therefore, would a judge write a fictitious judicial opinion and publish it, e.g. in a literary magazine, the opinion would never become a precedent for the solution of other cases, whatever its professional quality would be. Would, furthermore, a judge who has no jurisdiction over a case issue an opinion, this opinion would not become precedent and would not be able to render the law in force. However, would the parties not oppose this opinion and would it enter into force, then it would matter as a source of law. Apparently, procedural rules determine the quality of a text as a binding and valid judicial opinion. Statutes share the fate of judicial opinions in this respect. The best draft of a law prepared outside the legislative body remains a private initiative and cannot become law, even if it provides for highly persuasive and innovative solutions to social problems. Constitutional rules clearly determine its character as private and not binding in the public sphere. In terms of legal linguistics we could speak here about a text related to law rather than about a legal text. Juridical and other texts traditionally perceived as literary differ in the sense that they are engendered under boundaries imposed by different social institutions such as the literary world or the justice system.

Therefore, institutionality is their common characteristic feature. The texts produced within those institutions provide the missing material link between both areas. The materiality of a text is in essence linguistic (Todorov 2007: 9) and it is its most fundamental characteristic. Therefore, other cultures such as the Chinese did not distinguish formally between belles-letters, philosophy and legal scholarly writings. Instead, they relied on the most characteristic features of all these texts which is their linguistic basis. The European tradition of dealing with texts introduced distinctions which formally are well justified. However, one may ask oneself to what aim all these differentiations were actually undertaken? We therefore questioned here – not without a dose of personal courage – the traditional differentiation of texts and achieved results which challenge the received opinions about the nature of legal texts. Indeed, legal texts have been classified as a specific literary genre which has its own rules and conventions (Todorov 2007: 32). This is a particularly convincing approach. A judicial opinion differs from a novel like a poem differs from a detective story. None of them is or could become true in the sense of the correspondence theory of truth (cf. Todorov 2007: 74). They are based on the proper rules of their particular ontology. In fact, the structural difference between a judicial decision and a literary text is the reference to sources. In judicial decisions this reference is mostly explicit, especially in common law countries where court decisions abound in references to precedents. In literary texts which – as we already pointed out – are composed within textual traditions the explicit reference is rare. Sometimes, an understatement refers to the literary source, in other cases the textual parentage in recognizable only to an expert. Both, however, have one more feature in common, namely, that they cannot develop outside their textual reference.

4.3.8 What is then specific in legal texts?

Are legal texts specific in the sense that they are results of a specific reasoning? Basically, all texts are grounded in a specific reasoning, e.g. poetic texts are anchored in the specific reasoning of poets and other fictitious literary texts are created analogically. Science fiction novels follow the pattern of a science fiction reasoning, medical treatises follow patterns of the medical science etc. Texts of whatever sort are preconditioned by the specific material rules for their construction. The legal reasoning is specific in that it grounds in rules of legal argumentation which set limits to valid legal speech acts engendered in such operations. I have already mentioned such limitations. Among them are precedents issued by supreme courts and authoritative scholarly writings. Yet, all other texts, as we have seen, are equally limited in their constitution. Some constructivists therefore question even the distinctiveness of legal rules (Finnemore 2000: 701). Our result seems therefore to be trivial, because it suggests that legal texts are legal because they refer to law and medical texts are medical because they deal with medicine. Within the constructivist perspective upon law, Franck's 'compliance pull' for legal norms consisting of the elements: pedigree, determinacy, coherence and adherence may function as a test for the 'oughtness' in distinguishing norms (Finnemore 2000: 703). At the end, this test too concentrates on institutional criteria for distinguishing between norms and identifying legal norms among them. It seems to be explicitly pragmatic and therefore useful also for legal linguistics. It would mean that legal texts are determined as legal due to extra-linguistic factors. What is more, we have also identified the specific extra-linguistic factor that is responsible for the change in attitudes which writers and readers take when dealing with texts that are anchored in the institutionality of law. Writers write these texts and readers read them differently because both – at least ideally – are committed to *sincerity* as a condition of applying law and making the process of the application transparent in legal decisions. On the same reasons statutory provisions are received differently by their recipients than sonnets or science fiction. The sincerity as an ethical moment in law marks the distinction between fictitious texts and the legal ones. To put it short, legal texts create social facts whereas fiction does not. It may only influence the creation of such facts.

4.4 Literature about Law

Numerous literary texts, classic and contemporary, relate to law, its institutions and its application. These texts are frequently analyzed in the area of Law and Literature. For instance, Claire Bouglé-Le Roux (2013) put together quotes from French literary classics that explicitly deal with legal issues. For legal linguistics it is important to ask whether literary texts about law propose ontological, epistemological and aesthetic conceptions that might modify or broaden the legal-linguistic approach. I will try to answer this question in the following paragraphs. My point of departure will be, as so often, methodological.

4.4.1 Legal-linguistic interest in classics

Dealing with literature in legal linguistics presupposes a non-philological approach to literary sources. The legal linguist reads literary works in the legal-linguistic perspective and she filters out law from the texts in the multiple forms of its literary existence. While so doing, the legal linguist will commit acts of injustice and barbarity because no literary text is predominantly about law, yet the legal linguist is interested only in law in these texts. The approach will cause tensions and distortions when confronted with the philological reading of literary texts. The most advanced skill in writing about law in literature and in reading such writings is the acceptance of this distorted view upon artistic creation. Advantages gained from such readings outweigh by far disadvantages and this practical argument justifies also analyses such as the one that follows. For instance, some classical texts such as Hesiod's *Works and Days* (*Ἔργα καί Ἡμέραι*) do not concern directly the dominant legal-linguistic questions of emergence and application of law. Yet, the application of law gave rise to this classical text that would almost certainly not be framed in the textual opposition to injustice in court proceedings. Hesiod relates that he lost a suit initiated after his father's death by his brother Perses who claimed a bigger portion to the common inheritance than he could expect by right. Perses, so Hesiod, manipulated the court and bribed the judges who had issued a verdict detrimental to Hesiod. This result may be bitter, yet for the legal linguist other observations than those concerning Hesiod personally are particularly valuable in *Works and Days*. In Hugh G. Evelyn-White's translation Hesiod's impression of the ancient Greek court of law is one of *wrangles of the court-house* as well as *quarrels and courts*. The ancient court proceeding is a structured argumentative chaos that is dominated by a formal conclusion reached in the judgment. In Hesiod's view, the trial is unjust and manipulated, yet strict in the observance of formalities. Like the gods, the judges decide and their judgement is enforced: *So he ordered and they obeyed...* (*Works and Days*, II. 69). Thus, the court works within a formal, if not formalistic, juridical paradigm that is valid also in our times. Hesiod contrasts this paradigm with a critical view of justice that trumps formalistic law: *The better path is to go by on the other side towards justice; for justice beats outrage ...for oath keeps pace with wrong judgments* (*Works and Days*, II. 212–224). He constantly links justice to the quality of judgments: *There is a noise when Justice is being dragged in the way where those who devour bribes and give sentence with crooked judgments, take her* (*Works and Days*, II. 212–224). Justice as a legal-argumentative device is opposed in Hesiod's poem to textually formalistic law and manipulative legal argumentation. Interestingly, both textual forms of law are valid and productive also in the contemporary legal discourse. Additionally, Plutarch in his *Lives of the Noble Grecians and Romans* in the chapter on Solon argues that Solon in his legislation intentionally combined aspects of the exercise of power with law: *Overthrowing altogether and disordering the state...With force and justice working both in one.* Plutarch had clearly noticed the complexity of the legal discourse that is even today frequently reduced to mechanical jurisprudence, especially in the affirmative legal discourse. The legal-linguistic perspective uncovers the concept of ancient law in literary sources and establishes the link to contemporary understanding of law that might correspond to or contradict the contemporary concept of law.

4.4.2 Ancient, mainly Greek literary sources in legal linguistics

Textual diachrony that is relevant to legal linguistics finds its outer boundaries somewhere in ancient Chinese, Babylonian and Egyptian writings, which are mentioned here only in a way of example (cf. Notes and Commented Materials no. 6, Spiegelberg 1892/1907/1922, Lippert 2004) due to the inherent limits of this book. Pre-imperial ancient Chinese works have a special status in legal linguistics as they include concepts formed in an intellectual tradition that is occasionally distinct from the Greek. The Hebrew Bible was also a source of numerous law-related analyses. As an example one may quote the notion of *due process* and the situation of expulsion from paradise where Adam and Eve are given the possibility to explain and defend their action before they are expelled. Such textual patterns might have preformatted subsequent conceptual constructions of due process. Meanwhile, the ancient Greek sources seem to be closest to the Occidental, i.e. the Roman conception of law. In fact, contemporary law as a conceptual construct and as argumentative practice is in one way or another a prolongation and a modification of the Roman law. The Roman law constitutes a frame of reference for all contemporary legal traditions and it is to a different degree integrated into these legal traditions. The fundamentals of the Roman legal thought are Greek – *Romani primi Graecorum discipuli.* Meanwhile, the intellectual fundamentals of the Greek law are badly visible in this law. They have been always better grasped in the extra-legal perspective. For this perspective the pioneering work by Erik Wolf (vol. I–VI, 1950–1957) has been of unprecedented quality. It has been expanded by M. Gagarin's writings (Gagarin/Cohen 2005, Gagarin 2011). Other researchers concentrated mainly upon Homer's *Iliad* and *The Odyssey*, for instance upon the procedure of dispute settlement as displayed on the shield of Achilles (cf. Galdia 2014: 266). Additionally, *The Odyssey* in book XVI, 376–382 describes the procedure in which the assembly could force the pretenders into exile as a sanction for their attempt to misappropriate Telemachus' property. These classics and also Hesiod's *Works and Days* established the strict divide between *legality* and *lawlessness* in social action. In *The Odyssey* (book VI, 1–14) Ulysses evokes *the lawless Cyclopes* and he says about them again in book IX, 105–115: *lawless and inhuman Cyclopes.* Ulysses speaks in book XVI, 186–189 about suffering *from hands of lawless men.* Also Hesiod distinguishes between law as opposed to *violence* saying about the lawless and the violent: *might shall be their right and one man will sack another's city* (*Works and Days*, II. 170–201 and 274–285). Law is for the Greeks a rational creation: *he shall pay you all the damages that are held reasonable* (cf. *The Odyssey*, book VIII, 343–348), booty has to be *divided equitably* (cf. *The Odyssey*, book IX, 39–61). The last words of *The Odyssey* (book XXIV, 545) are conciliatory and framed in a legal mode: *Minerva...made a covenant of peace between the two contending parties.* Thus, law is perceived as a modern and advanced mechanism of social interaction, opposed to injustice, violence, inequality and irrationality of previous epochs. It is a characteristic feature of the human society; who is lawless is inhuman. Human law is spoken law: the Greeks discover its most salient legal-linguistic feature that is its discursiveness. For the Greeks, it starts with the enthymeme as a part of court pleadings (Saïd et al. 2013: 239). However, researchers also assume that many notional constructs of the Greek law such as *marriage, dowry* or *funeral rites* have their roots in Oriental social practices (Saïd et al. 2013: 31–32). Meanwhile, the ancient Greek literary sources should not be confused with the encyclopaedia of the Greek law. Some issues treated there, for instance *divorce* in Menander's comedies do not render the legal situation but rather the popular views upon this social institution (cf. Saïd et al. 2013: 302). Ancient literary texts are therefore best explored in the epistemological perspective that unfolds the processes in which emerge mental structures relevant to contemporary law rather than the ancient law itself.

4.4.2.1 Legal-linguistic issues in ancient Greek drama

The discursive practice of law is best rendered in the ancient Greek drama. Aeschylus's *The Suppliants* (*Ἱκέτιδες*) is the most prominent among the Greek dramatic writings in terms of the legal-linguistic interest. The philological research into this drama focused mainly on the female condition in the plot; meanwhile, legal linguists are attracted by the legal argumentation that permeates the dramatic action. The suppliant maidens, who are exiles, speak as if they were trained jurists and must answer legal questions in a way *founded on the law domestic* (cf. 360–399). Exiles, or refugees in contemporary parlance, have the right to be accommodated and a formal decision has to be rendered by the authorities. Due to the political complexity of the situation the authorities prefer to wait: *whether to act or not to act, /Or not to act and let fate her way.* The suppliant maidens insist that *to honor strangers* and to *reverentially protect them from wrong* is domestic law and that political expediency does not matter in the decision making (cf. 400–438). Finally, the people's assembly gives them right: *all freemen made this decision law, / Rustled with multitude of lifted hands* (cf. 579–612). P. Mazon translates these lines: *Dis-nous à quoi s'arrête la décision prise, selon la loi du scrutin populaire, où prévaut la majorité.* In this line *democracy* is meant and Mazon's translation is very clear yet conceptually cumbersome; also the above translation into poetic English by G.M. Cookson conceals the lexicological background of the original. Meanwhile, the drama has been translated as an artistic creation and not as a legal-linguistic document and the legal-linguistic reading uncovers some of its lost linguistic intricacies. It is also worthwhile mentioning that the above quote includes the eldest known reference to the concept of *democracy* in the Greek philology (604): δήμου κρατούσα χείρ όπη πληθύνεται (cf. Alaux 2003: vi, cf. also Haarmann 2013). Aeschylus's *Eumenides* (Εὐμενίδες) is another drama written as if it were for legal-linguistic purposes, also evoking *the life without law* (492–543). Legal and moral arguments are exchanged there with unusual exactness of legal argumentation. The text reflects also procedural aspects: *And it is sound law and justice both, that he/Who does prefer the charge shall first begin* (699–753). It quotes a verdict dressed in legal language: *The accused is found not guilty of the charge* (699–753). Aeschylus is surprisingly well informed about law and its procedural technicalities. It seems also that Aeschylus's public appreciated the strict legal argumentation in his plays as Aeschylus was perceived during his lifetime as one of the best dramatists in Athens. B. Holmes (2016: 24) identified in the Greek tragedies *combative quasi-legal speeches of the contest or "agon".* Also the antique chorus proceeds in its explanation of reality and myth "like a lawyer searching for precedent" (cf. Carson 2012). Oedipus is the "master of legal vocabularies that had been refined over the course of the fifth century" (Holmes 2016: 27). The development of legal vocabulary and its use in the Greek tragedy are related to the development of democracy and discursive interactions in law courts and other institutions (cf. Vernant/Vidal-Naquet 1988: 25–28). Thus law influences tragedy. B. Holmes (2016: 26) remarks in this context: "The appropriation of legal vocabulary by the tragedians is the main reason why Vernant put so much emphasis on the evolution of legal thought as a condition for the historical development of Athenian tragedy, which he located at the juncture of older religious paradigms of blame and punishment and fifth-century legal institutions." It is remarkable that law is instrumentalized as a facet of tragedy, for instance in Aeschylus's *Orestia* where law courts *appear to arrest the potentially interminable chain of harm*; yet literary tragedy cannot replace law (cf. Holmes 2016: 26–28). Sophocles' *Antigone* (Ἀντιγόνη) is less concerned with issues that interest the legal linguist; the drama is rather focused on issues central to the philosophy of law, such as disobedience to laws (cf. also Steiner 1984, Wilmer/Zakauskaite 2010, Carson 2012, Honig 2013). Sophocles is however more dramatic than Aeschylus, which may indicate that whoever spends too much time upon law risks missing an essential point. After all, law as it is practiced, concerns only a moral minimum that society imposes upon its members in order to function. Seen in this perspective, law is not a particularly fascinating area of study, especially not for poets and dramatists.

In Roman literature law is abundantly present, yet also less interesting for legal-linguists because explicit law is available, mainly in the form of the *Corpus Iuris Civilis* as a direct witness of the textuality of the Roman law. Meanwhile, Roman fiction such as Virgil's *Aeneis*, especially its book VI, and Aulus Gellius *Noctes Atticae* provide insights into Romans' awareness of law and their conception of legal thinking construed as distinct from other areas of social interaction (cf. Galdia 2014: 110).

4.4.3 Literary law

The relation of literature and law is indeed special and a glimpse of literature may facilitate the positioning of problems that we are trying to elucidate. In fact, law in its most technical sense has never really attracted poets, playwrights or novelists. Explicitly legal themes are rarely an issue for writers. Never a writer committed his artistic work to law unlike Lucretius who praised natural sciences in his De rerum natura. Historically, classical non-doctrinal texts about law such as Plato's Laws are in contemporary categories politics rather than law. Also Augustinus' De Civitate Dei develops a political vision of a Christian polis that includes yet is not limited to laws. Thomas of Aquino reflects in his Summa Theologica upon discursive aspects of law that are relevant to the contemporary discussion in his Treatise on Law (Part 1 of the Second Part of the Summa Theologica). After all, the Summa Theologica deals with received and revealed law that is pre-determined by a religious institution. Such a conception of law interests today only a minority of jurists. Overall, literature tends to focus more on topics such as power or justice that transgress or circumvent the technicality of law.

Paradigmatic for the interest in power and law are Christopher Marlowe's *Tamburlaine* (1587–1588) where the 'conqueror of the world' is in his right because he is a great victor and *Cambyses* (1569), attributed to Thomas Preston, which calls to 'punish the guilty'. Both works are typical of literature that tends to understand legal issues toward the background of social life and human condition. Literary works that were written within this paradigm are numerous. Richard Weisberg (1992: 117) spoke therefore in the context of Law and Literature studies of a "self-imploding canon" that would have to incorporate Dostoyevsky, Flaubert, Camus, Dickens, Faulkner and many others. Indeed, Law and Literature is not thinkable without F. Dostoyevsky's *Crime and Punishment* or *The Brothers Karamazov*, F. Kafka's *The Trial* or A. Camus's *L'étranger*. In positive terms, the first lesson that can be drawn from this circumstance is that dealing with law without taking account of power or justice as constitutive elements of discourses about law does not make much sense. Law deprived of its social extension is a sterile and repugnant enterprise not only for poets. Yet, some exceptions to the general lack of interest of writers in the technicalities of law are well known and they are not less instructive than the attempt to deal with law in a broader social perspective. By way of example, John Fortescue praised in his *De Laudibus Legum Angliae* (1468–70) the English Constitution and contributed to the formation of the 'national political pride' of the English people. Thomas Elyot in his educational essay *Governour*

(1531) admired the Romans' respect for law. Richard Hooker in *The Laws of Ecclesiastical Polity* (1593) argued that the Bible would not provide any strict standards for earthly legislation and that positive laws were susceptible of change. For him, existing laws that were enacted in societies must be obeyed and respected. William Shakespeare's *The Merchant of Venice* (1596) underwent a profound scrutiny in Law and Literature studies (cf. Weisberg 1992: 94–104, Sokol/Sokol 2000, Skinner 2014). Likewise, the legal matters of the crown of Denmark, and especially the conflict with the Norwegian prince Fortinbras and the tribute from England play only an insignificant and a largely incidental role in the plot of Shakespeare's *Hamlet* (ca. 1600). Equally incidental in the play is Hamlet's monologue over the skull of a presumed lawyer that becomes particularly significant, especially to legal linguists, in isolation from the main text:

> *There's another; why may not that be the skull of a lawyer? Where be his quiddities now, his quillets, his cases, his tenures, and his tricks? Why does he suffer this rude knave now to knock him about the sconce with a dirty shovel, Hum! This fellow might be in's time a great buyer of land, with his statutes, his recognizances, his fines, his double vouchers, his recoveries; is this the fine of his fines, and the recovery of his recoveries to have his fine pate full of fine dirt? Will his vouchers vouch him no more of his purchases, and double ones too, than the length and breadth of a pair of indentures? The very conveyances of his lands will hardly lie in this box, and must the inheritor himself have no more, ha?*

The ethical and legal contradictions in legal activities are well captured in the monologue. Yet, in the totality of the play the monologue remains insignificant: Lawyers might have impressed Shakespeare, yet they hardly would have amazed a Danish prince. Law has always been a subservient activity to the exercise of power. In power structures, law is used and the legal discourse flourishes. Meanwhile, and as a matter of fact, law does not enchant the rulers and their devotees. John Fletcher's comedy *The Little French Lawyer* (1619) passed largely unremarked. Thomas Hobbes' *Leviathan* (1651) remains basic to every theoretical speculation about law. John Lock treated in his essay *Some Thoughts Concerning Education* (1693) in a sober way both the civil law and the common law. In § 186 he wrote about the usefulness of civil law studies for young men:

> *When he has pretty well digested Tully's Offices and added to it Pufendorf's De officio hominis & civis, it may be seasonable to set him upon Grotius's De jure belli & pacis, or which perhaps is the better of the two, Pufendorf's De jure naturali & gentium; wherein he will be instructed in the natural rights of men, and the origins and foundations of society, and the duties resulted from thence. The general part of civil law and history are studies which a gentleman should not bear touch at, but constantly dwell upon and never have done with. A virtuous and well behaved young man that is well versed in the general part of the civil law (which concerns not the chicane of private cases, but the affairs and intercourse of civilized nations in general grounded upon principles of reason), understands Latin well, and can write a good hand, one may turn loose into the world with great assurance that he will find employment and esteem everywhere.*

Thinking about knowledge in terms of private utility and career is typical of Locke, who unlike Hobbes, avoided all too abstract ideas and ambitious intellectual goals. He does not underestimate intellectual efforts but sets educational goals prudently; not a prince or an academic shall be educated along his guidelines but a successful landowner who will stick with common sense his life long. Locke's guidelines concerning a gentleman's education in common law in § 187 are no more ambitious:

> *It would be strange to suppose an English gentleman should be ignorant of the law of his country. This, whatever station he is in, is so requisite that from a justice of peace to a minister of state I know no place he can well fill without it. I do not mean the chicane or wrangling and captious part of the law; a gentleman, whose business it is to seek the true measures of right and wrong and not the arts how to avoid doing the one and secure himself in doing the other, ought to be as far from such study of the law as he can concern diligently to apply himself to that wherein he may be serviceable to his country. And to that purpose, I think the right way for a gentleman to study our law, which he does not design for his calling, is to take a view of our English constitution and government in the ancient books of the common law and some more modern writers, who out of them have given an account of this government. And having not a true idea of that, then to read our history and with it join in every king's reign the law then made. This will give an insight into the reason of our statutes, and show the true ground upon which they came to be made and what weight they ought to have.*

One cannot avoid the impression that for Locke law is not really a subject to be studied by a gentleman. Some general law, international law and a sketch of the constitution would apparently do. It is interesting to recall that England in Locke's time did not have any written constitution that the young gentleman could actually study. The absence of all references to books that should be studied may therefore surprise. Unless one would grasp Locke's advice in negative terms: details of law should rather be avoided in education, unless one wishes to become a jurist. Yet law seems in Locke's conception not to be suitable for a gentleman's occupation because it includes ethically doubtful matters where right and wrong are twisted as it pleases people. And, men who deal with the 'captious part of the law' cannot be gentlemen. That far Locke's main idea about legal education reconstructed for any purposes. Daniel Defoe's *The Adventures of Robinson Crusoe* (1719) had been received as a book about destiny and struggle with nature; yet the Robinson myth is paradigmatic for the reflection about law (Galdia 2014: 320–323). Henry Fielding's *The History of Tom Jones, a Foundling* (1749) may also be mentioned here as a novel including numerous witty remarks about law. As it was written by a judge, it concerns also the technical part of the legal discourse. Meanwhile, *Tom Jones* is clearly not a novel about law. It has been exploited in my *Legal Discourses* (2014) at many places because it elucidates some allegedly paradoxical aspects of the legal discourse. The German dramatist Heinrich von Kleist dealt with some fundamental issues in law such as responsibility and rule of law (cf. Sohoudé 2010). Jane Austen in *Pride and Prejudice* differentiates between *offending* and *insulting* like a skillful jurist: *I might as well inquire, replied she, why with so evident a design of offending and insulting me, you chose to tell me that you liked me against your will, against your reason, and even against your character?* This sentence and very many others in here work are perfect examples of advanced legal rhetoric of her time. Some scholars devoted their research to the study of legal vocabulary in literary works (cf. Lambert 1997, Sokol/Sokol 2000). Among many sarcastic and ironical, yet also convincing remarks about law in Lewis Carroll's *Alice's Adventures in Wonderland* (1865) there is also a lyric that invokes the legal argumentation: *In my youth, said his father, I took to the law,/And argued each case with my wife;/And the muscular strength, which it gave to my jaw/Has lasted the test of my life.* Thus, law manifests itself as a school for life, in a somehow reversed order of things. This view may also facilitate the understanding of K. Kafka's *The Trial* where life is actually conceived as a legal procedure, in contradistinction to the routinely held view where law is perceived as the formal part of life lived under constraint and life itself is imagined as the residue of freedom that is separated from law. It may be therefore surprising to find such fundamental philosophy in a booklet written primarily for children. Furthermore, Charles Dickens's *The Pickwick Papers* (1836–37), *Bleak House* (1852–53) and *Great Expectations* (1860–61) reflect some legal problems of industrialized England. The last two novels have been analyzed by Richard Weisberg (1992: 34–36) who infers from them the way in which lawyers used to communicate. Also Herman Melville's *Billy Budd, Sailor* (published 1924) has been analyzed by Weisberg (1992, 104–116). R. Weisberg draws one more lesson from legal writings: jurists' work consists in manipulating language. Weisberg (1992: 54) argues:

> *All great literary lawyers have mastered the art of verbal communication. Storytellers may have otherwise satirized legal jargon, but when they portray successful lawyers, they endow these figures with the ability to control situations through language.*

In England, John Galsworthy's writings are an illustrative example of this sort of legal-linguistic strategy. J. Galsworthy (1867–1933) was a trained lawyer who was called to the Bar and also remained active as a critic of the English legal system. He authored several literary works with explicit legal focus. The most known is the *Forsite Saga* (1906–1921) that consists of several novels which were often published as a compilation. In the interlude to the *Forsite Saga* that bears the title *Indian Summer of a Forsite,* J. Galsworthy canvasses the limits of law. One of the background figures called by him Old Jolyon, on seeing a visitor who enters upon his land and whom he cannot identify spontaneously thinks: *She's trespassing – I must have a board put on.* In fact, the visitor is Irene, one of his preferred relatives, and he is glad about her unexpected visit. Old Jolyon is trapped by predominance of law in all his reflection about life. This law is of mechanistic type and all Forsites prefer it as such and practice it as a tool that protects 'property'. *The Man of Property* portrays the lawyer Soames Forsite who embraced law as an overarching worldview. For him, all principles of human action can be derived from this immutable set of rules. Thus, he claims the right to his wife as a matter of property and considers all human relations in terms of property rights. Significantly, though, *The Man of Property* refers through the choice of its motto "You will answer/the slaves are ours" to Shakespeare's *Merchant of Venice* that is another masterpiece based on hypostatized legal claims. Furthermore, in the Polish national epos *Pan Tadeusz czyli Ostatni zajazd na Litwie* (1834) by Adam Mickiewicz legal questions pertaining to the enforcement of civil judgments form one of the dominant and structuring currents of the plot (cf. also Lizisowa 2004). However, the epos is centered on a multitude of non-legal details that defer the legal element in the plot and make it less readable, especially to contemporary readers. This is also the reason why *Pan Tadeusz* cannot be perceived as a legal epos although legal aspects of the plot, which are clearly understandable to a jurist with a background in the history of law, make it a unique work. *Pan Tadeusz* refers in its superstructure to the technicalities of law, unlike most other literary works that avoid legal technicalities in the way they are stated in the legal doctrine and concentrate on questions of justice. Fundamental to such approaches is Miguel de Cervantes's *The History of Don Quixote de la Mancha* (1604/1615). Cervantes's protagonist construes law as natural law: He is *master and natural lord* of his squire. Meanwhile, natural law starts in his view with a paradisal social condition where people did not know *the two words 'mine' and 'thine'*. Pure justice dominated this society: *Justice held her ground, undisturbed and unassailed by the efforts of favor and of interest, that now so much impair, pervert, and beset her. Arbitrary law had not yet established itself in the mind of the judge, for then there was no cause to judge, and no one to be judged.* This reflection upon the stage of primeval law and the distributive kind of justice is an interesting narrative because literature and art regularly invoked the image of pure justice that once might have dominated the mankind. In Don Quixote's story this description is perverted by apparent contradictions between the abstract ideal law and Don Quixote's practice of it that is purely arbitrary as *by natural law all living are bound to show favor to knights-errant,* which means to him personally because he has *the right on his side.* Particular in Don Quixote's view upon law is his qualification of law as part of 'letters': *...(A)rms have need of the mind, as much as letters, let us see now which of the two minds, that of the man of letters or that of the warrior, has most to do...I speak of human letters, the end of which is to establish distributive justice, give to everyman this which is his, and see and take care that good laws are observed.* The literariness of law is for Don Quixote the sign of its weakness; chivalry is preferable as a means to establish justice in society because it is based on force that immediately rights the wrongs. Finally, legality and justice that are practiced in Don Quixote's world are also present amidst rascals: *Roque Guinart...made shares for the whole band so equitably and carefully, that in no case did he exceed or fall short of strict distributive justice* as they are absent under the rule of kings where *laws go as kings like.* As always in the text, the protagonist's views have an element of rationality in them, yet they initiate in a disturbed mind that reflects the contradictory social reality. Law is profoundly misunderstood in such a society where *the boys are disappointed when the man they are waiting to see hanged does not come out, because the prosecution or the court has pardoned him.* Cervantes's protagonist makes clear the inner contradictions in the social discourse about law and justice. This is a serious contribution to our understanding of law that as a subject was approached by Cervantes rather ambiguously and always ironically. In one of Cervantes's sources of literary inspiration, *Tirant lo Blanch* (1490) by Joanot Martorell, jurists are banned from the ducal court in England as they instigate fierce disputes and therefore deserve to end up in hell: (CAT) *Per cert, que hi va haver molta disputa...per culpa dels juristes de cada part...(el Duc) va ordenar que pengessin els juristes de cap per avall; i no va partir d'allí fins que van trametre les seves miserables ànimes a l'infern* (modernized Catalan version by Jordi Tiñera). Martorell depicts a scene of rare violence against jurists who pay with their lives for the exercise of their (specifically understood) profession, and who allegedly enrich themselves by destroying England and its people: (CAT) *aquests homes de lleis es fan rics destruint Anglaterra i el seu poble.* Even their corpses are objects of hatred: (CAT) *mano que restin aquí penjats fins demà i que després siguin esquarterats i els seus trossos, llençats pels camins.* F. Rabelais in his *Gargantua* (Part I, ch. 54) expressed an analogous thought sarcastically, if not humoristically: *Here enter not attorneys, barristers,/Nor bridle-champing law-practitioners;/Clerks, commissaries, scribes, nor pharisees,/Wilful disturbers of the people's ease;/Judges, destroyers, with an unjust breath,/Of honest men, like dogs, ev'n unto death,...*The poem in chapter 54, disguised by its author as an inscription upon a gate, combines satire and an acerbic critique of the practice of law in the Middle Ages.

More recently, George Orwell's political allegory *Animal Farm* (1945) and his novel *1984* (1949) were precursors of critical discourse analysis. In *1984* even a world without law is described: *The thing that he was about to do was to open a diary. This was not illegal (nothing was illegal, since there were no longer any laws, but if detected it was reasonably certain that it would be punished by death, or at least by twenty-five years in a forced-labour camp).* H.G. Wells's *A Modern Utopia* (1905) and Aldous Huxley's *Brave New World* (1932) were also influential, at least in the mentioned sense. Meanwhile, in Jack Kerouac's *On the Road* (1957), which is perceived as a critical piece of literature, law is approached ironically, if at all. Kerouac's protagonists tend to hide from it and avoid it by all means: *he spent days reading or hiding from the law...he yelled me the funniest stories about how he got around the law in every town...I think he was running away from something in New York, the law most likely... The blond kid was also quiet and he seemed to be running away from something, and it figured to be the law the way he looked straight ahead and wet his lips in worried thought...Most of them were running away from something – usually the law...*(quotes from the first sixty pages of *On the Road*). Law as confrontation with police forces definitely plays a role in the lives of the protagonists, yet it represents an oppressive and a foreign element in their biographies. The main protagonist has even some understanding for law, yet he prefers to keep a safe distance to it: *I knew that. I told him I wasn't cut out to be a cop...You can't compromise with things like this. Law and order's got to be kept. I did not know what to say; he was right; but all I wanted to do was sneak out into the night and disappear somewhere, and go and find out what everybody was doing all over the country.* The protagonist is disarmed by the arguments of the dominant discourse, yet he also unconsciously opposes the ideal of law and order as proposed in the affirmative discourse that he construes as hypocritical. Meanwhile, his reaction is argumentatively clearly ineffective as it is based on and expressed with purely emotional means. Finally, the affirmative discourse about law, marginal and ridiculed in *On the Road,* triumphs over the biographies of the protagonists, mainly due to its discursive professionalism: law may be displayed in it hypocritically, yet it is efficient due to the formal strength of arguments used in the discourse against which the non-professional protagonists have nothing to offer but their feelings. Being argumentatively weaker, they can only fail. Argumentative narratives with reference to law are not rare in contemporary literature (cf. Smith C.S. et al. 1983). Harper Lee's *To Kill a Mockingbird* (1960) and *Go Set a Watchman* (2015) document ambiguities in attitudes to human rights as a basis for law. David Foster Wallace's *The Pale King* (2011) is situated in a tax authority, perceived apparently and ironically as basic to the modern state and therefore represented as a background stage of the novel.

4.4.4 Aesthetic aspects of law

Law like whatever social phenomenon is most strikingly characterized in an artistic expression. Some of such artistic contributions to the broader legal discourse have been mentioned here. At the same time, one has also to maintain that a monumental artistic work that would treat law in an admirable way is still missing. However, a four-page-long praise of justice and legality in the town of Riga can be found in Basilius Plinius' *Encomium Inclitae Civitatis Rigae Metropolis Livoniae,* printed in Leipzig in 1595. Pathetically and in the style of Renaissance humanists Plinius composed his encomium in elegiac distichs (English translation by Pēteris Cedriņš): *Without the support of reverence and the blessing of Themis,/even the foundation of our common welfare would crumble.* He continues: *Truth is the spirit that quickens the soul of the city,/ guiding its citizens to temperance along the path of justice,* and characterizes his native town Riga as *Impervious to corruption, beyond reach to the conqueror,/ she stands by her laws, steady in her course.* Plinius develops hyperboles of this sort on several pages that finally illustrate wishful thinking rather than social reality in his native town in the 16th century. Meanwhile, the *Encomium* is not only a literary curiosity; as a document it bears witness to the expectations that people in the 16th century had cherished toward judicial institutions. As said, no Lucretius, who had devoted his artistic life to the admiration of natural sciences in his *De rerum natura,* ever existed in the realm of the legal sciences. Never a jurist came close to the achievements of Petronius, Dante, or scholars such as L. Wittgenstein. Even Descartes, who as a trained jurist described in his *Geometry* the fundamentals of analytical geometry in a way that approaches poetical language and where he reached rare clearness, high style and where he proved his commitment to the subject matter, never found any time to deal with law. No legal scholar ever has written a book on law that could compete with Descartes' exposition of analytical geometry in terms of clarity and philosophical depth. Arguably, also some other disciplines such as dentistry cannot proud themselves to possess any monumental admirable eposes about their subject, in casu the disinterested devotion of dentists to their patients. In sum, no general explicative and aesthetically appealing narrative on law that could explain law in a larger context of human culture and society has ever been handed down in history. Digressions on law are legion in literature; critical remarks are not difficult to find either. Law is present as a largely incidental reference in Robert Frost's poem *The Gift Outright.* This poem reached the status of a political symbol in America and was even read by the poet during the 1961 presidential inauguration ceremony of John F. Kennedy. Frost addresses constitutional issues of formation of the independent American state poetically: *We were withholding from our land of living,/And forthwith found salvation in surrender./ Such as we were we gave ourselves outright/(The deed of gift was many deeds of war)/ To the land vaguely realizing westward.* Finally, possession of the land is for Frost a question of will: *This land was ours before we were the land's.*" In *The Gift Outright* a complex legal question is expressed in poetical arguments that may be emotionally appealing to Frost's readers. It is however reduced to some images and metaphors that make plain the incidental character of law in the poem. Finally, Frost stresses the will rather than the law in the act of taking possession of the land. The volitive element in power acquisition was seized, although rather naively, by the Hungarian poet János Arany in *The Welsh Bards* (translated into English by Watson Kirkconnel): *Edward the king, the English king,/Bestrides his tawny steed,/'For I will see if Wales,' said he,/'accepts my rule indeed.* In the following verses the Welsh will not prove particularly cooperative. More than pure will seems to be necessary to gain power. The Swedish poet Victor Rydberg described in pathetic terms the constitutive role of law for society and its subsequent interpretation in his *Juris Prudentia* (cf. Notes and Commented Materials no. 68). Yet, laws may not be sufficient either. The American John Greenleaf Whittier (1807–1892) wrote in his *Song of the Negro Boatmen: The laws of changeless justice bind/Oppressor with oppressed;/And close as sin and suffering joined/We march to fate abreast.* In sum, law is of marginal interest for eminent thinkers and artists. No one reads books on law because they are interesting as books that display their authors' particular talents or their intellectual skills. Politics is central to writers, law is boring or oppressive. Is it that jurists are not really committed to law?

4.5 Literature and Law as Part of Legal Linguistics

I have scrutinized here Law and Literature, the sister discipline of Law and Language, in the hope to be able to learn from it and use some of its results. I have to admit that I looked at Law and Literature from a very specific point of view and that I focused mostly upon some methodological aspects concerning the law as expressed in the written textual form. To avoid misunderstandings I also modified the heading and called this part of the book Textuality of Law or Literature and Law. The sense of this modification has been foremost to signal that I will not discuss specific issues of Law and Literature such as the question of how law, i.e. its institutions or its professionals are rendered in novels. While focusing on the textuality as a common feature of law and of literature I was nevertheless able to identify some pertinent structural resemblance between both. It appears now more clearly that writing literature and writing law are kindred activities. Texts are produced in both according to specific professional rules. The rules and mechanisms in which they are applied differ; the procedure is the same. Moreover, argumentation in law is not limited to doctrinal issues. Facts described and evaluated in law are presented in judicial decisions toward the background of factual-linguistic imagery which is, in its core, argumentative. Additionally, legislative acts display narrative ambitions which can be meaningfully accessed by means of literary analysis. Therefore, in order to understand the language of the law and its use by legal professionals it is necessary to understand also this specific imagery. Since this imagery is embodied in texts which show a striking resemblance with literary fiction, methodological approaches developed in the literary criticism are equally operative in this field of legal linguistics. All these specific features make plain that textuality and its pragmatic consequences are part of the prolegomena to a pragmalinguistic theory of linguistic aspects of law. This result permits me to count Literature and Law – seen from the pragmatic perspective – as a part of legal linguistics.

Part 5: Toward Global Legal Linguistics

Law and legal linguistics are aim-oriented activities. Among the aims of legal linguistics are those of theoretical nature such as the clarification of the tantalizing relation between language and law in general as well as in all detail. The main part of this book was dedicated to these problems. Finally, legal linguistics has also a practical dimension which is no less important. It can be namely expected to contribute to the emergence of the global law. This practical activity may be duly perceived as one of the noblest tasks for the legal-linguistic research in the decades to come. Legal linguistics describes linguistic requirements of the globalization process in law from the diachronic and the synchronic perspective. Particularly, it scrutinizes the attempts to conceptualize law in competing national languages and it reflects upon the conceptual language of law, i.e. the language behind languages. It also looks back to times when the legal language has been formed in order to facilitate all attempts to advance the globalization process in law and to avoid unnecessary frictions. In the debate about global law numerous specialists representing many different branches of law will have their word to say. Ultimately, and predominantly, legal linguists should be among them.

5.1 Converging Laws and Converging Languages

5.1.1 Globalization of law

The expansion of transnational and international law ranging from trade to human rights as well as the creation of new worldwide legal institutions such as the International Court of Justice or the International Criminal Court are indicative of an emerging global legal order (Cassese 2005: 5). This process is a part or a tendency in the general process of globalization (Reus-Smit 2005: 358, Lang 2011). Because different legal cultures converge or merge in it, it also illustrates the main theoretical problems related to the general process of globalization, its advantages and disadvantages. The task of legal linguistics is to reflect upon linguistic presuppositions of the globalization process in law. For these reasons and more, one could assume that the merger of national laws, laws of supranational and international institutions into global law should not be particularly difficult. Laws are – as we have seen – made of words and include a volitive element. Their merger would mostly require a political commitment to conclude the process because practically only two main legal traditions, i.e. *civil law* and *common law* are productive in this sense (Mattila 2006: 106). However, work on the merger of these two systems has been sluggish and cumbersome. Presumably, the volitive element in law, i.e. that it is a mechanism through which power is exercised in society (cf. Mattila 2006: 31; Husa 2007: 1) impedes rather than supports the process. The globalization process in law was launched on different levels of international exchanges including informal *consultations*, more formal *co-operation*, formal *harmonization* and *uniformization*. All these steps in the international exchange relations aiming at an approximation of the two dominating systems of civil law and common law are political in essence, but there are also explicitly linguistic in nature. It is therefore necessary to find the appropriate language for this law. Comparative law deals with issues which are very close to this task. In its core, seen from the perspective of legal linguistics, comparative law is about comparing legal languages. This means, as we have seen in above chapters, mostly the comparison of legal argumentation applied in different legal traditions. We do not have until now any exhaustive repertoire of argumentative forms in the Western law, in its dominant traditions common law and civil law. We miss this sort of knowledge also regarding other cultures, which either totally or partially adopted Western approaches to law, such as the Japanese (cf. Notes and Commented Materials no. 39) or the Chinese one. Last but not least we do not know much about legal argumentation in traditions which developed differently from the Western legal culture. The practical work on the globalization in law concerns rules of substantive law, the procedural rules and the rules of the conflict of laws. Within substantive law the most crucial legal-linguistic question is connected to the textuality of law and to text types. It mostly concerns the issues whether it is useful to codify legal provisions, which means from the legal-linguistic perspective, to establish the *code* as a global text type. In some approaches to *uniform law* or (D) *Weltprivatrecht* the issue of the textuality of law is left open and harmonization of the content of provisions is stressed instead (Linhart 2005: 3, 13). It is nevertheless maintained that equal texts do not guarantee equal application due to differences in interpretation (Linhart 2005: 2). Legal linguistics can provide some input at this stage. The procedural rules, in turn, pose another sort of problems as they involve also non-lawyers. The way how people speak, describe facts, etc., is culturally different. It may be therefore risky to postulate without further research that one set of procedural rules could become operative globally. Yet, results of the international co-operation, such as the *Principles of Transnational Civil Procedure* prepared by UNIDROIT and the American Law Institute in 2006 are interesting initiatives which pave the way toward an effective international co-operation. Finally, the rules of the conflict of laws are rather easy to harmonize.

Under regular circumstances, language does not seem to be an obstacle to unification processes in law. Languages generally can be adapted to the received legal tradition. The Swiss Civil Code had been transformed into Turkish law (cf. 4.9.2). The Japanese and the Chinese contemporary legal terminology are based on the European tradition. The Chinese terminology has been successfully adapted to the international demand and to the systemic necessities of the Occidentalization of law against all fears to the contrary (cf. David 1978: 538). The languages of India adapted to the English common law terminology. South Korea adopted the German conception of administrative law including the administrative process. Unsurprisingly, some problems remain on the level of the understanding of these new texts by their readers and especially by those who shall apply them in cultures different from those in which these rules emerged. Laws refer to values and cannot be applied without them. However, legal provisions rooted in values expressed in general terms can be successfully applied in different, sometimes even diametrically opposed societies. This had been the case with the German Civil Code applied in West and East Germany until 1975, the year of the entry into force of the East German Civil Code that became obsolete after the German unification. The abstract general language of the law adapted by other countries in cultures different from the European legal culture shows that unification should proceed on the basis of the broadest common conceptual denominator. This strategy would not challenge the existing cultural diversity. It would, by necessity, focus on the common heritage rather than on differences. The results of unification of law will occasionally lead to differences in interpretation (Linhart 2005: 2). However, these differences can be easier overcome than conceptual dichotomy. Within our perspective on language – which is comparative – one more fundamental problem exists. It concerns the homogeneity of legal language in the comparative perspective. Apparently, the major legal languages have a lot in common, especially common technical terminology. However, they differ also in many respects. Legal German applies a more abstract language than legal Finnish (Galdia 2003: 18), legal Russian follows sometimes other paths than other languages (Mattila 2006: 93–96), some judges in Islamic law countries tend to a more solemn expression than for instance judges in Scandinavian countries. The style of judgments rendered by judges in the Anglo-American law tradition differs significantly from French or Scandinavian decisions. Sarcastic and even humorous remarks are not unusual in the common law decisions while on the European continent they could jeopardize the judicial decision that could be perceived as rendered by a biased judge (cf. OHG v. Kolodny in Notes and Commented Materials no. 46). These examples reflect pragmatic aspects of legal language use which may impede its uniformization.

5.1.1.1 Global law as guiding idea in legal linguistics

Legal linguistics to which these lectures are a contribution is not a pure theory of law. It has practical goals, and one of them is its possible contribution to the globalization process in law. Many perceive globalization as merely an economical phenomenon. Others, e.g. W. Menski (2006) or H.P. Glenn (2010) deny the possibility of legal globalization because for them law is a part of social and cultural traditions that differ regionally and therefore they cannot be united under one conceptual roof. Fundamental anthropology and political theory may however define these traditions and the possibility of their unification differently. For R. Domingo (2010) the unification of law is not only possible, but also unavoidable. The crisis of the modern national state and the crisis of the international law force the citizenry to reformulate the global body politic and its most efficient mechanism, the law. Globalization in the area of economical, penal and administrative law signals the trend toward the general globalization of law. J. Rawls's works (1993, 1999) in the area of political theory as well as J. Habermas's work (1996) on the transformation of the modern national state provide a theoretical foundation for this process.

Domingo calls this law *global law* or *derecho global*, sometimes also *ius commune totius orbis*, sometimes *ordo orbis*. Some other terms such as *iuris ordorum ordo* or *lex mundi* play the same role in the projects of legal globalization. They refer to the Roman conceptual world where the principles and techniques of the dominant law on the planet had been forged. Domingo (2010: xx) also quotes Harold J. Berman who used the term *world law*. H. Berman (1995: 1617) wrote: "The term world law will, I believe, become more and more widely used as humanity moves into a new century, and a new millennium. It will embrace, but not replace, both terms 'international law', introduced by Jeremy Bentham in 1789, and the term 'transnational law' introduced by Philip Jessum in 1956." R. Domingo searches not only for the content but also for the language of this new global law. In respect of the language he remarks: "...the law must serve as an effective catalyst and support for the new supranational language – interpreting it, shaping it, and drawing out its logical consequences" (Domingo 2010: 64). Language capable of expressing the new global law cannot be enslaved. Domingo (2010: 196) having in mind words such as 'nation' or 'sovereignty' writes about this issue: "The politicization of certain words and their constant political manipulation makes them unusable for the consolidation of the global law." In Rawls's, Habermas's and Domingo's conceptions the globalized law emerges around the *law of the people* that is a law centered on a person and its rights. At this point Rawls stresses rather the collective aspect and Domingo the individual aspect of the creation of new rights and principles. According to Domingo, this new law does not involve the idea of natural law. Meanwhile, as it is based on the person's dignity and not on the sovereignty of states, it refers to ethics unlike interstate law, "(t)he state by its very nature is coercive; that is to say, it generates its own enforced ethics" (Domingo 2010: 49). Domingo's new global law should not be confused with conceptions that replace the agonizing national states with multinational enterprises as sole agents able to finance and develop the globalized world. The new law is not a 'law of the jungle' but a democratic catalogue of principles universally agreed upon by the people, not by states. The most essential are: freedom, equality, independence and solidarity of peoples, observance of treaties, duty of non-intervention, the right to self-defense, and the protection of human rights (cf. Domingo 2010: 42). Its mechanism is one of general 'consent' as described by Held (2005: 12–14). Interestingly, Domingo (2010: 42) questions the necessity of independence in such a law of the cosmopolitan society. Domingo (2010: 53–97) developed a broad overview over the erosive trends in the modern national state that finally precipitate its decline.

At least, it seems to be sure that the principle of justice in which all other principles are anchored remains indispensable to any project of a cosmopolitan political community. Certainly, as a theoretical conception such a project also includes some elements of utopia. Meanwhile, its strong fundaments should be able to support the ongoing detailed processes in the globalizing law. Its fundamental idea is 'justice'. The rest is, in the view that is coherent with the main ideas of this book, taken care of in the general operations of law such as argumentation and interpretation that seem ubiquitous. The main material idea of justice and the legal-linguistic operations are the minimal prerequisites of the new global law. They undeniably correspond to traditional structural features of law. The difference is in the sincerity. The new global law is the law of peoples, not of states. It is meant as it is written and it is not a decoration for cynical cryptocracies that oppress silent majorities.

5.1.1.2 Non-legal aspects of the language of global law

Developing language is a matter of perspective. Examples from non-legal areas may make it clear. An encyclopaedia says: *The Portuguese Diogo Dias discovered 1500 Madagascar, where the Arabs had their trading posts since 12th century.* There is a linguistic perspective in the language of the encyclopaedia that is geographic and ideological at the same time. D. Dias could have '*discovered*' the isle of Madagascar exclusively for the Europeans. From the perspective of local people and the Arabs Madagascar has been '*discovered*' and occupied since ages. A formulation in another encyclopaedia comes closer to our aim: "Madagascar was known to Ptolemy under the name of Menuthias and it is certain that there were Arab settlements over a thousand years ago, for traces of Arab occupation are evident today in the Malagasy language." The same linguistic approach is traceable in *'Far East'* that may appear geographically and ideologically far away to Europeans, yet not to local people. The reflection upon such linguistic perspectivism enabled the shift in the perception of the geographic notion. Today, many speak of *'East Asia'* while referring to the territory formerly named *'Far East'*. Formulations such as *1610 Hudson discovered the bay that today bears his name* are positioned midway on the scale between particular and universal linguistic perspective. In the area of law examples of non-universal language are equally frequent. An author writes in her article on contracts in a work with international ambitions: "According to conventional contract law, the formation of a valid agreement ordinarily involves an offer, an acceptance, and consideration." This is definitely true in the area of common law contracts; civil law contracts require no consideration to be valid. Therefore, the utterance does not represent the universal language of law. More universal is the language of Art. 3 of The North Atlantic Treaty: *In order more effectively to achieve the objectives of this Treaty, the Parties, separately and jointly, by means of continuous and effective self-help and mutual aid, will maintain and develop individual and collective capacity to resist armed attack.* The first requirement for a language that pretends to universal use is this shift in perspective toward the objects of its reference. Global means universal, that is valid from whatever corner. However, language cannot display a neutral perspective, i.e. describe its objects of reference from nowhere. Legal language in use today is dominated by the Latin of the Roman law in one way or another. This domination determines somehow the perspective that the language of the global law is able to offer. It is doubtful whether a legal language could be developed soon without direct or indirect reference to the language of the Roman law.

Furthermore, the development of a more neutral legal terminology with English as its basis or with whatever other language is not necessarily the final solution to the problem of the global legal language. Crucial to the creation of law is the appraisal of linguistic processes which anticipate the interpretation and the use of arguments in the legal language. Central to the application of law is argumentation, and this theoretically universal operation is until now not universal in its application. Argumentation as such is an extremely complex linguistic speech act. The results and the profile chosen here for the analyses of the legal language lead to the conclusion that the argumentation research is substantial to the development and the transformation of comparative law in times of globalization. Differences and parallels in the argumentation in different legal traditions and among legal cultures have been discovered in the research and every contact of a comparatist with a legal decision rendered in a foreign country shows both the differences and the similarities in the use of arguments (cf. Galdia 2008: 24 regarding German and Greek court decisions). Also, the degree of formality involved in interpretive practices may differ (cf. Atiyah/Summers 1987: 15). However, intuitive conclusions are not satisfying anymore and comparative law as well as all other legal branches will have to turn to the argumentation research for fundamental advice how to develop their disciplines in times dominated by qualitative changes. Comparative research into the legal language must therefore aim at canvassing the argumentative mechanisms at work in the different national legal systems and in the international law. From the legal-linguistic perspective it is important to maintain that intertextuality is the constitutive principle of the global law. Should this principle be neglected, the future law would risk to become a law of a part of the globe imposed upon other legal traditions.

5.1.1.3 Globalization of law in comparative perspective

Comparative law is essentially committed to legal pluralism that is the conditio sine qua non of its existence as an academic discipline (Husa 2015a: 24). The possibility of globalization in law is construed there in the perspective of a harmonization or uniformization of legal rules all over the globe (Menski 2006: 16). The chances that the harmonization process would succeed in the near future or at all are perceived by many scholars rather sceptically, mostly due to the embeddedness of law in particular legal cultures. Menski (2006: 3) remarks: "It is rather unreal to expect that the whole world would ever follow one rule system, one language and culture, or one law." Others perceive the co-existence of legal traditions as natural. P. Glenn (2004: 358) remarked as regards the legal pluralism that it "looks like it will be with us for a long time. It is sustainable, and perhaps there should even be efforts to sustain it." Meanwhile, for Menski (2006: 14, 3) and some other scholars legal pluralism is not an end in itself. The same concerns also legal globalization that as such does not guarantee the end of social conflicts only due to the harmonization of legal rules.

It seems that the debate about legal globalization in comparative law concerns mainly the harmonization of legal provisions. Moreover, the shift from "a predominance of authoritative law-making" (Menski 2006: 16) toward a more democratic global law compiled by the citizens of the world is stressed as well (Domingo 2010). Other skeptical and critical voices are quoted and commented in Bauman

(2004: 64–65) where especially democratic deficits of the global law are underscored. The critics warn against a fluid, i.e. not really binding global law concept that blurs the borderline between the legal and the illegal that it sets up to the benefit of the powerful. Certainly, the acceptance of legal globalization in the global citizenry is bound on conditions and therefore it largely depends on its degree of openness to change and its commitment to democracy. This attitude in the citizenry can be influenced by the research. When this task is not addressed by the research someone else will provide citizens the argumentative framework they need to make decisions about right or wrong of globalization. Therefore, comparative law should inquire into the prerequisites of acceptance of legal globalization rather than legitimize legal inertia and the status quo in the evolving social reality on the planet. Paradoxically though, some researchers even identified an increase in the emergence of differing legal rules all over the world, "a further pluralisation of laws" (Menski 2006: 5). Yet, no tendency toward further diversification of legal interpretation standards or legal argumentation has been observed in the comparative research. Exactly at this point legal linguistics proposes another view upon legal globalization in that it stresses the globalization of legal-linguistic operations such as legal interpretation or legal argumentation. Legal linguistics is neutral to the view whether the complete harmonization of rules of existing legal systems should be envisaged as it concerns only the methodological and not the substantial level of law. This finally does not mean that legal linguists do not have any opinions about the wishful direction in the development of the global law.

5.1.1.4 Argumentation in lex mundi

Ubiquitous legal argumentation enables the development of a unified global law, a *lex mundi* or a *world law*. Constructive linguistic input into the discourse that supports and shapes the global law started early with concepts such as I. Kant's *lex cosmopoliticum* or the named *lex mundi* and with some other coinages. These concepts clearly do not exist as isolated creations of terms with the help of language. They are results of discourses about the necessity to overcome the diversity of laws on the planet. The background of these discourses is the goal to achieve *perpetual peace*, a notion that the international law incorporated already centuries ago. Other, less noble aims such as the reduction of purely commercial disadvantages, which in the language of economics are termed *transaction costs*, followed suit. Legal certainty in times of increased international migration is one more such argument in favor of the uniformization of laws. National states frequently perceive the emergence and the strengthening of globalized rules as a challenge to their sovereign rights. National states are, as a rule, constituted around dominating political forces that claim the right to leadership on a territory. They use the national law, which they also develop in order to strengthen their dominating role in state and society. They therefore stress in their political discourse the 'nationality' of law and the necessity for law to remain national. They use this aspect also for federative purposes. What is more, national political elites form global alliances to guarantee their power while paying allegiance to local constituencies. They think globally and act globally, although they recommend to others to think globally and act locally. Moreover, some people are excluded from these transformative processes; they become outcasts (cf. Bauman 2004). This is, in short, the basic discursive structure of the globalization process in law.

The argumentation used by national states is purely ideological as no fundamental structural features of law are known that would prevent the approximation or the uniformization of laws. Already H.L.A. Hart in his *Concept of Law* (1961: 3) stressed the unifying rather than the dividing features of law: "Most educated people have the idea that the laws in England form some sort of system, and that in France or the United States or Soviet Russia and, indeed, in almost every part of the world which is thought of as a separate 'country' there are legal systems which are broadly similar in structure in spite of important differences." These "important points of similarity" comprised for Hart: "(i) rules forbidding or enjoining certain types of behaviour under penalty; (ii) rules requiring people to compensate those whom they injure in certain ways; (iii) rules specifying what must be done to make wills, contracts or other arrangements which confer rights and create obligations; (iv) courts to determine what rules are and when they have been broken, and to fix the punishment or compensation to be paid; (v) a legislature to make new rules and abolish old ones." Although Hart's approach to law is rule-oriented and our's favors law's discursiveness, his perspective upon law in the world that looks for similarities rather than differences seems to be worth mentioning. Furthermore, J.L. Halpérin (2009: 1) referred to E. Zitelmann's *Die Möglichkeit eines Weltrechts* (1888) for the development of the general doctrinal shape of the global law. Also F. Galgano (2005: 35) perceives legal pluralism as a legal anachronism: "La statualità e la nazionalità del diritto non sono fattori di progresso, bensì di crisi del diritto." Indeed, in all other areas of knowledge the unifying tendency won the competition to shape knowledge. Galgano may be right in his assumption that the reluctance of the legal science to join the globalization process may be a sign of a crisis in law. Likewise, G. Ziccardi-Capaldo (2008) engaged in portraying the ongoing process of legal globalization that she understood as a transformation of the international law. In order to describe the ongoing process she used following criteria: verticality and sharing of decisional processes, legality principles and common global values, integration of legal systems in the direction of global law, and collective guarantees (cf. Ziccardi-Capaldo 2008: xvi). Problems of the descriptive framework of reference were also addressed by M. Delmas-Marty (1998). It seems that the comparative research did not identify any fundamental obstacles to legal globalization. Meanwhile, jurists remain divided on this issue.

The discourse about the globalization of law among jurists oscillates between skeptical and enthusiastic approaches (cf. Hargitt 2013: 430–435). In the middle of the spectrum one may identify descriptive positions whose authors elaborate criteria for measuring progress in the legal globalization process. As can be seen from the above overview, rare are contributions that create principles and rules of the global law. The main reason for this situation seems to be the positivist attitude toward law that reduces jurists' role to so-called systematization of provisions created and enacted by others. Thus, the legal profession depraves itself of participation in the process of norm creation and by so doing it risks losing its social relevance in a global reality propelled by rapid change. Also P. Schiff Berman (2012) described the paradigmatic constellation of public discourse about the global law as a discourse between nation-state sovereigntists and international law triumphalists. Gillespie et al. (2012) added to it a review of different perspectives that societies take in approaching legal transfers. These perspectives also include failures of global legal reforms because globalization of law as a contemporary trend in the development of humankind is exposed to countervailing actions of multiple origins (Raadschelders 2011: 216). Some experience may therefore be rather encouraging, as shown by Black and Bell (2011) or Woo and Gallagher for Asia (2011) or by Adamolekun (1999) for Africa. Institutions such as domestic courts play a role in the globalization process that may be impeded or facilitated by their actions (McLaughlin/Powell 2011). Public administration also globalizes in terms of 'conceptual convergence' (Caiden 1994). It means that governments tend to use the same words all over the planet such as: *'bureaucracy, accountability, civil service reform, combatting corruption, management, efficiency, decentralization, welfare state reform'* as key terms.

Researchers mention also that private law can be harmonized through commercial customs (Frisch/Bhala 1999: 6). Other researchers, such as Hofstede (1991: 182) and Aldrich (1979: 22) are sceptical as they stress cultural differences that in their view inhibit convergence. Raadschelders (2011: 217) makes the development dependent on the view upon social reality that people adopt; they may see it globally or tend to localize differences that impede a global view upon the world. Meanwhile, forced searches for identities that are based on cultivation of differences end up in civilizational retrocession. In such processes where ethnic and cultural differences are cultivated against all odds 'apophatic identities' are formed that may lead to unproductive voluntary seclusion or confrontation. Anthropologically, law makes part of the civic identity rather than of a tribal distinction. Culture, with all differences that it may comprise, cannot be an obstacle to attempts at structuring or re-structuring social reality. Humankind's progress has always been based on generalizing change. One may also keep in mind that the humankind arrived at a common government of Antarctica while overcoming the small scale perspective and adopting a 'grand design' (Raadschelders 2011: 216, 217). Raadschelders (2011: 216) also stresses the problem of differing application of similar concepts that finally would make legal globalization impossible: "The differences in national culture are not only apparent in how the study is conceptualized and perceived but also in how theory can be applied." Ajani (2005) showed however that the comparative microperspective that focuses on functionality and the comparative macroperspective that focuses on method may be used for the purposes of unification of legal terms notwithstanding their initial functional difference. Finally, Mattila (2014: 200) mentions that when a Finnish and an Indonesian lawyer discuss problems of private law they use the same conceptual language. Legal globalization is therefore a matter of unified method rather than of functional comparison. The method governs the comparison and therefore incongruent legal concepts can be easily turned into perfectly congruent provided the appropriate method has been adopted by the researcher. Argumentatively, law all over the world can always be described as profoundly diverse or as perfectly unified, depending on the method that structures the discourse about the law in the world.

5.1.1.5 Global law as American law

One of the typical questions asked in relation to the new global law is its possible American structure and content. Domingo (2010: 197) writes about the prospects of the Americanization of the future law that he considers probable: "In the same way that ius gentium was a Roman law and international law was effectively European, so could global law become an American law. The strategy of the United States is clear: to refuse to play the legal globalization card and establish itself de facto as the true champion of democracy in the world, using American law for this purpose. Everything that is not American law becomes civil law – that is, second-rate law, a non-American law." However, the U.S unlike the U.K., compromised when it ratified the CISG that also includes civil law concepts and a contract structure that does not know the structural element of 'consideration' that is typical of the common law. In fact, harmonization of the U.S. American law resembles in many respects the European development. However, in the U.S., convergence processes, e.g. within the adoption of the UCC, were easier because they took place in the same language and in the same political system, even if the legal tradition of Louisiana is different from most other U.S. federal states. In the confrontation between federal states and the Union a compromise has been achieved in the Erie-doctrine. According to this doctrine, federal courts apply the law in the limits of the federal state's law in which they function. Predominant in the development have been therefore the strategies developed by the federal government and some prominent lawyers within the American Law Institute to proceed piecemeal, yet to insist on progress. Likewise, the dynamic and the modern textuality of the American law as well as its practical accessibility exert an irresistible attraction on enterprises and legislators all over the world. The absence of true competition in the area of law leaves the American law on the global scene as the only influential player. Sometimes, it is difficult to blame the Americans for being successful in promoting their law and their world view. Clearly, therefore, the Americanisation of law in contemporary legislative and contractual practice is also the result of negligence, inertia, and disinterest in creative aspects of law in other parts of the world.

In more theoretical terms the risk of full Americanization of the global law depends on the approach to pluralism. Further, will this new law be applicable in a global state or within another structure? Some like Shaw (2000) propose the structure of the 'global state' to accommodate the new law. However, this issue that pertains to the traditional political theory, of which it is a prolongation, remains open as the postulate of universality of the global law may be difficult to reconcile with the doctrine of territoriality of states. Rawls (2005) characterized this challenge in a quote endorsed also by Domingo (2010: 184): "A modern democratic society is characterized not simply by a pluralism of comprehensive religious, philosophical and moral doctrines (...) Political liberalism assumes that, for political purposes, a plurality of reasonable yet incompatible comprehensive doctrines is the normal result of the exercise of human reason within the framework of the free institutions of a constitutional democratic regime." The main challenge to this political and theoretical desideratum is that the incompatible doctrines can coexist when they are also perceived as reasonable. It will probably not suffice that they originate in the human reason as too many ideas have their origin in this complex structure. Reasonableness of ideas is an issue of rational discourse. When a rational discourse is not possible, there is no reasonable idea. This conclusion may seem not very tolerant, but the global law cannot emerge as an amalgam of everything that the human mind is able to produce. Then the law of the jungle would be more appealing than this sort of unified law. Meanwhile, the global law remains "the main contribution that legal science can make to humanity" in response to the "irrepressible human desire to organize a global community" (Domingo 2010: 199, 92). It requires therefore a global input during the process of its formation.

5.1.2 Legal linguistics and comparative law

I am aware of the fact that the process in which global law is constructed will take quite a long time. And, as it is the case already today the international legal order will coexist with national laws all over the world (Cassese 2005: 21). Some researchers underline in this context the high level of internationality that has been already achieved in contemporary national legal systems (Pigolkin 1990: 11). This systemic duality makes the work of lawyers difficult because they are dealing with a changing object both on a national and international level. The content of legal regulation, of course, always changed. But, it was mostly an evolution of the national legal system which lawyers had to face. Today, the national legal systems still evolve and simultaneously they also disappear. Consequently, they are replaced by rules of supranational organisms such as the European Union or by the international legislation, for instance the CISG whose 'internationality' is limited to the states that ratified it. What is more, comparative lawyers and specialists in private international law (conflict of laws) are conscious of the fact that their special disciplines have one finality, i.e. that they will disappear. It is, in fact, an exciting task to participate in the destruction of one's own profession because is serves a good cause. This destruction will pass several stages until the final result will be attained. The named formalized processes of bilateral and multilateral consultations, co-operation between national states, harmonization and unification with formulas of opting-in or opting-out will gradually dissipate any need for the comparative law in its contemporaneous shape or the conflict of laws in the international arena. Therefore, a gradual transformation of comparative studies into comparative legal-linguistic and later on into legal-linguistic studies is recommendable because the legal language will resist change in the globalizing subject matter. Paradoxically, civil law and common law may differ in their methodology, as far as their language is concerned they seem far less remote. Comparative law showed that systemic difference does not play any particular role in the light of results achieved in both legal traditions. Methodological differences seem in practice to be much less decisive than in some theoretical explorations based – often artificially – on an opposition between civil law and common law. This opposition in description and analysis of both Continental civil law and the Anglo-American common law is an issue for legal linguistics. It is best addressed under the caption *Literature and Law* as it concerns problems of textual conceptualization in comparative legal research. Here, we shall maintain some of its possible consequences. As said, the long-term goal of legal globalization will not be achieved over night.

Therefore, the conception of legal linguistics as comparative legal linguistics in the sense proposed by Mattila (2006, 2013a) remains a realistic option for the research in the time to come. Comparative legal linguistics will have to develop a legal language which can be used in the forming of the global law. This language is first of all based on the morphology of law. It will have to cover all its morphological elements such as contracts, torts or delicts, property, etc., with their inherent structural elements. One could call this auxiliary language a meta-language of the law. But it concerns also the adaptation of the main natural language of international relations, the English language, to function in this role. Criticism on the English language as a tool able to express the conceptual totality of international law is not new. Due to its links to the common law tradition it tends toward retransformation of whatever conceptual apparatus into common law. Within the European Union considerable progress has been achieved to develop a more neutral legal English (cf. 5.1.5). The same concerns legal relations within private law, especially within the UNIDROIT, e.g. the *Principles of International Commercial Contracts* (Beveridge 2002: 77) and the draft of the *Principles of the European Contract Law* prepared 1999 by the Commission on European Contract Law. As an alternative to a natural language as bearer of the global legal language one can imagine an auxiliary language such as Esperanto to take over this role after all necessary adaptation. In comparative diachronic research the differences in development between different national and legal languages may lead to complications, especially in terms of terminology. This is, for instance, the case when in the diachronic research notions with long history, such as the German ones must be transferred into Finnish which is a language with relatively short tradition of specialized legal terminology (Letto-Vanamo 2002: 29). In such a case there is a risk that whatever new term used in the linguistic transfer could be perceived as anachronistic.

5.1.3 Are laws different?

A very substantial question in the dialogue between legal linguistics and comparative law, as can be seen from the above subsection, regards the alleged or existing differences between laws all over the world (cf. for modern approaches to comparative law Örücü 2004, Siems 2014, Husa 2015a). Menski (2006: 26) states:

"Arguments for recognizing the inherent plurality of law are well recognized in the theoretical literature on comparative law." The most striking point here is the 'inherent plurality' that apparently cannot be thought away without disintegrating the phenomenon. It would be difficult and also unwise to question the legal plurality in the world (cf. Fenrich et al. 2011). The other thing is to admit that this plurality is inherent in law. Speaking about the law in the abstract does not mean that there is only one law, namely the Occidental law. This speaking comes close to the linguistic perspective upon the plurality of languages that for a linguist makes it possible to speak about the language notwithstanding the differences among some thousands of languages spoken worldwide. Laws can differ as to their source that may be the state or a religion, as to their structure, or the way in which legal transplants from other legal systems are used in them. They, however, seem to have one feature in common. It is not known that a law would be able to cope with social problems without some of the legal-linguistic operations that we are dealing with in this book. Legal linguists can also compare these operations and look at the particular modes and results that are achieved in the particular legal systems. In this sense we can speak about the abstract law as we can speak about language in general while admitting legal and linguistic pluralism on the planet. Several examples may shed some light on this issue. In particular, tendencies toward combining traditional legalism with authoritarian rule are present today in Asia (Rajah 2012). Rajah mentions as typical of the legal discourse in Singapore the discrepancy between the liberal form and the illiberal content of its law. Law on such occasions is, as observed by Rajah, regularly limited to rigorous observance of legal procedure that is equated with the rule of law. For India, Sarangi et al. (2010) added an analysis of the interrelation of language and politics, especially focusing on the unfolding of this relation in the twentieth century. Practically, the LAMLO-method, i.e. lawyering across multiple legal orders that was developed at the Columbia University Law School tries to integrate the disparate elements of law in the global perspective toward the background of legal globalization that in the current situation practically means that there is no global law while global legal practice is boasting. These developments suggest that global law can be construed and practiced as non-State law.

Meanwhile, in the Islamic law, certain provisions may be perceived as discouraging any attempt at legal globalization. In Kern v. Dynalectron Corp. (577 F. Supp. 1196, N.D. Tex. 1983) a court in Texas had to deal with a complaint of an American pilot who was employed by the defendant to fly helicopters over crowds of Moslems making their pilgrimage to Mecca. Saudi Arabian law prohibits however the entry of non-Moslems to Mecca under penalty of death. As the plaintiff was a Baptist, and he was unwilling to convert to Islam, he could not perform the contract. The defendant offered him a less interesting job, yet he declined the offer. The rest of the lawsuit is not interesting in our context. Striking is the peculiar Saudi Arabian regulation that according to the jurists of this country in based on the Quran. It is doubtful, whether specific regulation of this sort could be overcome in the near future. Other court decisions under the sharia show however parallels in the legal development in the Islamic law and in the Occidental law. They witness to the common rational basis of legal principles. For instance, the sharia has been applied in a way corresponding to secular legal orders in the case Libyan American Oil Comp. v. Government of the Libyan Arab Republic (in: International Law Reports, 1982, vol. 62, p. 140). The legal problem in this case concerned the termination of long term concessions to extract and sell petroleum that the plaintiff acquired from the Government of Libya before the military coup of 1969. The new Libyan government nationalized the concessions although the contract provided that it "shall not be altered, except by mutual consent of the parties." The question whether the concessions have been lawfully nationalized has been decided according to Islamic law. The judge held that "the principle of the sanctity of property and contracts, the respect for acquired vested rights, the prohibition of unjust enrichment, the obligation of compensation in cases of expropriation and wrongful damage" made part of the precepts of Islamic law. The judge based his decision on Quran's chapter V, verse 1 that says: *You who believe, perform the contracts* and decided for the plaintiff. The quoted sura corresponds to the Roman legal maxim *pacta sunt servanda* and the common law principle of the *sanctity of contracts.* All three maxims in concert form a workable basis for the global law at least in the area mentioned in the above case.

5.1.3.1 Legal Traditions in the World

Law as a historical phenomenon developed in contacts and in contrasts among communities formed on this planet. Both isolation and cultural exchange formed the phenomenon law in historical processes marked by the dialectic of continuity and discontinuity. The geographically distinct areas of particular developments in the area of law are often called in comparative law 'legal traditions' in contradistinction to the law of the Occidental type that dominates the world today. These legal traditions developed their own language. The language of these legal traditions has been less researched than the legal language currently in use (cf. 5.2.1). The most important legal traditions are the Chinese legal tradition, the Hindu law, the Jewish law and the Islamic law. Legal culture is still influenced by these traditions notwithstanding the application of the Occidental law in countries previously dominated by this traditional, non-Occidental law.

Traditional Chinese Law is based on Confucianism. In his *Analects* Confucius introduced a system of rules that determined the behavior in state and society as well as the mutual obligations resulting from these rules. The *Analects* consist of maxims, e.g.: "The master said, the superior man thinks of virtues; the small man thinks of comfort. The superior man thinks of the sanctions of law; the small man thinks of favors which he may receive." Jurisprudence or legal philosophy as separate sciences did not exist in China. Instead, *lüxue* (study of imperial codes) had been perceived as the study and annotation of the successive imperial codes. The Chinese legal tradition that was based on Confucianism influenced the law in Japan, Korea, Vietnam, and practically all over East Asia. Nowadays, China and all other East Asian countries adopted legal systems of Western origins.

Hindu Law (*Dharmasastra,* in Sanskrit 'the doctrine of proper behavior') is a religious law. Classical Hindu law rests neither on civil codes nor on court decisions but on the works of private scholars that were passed along by oral tradition. These records were later collected in *smritis* (law books). Dharmasastra is rooted in divine revelation of *Veda* (collection of Indian religious songs, prayers, hymns, and sayings). Most Hindu law is concerned with family matters and the law of succession. After India became a British colony, British judges applied the combination of Hindu law and common law, called the Anglo-Hindu law, in solving cases. The Anglo-Hindu law was ousted when India became independent. In the mid-1950s, India codified the Hindu law by enacting the Hindu Marriage Act, the Hindu Minority and Guardianship Act, the Hindu Succession Act, and the Hindu Adoptions and Maintenance Act. Laws of India reflect also local particularities from the Occidental perspective. Art. 17 of the *Constitution of India* says: "Untouchability" is abolished and its practice in any form is forbidden. The enforcement of any disability arising out of "Untouchability" shall be an offence punishable in accordance with law." Outside India, the Anglo-Hindu law applies in most other countries populated by Hindus.

Jewish Law is based on the *Torah.* It prescribes comprehensive rules of religious, political, and legal life that together form the Jewish thought. Jewish law is decided by rabbis who are scholars of the *Torah* and other Jewish scriptures. Rabbinic jurisprudence, known as *Halakha,* is administered by rabbis, sitting in *Beit Din* (house of law).

Islamic Law (Sharia) is the only law in Saudi Arabia. In other Islamic countries, the Sharia forms the basis of family law but coexists with other laws. The Islamic law is derived from the *Quran,* the Sunnah (decisions and sayings of the prophet Muhammad), and reasonings by Islamic scholars. By the tenth century A.D., Islamic scholars had decided that no further improvement of the divine law could be made. By so deciding, they 'closed the door of *ijtihad* (independent reasoning), and froze the evolution of Islamic law at that point. Islamic law prohibits *riba,* or the making of unearned or unjustified profit (cf. Cases and Commented Materials no. 51). Making a profit from the sale of goods or the provision of services is permitted. The most important consequence of riba is that the payment of interest on loans is forbidden.

5.1.3.2 Evolution and converging tendencies between common and civil law

Civil law is one of the two major legal systems currently in use in the world. It is based primarily on the written codes of Justinian *(Corpus Iuris Civilis)* and influenced by the French Civil Code. The predominant feature of civil law is the attempt to establish a body of systematized rules in one systematized code, a single comprehensive legislative enactment for every area of law. In this system, judicial decisions (case law) are not a source of law, although judicial decisions may be useful in the decision of cases. Civil law remains the legal basis of the legal systems in Italy,

France, Spain, Germany, Monaco, Russia, Scandinavian countries and other parts of the world, esp. in Latin America.

England did not follow the comprehensive code approach to law. Legal disputes there were resolved on a case-by-case basis, binding judges in future cases. Common law is, therefore, the overall accumulation of judicial decisions, known as case law. Statutes play a limited role there. As common law developed, a judge confronted with a new case would search in the literature for a similar case to determine whether a precedent had been established. If so, the judge would follow the prior decision. The requirement that courts follow precedents is based on the legal principle of *stare decisis* (stand by the decision). The principle of *stare decisis* binds all of the lower courts of a jurisdiction to determinations rendered by the highest court in that same jurisdiction. Today England, U.S., Canada, Australia, New Zealand, Hong Kong, India, Nigeria, Kenya and others follow the common law. It is the second of the two major legal systems currently in use in the world.

Despite their shared inheritance, the civil and the common law traditions have developed in sufficiently different ways that they are now generally regarded as belonging to different legal families. In practical terms, this means that each system is, in important respects, inaccessible to a lawyer trained only in the other system. Meanwhile, converging tendencies dominate the development of both legal traditions.

5.1.3.3 An exercise in functional comparative law

A jurist interested in comparative law may proceed while using the comparative method. She may for instance focus on eligibility conditions for the U.S. President and for the President of Latvia. First, she will determine the relevant provisions in the legal acts of both countries. These will be Art. II of the U.S. Constitution and Art. 3 of the Latvian Constitution (LV *Satversme*). The mentioned constitutional provisions say: *No Person except a natural born Citizen, or a Citizen of the United States, at the time of the Adoption of this Constitution, shall be eligible to the Office of the President; neither shall any Person be eligible to that Office who shall not have attained to the Age of thirty five Years, and been fourteen Years a Resident within the United States.* (*US Constitution, Art. II, Sec.1*) And, (LV) *Par Valsts Prezidentu var ievēlēt pilntiesīgu Latvijas pilsoni, kurš sasniedzis četrdesmit gadu vecumu. Par Valsts Prezidentu nevar ievēlēt pilsoni ar dubultpilsonību.* (*LR Satversme 3. no, 37p.*) (Trans. *A major citizen of Latvia who has accomplished forty years of age can be elected President of the State. A citizen with double citizenship cannot be elected President of the State.*) Second, the comparison of elements relevant to eligibility shows differences in the age limit, residency, naturalization and double citizenship. Based on these textual elements the comparatist can develop an argument concerning the eligibility conditions in both constitutions. The legal linguist would be additionally interested in the way the U.S. and the Latvian legislators state the eligibility conditions and in the legal argumentation in texts that apply these provisions. Full understanding of law comprises both the functional-comparative and the legal-linguistic analysis.

5.1.4 Legal terminology and cultural diversity

Nowadays, the legal terminology – seen from the global perspective – develops under a strong influence from the civil law and the common law traditions. This concerns also countries which are not perceived as European or having strong cultural links to the European culture. I already mentioned that the legal terminology had been perceived by many as the heart of legal linguistics. It could be analyzed in many different ways. First, it could be approached in a monolingual scheme and be based on the contrast between the special register and the ordinary language or second, it could be instrumentalized in the same perspective while including two or more natural languages. Third, it could focus on an exclusive comparative analysis of the special registers. Fourth, it could include the diachronic perspective and focus on changes in the special register in time or fifth, it also could concentrate on language contacts concerning the emergence of the special register, be it synchronic or diachronic or both. Very often, and rightly so, the named perspectives are combined in the research and they lead to substantial results. Generally, legal terminology developed within one cultural tradition in the process of linguistic contacts. In the Turkish legal language Persian loan words such as (TR) *şartname* (document containing terms and conditions) are frequent. This holds also true for the Chinese signs used in Japanese (Okawara 1998: 199). The same process concerns legal English or legal French which were influenced by the Latin terminology and to some extent by the Greek language (cf. Husa 2007: 97). Terminological influence from outside the cultural reference in Europe is rare. In the legal French words rooted in Arabic or Persian like *douane* or *avarie* (Cornu 2005: 142), in the legal Russian Tatar words like *tamozhnja, kazna, jarlyk* or *karaul* (Pigolkin 1990: 45) have been identified in the research. One could add to them also (FR) *tarif* from Arabic *tarif (notification)*. The legal terminology in former Yugoslavia had been influenced by Turkish, e.g. (MAC*) ortach (partner)*. Furthermore, for legal English the process of introducing Islamic legal terminology into legal texts written in English in Pakistan is characteristic (Mattila 2006: 249). In Chinese, one of the legal terms meaning *sale*, (CN) *mǎimai* corresponds literally to (LAT) *emptio-venditio*. However, this linguistic contact is a one-sided process.

The multilingual perspective has the advantage that it paves the way toward developing a legal language for the emerging global law. English language terms rooted in the constitutional system of the common law countries such as *state of law, good governance*, or *checks and balances* find their way into legal languages which belong to civil law. Specifically, *corporate governance* may be rendered as (D) *verantwortungsvolle Unternehmensführung*. One can also follow this lexical creation in a broader comparative perspective. To illustrate, *parent company* corresponds in (S) to *moderföretaget* as a pendant to (S) *dotterföretaget* and to (D) *Muttergesellschaft* and (D) *Tochtergesellschaft* respectively. The distinction in the German terminology is due to the feminine gender of (D) *Gesellschaft* (company) whereas the Swedish language terminology is based on (S) *företaget* and sometimes (S) *bolaget* which are both of neutral gender. Therefore, the Swedish form – unlike the German terms – seems to be a calque, a foreign borrowing rather than a linguistic creation anchored in the linguistic system. In the Japanese terminology (JAP) *oyagaisha* (i.e. parent company) and (JAP) *kogaisha* (i.e. child company) are used respectively. Comparative law studies began in some cases with the process of emerging of the legal terminology. R. David (1978: 554) reports that during the Meiji era in Japan (beginning 1868) Japanese terminology has been invented in the process of translation of the European codes into Japanese. Terms such as (JAP) *kenri* for *subjective right* and (JAP) *gimu* for *legal obligation* date from this period. Less interest had been brought toward the existing legal Japanese terminology before the time of Europeanization of Japan's legislation. Igarashi (1990) accounts for a specific Japanese legal vocabulary or vocabulary with legal connection including terms such as: *assen, horei, iriai, iriai-ken, jori, kaisha, kanji, kankai, karitoki-tampo, kojoryo-zoku, kokutai, kumiai, mansion, meinin-hoko, menso, nainen, ne, onsensarakin, shiho-shoshi, shinpan, shinto, tenno.* They are difficult to translate; sometimes a description is necessary as in the case of *jori* which may be translated as *customs* or the *nature of things* (Igarashi 1990: 2). Analogous remarks can be found concerning the legal Chinese terminology (Escarra 1936: 55) as independent terminology, e.g. (CN) *yong dian quan* (eternal lease) is rare there. The development of the modern Chinese terminology in the international law (*ius gentium sinense*) was sketched by Zhang (2002). He concentrated on concepts such as *international law, state, nation, international, inter-state* (all p. 4), *war* (p. 233), *immunity* (p. 54), *human rights* (p. 47), *treaty* (p. 185), *larger freedom* (p. 211), *obligation* (p. 177), *ius cogens* (p. 212), *security* (p. 209), *individual* (p. 53), *person* and *thing* (p. 53), *extradition* (p. 74), *hot pursuit* (p. 128) or *self-executive* (p. 24) and demonstrated that these concepts can be clearly termed in the Chinese language.

5.1.4.1 Swahili legal vocabulary

All legal languages developed in a way that favors globalized legal language. In Swahili, the African lingua franca used predominantly south of the Sahara, most lexical units that pertain to law are borrowings from Arabic. This is particularly striking in *sheria* for *sharia* and the related syntagma *peleka sheriani* (to sue in the court); *shahidi* (witness) with the corresponding syntagma *shahidi ya uwongo* (false witness). The same holds true for *sharti*, pl. *shuruti* (condition, regulation or constraint) or *shauri* (plan, intention, advice) or *haki* for justice or *halali*, furthermore *hukumu* and *mamlaka* for administration and the verb *hukumu* (to govern), *namna ya taarifu* (customs declaration), *wakili* (trade) representative follow this pattern. A particularity of the Swahili law-related vocabulary is its free combination between the Arabic superstrate and the Bantu substrate, visible in e.g. *shahidi ya uwongo* where only the legal term witness is Arabic or *peleka sheriani* where only the reference to sharia is truly Arabic, while the syntagmatic structure, including its syntax remains rooted in the Bantu linguistic model. Likewise, *shauri moja* (univocally) or *fanya shauri* (to decide) or *fuata shauri* (follow an advice) or *fanya haki* (make justice), *jeshi la askari* composed of Bantu *jeshi* for herd or flock and Arabic *askari* for soldier, both united by the Swahili genitival preposition *la* manifest this regularity.

Other most common Arabic borrowings include *ada* (custom, fee paid to a worker or a physician); *adhabu* (punishment) and the corresponding verb *adhibu* (to punish); *adili* (just or righteous). Originally Bantu in terms of legal anthropology seem to be *fichuo* (gift for a newly married woman); *fisha* (condemn to death); *haramu/ maharamu* (forbidden relation between closely related persons); *iba* or *kwiba* (to steal), *mwenyi kwiba* (thief), *mwenyi kwibiwa* (victim of theft), *jambo* (thing or matter), *konde* (field), *kopa* (borrow), *mali* (property or goods), *malipo mbele* (advance payment), *mfanya maovu* (perpetrator of crime), *mweni* (owner), *mwamua* or *mwamuzi* (judge), *mweni kulipa* (debtor), *punja* (deceive), *ua* (to kill), *uza* (to sell), *vita* (war). However, some other basic vocabulary such as *jamaa* (family or reunion) are clearly Arabic. Much more problematic are general terms such as *pasa* (to be obliged) that have also many daily connotations that are visible in *inanimpasa* (it belongs to me) or *imekupasaje?* (why do you care for it?). *Wajibu* for obligation is used also in *ndio wajibu wako* (how nice from you).

Legal language in Sub-Saharan Africa is not well researched, if European languages such as English or French are set apart. Local legal terminology is better known. Some Swahili vocabulary that is connected to law is not clear in terms of its etymology. It might be of Bantu or of Arabic origin: *agana* (agree), *agano* (contract, cf. *agano jipya*), *agano la Kale, andika (askari), amrika (askari), chuma mali, deni* (cf. *lipa deni*), *desturi, dhamana, dhamini, dhambi, dola, fidia, gawanya, haka, hati, hatia, milki, nauli* (fright), *mirathi, pata, patina, pangisha* (rent, cf. *una nyumba ya kupangisha; nataka kupanga), rahani, shtaki, singizia, singizio, stakabadhi, ufilisi, uizi, ukahaba, ungama, ungamo, uovo, uozi/wozi, wasia.* African terminology may further encompass custom *fomba* or *heer* in Somalia (Menski 2006: 409). These terms maintain their linguistic presence in the legal culture like the Japanese *giri* for custom. The acceptability of international legal terminology which is written mostly in English and subsequently translated into some official languages could be increased through loan words borrowed from beyond the borders of the European culture. Rules for such a linguistic policy should be preferably developed by international organizations. They could, for instance, include also percentage limits for vocabulary representing different legal traditions and cultures, as is the case with rules for the development of Esperanto.

5.1.5 Linguistic aspects of the E.U. law and the law in the U.S.

Convergence processes in law can be well observed on the example of the European Union and the U.S. Within the European Union, linguistic issues and matters of policy intertwine (cf. Paunio/Lindroos-Hovinheimo 2010). Political decisions are necessary for any legislative break-through. Attempts had been undertaken in the research to determine the nature of the law ruling the European Union. Apparently, the law of the European Union does not develop toward a conceptual background which would guarantee its fundamental cohesion. In particular, text types were perceived to be mostly of French origin. Most leading concepts like (FR/EU) *acquis communautaire* are of French origin or new coinages made initially in French.

However, some interpretive approaches are perceived as typical of the common law. The European Union tried therefore to develop a more coherent legal terminology (Mattila 2006: 102). These efforts culminated in the Inter-institutional agreement on common guidelines for the quality of drafting of Community legislation from December 22, 1998. The Inter-institutional Agreement on common guidelines for the quality of drafting of Community legislation (Official Journal C 073, 17/03/99) recommends in its Section 5: "Throughout the process leading to their adoption, draft acts shall be framed in terms and sentence structures which respect the multilingual nature of the Community legislation; concepts or terminology specific to any one national legal system are to be used with care." Likewise, the Principles of European Contract Law (PECL) reflect the spirit of the drafting instruction. J. M. Smits (2005: 568) characterizes the PECL as an attempt to draft a common European private law code. He also stresses that the PECL create a common language through which the European scholars can communicate and European students be educated (Smits 2005: 573). However, provisions in plain English that is largely independent of the common law are difficult to draft even if their neutrality is expressly postulated (Smits 2005: 568). For instance, a linguistic plan scheduled in steps for a regulated action is developed in PECL Art. 6: 111 (*Change of Circumstances*):

> (1) *A party is bound to fulfil its obligations even if performance has become more onerous, whether because the cost of performance has increased or because the value of the performance it receives has diminished.*
> (2) *If, however, performance of the contract becomes excessively onerous because of a change of circumstances, the parties are bound to enter into negotiations with a view to adapting the contract or terminating it, provided that:*
>   (a) *the change of circumstances occurred after the time of conclusion of the contract,*
>   (b) *the possibility of a change of circumstances was not one which would reasonably have been taken into account at the time of the conclusion of the contract, and*
>   (c) *the risk of the change of circumstances is not one which, according to the contract, the party affected should be required to bear.*
> (3) *If the parties fail to reach agreement within a reasonable period, the court may:*
>   (a) *end the contract at a date and on terms to be determined by the court; or*
>   (b) *adapt the contract in order to distribute between the parties in a just and equitable manner the losses and gains resulting from the change of circumstances.*
>
> *In either case, the court may award damages for the loss suffered through a party refusing to negotiate or breaking off negotiations contrary to good faith and fair dealing.*

In the above provision notions such as *performance* or *agreement* may, even if read independently of their meaning in the common law, nevertheless cause in the common law reader connotations that are different from the civil law perspective. Moreover, this risk of misunderstanding increases when notions typical of the common law such as *good faith and fair dealing* are included in a language that purports to be neutral. In addition, the formulation in Art. 9: 201 PECL *Withholding Performance* or Art. 9: 303 PECL *Anticipatory Non-Performance* are probably understandable only to lawyers who know the respective common law and civil law equivalents of this concept. Furthermore, the *prescription* of PECL 14th chapter that corresponds to the common law *statute of limitations* is clearly grounded in the civil law terminology. It is therefore not really neutral, although it pretends to be it. In fact, a drafted language may be free from specific denotations due to explicit drafting guidelines that are known also to the users; language-specific connotations remain however unavoidable. Some expressions in Art. 6: 111 PECL such as *to fulfil the obligation*, *excessively onerous* or *within a reasonable period of time* will usually be construed within language-specific limits of use by the English speakers. Alleged neutrality of language use in drafting different and often contradictory legal provisions in one language, e.g. CISG, UCC, PECL or EU legislation in English will always lead to interpretive divergences because language cannot be used out of its context. If the context is overburdened by too many interpretive guidelines then the language will not fulfill its goal to function as a means of effective communication. Instead, misunderstandings that cause harm to legal certainty will emerge. More specifically, most problems concern the legislative drafting of the EU secondary law (Cordeiro 2004). Meanwhile, the legislative drafting concerns all sorts of official documents, beginning with the constitutional provisions, laws, decrees and ending with the particular decisions taken in singular cases. Another aspect concerns the correctness of language use – which doubtlessly exists in language – that is also part of language use in law and therefore part of legal linguistics. Text editing has also its part to play there. The full stop or the colon should be put in a legal text at the right place and no adventurous spelling can be allowed in official texts. Official texts, and legal texts are official *par excellence*, are characterized by increased level of intersubjectivity. They are aimed to be read, understood and enforced by other persons than their authors. They must therefore follow as close as possible the rules of linguistic correctness in order to avoid subjective or individualistic, hermetically close language use. Banalities such as correct spelling or right use of diacritic signs are part of this sort of correctness, and therefore also of the legal language, although they definitely are not its most fascinating part. Editing legal texts comprises these tasks – as trivial as they may seem – and it constitutes a link between both involved disciplines, i.e. national language philology and legal linguistics.

Translation of EU law into official languages of the member states is not unproblematic either although the relevant legal languages refer basically to the same object (cf. Baaij 2012). The databank IATE (Inter-Active Terminology for Europe) recently created within the agencies of the European Union unified the existing terminological databanks (Mattila 2010a: 727). However, it seems to be difficult to find the appropriate national legal language for this task. For instance, the Swedish language version of laws drafted in Finland is as a rule a translation from Finnish. However, according to the Finnish Constitution's Section 79 all legal acts are to be enacted and published in the Finnish and Swedish languages. According to the Government Bill concerning the new Constitution (no. 1/1991, p. 131) the enactment of the legislation in two languages means that both linguistic versions have an equal legal status. Thus, due to the enactment procedure the translated text acquires a legal status which in terms of law transforms its very nature from a translated text into an original text (Palmgren 2002: 157). Nevertheless, in terms of text type the Swedish text will remain a translation. The EU develops a type of Swedish terminology which is common for Finland and Sweden (Palmgren 2002: 159) despite persisting differences between the legal Swedish language terminology in Sweden and in Finland.

Where the EU insists upon *transparency*, the U.S. Government stresses the necessity of *plain language* use. In the U.S., the *plain language* of the legislation dominated the linguistic discussion of legislative problems. Already 1978 the U.S. President J. Carter issued an executive order to all government departments regarding the use of plain language. Likewise, U.S. President W. Clinton issued 1998 an administrative order requiring that laws be drafted in plain language as of January 1999. For instance, the (US) Securities and Exchange Commission adopted 1998 amendments to the Securities Act Rule 421 and required that the prospectus disclosure comply with the principles of plain English, including the use of active voice, short sentences, definite, concrete everyday words, tabular presentation or bullet lists, without legal or highly technical business terminology or multiple negatives (cf. Sec. Act Rel. 33–7380/1997). Furthermore, the U.S. Congress passed the Plain Writing Act of 2010. In the Act, the term *plain writing* is defined as writing that is clear, concise, well-organized, and follows other best practices appropriate to the subject or field or intended audience.

The *plain language* requirements in Europe concern mostly the UK and the Scandinavian countries (cf. Hadryan 2015). Elsewhere, the postulates for the understandability of the legal language are expressed in less assertive terms. Comparatively, the guidelines developed in Finland in regard of the use of plain Swedish language include following recommendations (cf. Palmgren 2002: 158):

a) *The official texts (including legislation) are written for the citizen's sake;*
b) *They must therefore have a linguistic style that is understandable at least for people who are willing to enter deeper into the substance;*
c) *The linguistic style is 'present-day, ordinary Swedish prose'.*

Within the *plain language* tendency legal linguists could have a role to play. They could develop linguistically founded mechanisms for legislative drafting in a way which takes account of understandability and avoids the banalization of the legal language.

5.1.6 Lessons learned

Searching for the language of the emerging global law may happen on different levels. First, the conceptual language, i.e. the language behind national languages must be defined. The task includes the identification of textual forms for this language, e.g. *codes, legal commentaries* or *legal dictionaries*. Its basis is the *meta-language of law* that is scrutinized and developed in the linguistically oriented comparative law. Second, a national language or a set of national languages must be defined to carry the concepts of the global law. Alternatively, an artificial language like Esperanto or Legal Latin may function in this role. This language must be neutral enough in order to cope with the autonomous terminology of the global law. Third, as the linguistic operations in law are dominated by argumentation, the argumentative specifics in different legal cultures must be reflected upon while drafting common provisions of substantive and procedural law. Fourth, linguistic strategies for legislative drafting should be developed in order to put in line the language of law with the realities of communication, especially as far as understandability and acceptability are concerned. Increasing the overall level of internationalization in drafting will also improve the acceptability of political decisions among citizenry. Research into legal argumentation in different legal cultures would also show which parts of the language use in law are particularly resistant to unification efforts and which parts fit smoothly into innovative conceptualizations of law.

5.2 *Épistémologie* of Law as Search for the Original Legal Language

The above scrutiny of some pertinent linguistic problems in the process of globalization of law ended with the postulate to adopt a coherent set of legal-linguistic strategies adapted to the requirements of modern societal conditions. Additionally, we could also ask whether the legal linguist may be able to learn something essential from past laws. The answers will often be elusive as we have also experienced the limits of cultural phenomena such as Greek philosophy, Roman law or the Biblical texts which are perceived by many as essential foundations of the Western culture. It seems that the retrospective upon the Biblical tradition is the least promising for law because ethical and legal issues are treated there authoritatively as received law (Gaudemet 2001: 10). They are not subject to deliberation which is the essence of law as it functions nowadays. But we can assume that the Greek philosophy as the fundamental discourse about man and the world could provide some insights into the discursive operations in law. The Roman law as a discourse of jurists about the content of law – especially in the textual form of the *Corpus Iuris Civilis* – is a deliberation which did not lose its impact until today. However, theoretically more giving are epistemological inquiries into the linguistic side of law. They show its initial grammar, i.e. processes of the emergence of legal speech acts, their terminology and textual forms which turned them into a success story in the Western world. Knowledge of epistemic regularities may help avoid disorientation, frustration and reluctance to the new legal language of the globalized world. This task can be approached from different perspectives. I will remain close to the method developed mostly for the scrutiny of humanities by Michel Foucault that in the French scientific tradition is called *épistémologie* (cf. also Galdia 2014: 65–68). I call it also in the following by an English name *epistemology* although mainly another philosophical discipline claims this denomination in the English speaking academia. Moreover, I limit myself to law and will therefore speak only about *legal epistemology*. Legal epistemology (FR *épistémologie juridique*) has been developed in France foremost by Christian Atias (1986) who referred to the work by Fr. Gény (Atias 1994: 24) as far as the coinage of the term is concerned. In parenthesis, I may mention that in the same work Fr. Gény also used the term *linguistique juridique* which was transformed here into *legal linguistics* (cf. 2.1.2). Atias sees the role of the legal epistemology in tracing the legal knowledge in terms of its scientific formation. However, he relies on the conceptual foundations set by G. Bachelard (Atias 1994: 44) and G. Canguilhem rather than on the discursive approach developed by M. Foucault and expounded by Fr. Ewald. Also the common law has been exposed to analyses that methodically represent legal epistemology. R.C. Berring (2002: 1684) described the myth of the common law with reference to the legal practice at the end of the nineteenth century: "The myth of the common law as a beautifully constructed, logically consistent, Ptolemaic system of unwritten law was still very much alive." The largely demystified law is today construed as representing in essence the legal reasoning. R. Khurana (2007: 398) remarks about this shift in the perception of law in the U.S.: "The study of law in America today remains rooted in the centuries-old traditions of Roman and Anglo-American law as systematized and interpreted by the disciplines of legal philosophy or jurisprudence. Law students now learn "the law" not as a collection of statutes but rather as a set of principles, doctrines, and rules that have evolved over the course of centuries and are said to constitute legal reasoning itself." Meanwhile, discursiveness as a steering idea dominates many theoretical approaches to law.

5.2.1 Épistémè in law

Legal epistemology is equally deep as is the legal language. To create notions such as *plaintiff* or *defendant* a linguistic and legal practice of a court procedure is necessary. The emergence of this practice, which reflects exactly the general linguistic patterns of emergence of speech acts in forms of life proves the interdependence between the legal language and the legal institutions. In this circularity there is method and it consists in introducing or modifying the linguistic practice along the societal evolution where changes in the perception of values and norms occur. In the research, it has been regularly stressed that the process of emergence of the legal language is central to every perspective upon the legal language (Hałas 1995: 6). In fact, the reconstruction of the original language of law, which in the Western tradition had been expressed in Latin is one of the most fascinating projects within legal linguistics. It fascinates not because of nostalgia or its backward orientation toward a better or more reliable law of times past. It fascinates because it makes language used in contemporary legal practice transparent, it provides for its inner motivation. Law has qualitatively never been as efficient or humane as it is today. There is, therefore, no reason to glorify the past of the law.

Research into old law also includes other legal languages and cultures than Latin and the Roman law. It starts with ancient Chinese (Escarra 1936), Babylonian (Gaudemet 2001: 3–8, cf. also Notes and Commented Materials no. 5), Egyptian (Spiegelberg 1892, 1907, 1922; Lippert 2004), Hebrew (Gilmer 1975, Sonsino 1980, Sperber 1984, Gaudemet 2001: 8–10), Greek (Gaudemet 2001: 11–24, 28–29; Thür 2003, Husa 2013), Nordic (Amira 1882/1895), and Mediterranean (Ladjili-Mouchette 1990). The note no. 5 shows that textual forms typical of law, such as contracts have a long epistemological history of continuity and discontinuity. Although religious traditions may deny creative elements in law because they perceive it as received (e.g. Bible, Quran), they use rhetorical elements in the discourse about law. Hebrew rhetorical tradition produced neither theoretical works nor handbooks on rhetoric; meanwhile the Hebrew Bible as well as commentaries thereto abound in rhetoric figures (cf. Sloan 2001: 325).

Nowadays, Western-type societies reached a level of reasoning upon law which provides the most appropriate solutions to legally relevant social problems. These solutions may not be perfect, but they have never been as perfect as they are today. Some legal constructs have reached particular importance: *state* as distinct from citizenry, *crime* isolated from its social background and *contract* as a utopian place where the minds of the parties used to meet. *Civil society* – a term with an unclear legal status – is contrasted with *state*. *State* as a legal concept includes the following: a territory with defined boundaries, a population (with or without a national or common identity), a government or administration, recognition as a sovereign state by other sovereign states. *Sovereignty* – a claim to political authority to make policy or take action at home or abroad based on territory and autonomy, is historically associated with the modern state. Equally, *war*, even cold war is the domain of states. The corresponding '*cold peace*' is not a legal notion, yet it accompanies discourses about law (cf. Blumenberg 1968: 122). *Global governance* is one more such notional coinage. Semantic fields that emerge in legal discourses are broad. Some examples may elucidate this statement: *Contract* has been perceived as a misnomer for contemporary cell phone services because they are not results of bargain between the parties (Resnik 2014: 17). Contracts called '*cellular service agreements*' are accompanied by patronizing advice such as: "Please read carefully before filing in a safe place" (Resnik 2014: 18). Such well-intentioned hints strengthen the suspicion that one party clearly wishes to dominate another. *Household* (*domestic*) *violence* corresponds to restraining order as legal remedy. This restraining order is obtained from a court. *Financial derivatives* can be perceived as intangible commodity. Further, in the Polish terminology difference is made between (PL) *opóźnienie* ordinary delay (Art. 477 and Art. 481 of the Civil Code of Poland) and (PL) *zwłoka* qualified delay that is marked as belonging to the legal language by a qualifier *bez odpowiedzialności* for the first term and *o ile ponosi odpowiedzialność* for the second. Hence, the epistemological conception of law and the discourse about law concern different linguistic practices. The linguistic aspects of the law of Occidental type are, however, best reconstructed through the Roman law to which the Occidental law is directly tied.

5.2.2 Legal-linguistic aspects of the Roman Law

Legal epistemology in the sense of identifying legal-discursive practices and their roots is historically based upon the Roman law. The Roman law is for jurists what the Greek philosophy is for philosophers. It means that both jurists and philosophers may exercise their respective professions without knowing the Roman law or the Greek philosophy but they will never understand why their disciplines became what they are, should they decide to ignore their epistemological foundations. Moreover, one could claim that the beginning of the research into the Roman law marks also the beginning of legal linguistics. It included at least studies of legal vocabulary, categories and concepts used in law (David 1978: 51). In the sense of the above, the legal theory of the Roman law is archaeology of linguistic forms rather than other phenomena. Archaeology of thought is most effective under the criteria introduced by M. Foucault (1969). I will try to identify some forms that shaped this discursive reality and I will again strongly rely on terminology. In this context, R. Arntz (2002: 39) remarks that influences from the Roman law on the terminology are not always immediately apparent. Sometimes the terminology may have undergone fundamental changes and it may have been transformed into the national language in form of a *calque* or a neologism which is not perceptible as such any more. Therefore, it is necessary to look into the 'inner form' of the language in order to discover the conceptual and terminological legacy of other languages (Arntz 2002: 44). Yet, what does it mean to understand the inner motivation of a language? It means to be able to follow its conceptualization and lexicalization patterns. For instance, expressions like *to subpoena someone* show that the motivation in the special register is not understood by the speakers any more.

5.2.2.1 Romans conscious of legal language

The specialized language creation in law includes practices of language creation on different levels of linguistic exchange. A specific pronunciation or use of antiquated vocabulary, use of honorifics, etc., are examples regularly quoted in legal linguistics. Cicero complains in his *De Oratore* (I-193) about the antiquated language in the Law of the Twelve Tables, which sometimes was difficult to grasp for his contemporaries. Others do not complain but rather contribute to the specialized legal register and they increase its complexity but also its optimal use in legal-linguistically relevant situations. The list of abbreviations, known as *De Juris Notarum* by Valerius Probus or Gaius Aelius Gallus' lexicon *De verborum quae ad jus pertinent significatione* (Mattila 2006: 7, Mac Aodha 2014: 1) are artifacts of the later type. Gallus' work was appreciated in Rome and it was also commented upon (cf. Auli Gellii Noctes Atticae, Liber XVI in Notes and Commented Materials no. 11). Valerius Probus justifies the reasons for the existence of his work and he elaborates with a theoretical ambition unusual for the Roman jurists upon the use of abbreviations in legal texts, including both legal acts and legal actions. His short text could be perceived as one of the first legal-linguistic treatises in the development of legal linguistics. I render therefore its entire theoretical part which constitutes its introduction in a note (cf. Notes and Commented Materials no. 7). One reason for the express theoretical ambitions in *De Juris Notarum* could have been that its author had been a grammarian, not a jurist. We can assume that a Roman jurist, had he been the author of the list of abbreviations would have set up an uncommented register, and by so doing, he would expose us to one more riddle about the origins of the Roman law and its language. As for Gallus and his successors, Mattila (2006: 7) remarks that the lexicographic method once established remained productive later on in Byzantium and in the Western Europe of the Middle Ages (cf. also Barenot 2014: 11–12).

5.2.2.2 Formal legal education

Professional legal language is closely related to the emergence of formal legal education in ancient Rome. Aulus Gellius mentions in his *Noctes Atticae* the beginnings of this rudimentary and adventurous education in same places in Rome, (LAT) *in plerisque Romae stationibus* (cf. Notes and Commented Materials no. 12). Besides, from this quote it becomes plain why even today young lawyers in Germany used to article in courts in (D) *Stationen*, such as (D) *Zivilstation* or *Strafstation*. In CIC, book I. 2. (Pomponius libro singulari Enchiridii) the subsequent phases of the legal education are presented under the broader heading of the chapter *De origine iuris et omnium magistratuum et successione prudentium*. This succession of experts is possible only when there exists a notion of formal education based on the transfer of knowledge in a systematic way (Ladjili-Mouchette 1990: 423, cf. also Notes and Commented Materials no. 8). Furthermore, the Constitution *Omnem* from 16 December 533 includes even a more binding scheme with a complete curriculum for the legal education in the Byzantine Empire under Justinian. This education is based on the studies of texts in Latin and Greek and survives in the medieval legal education revigorated in Bologna in a form reduced to commentaries upon foremost Latin legal classics (Berman 1977: 903). However, it would be a risky undertaking to pretend that the details reported in the ancient sources quoted above can all be taken for face value. For us, they are interesting mostly as a testimony of an epistemological tendency in the upcoming legal reasoning. This legal reasoning was construed as "a conceptual system of law, which presupposes clarifying connections between specific legal concepts" and, consequently, also makes the defining of terms for the expression of legal concepts unavoidable (Mattila 2006: 7). Mattila (2006: 108) also persuasively showed the interrelation of term and concept in law. In its application it has been perceived mostly as forensic rhetoric. This formal division of tasks survived in the legal sciences in a slightly modified and occasionally even modernized form until today. The division of tasks in the research into legal reasoning between the legal doctrine and the legal theory has been complemented by the legal rhetoric which in the views of some would be the domain of legal linguistics of today. This is an unhealthy dichotomy as it splits what should not be divided, namely reasoning and language (cf. Recanati 2008: 10).

5.2.2.3 Use of legal Latin in contemporary statutes and court decisions

After the Norman conquest, the English statutes were written in Latin. This linguistic circumstance is less visible today as most texts of this time are quoted in publications in their English translations. So is *Magna Carta* (1215) generally known as an English language text although its original is written in Latin. Some of its provisions, such as its Art. 39 *No free man shall be seized or imprisoned, or stripped of his rights or possessions, or outlawed or exiled, or deprived of his standing in any other way, nor will we proceed with force against him, or send others to do so, except by the lawful judgment of his equals or by the law of the land* are frequently quoted in their English language version that contributed to the formation of English legal syntagmas such as *the law of the land*. The *law of the land* appears in the original as *lex terre* (*terrae*): *Nullus liber homo capiatur, vel imprisonetur, aut disseisiatur, aut utlagetur, aut exuletur, aut aliquo modo destruatur, nec super eum ibimus, nec super eum mittemus, nisi per legale judicium parium suorum vel per legem terre.* Such texts are invaluable sources for the research into the processes in which the English legal language emerged.

Nowadays, classical studies which traditionally comprise Latin and Ancient Greek are no longer perceived as an obligatory part of the academic education. However, the Latin legal terminology is still present in many statutes or precedents. One can find legal Latin used in an international instrument such as the Geneva Convention on the Status of Refugees which is applicable also in countries remote from European educational traditions. The use of Latin terms in an international instrument indicates that legal Latin is perceived as part of the general legal cultural tradition and education. The Convention Relating to the Status of Refugees states in its Article 16 (2): *A refugee shall enjoy in the Contracting State in which he has his habitual residence the same treatment as a national in matters pertaining to access to the Courts, including legal assistance and exemption from* ***cautio judicatem solvi*** (emphasis added). In this respect, legal Latin, like Greek philosophy, succeeded to overcome traditional cultural boundaries.

Also in the legal acts of the European Union legal Latin is present. For instance, Art. 16 of the European Takeover Directive (2004/25/EC) refers to the right of the sell-out of securities and it provides in its paragraph 3: *Article 15 (3) to (5) shall apply* ***mutatis mutandis*** (emphasis added). The Latin expression is printed in italics in the English language text of the directive. It is risky to interpret such language use. However, it seems possible to assert that the European legislator assumes the knowledge of basic Latin among the users of the directive. It is not possible to assess how realistic the assumption is. In turn, it is well founded to assert that it reflects the legislator's conviction that the knowledge of the legal Latin makes part of the general legal culture. In English and American court decisions Latin formulas and expressions are still occasionally used. In the Maldonado-cases (quoted in Notes and Commented Materials as text no. 61) the formula *mobilia sequuntur personam* or the terms *bona vacantia* and *jus regale* are quoted without any English translation although they are central to the decision and without the knowledge of their meaning the court opinion cannot be understood properly. Also in the heading of Art. 292

of the Constitution of India the term is used without translation: *Property accruing by escheat or lapse or as bona vacantia.* Furthermore, Art. 32 (2) of the *Constitution of India* mentions certain procedural acts in their Latin form exclusively: *The Supreme Court shall have power to issue directions or orders or writs, including writs in the nature of habeas corpus, mandamus, prohibition, quo warranto and certiorari, whichever may be appropriate, for the enforcement of any rights conferred by this Part.* This language use again presupposes the assumption of the authors that the readers know these Latin expressions. In sum, the use of Latin in current legislation and court opinions allows the conclusion that the Latin legal language is still perceived by many jurists as part of their professional culture.

5.2.2.4 *Incorporation of legal Latin into national legal languages*

Latin maxims and Latin legal terminology are incorporated into texts in other languages than Latin in different ways. In the Maldonado-case (quoted in Notes and Commented Materials no. 61) the mentioned Latin expressions and maxims such as *mobilia sequuntur personam* or by virtue of *jus regale* over *bona vacantia* (p. 1582) are quoted without translation and are not even italicized in the main English language text. Sometimes their use is adapted to their English language syntactic surroundings, e.g. a *persona ficta* (p. 1581), such *personae* (p. 1581), claiming *jure regali* (p. 1585), not as *ultimus heres* but *jure regali* (p. 1582), or (B)ut *non constat* that (p. 1586).

In some cases the Latin expressions were put between quotation marks, in others left unmarked in the English text. The differences in the treatment of the Latin expressions and maxims show that the judges sometimes perceive these lexical units as foreign and wish to mark this impression in the text. In other cases, they may identify these expressions with the national legal language which does not necessitate any differentiation. This comes close to the terminology which grounds in the legal Latin and which provides for the multitude of variations in national languages: *avocat, advokat, advokaat, advocate, avvocato, advogado, abogado* for *attorney-at-law.* The created concepts refer to the original (LAT) *advocatus* that is transformed in line with the phonetic rules of the involved languages. This procedure for creation of legal-linguistic vocabulary is relatively simple. More complicated are notional correspondences such as (D) *Rechtsanwalt* or the English *attorney-at-law* which function in the textual contexts of (LAT) *advocatus.* Moreover, it is challenging to trace and to prove the genetic link between, e.g. (LAT) *persona legalis* and (CN) *fărén* or (LAT) *emptio-venditio* and (CN) *măimai* that correspond literally. The Latin terminology survives in the legal language apparently in times and places remote from the space where it emerged.

5.2.2.5 *Systematization in the Roman law*

In legal linguistics aspects of systematization that are related to language must be analyzed because the systematization is one of the fundamental legal-linguistic operations. In the diachronic perspective the systematization is primarily related to the formation of concepts. It is linked on the synchronic level to the legal argumentation (cf. 3.1.2). In the diachronic perspective upon law, the Roman law is central to this undertaking. Indeed, the idea that something different from 'systematization' had been in the center of the Roman legal thinking was often claimed in the research. In this context especially the 'casuistic nature' of the early Roman law had been stressed. As J. Gaudemet (1986: 11) put it: *Que les Romains aient envisagé le droit sous son aspect casuistique, nul ne saurait le contester.* Nevertheless, the Roman law offers more than a casuistic inventory and this is the reason why it has fascinated generations of jurists from the very Middle Ages until our own day. The ancient Roman lawyers developed the notion of a contract toward the background of a metaphor of a link or a bound of law (*iuris vinculum*). In *Digesta Iustiniani* and in *Institutiones* this image is invoked to make clear the binding nature of the contractual relation: *Obligatio est iuris vinculum, quo necessitate adstringimur alicuius solvendae rei secundum nostrae civitatis iura* (cf. D 44.7.3 and I 3,13). The medieval legal commentator Bartolus de Saxoferrato glossed upon this metaphor: *Dicit ergo littera: Obligatio est iuris vinculum. Exponitur iuris vinculum, i.e. ius vinciens. Sicut enim boves finibus ligantur, ita et homines verbis obligantur. Iuris vinculum* has been also interpreted in *Institutiones Iustiniani* (I. 2,2) toward the distinction between material and immaterial things: *Ut enim boves funibis visualiter ligantur, sic homines verbis ligantur intellectualiter.* This interpretation stresses the immaterial character of an obligation and starts the intellectual legal-theoretical tradition of invisible law. Bartolus opposes this crude image regularly used by the ancient Romans and later commentators of the Roman law and stresses the factual element of performance of a contract rather than the metaphorical bound between the parties tied to each other by words like cattle that is tied by cords: *Nascitur illa obligatio ex facto vel ex beneficio, cum ad vinculum illius iuris naturalis suo modo, cuius iuris aequitas dictat bene facienti bene facere. Illa autem obligatio, quam ius recepit, sicut est in nudis pactis, est introducta de iure gentium.* These historical views are present even today in the legal doctrine as remnants of the theoretical discussion about the nature of the contract that has been construed in the mutually exclusive essentialist and constructivist perspectives. One of the particular reasons for this fascination with the nature of concepts has been the presence of many concepts used nowadays in the writings of classical Roman legal writers such as Gaius, Ulpianus and Paulus or in the *Corpus Iuris Civilis.* The Roman law seems to be edified as a legal system when seen in the retrospective taken from the CIC (Ladjili-Mouchette 1990: 421). The Roman jurists did not explain in their writings – at least in those disponible to posterity – their conceptual method (Glendon 1999: 39, Husa 2013: 13–15). Thus, it has to be reconstructed.

5.2.2.5.1 Possible reconstructions

The roots of such a reconstruction are far reaching. For instance, a concept such as *res publica* has been used by the Romans without any distinction of the regime. Its lexical form is strikingly simple and is therefore apt to cover whatever form of governance. Concepts, however, function in contrast. The networks in which these contrasts can be observed are the basis for their linguistic and epistemological reconstruction. The epistemological reconstruction of the Roman law would have to start in the private law with the dichotomy of *actor/reus* as the dialectical source of litigation perceived by the Romans as contradictory and its instrument, actions of different sorts. Thus, where the *actor* (plaintiff) brings the suit, there should also be a *reus* (defendant) to be held liable. Furthermore, a specific procedure is needed which includes the *actio* as its main argumentative element. *Actor* does not simply complain to the *praetor* about someone; he starts a litigation with *reus*, who in case of a contested demand *(exceptio)* becomes himself *actor* (cf. the rule *excipiendo reus fit actor* in a case of *probatio*). The litigation continues until the claim or the exception is proven. That *reus* must correspond to *actor* may be understandable, the necessity of *actio* will forever remain a special feature of the Roman law, which interfered with and sometimes even confused the legal thinking until our times.

Furthermore, the background and the emergence of one of the most important concepts of private law, *obligatio,* are documented in the sources. Gaius (3, 88) says about it: *Omnis enim obligatio vel ex contractu nascitur vel ex delicto. Obligatio est iuris vinculum, quo necessitate adstringimur alicuius solvaendae rei secundum nostrae civitatis iura.* Gaius' words were additionally commented in *Corpus Iuris Civilis* (I. 313). Max Kaser (1983: 149) claims that Gaius' words were a description rather than a definition. However, the more the concept was used the more it was commented upon. Paulus (D 44, 7, 3) says: *obligationum substantia non in eo consistit, ut aliquod corpus nostrum aut servitutem nostram faciat, sed ut alicui nobis obstringat ad dandum aliquid vel faciendum vel praestandum.* This approach comes already very close to the later commentary (interpretation) of concepts before they were applied in practice. The analysis of the dialectical procedure for emerging concepts is different from anthropological or ethnological analysis of *obligatio* as a mental state of being bound by a promise which may not be accessible to all minds in all cultures. Undoubtedly, somewhere in the deepest layers of our and Roman legal consciousness there must have been an identification with the idea of *obligatio,* although even today not everyone and not everywhere feels equally bound by a promise. The same concerns the tendency to create concepts out of common language, such as *possessio* (...) or *dominium/proprietas* (...) (cf. also Aikhenvald et al. 2015). In this context, Ulpian (D 43, 17, 1, 2) stresses the necessity to distinguish between these legal concepts and the daily use which apparently differed from it:... *separata esse debet possessio a proprietate: fieri etenim potest, ut alter possessor sit, dominus non sit; possessor vero non sit: fieri potest, ut et possessor idem et dominus sit.* Legal concepts, once created, could have been replaced by others, such as *pignus* which was later replaced by *hypotheca* in most contexts whereby its meaning was again modified in Institutiones Iustiniani (I 4, 6, 7). Nowadays uncertainty reigns as to the scope of both concepts (Kolańczyk 1986: 328). The Romans had apparently less problems with understanding them. As mentioned above, the Roman jurists did not teach us their methodology. We used to learn their concepts as we go along reading the ancient sources. There, systematization efforts increase with time. A typical procedure in Rome was to enter *in medias res*, and, for instance, introduce a sale of goods contract (*emptio venditio)* without defining it otherwise than by the description of its components. It was stated that parties of the contract *(conventio)* had to agree about the price *(pretium)* and the object of the contract (*res*), (cf. Gaius 3, 139–141: *Emptio et venditio contrahitur, cum de pretio convenerit, quamvis nondum pretium numeratum sit, ac ne arra quidem data fuerit; nam quod arrae nomine datur, argumentum est emptionis et venditionis contractae...et I. 3, 23: Emptio et venditio contrahitur, simulatque de pretio convenerit...*).

5.2.2.5.2 Case study 'res incorporales'

The concepts of the Roman law usually emerge in the form of a simple introduction which coincides with their creation. We are not told how they came about nor can we know what their theoretical origins were. Gaius' writing is the most striking example of such a procedure. In his *Institutes* 2,12 and 2,14 he introduces the distinction between corporeal and incorporeal things: *12. Quaedam praeterea res corporales sunt, quaedam incorporales. Corporales hae sunt quae tangi possunt, velut fundus, homo, vestis, aurum, argentum et denique aliae res innumerabiles...14. Incorporales sunt quae tangi non possunt, qualia sunt ea quae jure consistunt, sicut hereditas, ususfructus, obligationes quoquo modo contractae.*

Whereas some of the named institutions in sentence 14 may be perceived as pre-legal and thus not particularly interesting in the context of the emergence of legal terminology, the statement that also *obligationes* were among incorporeal things provides insight into the methods of concept creation in the Roman world. However, some scholars such as M. Kaser (1983: 90) claimed that the above distinction proved to be without any particular influence upon the Roman law: "Praktische Bedeutung hat diese schulmäßige Einteilung in Rom nicht gehabt." This opinion may surprise because the distinction and the example of *obligatio* as an incorporeal thing enabled various transactions related to them in analogy to corporeal things. Thus, it became possible to sell *obligationes*, to claim rights to them in an action or to assign them. Furthermore, the distinction allowed jurists such as Gaius, and later on also Justinian's compilators, to treat both in one chapter as *ius quod ad res pertinet*. Therefore, the importance of this distinction cannot be overestimated. According to Gaius the incorporeal things existed through the law in force (*...quae in iure existent,* Gaius 2.2). This is amazing as a sophisticated, if not a Greek, idea. And indeed, the traditional research into Roman law stresses the Greek character of this thought (Kolańczyk 1986: 262). The French classic of the Roman law research Stroux refers in this context to the work of the grammarian Charisius. In fact, the scarce sources of the classical Roman law do not allow claiming Gaius's authorship of the concept. However, in the discussion about the distinction it can be treated as one introduced by Gaius, at least for the audience of later centuries. It had been assumed that until Gaius the Romans did not make any distinction of this kind (Girard 1928: 273). Moreover, it had been claimed that this distinction may have been opposed by Cicero in his *Topica* (27). Cicero's words may rather prove his ignorance of the concept. They do not prove his criticism on it. In his philosophical analysis Cicero rather concedes the possibility of existence of incorporeal things: "26. Definitio est oratio, quae id, quod definitur, explicat, quod sit. Definiendum autem due sunt genera prima: unum earum rerum, quae sunt: alterum earum, quae intellegitur. 27. Esse ea dico quae cerni tangire possunt, ut fundum, aedes, parietem, stillicidum, manicipium, pecudum, supellectilem, penus, cetera; quo ex genere quaesdam interdum nobis definienda sunt. Non esse rursus ea dico, quae tangi demonstrarivae non possunt, cerni tamen animo, atque intellegi possunt. Ut, si usucapionem, si tutelam, si gentem, si agnationem definias: quarum rerum nullum subest quasi corpus: est tamen quaedam conformatio insignita et impressa intelligentiae: quam notionem voco."

All above findings show that it is possible to trace the lexicalization of concepts undertaken in the ancient Roman law. Overall, the creation of the concept 'res incorporales' is what G. Deleuze and F. Guattari call *l'art de former des concepts* in their work where they characterized the way how philosophical concepts were formed. They posited that *la philosophie est l'art de former, d'inventer, de fabriquer des concepts* (Deleuze/ Guattari 1991: 8 ; cf. also Searle 1999: 159). In philosophy this view may be controversial, but in classical Roman law it hits the nail on the head. Consequently, we encounter here a process deemed as philosophical by its nature, namely creating concepts. It is aiming at tracing the way how concepts of which many still remain essential to our law were invented by Roman jurists and applied in the Roman jurisprudence.

5.2.2.5.3 The rule *in Roman law*

The Roman jurists did not display any particular interest in the idea of a system; they also omitted the reflection upon another central legal concept of modern jurisprudence – the rule. However, the CIC (50. 17.1) provides Paulus' definition of a rule: *Regula est, quae rem, quae est, breviter enarrat. Non ut ex regula ius sumatur, sed ex iure, quod est, regula fiat.* As is so often the case, they lay the ground for future elaboration of theories (Ladjili-Mouchette 1990: 456). The Roman legal rule that is rooted in interpretation emerges at a point where the disparate rules are positioned in a context (cf. Ladjili-Mouchette 1990: 423); they function as the epistemological background of systematization. This extraordinary intellectual capacity has been soon instrumentalized politically; the personal authority of the interpreter to determine the meaning of legal rules on behalf of public authorities (LAT *jurisconsultum*) has been replaced by an officially attributed privilege (LAT *ius publice respondendi*, cf. CIC 1.2.2.47). In modern legal thinking *system*, *rule* and *concept* compete with each other for the supremacy in the realm of jurisprudence. Indeed, creating legal concepts appears to be its very essence and applying these concepts remains the main task of the legal practice. Applying the law – or its concepts – includes interpretation (lege artis) of its rules; creating concepts involves knowledge of specific techniques which by their very nature are extra-legal. That *concept* attracted the Roman jurists more than rules may be connected with the partition of tasks among the legislator and the legal writers. The legislator usually does not introduce self-made concepts, e.g. *negotiorum gestio*. He rather decides that in the case of *negotiorum gestio* the costs of an operation of law shall be borne by one of the parties concerned. This means that he sets up a rule.

5.2.3 Following ancient Greeks or Romans and their law?

In a work perceived as prolegomena to an emerging branch of legal science and/or linguistics, I spent a lot of time upon issues which are perceived as belonging to history. And indeed, the reflection upon the Roman law or the development of rhetoric in ancient Greece are definitely topics which can be perceived as historical. I nevertheless mentioned that I perceive historical experience and testimony, especially the written one, in a specific perspective. I concentrated on them from the epistemological point of view and I tried to understand how legal terms or concepts as well as forms of legal argumentation emerged and developed as parts of the legal language. I also mentioned that interpretive methods in law which have a long history can be perceived as a part of the legal metalanguage in that they enable the understanding of utterances formulated in a special register which is different from that in daily use. The epistemological interpretation made it possible to grasp some aspects of this development. Therefore, the retrospective made sense for me in a research which is not predominantly historical but rather methodological. Could this retrospective contribute also to a prospective view, to the view of the law of the future? Does it allow the identification of tendencies in the development of the prospective law and its language? I think it does. The retrospective taught us, roughly speaking, that the Romans concentrated their efforts on constructing their law upon concepts. The ancient Greeks stressed rather the legal argumentation. Of course, this assertion, when expressed that sweepingly, invites opposition. Were not the Greeks also masters of concepts? Yes, they were. Were not the Romans among the best court orators? Yes, without any doubt. Nevertheless, in our epistemological perspective upon the law and the legal language in the Antiquity they pertain to two conceptions of law. Ancient Greeks were also critical of pure rhetoric. Paul Woodruff (2011) demonstrated that the idea of justice prevailed in Greek culture over the less complex fairness of daily practice. No social management or common sense fairness could meaningfully compete with philosophically and discursively engendered just decision. Likewise, the ancient Greeks opposed in the fundamentals of their culture algorithmic solutions to social problems. Meanwhile, the ancient Greek court procedure appears at times as very 'Roman'. The propositions of law have been clarified differently in both traditions of Western antiquity. The Greeks maintained that what is right or wrong in their society is defined in the agora (GR αγορά) as a result of free deliberation among citizens. Their legal reasoning had been based on ideas of justice and coherence (Ladjili-Mouchette 1990: 421) that grounded in the Greek dialectics. Additionally, J. Mansfeld (1964) analyzed and reconstructed the fundamental language of the Greek court decision. The judge finds out *dike* (Δίκη) that is the right of persons that appear before him. He establishes a *judgment* (κρίσις) that in the Greek language means also *discernment*. The legal person is according to Mansfeld defined through its property right. Therefore, when a person is injured the perpetrator is obliged to shift a part of his property upon the injured as compensation. Constitutive of such a judgment is the adjudication of the property right to another person. The judgment has obligatory force, it binds the parties (πειράς means *bound*). The judgment is *communicated* (δείκνυμι). The process and its language may have according to Mansfeld a religious background.

The Romans, in turn, discovered the law through conceptual analysis based on the scrutiny of legal texts. What can we learn from this experience? We have seen that legal concepts and legal terms which represent them in legal texts have an essential role to play in the legal argumentation. Legal argumentative texts, oral or written, are centered on crucial legal terms which condition their structure. Legal argumentation and legal systematization are therefore not opposite, they are complementary operations. In both of them, the Roman and the Greek legal landscapes merge into a law that is understood as a discursive practice. I do not pretend that the ancient Greeks or Romans did not understand this ontological implication of law and its language. However, I argue that nowadays we (which means here not only the author of these lines but persons dealing with legal theory and legal linguistics) understand these two landscapes in a particular way. It means that we are able to explicitly describe them in an epistemological perspective. Our inquiry ends, therefore, with a happy end.

Part 6: Law of Linguistic Communication

Human communication takes place in processes of creation and interpretation of interconnected signs. In the area of law the most interesting signs are legal signs, yet other signs accompany them. They enable the emergence of meaning in law and are constitutive of the legal discourse. More often than not these legal and non-legal signs are not strictly linguistic (e.g. gestures such as handshakes or design of courts of law or design of courtrooms). Meanwhile, they may also be perceived as a background to linguistic communication in law as the understanding of legal discourses is exhaustive only toward the background and within the interplay of legal and non-legal verbal and non-verbal sign systems. However, the importance of strictly linguistic communication in law cannot be put aside; speaking, reading, and writing are activities that technically dominate professional and non-professional activities in the area of law. Legal linguistics researches the way legislators and other jurists influence communication processes through legislative acts. It asks whether law structures linguistic communication in line with our knowledge about the functioning of linguistic processes. When jurists' approaches to communication correspond to linguistic insights the legal linguist can withdraw from the field as his further involvement would be obsolete. When however the legal linguist discovers a discrepancy between the linguistic and the legal understanding of communication, he has to get involved in the best interest of speakers. Law as a discursive practice cannot work differently from other productive discourses in our societies. In these discourses, law and language are interdependent. Wherever law functions differently than language it becomes dysfunctional as a practice that should inspire and steer society. Moreover, as law regulates also its own language and the use of language in society, legal linguistics has also the task to assist the legislator at this point and to contribute a linguistically acceptable structure for linguistic legislation. The mentioned problems can be discussed under the label of Law of Linguistic Communication that is perceived here as a research area integrated into legal linguistics.

6.1 Communication and Information in Legal Linguistics

The concept of communication as well as the related concept of information are perceived as controversial in the branches of science that deal with them predominantly. Communication may be understood as the aim of the discursive action, information as the content of communicative acts. In the legal-linguistic perspective both concepts acquire a specific meaning because law also regulates communication and information (cf. van Hoeke 2002: 8). However, the traditional concept of communication that is based on pure sound emission and its reception (Badura 2007: 17) is not interesting in our context. Equally, information that is defined around the concept of code will not do either in our approach to human speech (cf. van Peursen et al. 1984: 66–70). Likewise, some definitional aspects will remain problematic in this area. For some theorists of communication, a *monologue* or a *diary note* are no acts of communication because the interlocutor is missing in them. In law, however, such communicative constellations are interesting because the missing receiver may emerge at whatever moment and take note of them. Therefore, for legal linguistics also potential communicative acts are interesting as long as they are regulated by law. The area of social practices that is concerned by our topic is immense. It includes, for instance, legal issues such as what can be legally written in this book, what can be legally written about this book by reviewers, how much of the book can be quoted in other works without the permission of the copyright holder etc. The same concerns oral speech: What can I say to hearers of my lectures on legal linguistics within the limits of legal regulation? Where are the limits set by legislation to my public speaking about law? Therefore, when I ask: What can I write in my articles and which opinions about my writing talents am I obliged to accept as matters of law? I pose a question that has legal-linguistic implications. This is mainly the case because legality seems to be one of the steering mechanisms in legal discourses.

The central moment in the regulation of communication and information, at least in Western democracies, is an overall positive approach of legislators to the issue. Communication is perceived in law as a natural activity of humankind and it enjoys constitutional protection as a human right. Freedom of speech is a quintessential concept that has been created for this purpose. Its role is to further define legality of speech in social contexts. This mechanism implies also the legal principle that there cannot be any unlimited freedom of speech. In the area of the law of linguistic communication the main tension that challenges legal discourses is the relation between legally approved and illegal speech acts. Law of Linguistic Communication concerns the legal range of communicative situations. These communicative situations are regulated in law where limits of the freedom of speech are set in statutory law and in precedents. This area of law marks the legal limits of public communication. As a rule, law does not interfere with private communication, especially among family members. However, one may notice that nowadays some boundaries emerge in respect of language used among spouses or between parents and their children. Overall, one may maintain that it is by far not evident any more that vulgar, intimidating, humiliating or degrading language be used in communication among family members without legal sanctions. In penal law, certain communicative situations can nowadays be even perceived as exercise of violence, for instance in cases when recurrent use of degrading or humiliating speech by a spouse causes the suicide of the other spouse. Yet, as of now regulation of public speech dominates legal acts that interest us here.

6.1.1 Legal discourse and legal communication

The above remarks signal also a narrow relation between the legal discourse and the legal communication. The legal discourse represents the acts of legal communication (cf. Goodrich 1987; Mattila 2013: 41). It embraces in a structured way messages that were communicated in legally relevant situations. Traditionally, specific aspects of legal communication have been dealt within legal rhetoric (Galdia 2009: 157). Subsequently, the discovery of broader textual structures such as legal texts and legal discourses shifted the interest in this domain toward explicitly communicational conceptions. Therefore, contemporary legal communication as research object is rooted either in the broad conception of the legal text and its components or in the parallel broad conception of the legal discourse with its constitutive elements that are the subject of this book. For instance, Mattila (2013a: 41–85) discusses many such discourses under the headline of '*functions of legal language*'. On the other side, in logically founded approaches to legal discourses the main stress is set upon the juridical reasoning. Language in its broader setting is analyzed there in order to infer laws of juridical reasoning from it. This approach to legal discourses is typical of the mainstream legal theory. In linguistically founded approaches the legal discourse is the most complex structure constituted of the legal language. It is approached from the perspective of its communicative function. In general linguistics, communication is since the work of Roman Jakobson perceived as the main function of language (cf. Mounin 1968: 80). Legal linguists may therefore rely on it when approaching legal language. In legal language it cannot happen that a message is there, yet it lacks communicative value. Legally relevant texts are always interpretable in terms of communication because an element of intention is always included in them, be it only in the negative. This happens in semantically evasive or purposefully imprecise legal texts that are typical of the modern state under the rule of law (Engberg 2007: 76–77).

Legal information is communicated with the help of argumentative speech acts. Legal argumentation is simply communication related to legal messages. The legally relevant message may be structured in a relatively simple way. The road signs used on the European Continent are a good example of such apparently simple structure. Round signs stand for prohibited action, triangles for danger, blue signs signal obligation or permission. The combination of shape, color and some additional distinctive elements makes the production of numerous acts of obligation or prohibition possible. Yet, the situation is not as simple as that. In order to understand that a white triangle with a red margin stands for the prohibition of certain acts in traffic one has to know quite a lot about signs. It would probably be easier to write: *No entrance* instead of deciphering the sign that conveys this meaning. A sign in general, not only a traffic sign, is arbitrary to its message. It could mean whatever, yet also what it means. Even a road sign that announces the curve and that instrumentalizes a simplified drawing of the curve is only partly symbolical and immediately readable. Interpretive skills, context and background knowledge will be still necessary to decipher the meaning hidden behind it. The communicative situation, i.e. that road signs are read in traffic necessitates the use of an abbreviated code that as such is only apparently simple. A road sign therefore transfers a message, yet it does not communicate it. Communication emerges when the procedural knowledge that the recipient possesses is used in order to grasp the meaning of the transmitted message. Thus, even the most visualized signs in law do not communicate automatically. Their simple meaning is engendered in relatively complicated semiotic operations of apprehension and interpretation. Modern media and especially the internet add examples to this already disparate picture. While informal modes of communication are normal even in public institutions such as governments, one may bear in mind that these institutions are based on formal rules and formalized relations (cf. Berring 2000; Craig 2013: 120). Therefore, communication is a very complex situation of language use in law. One could ask whether it can be treated as a speech act at all or whether it is too heterogeneous to be integrated as a working concept into the legal-linguistic research related to discursive practices.

6.1.1.1 Defining speech

The visual and the linguistic aspects of law have at least one common feature that is their expressiveness. Whenever something is expressed, the law approaches it as speech. Speech is in the American law protected by the First Amendment of the U.S. Constitution. Many other countries also perceive speech as expression of thought, not only the linguistic variety of thought. In the American law, pictures, graphic design, concept art, sounds, music, stories, and narrative present in video games are speech in the sense of the First Amendment (cf. C.B.C. Distribution and Marketing, Inc. v. Major League Baseball Advanced Media, LP, 505 F.3d 818, 2007). Expressiveness connects rather than divides the visual and the linguistic elements of law. Therefore, discourses about visual aspects of law are possible and they also take place. They are part of law as a discursive practice. In the extreme ambiguity of the image they challenge the rationality in law. After all, challenging the rationality of law is a justifiable and even helpful enterprise. It should, however, not be confused with the idea that there is no rationality in law. Furthermore, showing how complex is the legal rationality is one thing. Claiming that because of ambiguity and fluidity of the iconic message there is no rationality in law, is another thing. As legal rationality can be engendered only with linguistic means, the iconic challenge remains a trigger point in the legal discourse, not its basis. This interrelation clearly favors the linguistic element over the iconic. It is therefore doubtful whether significant changes could occur in this submission of one semiotic process under another in the future. Also, or even predominantly, in terms of semiotics, law is a quest for rationality in obtaining justice. Would it be redefined in a way that would stress its purely iconic character, it would become uninteresting as a social mechanism that has to fulfill a regulative task in society (cf. also Kocher 1992, Feigenson 2006, Modéer et al 2012). Therefore, the linguistic turn is a valuable goal to be envisaged in the legal science and the discourses around it. The iconic turn is welcome, as long as it does not pretend to introduce a post-linguistic period in law.

6.1.2 Truth and lies

Communication depends on contents and contents are meaningful when they are true. In some areas of law, truth is only a guest as communication is dominated by manipulative practices that oscillate between true and false. Legal linguistics researches this specific area of societal discourse and especially the linguistic inadequacies engendered by the use of such communicational devices. Lies are the stronger form of linguistic inadequacies (cf. Weinrich 1966). They are stronger than over-interpretations because they ground in intentional manipulation of truth that is usually not the case with over-interpretations. Semiotically, lies have been characterized as speech acts that are easy to accomplish verbally, while displaying considerable problems in terms of paraverbal (e.g. tone of voice) or nonverbal (e.g. body language, facial expression) communicative components (Watzlawick et al. 1974). Paraverbal and non-verbal components of lies are therefore particularly challenging for liars because they are regularly unmasked with the help of communicative parameters based on extra-linguistic communicative components. Lies are frequently represented in legal-linguistic contexts and it is therefore surprising that they did not attract much attention in the research. Especially, lies may constitute the factual basis for cases and dominate witness testimony. Sometimes also lawyers provide in their briefs objectively non-existent information about the law, e.g. reference to precedents which allegedly prove their contentions while knowing that this is not the case. Lies are particularly dangerous in the witness testimony because the proof of the contrary is frequently impossible since the witness may have been the only person who has acquired factual knowledge about a past event. Sometimes, lies can be detected through the linguistic analysis of coherence in the testimony. However, illogical formulations, especially the contradictory ones do not necessarily prove that the witness is lying because he/she may not be a good speaker but they signal that the witness should be asked further questions in order to clarify unclear formulations (cf. Bronston v. U.S. in Notes and Commented Materials no. 56). Needless to mention that a skillful liar usually has no linguistic problems to lie successfully in a court of law and to remain unmasked. In terms of linguistic pragmatics lies are speech acts characterized by the abuse of the communicational procedure. They are possible because no biological linguistic mechanism hinders the formulation of utterances about facts performed with the speaker's intention not to state the facts but their contrary while pretending to state the facts. Pragmatists were not particularly interested in such cases because the speech act theory is based upon felicity conditions for speech acts which are fulfilled only when the speaker says what he intends to say and when he is convinced that what he is saying is true (Baylon 1991: 238; Davidson 2001: 273). Speech acts may also be formulated under less prosperous circumstances but then these circumstances make explicitly part of an utterance. Thus, in such situations the speaker would say *I doubt, I could imagine that...* etc. These formulations guarantee that the speech act is felicitous even in less determinate situations. The same concerns other deliberately unclear formulations applied with the goal to deceive, especially when they are not easily identifiable as unclear or are not identified as unclear by certain recipients. A typical communicative situation of this sort is illustrated by the mentioned case Bronston v. U.S. In law, misrepresentation is the most prominent example of such a speech act. N. Jareborg (1972: 445) and G. Falkenberg (1982) described this type of misrepresentation in their research. The contrary constellation is *self-deception*

(Searle 1999: 71) where the speaker deceives himself, e.g. claiming not to be jealous although the contrary is evident to every observer. Related errors such as *misinterpretations* and *temporary infatuations* (Searle ibid.) follow suit. Meanwhile, truth in law is procedural. Bańkowski (1981) speaks of a *truth certifying procedure* that is formalized in the verdict. What is said in the procedure is taken as an established truth for all ulterior purposes of the law, unless and until it is quashed on appeal (Bańkowski 1981: 129). Therefore, objectively false declarations of the parties that may both wish to avoid the confrontation with the truth in a court of law become true through the procedure in which they function as a basis for the application of law. As indicated, it seems that lies do not have any future in the pragmatic research. They do not interest particularly because they are preconditioned by the sincerity requirement; without the hearer's trust in what is said there is no possibility of lying (Baylon 1991: 238). The case Bronston v. U.S. shows this interpretive mechanism in action. In law, however, lies matter in a specific way. The legal process based on lies makes of law a hopeless enterprise. When lies remain undiscovered, law loses any sense and perturbs society which it is expected to guide and to protect. Researching lies is therefore extremely important for legal linguistics.

6.1.2.1 Half-truths

In the legal practice, the so-called *half-truths* are particularly common in witness testimony and in utterances made by corporate officers, especially in forward looking statements. Cases such as First Virginia Bankshares v. Benson (559 F.2d 1307, 1314; 5th Cir. 1977), Backman v. Polaroid Corp. (910 F.2d, 10; 1 Cir. 1990), Cooperman v. Individual Inc. (171 F.3d 43; 1st Cir., 1999) illustrate the discrepancy between the legal obligation to speak completely when making a statement and the strategy to avoid the plain disclosure of material facts. Therefore, in law, the half-truths emerge in situations where the duty to speak completely is violated (Langevoort 1999: 87, Anderson/Furberg 1977: 161, cf. also Bacewicz 2003). Close to the duty to speak completely is the duty to update relevant information which has been made public (Cox 2006: 690). The test of factual materiality in such a case is that the disclosed information is still relied upon by the third party, that it is 'alive' (Weiner v. Quaker Oats Co., 129 F.3d 310; 3d Cir., 1997). A further constellation concerns a duty to correct when information disclosed was objectively false but relied upon by the maker of the statement who only later discovers its falsehood. The legal consequences, at least in securities litigations, should be the same as in cases concerning the duty to update (Cox 2006: 691). False information can be furthermore disseminated by or through third parties. Again, especially in securities litigations, when the party endorses statements done by third parties that subsequently turn out to be wrong, it may have the duty to correct them (Elkind v. Ligget & Myers Inc., 635 F.2d 156, 2d Cir. 1980). This can occur today through the creation of a hyperlink connection to the information (e.g. a report) issued by a third party. The situation becomes even more complicated when the party which establishes the link to an electronically available report which is favorable to its economic interests (and which is objectively false, e.g. too favorable) simultaneously places a warning or a disclaimer that it is not responsible for the information provided by the third party. This again comes close to a constellation that a party is disseminating false information through the third party. Overall, the requirements for a complete testimony developed by the legal science correspond to the principle of exhaustivity in discourse that requires the information maximally compatible with the truth (Baylon 1991: 239). Classical rhetoric knows a corresponding figure called *litotes* which consists in saying less than one would like to be understood. Through the *litotes* the thought is often expressed by its opposite, especially by adding *not* to the speech act. Moreover, in a declaration *I have three children*, the existence of the fourth child or even more children is logically not excluded; nevertheless the declaration will be understood in this narrower sense under the circumstances of testimony, i.e. as limited to three children. Such utterances modify the application of the principle of discursive exhaustivity. Summing this up, the pragmatic conditions of a speech act aiming at avoiding the half-truth are: speaking completely within the boundaries of confidentiality and making clear that some information may be hold back due to its confidentiality, updating and correcting issued information when the information is material and is still relied upon, possibly also correcting and updating information provided by third parties and avoiding any reference to it which is limited by disclaimers. Disseminating misleading and false information through third parties is the most blatant example of the violation of the procedure to speak completely when making a statement which is relevant to the public.

6.1.2.2 Controlling lies

Lies are rarely named as such by courts. Nevertheless, the way in which judges evaluate witness testimony frequently suggests that they perceive the party or witness depositions not as inadequacies or misunderstandings, but as lies. Courts apply rationality tests based on linguistic and extralinguistic knowledge to detect lies. In MCC-Marble Ceramic Center v. Ceramica Nuova d'Agostino, S.P.A. (144 F 3rd. 1384, 11th Cir., 1998) the court had to decide whether the parties agreed upon the application of the defendant's terms and conditions of sale. The terms of the sale contract between the parties were set upon a pre-printed order form provided by the defendant with terms and conditions on the reverse side. The plaintiff provided affidavits by three of his employees. In these documents, the court was ensured that the employees involved in the signing of the contract on behalf of the plaintiff did not take notice of defendant's terms and conditions because they were entirely in the Italian language. The court remarked:

> *We find it nothing short of astounding that an individual, purportedly experienced in commercial matters, would sign a contract in a foreign language and expect not to be bound simply because he could not comprehend its terms. The general proposition is that they will bind parties who sign contracts regardless of whether they have read them or understand them. ... Affidavits of MCC acknowledged that D'Agostino's representatives were aware*

of MCC's subjective intent not to be bound by the fine print terms...What a judge or a jury does with the parol evidence once it is entered into evidence is within their discretion as the weighers of the evidence. A reasonable finder of fact is free to disregard the parol evidence that conflicts with the written contract. Thus, it may disregard testimony that sophisticated international merchants signed a contract without intending to be bound as simply too incredible to believe and hold MCC to the conditions printed on the reverse side of the contract. However this is for the trier of fact to determine.

Further, in Finnish Fur Sales Co., Ltd. v. Juliette Shulof Furs, Inc. et al (770 F. Supp. 139, S.D.N.Y., 1991) one of the defendants denied liability under the contract and claimed that conditions of the public sale did not become part of the contract due to their unconscionability. The defendant took part in a fur auction and was given there a booklet with sale conditions which a.o. provided for personal liability of bidders in the auction until the full payment of the price by the represented party. The court remarked: "Nevertheless, the perusal of the Conditions reveals that their entire text is only a single page long, and that all of the Conditions, including section 4, are printed in the same size print, which, although small, is legible. Under these circumstances, it seems unlikely that a New York court would refuse to enforce Section 4 in an arm's-length commercial transaction involving a sophisticated defendant accustomed to bidding at fur auctions." Here, the defendant did not argue that he did not know about the contractual condition providing for his personal liability. Instead, he challenged the legality of the clause. The situation is nevertheless similar to the preceding case. The resemblance is situated in the denial to properly qualify the facts of an event. The court's opinion therefore resembles the preceding one, especially in that it underscores the commercial experience of the party denying the facts which underlie the legal defense. Overall, the contentions analyzed here are in terms of private law and procedure defenses against claims. In the pragmatic perspective they become interesting because they show how parties manipulate the choice of facts they present to the court. By doing so, they abuse the legal procedure. This abuse is discovered by courts and sanctioned such that the parties lose their cases. It happens because they do not play according to the rules of the procedure. The underlying rule of the procedure is that facts presented by the parties must correspond to reality. Their quality of being an efficient defense is not decisive in a legal process. Lies discovered in private litigations rarely lead to criminal prosecution as *perjuries*. Regretfully, oath is rarely sworn in courts on such occasions.

6.1.2.3 Commercial lies

Limits to the freedom of speech in the commercial sphere reflect the tendency among the professionals of commerce to blur the distinction between truth and lie. Lies in the commercial sphere are mostly half-truths, for instance when a 'tax deferred' investment is described by a broker as 'tax-free'. Less offensive lies are known as puffery, for instance when a fast food restaurant praises its French fries as 'best in the world'. In Pizza Hut, Inc. v. Papa John's International, Inc. (227 F.3d 489, 2000) an American court of appeals had to decide whether the advertisement *Better Ingredients. Better Pizza* in a comparative advertising campaign was false advertising. As a speech act, false advertising is a lie. Lies must relate to statements of facts, otherwise Section 43(a) Lanham Act that prohibits false advertisement would not apply. In the context of this provision, general opinions such as puffery are not perceived as statements of facts. The court defines puffery as: "1) an exaggerated, blustering, and boasting statement upon which no reasonable buyer would be justified in relying; or 2) a general claim of superiority over comparable products that is so vague that it can be understood as nothing more than a mere expression of opinion." As to the qualification of puffery as lie the court quoted the legal writers Prosser and Keeton who in the fifth edition of their *Law of Torts* characterize puffing as: "a seller's privilege to lie his head off, so long as he says nothing specific, on the theory that no reasonable man would believe him, or that no reasonable man would be influenced by such talk." The court divided the advertisement slogan in two parts. First, to make a 'Better Pizza' is as an assertion a general statement of fact (cf. also Brown/Cappelen 2014). Second, 'having better ingredients' is likewise a general opinion, because the assertion cannot be further quantified, as no ingredients are mentioned. Thus, the advertisement slogan appears as non-actionable under the Lanham Act. The situation is different when material proof is available, as in Kraft, Inc. v. Federal Trade Commission (970 F. 2d 311, 7th Cir., 1992). The American enterprise Kraft, Inc. brought on the U.S. market "Kraft Singles" that are process cheese food slices. Generally, individually wrapped slices of cheese and cheeselike products come in two major parts: process cheese food slices, which according to federal regulation must contain at least 51 percent natural cheese, and imitation slices, which contain little or no natural cheese. In its advertisement Kraft pretended that Kraft Singles cost more because each slice is made from 5 ounces of milk. In the broadcast version of the Singles' advertisements, a woman stated that she bought Kraft Singles for her daughter rather than "skimping" by purchasing imitation slices. She pretended that: "imitation slices use hardly any milk. But Kraft has 5 ounces per slice. Five ounces. So her bones get calcium they need to grow." The commercial also showed milk being poured into a glass that bore the label "5 oz. milk slice." The glass was then transformed into part of the label on a package of Singles. Later, Kraft added as a subscript in the television commercial: "one ¾ ounce slice has 70% of the calcium of five ounces of milk." Another commercial said: "Half of the school kids in America don't get all the calcium recommended for growing kids. That's why Kraft Singles are important." The Federal Trade Commission instituted a deceptive advertising proceeding against Kraft, Inc. under § 5 of the FTC Act. § 5 FTC Act prohibits material deceptive practices in commercials. The FTC regarded the milk equivalency claim used by Kraft as false even though Kraft actually uses 5 ounces of milk in making each Single slice because roughly 30 percent of the calcium contained in the milk is lost during the processing. With reference to this circumstance the court perceived Kraft's factual statement as deceptive. Thus, Kraft used a lie that has been determined as such in a formal, and not in a legal-linguistic procedure. From the legal-linguistic perspective, both cases that were analyzed in this paragraph are very close and it could be even posited that they represent the same type of speech act. In the formal, legal procedure difference is made between quantifiable data and other vague linguistic data. In turn, ordinary language avoids this sort of distinguishing. Its mechanisms seem therefore better adapted to tracing abusive speech. Meanwhile, lies are only one of many examples of legal speech acts that display anthropological intricacies. Some of them will be discussed in the following paragraphs.

6.1.3 Freedom of academic speech

Essential to academia is the scope of the freedom of expression in educational and research institutions, especially in times of growing inclination to censorship from the part of students. Historically, at least in the Western educational tradition, attempts to limit the academic freedom of speech came from public or religious authorities, i.e. from outside the educational institutions. Today, mainly in U.S., yet also in Western Europe, the tendency to impose oneself discursively with means of formal censorship is also increasingly attracting students. Some universities reacted to this tendency by setting up explicit standards that aim at clarifying the range and the rationale of the academic freedom to express one's views or to analyze views of others. For instance, the University of Chicago published in 2015 the so-called *Chicago Statement* that has been adopted in the meantime also by many other universities. Freedom of speech is based there on the conviction that "it is not the proper role of universities to attempt to shield individuals from ideas and opinions they may find unwelcome, disagreeable, or even deeply offensive." More often than not, in confrontations about the expressed ideas mainly formal arguments are used in order to censor speech. Therefore, and rightly so, the statement mentions that "concerns about civility and mutual respect can never be used as justification for closing off discussion of ideas, however offensive or disagreeable". Academic institutions have to promote and to protect "the fearless freedom to debate." Meanwhile, limits to the exercise of the freedom of speech in academic institutions, such as the ban on hate speech and other legally imposed boundaries, clearly exist. The academic institution regulates "time, place and manner of expression" and makes clear that its personnel and not the audience have the lead in the pursuance of academic objectives; it may also ban and sanction confrontational speech coming from students. It will, as a rule, prohibit expressions that "invade substantial privacy" or "constitute a genuine threat."

6.1.4 Censorship and rubbernecking

The most effective legal tool that challenges the freedom of expression is censorship. In many countries complex legislation exists that controls the freedom of speech. The question whether such laws are actually more dangerous than the incriminated printed matters is mentioned already in a legal commentary by W. Becker and

H. Seidel (1953: 22). Furthermore, institutions that supervised communication of dangerous materials were established. Such acts institutionalized this part of the legal discourse. Specific tasks of censorship engendered terminology related to works perceived as (FR) mauvais livres, or licencieux, obscene, lascif and lubrique, pornographique (cf. Goulemot 1991), (D) jugendgefährdende Schriften, anstößige Schriften, Schmutz und Schundschriften, gemeine oder niedrige Gesinnung, Dauerschädigung, Verbildung des Geschmacks, Primitivliteratur, das Gefühl für Scham und Sittlichkeit verletzenden Verstöße (cf. Becker/Seidel 1953). Also copyright can be used as a means of censorship (cf. Vaidhyanathan 2001: 249).

Close to censorship, yet different as to its rationale, are measures taken by authorities to prevent bypassers from seeing others in vulnerable and helpless conditions, e.g. victims of traffic accidents. Some legal provisions, for instance Art. 201a I, 2 of the German Penal Code prohibit photographing scenes perceived as covered by privacy, (D) *höchstpersönlicher Lebensbereich.* Likewise, gaping (rubbernecking) is prohibited in such situations and the scene of crime or traffic accident is frequently covered and accompanied by banners fixed by the police with texts such as *Do not rubberneck, we are about to rescue life,* (D) *Nicht gaffen, wir retten!* Sometimes, however, citizens' interest in tragical events is perceived by authorities all too eagerly as excessive and intrusive and as a sign of unhealthy curiosity. Meanwhile, for our orientation in life and in society we need information, also in situations when it involves unusually cruel and tragical events because they also are part of the reality in which we live. Socially fashionable and politically correct measures tend to obstruct these crucial epistemic processes where knowledge about the world emerges in our minds. Incidentally, after the EU countries agreed 2016 to a controversial deportation of refugees from Greece to Turkey, the Turkish authorities ordered to cover the first ship arriving in Dikili (Turkey) with tarpaulins "to prevent journalists from seeing inside" and enquiring into the fate of the first group of 202 deportees (The Economist, April 9th, 2016, p. 24). Viewing public events also enables social control of public services. Inappropriateness may not be the best argument to be used in limiting access to public events.

6.1.5 Intellectual property and legal linguistics

First printed book known (or first that was dated) was the Chinese translation of the Sanskrit treatise Vajracchedikaprajn-a-pa-ramita, the so-called Diamond Sutra. It was translated into Chinese by the Buddhist scholar Kuma-raji-va in 402 CE and the manuscript was printed 868 (Sen 2005: 82). The introductory note that made part of the volume made clear that it was conceived for 'universal free distribution' (Sen 2005: 82). Since that time habits of dealing with intellectual creation changed profoundly. Creation is perceived as a property right and is treated accordingly. The U.S. copyright system is based on some fundamental principles that shall guarantee the right balance between private interests and public interests in advancement of arts. These principles are: *fair use* that allows for restricted quotations of original works in scholarly works or in parodies, *first sale* that allows the use of purchased items (lending libraries are based on this principle), copyright protection for the *expression of ideas* but not for the ideas themselves, and the constitutional principle of protection *'for limited times'* (cf. Vaidhyanathan 2001: 250). These fundamental principles are occasionally also called doctrines. This has the consequence that all other statutory provisions are based on them or shall be interpreted in the light of these doctrines. Public interest is for example manifest in the *fair use doctrine* that enables to make use of copyrighted materials for otherwise unwelcome criticism that definitely would not be allowed by the copyright holder. Other forms of illegal interest in works developed by others are discussed as problems of *piracy* (Dreier et al. 2013).

What is the best possible copyright system? Apparently, such a system would be based on an idea of monopoly granted for a certain period of time rather than on the ideologically overburdened concept of property that misleads through its association with real property (cf. Vaidhyanathan 2001: 252). Another approach is based on Law and Economics arguments where generally conservative views anchored in the property-discourse are reflected toward the background of transaction costs. According to this school, broad appeals to values beyond material concerns – culture, beauty, dignity, democracy – invite inefficiency into social, political and economic systems (Vaidhyanathan 2001: 151). Many authors in Law and Economics are of the opinion that an overall leak-proof system of protection is counter-productive because the numerous small violations of property rights generate costs that are unproportional to the economic damage actually suffered; they therefore champion the enforcement of grave violations of property rights (cf. Vaidhyanathan 2001: 151). These views are actually rather narrow as they do not reflect the public interest inherent in the policy such as educational purposes.

What is more, the *digital moment* – a term introduced by Vaidhyanathan – is a particular challenge for the legislator. Digitization of intellectual creation as an opposing method to analogical technologies that are the basis for most intellectual property regulations remain a puzzle for jurists. The U.S. Digital Millennium Copyright Act of 1998 that was construed as the legislator's response to new challenges has been largely criticized as prohibitive and counter-productive (Vaidhyanathan 2001: 174). The U.S. Patent Office originally perceived computer software as protected by copyright, later started issuing patents for algorithms (Vaidhyanathan 2001: 153, cf. also State Street Bank & Trust Co. v. Signature Financial group, 149 F. 3d 1368, 1998). Nowadays, the software protection is based on patents, trademark, trade secret and contract law, especially when licensing is concerned. This confusion is symptomatic of this branch of law and it shows that the traditional conceptualization should be revised. It is worth mentioning that the WIPO Copyright Treaty protects computer programs as literary works. The World Intellectual Property Organization WIPO revised already the Bern Convention for the Protection of Literary and Artistic Works. The U.S. ratified the convention only 1989. Interestingly, by ratifying the WIPO Performances and Phonograms Treaty it also incorporated the French concept of 'moral rights' for composers into its copyright law that was until now unknown there (Vaidhyanathan 2001: 162). The U.S. composer can now oppose any attempt to distortion, mutilation or other modification of his performances that would be prejudicial to his reputation. There is, therefore, progress in this asystemic incorporation.

6.1.6 Law of Linguistic Communication and Law of New Technologies

More often than not contemporary linguistic communication functions with the help of technological devices such as telephone, cell phone, internet and classical media such as printed press, books, radio, television, film, theatre, etc (cf. also Tiersma 2010). The use of technological tools of communication is regulated in the area of the law of new technologies and the more classical problems are governed by the law of communication, general regulation of the freedom of speech and other regulation concerning cultural performance. Therefore, for our purposes this chapter stresses the law of *linguistic* communication and it excludes from the subject all regulation that concerns the technical part of the use of classical and new media for communicative goals that is often called *law of communication*. Only in cases where is seems impossible to describe a linguistic issue without reference to the underlying technological aspects the regulation on the use of technology is mentioned here. In reality, both areas are of course closely connected.

6.1.6.1 Law of Internet

In times of internet, all legal-linguistic issues connected to modern means of communication acquire an unprecedented importance (Féral-Schuhl 2010: 34, Craig 2013, cf. also Reed 2011). Use of language in the cyberspace of communication and information blended old and new views on language and law. First, the term *cyberspace* had been invented. A science fiction author, William Gibson, is credited for having coined the term cyberspace in his novel *Neuromancer*. The term entered the U.S. American legal language smoothly, e.g. Gorman v. Ameritrade Holding Corp. (293 F.3d 506 D.C. Cir. 2002) uses it as a background concept for modern internet legislation: *Cyberspace, however, is not some mystical incantation capable of warding off the jurisdiction of courts built from bricks and mortar.* Then a view emerged that this new space were law-free. This view has been immediately corrected by courts. Indeed, law applies also to the cyberspace that is structured linguistically. IT-specialists needed time to adapt to this rather simple truth. Also the adaptation of law and linguistics to the technical innovation in communication and information will apparently take time. The introduction of telephone and broadcasting also led to some turbulence, mainly in the legal sphere. Yet, the legal equilibrium had been relatively quickly attained. Meanwhile, even if the total integration of the cyberspace into traditional law would take place timely, legal-linguistic implications of the cyberspace will doubtlessly last longer due to the mass character of the phenomenon. The normativity as steering mechanism concerns predominantly law, it is however less easily applicable to language where speakers constantly and spontaneously create norms that are at times contradictory. In this sense, legal informatics is the closest discipline to the Law of Linguistic Communication.

In terms of the legal discourse, law of internet is not unproblematic as an area of regulation because it tends to differentiate between the off-line world and the on-line world. Meanwhile, our rationality does not allow us to live simultaneously in a real world and in a virtual reality. Therefore, rules for legal action have to be equal for the on-line and the off-line world. To put it brief, what is not allowed in the public sphere off-line cannot be allowed on-line. Coherence of legal argumentation requires that both spheres are treated equally and that legality of an on-line action can be inferred from regulation dealing with the off-line world. This would also mean that the future law of linguistic communication could become uniform in terms of its textuality. No discursive split between the on-line and the off-line world would be conceptually needed any more to draft legal provisions. An additional problem in attempts at the uniformization of the on-line and the off-line regulation is the globalization process in law. Internet is a global phenomenon, yet it is regulated in acts of domestic legislation, if at all. As standards of the freedom of speech practised all over the world differ, the only textual reference for uniform internet legislation are existing UN instruments which are formally accepted by the international community as valid benchmarks for the protection of the freedom of speech worldwide. Meanwhile, in this respect the law of internet shares the imponderables of the legal globalization process.

6.2 Legal Regulation of Language Use

Language has been regularly the object of legal regulation. Therefore, within legal linguistics issues concerning regulation of language use are perceived as belonging to its realm (Mattila 2006: 18). Three issues have attracted particular interest in the research. They are: *linguistic legislation*, *language risk* and *professional liability of translators*. The three issues have a pragmatic dimension in that they show law in action. In our context of emerging global law they also provide insights into some particular problems related to this process and especially to the distribution of languages in the globalization process. The dominating topic in this special area of legal linguistics has been linguistic legislation. Studies in linguistic legislation have at least a two-fold goal. First, from the point of view of applied linguistics, they should prepare a model of linguistic legislation which would reflect linguistic presuppositions of such a type of legislation. Second, from the point of view of human rights protection, they should advance the level of international standards and their application in national legislative projects. A successful piece of national linguistic legislation has to combine both perspectives. In addition to these issues, it is worthwhile mentioning that research related to clarity and *understandability of the legal language* for ordinary citizens is perceived by some researchers as belonging to linguistic legislation because it posits a right to clear language (Mattila 2006: 18).

In the following, this issue will not be treated because it has been discussed passim in other chapters and in different contexts. Language risk and professional liability of translators may appear to be purely legal issues as they pertain to legal questions. The legal-linguistic interest in them is equally two-fold as is the legal-linguistic position toward linguistic legislation that is doubtlessly also legal in its essence. In both areas, it is necessary to show the linguistic element in the legal debate and stress the professional linguists' input into it. Moreover, the specialists' view on language should be taken into consideration while solving language-related cases in courts. This happens only rarely nowadays (cf. Salmi-Tolonen 2008a: 391). Linguistic legislation developed around areas of linguistic diversity, protection of script and name giving. Rationally, language as a sign system corresponds to script as its technology of fixation of meaning. Language and script are not naturally connected; language can exist without script, script being a pure technical sign system that refers to another sign system, namely to natural language. In the linguistic legislation, however, next to natural language, which is the source of culture and personal experience, we also protect script. Both are socially created cultural phenomena that are constitutive of life forms that create individual biographies. Therefore, although rationally we as humankind need only one language to cope with the complexity of life on the globe and only one corresponding script system, we nevertheless tend to protect cultural phenomena expressed in different languages and through different scripts. The human condition, the psychological dependence of individuals on their native languages and scripts justify the legal protection of linguistic and script diversity.

Furthermore, legislation regulates also the freedom of name giving. Freedom to give names to children has been in many countries regulated by laws (cf. Kangas 1991). In recent years, the French authorities refused to register following names that were perceived as not suitable for children (FR *non recevables*): *Titeuf, Fraise, Nutella, Mini-Cooper, Prince-William, MJ, Anal* and *Anus*, yet they registered as admissible *Tarzan, Mowgli, Pomme, Prune, Fraisine.* Recently, a British Court of Appeal prohibited a mother to name her child *Cyanide* perceiving the name as '*objectionable*' (cf. The Spectator, June 4, 2016, p. 13). Meanwhile, in China, the use of Western names as unofficial names is not regulated. Recently, names such as *Cinderella, Dreamjazz, Angelababy, Ultraman, Yes* have been reported (Liu 2016). Choice of family names is equally problematic (cf. In re Standesamt Niebüll, in Notes and Commented Materials no. 65).

6.2.1 Linguistic legislation

Linguistic legislation has been perceived in the academic research as either belonging to legal linguistics or to the area of international law and human rights protection. For legal linguists such as G. Cornu (2005: 11) linguistic legislation is a necessary part of legal linguistics because it deals with the norming of language use. For Cornu, legal language cannot be characterized efficiently without taking into consideration the operation in which linguistic elements, words, phrases as parts of the legal discourse became elements of the legal discourse by a legislative decision. In this sense, linguistic legislation would comprise not only issues of the distribution of language use in society that is linked to human rights protection but would reach much further and include legislation relating to the creation and the interpretation of law. Pigolkin (1990: 5) adds to it the determination of the authentic linguistic version of a piece of legislation, both national and international. In this context, Chinese legal linguists stressed that language in law is power that must be regulated (Zhou 2003: 2). Cornu's vision is helpful in shaping a coherent conception of legal linguistics. It does not impede the research into specific aspects of linguistic legislation under other topics, especially in the public international law (cf. Mattila 2006: 18). Generally, issues addressed in legal linguistics are also topics of research in the specialized branches of law such as human rights protection and they are addressed there in a methodologically different way. Purely technical legal issues may also be better settled there. The legal linguist has an interest in contributing her professional knowledge about the role and the use of language to the linguistic legislation.

The part of linguistic legislation which focuses upon the societal distribution of language use emerged toward the background of a multilingual world that is divided into national states. This state of affairs resulted in linguistic or religious conflicts in many parts of the world. There is no tendency perceptible on the international arena toward a more distanced approach to ethnic issues and language use in multilingual societies. Linguistic legislation seems therefore to be necessary in countries in which linguistic problems persist and occupy the citizens. In countries where problems with language choice and language use do not exist (such countries are not particularly numerous) no linguistic legislation is necessary. In the U.S., no legislation concerning the official language of the country exists on the federal level. Nevertheless, most citizens concerned do not have any problems with identifying English as the official language of their country. In Germany, the main language is of course German although no legal guarantee exists to this effect there. Elsewhere, countries such as France opted for precise legislative regulation of language use. Other multi-ethnic states, like the Russian Federation, have federal and regional legislation on language use. Multilingual states such as Switzerland regulate the use of languages regionally, while others, for instance Finland or Belgium adopted a functional approach. In India, the language planning evolved since the declaration of independence. Its main principle is laid down in the Constitution of 1947–50; it is directed toward acceptance of the use of the English language as a lingua franca notwithstanding the initial attempts to introduce Hindi as the language of the communication in the subcontinent. Due to the resistance coming from the Dravidian speaking territories in the south of the country the transitory period for the change from English to Hindi scheduled to take place between 1950 and 1965 has been reported sine die. The idea of linguistic transfer is still supported by the official linguistic policy of the Indian government and enhanced by the activities of the Hindi Directorate according to Art. 351 of the Constitution of India. The Constitution of India includes as Part XVII (Art. 343–351) provisions regulating official language that has to be used in the Parliamentary work, in courts and in administration as well as languages used in the States of the Union. The People's

Republic of China recognizes 56 nationalities on its territory and it perceives itself as a multinational state with the Han majority constituting 92% of the population. Therefore, numerous legal acts regulate the use of languages on its territory. The Law of the People's Republic of China on the National Commonly Used Language and Script of July 5, 2000 regulates the use and the norm for Putonghua based on the language of Beijing that is used as lingua franca in the country. The legislation is tolerant of the use of local languages in daily communication, yet it promotes the standards Mandarin and the simplified script. Governmental policy also supports the exclusive use of Mandarin in all official activities, educational institutions, and the media. Overall, consequences of these different approaches to linguistic legislation are visible in the respective national linguistic policies and in daily attitudes to multilingualism in these countries.

6.2.1.1 Idea of linguistic legislation

The fact that some countries introduced linguistic legislation into their legal systems while others did not indicates that such decisions are not unproblematic. The importance of linguistic legislation and its connection with the rising of social tensions and violent conflicts in societies and states has been recently recognized also in the area of conflict prevention. However, the idea that minority or linguistic legislation can have a negative impact on societies and states and even on interstate relations is definitely not new. The history of bilateral treaties dealing with the status of ethnic minorities is proof of the relevance of this issue as it can be traced back to the 16th century (Varennes 1996: 24). Yet, in the 20th century the issue gained renewed importance because of increasing tensions and conflicts directly related to ethnicity and language use. This was the reason why within the field of international law, in preventive diplomacy and in the non-governmental sector attention has been paid to this issue especially over the last two decades. As a result, the need arose to develop mechanisms which could facilitate conflict prevention work in this area. Therefore, the contemporary approach to the issue includes also the socio-political background of linguistic legislation. Below, some developments in this area shall be traced. Additionally, mechanisms for practical work in the area of international law, such as preventive diplomacy, especially conflict prevention, or non-governmental action will be canvassed.

6.2.1.2 Minority legislation and cultural heritage

The emergence of minority legislation and the development of linguistic legislation is a case study in and of itself. Historically, multicultural contacts, migration and the reception of cultural achievements or linguistic proficiency must be perceived as almost natural phenomena in the European or Asian context. Cultural exchange shaped the life form of modern day European and Asian nations while daily language contacts formed the languages spoken today in Europe and in Asia. Therefore, it comes as a surprise how any tensions or conflicts could arise on a basis that constitutes a common denominator in the development of the European and the Asian culture and one of the most fruitful processes in the development of humankind. Meanwhile, conflicts of interests and social contradictions need not necessarily end up in violent conflicts. Civilized societies and well governed states establish mechanisms which enable social cohesion under circumstances which may be perceived as antagonistic. In order to guarantee the effective functioning of state and society social practices must additionally include a culture of conflicts with elements of protection against acting in the heat of the moment. These tasks seem to have been neglected in some parts of the world. In addition, it has become pertinent that some conflicts are not based on aggressive motivation but on purposely calculated uses of force and manipulation of emotions. However, research into linguistic legislation also shows that the regulation of language use had in certain societies a selective and even a discriminatory role to play (Varennes 1996: 32). The character of linguistic legislation in many countries is perceived as repressive in terms of linguistic diversity (Mattila 2006: 18). Again, this result could surprise given the European and the Asian history that bears witness to the multiethnic and multicultural development of these continents. Likewise, some negative historical experience that might also be traced in the history of both continents need not necessarily determine the action of successive generations. Rather a reflected reaction to dysfunctional social practices could be expected in a world which is increasingly governed by laws and international standards.

6.2.2 Social and scientific perspectives on multilingualism

Societal multiculturalism and multilingualism have a long and only partly examined history. Some researchers have tried to reconstruct our historical perspective on multiculturalism and multilingualism, an inquiry typical of our reasoning which asks for (GR) *αρχή*, i.e. the beginning of things. Some connect it even to the biblical myth about the Tower of Babel. Others, still interested in the very beginning of things, thought about the multiplicity of languages on the planet and speculated about an original language of mankind. Some others have reflected the fears of peoples confronted with multilingualism which sometimes came up even in monolingual societies. Many of them have tried to advocate monolingualism, but in vain. It has been, for example, the case in Finland where the statesman J.V. Snellman (1806–1881) tried to disseminate his ideas with the help of the slogan (FIN) *yksi kieli, yksi mieli*, i.e. one language, one mind. As different as these approaches may be, they show that language use and societal interaction are closely connected. And indeed, the linguistic community has overcome a long time ago the view of primal linguistic confusion in the linguistic landscape and perceives it nowadays as transparently structured. The linguistic landscape includes some monolingual areas and vast multilingual regions with or without diglossia (Hoffmann 1991: 157). However, certain social groups have been always multilingual, if the ancient Greek scholars are left unconsidered (cf. Wandruszka 1997: 41–50). This concerns also Byzantine jurists (Husa 2013: 53). Meanwhile, monolinguality can be exceptionally beneficial.

P. Torop mentions in his note on the development of the Tartu school of semiotics that it developed in a situation of linguistic isolation from the Estonian speaking majority of the town (Torop 1992: 13). Russian speaking scholars were by necessity limited in their choice of social contacts and had to concentrate on their theory building within a limited group of interlocutors. Meanwhile, such experience, which may also have a positive impact, is exceptional and definitely not recommendable.

Thus, in the historical perspective multiculturalism and multilingualism involve in our context a structured language use and a cooperative social interaction rather than social chaos introduced by cultural and linguistic plurality. Nevertheless, linguistic conflicts continue to be a part of political developments all over the world. Speakers react to linguistic issues and they react often in a different way than scholars would recommend. They sometimes share views about language use concerning, for example, the prestige or usefulness of a language which may seem controversial to linguists. In our scientific tradition particular languages were for a long time perceived as pure sign systems and also analyzed as such. This perspective seemed to have been sufficient for academic research. Only recently linguistic research realized that languages and their use have an emotional component for their speakers as well as their listeners and began to reflect upon these aspects. Speakers have namely a tendency to identify with sign systems such as languages, however unscientific or irrational this tendency may seem. The consideration of the behavior of speakers led to a shift in attention or at least to the broadening of the linguistic research perspective. This modification, in turn, resulted in the interference of emotional aspects of language in such austere areas as international and domestic legislation.

6.2.2.1 Minority legislation and linguistic legislation

Linguistic legislation is a part of a bigger legislative branch of minority legislation. This legislation comprises, in addition to linguistic legislation, legislation governing education and legislation affecting the participation of ethnic minorities in public life. Additionally, it includes international and domestic legislation concerning statelessness and obtaining citizenship, migration, and protection of stateless children. Also the legislation on the status of foreigners provides a broader legal perspective in which the problems of ethnic minorities are embedded. The traditional approach to this part of legislation which distinguishes between the subjects and the objects of rights and their legal protection shows already some characteristic features of this branch of law. The subject of the law may be a person or another legal entity, like a group and this issue constitutes a new problem in minority legislation (Giordan 1992: 12–15). The issue is further made difficult since a definition of a national or ethnic minority is not resolved in the professional discussion. Capotorti (1991: para. 568) defined it as "a group numerically inferior to the rest of the population of the state, in a non-dominant position, whose members – being nationals of the State possess ethnic, religious or linguistic characteristics differing from those of the rest of the population and show, if only implicitly, a sense of solidarity, directed towards preserving their culture, traditions, religion or language." This definition, which has been developed for the purposes of Art. 27 ICCPR, had been watered down considerably in the academic research (Engel 2002: 57). The aspect of the object protected by the state is also difficult to determine as obligations of a state are often described in an ambiguous way, e.g. the states *should as far as possible* or *under specific circumstances* guarantee specific minority or linguistic rights (Yacoub 1998: 173). This aspect is reflected also in the area of monitoring and protection of minority rights where blurred provisions lead to uncertainty in their interpretation and application. Moreover, national legislative acts are often incompatible in their structure and terminology and therefore difficult to compare or to evaluate (Engel 2002: 31).

Legal standards for the minority legislation are set in international instruments. The most important international legal instruments in this area are: the Universal Declaration of Human Rights (1948), the International Covenant on Civil and Political Rights (1966), the International Covenant on Economic, Social and Cultural Rights (1966), the International Covenant on the Elimination of All Forms of Racial Discrimination (1965), and the Declaration on the Rights of Persons Belonging to National or Ethnic, Religious and Linguistic Minorities (1992). For the member states of the Council of Europe the European Convention on the Protection of Human Rights and Fundamental Freedoms (adopted in 1950) is the basic document. Within the Council of Europe the possibility to appeal to the European Court of Human Rights in Strasbourg constitutes one of the most effective mechanisms of implementation of the Convention (Wildhaber 2002: 72). Furthermore, in the European Union a relevant role is played by Article 13 of the Treaty establishing the European Community, Article 21 of the Charter of Fundamental Rights of the European Union, the anti-discrimination directives 2000/43/EC implementing the principle of equal treatment between persons irrespective of racial or ethnic origin, 2000/78/EC establishing a general framework for equal treatment in employment and occupation and 2003/9/EC laying down minimum standards for the reception of asylum seekers and the Council Decision 2000/750/EC establishing a community action program to combat discrimination.

Another group of sources with legal impact consists of political documents which due to their practical importance in shaping international relations have reached a position similar to that of legal acts. Those documents belong to the area of the so-called *soft law* and are becoming more and more influential in this sphere. Among them are: The Final Act of the CSCE Conference in Helsinki (1975), the Copenhagen Document on the Human Dimension of the OSCE (1990) and several OSCE HCNM recommendations. Recently, these documents, which were meant as interpretive guidelines that belong to the soft law, have attained a status of much more practical importance (Kemp 2001: 28). Among the most frequently used documents are: The Hague Recommendations Regarding the Education Rights of National Minorities issued in October 1996, The Oslo Recommendations Regarding the Linguistic Rights of National Minorities dating from February 1998, and the Lund Recommendations on the Effective Participation of National Minorities in Public Life, regarding participation in governance of the state as well as self-governance, adopted in 1999. Additionally, Guidelines on use of minority languages in broadcast media were launched in October 2003. These documents were issued by the OSCE HCNM and are based on well founded and balanced expert opinions. Presumably, this is the reason why – in a relatively short time – they have reached the position of standing as reliable reference works when both standard and exceptional legal problems concerning ethnic minorities are at stake. Excerpts from these documents are quoted in Notes and Commented Materials no. 32.

Overall, minority legislation is already a vast area of legal provisions, which can be in their majority applied by courts to protect rights established by the provisions. Although some criticism has been expressed as to the extent of these rights, one has to admit that considerable progress has been achieved in this domain since the establishing of the UN and some regional organizations such as the Council of Europe or the OSCE. Another issue is, to what extent additional measures can be claimed in courts. In legal terms, the question how far a state can be forced to take positive action on behalf of linguistic minorities is here at stake. This is to a large extent a question of domestic legislation. Moreover, one should not forget that linguistic legislation provided in domestic and international instruments is a part of an ongoing legislative evolutionary process with a determined direction toward ever more generous improvement of these standards. The last word on its content and implementation has by no means been spoken yet. While working with international instruments one should therefore bear in mind that they are a product of political compromises among states on issues perceived as problematic and that they reflect a legal minimum of rights rather than a full-fledged system of minority protection. The domestic legislator should therefore never feel limited in an attempt to provide a more generous legal status to minorities and further develop this area of legislation. By doing so, the domestic legislator contributes also to the development of international standards and paves the way for the emergence of new tendencies that are reflect better the needs of new generations.

6.2.2.2 Nature of linguistic rights and their background

Linguistic rights are by their very nature human rights. The concept of linguistic human rights is widely used and rightly so (Skutnabb-Kangas 1995: 1). Nowadays, the commitment to non-discrimination on the basis of language is general and as such a major standard of linguistic legislation. In most developed societies the idea that exceptions from the rule must be made to protect minorities has been understood and accepted (Kymlicka 1995). No substantial discussion about *equal rights for all* can be expected under these circumstances. The new dimension in the discussion is represented in the research concerning language death (Crystal 1997; Nettle and Romaine 2000; Skutnabb-Kangas 2000). As many languages are disappearing the discussion about language protection introduces a new and unexpected component into the area of linguistic legislation. The current discourse on linguistic human rights has also other characteristic features which are worth to be mentioned. First, if we don't consider the marking events associated with the adoption of bilateral treaties, the area lacks a history and a tradition. Second, it concerns mostly linguists as lawyers often refuse to participate in it due to the alleged linguistic character of the problem which is approached with purely political means. Furthermore, it starts on the highest possible level – which in terms of human political organization as a species is the UN – and works downwards reaching sometimes the grass root level, but this is rare. Add to it that initiative for legislative measures comes often from the states and not from the speakers concerned. This circumstance will not change until legal aspects of the minority problematique reach a higher level of knowledge in the societies concerned, mainly through the strengthening of the linguistic component in the discussion. Due to its novelty, there is a far-reaching confusion between arguments *de lege lata* and *de lege ferenda* which unfortunately contributes to uncertainty in the resulting debate. This uncertainty may also arise from the fact that the discourse is inter-disciplinary and methods implemented in it may vary. Textually, linguistic rights are mostly formulated in a negative way as non-discrimination prescriptions. Sometimes, however, the states take upon themselves the obligation to ensure specific rights. This formulation may, when taken concretely and not only as a programmatic phrase, enable both sorts of implementation of rights, negative as well as positive.

Linguistic rights are scattered around various international agreements, but this fact does not impede their application. The lack of one binding codification is caused by the fact that several international – universal and regional – organizations are in charge of different aspects of minority legislation. As a result, some globally valid legal instruments were constructed within the UN and supported by provisions issued, for example, by European organizations. Among them are the OSCE and the Council of Europe, which has a slightly more legalistic approach to the issue than the OSCE, which works with political instruments and soft law measures. When applying these norms it is necessary to verify whether the state in question has ratified the specific document. Most important among the international legal provisions are: Articles 25 and 27 of the International Covenant on Civil and Political Rights according to which persons belonging to ethnic, religious or linguistic minorities shall not be denied the right to use their language. The same right is guaranteed to children belonging to minorities in Article 30 of the Convention on the Right of the Child (1989). The UNESCO Convention against Discrimination in Education (1960) provides in Article 5 para.1 lit. c) for the right to use the person's own language in education. Article 5 para. 1 of the Framework Convention for the Protection of National Minorities (1995) obligates the states to protect language as part of the identity of persons belonging to minorities. Further relevant provisions are Articles 12, 13 and 14 regarding education. Furthermore, the European Charter for Regional and Minority Languages (1992) regulates the right to use a minority language in its Articles 2, 7, 9 and 10. In addition, the European Convention on Human Rights concerns also the protection of language use, e.g. in Article 8 para. 1 in conjunction with Article 14 and another Article 10 concerning the freedom of expression and Article 11 concerning names, language signs and other inscriptions. Still further, the Copenhagen Document of the OSCE as a part of the soft law includes in its par. 32 regulation regarding linguistic guarantees to minorities.

Following the systematics developed by Francesco Capotorti (1991), it is essential to distinguish in a legal analysis at least four spheres: language use in the private sphere, language use in the public sphere, language use in media and language use in the educational system. It goes without saying that no state can interfere in the use of any language in the private sphere (Engel 2002: 81). Language use in the public sphere may be subject to limitations when there is a clearly proven need for such measures. In such a case the burden of proof must be carried by the state. Language use in education and media can be limited in certain cases and it is decisive to determine the cases in which this limitation is admissible. Researchers are of the opinion that only the official status of a language can secure to its speakers the enjoyment of all linguistic human rights. This argument is used when linguistic legislation is planned. On the other side, countries without linguistic legislation exist and no significant legal problems with the protection of their languages are reported there. Occasionally, especially when it is politically impossible to provide a strong legal status for a language, the determination of its linguistic status can be replaced by a *guarantee of development* for the language in question (Wydra 2008: 86). However, this formulation seems to function only as a temporary solution. What is more, the specific structure of minority problems and their relation to majorities may demand additional efforts, such as *affirmative actions* or development of *integration strategies* which are worthwhile considering within the scope of linguistic rights. They may include: a broad discussion of minority-majority issues in society in the situation where there is a lack of, or confusion in respect of information that society receives from state agencies about the possibilities of creation of multicultural and multilingual biographies.

Toward the background of the concept of linguistic human rights, linguistic legislation with its topics concerning prescribed language use in different spheres emerged at the same time on different levels of hierarchy in international and domestic law. The more effective and substantial the legislative measures in the area of linguistic legislation have been, the more specific terminology they engendered. Most concepts introduced into linguistic legislation have their origin either in linguistics or in ethnology/anthropology. This is why the current discussion about linguistic legislation is dominated by infiltration of conceptual instruments of different scientific disciplines (esp. linguistics, socio- and psycholinguistics, ethnology and others) into the legal language. The discussion about prescribed or guaranteed language use – and this is the essence of linguistic legislation – has to follow its own methodological rules as it is a legal discourse, i.e. a discussion about the content of law which has to follow the interpretive guidelines of this art. Unfortunately, often methodological aspects of disciplines which willingly offer their concepts to lawyers are disregarded. The most striking feature in it is that the linguistic and the ethnological terminology is mostly descriptive, legal terminology in turn is a part of prescriptive texts. While entering legal texts ethnological or linguistic concepts become legal concepts with all consequences (e.g. application by authorities, interpretation by judges, etc.) Thus, when the Canadian legislator passed the Official Languages Act or the Canadian Multiculturalism Act (1988) he simultaneously introduced new legal concepts like *official language* and *multiculturalism* into the domestic legal system. Furthermore, what remains unclear is the question as to what extent the legislator is bound by the achievements of scientific research in the field of different scientific disciplines like linguistics or ethnology. The answer may be surprising; it seems, to some extent. This is because of the fact that the state has an overall and a long-term policy to follow in which the inter-ethnic relations are only a segment. The state understandably has multiple tasks and has to balance different, often contradictory interests. It cannot always reflect upon and react immediately to the state of the art in one particular discipline, especially when consensus among scientists has not been reached in that area. Yet, in accordance with the principle of good governance, the state should have an interest in following closely the development of scientific research and it should also consider the results of new research studies.

6.2.2.3 Structure of linguistic legislation

In states where it is deemed useful or politically expedient, language use in the linguistic legislation is determined along the lines of linguistic policy of such states. This policy, which may be formulated explicitly or be implicitly identifiable, is reflected in the legal norms and it constitutes their contextual background. This policy is also determinative of the legislative process in which the prospective legal norms are construed and voted. Through linguistic legislation the state influences communication processes in the given society by attributing certain functions to specific languages. By so doing, it often relies on domestic legislative techniques and foreign and international experience. Thus, certain concepts and topics can be perceived as characteristic instruments of domestic linguistic legislation which underlie its structure. The conceptual instruments traditionally associated with this legislation include the following: *national language* – an elderly formulation still in use, sometimes used in association with the situation in the U.S., where no specific federal legislation on the status of the English language exists, *official language* (*state language*) – language of intra-state communication, language of official acts and administration, so to say the language in which the state speaks to its citizens and vice versa, *official state language* – a European Union term regarding a language used in an E.U. country which is at the same time an *official language* of the E.U., *administrative language* – language used by public authorities and regularly also courts, *working language* – a subset of the term official language which encourages the use of other languages, e.g. *conference language, regional language, minority language* – a concept closely connected to different definitions of minority, *lesser used languages, language of international communication* – language used in formal contacts among states. Other forms also exist, but they are rarely used in European settings, such as: *language of court decisions or pronouncements, literary language defined in laws, religious language,* and *language of alphabetization.* The use of the above terminology is closely linked to the policy of states and international organizations like the U.N. and the E.U. Consequently, it is linked to priorities clearly defined by the drafters of the legal acts. Some concepts, such as *working language* provide an elastic tool for the shaping of the legislation and help avoid dogmatism. This issue is particularly important when linguistic norms are shaped in a conflict-like atmosphere. Through the use of elastic concepts the legislator may avoid many problematic decisions and refer to particular situations in which interlocutors involved can freely choose the language to be used in their public communication. These concepts bear in themselves a great potential for future legislation. International organizations use the concept of *working languages* already in their political practice in order to avoid frictions and to increase their daily practical operational efficiency. Linguistic legislation all over the world follows a pattern where the above terminology is used and sometimes specifically defined. Furthermore, special topics like language use in the public sphere, jurisdiction, education, broadcasting and advertisement as well as sanctions for the violation of the law are included in it. A model language law could be easily developed on the basis of analysis of the existing legislation. However, it would be premature to cherish high expectations regarding such piece of legislation and to believe that linguistic problems in a state or a society can be solved solely through using certain sterile legislative techniques. Therefore, no legislator will be able to hide behind these concepts without presenting a clear linguistic policy. One could pretend that linguistic legislation is blind when there is no linguistic policy to refer to. It is conceivable that a multilingual state might not have any linguistic legislation at all, but should it decide to introduce it, it will have to develop an explicit linguistic policy upon which it may rely when shaping the law and implementing it. Thus, linguistic legislation provides for a framework of formal rules and concepts concerning the status and the use of languages in a society which are necessary prerequisites for the implementation of a state's linguistic policy.

6.2.3 Linguistic policy

International instruments such as Art. 1 of the U.N. Charter and other provisions named above prohibit any discrimination based on language use. In addition, international practice of shaping and implementing the linguistic legislation provides reliable guidelines to tackle the most upcoming issues. The blindness mentioned above is therefore curable because there exist many examples of successful linguistic policies and integration strategies for ethnic minorities developed along the lines of some descriptive and prescriptive properties.

The linguistic policy should:

1. *reflect common views on language use in the linguistic community (descriptive element),*
2. *encourage social debate on issues concerning inter-ethnic relations and provide the appropriate conceptual framework for it (integration of minorities, multiculturalism, multilingualism),*
3. *include an overall strategy regarding the use of language and inter-ethnic relations involving both minorities and the majority,*

4. *propose measures of active promotion of language (prescriptive element) where inadequacies formed in historical processes can be compensated for,*
5. *increase public awareness about issues concerning multiculturalism and multilingualism in the educational system,*
6. *develop professional skills among legal professionals and state officials dealing with multiculturalism and multilingualism*

It is advisable that a linguistic policy of a country closely follows the state's linguistic realities (cf. also Moraldo et al 2012, Stephens/Boyce 2014, Weerts 2015, Piller 2016). In a stable multilingual landscape official multilingualism is usually the best adapted basis for the development of a long-term linguistic policy. Countries such as Finland or Switzerland have proved that official bi- or multilingualism is neither a burden to the state nor to society. Tensions with linguistic background in the post-Soviet area, however, show that the non-application of this concept leads unavoidably to serious social frictions. In areas where bi- or multilingualism appears in regional boundaries, appropriate measures like establishing locally limited bilingual areas should be implemented. Once again, the experience, for instance in Canada or Finland, shows that introducing and implementing official regional bi- or multilingualism does not confound the state structure nor society but makes it more stable and efficient. Undeniably, situations can occur where the linguistic landscape of a country may become inadequate due to former linguistic policy which may even have been introduced forcibly. In such situations measures to compensate linguistic losses, such as the active promotion of a formerly suppressed language by state agencies and increased teaching of the language in the educational institutions should be taken. An additional problem is the legal status to be given to a linguistic policy which may appear to be a purely political document binding solely the government in power. Rather, it is advisable that the policy is endorsed by the Parliament as a document binding the state or that it is passed as a framework law on language use in the state (cf. Strategy of the governmental policy on ethnic issues for the period until 2025 of the Russian Federation, adopted 2012). This issue is decisive because without a legal status the linguistic policy risks becoming a short-lived phenomenon.

6.2.3.1 Role of legislation in conflict prevention

Recent experience from the conflict prevention work, especially in the OSCE and in the Council of Europe region, shows that legislative initiatives in the area of minority legislation and foremost in the linguistic legislation have to be based on a solid linguistic policy developed by state agencies in a dialogue with minorities concerned and the broader interested public. Most tensions concerning linguistic legislative initiatives emerge due to one-sided and uncompromising approaches by legislative bodies, which have preferred quick action instead of a long-term policy and broad social dialogue. An assessment of this type of action makes the development of preventive mechanisms necessary. Many preventive measures have been developed to this aim. First of all, *early warning* based on systematic monitoring and awareness rising about issues concerning minorities enables an efficient early response to the upcoming tension and blocks a possible escalation into a conflict. Concrete and determined political action must be taken as well. Here, steps taken within the *quiet diplomacy* seem to be particularly efficient. In order to prevent tensions and even conflicts around legislative initiatives it is essential to interfere at the earliest possible stage of the development so that legislative initiatives can be stopped early, preferably before their first reading in the Parliament takes place. A series of consultations with national and international experts can be proposed to legislative bodies with the aim to work out a coherent approach to the planned piece of legislation. Such an approach must be based on strict observance of human rights and especially on international instruments concerning the rights of national minorities and international standards which proved to be effective during longer time in the practical work of the application of linguistic legislation.

Furthermore, harmonization of domestic legislation with international standards can help avoid tensions as it shows to the minorities that work is done on their issue and that their legal situation shall reflect the general standards of legislation which, even if sometimes perceived as insufficient, guarantees their equal treatment in international comparison. Awareness rising among minorities and in the majority about existing international standards in minority and language protection is one of the fundamental tasks within conflict prevention activities. It goes even beyond pure information about legal issues, because due to the quality of some standards the impression of discrimination may persist in a case where specialists are of the opinion that international and domestic legislation have been observed but the minority does not share the view of the experts. Here, political measures like reconciliation activities and strengthening social dialogue can help. Minorities concerned must take into account the well-founded advice to learn the state language in order to better integrate into the life of their surroundings that is structured by the linguistic needs of the majority. On the other side, majorities should be informed in the educational system about the situation of neighboring minorities. Occasionally, it is worthwhile to consider teaching minority languages to majorities as they constitute languages of closest cultural neighbors and enable the speakers belonging to a linguistic majority to cope much better in their social surroundings. Problems concerning migrants, especially those undocumented or those perceived as illegal residents, must be addressed by the legislator and should not be shifted to the police or the broader society. Migrants must be provided a clear legal status (even gradually) and should be involved in integration measures, as well as integration courses on civic education and the language of their new country of residence. It is naive to believe that migrants will out of themselves develop the most appropriate behavioral strategies for their integration. Additionally, it is not reasonable to expect the majority of traditional residents to be prepared for life in changing ethnic circumstances. Work in the educational sector and work with media can help stabilize the situation. In fact, the experience shows that when linguistic legislation is a part of a coherent linguistic policy of the state and when it reflects international standards the risk of social tensions or violent conflicts diminishes radically or can be assessed as highly improbable.

6.2.3.2 *Soft law, recommendations and promotional measures*

Laws are the strictest instrument of governing in a society, if arbitrariness is set aside. In a democratic state, exclusively legalistically defined decisions are perceived as largely admissible. Such decisions are deemed as a sufficient protection against arbitrary, i.e. undemocratic decisions. Indeed, arbitrariness has an opposite side which is rationality. Both legality and rationality must coincide in order to produce efficient legislation. However, in the course of the development of social techniques of governing other instruments close to the legal ones came up and were used with some success. For instance, *soft laws* are sometimes mentioned as one example of such modern and effective means of governing. Other tools, such as *promotional programs* and *promotional projects* are still not sufficiently used to be perceived as an appropriate counterweight to laws. Meanwhile, laws in their very essence are coercive by their structure, tone and even more, they are coercive in their application. This may make them less popular among citizens who are rather surprised by changes in society and in its leading scientific institutions. This seems to be the case in many areas concerning law and ethnicity, and especially with the legislation pertaining to language use. Changes in our views upon ethnicity which had happened in the last century, changes in our comprehension of the cultural diversity and multiculturalism/multilingualism as a mass phenomenon became sometimes more visible in the political and legislative processes than in the social practice. Here, informal, educational and promotional measures can reach more than coercive mechanisms which involve state structures and which in the end force them to sanction those who act in disaccord with the coercive legal mechanisms. Alternative measures make this approach unnecessary and fill the gap between coercive measures and arbitrary action in society. They are not neutral as they show the direction recommended by the state and make ethically determined choices toward multilingualism and cultural diversity and against ethno-nationalism or allegedly existing monoculturalism. *Promotion of multiculturalism*, especially in a situation where local languages appear in a disadvantageous situation was undertaken in the Republic of Ireland and in Welsh speaking areas of the U.K. The results of these measures expressed in figures may be perceived as limited but coercive measures of language use would scarcely bring about better scores, especially when their destructive impact upon society is taken into account. In addition, setting up laws without sanctions makes no sense as they rest programmatic and decorative. Actions increasing the public awareness such as the granting of the Cultural Harmony Award by the Canadian town of Vancouver or E.U. programs promoting tolerance can under specific circumstances influence society more than legislative or purely political measures.

Specific help for interpretation is provided in guidelines and recommendations developed to support the work of lawyers applying the linguistic legislation. Often such documents are classified as *soft law* (Lukashuk 1996: 104), a term which may prove useful in determining the legal character of a document without changing the concept of law. Sometimes, they may play a role of temporary guidelines until a formal solution is found and incorporated into law. In this spectrum other documents of purely consultative character such as the OSCE HCNM *recommendations* have gained substantial practical importance. They are as a rule drawn up for issues deserving particular elucidation and care. For the area of the linguistic legislation the OCSE accumulated serious experience in dealing with tension-loaded issues due to its involvement in preventing ethnic conflicts (Kemp 2001: 28). The task of drafting guidelines has been addressed by a group of experts upon the request of the OSCE HCNM. This group set up in 1998 the Oslo Recommendations regarding the Linguistic Rights of National Minorities. These recommendations are further elucidated in an explanatory note. The international legal standards on language use in minority contexts concern first of all issues linked to names, religion, community life and NGOs, media, economic life, administrative authorities and public services, independent national institutions, judicial authorities and deprivation of liberty. The issues highlighted in the recommendations represent the areas in which problems used to occur in the national legislation of numerous countries.

6.2.4 Interpreting minority and linguistic legislation

As already noted, no international legal standards oblige states to adopt linguistic legislation. Many countries, such as Germany and the United States do not have any such legislation. Unlike in many others branches of law, e.g. in the penal or in the family law, there is no international standard of norm setting which would provide for the introduction of linguistic legislation into the legal system of the country. Thus far, a state can decide whether it needs linguistic legislation or not. Such a choice should be a matter of profound analysis of needs by the legislative body in a given society. Some countries such as Latvia have a history of linguistic legislation (cf. Kuzmins 2015: 134–159). Usually, it is worthwhile considering other instruments of language promotion and strengthening the position of one selected language than to determine the use of a language which in practice means also to limit the use of other languages than the promoted one. It is difficult to say in which way the existing linguistic legislation all over the world has proven useful or unavoidable. Nevertheless, the impact of this specific legislation on human behavior is unquestionable. On the other side, it goes without saying that states act within their sovereign rights when they adopt such legislation, should they deem it necessary. The approach of states toward this topic is apparently as different as is their experience with or without this type of legislation. At the end of the day, the matter concerns a legitimate purpose of legislation and the adoption of such laws by a state is, therefore, generally speaking legitimate.

Another problem concerns the interpretation of language laws. It is, of course, first of all limited by professional procedures. Interpretation of laws is a part of everyday activities of members of the legal profession, and such work does not take place in an empty space. As stressed in the main part of this book, interpretation of laws has its own premises and consequences. This is especially important in our context where many non-lawyers have to deal with the interpretation of laws. Regarding the language laws, one must take into account their concrete background. The primary purpose of this kind of law is to protect and to promote language as a part of the protection of human rights. Human rights are closely connected to linguistic, educational, and political rights. This helps understand the background of the interpretive activity. The protection of human rights and the fulfillment of the specific obligations guaranteed in international instruments must also be guaranteed as the primary goal of the interpretive process. While interpreting we have to bear in mind that international standards reflect a legal minimum and thus their *restrictive interpretation* would be unfortunate as it would contradict their main aims. It is also important to distinguish between legal obligations based on international instruments and other social goals. The question is to determine what is allowed by international or domestic law and which measures seem to be aim-oriented in terms of policy or the everyday practicalities of the given society. First of all, it must be made clear what is legally allowed, and then it has to be decided which restrictions are imposed on a person's professional activities. These requirements must be reasonable and correspond to the principle of legality. In fact, interpretation of legal norms is an unavoidable activity. It is therefore necessary to choose an appropriate approach to it. Purely structural or linguistic interpretation of legal provisions proved to be insufficient when changing needs of a complex society are at stake. The interpreting person will have to go a step further and courageously define the goals of the legislation in an attempt to interpret it. The constructive interpretation, which has been characterized in the foregoing chapters of this book, is vital if the provisions with human rights character shall remain efficient in society (Dworkin 1991: 87). Terminology plays a special role in it. We may speak about terminology at the political level or handle it in legal terms, we may speak of national majorities at the cultural, historical or political levels but first of all it is important to determine from which definition we proceed. Legal standards and definitions differ very much from those used in historical-political or other contexts.

6.2.4.1 Specific aspects in the interpretation of linguistic legislation

Linguistic legislation is determining the use of languages in society. Its background is rooted in the public policy on language use in state structures and society. It is formed like all other acts of legislation in the Parliamentary legislative process, and is afterwards implemented through competent state agencies. The two sides of the phenomenon, i.e. the legislative one (norm setting) and its subsequent application are closely interrelated. In fact, deficiencies in the legislative process regularly show up within the application of the law. Thus, the overall linguistic policy must anticipate problems of law setting and its subsequent application, if the linguistic legislation is to be efficient. In the theoretical perspective, the problems of application coincide with the problem of interpretation of legal norms. They focus upon the issues which have to be considered in this specific legislation toward the background of international legal standards. These standards form – next to the public linguistic policy – the landmarks for the domestic linguistic legislation and its interpretation. At first, the interpretation of norms perceived as belonging to linguistic legislation follows the general procedures of professional interpretation of legal norms. Due to the characteristic features of legal-linguistic norms, some specifics must be also borne in mind. In fact, only a skillful interplay between the general rules of interpretation and the specific features of their subject matter guarantee a solid and convincing result of the interpretation of norms belonging to the linguistic legislation. Here, once again, the creative interpretation of norms proves to be a reliable instrument in dealing with a subject which frequently gives rise to tensions and conflicts.

All too often, the legislator tries to determine the language use in all spheres of the societal life. As far as the public sphere is concerned, this approach is in many cases understandable. Problems usually emerge when the legislator interferes in the private sphere, be it business life, private mass media, private schools, or other cultural institutions. Here, interference is legally allowed only within limits. Moreover, the legislator can be advised not to enter this field when avoidable. In the legislation of many states, especially in transition economies, separation of public and private sectors, which may indeed be complicated in certain cases, is very important. A clear definition of private and public sector is possible and it is important to interpret the provisions accordingly. At the same time, standards valid in the public sphere cannot be transferred automatically into the private sector. This concerns e.g. private and public schools which are often organized differently and have specific goals. Any analogy should be applied extremely cautiously. At the same time, the social background of some provisions must be considered when legal acts are developed in a legislative tradition of a country involved in a systemic transition and they shall function under the conditions of market economy. The language used in the linguistic legislation is an additional problem. Especially, very general norms granting rights *within the possibilities of the State, or as far as possible* are not particularly effective and should be omitted. It goes without saying that the inclination for this sort of formulations is of a political rather than of linguistic nature. However, the flawed language of such norms results regularly in problems of interpretation. To be able to interpret this kind of legislation additional background information is needed which can be found either in recommendations or guidelines of specialized bodies or in soft laws providing general rules for understanding and application of this type of legislation.

6.2.4.2 Interpretive methods

Research into legal interpretation brought about not only specific methods but also a distinguished set of legal texts which differ in content and due to these circumstances also demand different interpretive techniques. Consequently, we used to interpret statutes differently than precedents and these again differently than contracts. Still, the classical list of interdependent methods is traditionally referred to as the canon of interpretation. The traditional techniques of interpretation, (i.e. grammatical, logical or systematic) are of limited importance for the linguistic legislation. Some role could be ascribed to the teleological (aim-oriented) technique, but even there limits clearly show up very soon. The linguistic legislation is rarely unclear in grammatical or logical terms and its systematics is rather limited. Nevertheless, some help can be provided via the analysis of the legislative intention when exploring the aim of the statute. As said, it is impossible to avoid interpretive attitudes while dealing with laws (Dworkin 1986: 46). These attitudes are inherent in our dealing with social practices. We interpret unclear statutes always from a determined point of view; we rely on our interpretive attitudes with all implied values and experience.

Roughly, interpretive problems include:

- unclear concepts due to limited legal tradition or their roots in either ethnology or linguistics (e.g. *multilingualism/multiculturalism, official bilingualism, ethnic/national minority*)

Unclear concepts can be clarified by using recommendations and guidelines issued by specialized state agencies and expert bodies.

- clearly sounding concepts which are often of unlimited scope such as *state language*

Above general concepts pertaining usually to the constitutional law can be clarified within domestic procedures set up for solving such legal interpretive problems. Hereby, the main principles of democratic legal systems, especially the rule of law and good governance as well as the goals of the state policy such as strengthening multiculturalism provide guidelines which enable to find a workable interpretive variety of a general concept.

- a special case of the linguistic legislation form open-ended formulations like *The state shall whenever possible enhance...*

These formulations constitute a real challenge for the interpreter. They are the classical area for the creative interpretation. They shall be interpreted toward their background in human rights. This background and the aim of this type of legislation pertaining to the protection and to the strengthening of human rights in society will show the interpreting lawyer the appropriate criteria for his work. Within the problematic type of formulations some changes are necessary in the course of times. Aims and principles once accepted such as *affirmative actions* may not be productive any more. This is one of the reasons why the reference to legislative intent does not always lead to acceptable results. It is also worthwhile to make the interpretive principles visible in the final result. The interpretation gains on legitimacy and acceptability when rules and principles upon which it has been based are clearly stated in it. Furthermore, it should be stressed that the result of the interpretation is not only a recommendation of "a certain notion or meaning" (Juhl 1986: 3). It is also the best possible result of the interpretation that can to pass the constitutionality test, and that finally corresponds with international standards. In sum, interpreting linguistic legislation is a challenging task. Nevertheless, it can succeed when the aims of the legislation are clearly understood and their interference with the international instruments and the broader background of human rights protection finds an appropriate place in the constructive work of the interpreter.

6.2.5 Comparative language law

Due to the amount of statutes pertaining to language use the establishing of a new discipline called comparative language law has been suggested in the academic research (Turi 1995: 111). This discipline should support further systematization of the legal material in the international settings and elaborate general principles of linguistic legislation. Case studies upon which such a comparison is to be based would make a model linguistic law possible and prescribe law setting standards in the international legislative practice. Within the comparative studies, Finnish and Swiss legislation have gained particular importance. Furthermore, Canadian and Russian legislation which reflect an extreme cultural variety on their political territories were also considered. French linguistic legislation gained momentum in recent years as well. A closer look at different legal conceptions of determining language use makes some general remarks possible. It signals also possible interpretive problems inherent in the structure of the statutes. Below the French, Russian, and Finnish linguistic legislative approaches are contrasted to illustrate the role which comparative linguistic legislation could play in future.

6.2.5.1 French linguistic legislation

French linguistic legislation has been approached with some reservation by the experts (Baylon 1991: 190). It is nevertheless worthwhile studying because it displays some structural problems of classical treatment of this subject by national legislators. The first structural problem is the determination of the goal toward which such legislation should be interpreted and applied. In France, it has traditionally been the protection of the French language (Cornu 2005: 422). Never any other goals have been advanced in the legislative materials or in the public policy statements. Therefore, all statutory provisions and court decisions relating to them are structured around the idea of protection of the French language. This fact may be surprising as in France no serious challenge to the preponderance of the French language in the public sphere (be it political or cultural) has been perceived since the French revolution, the obligatory point of reference of any thought about the French Republic. Usually, reference has been made – mostly by French researchers – to regionalist and autonomist political claims in areas where Occitan, Breton, Alsatian, Basque or Corsican are spoken (Cornu 2005: 427). However, no political evaluation of these movements has been undertaken. Such an evaluation would probably show their rather folkloristic character and limited political impact as well as their isolation among the majority of citizens. Furthermore, it would attenuate the legislative fervor and fears based on the illusionary assumption that a risk exists for the position of the French language within the French state and the French society.

The history of the French linguistic legislation and the linguistic policy is visible in its contemporary legislation. With the ordinance of Villers Cotterêts from 1539 France embraced the linguistic legislation which for centuries remained basically oriented toward the strengthening of the French language as spoken in the capital and the surrounding provinces. The ordinace replaced Latin by French in legal matters including court proceedings. Moreover, 1694 the first normative *Dictionnaire de l'Académie française* drew the final line under the attempts to control language use by the state. Hence, historically, two perspectives on language have been anchored in the French legislation, i.e. the necessity of one state language and the right of the state to determine this language and survey its development. The mentioned goal of protection of the French language structures basically the whole legislation. In addition, the goal to make France a unilingual country is manifest as well (Cornu 2005: 425). Art. 2 of the French Constitution states since 1992 that French is the language of the Republic: *La langue de la République est le français.* Surprisingly, it does not perceive the French language as a national language, unlike its national anthem *Marseillaise* or its national flag, the *tricolore.* This circumstance has also been interpreted in the sense that the French language still plays a role in international communication (Cornu 2005: 424). It is interesting to compare the formulation of Art. 18 of the Swiss constitution from 1999 applied in a country where the French language is one of the dominating idioms: The freedom of language is guaranteed – *La liberté de la langue est guarantie.* As a result, it can be inferred from the comparison of the two fundamental constitutional provisions that in the Swiss legislation the use of the language is not connected to politically determined preponderance of a language. Neither is in a profoundly multilingual country, that Switzerland undeniably is, any reference been made to the necessity to protect a language against others or to the risk for a language, imagined or proven. Regional languages did not play any particular role in the French legislation. However, in 2008 regional languages have been declared a part of the national heritage (FR *patrimoine de la France*) and a provision with the corresponding content has been introduced into the French constitution's Art. 75. The position of the regional languages is still unclear as governmental directives mostly deal with facultative teaching of those languages in public schools. The *Conseil Consititutionnel* decided 1999 that the European Charter on Regional and Minority Languages is not compatible with the French constitution and therefore should not be ratified by France (Dec. nr. 99–412 DC, dated June 15, 1999). The *Conseil Constitutionnel* referred to the indivisibility of the Republic, the unity of the French people and the equality of all citizens while rejecting the aims underlying the European Charter as well as the spirit of the Charter altogether. A further Parliamentary Act, the Law on the Use of the French Language no. 94–665 (*Loi relative à l'emploi de la langue française)* from 1994 determines the use of the French language in the public sphere which is however rather broadly conceived in the act. It includes certain contracts and publications as well as public advertisements and notifications accessible to the broad public. The application of this law became controversial in matters concerning internet that is operated internationally.

Additional and very specific aspects of the French linguistic legislation concern issues such as neologisms and orthography reforms which are dressed in legislative forms, decrees or laws. Orthography reforms have been regularly initiated by the *Académie française* in 1694, 1718, 1740, 1762, 1798, 1835, 1878, 1932–35 and also recently, in 1990. The recently proposed changes have a character of recommendations; however, they are mandatory for the public educational institutions. As a result, orthography reforms remain within the State domain and the reforms are undertaken on behalf of the government. Spelling is not perceived as a private matter or a question which should be decided among cultural elites, scholars and writers, mostly interested in such issues. Lists of neologisms are prepared by state agencies, predominantly within the Ministry of Culture. Moreover, France's linguistic policy embraces the idea of *francophonie* which makes also clear why the constitution does not perceive the French language as a national medium of communication. Promotional measures are developed within *francophonie* which has also a pronounced political dimension. The *francophonie* as an idea is of interest because it reflects the international perspective in the linguistic legislation. Unlike in France, in most other countries the linguistic legislation relates exclusively to the internal distribution of language use. The French linguistic legislation is an illustrative example of the initial presupposition advanced here that in the linguistic legislation the politically determined goal pre-structures all further legislative efforts. It shows furthermore that the argumentative practice in the application of this legislation is clearly determined by its initial goal.

6.2.5.2 Russian federal linguistic legislation

Overall, the linguistic legislation of the Russian Federation has been deemed as acceptable in the light of international standards (cf. Galdia/Wydra, in: Voronina/Galdia 2004: 334, Wydra/Galdia 2010, Filippova 2013, Zamyatin 2014). Basically, only the provision of Art. 3 (6) of the Language Act prohibiting the use of other alphabets than Cyrillic for languages spoken in the Russian Federation have been qualified as clearly violating international standards. However, acceptability of a set of norms in the international perspective does not automatically mean that the legislation perfectly fits local needs or does not lead to problems in application. Particular problems connected to the Language Act reflect its roots in the Soviet legal techniques which produced overlong laws in flawed terms and little essence. Clearly, the intention of the legislator has been to describe the linguistic use in the country and mark more or less precisely to what extent the free choice of the language is permissible. As the law is overburdened with situational descriptions it is difficult to interpret and to apply. Moreover, terms in provisions referring to permitted use of a language other than Russian are formulated in extremely general wording, e.g. Art. 21 (RUS) *с учетом местного населения* (while taking into account the local population), Art. 16 (3) (RUS) *в необходимых случаях* (in necessary cases), or 15 (3) (RUS) *в случае необходимости* (in case of necessity). In situations, in which this wording may lead to difficulties in determining the scope of the application of the concerned provisions a broad interpretation can be recommended. Indeed, in the domain of human rights when the legislator is using terms which are difficult to interpret, he will also have to accept the risk that more rights can be attributed to citizens than he actually intended to provide them. In all countries, Russia included, the general rule should be that human rights cannot be interpreted restrictively.

6.2.5.3 Finnish linguistic legislation

Finnish linguistic legislation has been perceived by many as an advanced system of norms regulating language use in a satisfying way and rightly so. Approaches to address language use issues in Finland date back to 19th century (Mattila 2002: 156). The long legislative tradition in Finland and the experience made with the linguistic legislation there led to a model-like language law which is interesting in several ways. The new language law (FIN Kielilaki 6.6.2003/423) entered into force on January 1, 2004. It develops the main contents of Art. 17of the Constitution stating that Finnish and Swedish are national languages of the Republic. It may at the first glance appear surprising as this law does not address very many questions which use to come up in numerous other countries, at least in the last decade. This is definitely not a coincidence, but rather the result of experience made in a bilingual country in the last century. Indeed, efficient linguistic legislation requires first of all limitation. Once the needs for legal regulation are explored and determined, it is possible to curtail the legislation which suits the country best and responds to legitimate social needs in the society. The legislator must ask himself, which part of linguistic relations between the state and its citizens and the relations among citizens shall be determined in laws. By far, no speculative range of situations or a general approach aiming at regulating everything everywhere makes sense. This is the lesson learned by the Finnish legislator who introduced a streamlined set of rules which correspond to situations that must be regulated in the Finnish society. They are as a matter of fact fundamental, but not particularly numerous. Thus, the law determines in its Art. 1 the state languages and in its Art. 2 the scope of the regulation which is the use of the state languages in courts and administrative bodies. Additional acts such as the Act on the Knowledge of Languages Required of Personnel in Public Bodies (424/2003), the Church Act (1054/1993), the Act on Judicial Appointments (205/2000), and the Act on General Language Examinations (668/1994) address specific issues relevant to the civil service. This legislative program may appear from the perspective of the linguistic legislation passed in the last years in many European countries as very reduced. However, it may also pave the way for the development of modern linguistic legislation in other countries.

6.2.6 Global English and Global Legal English

Linguistic changes in recent decades all over the world strengthened the position of the English language as a generally accepted vernacular (cf. Cagliero et al. 2010). Meanwhile, some specific conditions of language use led to the emergence of International or Global English that refers in its formal structure to standard English while introducing unstable modifications to its phonetics, semantics and pragmatics. Reasons for these processes are multiple. First and foremost, at least currently, time and efforts invested in learning and teaching English do not allow for reaching a native or native-like proficiency for the majority of users who by necessity use this language regularly, mostly in professional settings. Second, International English is used in contacts with non-native speakers of this language rather than with native speakers of English who represent a minority among the speakers of English worldwide. Specialists maintain that International English is formed along the North American variety of English. It is further characterized by fluidity of standards that may differ from speaker to speaker and a strong influence from native languages of speakers upon semantics and pragmatics (cf. also Wierzbicka 2013). Last but not least, International English is clearly recognizable by phonetic particularities. International English differs from English as a second language that aims at mastering the English standard language coined by the native speakers of English. There, for instance, considerable efforts are spent to ensure the type of pronunciation that comes as close as possible to native pronunciation. International English speakers, instead, while reflecting pronunciation standards set by the native speakers, do not strive to achieve this level of phonetic adequacy; they are not under the obligation to sound like native speakers or to be taken for natives. This feature enabled the English language to be transformed into International English that does not require the speaker to join the Anglo-American culture or to imitate native speakers; it leaves the speaker his linguistic and cultural identity as a non-native speaker of English. International Legal English, a variety of International English, is used regularly in international legal exchanges. Legal problems that emerge due to the use of English in the public sphere are multiple. The most problematic issue is the non-regulated yet dominant use of English in international institutions and international contacts. English is de facto the language of almost all activities of the European Union, yet the policy and the legislation of the E.U. are based on strict formal multilingualism. Also in most E.U. countries the English language has no official status although it is regularly used there.

Internationalization of the use of the English language is a global phenomenon. Even China, which is not a country where English had been used as a second or as an administrative language considers its institutionalization. The chief justice of the Chinese Supreme People's Court Jiang Qibo expressed support for introducing English language services in Chinese courts for lawsuits filed by foreigners. He has been quoted as saying: "It is necessary to establish an English lawsuit service platform nationwide, and we are considering this" (cf. China Daily, December 18–24,

2015). This statement has been interpreted as supporting English language services in Chinese courts. Such measures could be also used in the European Union as introductory steps toward institutionalization of the English language as a second language of the EU or in Europe in general.

While some refer to growing cultural imperialism through the worldwide spreading of English, P. van Parijs (2011) stressed the democratic element in the use of one language, i.e. English, worldwide. Being aware of the criticism on the pre-dominance of English that might be perceived by some as anti-democratic he discusses possible mechanisms that would enable linguistic justice. It goes without saying that whatever lingua franca provides unjust and unjustified privileges for its native speakers. Meanwhile, as linguae francae as socio-linguistic phenomena are unavoidable, it seems more appropriate to develop distributional and compensatory mechanisms that would ensure linguistic justice within the given linguistic settings dominated by a lingua franca.

6.2.7 Conclusions on linguistic legislation

At least one result emerges from our analysis of the comparative language law. It seems that the limitation of the scope of the legislation has a positive effect upon the application of statutes and on their acceptability in societies concerned. On the other side, it becomes also plain that the differentiated structures of the legislative acts in the three countries in question make comparative efforts difficult. Therefore, the mentioned model linguistic legislation would also provide a useful basis for comparison of existing national legal acts. Moreover, the recommendation "the best laws are those that legislate the least, especially regarding unofficial use of language" (Turi 1995: 114, 116) remains a reliable guideline for the legislators in this domain. Linguistic legislation is a double edged sword; it may lead to solving problems in society or instigate tensions and ethnic conflicts. Therefore, the state has to consider twice the necessity of legislative acts regarding language use and set up a linguistic policy which accompanies the implementation of such acts. A legislation that regulates language use must be shaped also by linguists. Their advice that multilingualism and multiculturalism are characteristic features of developed societies must be heard. Linguistic legislation must reflect the structure of linguistic landscapes which it regulates. Historical inadequacies must be balanced by soft law and promotional measures. In sum, linguistic legislation after having reached the phase of an apparent triumph, which culminated in abounding legislation regulating all thinkable details of language use, may become in future a domain of limited and much more relaxed application. The growing acceptance of principles of multiculturalism as guidelines for state and society among legislators might in some time from now lead to less tense relations between ethnic groups and limit the necessity of decisions regarding language use in legislative bodies. The interpreters of the linguistic legislation could reflect this tendency in their works and influence the further development of interpretive standards along the lines of cultural diversity. Thus far, it is the legislation which relies upon the cultural diversity and not the other way round.

6.3 Language Risk

The tendency toward developing legislation which could be some day called global law is in our view not questionable. Problematic are, however, methodological insufficiencies in practical and theoretical approaches to this task. Especially, frustrations caused by the globalization in some countries may hinder the legislative progress. Certainly, they will not be able to impede significantly the development of the global law. The emerging globalized world is multicultural and multilingual and this fact cannot be changed. The global law will be therefore a multilingual law. This is one of the reasons why in this book problems of the legal translation were discussed as central issues of legal linguistics. Other consequences of this fact are the legal liability related to the use or the omission to use a language, called especially in the private international law *language risk*. Until now, no clear rules exist for cases concerning the language risk. In times, when the population on a territory was culturally relatively homogeneous and migrants played only a peripheral role, linguistic problems in law, be it in the public or in the private sphere, were not perceived as crucial. Today, it would be simplistic to claim that the knowledge of the main language of the country is a practical necessity if not a legal obligation for every resident upon its territory. The diversity of biographies and the diversity of cultures make clear even for uninterested lawyers that such a rule would oversimplify the social reality in an inadmissible way. Finally, as a result of this uncertainty about right or wrong language use the language risk became an increasing issue in law. The most problematic cases in multilingual contacts concern negotiations in a language which is less understandable to one party than to another or when one party uses a language dominant in a specific branch which is also its native language whereas this language is a foreign language to the other party. The basic constellation can be more complicated; due to cases which emerge in such situations we are able to distinguish between situations where the linguistic incompetence of one party is (manifestly) recognizable and where it is well hidden in the subject matter and manifests itself as misunderstanding, e.g. after a contract has been concluded. The first constellation concerns mostly consumer related issues (cf. Dreißigacker 2002), the second is rather specific to advanced business practices such as negotiations between enterprises.

The first constellation can be exemplified with the help of the court opinion Ramirez v. Plough, Inc. (15 Cal. App. 4th 1110, 12 Cal. Rptr. 2d 423, 1992, cf. also Notes and Commented Materials no. 60) where the Court of Appeal of California had to decide a product liability case. A Spanish-speaking mother of a sick baby bought aspirin in a pharmacy. On the package the standard Reye's syndrome warning was printed in English only. The mother administered the drug to her baby who developed the Reye's syndrome and was damaged for life. She sued the manufacturer for damages. The manufacturer argued that no duty to warn in any other language than English existed in the U.S. and insisted on this practice pointing to the fact that ca. 148 languages were spoken in the U.S. The court however adopted a differentiated point of view and asked whether the warning given in English only was adequate under the circumstances of the case. It stressed that the public policy in the U.S. is directed toward the treatment of English as official language of the Union. However, "nothing compels the conclusion that a manufacturer of a dangerous or defective product is immunized from liability when an English-only warning does not adequately inform non-English literate persons likely to use the product". In this case, the manufacturer was aware of the fact that the product was distributed also in pharmacies situated in areas where Spanish-speaking population dominates. Moreover, he even advertised it in Spanish-language media. Therefore, the court denied Plough the summary judgment without stating, however, that a warning in foreign languages is necessary on certain products: "In deciding that Plough did not establish its right to judgment as a matter of law, we do not hold that manufacturers are required to warn in languages other than English simply because it may be foreseeable that non-English literate persons are likely to use their products. Our decision merely recognizes that under some circumstances the standard of due care may require such warning."

The second constellation can be illustrated with the help of the already cited case MCC – Marble Ceramic Center v. Ceramica Nuova d'Agostino, S.I.A. (144 F3d. 1384, 11th Cir. 1998) where a more stringent standard is developed (cf. 3.6.4.5, cf. also Notes and Commented Materials no. 67). The parties, an American enterprise as buyer and an Italian enterprise as seller agreed to terms and conditions of a contract that were preprinted on the reverse side of the order form prepared by the seller in the Italian language. Later, the buyer pretended that he did not understand the clauses written in Italian and that the parties agreed to remove them from the contract. The court however assumed it as improbable that a professional buyer would sign a contract including terms and conditions in a foreign language that he did not understand. MCC had therefore to bear the language risk. In Ramirez, the approach to the language risk issue is based on circumstantial appreciation and this seems to be an effective criterion for a liability test. In MCC v. Marble, the test is more formal as it can be based on commercial practices among enterprises involved in international business; nevertheless, it also stresses the role of circumstances for answering the question as to who bears the language risk. It may be assumed that in future decisions in this area the differentiating test will be applied which would enable to avoid a rigid legislation on the matter.

6.4 Professional Liability of Translators

Translators are, like all other professionals, liable for damages caused by their products, i.e. texts in the target language (Mattila 2002b: 487). However, the legal issue regarding the liability of translators is complicated due to the nature of the legal texts and problems of legal translation which were discussed above (cf. also Kinnunen 2006: 25). Therefore, the question when a translation is erroneous is not always easy to decide. Legal texts may lead to misunderstandings, and cause damage due to formulations in the source text which deliberately or negligently might have been formulated in an ambiguous way. Is the translator obliged to discover such ambiguities and signal them to his client? Is this his legal or professional obligation? Where is the borderline between translating and detective work to be drawn? Another set of problems concerns translations into lesser used languages with underdeveloped or missing legal terminology such as some Uralic languages spoken in Russia. There, a general description of the meaning included in the source language document or direct borrowings from Russian are used to render the meaning (Galdia 2013, cf. also for Maori Stephens et al. 2014). The third possibility is to shape neologisms in the hope that they will be understood properly by the readers. In many other languages the description with words from the ordinary language is preferred to the forming of neologisms. The translation of a promissory note from English into Hawaiian from 1917 is an example of such a procedure (cf. Notes and Commented Materials no. 16). Another legal-linguistically relevant problem is the translation of international conventions into languages that lack the necessary legal terminology and where the terminology is invented by their first translators. Are these new coinages binding also on future translators of international instruments related to these documents even when the new translators have better proposals for rendering the original terminology in the texts that they develop? The standards for professional translation are unclear at this point. In all such cases the central legal question is whether the lack of equivalent terminology or legal-linguistic features in a language increases or diminishes the translator's professional liability. Liability standards in some countries may suggest increased liability linked to the contractual acceptance of an offer to translate. Indeed, who accepts an offer, accepts also the risk inherent in it. The nature of the legal translation would, however, require rather an increase in tolerance toward legal translation into languages that are problematic from the point of view of their legal-linguistic features. The proper test for such translations must therefore focus on the essentials of the message, and not on the legal terminology.

In the legal-linguistic research, work concerning the standards of a correct legal translation in the light of professional liability has only begun. The most reliable criterion to determine professional liability would be court decisions about the acceptability of variations in legal translations. However, very few legal translations have been challenged in courts of law (Gémar 2004: 743). Therefore, the limits of interpretive creation in the translation of legal texts remain the professional risk of translators. In some cases, such as Falcoal, Inc. v. Kurumu (660 F. Supp. 1536 S.D. Texas, 1987) the translation error is evident. In casu, the Turkish language clause in the contract between the Turkish and the U.S. American parties – here retranslated into English – provided that "the final jurisdiction for the settlement of any disputes, in the case of the Purchaser submitting a claim, lies within the jurisdiction of the Houston commercial courts and, in the case of the Supplier submitting a claim lies within the jurisdiction of the Ankara commercial courts." The English version of the clause stated that any dispute "shall be settled in Houston and submitted to the jurisdiction of the courts of the U.S.A. if the claim is put forward by Supplier and in Ankara, Turkey, and submitted to the Turkish Courts if the claim is put forward by Buyer." Hence, the forum selection clauses in the source and in the target language directly contradicted each other. This resulted in the impossibility for the plaintiff to sue in Houston which led to damages. In such a case where the translation error is evident also to a non-specialist, the determination of liability is not problematic.

Liability issues may emerge also in the case of a translation that does not comply with professional standards of language knowledge and which includes numerous grammatical errors. Such a translation may not lead to direct damage because it is usually understandable notwithstanding its numerous grammatical errors but may indirectly tarnish its user's image. The liability claim would in such a case be based on bad quality of work provided by the translator. The translation into the German language of a Turkish court decree (cf. Notes and Commented Materials no. 19) that was mentioned here in another context is illustrative of this set of problems. The translator of this text would almost certainly not be able to claim her fee for the work done because her work does not even approach the lowest standards set up for a professional translation. Overall, at this stage of the legal-linguistic development one would have to ask whether different standards of professionalism should be accepted within the evaluation procedure of the legal translation depending on the languages from and into which the texts are translated. Today, practically, different standards govern the translation from French into English and from Russian into Mari or Italian into Hawaiian. Should a more differentiated standard for the evaluation of the professional work emerge among the professionals themselves, it would also become easier to determine who shall bear the risk for misunderstandings caused by translation into languages with limited legal terminology.

Part 7: Conclusions: Legal-Linguistic Prospects and Limits

The foregoing parts of this book could be summarized as follows: While developing a discourse about the role of language in the area of law a shift in perspective from elucidating isolated words to words in contexts has been achieved in these lectures. Speech acts and not words dominate our language and legal language is not an exception in this sense. Speech acts, in turn, do not function in isolation either. They are parts of the legal discourse that represents the overarching structure within which we used to speak about law. In this complex communicative structure legal meaning emerges as a result of exchanges between professionals and non-professionals of law. This legal discourse is therefore part of a broader communicative structure that may be called social discourse. Furthermore, meaning in law is constructed and not deciphered or deducted from legal texts. This is the consequence of legal discursiveness, i.e. the fact that law is a discursive practice and not something else. Legal linguistics researches legal discourses with all their extra-legal implications. It also uses its expertise about the functioning of language in society to contribute to a better law. Let us now look closer at further reaching consequences that follow from this summary.

7.1 Linguistic Turn in Law

In this study I proposed a *linguistic turn* in dealing with issues of creation and application of law (cf. 1.2.11). As a matter of fact, my initial idea is not totally new. Generations of researchers, lawyers, philosophers and other scholars were perfectly aware of the specific relation that law entertained with language – here I allow myself to use the metaphor one last time. Indeed, law and language cannot but artificially be separated. Until now, much too frequently this artificial separation took place. Law was perceived as a logical system where systematization of provisions and concepts had to prevail. The civil law tradition devoted itself sometimes even excessively to the task of conceptual systematization at the risk of losing connection to social practice. The alleged logical legal system represented by systematized provisions, legal concepts, and their constitutive elements dominated positivist legal research and positivist legal education. In the common law tradition the importance of court procedures and judicial decisions for the development of law prevented to some extent the exaggerated interest in pure systematization of legal concepts. In fact, it takes time to understand the consequences of this state of affairs, as it took time to discover this anomaly in the perception of essential features in the creation and in the application of law. The time factor is particularly beneficial to the proposed shift in attention to the subject. The past century was dominated by the linguistic turn in philosophy, the ordinary language philosophy, and the following developments in philosophical and linguistic pragmatics. Time has shown the limits of these approaches as well. Nevertheless, the achievements of the academic research based on pragmatic conceptions are undeniable, although other concurring or even contrary movements also contributed to the renewal of the perspective in which we used to perceive social reality. Meanwhile, our material analysis allows the first important conclusion that legal argumentation prevails over conceptual systematization in law. It must therefore be perceived as central to legal research as well as to legal education. I am not inclined to deny the necessity of systemizing work in law as systematized concepts provide a reliable matrix for legal argumentation. My idea is limited to the necessary shift in the attention to law. The shift in the attention to linguistic implications of law occurs due to the fact that legal argumentation is as such a linguistic phenomenon. Therefore, while undertaking the linguistic turn in law I actually re-establish the necessary balance of cognitive interests in law. My analysis has also demonstrated that jurists have been always dealing with language but did not take law's linguistic foundations seriously. They rather construed language as a decoration which was added to the legislative or to the judicial decision after the legal work was accomplished. In order to balance this inadequacy, the focal point must shift to legal argumentation. This, in essence, is the linguistic turn in law.

Meanwhile, the linguistic turn in law would be truly accomplished only in a process of a profound transformation of law in accordance with the rules of language use. Wherever in these lectures a discrepancy between socially dominant discursive practices and linguistic practices in legal institutions has been discovered in the analyzed materials a transformation process would have to start. Its final aim would be to harmonize the rules governing the use of language in society and the rules according to which language is used in juridical and other institutions relevant to law. As the common communicative denominator for multiple social discourses is the ordinary language, this language would be used as a tool in the transformation processes of law. This means that professionals and non-professionals would be using ordinary language in communicative situations that are dominated today by the legal language as it is defined by most researchers, i.e. as a language for special purposes fully understandable only to legal professionals. The findings of my long lectures did not uncover any theoretical obstacles that would contradict the above postulate. Laws and administrative acts could be written in ordinary language, lawsuits could be conducted in this language and jurists could generally use ordinary language in all their activities. This means also that laws would have to be re-written in accordance with the above postulate. While using the ordinary language as the main means of their professional communication jurists would also have to follow another central postulate that is connected to ordinary language use, namely the recommendation to use explicit language. Thus, jurists would be professionally committed to the communicative strategy of saying what they mean. Moreover, legal discourse expressed in explicit ordinary language seems to me a conception of law that would enable the creation of a law of better quality. This result would also shift the legal-linguistic interest in law toward other, possibly more relevant theoretical issues than those discussed today.

7.2 Conception of Legal Linguistics

The conception of legal linguistics proposed here is based on language use in opposition to studies of linguistic utterances, for instance particular legal provisions or legal notions without reference to their context of use. This approach has the advantage to be broad enough to capture not only the legal language but also the law as a social phenomenon. Law's most distinctive features, i.e. its link to power as well as to language, are best understood when the use of linguistic devices and not the use of abstract declarations of legislative intent is perceived as the central field of the legal-linguistic research. Theoretically, the choice exercised here means the preference for the pragmatically oriented perspective over the semantic one that is dominated by the tendency to denote meaning in legal concepts. Many semantic problems can be solved or they simply disappear when the shift from the semantic to the pragmatic perspective occurs because in law meaning is created in the processes of application of legal rules within complex linguistic operations. Therefore, meaning cannot be simply decoded or distilled from legal provisions or court opinions.

With this result in mind, I tried to expand the core legal theory by explicitly linguistic elements. I started with the question how are laws made with words and ended with a more complicated problem setting, namely how we speak about law. Legal terms which we have analyzed turned to be vantage points for arguments, the later being elements of a discourse about law which takes place in different professional and less professional settings (cf. also Galdia 2014). Complex speech acts such as legal argumentation, legal interpretation or legal translation proved to constitute such discourses. The main field of legal linguistics are legal operations in law developed around legal speech acts. Legal speech acts are qualitatively different in that they reach from simple utterances like a promise to complex argumentative and interpretive structures. Legal terms that represent legal concepts function as focal points for these complex structures. Linguistic operations are organized within legal discourses on different levels of discursiveness as they involve legal professionals, professionals and laypersons or laypersons solely. These legal discourses take place in preformulated textual patterns; the stricter is the discursive pattern organized, the more professional the discourse will be. Laypersons' discourses about law are less strict in the choice of argumentative or interpretive devices, but they are also less effective in their impact upon the creation and the application of law. In such discourses, formal aspects may dominate the debate to the detriment of the subject matter. In turn, they are less exposed to the risk of reification of language than professional discourses about law. These discourses demonstrate that law seen from the linguistic perspective appears to be a discursive practice that is subject to institutional limitations. I would wish to provide an exhaustive overview over legal arguments used in the discursive practice. Yet, legal linguistics in the modern sense of the term is only in its beginnings.

7.2.1 Methodology of legal linguistics

At the initial stage of theory building, legal linguistics has to answer two fundamental questions. First, what is law and second, how is language used in law. In the first task it is assisted by general legal theory while it remains a particular theory of law. The second task is best performed with the help of pragmalinguistic approaches because they show the closest affinity to law among all linguistic perspectives. I have therefore adapted the analytic conceptual apparatus of the speech act theory and the discourse theory and I have shown that it serves perfectly its purpose also in law. Law and language seen in the perspective of the speech act theory are not artificially separated any more. Creation and application of law as explicitly linguistic operations can be described with theoretical means of the linguistic research. This description is justified because it touches upon the most essential feature of law, i.e. its embeddedness in institutionalized discursive social practices. These social practices remain unclear until perceived as argumentative practices. This result may, at first, disappoint because it seems to concern the scientific paradigm in legal theory rather than the social practice. However, through the shift in perspective we will be gradually able to improve rationality tests for legal argumentation and subsequently we will be able to produce law of better quality. This result, which may seem limited to theory, satisfies the demand expressed in society for good governance, which means in essence a demand for law created along the principles of an advanced democracy and the application of modern law according to principles of rationality in which the best available arguments will be used.

Incidental to my efforts aimed at clarifying the structure of the legal discourse has been the elucidation of the concept of the legal language. I can finally define the legal language as language used in legally relevant communicative situations. Its quality as ordinary language or special register does not matter under pragmalinguistic descriptive requirements; the context of use determines the status of a language as legal language. It is equally clear that this legal language covers professional use of language in different communicative situations (e.g. criminal investigation, trial, examination of law students, informal talk of judges about their work at a party) and the non-professional language use (e.g. witness testimony, laypersons' comments on judgments or legislation, media reports about legal matters). Meanwhile, the legal language appears as an institutionalized social practice as it refers to institutionally regulated use of language where status issues that have an impact upon the validity of legal speech acts are determined in institutional (political) hierarchies. In fact, the closer the speaker is able to approach the institutional requirements of the use of language the higher will be – paradoxical situations excluded – the effectiveness of the use of arguments by the speaker. In this context, the knowledge of professional (i.e. institutionally approved) arguments by the speaker is decisive as the professional legal discourse where legal decisions are made depends on and is steered by received legal arguments. What is more, legal-linguistically valuable and particularly interesting are situations where new legal arguments that may have their origin in non-professional discourse break the protective walls of the institutionalized discourse and establish themselves as a new legal doctrine in the legal-argumentative landscape. Yet, such situations are rare. Law being a mechanism of the exercise of power in society is not primarily dominated by disinterested rational argumentation.

Furthermore, when the use of language in legally relevant communicative situations is not intrinsically related to special registers but can be equally functional when expressed with means of the ordinary language another important research problem may be perceived as elucidated: The future of the legal language can be perceived through the prism of ordinary language. Meanwhile, establishing ordinary language in a role of legal language is only a partial victory in breaking unjustified social monopolies. As has been demonstrated in these lectures, not a linguistic register but legal-linguistic operations are responsible for the emergence of meaning in legal discourses. This means that even if law would be expressed in ordinary language it would still have to be interpreted, justified, described and stated in already known legal-linguistic mechanisms. These mechanisms called by me legal-linguistic operations are ubiquitous and until know no type of law that would be independent of them has manifested itself in discursive social practices on this planet. Meanwhile, ordinary language cleans law from meaningless and deceiving speech in analogy with the impact of analytical philosophy upon metaphysics. Certain discursive formations disappear from law when its language becomes accessible to everyone. Abusive linguistic exercises are less probable under such circumstances, for instance in the justification of court decisions. Law in its primary textual form becomes accessible to citizens who are expected to know it and to act accordingly. Last but not least, the governmental monopoly of power in the enforcement of law depends upon the general knowledge of law in the citizenry as a requirement of the legally justified exercise of power toward those who break the law. Understanding law is therefore not like understanding nuclear physics. One may deplore the generally rather low level in the understanding of fundamental issues of the standard model of modern physics among citizens. Yet this lack of knowledge has other consequences for society that the lack of legal knowledge due to the limited linguistic accessibility of legal sources. However, access to legal sources does not automatically engender the understanding of law. As said, the understanding of law emerges in legal-linguistic operations. These operations enable speakers to process legal texts in legal discourses with the aim to shape appropriate law in a particular situation of its application. Today, legal-linguistic operations are taught solely to law students and this only implicitly. Society would have to establish educational mechanisms that would enable citizens to handle consciously legal-linguistic operations and to put them on equal footing with jurists in this respect. In this constellation, however, citizens would not become jurists as the knowledge of law includes also the systematic knowledge of legal regulation that is vast and that can be mastered only within year-long legal education. Meanwhile, mastery of legal-linguistic operations is the prerequisite of legal literacy; their constant skilful use in legal discourses makes a jurist of a citizen.

Finally, ordinary language use in law establishes also the postulate of explicit language use in legislation and in court decisions. In fact, speech acts of the ordinary language can function meaningfully only when all speakers say what they really mean. This postulate has a far reaching consequence for law. Implicit elements of law that guarantee its elastic application and impede its immediate understanding would disappear from a type of law that comes about and is applied under the strict requirement of linguistic explicitness. Processing explicitly formulated legal texts in legal-linguistic operations is an activity of different quality than the multi-layered interpretation of provisions that simply mean too much. Law becomes inefficient when it is overburdened with semiotic processes. For the legislator to say clearly what is actually meant in a piece of legislation may appear problematic due to a century-long tradition of inexplicit speaking and intentional avoidance of clear statements about the semantic range of legal provisions. For judges, the same problem may emerge in their use of language that for many equals the constant use of pre-formulated bleak formulas that fit whatever case constellation. Legal certainty suffers under such circumstances of language use. It is also difficult to require from citizens to respect the law when this law is stated in nebulous formulations that mean everything and nothing. Pragmalinguistic requirements of language use include therefore the postulate of adequate use of language in legally relevant communicative situations. This means the commitment of all speakers to explicit and true statements in their linguistic input into legal discourses.

7.3 Legal Discourse is not Autonomous

One of the central conclusions that can be drawn from this book and also from my *Legal Discourses* (Galdia 2014) is the thought that the legal discourse is embedded in broader argumentative activities that can be called social discourse. The legal discourse cannot be grasped or made instrumental in society in isolation from the main discourse and some minor contributive discursive practices such as political discourse or academic discourse because it is not autonomous. Previously, the concept of law as it had been developed by legal positivists was based upon the paradigm of an independent legal discourse and upon the idea of an isolated legal language perceived as a special register that could be approached in a methodologically reduced way as allegedly pure law. Parts of legal linguistics, especially at the beginning of its development, followed the positivist paradigm and focused upon the legal language in splendid isolation from other linguistic practices that accompany strictly legal language use. This approach impoverished legal linguistics as it suggested to the users of the legal-linguistic research that legal language is an independent linguistic code in which meaning is encoded according to some professional rules that cannot be understood by non-jurists. Relevant research made also clear that legal institutions have the tendency to stress the autonomy and the specific legal rationality in the discourse (Zieliński 1972, Tammelo 1978, Cover 1983). Today we know that meaning is not encoded in legal texts and that it emerges in complex argumentative and interpretive legal-linguistic operations. Specific to those most interesting among them is the element of institutionalization, i.e. that the emergence and the use of the legal language depend upon the existence of judicial institutions that are in many constellations, for example in the case of a court judgment, the preconditions of its valid use. Meanwhile, language is used in respect of legally relevant contexts also outside judicial institution and its use there is no less rational, yet it is clearly less efficient because it is not institutionalized, i.e. non-professional. The legal discourse is an argumentative practice centred on the exercise of power and therefore it cannot be expected that the professional, institutionalized legal discourse and the non-professional and institutionally unfettered discourses would display the same degree of efficiency in society.

7.3.1 Narratives and information in law

The most interesting and practically important part of the legal discourse is its immediate content. This can be the story told by a witness in court proceedings or the description of a legal provision developed by a judge in the context of the application of this provision in his written judgment. More complex legal narratives concern legal regulation, i.e. statutory provisions that state the law. Regulation gives rise to most particular narratives in law such as *commentaries* or *scholarly writings*. Legal linguistics researches the types of legal narratives and the rules of their composition. It classifies legal narratives and is able to distinguish fundamental legal narratives such as *constitutions* and accompanying narratives such as *accusation acts*. It furthermore studies how the legal-narrative materials overlap with novelistic and poetic narratives (cf. 4.1.1). Legal linguistics also discovers rules that inform lawyers what to do with legal narratives, i.e. how to apply law. It stresses in this context mainly legal-linguistic operations such as legal argumentation, legal justification and many others. A skilful jurist is someone who masters these operations that take place with reference to legal narratives. Legal narratives and legal information, i.e. the professional knowledge what is to be done with legal narratives constitute the knowledge of law. Broader than this knowledge is the structure of the legal discourse that unites professional and non-professional socio-linguistic interaction with reference to law.

Meanwhile, the idea to broaden the material range of the legal discourse is not new. In the U.S., the use of social science and statistics by the judge Louis Brandeis, for instance in the case Muller v. Oregon (1908), has been perceived as paradigmatic in this respect (cf. Berring 2000: 1688, Khurana 2007: 54). Brandeis used data from social sciences to coin the aim of social welfare as governmental policy under the Constitution. Equally, in Brown v. Board of Education information that was meant as evidence was provided from sources that were viewed by some as not strictly legal but rather social (cf. Berring 2000: 1688). R.C. Berring (2000: 1690) also contends that the contemporary U.S. Supreme Court is not committed to any final and primary authority; the court refers to a kaleidoscope of sources to justify its decisions that can "provide any of a number of pictures." Some authors described this tendency as a 'delegalization of law' (cf. Schauer & Wise 1997 and 2000). One could also claim that law that emerges in its broader surroundings is a law of better quality, a relegalized rather than a delegalized law. These examples also illustrate the change in the perspective upon the legitimate sources of law.

7.3.2 Diachronic aspects of legal discourse

Legal discourse displays next to the synchronic dimension that is immediately accessible to all its participants also a historical dimension that has to be reconstructed in order to be grasped. The legal discourse is regularly analyzed in its historical dimension, also in this book. First of all, legal discourse is embedded in history and its proper understanding requires the knowledge of its historical context. For instance, the Roman law deals regularly with the concepts of equality and freedom. The emergence and the application of these concepts can be properly understood only within the historical context of the ancient Roman legal discourse. In this discourse equal citizens were always treated equally, yet the discourse defined in a very specific way and differently from the contemporary legislators those groups of equals who had to be treated equally and were allowed to act freely. The misunderstanding of the historical embeddedness of the legal discourse causes anachronistic readings of ancient sources that constituted the legal discourse of past times. Particularly, it might lead to the misunderstanding that ancient Romans in fact treated people in an unequal and arbitrary way unlike the modern legislator who discursively insists upon equality and freedom. Meanwhile, also the modern legislator defines specifically the social groups that he wishes to treat equally and regularly excludes foreigners, children, other primates and some less distinctly constituted social groups from equal treatment. Legal-linguistic reconstructions of the diachronic elements of the legal discourse that in this book as well as in my *Legal Discourses* (Galdia 2014) are based mainly on Michel Foucault's *épistémologie* prevent this sort of aberrant readings. Another striking result of this research for legal linguistics are anti-essentialist conclusions where it is maintained that law is a social construct and not the reflection of a petrified and allegedly natural order of things and values. The understanding of this structural property of law is fundamental to the legal argumentation and all other legal-linguistic operations. Work on law looks differently when jurists and non-jurists are convinced that they construct and not simply decipher law in the acts of its institutional application. Equally, work on legal terminology and references to etymology of legal terms appear in another perspective when the constructivist nature of the legal practice as a discursive practice is taken into consideration. Additionally, the textological aspect of the legal discourse when seen in the diachronic perspective uncovers a web of intertextual connections that make the legal discourse as social discourse possible. This discourse requires language and this complex language comes about in the interdependence of texts. This process has a historical dimension that is even more visible in the legal language than in ordinary linguistic registers. Legal language is institutionalized and close to power structures; therefor it tends to display social practices of past time and to preserve the language of that time. Legal linguistic research clearly shows this regularity. Less clear is the future-oriented dimension of law that is textually manifest for instance in texts such as dissenting opinions that aim at shaping *better law* (cf. 3.4.2). The nexus between the diachronic and the futuristic dimension of law is neglected in the legal and legal-linguistic research. Meanwhile, better law is thinkable and legal linguists should be interested in researching the prerequisites of this law.

7.3.3 Morals in law and morals of law

I have equally shown the importance of moral values in law. This holds true for society as a whole as well as for the social group of lawyers who create and apply the law. This circumstance is actually the guarantee of operationability of law in whatever democratic society. Again, while making it clear I did not express anything particularly new. I simply made plain that values and value-laden language are integrated into law. They are so deeply merged that law cannot be perceived or applied *more geometrico,* i.e. without taking into consideration the values which underlie legislation or legal decisions in the general and in the professional discourse about law. By identifying values embedded in law I approached legal argumentation which differs in many ways from other types of language use. Arguments used in it are of volatile nature; they are grounded in the plurality of views on ethical issues (ethical diversity). Modern legal linguistics supports argumentative and interpretive strategies that further socially relevant issues and it does not focus any more on discovering devices that engender success in litigation within formal procedures. It also reflects upon the quality of arguments. Legal linguistics is therefore not neutral in terms of morals.

7.3.4 Normativeness in legal linguistics

Some parts of this book might indicate that legal linguistics is a much more innovative academic undertaking and a more radical social practice than many readers had expected. Its outreach seems to transgress the limits of a Masters' program or the boundaries of a subject taught to law students in order to broaden their intellectual horizons. Indeed, legal linguistics positions itself on the scale of academic disciplines not only as a part of linguistics or a part of law. It emerges from these disciplines as a specific theory of law; it claims to be able to explain law. To reach this goal it uses linguistic knowledge, in our case mainly linguistic pragmatics. Research results outlined in this book suggest that the legal-linguistic approach to law, when taken seriously, might have profound consequences for law as a teaching subject, as a research object, and especially as a practice of adjudication. Readers of the above chapters may have the impression that even if some or many of legal-linguistic findings are actually convincing they have no chance to be implemented in the social practice due to structural and ideological limitations of traditional positivist and the neo-positivist legal science and the practice of adjudication based upon this type of the legal science. This view may not be wrong, yet this is not the decisive point. Legal linguistics is a theoretical subject and as such it is the bearer of social and cultural normativeness and it transfers its knowledge over generations. Like whatever academic enterprise it is not directed at immediate application; materialization of theories has always been a hopeless expectation in the academia. Meanwhile, in that legal linguistics rises a claim to the validity of its findings it may expect changes to happen in future. Its main task is therefore to remain normative and not to step behind its main claims and to refer to expedient means and compromises. It is acceptable to deposit and to transfer knowledge in a situation when its implementation can occur only in better times.

7.4 Legal Futurology

Many issues discussed in these lectures are connected to legal futurology. Legal futurology is mainly concerned with future law that is understood as a law of better quality than the existing law. Legal futurologists do not guess or speculate about the future law. The task of legal futurology is to research contemporary tendencies in law that may influence future developments and that could engender a better law. One such identified tendency is legal globalization. Practically, it follows from such futurologist analyses of fundamental developments in law that the identified tendency should be supported by legal linguists and that they should contribute to the development of global law. Equally, it would be less advisable to support efforts toward legal isolationism as they are not dominant nowadays in the international legal practice and they do not represent any better law. It follows also from these lectures that future law cannot be simply designed by an author as law is a common, a social enterprise. Using more theoretical language I used to say that law is a discursive practice. Meanwhile, also other tendencies toward improving the quality of law can be identified in the social practice and they should be strengthened by legal linguistics. As a lot of effort has been spent in legal science on past law it is now time to balance the distortion caused by this one-sided perspective through the change of perspective. Legal futurology is the most practical of all areas of legal linguistics as it shapes law and not only our views upon it. One of its most important areas is, as mentioned, legal globalization that has been treated here exhaustively. Another example is linguistic regulation that has been discussed within the law of linguistic communication. Thus, legal futurology proposes a linguistically founded conception of future law as better law.

7.4.1 Future issues in legal linguistics

Creation of language used in the public sphere will remain one of the central issues for the future legal-linguistic research. Notions such as *intentional infliction of emotional distress* or *common heritage of mankind* will be elucidated in respect of the way in which they are constituted. Traditionally, signification processes had been characterized only in general epistemological terms. The reason for this shortcoming has been that only limited data was available allowing research into linguistic processes of their immediate constitution. Today, in the public sphere it is occasionally even possible to identify the creator or the first group of users of a specific legal term as well as the strategies which guaranteed the use of the new legal term in the language of the public sphere. Similarly, interpretive strategies directed toward these texts as well as argumentative strategies used by the issuers of texts composed in a language that is specific to the public sphere and especially to legal contexts will remain essential to the research. The part of conversational analysis will probably increase as access to and recording of oral sources within legal institutions are nowadays technically and legally less prohibitive. Under these circumstances, the legal discourse will be characterized materially and enable further theoretical insights into law which may become useful for the purposes of legal theory.

7.4.2 Future of comparative research in legal linguistics

I have used frequently, if not predominantly, contrastive and comparative methods in the whole book. The result of the analyses based on these methods is somehow chilling: The language of law seems to be uniform, notwithstanding regional developments that might introduce new aspects into the history of development of the legal language, especially into its terminology and into its textual forms. Meanwhile, legal language emerges, last but not least, as an exercise in legal-linguistic operations that steer the legal discourse. All contrastive and comparative examples provided in this book support this finding. Strictly speaking, this result means that the legal language has a ubiquitous structure that does not differ even if some characteristic terminological or textual features might be identified in the analyzed particular linguistic samples. This result may appear paradoxical as it might call into question the mere rationale behind comparative research in legal linguistics. This dilemma is not limited to legal linguistics. Also in linguistics proper the attention paid to comparison and cultural differences that language may or may not display begins to shift. Since John McWhorter's *The Language Hoax: Why the World Looks the Same in Any Language* (2014) linguists became more aware of the most vulnerable claims of Whorfianism. Whorfianism or the theory of linguistic relativity, which goes back to B.J. Whorf's views about the influence of language upon our perception of the world, presupposes that we think differently in different languages due to cultural specifics that are present in natural languages. In fact, cultural differences definitely exist yet our reasoning about the world and our perception of it is first of all human, and only then particular in terms of a specific culture. The reason for this regularity is relatively simply stated: human reasoning in human brains that is expressed in human language cannot be expected to be all too different (cf. Berwick and Chomsky 2016). Anthropologically, the human being is the same all over the planet. Due to previously prevalent isolation of human groups culture developed slightly differently among these groups while it remains anthropologically one human culture. Diachronic and synchronic cultural differences clearly matter to societies and they also have consequences for them. Yet they do not manifest any further going implications than those of variation. Like airlines that use different names and different business strategies, yet finally operate airplanes that fly according to principles of aerodynamics, cultures engender particular languages that function in the same way. The legal language is no different in this respect. It appears on its face as particular, yet behind its cultural particularities there are the same operative legal-linguistic (discursive) mechanisms. These cultural particularities matter practically because in daily work jurists and legal linguists deal mainly with these particular varieties of the legal language and they may perceive as less helpful the reduction of all legal-linguistic varieties to one legal language. And it seems to me that future comparative research will have to operate in this practically unavoidable area. Valuable and methodologically well-founded legal linguistics of the future will have to strike the right balance between the general and the comparative aspects of legal language in order to remain informative beyond fashions and whimsical trends of the moment. However, and as often stressed in this book, legal globalization will have its last word also on this issue.

7.5 Author's Final Words

In these lectures I have focused upon issues which I perceive as central to law, and I have determined legal argumentation as methodologically fundamental to all reflection upon law. In this sense, law is for me a matter of language. I have also proposed a vast research program into argumentation in the area of national and international law. Finally, it is tempting to ask whether, provided exhaustive results of such a research program would become available, legal problems, i.e. problems of legal theory would be perceived as solved. Is it realistic to assume that we would be able to reach a stage where we would know everything about law and witness the end of the reflection upon it? There exist several hindrances to this result. The first is inherent in the phenomenon law itself. Indeed, I have excluded from this study material issues of law, i.e. questions why law is as it is or why it says things it says. I do not underestimate these questions, yet legal linguistics deals primarily with the language in which propositions about law are expressed. Nevertheless, even in legal linguistics we would be theoretically able to address the issue from a praxiological point of view. We would argue that law has to address subject matters it aims to regulate in an efficient way because efficiency is the central principle of activities in social contexts. This efficiency can be construed in different ways. One would nevertheless have to insist on the legislation that is adequate, i.e. which matches best the standards of modern democratic society. Our claim for efficiency would be therefore satisfied by the adequacy reached in institutionalized argumentative processes. The second inherent hindrance is of legal-linguistic nature. As constantly stressed in these lectures, material issues in law are inseparable from legal arguments. There is no limit to our inventiveness of legal arguments so far. Moreover, in a modern society it does not make much sense to use whatever arguments. A reliable reservoir of modern legal arguments are human rights which suggest subject matter related solutions. Yet, again, these recipes are argumentative in nature. In fact, also many limits to human rights have been obtained through reference to human rights.

Therefore, strategies adopted in argumentative reference to human rights or other central issues in the discourse about the *appropriate law* are equally relevant as is their material basis, i.e. what the legal provisions actually say. Therefore, in order to avoid traps in argumentation we have to master its most fundamental mechanics. The third hindrance is anthropological in essence. Law is an ongoing project in the development of humankind. One of the most impressive achievements in its long history is the understanding of its discursive nature. Laws are nowadays lesser imposed than they are agreed upon. Therefore, the discourse about the content of law will definitely continue. To reduce tensions in the battle of arguments and to transform it into a discourse about good governance and effective sustainable economic development and protection of human rights would be a step forward. Legal linguists can assist citizens in their efforts to participate in legal discourses in a more civilized and rational way than it has been the case to date. As for myself, I would humbly wish to claim credit for having developed in these lectures the theoretical and the practical contours of legal-linguistic activities in some detail.

Part 8: Notes and Commented Materials

In Notes and Commented Materials the reader will find some general remarks about legal-linguistic and related issues that are connected to the main topics of this book. They should be consulted by the reader upon indication in the main text (cf. Notes and Commented Materials no. xx). They are not construed as an ongoing text and should therefore not be read separately. All notes presented here are in a way relevant to legal linguistics although they do not necessarily make a part of it. Additionally, commented quotes from academic research as well as some longer statutory texts, which were not introduced into the main text due to their length can be found here. Furthermore, legal decisions issued by French, Italian, German, Japanese, English, Canadian, Argentinian, Pakistani, E.U. and U.S. courts, which were analyzed in the main text are quoted here at length. Some of them, especially those which manifest interesting legal-linguistic features irrelevant to the particular topic dealt with in the main text, are provided with additional comments. Other decisions are quoted in selected paragraphs which are of interest for legal linguists. Meanwhile, the main text of the book refers in its analyses exclusively to original versions of the materials used. Therefore, no translation of these texts into English has been supplied here, with the exception of languages that are less frequently used in Europe and in the U.S. Otherwise, new interpretive problems resulting from the linguistic diversity could emerge. They would, probably, necessitate further theoretical comments. In the end, such a procedure would not be in the reader's interest.

(1) On the relation between pragmatics and semantics

The relation between pragmatics and semantics has been addressed by many researchers in different ways (cf. Börjesson 2014). Levinson's classical textbook *Pragmatics* focuses in its introductory part upon the distinction between pragmatics and semantics. It emphasizes pragmatic contributions into the area that has been perceived by many as the realm of semantics. Moreover, Levinson (1983: 372) stresses in his conclusions that pragmatics can even simplify semantic analyses or broaden the ambit of understanding of linguistic phenomena. Other prominent researchers attempted at defining this distinction or at least tried to make plain the ambit of pragmatics. As can be seen from the quotes below it would be difficult to construct an integrative definition of pragmatics based on these views. Some of the views rendered below are of conciliatory nature, e.g. (Verschueren/Östman 1995), some perceive pragmatics rather as an appendix to systematic linguistics (Akmadjan et al. 2001), while others plead for autonomous pragmatics (Bülow 1988). This diversity of views is encouraging because it shows that the area of pragmatic research is actually quite broad. I am not interested here in counteracting this tendency that strives toward an integrative conception of pragmatics and keeps its ambit as open as methodologically admissible.

Morris, Ch. *Foundations of the Theory of Signs. In: Writings on the Theory of Signs, The Hague: Mouton* (1938/1971: 35, 43): Semantics deals with the relation of signs to...objects which they may or do denote... Pragmatics concerns the relation of signs to their interpreters. R. May (1980: 195) characterized Morris' semiotic distinction of linguistic dimensions as follows: An den allgemeinen Zeichencharakter von Sprache anknüpfend, können drei Dimensionen bezeichnet werden, die pragmatische, die syntaktische und die semantische Sprachdimension. Unter der pragmatischen Dimension ist der externe Beziehungsbereich zwischen Zeichen und Zeichenbenutzer in unbeschränkter Rücksicht auf den gesamten situativen Zusammenhang der Zeichenbehandlung zu verstehen. Demgegenüber be-inhaltet die syntaktische Dimension die Beziehungen zwischen Zeichen, währ-end die semantische Dimension den internen Beziehungs- und Deutungsbereich zwischen Zeichen und Bezeichnetem ausweist. R. May stresses the pragmatic dimension in his characterization of Morris' conception primarily through quoting it in the first place. This is definitely not a cosmetic shift of phrases. Instead, it comprises the fundamental idea that pragmatics has the first as well as the last word in language. Language without pragmatic dimension is an empty hull. No natural language has been meaningfully characterized without the pragmatic dimension nor can a language be properly spoken without it. Our lack of knowledge about this dimension makes a full characterization (and also the full command) of ancient languages like Latin or Greek impossible. This theoretical problem is even more manifest in the case of artificial languages such as Esperanto which cannot be fully determined in terms of pragmatics simply because they are artificial. An artificial pragmatics, in turn, would not make much sense.

Stalnaker, R. *Pragmatic Presuppositions, in: Munitz, M. and Unger, P. (eds.) Semantics and Philosophy, New York University Press: New York* (1972: 383): Syntax studies sentences, semantics studies propositions. Pragmatics is the study of linguistic acts and the contexts in which they are performed. There are two major problems to be solved within pragmatics: first, to define interesting types of speech acts and speech products; second to characterize the features of the speech context which help determine which proposition is expressed by a given sentence... It is a semantic problem to specify the rules for matching up sentences of natural language with the propositions that they express. In most cases, however, the rules will not match sentences directly with propositions, but will match sentences with propositions relative to features of the context in which the sentence is used. These contextual features are part of the subject matter of pragmatics.

Katz, J. *Propositional Structure and Illocutionary Force, Crowell: New York* (1977: 14): (I) draw the theoretical line between semantic interpretation and pragmatic interpretation by taking the semantic component to properly represent only those aspects of the meaning of the sentence that an ideal speaker-hearer of the language would know in an anonymous letter situation,...(where there is) no clue whatever about the motive, circumstances of transmission, or any factor relevant to understanding the sentence on the basis of its context of utterance.

Gazdar, G. *Pragmatics: Implicature, Presupposition and Logical Form, Academic Press: London* (1979: 4–5): What we need in addition is some function that tells us about the meaning of utterances...The domain of this pragmatic function is the set of utterances, which are pairs of sentences and contexts, so that for each utterance, our function will return as a value a new context – the context as changed by the sentence uttered... And we can treat the meaning of the utterance as the difference between the original context and the context arrived at by the sentence.

Bülow, E. *in a duplicated commentary to her lectures* (1988): Die Pragmalinguistik (PL) ist das zentrale wissenschaftstheoretische Paradigma, das die "Nach-Chomskysche Linguistik" charakterisiert. Sie markiert den Paradigmawechsel von der „C-(=Chomsky)-zur P-(=Pragmatik) Matrix" und hat die wissenschaftstheoretische Selbstreflexion der Linguistik wesentlich vorangetrieben. Die PL versteht sich als eine Performanzlinguistik, die den Sprachgebrauch, das sprachliche Handeln von Sprechern in den unterschiedlichen gesellschaftlichen Gruppen und deren kommunikativen Handlungsspielen sowie deren Regelsysteme untersucht. Sprechakttheorie, sprachliche Handlungstheorien und Interaktionstheorien allgemein (Sozialpragmatik), Konversationsanalyse, und Kommunikationstypologien bilden den Kern der PL.

Kempson, R. *Grammar and Conversational Principles, In: Newmeyer, F. (ed.): Linguistics vol. II, Cambridge University Press: Cambridge* (1988: 139): Semantics provides a complete account of sentence meaning for the language, by recursively specifying the truth conditions of the sentences of the language...Pragmatics provides an account of how sentences are used in utterances to convey information in context.

The Oxford Companion to Philosophy (Fotion 1995: 709): Pragmatics is the study of language which focuses attention on the users and the context of language use rather than on reference, truth, or grammar.

Verschueren, J., Östman, J.-O. et al. *op. cit.* (1995): Pragmatics is the cognitive, social and cultural study of language and communication.

The Cambridge Dictionary of Philosophy (Lycan 1995: 588): Pragmatics studies the use of language in context, and the context-dependence of various aspects of linguistic interpretation...(Its branches include the theory of how) one and the same sentence can express different meanings or propositions from context to context, owing to ambiguity or indexicality or both,...speech act theory, and the theory of conversational implicature.

The Blackwell Companion to Philosophy (Davies 1996: 124): The distinction between semantics and pragmatics is, roughly, the distinction between the significance conventionally or literally attached to words, and thence to whole sentences, and the further significance that can be worked out, by more general principles, using contextual information.

Akmajian *op. cit.* (2001:361) Therefore, we will take the term pragmatics to cover the study of language use, and in particular the study of linguistic communication in relation to language structure and context of utterance.

Gémar *op. cit.* (2004 : 738, 739): Si l'usage confère sa valeur sémantique première à un mot, c'est le contexte de son emploi, le mot mis en discours, qui en détermine toutefois sa signification réelle. De là l'importance du processus d'interprétation de textes, particulièrement poussé chez les juristes…Ce que presque tous les spécialistes appellent « le language du droit » posséderait au moins trois éléments fondamentaux analysable dans tous leurs aspects, soit un lexique…une syntaxe…et une sémantique (sens des unités significatives/mots et morphèmes : signifiés) ; ou encore, selon le point de vue (linguistique, sociologique, communicatif, sémiotique, philosophique, littéraire, etc) une « pragmatique », soit l'étude du language par l'usage qui en est fait, autrement dit l'étude des phénomènes énonciatifs.

Yan Huang in his *Pragmatics* (2007: 2) defines his subject within a reductive approach that invokes the Anglo-American component view of pragmatics in contradistinction to pragmalinguistics construed as "a theory of linguistic communication" (cf. Huang 2007: 4): Pragmatics is the systematic study of meaning by virtue of, or dependent on, the use of language. The central topics of inquiry of pragmatics include implicature, presuppositions, speech acts and deixis. The strict limitation of research areas proposed by Huang allows for a clearer "research agenda for pragmatics" (cf. Huang 2007: 5). Yet, the focus upon the known and better researched phenomena perceived by Huang as central to the field may blur the perspective upon the pragmatically relevant linguistic reality that might include many other, partly unknown phenomena, especially within less researched discursive practices. Pragmatic research is, unlike syntax and semantics, still in its beginnings. Therefore, today it seems to be difficult to determine its particular issues as such a determination might be applied to the detriment of the ongoing or future research. Furthermore, studies of language use *by virtue of* or *dependent on* the use of language might in terms of Huang's definition seems methodically elusive. The approach by F. Recanati, which follows, provides alternatives to the above restrictive definition.

Recanati *op. cit* . (2008: 93): Dans la conception traditionnelle inspirée des idées de Carnap et de Morris, la pragmatique (l'étude de l'emploi des formes linguistiques) présuppose la sémantique (l'étude de leur sens, identifiée à l'étude de la relation entre les mots et les choses qu'ils représentent), et la sémantique présuppose la syntaxe. En revanche, la syntaxe ne présuppose pas la pragmatique. Recanati (2008: 95) refuses this conception: … on ne peut accorder un contenu représentationnel aux phrases types, indépendamment du contexte; however, he maintains the distinction between semantics and pragmatics in the notion of *sémantique pragmatique* where functions or types of use are assigned to utterances. This, in turn, results in a partition of tasks: L'explication pragmatique a donc besoin des résultats de l'analyse sémantique, et c'est en ce sens qu'on peut dire de celle-ci qu'elle est présupposée par celle-là (Recanati 2008 : 98–99). This view is in our reading compatible with the conception of *integrative pragmatics* that embraces semantic questions in its conceptual framework, as is the case in this book.

(2) Discourse and discursiveness

The notion of *discourse* is used in philosophy and in linguistics in different contexts with broader or narrower meaning that comes close to *text* or *utterance*. Baylon (1991: 235–236) has identified some of them:

"Le mot *discours* est:

- synonyme de la parole saussurienne dans la linguistique structurale ;
- une unité linguistique de dimension supérieure à la phrase (transphrastique), un message pris globalement, un énoncé ;
- l'ensemble des règles d'enchaînement des suites de phrases composant l'énoncé (Harris)
- ce qui s'oppose à l'énoncé : « L'énoncé, c'est la suite des phrases émises entre deux blancs sémantiques, deux arrêts de la communication ; le discours, c'est l'énoncé considéré du point de vue du mécanisme discursif qui le conditionne » (L. Guespin, Language 23, « Le discours politique », sept. 1971, p. 10) ;
- « toute énonciation supposant un locuteur et un auditeur, et chez le premier l'intention d'influencer l'autre en quelque manière » (E. Benveniste, Problèmes de linguistique générale, I, Gallimard, 1966 ; p. 242)
- ce qui s'oppose à la langue. La langue s'oppose alors, comme ensemble fini, relativement stable d'éléments, au discours entendu comme lieu où s'exerce la créativité, lieu de la contextualisation imprévisible qui confère de nouvelles valeurs aux unités de la langue."

Swiss authors A. Linke, M. Nussbaumer, and P.R. Portmann mention in their *Studienbuch Linguistik* (5th ed. Niemeyer, Tübingen 2004, p. 290) the broader version of the concept of *discourse* that I follow in this book :

- « Unter dem Terminus *Diskurs* wird..., oft in Anlehnung an den französischen Philosophen Michel Foucault, das Netz aller in einer Gesellschaft möglichen Aussagen zu einem bestimmten Thema verstanden. Der Diskurs widerspiegelt so das Wissen über ein Thema einschliesslich der gesellschaftlichen Perspektiven, Normen, Interessen und Machtverhältnisse. Dabei weist der Diskurs historisch und sozial bedingte, inhaltliche und formale Strukturen auf, bestimmte Muster der kommunikativen Praxis, welche sich in den einzelnen Texten, die ihm zugeordnet werden können, niederschlagen. Zur Eruierung dieser Muster wird in der Diskursanalyse aus der Gesamtheit aller Texte, die zu einem Diskurs gehören, eine Auswahl zusammengestellt, das Diskurskorpus. »

Following the Saussurian concept of (FR) *langue* as a limited domain of the linguistic science and (FR) *parole* as a residue of a speaker's liberty, the discourse analysis in pragmatic sense concerns rather the *parole*. It concentrates on elaborating constraints or regularities of such a discourse and envisages the way in which things are said rather than what is said (Baylon 1991: 237). They can be found in the language itself, in history, ideology, habitus, mentality, and since M. Foucault's works also in the knowledge (FR *savoir*). This broader conception of discourse, especially in the sense introduced by Foucault, combines linguistic and extra-linguistic elements. Therefore, Foucault (1966: 102) stresses the discursiveness rather than the discourse: « Ce que nous laissent les civilisations et les peuples comme monuments de leur pensée, ce ne sont pas tellement les textes, que les vocabulaires et les syntaxes, les sons de leurs langues plutôt que les paroles qu'ils ont prononcées, moins leurs discours que ce qui les rendit possible : la discursivité de leur langage. » When applied to law, the broader conception of discourse provides for an overarching analytic concept apt at integrating the two most significant ingredients of law, i.e. power and language.

(3) Context in legal linguistics

The notion of *context* is no less ambiguous than the one of *discourse*. It can mean interpersonal (FR *contexte interpersonnel)* or social context (FR *contexte social*). *Context* may also extend to the physical environment and it can encompass general knowledge (Akmajian 2001: 388). Gottlob Frege in his *Grundgesetze der Arithmetik* introduced into the analytical philosophy the principle of *context* in the understanding of meaning. M. Marion (2000: 143) writes about Frege's principle of *context*: ...Frege se devait de fournir une nouvelle explication de cette connaissance arithmétique. C'est alors qu'il invoque au § 62 des *Fondements de l'arithmétique* son fameux principe du contexte, en vertu duquel le sens d'une expression telle que « quatre » ne peut être déterminé que par l'intermédiaire du sens des propositions, telles que « Jupiter a quatre lunes », dans lesquelles elle apparaît. Baylon (1991: 236–237) stresses that the research in the English speaking countries favors the interpersonal context, whereas the French linguistic research, represented mainly by D. Maingueneau and O. Ducrot relies more on social contexts in the tradition initiated by the writings of Mikhail Bakhtin. It has been also claimed that the context should not be specified in advance but rather discovered in a pragmatic analysis (cf. Levinson 1983: 22). Yan Huang defines in his *Pragmatics* (2007: 13) the context as follows: "From a relatively theory-neutral point of view,..., context may in a broader sense be defined as referring to any relevant features of the dynamic setting or environment in which a linguistic unit is systematically used." For legal linguistics a broad notion of context is needed due to the involvement of institutionalized and non-institutionalized elements that compete or coexist in legal discourses.

(4) A. M. Honoré and P. Strawson on the way how people speak and write

A.M. Honoré, Real Laws, in: P.M.S. Hacker and J. Raz (eds.) Law, Morality and Society (Oxford, 1977: 117): In the balmy days of the 1950s Hart was a central and I a peripheral figure in the movement called 'linguistic philosophy' which has since passed from fashion but from which lawyers can still learn much. We learned to pay precise attention to the way people speak and write. We repeated to ourselves and to anyone who would listen to the salutary maxim that everything is what it is and not something else.

P. Strawson (1992: 4–6): We got into this muddle, encounter those problems, only when we allow the concepts or the words to become detached from their actual use, from the practical or the concrete which give them their significance; when we allow them to float or race idly through our mind.

(5) Sale contract from Mesopotamia

A contract for the sale of a slave, dating from the reign of Rim-Sin, c. 2300 B.C. says in its English translation:

Sini-Ishtar has bought a slave, Ea-tappi by name, from Ilu-elatti, and Akhia, his son, and has paid ten shekels of silver, the price agreed. Ilu-elatti, and Akhia, his son, will not set up a future claim on the slave. In the presence of Ilu-iqisha, son of Likua; in the presence of Ilu-iqisha, son of Immeru; in the presence of Likulubishtum, son of Appa, the scribe, who sealed it with the seal of the witnesses. The tenth of Kisilimu, the year when Rim-Sin, the king, overcame the hostile enemies.

(in: George Aaron Barton, "Contracts," in: *Assyrian and Babylonian Literature: Selected Transactions, With a Critical Introduction by Robert Francis Harper* (New York: D. Appleton & Company, 1904: 256) quoted after *Ancient History Sourcebook: A Collection of Contracts from Mesopotamia, c. 2300–428 BCE;* www.fordham.edu)

The text enables to distinguish purely linguistic and legal-technical mechanisms of law in interaction. It identifies the legally relevant action *S-I bought x* and establishes a legal mechanism to guarantee the property of the new owner by the seller's guarantee *not to claim the slave back*. To ensure the enforcement of the guarantee the written form of the contract is chosen and the presence of witnesses is assured. Unlike in modern contracts, all actions undertaken are reflected or commented upon; e.g. *ten shekels of silver* is commented as *the price agreed* and fixed in writing. The seal is not only put on the document, the action of putting the seal is also mentioned in it. This procedure of reference to action taken seems to be characteristic of early periods of meaning constitution in law where everything must be explained because law is only emerging. Our short commentary is obviously influenced by the English translation, its presumably anachronistic language, spelling etc. The legal linguist shall never work with translations alone. I take here the risk of linguistic misconception in order to show that textual forms such as contracts to which I frequently refer in the main text of this book are deeply rooted in the history of linguistic conceptualization.

In terms of comparison one may recall Hesiod who says in his *Works and Days* (II. 370–372): *Let the wage promised to a friend be fixed; ...and get a witness; for trust and mistrust, alike ruin the man.* In *The Iliad,* which displays more ancient sources, testimony is still pathetic. Agamemnon says in book XIX 249–265: *I call Jove the first and mightiest of all gods to witness, I call also Earth and Sun and the Erinyes who dwell below and take vengeance on him who shall swear falsely...*Contract law seems to be immunised against such a lofty wording.

(6) Hammurabi Code

In the history of humankind law is perceived as a relatively new phenomenon, it might have emerged circa five to six thousand years ago. The eldest written documents show already linguistic forms that are still in use in contemporary legislation. The eldest known compilation of laws is the Mesopotamian text called *Hammurabi Code* after its originator, the Babylonian king Hammurabi (ca. 1792–1750 B.C.). J. Gaudemet (2002: 5) criticized the use of the term 'code' in respect of the compilation, calling it (FR) œuvre législative, que l'on qualifie abusivement de "Code". Some provisions of the Hammurabi (also Hammurapi) Code are rendered below in the antiquated original translation borrowed from: *The Sacred Books and Early Literatures of the East, vol. 1 Babylonia and Assyria* (1917), ed. by Ch. F. Horne (New York, London: Parke, Austin and Lipscomb, Inc.). Only obvious printing mistakes have been corrected. The editor characterizes the code as (p. 107): "the earliest known example of a ruler proclaiming publicly to his people an entire body of laws, arranged in orderly groups, so that all men might read and know what was required of them." Meanwhile, the Code was not the earliest collection of laws, the editor remarks on p. 108: "Hammurapi's code was not really the earliest. The preceding sets of laws have disappeared, but we have found several traces of them, and Hammurapi's own code clearly implies their existence. He is but reorganizing a legal system long established." There existed codifications before Hammurabi (Charpin 2008). Some indirect and fragmentary knowledge is available about the codes of king Ur-Nammu (2112–2095 B.C.), king Lipit-Eshtar of Isin (1934–1924 B.C.) and about the laws of the kingdom of Eshnunna (ca. 19th century B.C.). Indeed, in terms of legal linguistics the study of ancient documents is important as it shows how text types and legal terms and concepts emerge and how they are employed in contexts related to legitimization of established power structures. However, the study of such texts has to be undertaken in original to avoid doubtful associations of thought that translations regularly cause. Therefore, in order to avoid methodologically doubtful research, in this study such texts are used only with the author's intention to mark their role at a specific place in future legal-linguistic studies. Texts of Ancient Mesopotamian cultures, ancient Egypt and India, and ancient Chinese texts, to mention but a few, are critical in this respect. For China, D. Cao (2004) included an appendix of texts that can be studied along with her legal-linguistic analysis. Last but not least, also the Hebrew Bible and the Greek legal philosophy are fundamental to the understanding of the emergence of the legal thought expressed in language. The ancient texts make also clear that text types used in law are particularly time resistant. The Hebrew Bible contains a compilation of laws in its part called *Exodus*. The first part, *Genesis*, is known as a world without law. Many of its parts formed the modern understanding of law. The Greek legal culture, although less visible in daily reflection about modern law, is the origin of this very reflection. Without the ancient Greeks a book like this one would not have been written.

In terms of text structure, the articles of the Hammurabi Code come close to judgments as they often refer to singular cases (cf. also André-Salvini 2008). However, some of them reach the level of generalization that qualifies them as statutory provisions. This legislative technique has been also practiced by the ancient Romans. They focused on casuistry and subsequently reformulated the solution of a particular case in a more abstract linguistic dress using legal notions developed to this aim. Written laws also enabled the formalization of legal concepts that can be further discussed and rendered more precise through their analysis. For instance, scribes learned the Sumerian and the Acadian legal terms from bilingual tablets, where also legal terminology was included, i.e. Sumerian *Har.ra* – Akkadian *hubbulu* (loan with interest payment). Script reinforced therefore the stability of legal terminology and enabled its further research. It also promoted the use of juridical formulas that were in common use in ancient Mesopotamian legal texts. They were used in substantive law, for instance in the above example of the sale contract as well as in legal procedure: After the judgment has been issued, the losing party had to provide the winner a tablet where the waiver of the claim was explicitly stated (cf. comments to (FR) *tablette de non-revendication* in Charpin, 2008). It might seem that a step toward rationalization of legal acts has been taken by these measures. Yet, also the contrary view that stresses magic as the starting point for legal acts is not less convincing (cf. Charpin 2008). Acts of describing the property to be transferred and its price, the transfer of property in presence of witnesses, the use of formalized and unchangeable formulas that accompanied the physical acts may have its roots in ancient magical practices. These practices could have been used to mark and to perpetuate the transfer of *mine* into *thine* that is as fundamental to law as it is by far not obvious.

Let us look now at some excerpts from the *Hammurabi Code*. My comments are put in brackets.

> ...When Marduk sent me to rule over men, to give protection of right to the land, I did right and righteousness in..., and brought about the wellbeing of the oppressed.
>
> 1. If any one ensnare another, putting a ban upon him, but he cannot prove it, then he that ensnared him shall be put to death.

10. If the purchaser does not bring the merchant and the witnesses before whom he bought the article, but its owner bring witnesses who identify it, then the buyer is the thief and shall be put to death, and the owner receives the lost article.

11. If the owner do not bring the witnesses to identify the lost article, he is an evil-doer, has been traduced, and shall be put to death.

(Provisions 1, 10 and 11 are formulated in a textual type of a norm, beginning with 'if'. It remains the most popular form of shaping statutory provisions until our own day.)

35. If anyone buy the cattle or sheep which the king has given to chieftains from him, he loses his money.

36. The field, garden, and home of a chieftain, of a man, or of one subject to quit-rent, cannot be sold.

102. If a merchant entrust money to an agent (broker) for some investment, and the broker suffer a loss in the place to which he goes, he shall make good the capital to the merchant.

103. If, while on the journey, an enemy take away from him anything that he had, the broker shall swear by God and be free of obligation.

137. If a man wish to separate from a woman who has borne him children, or from his wife who has borne him children: then he shall give that wife her dowry, and a part of the usufruct of field, garden, and property, so that she can rear her children. When she has brought up her children, equal as that of one son, shall be given to her. She may then marry the man of her heart.

138. If a man wishes to separate from his wife who has borne him no children, he shall give her the amount of her purchase money and the dowry which she brought from her father's home, and let her go.

(The 'purchase money' refers to the amount paid to the bride's father. The purchase money had not always been paid. Under 139 the Code says: If there was no purchase money he shall give her one mina of gold and let her go. The language used is already legal, yet also a redundant formulation appears: "...dowry which she brought from her father's home...")

273. If any one hire a day laborer, he shall pay him from the New Year until the fifth month six gerahs in money per day; from the sixth month to the end of the year he shall give him five gerahs per day.

(The first part of the year comprises the period from April to August, when days are long and there is therefore more work to do. In the second part of the year, there is less work and also lower pay. The rule follows a casuistic pattern, no attempt at generalization and efficiency is made, e.g.: Day laborers receive in the first part of the year the amount x, in the second part the amount y.)

(7) Valerius Probus' *De Juris Notarum*

Valerius Probus' note on legal abbreviations is known in the classical literature under the heading *De Juris Notarum*. It consists of a short note of a few lines quoted below and a list of abbreviations with their explanations.

Valerii Probi DE JURIS NOTARUM

1.- Est etiam circa prescribendas vel paucioribus litteris notandas voces studiorum necessarium. Quod partim pro voluntate cujusque fit, partim pro usu publico et observatione communi. Namque apud veteres cum usus notarum nullus esset, propter scribendi difficultatem, maxime in senatu qui scribendo aderant, ut celeriter dicta comprehenderent, quaedam verba atque nomina ex communi consensu primis litteris notabant, et singulae litterae quid significarent, in promptu erat. Quod in praenominibus legibus publicis pontificumque monumentis et in juris civilis libris etiam nunc manet. Ad quas notationes publicas accedit etiam studiosorum voluntas. Sed unusquisque familiares sibi notas pro voluntate quas signarit, comprehendere infinitum est: publicae sane tenendae, quae in monumentis plurimis et in historiarum libris sacrisque publicis reperiuntur, ut: P. Publius: C. Gaius: M. Marcus: CN. Gnaeus: Q. Quintus: NV. Manius: TI. Tiberius: CL. Claudius: SP. Spurius: SEX. Sextus: SER. Servius: OP. Opiter: A.V.C. ab urbe condita: P.R.E. post reges exactos: P.C. patres conscripti: S.P.Q.R. senatus populusque Romanus: EQ. R. eques Romanus: V.R. urbs Roma: C.R. civis Romanus: COL. Coloniae vel coloni: MVN. Municipia vel municeps: N.L. nominis Latini: L.C. Latini colonari: S.N.L. socii nominis Latini, et similia. Secundum haec curiarum nomina, tribuum, comitiorum, sacerdotiorum, potestatum, magistratuum, praefecturarum, sacrorum, ludorum, rerum urbanarum, rerum militarium, collegiorum, decuriarum, fastorum, numerorum, mensurarum [juris civilis] et similium ceterorum notationes proprias habent.

LITTERAE SINGULARES IN JURE CIVILI DE LEGIBUS ET PLEBISCITIS ET SENATUS CONSULTIS.

1. – 1 P.I.R.P.Q.I.S.I.F.P.R.E.A.D.P. populum jure rogavit populusque jure scivit in foro pro rostris ex ante diem pridie.
2.E.H.O.L.N.R. ejus hac omnibus lege nihilum rogatur.
3.S.R.L.R.I.C.Q.O.R.E. siremps lex res jus causaque omnium rerum esto. (...)

(in: F. Girard (1923): Textes de droit romain)

(8) Excerpts from *Corpus Iuris Civilis*

Systematic legislation and systematic research into law began with the Roman law. Roman jurists established a collection of written legal sources, which enabled the emergence of the most efficient mechanism to steer society. The aim of the written law was to enable a predictable and rational application of law. This is the role of the Roman law in terms of pragmatics. As to its structure, the Roman law is best stated in the *Corpus Iuris Civilis* (CIC), compiled under Emperor Justinian (cf. Husa 2013). The CIC consists of *Institutes*, *Digest* (also called *Pandects*), *Codes* and *Novellae* (which supplement the *Institutes*). The Roman jurists developed in their Latin language a legal terminology that is the basis of concept formation in law even today (cf. Mattila 2002: 201–203, Ladjili-Mouchette 1990). This task has been facilitated by the reception of the Greek philosophy by the Romans: *Romani primi Graecorum discipuli.* The excerpts from the CIC rendered below illustrate the process of emergence of the Roman law and its understanding from the perspective of the Roman jurists.

DIGESTORUM SEU PANDECTARUM
Liber Primus

1. DE IUSTITIA ET IURE

1. Ulpianus *libro primo institutionum* Iuri operam daturum prius nosse oportet, unde nomen iuris descendat. Est autem a iustitia appellatum: nam, ut eleganter Celsus definit, ius est ars boni et aequi. (...) 2. Huius studii duae sunt positiones, publicum et privatum. Publicum ius est quod ad statum rei Romanae spectat, privatum quod ad singulorum utilitatem: sunt enim quaedam publice utilia, quaedam privatim. Publicum ius in sacris, in sacerdotibus, in magistratibus constitit. Privatum ius tripertitum est : collectum etenim est ex naturalibus praeceptis aut gentium aut civilibus. 3. Ius naturale est, quod natura omnia animalia docuit : nam ius istud non humani generis proprium, sed omnium animalium, quae in terra, quae in mari nascuntur, avium quoque commune est.(...) 4. ius gentium est, quo gentes humane utuntur. Quod a naturali recedere facile intellegere licet, quia illud omnibus animalibus, hos solis hominibus inter se commune sit.

5. Hermogenianus *libro primo iuris epitomarum* Ex hoc iure gentium introducta bella, discretae gentes, regna condita, dominia distincta, agris termini positi, aedificia collocata, commercium, emptiones venditiones, locationes conductiones, obligationes institutae: exceptis quibusdam quae iure civili introductae sunt.

10. Ulpianus *libro primo regularum* Iustitia est constans et perpetua voluntas ius suum cuique tribuendi. 1. Iuris praecepta sunt haec: honeste vivere, alterum non laedere, suum cuique tribuere. 2. Iuris prudentia est divinarum atque humanarum rerum notitia, iusti atque iniusti scientia.

II. DE ORIGINE IURIS ET OMNIUM MAGISTRATUUM ET SUCCESSIONE PRUDENTIUM

Pomponius *libro singulari Enchiridii* Necessarium itaque nobis videtur ipsius iuris originem atque processum demonstrare. 1. Et quidem initio civitatis nostrae populus sine lege certa, sine iure certo primum agere instituit omniaque manu a regibus gubernabantur. 2. Postea aucta aliquem modum civitate ipsum Romulum traditur populum in triginta partes divisisse, quas partes curias appellavit propterea, quod tunc rei publicae curam per sententias partium earum expediebat.

(9) Gaius *Institutiones*

The Roman jurist of the 2nd century, Gaius, is remembered foremost for his textbook *Institutiones* (cf. Honoré 1962, Behrends 1978). His textbook was also the basis for Emperor Justinian's Byzantine *Institutiones.* In his textbook he attempts at stating the Roman law systematically; therefore many jurists (mainly positivists) perceive it as a milestone of legal thinking that enabled to shape law as a closed system of notions and rules. Needless to mention that my conception of law, which is based on discursive practices, manifests the opposite tendency in legal-theoretical thinking that views such positivist approaches rather sceptically. In the ancient Roman law the tendency opposite to Gaius is documented in *Institutiones* by Ulpianus who admits the philosophical foundations of law and its ethical background (*ius naturale*). Both share the two central notions for the concept of the ancient Roman law, i.e. *ius civile* and *ius gentium.* For legal linguists, Gaius's *Institutiones* is central as it marks the moment of institutionalization of terminological coinages in law that influenced the whole subsequent work on legal terminology practically all over the world.

Commentarius Primus:

(I. De iure civili et naturali) 1. Omnes populi qui legibus et moribus reguntur, partim suo proprio, partim communi omnium hominum jure utuntur; nam quod quisque ipse sibi jus constituit, id ipsius proprium est vocaturque jus civile, quasi jus proprium civitatis; quod vero naturalis ratio inter omnes homines constituit, id apud omnes populos peraeque custoditur vocaturque jus gentium, quasi quo jure omnes gentes utuntur. Populus itaque Romanus partim suo proprio, partim communi omnium hominum jure utitur. Quae singula qualia sint, suis locis proponemus. 2. Constant autem jura populi Romani ex legibus, plebisscitis, senatusconsultis, constitutionibus principum, edictis eorum qui jus edicendi habent, responsis prudentium. 3. Lex est quod populus jubet atque constituit. Plebiscitum est quod plebs jubet atque constituit. Plebs autem a populo eo distat, quod populi appellatione universi cives significantur connumeratis etiam patriciis; plebs autem apellatione sine patriciis ceteri cives significantur; unde olim patricii dicebant plebiscitis se non teneri, quia sine auctoritate eorum facta essent; sed postea Lex Hortensia lata est, qua cautum est ut plebiscita universum populum tenerent: itaque eo modo legibus exaequata sunt. 4. Senatusconsultum est, quod senatus jubet atque constituit : idque legis vicem obtinet, quamvis fuerit quaesitum. 5. Constitutio principis est, quod imperator decreto vel edicto vel epistula constituit. Nec umquam dubitatum est, quin id legis vicem obtineat, cum ipse imperator per legem imperium accipiat. 6. Jus autem edicendi habent magistratus populi Romani; sed amplissimum jus est in edictis duorum praetorum, urbani et peregrini, quorum in provinciis jurisdictionem praesides earum habent; item in edictis aedilium curulium, quorum jurisdictionem in provinciis populi Romani qaestores habent; nam in provincias Caesaris omnino qaestores non mittuntur, et ob id hoc edictum in his provinciis non proponitur. 7. Responsa prudentium sunt sententiae et opiniones eorum quibus permissum est jura condere. Quorum omnium si in unum sententiae concurrunt, id, quod ita sentiunt legis vicem obtinet; si vero dissentiunt, judici licet quam velit sententiam sequi; idque rescripto divi Hadriani significatur. (II. De juris divisione) 8. Omne autem jus, quo utimur vel ad personas pertinet, vel ad res, vel ad actiones. Et prius videamus de personis. (III. De condictione hominum) 9. Et quidem summa divisio de jure personarum haec est, quod omnes homines aut liberi sunt aut servi. 10. Rursus liberorum hominum alii ingenui sunt, alii libertini. 11. Ingenui sunt, qui liberi nati sunt; libertini, qui ex justa servitute manumissi sunt. 12. Rursus libertinorum tria sunt genera; nam aut cives Romani aut Latini aut dediticiorum numero sunt; de quibus singulis dispiciamus; ac prius de dedicticiis...

(10) Gaius on legal-linguistic origins of (LAT) *obligatio*

Gaius examined the legal-linguistic origins of obligation in his *Institutiones* (3.92–3.96). These paragraphs include also his famous assumption of untranslatability of the Latin legal idiom *Dari spondes? Spondeo* into Greek. In his analysis Gaius discovered the pragmatic principle of institutionalization of the legal language. In his view, the Latin idiomatic formula can be translated literally into Greek, yet it will not engender any binding effect of the Latin formula because it is not anchored in the Greek legal practice:

> 92. Verbis obligatio fit ex interrogatione et responsione, veluti: DARI SPONDES ? SPONDEO; DABIS ? DABO ; PROMITTIS ? PROMITTO; FIDEPROMITTIS? FIDEPROMITTO; FIDEIUBES? FIDEIUBEO; FACIES? FACIAM. 93. Sed haec quidem verborum obligatio: DARI SPONDES? SPONDEO propria civium Romanorum est; ceterae vero iuris gentium sunt, itaque inter omnes homines, sive cives Romanos sive peregrinos, valent; et quamvis ad Graecam vocem expressae fuerint, veluti hoc modo: Δώσεις; Δώσω˙ Όμολογείς; Όμολογω˙ Πίστει κελεύεις; Πίστει κελεύω ˙ Ποιήσεις; Ποιήσω (etiam haec) tamen inter cives Romanos valent, si modo Graeco sermonis intellectum habeant; et e contrario quamvis Latine enuntientur, tamen etiam inter peregrinos valent, si modo Latini sermonis intellectum habeant. At illa verborum obligatio; DARI SPONDES? SPONDEO adeo propria civium Romanorum est, ut ne quidem in Graecum sermonem per interpretationem proprie transferri possit, quamvis dicatur a Graeca voce figurata esse. 94. Unde dicitur uno casu hoc verbo peregrinum quoque obligari posse, veluti si imperator noster principem alicuius peregrini populi de pace ita interroget: PACEM FUTURAM SPONDES? vel ipse eodem modo interrogetur. Quod nimium subtiliter dictum est, quia si quid adversus pactionem fiat, non ex stipulatu agitur, sed iure belli res vindicatur. 95. Illud dubitari potest, si quia (MG: here follow ten unreadable lines – 95a. Sunt et aliae obligationes) item si debitor mulieris iussu eius, dum...doti dicat quod debet : alius autem obligari hoc modo non potest. Et ideo si quis alius pro muliere dotem promittere velit communi iure obligare se debet, id est stipulanti viro promittere. 96. Item uno loquente et sine interrogatione alii promittente contrahitur obligatio, si libertus patrono aut operas se daturum esse iuravit, sed haec sola causa est, ex qua iureiurando homines obligantur, utique cum quaeritur de iure Romanorum. Nam apud peregrinos quid iuris sit, singularum civitatium iura requirentes aliud intellegere poterimus in aliis valere.
>
> (in: P. Girard, 1923: 302)

(11) Aulus Gellius on legal vocabulary

Auli Gellii Noctes Atticae Liber XVI :

V. Vestibulum quid significet; deque eius vocabuli rationibus...

III. C. Aelius Gallus in libro de significatione verborum, quae ad ius civile pertinent, secundo vestibulum esse dicit non in ipsis aedibus neque partem aedium, sed locum ante ianuam domus vacuum, per quem a via aditus accessusque ad aedis est, cum dextra sinistraque ianuam tectaque sunt viae iuncta atque ipsa ianua procul a via est area vacanti intersita.

(12) Aulus Gellius on legal education

Auli Gellii Noctes Atticae Liber XIII :

XIII. Quod in libris humanarum M. Varronis scriptum est aediles et quaestores populi Romani in ius a privato ad praetorem vocari posse. I. Cum ex angulis secretisque librorum ac magistrorum in medium iam hominum et in lucem fori prodissem, quaesitum esse memini in plerisque Romae stationibus ius publice docentium aut respondentium, an quaestor populi Romani ad praetorem in ius vocari posset.

(13) Legal text in Old English

The text in Old English which follows describes the circumstances of collection of ancient laws and the motivation for collecting them. The ancient laws were written down, and no new laws have been instituted by the king but rather a selection was preferred where the most suitable laws were collected and other ancient laws discarded. The translation of this text into modern English is provided in Hiltunen (1990: 22).

Old English: Ic đa Aelfred cyning Þas togaedere gegaderode awritan het, monege Þara Þe ure foregengan heoldon, đa đe me locodon; manege Þara Þe me ne licodon ic awearp mid minra witena geđeahte, on ođre wisan bebead to healdanne. Forđam ic ne dorste geđristlaecan Þara minra awuht fela on gewrit settan, forđam me waes uncuđ, hwaet Þaes đam lician wolde đe aefter us waeren. Ac đa đe ic gemette awđer ođđe on Ines daege, mines maeges, ođđe on Offan, Mercna cyninges ođđe on Aelelbryhtes, Þe aerest fulluhte onfeng on Angelkynne, Þa đe me ryhtoste đuhton, ic Þa heron gegaderode, Þa ođre forlet.

(in: Whitelock, D. (1979: 49, 9) (ed.): *English Historical Documents*, vol. I (London: Eyre Methuen).

(14) Strasbourg oaths in Old Romance and Old Germanic

Another medieval text, Nithardus' *Historiarum liber III*, 5 quotes the Romanic and the Germanic versions of the *Strasbourg oaths*, (FR) *Serments de Strasbourg*, in their

Latin textual context. The mutually exchanged oaths constitute a pledge to assist in a military alliance. The use of popular vernaculars in them is not coincidental; it enables the understanding of the essential obligations of the pledge for lower strata of combatants on both sides who might have mastered Latin only partly or not at all (cf. Becker 1972, Beck 2014, Galdia 2014: 145–150):

> Lodhuvicus, quoniam maior natu erat, prior haec deinde se servaturum testatus est: Pro deo amur et pro christian poblo et nostro commun salvament, d'ist di in avant, in quant deus savir et podir me dunat, si salvarai eo cist meon fradre Karlo et in aiudha et in cadhuna cosa, si cum om per dreit son fradra salvar dist, in o quid il mi altresi fazet, et ab Ludher nul plaid nunquam prindrai, qui meon vol cist meon fradre Karle in damno sit.
>
> Quod cum Lodhuvicus explesset, Karolus Teudisca lingua sic haec eadem verba testatus est: In godes minna ind in thes christiânes folches ind unsêr bêdhero gehaltnissî, fon thesemo dage frammordes, sô fram sô mir got gewizci indi mahd furgibit, sô haldih thesan mînan bruodher, sôso man mit rehtu sînan bruodher scal, in thiu thaz er mig sô sama duo, indi mit Ludheren in nohheiniu thing ne gegango, the mînan willon imo ce scadhen werdhên.
>
> Sacramentum autem, quod utrorumque populus quique propria lingua testatus est, Romana lingua sic se habet: Si Lodhuvigs sagrament, que son fradre Karlo iurat, conservat, et Karlus meos sendra de suo part non lo tanit, si io returnar non l'int pois: ne io ne neuls, cui eo returnar int pois, in nulla aiudha contra Lodhuvig nun li iu er.
>
> Teudiska autem lingua: Oba Karl then eid, then er sînemo bruodher Ludhuwîge gesuor, geleistit, indi Ludhuwîg mîn hêrro then er imo gesuor forbrihchit, ob ih inan es irwerden ne mag: noh ih noh thero nohhein, then ih es irwerden mag, widhar Karlo imo ce follusti ne wirdlxit.
>
> Quibus peractis Lodhuwicus Reno tenus per Spiram et Karolus iuxta Vuasagum per Vuîzzûnburg Vuarmatiam iter direxit.

(15) Legal text in Old Portuguese

The last will by King Alfonso II (1214):

> E(n) nome de Deus. Eu, rei don Alfonso, pela gracia de Deus rei de Portugal, seendo sano e salvo, temēte o dia de mia morte, a saude de mia alma e a proe de mia molier raina dona Orraca e de meus filios e de meus vassalos e de todo meu reino, fiz mia māda per que, depos mia morte, kia molier e meus filios e meu reino e meus vassalos e todas aquelas cousas que Deus mi deu en poder, sten en paz e en folgãcia.
>
> Primeiramente mãdo que meu filio Infante Don Sancho, que ei da raina Dona Orraca, agia meu reino entegramente e en paz. E ssi este for morto sen semmel, o maior filio que ouver de raina Dona Orraca agia o reino entegramente e en paz. E ssi filio barõ nõ ouvermos, a maior filia que ouvermos, agia-o. E ssi no tĕpo de mia morte meu filio

ou mia filia que devier a reinar nõ ouver revora, segia en poder da raina sa madre, e meu reino segia en poder da raina e de meus vassalos ata quando agia revora. E ssi eu for morto, rogo o apostoligo come padre e senior, e beigio a terra ante seus péés, que el recebia en sa comĕda e so seu difindemento a raina e meus filios e o reino. E ssi eu e a raina formos mortos, rogo-li e prego-li que os meus filios e o reino segiã en sa comĕnda.

E mãndo da dezima dos moravidíís e dos dieiros que mi remaserũ de parte de meu padre que sũ en Alcobaza, e do outr'aver movil que i posermos pora esta dezima, que segia partido pelas manus do arcebispo de Bragáá e do arcebispo de Santiago...

(16) Promissory note in English and Hawaiian

Legal terminology is introduced into languages that did not develop any specific legal language in the sense of the Western legal culture through neologisms and descriptions. The following text of a promissory note displays such translation problems from English into Hawaiian in 1917. The unequal length of both texts signals that many terms of the English text have been described in the Hawaiian translation, e.g. the term *promissory note* is rendered by a lengthy *he palapala hooia e uku aku.*

Promissory note, Honolulu, May 20, 1917

Twelve month after date, I promise to pay Henry Philip, the sum of One Hundred Dollars, with interest at 1 per cent, per month, value received.

John Kapena

He Palapala Hooia e Uku Aku, Honolulu, Mei 20, 1917

He umikumamalua malama mahope aku o keia la, ke hooia nei au e uku aku ia Hanale Pilipo, i na Kala Hookahi Haneli, me ka ukupanee ma ka 1 pakeneka no ka malama, no ka waiwai i loaa mai.

Ioane Kapena

(17) Excerpts from Japan's Constitutions

The Occidentalization of the Japanese legal language and its law is manifest in text samples from the different Constitutions of Japan which are in terms of language and legal thought typical of the different time periods in which they emerged (cf. Upham 1990: 304):

(1889)

Art. I The Empire of Japan shall be reigned over and governed by a line of Emperors unbroken for ages eternal.

Art. III The Emperor is sacred and inviolable.

(1908)

A. The prerogatives of the monarch

1. The Ta Ch'ing Emperor will rule supreme over the Ta Ch'ing Empire for one thousand generations in succession and be honored forever.

(1947)

Art. 1 The Emperor shall be the symbol of the State and of the unity of the people, deriving his position from the will of the people with whom resides sovereign power.

Art. 3 The advice and approval of the cabinet shall be required for all acts of the Emperor in matters of State, and the Cabinet shall be responsible therefore.

Art. 4 The Emperor shall perform only such acts in matters of State as are provided for in this Constitution and he shall not have powers related to government.

The magical rhetoric of eternity of power is there to justify the exercise of this power. For instance, the *Royal List of Sumer* says: After the kingdom descended from heaven, it went to Eridu. At Eridu, Alulim became king and ruled for 28 800 years.

(18) Excerpts from the Constitution of the People's Republic of China

Art. 33 All citizens of the People's Republic of China are equal before the law.

Art. 34 All citizens of the People's Republic of China who have reached the age of 18 have the right to vote and stand for election, regardless of ethnic status, race, sex, occupation, family background, religious belief, education, property status or length of residence, except persons deprived of political rights according to law.

Art. 35 Citizens of the People's Republic of China enjoy freedom of speech, of the press, of assembly, of association, of procession, and of demonstration.

Art. 36 Citizens of the People's Republic of China enjoy freedom of religious belief. No state organ, public organization or individual may compel citizens to believe in, or not to believe in, any religion; nor may they discriminate against citizens who believe in, or do not believe in, any religion.

Art. 40 Freedom and privacy of correspondence of citizens of the People's Republic of China are protected by law. No organization or individual may, on any ground, infringe upon citizens' freedom and privacy of correspondence, except in case where, to meet the needs of state security or of criminal investigation, public security or procuratorial organs are permitted to censor correspondence in accordance with procedures described by law.

Art. 41 Citizens of the People's Republic of China have the right to criticize and make suggestions regarding any state organ or functionary.

Art. 48 Women in the People's Republic of China enjoy equal rights with men in all spheres of life, in political, economic, cultural, social and family life.

Art. 54 It is the duty of the citizens of the People's Republic of China to safeguard the security, honor and interests of the motherland; they must not commit acts detrimental to the security, honor and interests of the motherland.

(19) A translation from Turkish into 'German'

The following text, published August 9, 2001 in the German newspaper *Hamburger Abendblatt* could be characterized as an attempt to translate a Turkish court decree into legal German. The linguistic errors are not marked in it due to their overburdening number; the initial asterisk marks therefore the general quality of this linguistic experiment. The text as such is nevertheless understandable and is clearly identifiable as representing a legal text type. The Turkish court wishes to communicate through its decree to the defendant who is presumably residing in Germany that her marriage was dissolved in Turkey and that she can appeal against this decision within 15 days counted from the day of publication. The text is apparently binding in terms of law because its legally relevant sense is intelligible also to a layperson with some effort. For purposes of the below quotation, family names that are rendered in full in the decree were reduced to initials, also some addresses were omitted as irrelevant.

(*) Republik Turkei

Karakoçan

Juristischerechtgericht

Grund Nr. : 1997/126

Urteil Nr. : 2000/30

Ankläger : Ziyattın D., Sohn von Şeyho und Hanife, 1967 geb. Karakoçan, Elaziğ/ Karakoçan-Bazlamköyü gemeldet.

Vertreter : Rae. Aziz K., A. Cad. Nr: 137/a Karakocan

Beklagterin : Adriane M..., Tochter von Roswit, 1969 geboren

Klage Art : Von heftigen Ehestreit Scheidung.

Klagedatum: 29.07.1997

Urteildatum: 22.03.2000

Durch den Vertreter von Ankläger gegen die Beklagterin gegebene Scheidungsantrag, das Gericht hat zwischen den Parteien haben heftigen Ehestreit. Nach dem Zivilgesetz (M.K.) 134/1 das Gericht hat die Parteien scheiden gelassen. Die Adresse von Beklagterin ist unbekannt, das Gerichtsurteil konnte an sie nicht mitteilen können, darum die Mitteilung durch öffentliche Bekanntmachung Urteil gegeben. Die Frist von öffentlichen Bekanntmachung von 15 Tagen und nicht Widersprucheinlegung, das Gerichtsurteil wurde rechtskräftig gerechnet und mitteilen. 24.05.2000

Stempel und Unterschrift

Richter-34006

(20) Abbreviated language of a German code

The Palandt Commentary to the German Civil Code, (D) *BGB Kommentar*, is written in an abbreviated language. In the comment to Article 29 BGB abbreviations of legal terms and words belonging to the ordinary langage are used in order to save space. As a result, the text is readable only for jurists and persons with full command of the German language because many words must be reconstructed from the context of their use. The connotation is provided below in the original quote and, subsequently, with the transformation of the abbreviations into the full text with deciphered abbreviations.

Original text of Sec. 29 BGB:

Fassg des RPflG 1957. Zust is das AG, das gem § 55 das Vereinsregister führt. § 29 ist, sow keine SonderVorschr bestehen, auf alle JP des PriR anwedb, so auf die GmbH, Genossensch, bergrechtl Gewerksch, wg Akt 85 nicht auf die AktGes.

Full text in German:

Fassung des Rechtspflegergesetzes 1957. Zuständig ist das Amtsgericht, das gemäß § 55 das Vereinsregister führt. § 29 ist, soweit keine Sondervorschriften bestehen, auf alle juristischen Personen des Privatrechts anwendbar, so auf die GmbH, die Genossenschaft, die bergrechtliche Gewerkschaft, wegen § 85 Aktiengesetz jedoch nicht auf die Aktiengesellschaft.

(21) Italian *massime di giurisprudenza*

Italian synthetic versions of court decisions (IT. *massime di giurisprudenza*) are frequently worded in over-long phrases, e.g.:

(a) Nel caso di danno cagionato dall'alunno a se stesso, la responsabilità dell'istituto scolastico e dell'insegnante non ha natura extracontrattuale, bensì contrattuale, atteso che – quanto all'istituto scolastico – l'accoglimento della domanda di iscrizione, con la conseguente ammissione dell'allievo alla scuola, determina l'instaurazione di un vincolo negoziale, dal quale sorge a carico dell'istituto l'obbligazione di vigilare sulla sicurezza e l'incolumità dell'allievo nel tempo in cui questi fruisce della prestazione scolastica in tutte le sue espressioni, anche al fine di evitare che l'allievo procuri danno a se stesso; e che – quanto al precettore dipendente dell'istituto scolastico – tra insegnante e allievo si instaura, per contratto sociale, un rapporto giuridico, nell'ambito del quale l'insegnante assume, nel quadro del complessivo obbligo di istruire ed educare, anche uno specifico obbligo di protezione e vigilanza, onde evitare che l'allievo si procuri da solo un danno alla persona. (*Supreme Court of Italy, June 27, 2002*)

(b) La responsabilità nei confronti del beneficiario di un assegno circolare non trasferibile in cui incorre la banca girataria per l'incasso qualora, violando l'obbligo di diligente accertamento dell'identità e della legittimazione del presentatore del titolo, paghi l'assegno a persona diversa dal predetto (artt. 43 ed 86 del r.d.n. 1736 del 1933), non ha natura né extracontrattuale, in quanto non consegue dalla violazione di una norma di condotta, né contrattuale, poiché non sussiste tra dette parti alcun rapporto negoziale, dato che detta banca è estranea sia alla convenzione di assegno sia al rapporto di emissione del medesimo, bensì constituisce violazione di un'obbligazione "ex lege", riconducibile, in base all'art. 1173 c.c. ad ogni altro atto o fatto idoneo a costituire fonte di obbligazione in conformità dell'ordinamento giuridico, siccome derivante dalla violazione dell'obbligo posto a suo carico dall'art. 43 r.d. cit., di pagare l'assegno esclusivamente all'intestatario, titolare del diritto di agire per il risarcimento del danno eventualmente subito, con la conseguenza che siffatto diritto è soggetto alla prescrizione ordinaria decennale. (*Supreme Court of Italy, October 6, 2005*)

(c) Mentre la convenzione contenente una promessa di attribuzione di propri beni a titolo gratuito configura un contratto preliminare di donazione che è nullo, in quanto con esso si viene a costituire a carico del promittente un vincolo giuridico a donare, il quale si pone in contrasto con il principio secondo cui nella donazione l'arricchimento del beneficiario deve avvenire per spirito di libertà, in virtù cioè di un atto di autodeterminazione del donante, assolutamente libero nella sua formazione; diverso è, invece, il caso in cui un coniuge, in sede di separazione consensuale, assume l'obbligo nei confronti dell'altro coniuge di provvedere al mantenimento del figlio minore, impegnandosi a tal fine a trasferirgli un bene immobile, ponendo in essere con il detto coniuge un contratto preliminare a favore del figlio, con la conseguenza che l'atto scritto con cui il coniuge obbligato, in esecuzione di tale contratto, dichiara di trasferire al figlio quel bene, essendo privo dello spirito di liberalità, non configura una donazione, ma una proposta di contratto unilaterale gratuito e atipico, che, ai sensi dell'art.1333 c.c., in mancanza del rifiuto del destinatario in un termine adeguato (alla natura dell'affare o stabilito dagli usi), determina l'irrevocabilità della proposta e quindi la conclusione del contratto, nonostante che la volontà di accettazione non risulti da atto scritto, dovendosi ritenere assolto l'obbligo della forma attraverso le modalità con cui è stata formulata la proposta. (*Court of Appeals, Rome, June 15, 2005*)

The culture of long sentences in the Italian legal language clearly reflects the general cultural and linguistics standards of written academic Italian. Italian *massime di giurisprudenza* are unthinkable without long sentences used in Italian scholarly writings. For instance, the editor of Dante Alighieri's *Divina Commedia*, G. Vandelli writes with reference to his predecessor, the philologist G.A. Scartazzini:

> "Ma anche quel nome s'è voluto che ivi seguitasse ad apparire quale meritato omaggio alla memoria dello Scartazzini e perché l'opera, sebbene rinnovata così radicalmente che non una pagina, non un colonnino vi ricompare più quale uscì dalla penna di lui, conserva tuttavia certe linee fondamentali della primitiva struttura e certe originarie caratteristiche ch'ebbero lode anche da critici non del tutto benevoli e che solo una smania inconsulta di tutto trasformare e innovare senza discrezione ci poteva indurre ad abbandonare." (op.cit. Milano, ed. Hoepli, 1965, p. vii).

(22) French court maxims

Longer maxims phrased in one sentence are also used in French courts; the (FR) Cour de cassation synthesized in its decision no. 04–44713, dated 7.11.2006 the main issue as follows:

> La court de cassation a renvoyé la question préjudicielle suivante à la CJCE aux fins de dire a) si le principe de compétence spéciale énoncé à l'alinéa 1 de l'article 6 du Règlement Bruxelles I est applicable à un litige engagé par un salarié devant une juridiction d'un Etat membre contre deux sociétés appartenant au même groupe, dont l'une, qui est celle qui a embauché ce salarié puis refusé de le réintégrer, a son siège dans cet Etat membre et l'autre, pour le compte de laquelle l'intéressé a travaillé en dernier lieu dans des Etats tiers et qui l'a licencié, a son siège dans un autre Etat membre, alors que ce demandeur invoque une clause du contrat de travail pour faire valoir que les deux défenderesses étaient ses co-employeurs auxquels il demande l'indemnisation de son licenciement, b) ou si les dispositions de l'alinéa 1 de l'article 18 de ce même Règlement excluent l'application de ce principe.

In some other jurisdictions, for instance in the European Court of Justice, court maxims are distinctive as a feature of translation language:

> The (ESP) Tribunal Superior de Justicia de Castilla y León referred within the procedure for preliminary ruling in the matter Anacleto Cordero Alonso v. Fondo de Garantía Salarial (C-81/05, 7 September 2006) the following question to the European Court of Justice : Do the obligations imposed on a Member State to take all appropriate measures, whether general or particular, to ensure fulfilment of the obligations arising out of the Treaty establishing the European Community or resulting from action taken by the institutions of the Community (Article 10 EC), and the principle of the primacy of Community law over national law imply, of themselves and without the need for specific provisions of national law, that national courts have the power to disapply all provisions of the national law which are contrary to Community law, irrespective of the status of such provisions in the hierarchy of norms (regulations, laws and even a Constitution)?

(23) French annotated codes

In French codes, in which statutory provisions can be annotated (FR *annoté*) or commented (FR *commenté*), text composition that is limited to one sentence is the rule:

Two quotes relating to Art. 222–33 of the French Penal Code may illustrate this procedure:

(1) Un président-directeur général ne se rend pas coupable de harcèlement sexuel envers une salariée en lui manifestant des sentiments amoureux à l'aide de lettres et de poèmes sans pour autant abuser de son autorité par ordres, menaces, contraintes ou pressions dans le but d'obtenir des faveurs sexuelles, dès lors que ces poèmes et ces lettres ne traduisent que l'émoi sentimental de son auteur, sans contenir aucun terme indècent ou obscène dépassant la simple expression d'une passion amoureuse et pouvant affecter la dignité de la salariée dans sa vie professionnelle (Court of Versailles, June 30, 1993: D. 1993. IR 228).

(2) Dès lors qu'un employeur a adopté, à l'égard de sa secrétaire, une attitude de séduction exempte de tact et non dénuée d'arrière-pensées, assortie de manières et de propos grivois ou grossier, mais qu'aucun élément objectif ne vient cependant caractériser les contraintes résultant d'un abus d'autorité, en vue de faveurs de nature sexuelle, ce comportement, qui a pu paraître insupportable à la partie civile et faire naître, en elle, un sentiment de contrainte, mais dont il n'est pas prouvé qu'il ait mis en œuvre objectivement le rapport d'autorité existant entre l'un et l'autre, n'entre pas dans les prévisions de l'art. 222–33 c. pén. réprimant le harcèlement sexuel (Court of Versailles, November 29, 1996: Bull. inf.C. Cass. 1997, no. 711).

A note to Art. 9 of the French Civil Code says:

> Après avoir constaté la révélation de l'orientation sexuelle de l'intéressé, secrétaire général du Front national, et l'atteinte portée à sa vie privée, l'arrêt retient que l'évocation de cette orientation figure dans un ouvrage portant sur un sujet d'intérêt général, dès lors qu'il se rapporte à l'évolution d'un parti politique qui a montré des signes d'ouverture à l'égard des homosexuels à l'occasion de l'adoption de la loi relative au mariage des personnes de même sexe ; qu'ayant ainsi apprécié le rapport raisonnable de la proportionnalité existant entre le but légitime poursuivi par l'auteur, libre de s'exprimer et de faire état de l'information critiquée, et la protection de la vie privée, la cour d'appel a légalement justifié sa décision de rejeter la demande d'interdiction de la diffusion à venir et la saisie du livre intitulé « Le Front national des villes et le Front national des champs » (French Supreme Court, Cass. 1re civ.,). April 9, 2015)

A note to Art. 226–4 of the French Penal Code says:

> Lorsque certaines dispositions des lois et règlements en vigueur, concernant les locaux d'habitation, déclarent les occupants déchus de leur droits au maintien dans les lieux, ou considèrent les locaux comme inoccupés, ses dispositions exceptionnelles se bornent

à ouvrir aux ayants droit des recours judiciares ou à l'Administration un droit de réquisition, mais n'autorisent personne, fût-ce un magistrat municipal, à pénétrer dans ces locaux sans titre et par voie de fait, et ne modifient en rien les articles du code pénal qui protègent, contre toute violation arbitraire, le domicile des citoyens (Crim. 12 mars 1958).

(24) Excerpts from the CISG

United Nations Convention on Contracts for the International Sale of Goods

Article 1 (1) This Convention applies to contracts of sale of goods between parties whose place of business are in different States:... (2) The fact that the parties have their places of business in different States is to be disregarded whenever this fact does not appear either from the contract or from any dealings between, or from information disclosed by, the parties at any time before or at the conclusion of the contract. (3) Neither the nationality of the parties nor the civil or commercial character of the parties or of the contract is to be taken into consideration in determining the application of this Convention.

Article 3 (2) This Convention does not apply to contracts in which the preponderant part of the obligation of the party who furnishes the goods consists in the supply of labour or other services.

Article 4 This Convention governs only the formation of the contract of sale and the rights and obligations of the seller and buyer arising from such a contract.

Article 7 (1) In the interpretation of this Convention, regard is to be had to its international character and to the need to promote uniformity in its application and the observance of good faith in international trade.

Article 8 (2) If the preceding paragraph is not applicable, statements made by and other conduct of a party are to be interpreted according to the understanding that a reasonable person of the same kind as the other party would have had in the same circumstances. (3) In determining the intent of a party or the understanding a reasonable person would have had, due consideration is to be given to all relevant circumstances of the case including the negotiations, any practices which the parties have established between themselves, usages and any subsequent conduct of the parties.

Article 18 (1) A statement made by or other contract of the offeree indicating assent to an offer is an acceptance. Silence or inactivity does not in itself amount to acceptance.

Article 20 (1) Official holidays or non-business days occurring during the period for acceptance are included in calculating the period.

Article 24 For the purposes of this Part of the Convention, an offer, declaration of acceptance or any other indication of intention "reaches" the addressee when it is made orally to him or delivered by any other means to him personally, to his place of business or mailing address or, if he does not have a place of business or mailing address, to his habitual residence.

Article 38 (1) If the goods are redirected in transit or redispatched by the buyer without a reasonable opportunity for examination by him and at the time of the conclusion of the contract the seller knew or ought to have known of the possibility of such redirection or redispatch, examination may be deferred until after the goods have arrived at the new destination.

Article 43 (2) The seller is not entitled to rely on the provisions of the preceding paragraph if he knew of the right or claim of the third party and the nature of it.

Article 80 A party may not rely on a failure of the other party to perform, to the extent that such failure was caused by the first party's act or omission.

(25) Excerpts from the UCC

Uniform Commercial Code (2000 Official Text), Article 2:

2–101 Short Title. This Article shall be known and may be cited as Uniform Commercial Code – Sales.

2–301 General Obligations of Parties. The obligation of the seller is to transfer and deliver and that of the buyer is to accept and pay in accordance with the contract.

2–316 Exclusion or Modification of Warranties.

(1) Words or conduct relevant to the creation of an express warranty and words or conduct tending to negate or limit warranty shall be construed wherever reasonable as consistent with each other, but subject to the provisions of this Article on parol or extrinsic evidence (Section 2–202) negation or limitation is inoperative to the extent that such construction is unreasonable.

(3) Notwithstanding subsection (2)

(a) unless the circumstances indicate otherwise, all implied warranties are excluded by expression like "as is", "with all faults" or other language which in common understanding calls the buyer's attention to the exclusion of warranties and makes plain that there is no implied warranty; and...

2–711 Buyer's Remedies in General; Buyer's Security Interest in Rejected Goods.

(1) Where the seller fails to make delivery...the buyer may...

(a) "cover" and have damages under the next section as to all the goods affected whether or not they have been identified to the contract; or

2–712 "Cover"; Buyer's Procurement of Substitute Goods.

(1) After a breach within the preceding section the buyer may "cover" by making in good faith and without unreasonable delay any reasonable purchase of or contract to purchase goods in substitution for those due from the seller.

(3) Failure of the buyer to effect cover within this section does not bar him from any other remedy.

2–305 Open Price Term.

(2) A price to be fixed by the seller or by the buyer means a price for him to fix in good faith.

(3) When a price left to be fixed otherwise than by agreement of the parties fails to be fixed through fault of one party the other party may at his option treat the contract as cancelled or himself fix a reasonable price.

(26) Statutory provisions (Truth in Music Advertising Act)

The statute rendered below has been prepared for publication by the Office of the Revisor of Statutes of the U.S. State of Maine in September 2007. The text begins with the characterization of the statute by the staff of the Office as belonging to public law. Technical details which enable to incorporate the statute into the collection of Maine laws are included as well. Following the American legislative tradition the statute has a long name (*An Act to Ensure Truth in Music Advertising*) and a short one (*The Truth in Music Advertising Act*) which is usually quoted in court decisions and in research papers. The text ends with the indication of the day on which the statute enters into force. The text including the Maine statute reads as follows:

Public Law

123rd Legislature

First Regular Session

Chapter 171

H.P. 517 – L.D. 686

An Act to Ensure Truth in Music Advertising

Be it enacted by the People of the State of Maine as follows:

Sec. 1.10 MRSA c. 202-E is enacted to read:

CHAPTER 202-E

TRUTH IN MUSIC ADVERTISING

§ 1156. **Short title**

This chapter is known and may be cited as "the Truth in Music Advertising Act."

§ 1157. **Definitions**

As used in this chapter, unless the context otherwise indicates, the following terms have the following meanings.

1. **Performing group.** "Performing group" means a vocal or instrumental group seeking to use the name of another group that has previously released a commercial sound recording under that name.
2. **Person.** "Person" means any individual, partnership, corporation or association.
3. **Recording group.** "Recording group" means a vocal or instrumental group at least one of whose members has previously released a commercial sound recording under that group's name and in which the member has a legal right by virtue of use or operation under the group name without having abandoned the name or affiliation with the group.
4. **Sound recording.** "Sound recording" means a work that results from the fixation on a material object, such as a disc, tape or other phonorecord, in which the sounds are embodied.

§ 1158. **Production**

A person may not promote, advertise or conduct a live musical performance or production in this State through the use of a false, deceptive or misleading affiliation, connection or association between a performing group and a recording group unless:

1. **Authorized; federal service mark.** The performing group is the authorized registrant and owner of a federal service mark for that group registered in the United States Patent and Trademark Office;
2. **Legal right.** At least one member of the performing group was a member of the recording group and has a legal right by virtue of use or operation under the group name without having abandoned the name or affiliation with the group;
3. **Salute or tribute.** The live musical performance or production is identified in all advertising and promotion as a salute or tribute and the name of the performing group is not so closely related or similar to the name used by the recording group that it would tend to confuse or mislead the public; and
4. **Expressly authorized.** The performance or production is expressly authorized by the recording group.

§ 1159. **Restraining prohibited acts**

1. **Injunction.** Whenever the Attorney General or a district attorney has reason to believe that a person is promoting, advertising or conducting or is preparing to

promote, advertise or conduct a live musical performance or production in violation of section 1158 and that proceedings would be in the public interest, the Attorney General or district attorney may bring an action in the name of the State against the person to restrain that practice by temporary or permanent injunction.

2. **Payment of costs and restitution.** Whenever any court issues a permanent injunction to restrain and prevent violations of this chapter as authorized in subsection 1, the court may in its discretion direct that the defendant restore to the recording group any money or property, real or personal, that has been acquired by means of any violation of this chapter, under terms and conditions to be established by the court.

§ 1160. **Penalty**

In addition to any other relief that may be granted under section 1159, a person who violates section 1158 commits a civil violation for which a fine of not less than $500 per violation may be adjudged. Each performance or production advertised or conducted in violation of section 1158 constitutes a separate violation.

§ 1160-A. **Exemption**

This chapter does not apply to any nonprofit corporation incorporated under the laws of this State and subject to the provisions of Title 13, chapter 81 or 93 of the Maine Nonprofit Corporation Act.
Effective September 20, 2007

(27) French, Italian, German, Spanish and international statutory provisions on interpretation

The French *Code civil* includes in its Articles 1156–1164 provisions about the interpretation of contracts:

De l'interprétation des conventions.

Art. 1156 On doit dans les conventions rechercher quelle a été la commune intention des parties contractantes, plutôt que de s'arrêter au sens littéral des termes.

Art. 1157 Lorsqu'une clause est susceptible de deux sens, on doit plutôt l'entendre dans celui avec lequel elle peut avoir quelque effet, que dans le sens avec lequel elle n'en pourrait produire aucun.

Art. 1158 Les termes susceptibles de deux sens doivent être pris dans le sens qui convient le plus à la matière du contrat.

Art. 1159 Ce qui est ambigu s'interprète par ce qui est d'usage dans le pays où le contrat est passé.

Art. 1160 On doit suppléer dans le contrat les clauses qui y sont d'usage, quoiqu'elles n'y soient pas exprimées.

Art. 1161 Toutes les clauses des conventions s'interprètent les unes par les autres, en donnant à chacune le sens qui résulte de l'acte entier.

Art. 1162 Dans la doute, la convention s'interprète contre celui qui a stipulé et en faveur de celui qui a contracté l'obligation.

Art. 1163 Quelque généraux que soient les termes dans lesquels une convention est conçue, elle ne comprend que les choses sur lesquelles il paraît que les parties se sont proposé de contracter.

Art. 1164 Lorsque dans un contrat on a exprimé un cas pour l'explication de l'obligation, on n'est pas censé avoir voulu par là restreindre l'étendue que l'engagement reçoit aux cas non exprimés.

The Italian *Codice civile* provides numerous explicit provisions regarding the interpretation of legal provisions and the interpretation in law:

Art. 12. Interpretazione della legge. (1) – Nell'applicare la legge non si può ad essa attribuire altro senso che quello fatto palese dal significato proprio delle parole secondo la connessione di esse, e dalla intenzione del legislatore.

Se una controversia non può essere decisa con una precisa disposizione, si ha riguardo alle disposizioni che regolano casi simili o materie analoghe; se il caso rimane ancora dubbio, si decide secondo i principi generali dell'ordinamento giuridico dello Stato.

Capo IV *Dell'interpretazione del contratto*

Art. 1362. Intenzione dei contraenti. – Nell'interpretare il contratto si deve indagare quale sia stata la comune intenzione delle parti e non limitarsi al senso letterale delle parole.

Per determinare la comune intenzione delle parti, si deve valutare il loro comportamento complessivo anche posteriore alla conclusione del contratto.

Art. 1363. Interpretazione complessiva delle clausole. – Le clausole del contratto si interpretano le une per mezzo delle altre, attribuendo a ciascuna il senso che risulta dal complesso dell'atto.

Art. 1364. Espressioni generali. Per quanto generali siano le espressioni usate nel contratto, questo non comprende che gli oggetti sui quali le parti si sono proposte di contrattare.

Art. 1365. Indicazioni esemplificative. Quando in un contratto si è espresso un caso al fine di spiegare un patto, non si presumono esclusi i casi non espressi, ai quali, secondo ragione, può estendersi lo stesso patto.

Art. 1366. Interpretazione di buona fede. – Il contratto deve essere interpretato secondo buona fede.

Art. 1367. Conservazione del contratto. – Nel dubbio, il contratto o le singole clausole devono interpretarsi nel senso in cui possono avere qualche effetto, anziché in quello secondo cui non ne avrebbero alcuno.

Art. 1368. Pratiche generali interpretative. – Le clausole ambigue s'interpretano secondo ciò che si pratica generalmente nel luogo in cui il contratto è stato concluso.

Nei contratti in cui una delle parti è un imprenditore, le clausole ambigue s'interpretano secondo ciò che si pratica generalmente nel luogo in cui è la sede dell'impresa.

Art. 1369. Espressioni con più sensi. – Le clausole inserite nelle condizioni generali di contratto o in moduli o formulari predisposti da uno dei contraenti s'interpretano, nel dubbio, a favore dell'altro.

Art. 1370. Regole finali. – Qualora, nonostante l'applicazione delle norme contenute in questo capo, il contratto rimanga oscuro, esso deve essere inteso nel senso meno gravoso per l'obbligato, se è a titolo gratuito, e nel senso che realizzi l'equo contemperamento degli interessi delle parti, se è a titolo oneroso.

The Italian Law on the Conflict of Laws (L. 31 maggio 1995, n. 218) includes following interpretive provisions:

2. Convenzioni internazionali. – 1. Le disposizioni della presenta legge non pregiudicano l'applicazione delle convenzioni internazionali in vigore per l'Italia. – 2. Nell'interpretazione di tali convenzioni si terrà conto del loro carattere internazionale e dell'esigenza della loro applicazione uniforme.

15. Interpretazione e applicazione della legge straniera. – 1. La legge straniera è applicata secondo i propri criteri di interpretazione e di applicazione nel tempo.

The Spanish *Código civil* stipulates:

CAPITULO IV

De la interpretación de los contratos

1.281. Si los términos de un contrato son claros y no dejan duda sobre la intención de los contratantes, se estará al sentido literal de sus cláusulas.

Si las palabras parecieren contrarias a la intención evidente de los contratantes, prevalecerá ésta sobre aquéllas.

1.282. Para juzgar de la intención de los contratantes, deberá atenderse principalmente a los actos de éstos, coetáneos y posteriores al contrato.

1.283. Cualquiera que sea la generalidad de los términos de un contrato, no deberán entenderse comprendidos en él cosas distintas y casos diferentes de aquellos sobre que los interesados se propusieron contratar.

1.284. Si alguna cláusula de los contratos admitiere diversos sentidos, deberá entenderse en el más adecuado para que produzca efecto.

1.285. Las cláusulas de los contratos deberán interpretarse las unas por las otras, atribuyendo a las dudosas el sentido que resulte del conjunto de todas.

1.286. Las palabras que puedan tener distintas acepciones serán entendidas en aquella que sea más conforme a la naturaleza y objeto del contrato.

1.287. El uso o la costumbre del país se tendrán en cuenta para interpretar las ambigüedades de los contratos, supliendo en éstos la omisión de cláusulas que de ordinario suelen establecerse.

1.288. La interpretación de las cláusulas oscuras de un contrato no deberá favorecer a la parte que hubiese ocasionado la oscuridad.

1.289. Cuando absolutamente fuere imposible resolver las dudas por las reglas establecidas en los artículos precedentes, si aquéllas recaen sobre circunstancias accidentales del contrato, y éste fuere gratuito, se resolverán en favor de la menor transmisión de derechos e intereses. Si el contrato fuere oneroso, la duda se resolverá en favor de la mayor reciprocidad de intereses.

Si las dudas de cuya resolución se trata en este artículo recayesen sobre el objeto principal del contrato, de suerte que no pueda venirse en conocimiento de cuál fue la intención o voluntad de los contratantes, el contrato será nulo.

The German civil code (*BGB*) also includes analogous interpretive regulations:

Art. 133 BGB Auslegung einer Willenserklärung – Bei der Auslegung der Willenserklärung ist der wirkliche Wille zu erforschen und nicht an dem buchstäblichen Sinne des Ausdrucks zu haften.

Art. 157 BGB Auslegung von Verträgen – Verträge sind so auszulegen, wie Treu und Glauben mit Rücksicht auf die Verkehrssitten es erfordern.

Some international instruments such as the UNIDROIT Principles, CISG or PECL also include provisions concerning interpretation:

UNIDROIT Principles of International Commercial Contracts (1994), Chapter 4 – Interpretation:

Art. 4.1 – Intention of the parties

1. A contract shall be interpreted according to the common intention of the parties.
2. If such an intention cannot be established, the contract shall be interpreted according to the meaning that reasonable persons of the same kind as the parties would give to it in the same circumstances.

Art. 4.2 – Interpretation of statements and other conduct

1. The statements and other conduct of a party shall be interpreted according to that party's intention if the other party knew or could not have been unaware of that intention.

2. If the preceding paragraph is not applicable, such statements and other conduct shall be interpreted according to the meaning that a reasonable person of the same kind as the other party would give to it in the same circumstances.

Art. 4.3. – Relevant circumstances

In applying Articles 4.1. and 4.2. regard shall be had to all circumstances, including:

(a) preliminary negotiations between the parties; (b) practices which the parties have established between themselves; (c) the conduct of the parties subsequent to the conclusion of the contract; (d) the nature and the purpose of the contract; (e) the meaning commonly given to terms and expressions in the trade concerned; (f) usages.

Art. 4.4. – Reference to contract or statement as a whole

Terms and expressions shall be interpreted in the light of the whole contract or statement in which they appear.

Art. 4.5 – All terms to be given effect

Contracts shall be interpreted so as to give effect to all terms rather than to deprive some of them of effect.

Art. 4.6 – Contra proferentem rule

If contract terms supplied by one party are unclear, an interpretation against that party is preferred.

Art. 4.7 – Linguistic discrepancies

Where a contract is drawn up in two or more language versions which are equally authoritative there is, in case of discrepancy of the versions, a preference for the interpretation according to a version in which the contract was originally drawn up.

Art. 4.8 – Supplying an omitted term

1. Where the parties to a contract have not agreed with respect to a term which is important for a determination of their rights and duties, a term which is appropriate in the circumstances shall be supplied.
2. In determining what is an appropriate term regard shall be had, among other factors, to:
   (a) the intention of the parties; (b) the nature and purpose of the contract; (c) good faith and fair dealing; (d) reasonableness.

Art. 7 CISG: In the interpretation of this Convention, regard is to be had to its international character and to the need to promote uniformity in its application and the observance of good faith in international trade.

The PECL include in chapter V *Interpretation* following provisions regarding contract interpretation:

Art. 5: 101: *General Rules of Interpretation*

(1) A contract is to be interpreted according to the common intention of the parties even if this differs from the literal meaning of the words.
(2) If it is established that one party intended the contract to have a particular meaning, and at the time of the conclusion of the contract the other party could not have been unaware of the first party's intention, the contract is to be interpreted in the way intended by the first party.
(3) If an intention cannot be established according to (1) or (2), the contract is to be interpreted according to the meaning that reasonable persons of the same kind as the parties would give to it in the same circumstances.

Art. 5: 102: *Relevant Circumstances*

In interpreting the contract, regard shall be had, in particular, to:

(a) the circumstances in which it was concluded, including the preliminary negotiations;
(b) the conduct of the parties, even subsequent to the conclusion of the contract;
(c) the nature and purpose of the contract;
(d) the interpretation which has already been given to similar clauses by the parties and the practices they have established between themselves;
(e) the meaning commonly given to terms and expressions in the branch of activity concerned and the interpretation similar clauses may already have received;
(f) usages, and
(g) good faith and fair dealing.

Art. 5: 103: *Contra Proferentem Rule*

Where there is doubt about the meaning of a contract term not individually negotiated, an interpretation of the term against the party who supplied it is to be preferred.

Art. 5:104: *Preference to Negotiated Terms*

Terms which have been individually negotiated take preference over those which are not.

Art. 5: 105: *Reference to Contract as a Whole*

Terms are to be interpreted in the light of the whole contract in which they appear.

Art. 5: 106: *Terms to Be Given Effect*

An interpretation which renders the terms of the contract lawful, or effective, is to be preferred to one which would not.

Art. 5: 107: *Linguistic Discrepancies*

Where a contract is drawn up in two or more language versions none of which is stated to be authoritative, there is, in case of discrepancy between the versions, a preference for the interpretation according to the version in which the contract was originally drawn up.

(28) French governmental instruction on counting paragraphs in legislative drafts

A French governmental instruction dating from 2000 regulates the mode in which paragraphs in legal texts should be counted. It has been issued, according to its declared *raison d'être,* in order to harmonize and to simplify the structure of legal texts. However, the Secretary General of the Government in charge of this instruction self-critically invokes the risk that through new formal measures such as those reprinted below the texts may not become easier to draft or to grasp. Therefore, the instruction illustrates rather the problem of formalized measures aiming at structuring the legal texts. In the main text of this research language use strategies have been favored to the detriment of such formal, if not formalistic rules. The instruction stresses in the last phrase of its sec. 5 the strategy to express in an article only one rule and not to overburden it with paragraphs. Such strategic rules are more efficient when introduced in a coherent body of rules about legislative drafting. Despite the efforts undertaken in the instruction, the impression comes up that it replaces one formal system by another and that it does not improve the overall quality of legislative texts. It goes without saying that a certain order in the drafting of legal texts or in the usage of abbreviations in them is absolutely necessary. However, from the legal-linguistic point of view it is the approach taken to these issues which is decisive. Legal linguistics cannot support blind approaches which ground in mechanistic development and application of formalized rules for the drafting of legal texts. Rules for language use in texts which convey orders must be embodied in general strategies of language use in the social sphere in which they emerge and are applied. When this is not the case, new rules remain ineffective or are perceived, at best, in a comical perspective.

Circulaire du 20 octobre 2000 relative au mode de décompte des alinéas lors de l'élaboration des textes

J.O. n° 253 du 31 oct. 2000, p. 17302.

Le secrétaire général du Gouvernement à Mesdames et Messieurs les ministres et secrétaires d'Etat.

Référence : circulaire du 30 janvier 1997 relative aux règles d'élaboration, de signature et de publication des textes au Journal officiel et à la mise en œuvre de procédures particulières incombant au Premier ministre.

1. Le Parlement et le Gouvernement utilisaient jusqu'ici des règles différentes pour décompter les alinéas composant un article de loi ou de décret. Les assemblées parlementaires ont pour usage de compter come un alinéa tout mot ou ensemble de mots qui commencent à la ligne, alors même qu'ils ne constituent pas, à eux seuls, une phrase, et quels que soient les signes de ponctuation dont ils sont précédés. De son côté, le

Gouvernement avait fait sien le mode de computation préconisé par le Conseil d'Etat. Selon ce dernier, il n'y avait lieu de compter un nouvel alinéa que lors de chaque passage à la ligne faisant suite à un point. A contrario, étaient regardés comme la suite du même alinéa les termes venant après une phrase introductive qui étaient renvoyés à la ligne, soit qu'ils constituent les éléments d'une énumération, soit que, placés entre guillemets, ils fussent destinés à s'insérer dans un autre texte.

2. Ce double décompte était peu satisfaisant, à deux égards. D'une part, dans le cas des projets de loi comportant des renvois à des alinéas, il conduisait à une modification systématique, lors du passage devant la première assemblée saisie, du texte préparé par le Gouvernement. D'autre part, l'existence d'une dualité de règles, selon que le texte était de forme législative ou réglementaire, n'était pas de nature à faciliter la consultation des textes et l'accès à la règle de droit. Ce sont sans doute ces considérations qui ont récemment conduit le Conseil d'Etat à faire sien le mode de comptation utilisé par le Parlement.

3. Les administrations chargées de la préparation des textes doivent évidemment tirer sans tarder les conséquences de cette évolution, qui rend caduques les indications figurant au point 1.1.3.5. de la circulaire du 30 janvier 1997 susmentionnée.

Il conviendra donc, désormais, de compter pour un alinéa tout mot ou groupe de mots renvoyé à la ligne, sans qu'il y ait lieu d'établir des distinctions selon la nature du signe placé à la fin de la ligne précédente (point, deux-points ou point-virgule) ou au début de la ligne nouvelle (chiffre arabe ou romain, tiret, guillemets...).

Il va de soi que, dans un souci de simplicité, l'application de cette règle ne saurait être limitée aux seuls textes soumis au Conseil d'Etat. Vous en ferez usage pour l'ensemble des textes préparés par votre département ministériel, décrets, arrêtés ou circulaires.

4. La simplification ainsi obtenue trouve, il est vrai, ses limites dans le fait que coexisteront, dans le droit positif, des textes réglementaires appliquant l'une et l'autre décompte, selon la date à laquelle ils auront été adoptés.

Aussi est-il souhaitable qu'à l'occasion des modifications qui seraient apportées à un texte rédigé sous l'empire de l'ancienne règle, vous vous assuriez que sa lecture ne prête pas à l'ambiguïté selon que l'on applique l'ancien ou le nouveau mode de décompte des alinéas. Si tel était le cas, il conviendrait de revoir cette rédaction, par example en recourant à la numérotation des dispositions auxquelles il est renvoyé.

En tout état de cause, vous veillerez à éviter la coexistence, au sein d'un même texte, de dispositions utilisant alternativement l'un et l'autre mode de décompte. Cette alternance pourrait d'autant plus dérouter le lecteur que l'ensemble des décrets devraient prochainement être mis à la disposition du public sous une forme consolidée, par le site Légifrance. S'agissant des dispositions dont l'ampleur est telle que ce travail de révision n'apparaît pas possible, notamment le code général des impôts et les codes dont la partie réglementaire a déjà été adoptée, vous vous efforcerez, à tout le moins, de rédiger les modifications à venir de telle sorte qu'il n'existe pas d'ambiguïté dans les renvois opérés.

5. Plus généralement, je vous invite, lorsque vous élaborez un texte procedant à des renvois, à n'utiliser qu'avec circonspection la notion d'alinéa. Cette technique de rédaction, s'il en est fait un usage trop libéral, rend la lecture du texte malcommode et peut, en outre, être à l'origine d'interrogations ou même d'erreurs sur l'exacte portée de ses dispositions.

Aussi vous efforcerez-vous d'agencer le contenu des articles de telle sorte que le renvoi à certaines des dispositions qui y sont contenues puisse se faire par référence à un chiffre ou une lettre. Par ailleurs, ces références à des parties d'articles peuvent être elles-mêmes plus souvent évités, grâce à une meilleure application du principe qui veut qu'un article ne contienne l'énoncé que d'une seule règle.

(29) Spanish Royal Decree on National Anthem

The (ESP) *real decreto* that follows concerns the mode of use of the Spanish National Anthem. It is as a legal text type interesting because it includes a text written in another code, i.e. in notes. The score of the *Himno Nacional* is rendered as the last part of this text and takes several pages in original printed in the Spanish Legal Gazette. This part is not included here because of technical problems.

Real Decreto 1560/1997, de 10 de octubre, por el que se regula el Himno Nacional.

De conformidad con lo previsto en el artículo 97 de la Ley del Patrimonio del Estado de 15 de abril de 1964, y en el artículo 43 de la Ley de Propiedad Intelectual de 12 de abril de 1996, el Real Decreto 1543/1997, dispuso la adquisición de la obra tradicionalmente conocida como « Marcha Granadera » o « Marcha Real Española ». Dada la naturaleza de esta obra, resulta oportuno regular, asimismo, su carácter y utilización como himno nacional de España y establecer, formalmente, la partitura oficial, sus diferentes versiones y las distintas modalidades de interpretación. En su virtud, a propuesta de Presidente del Gobierno y previa deliberación del Consejo de Ministros en su reunión del día 10 de octubre de 1997,

DISPONGO :

Artículo 1.

El himno nacional de España es el conocido tradicionalmente por « Marcha Granadera » o « Marcha Real Española». Su partitura oficial será la que figura en el anexo del presente Real Decreto.

Artículo 2.

El himno nacional de España se interpretará de acuerdo con las siguientes directrices:

a). Constará técnicamente de una frase de dieciséis compases, dividida en dos secciones, cada una de las cuales tendrá cuatro compases repetidos. La indicación metronómica será de negra igual a setenta y seis y la tonalidad de Si b mayor. Sus duraciones serán de cincuenta y dos segundos para la versión completa y de veintisiete segundos para la versión breve. b). Se entenderá por versión breve la interpretación de los cuatro compases de cada sección, sin repetición. c). Las partituras de banda, de orquesta y de redución para órgano son las que se contienen en el anexo de este Real Decreto y servirán de referencia para cualquier versión de grupo de cámara. d). El himno nacional de España, en cualquiera de sus dos versiones, se interpretará siempre íntegramente y una sola vez.

Artículo 3.

El himno nacional será interpretado, cuando proceda :

1. En versión completa:
   a) En los actos de homenaje a la Bandera de España.
   b) En los actos oficiales a los que asista Su Majestad el Rey o Su Majestad la Reina.
   c) En los actos oficiales a los que asista la Reina consorte o el consorte de la Reina.
   d) En los demás actos previstos en el Reglamento de Honores Militares.
2. En versión breve :
   a) En los actos oficiales a los que asistan Su Alteza Real el Príncipe de Asturias, Su Alteza Real la Princesa de Asturias o Sus Altezas Reales los infantes de España.
   b) En los actos oficiales a los que asista el Presidente del Gobierno.
   c) En los actos deportivos o de cualquier otra naturaleza en los que haya una representación oficial de España.
   d) En los demás casos previstos en el Reglamento de Honores Militares.

Artículo 4.

La actitud de respeto al himno nacional de los asistentes a los actos en los que sea interpretado se expresará, en el caso del personal uniformado de las Fuerzas Armadas y de las Fuerzas de Seguridad, efectuando el saludo reglamentario.

Artículo 5.

De acuerdo con la costumbre y usos protocolarios habituales, cuando las Personas Reales o Autoridades a que se refiere el artículo 3 del presente Real Decreto asistan a actos oficiales de carácter general, organizados por una Comunidad Autónoma o Corporación Local, siempre que la naturaleza del acto requiera la interpretación del himno nacional, ésta se realizará de acuerdo con los siguientes criterios:

a) Cuando al iniciarse el acto esté prevista la ejecución de los himnos oficiales de las Comunidades Autónomas o de las Corporaciones Locales, el himno nacional de España se interpretará en primer lugar.
b) En los casos en que esté prevista la ejecución de los expresados himnos al finalizar el acto, el himno nacional de España se interpretará en último lugar.

Artículo 6.

1. En los actos y visitas oficiales de carácter internacional celebrados en territorio español, cuando deba ejecutarse himnos nacionales, se interpretarán, en primer lugar, los himnos extranjeros y después el himno nacional de España. En las despedidas, se interpretarán en orden inverso. Igual orden se observará en las visitas oficiales de buques de guerra extranjeros.
2. En puertos extranjeros, a bordo de los buques de la Armada, se interpretará en primer lugar el himno nacional de España y a continuación el de la nación anfitriona.
3. En todo caso, la interpretación de himnos nacionales extranjeros irá acompañada siempre del himno nacional de España.

Disposición transitoria primera.

1. En el plazo de dos meses a partir de la publicación del presente Real Decreto, los distintos organismos e instituciones, tanto públicos como privados, adaptarán la interpretación del himno nacional de España a la partitura oficial.
2. Durante el plazo señalado, las modalidades y tiempos de duración de la interpretación del himno nacional se podrán ajustar a la versión vigente hasta la entrada en vigor del presente Real Decreto o, en su caso, a lo establecido en la costumbre.

Disposición transitoria segunda.

Hasta tanto se modifique el Reglamento de Honores Militares, y a los efectos previstos en el artículo 3 del presente Real Decreto, las referencias que el expresado Reglamento contiene al "himno nacional completo" y "la primera parte completa" se entenderán hechas a la versión completa. Igualmente, las referencias de esta misma disposición a la "primera parte sin repetición" se entenderán hechas a la versión breve.

Disposición final única.

El presente Real Decreto entrará en vigor el mismo día de su publicación en el "Boletín Oficial del Estado".

Dado en Madrid a 10 de octubre de 1997.

JUAN CARLOS R.

El Presidente del Gobierno,

JOSÉ MARÍA AZNAR LÓPEZ

(30) German Presidential Order on National Anthem

The German Presidential decree from 1952 that introduced the third strophe of Hoffmann von Fallersleben's text is concise; it does not include any quotes of the text or the score. Unlike the Spanish national anthem, the German anthem became official through a legally informal exchange of letters between Chancellor K. Adenauer and president T. Heuss in 1952. When contrasted, the Spanish and the German procedures make plain the ambit and the limits of legal regulation. The letter by President Heuss re-introduces the national anthem informally into the social practice and stresses the intention to do so. No 'festive proclamation' shall take place; mentioning the controversial matter in an exchange of letters must do. It is remarkable that the speech act of 'proclamation' is no less binding than are formal acts of proclamation although the usual textual form is neglected. Meanwhile, no attempt has been undertaken by the German government to re-introduce the anthem factually, without proclamation. Indeed, for legal acts their proclamation is essential; the performative excludes, unlike the pure act of singing or making sing the anthem, any ambiguity as to its legal status (cf. Galdia 2014: 272–274).

Bundesrepublik Deutschland Bonn, den 29.4.52

Der Bundeskanzler

An den

Bundespräsidenten der

Bundesrepublik Deutschland

Herrn Prof. Dr. Theodor Heuss

Bonn

Sehr geehrter Herr Bundespräsident!

Die Frage einer „National-Hymne" ist in den vergangenen zwei Jahren wiederholt zwischen uns besprochen worden. Ich achtete, wenn auch mit Zweifel an dem Gelingen, Ihren Versuch, durch einen neuen Text und durch eine neue Melodie über die unliebsamen Zwischenfälle hinwegzukommen, die bei der Wiedergabe oder bei dem Absingen des „Deutschland-Liedes" sich ereignet haben; es sollte vermieden bleiben, hier einen neuen Streit in unser Volk zu tragen.

Sie haben mir selber gelegentlich zum Ausdruck gebracht, dass Sie das Bemühen als gescheitert betrachten müssen. Die Gründe mögen jetzt unerörtert bleiben. Als das Kabinett Sie vor Monaten durch mich bitten ließ, sich für die dritte Strophe des „Deutschland-Liedes" zu entscheiden, gab ich zu, dass Ihre damaligen Gegenargumentation eine innere Berechtigung besaß.

Inzwischen ist nun die Frage dringend geworden, und ich muss den Wunsch der Bundesregierung darum pflichtgemäß wiederholen. Sie wissen selber um die Lage, in der bei amtlichen Veranstaltungen unsere ausländischen Vertretungen sich befinden. Ich will in diesem Augenblick die innerdeutschen Gefühlsmomente, deren Gewicht von uns beiden gleich hoch gewertet wird, gar nicht in Anschlag bringen. Es ist wesentlich der außenpolitische Realismus, der uns, Ihnen wie mir, nahe legen muss, die Entscheidung nicht weiter hinauszuzögern; ich möchte auch hoffen dürfen und glaube, dazu Grund zu haben, dass die innenpolitischen Vorbehalte, die sich auf den Missbrauch des „Deutschland-Liedes" durch die Vernichter des alten Deutschland beziehen, an

Schärfe verloren haben – war es doch der Reichspräsident Friedrich Ebert, der das „Deutschland-Lied“ durch eine staatsmännische Entscheidung zur Nationalhymne erklärte.

Daher die erneute Bitte der Bundesregierung, das Hoffmann-Haydn'sche Lied als Nationalhymne anzuerkennen. Bei staatlichen Veranstaltungen soll die dritte Strophe gesungen werden.

Mit freundlichen Grüßen

Ihr

(gez.) Adenauer

The answer:

Der Präsident der Bundesrepublik Deutschland

Bonn/Berlin 2.5.1952

Sehr geehrter Herr Bundeskanzler!

Sie haben recht: ich wollte vermieden wissen, dass in öffentlichen Veranstaltungen mit einem vaterländischen Akzent, gleichviel wie ihre Ausdehnung oder wie ihr Rang sei, ein Missklang ertöne, weil sehr, sehr viele Menschen unseres Volkes Haydns große Melodie nur eben als Vorspann zu dem „dichterisch“ und musikalisch minderwertigen Horst-Wessel-Lied im Gedächtnis haben, dessen banale Melodie den Marsch-Takt in ein Volksverderben abgab.

Doch das ist es nicht allein. Als mich die Frage nach einer Nationalhymne bewegte – und es liegt innerlich längst vor meiner Wahl zum Bundespräsidenten – glaubte ich, dass der tiefe Einschnitt in unserer Volks- und Staatsgeschichte einer neuen Symbolgebung bedürftig sei, damit wir vor der geschichtlichen Tragik unseres Schicksals mit zugleich reinem und freiem Herzen, in klarer Nüchternheit des Erkennens der Lage bestehen werden. Ich weiß heute, dass ich mich täuschte. Ich habe den Traditionalismus und sein Beharrungsbedürfnis unterschätzt. Man hat mir wegen meines Planes manche herzhafte Zustimmung gegeben, und zwar aus schier allen heute wesentlichen politischen Gruppen, man hat mich bewegend, entrüstet, töricht, banal in zahllosen Briefen, Telegrammen, Resolutionen belehrt, dass man in der Not die Vergangenheit nicht verleugnen usf. usf. Wenn mich jemand über geschichtliches Würdegefühl belehren wollte, habe ich das kühl auf die Seite geschoben. Denn ich bin stolz und selbstbewusst genug, zu meinen, dass einige meiner in der Vergangenheit liegenden literarischen und wissenschaftlichen Arbeiten der deutschen Würde bekömmlicher waren als die Leistung mancher „prominenter“ Protestler von heute, die besser schweigen.

Da ich kein Freund von pathetischen Dramatisierungen bin und mit mir selber im reinen bleiben will, muss ich nach meiner Natur auf eine "feierliche Proklamation" verzichten. Wenn ich also der Bitte der Bundesregierung nachkomme, so geschieht das in der Anerkennung des Tatbestandes.

Ich möchte daran zwei Erwartungen und Wünsche knüpfen:

In den letzten Jahren habe ich, zum Teil durch recht prominente Mitglieder aus den Reihen der CDU, der FDP, der SPD Versicherungen erhalten, wie richtig, wie falsch das sei, was ich versucht habe – es wäre ein Glück, wenn nun das Kapitel der Parteiauffassungen abgeschlossen wäre, das auch in einigen Landtagen abgehandelt wurde. Zum anderen: Man hatte mir nahegelegt, bei der Freigabe von Helgoland den erwarteten Akt der „Proklamation" zu vollziehen, weil bekanntlich auf dieser Insel Hoffmann seine Verse gedichtet hat. Das ist nun so: Hoffmann von Fallersleben war ein Schwarz-Rot-Goldener, sogar leicht verärgert, dass nach 1870 sein Gedicht gar nicht in Aufnahme kam. Ich würde sehr froh sein, wenn alle, die sich jetzt in Briefen und Entschießungen und Artikeln so lebhaft zu ihm bekannt haben, auch die Folgerungen daraus weiter ziehen, und es wäre verdienstlich, Herr Bundeskanzler, wenn die Bundesregierung mit dafür sorgen könnte, dass diese Farben bei festlichen Anlässen, da man die Worte von Hoffmann von Fallersleben singen will und singen wird, nicht bloß an den Amtsgebäuden wehen, sondern von den Mitgliedern der Gruppen, die sich dafür in Beschlüssen erklärt haben, als das Symbol unseres Staates auch öffentlich bekannt würden.

Mit guten Grüßen,

Ihr gez. Theodor Heuss

After die German reunification, the issue has been regulated again through the exchange of letters dated August 19/23, 1991 between the Federal Chancelor, H. Kohl und the Federal President, R. von Weizsäcker (cf. *Bulletin des Presse- und Informationsamtes der Bundesregierung Nr. 89/1991, August, 27, 1991*).

(31) Law of the Allied Control Council (1947)

The statute provides for the dissolution of the State of Prussia and refers to Prussia's factual brackdown in 1945, before the legal decision about its dissolution has been taken. Thus, the performative act is embedded in the facticity of exercising power by a state. In fact, the statute misunderstands the constructive nature of legal provisions where linguistic performativness overdoes political facts. After all, a state exists or ceases to exist by a normative decision and not by brute facts. This circumstance is clearly underestimated in the texts of the statute.

Gesetz des Allierten Kontrollrats (from 15 February 1947)

Der Staat Preußen, der seit jeher Träger des Militarismus und der Reaktion in Deutschland gewesen ist, hat in Wirklichkeit zu bestehen aufgehört. Geleitet von dem Interesse an der Aufrechterhaltung des Friedens... (bestimmt) der Kontrollrat...Art. I: Der Staat Preußen, seine Zentralregierung und alle nachgeordneten Behörden werden hiermit aufgelöst.

(32) Excerpts from OSCE Recommendations on Minority and Linguistic Rights

Excerpts from *The Hague Recommendations regarding Minority Education Rights*:

The spirit of international instruments

1) The right of persons belonging to national minorities to maintain their identity can only be fully realised if they acquire a proper knowledge of their mother tongue during the educational process. At the same time, persons belonging to national minorities have a responsibility to integrate into the wider national society through the acquisition of a proper knowledge of the State language.
2) In applying international instruments which may benefit persons belonging to national minorities, States should consistently adhere to the fundamental principles of equality and non-discrimination.
3) It should be borne in mind that the relevant international obligations and commitments constitute international minimum standards. It would be contrary to their spirit and intent to interpret these obligations and commitments in a restrictive manner...

Excerpts from *The Lund Recommendations on the Effective Participation of National Minorities in Public Life*:

General Principles

1) Effective participation of national minorities in public life is an essential component of a peaceful and democratic society. Experience in Europe and elsewhere has shown that, in order to promote such participation, governments often need to establish specific arrangements for national minorities. These Recommendations aim to facilitate the inclusion of minorities within the State and enable minorities to maintain their own identity and characteristics, thereby promoting the good governance and integrity of the State.
2) These Recommendations build upon fundamental principles and rules of international law, such as respect for human dignity, equal rights, and non-discrimination, as they affect the rights of national minorities to participate in public life and to enjoy other political rights. States have a duty to respect internationally recognized human rights and the rule of law, which allow for the full development of civil society in conditions of tolerance, peace and prosperity.
3) When specific institutions are established to ensure the effective participation of minorities in public life, which can include the exercise of authority or responsibility by such institutions, they must respect the human rights of all those affected.
4) Individuals identify themselves in numerous ways in addition to their identity as members of a national minority. The decision as to whether an individual is member of a minority, the majority, or neither rests with that individual and shall not be imposed upon her or him. Moreover, no person shall suffer any disadvantage as a result of such a choice or refusal to choose.

5) When creating institutions and procedures in accordance with these Recommendations, both substance and process are important. Governmental authorities and minorities should pursue an inclusive, transparent, and accountable process of consultation in order to maintain a climate of confidence. The State should encourage the public media to foster intercultural understanding and address the concerns of minorities...

(33) Structure of French court decisions (1)

Cour de Cassation (Ch. Civ. 1re sect. Civ.) 20 janvier 1964

(Dame Blum C. Dlle Lassus) – Arrêt

La Court ; – Sur le premier moyen, pris en sa première branche. – Vu l'art. 1382 c. civ.; – Attendu que l'exercice du droit de propriété, qui a pour limite la satisfaction d'un intérêt sérieux et légitime, ne saurait autoriser l'accomplissement d'actes malveillants, ne se justifiant par aucune utilité appréciable et portant préjudice à autrui ; – Attendu que la cour d'appel a refusé d'ordonner la suppression d'un rideau de fougères de 1,70 m de hauteur, planté par demoiselle Lassus, à environ 0,85 m du mur de la maison de dame Blum et empêchant le passage de la lumière par une ouverture à verre dormant dont l'aménagement avait été judiciairement autorisé pour l'éclairage d'une cuisine ; que pour statuer ainsi, l'arrêt informatif attaqué (Agen, 28 mars 1962) se fonde sur ce que s'il était fait droit à la prétention de dame Blum, l'héritage voisin se trouverait grevé « d'une véritable servitude d'éclairement...contractuellement inexistante » ; -Mais attendu que la même décision, après avoir rappelé et déclaré constantes les constatations de fait de premiers juges, a relevé « qu'il apparaît bien des éléments de la cause que les parties vivent dans une mésintelligence certaine » et que « l'instance...reflète et caractérise la psychologie de demoiselle Lassus, recherchant la satisfaction d'un mobile malicieux » ; – Attendu qu'en se refusant, dans de telles circonstances, à accorder à dame Blum réparation du préjudice dont elle se plaignait alors qu'ils constataient, en même temps, à la charge de demoiselle Lassus, un exercice purement malicieux, partant, abusif, de son droit de propriété, les juges du second degré ont violé le texte visé par le pourvoi ;

Par ces motifs, et sans qu'il y ait lieu de statuer, soit sur les autres branches du premier moyen, soit sur le deuxième moyen, casse..., renvoie devant la cour d'appel de Bordeaux.

(34) Structure of French court decisions (2)

Sur la recevabilité du pourvoi:

Attendu que selon les articles 1 et 2 du décret no 67–1210 du 22 décembre 1967, le pourvoi en cassation est formé au plus tard dans un délai de deux mois à compter de la signification de la décision attaquée ;

Qu'en vertu des dispositions de l'article 46 du décret susvisé du 22 décembre 1967 et des articles 6 et 7 du décret no 72–788 du 28 août 1972, alors applicable, ce délai expire le jour du dernier mois qui porte le même quantième que le jour de l'acte qui fait courir le délai, à vingt-quatre heures ;

Attendu qu'en l'espèce le pourvoi a été formé par la dame Benet le 4 septembre 1975 contre l'arrêt rendu le 27 mai 1975 par la Cour d'appel d'Aix-en-Provence ; que, cet arrêt ayant été signifié le 3 juillet 1975 à la dame Benet, le pourvoi est tardif et doit être déclaré irrecevable ;

PAR CES MOTIFS :

DÉCLARE IRRECEVABLE le pourvoi formé contre l'arrêt rendu le 27 mai 1975 par la Cour d'appel d'Aix-en-Provence.

(35) Composition of French court decisions

The French decision quoted below illustrates the *attendu que* -technique used by French and Belgian courts (cf. also a less formal application of this technique (*considerando que*) in the Argentinian decision below, no. 37). There, every paragraph in which the views of the parties and the facts provided by them are discussed, begins with the quoted formula. At times, this technique may be perceived as tiresome, especially when the *attendu que*-formula is used several times in one sentence as illustrated here by an excerpt from the decision of the French Supreme Court. Also the decision Dame Blum C. Dlle Lassus (quoted above as no. 33) uses the *attendu que*-technique. Some other courts such as the French *Conseil d'Etat* use the formula *considérant que* instead of *attendu que*, but the technique of text composition remains the same. The French Supreme Court, (*Court de cassation*, 1ère Chambre civile), in a decision rendered on July 4, 2007, no. 05–14918, formulated one of the main complaints of the appeal which it had to decide in two paragraphs following strictly the *attendu que*-technique:

> Attendu qu'il est fait grief à l'arrêt attaqué d'avoir rejeté la demande de sursis à statuer et d'avoir en conséquence déclaré exécutoires en France les décisions des juridictions suisses alors qu'une décision pénale, de nature à révéler que les décisions étrangères ordonnent l'exécution de conventions constituant l'instrument d'une infraction pénale, est susceptible d'influer sur l'instance civile en exequatur; qu'en refusant de surseoir à statuer au motif inopérant que la licéité des conventions fondant les condamnations ne pouvait être discutée au regard de l'ordre public français et que la validité de ces conventions ne pouvait être remise en cause au stade de l'exequatur, sans rechercher si la décision à intervenir sur l'action pénale était susceptible d'avoir une influence sur décision à intervenir sur la demande d'exequatur, la court d'appel a privé sa décision de base légale au regard des articles 4, alinéa 2, du Code de procédure pénale et 27 alinéa 1 de la Convention de Lugano du 16 septembre 1988 ;

Mais attendu qu'après avoir rappelé que le contrôle de la conformité des décisions suisses à l'ordre public international français est exclusive de leur révision au fond, l'arrêt retient à juste titre qu'un sursis à statuer sur le fondement de l'article 4, alinéa 2 du Code de procédure pénale ne pourrait être décidé qu'en cas d'incidence prouvée de la procédure pénale sur la licéité des engagements, souscrits par Y Congo à l'égard de X, fondant les condamnations prononcées par les décisions dont l'exequatur est demandé ; que l'arrêt relève que Y Congo, qui ne s'est pas constituée partie civile, n'apporte aucun élément sur l'état de la procédure pénale, dans laquelle MM. A... et B... aurait été mis en exament, portant sur des suspicions de versement de commissions au profit de personnes physiques autres que les persones morales en cause devant les juridictions suisses; que la court d'appel, qui avait constaté un engagement irrévocable de Y Congo à l'égard de X, dont la licéité ne pouvait être discutée au regard de la conception française de l'ordre publique international, dont la validité ne pouvait être mis en cause au stade de l'exequatur, et dont l'inexécution partielle par Y Congo avait été sanctionnée par les juridictions suisses à statuer dès lors que la République du Congo et Y Congo, sur lesquelles pesait la charge de la preuve, n'établissaient pas l'incidence de la procédure pénale sur l'instance civile; ...

PAR CES MOTIFS :

REJETTE les pourvois...

The structural split between *attendu que*-arguments and *mais attendu que*-arguments is marked in the text by grouping arguments in paragraphs. The technique may seem formalistic as it is exercised with rare consequence. In the decision of the French Supreme Court which follows this technique is strictly observed. It could however be that both decisions were written by the same judge. The contrasting argumentation or rather the grouping of arguments along the mentioned split prepares also here a negative decision for the requesting party:

Cour de cassation, 1ère chambre civile, March 27, 2007, no. 05–1048

Attendu que la société X fait grief à l'arrêt d'avoir appliqué le droit français à l'action en responsabilité engagée contre elle par la société d'assurance alors qu'en l'éspece la companie Z se prévalait exclusivement des manquements aux obligations découlant de la convention conclue entre la société X et l'armateur ; qu'en statuant comme ils l'ont fait, sans s'interroger au préalable sur le droit applicable à cette convention, les juges du fond ont privé leur décision de base légale au regard de l'article 3 du Code civil et de la règle de conflit de lois applicable en matière de responsabilité quasi-délictuelle ;

Mais attendu que l'arrêt relève que le manquement du X à ses obligations contractuelles vis-à-vis de l'armateur, a causé un préjudice dont la compagnie Z pouvait demander réparation; que l'action étant de nature délictuelle, la loi applicable au contrat entre la société de classification et l'armateur, d'ailleurs non invoquée devant les juges au fond, était sans incidence sur la détermination de la loi applicable à l'action ; que le moyen n'est pas fondé ;

...

PAR CES MOTIFS:

REJETTE les pourvois...

(36) Composition of Italian court decisions

Italian court decisions are structured less strictly than the French ones and come close to the German and Spanish court decisions. Arntz (2002: 35, 37) provides a formal textual structure of these decisions. However, their textual structure is still more rigid than the individualistic form and style of common law court opinions. Furthermore, as in the (IT) *massime di giurisprudenza,* which are also quoted in these Notes and Commented Materials under no. 21, over-long sentences occur with systematic regularity. In the decision rendered below in some relevant parts the Italian *Corte di Cassazione* had to decide the dispute between a French and an Italian enterprise concerning the appropriate jurisdiction for a claim regarding unpaid invoices.

Corte di Cassazione 27.9.2006 – n. 20887

Excerpts from the decision

Provvedendo sul ricorso, rilieva questo giudice di legitimità che deve essere dichiarato il defetto di giurisdizione del giudice italiano.

Al riguardo, si osserva preliminarmente che – contrariamente a quel che assume la società francese S. s.a. ed a quanto sostiene anche il P.M. nelle sue conclusioni – nella specie deve, ratione temporis, farsi applicazione della disciplina prevista dal Regolamento 44/2001 CE, che è entrata in vigore in data 1.3.2002, successivamente alla stipulazione dei due contratti per i quali è causa, ma anteriormente alla notificazione della citazione in data 15.5.2002.

Dispone, infatti, in proposito l'art. 66, primo comma, che "le disposizioni del presente Regolamento si applicano solo alle azioni proposte ed agli atti pubblici formati posteriormente alla sua entrata in vigore", per cui, dovendo il momento della proposizione della domanda essere determinate in rapporto al diritto processuale del foro adito, deve ritenersi che la domanda al giudice italiano, che è stata introdotta con l'atto di citazione notificato il 15.5.2002, rientra tra le "azioni proposte" successivamente all'entrata in vigore del Regolamento (obbligatorio per tutti gli Stati membri della Comunità Europea, fatta eccezione per la Danimarca nei previsti casi), la cui disciplina ha sostituito, quando alla "materia civile e commerciale", quella della Convenzione di Bruxelles relativamente alla competenza giurisdizionale ed alla esecuzione di decisioni nella predetta materia.

La questione di giurisdizione, in relazione al primo dei profili dedotti, deve essere esaminata con riguardo alla sussistenza della clausola di deroga pattizia a favore del giudice francese, deroga che, secondo la prospettazione della società ricorrente, dovrebbe derivare per le seguenti ragioni:

1) la clausola n. 11 di attribuzione delle controversie al giudice francese, inserta nelle condizioni generali del contratto predisposte dalla società francese, sarebbe stata accettata dalla società italiana per il fatto che, conoscendole, la società T. srl aveva dato successiva esecuzione al contratto;
2) le medesime condizioni generali erano riportate sul retro delle fatture, rimesse dalla società francese a quella italiana e da questa pagate, per cui la mancata formulazione di obiezioni al riguardo costituirebbe la prova dell'esistenza di un accordo sulla deroga della giurisdizione a favore del giudice francese;
3) la mancata espressa sottoscrizione della clausola da parte della società T. srl non impedirebbe l'operatività della deroga, poiché l'attribuzione di competenza al giudice francese dovrebbe farsi rientrare nell'ambito degli abituati rapporti commerciali tra le parti.

Premesso che in tema di giurisdizione questa Corte giudica anche del fatto e deve procedere all'apprezzamento diretto delle risultanze e degli atti di causa, in modo indipendente dalle deduzioni delle parti, si osserva che, nel caso in esame, la norma che disciplina il patto derogatorio è quella dell'art. 23 del Regolamento 44/2001 CE, che, con disposizione sostanzialmente analoga a quella dell'art. 17, primo comma, della Convenzione di Bruxelles 27.9.1968, stabilisce che la clausola attributiva di competenza "deve essere conclusa: a) per iscritto o oralmente con conferma scritta, o b) in una forma ammessa dalle pratiche che le parti hanno stabilito tra di loro, o c) nel commercio internazionale, in una forma ammessa da un uso che le parti conoscevano o avrebbero dovuto conoscere e che, in tale campo, è ampiamente conosciuto e regolarmente rispettato dalle parti di contratti dello stesso tipo nel ramo commerciale considerato"...

La questione di giurisdizione è, invece, fondata in relazione al secondo dei profili esposti dalla società ricorrente, la quale ha dedotto che il difetto di giurisdizione del giudice italiano, deve essere ritenuto in applicazione, comunque, della regola di cui all'art. 5 n. 1 del Regolamento 44/2001 CE, secondo cui nella materia contrattuale, analogamente alla previsione della Convenzione di Bruxelles (art. 5 n.1), consente all'attore di citare il convenuto, domiciliato nel territorio di uno Stato membro, davanti al giudice di un altro Stato membro se questo corrisponde con il "giudice del luogo in cui l'obbligazione dedotta in giudizio è stata o deve essere eseguita"...

Ritiene questa Corte che non si è realizzata nessuna delle tre previste ipotesi di patto derogatorio.

In accogliamento del ricorso va, pertanto, dichiarato il difetto di giurisdizione del giudice italiano.

La società resistente è condannata a pagare le spese del presente procedimento di cassazione nella misura indicata in dispositivo…

(37) Previfort S.A. c/ Banco de la Provincia de Buenos Aires (AR)

(Supreme Court of Argentina)

Recursos de hecho

Buenos Aires, 15 de junio de 2010

Vistos los autos : « Recursos de hecho deducidos por la actora y la demanda en la causa : Previfort S.A. c/ Banco de la Provincia de Buenos Aires s/ordinario », para decidir sobre su procedencia.

Considerando :

Que esta Corte comporte los fundamentos expuestos por la señora Procuradora Fiscal en su dictamen al que cabe remitirse en razón de brevedad.

Por ello, se hace lugar a la queja deducida por la demanda, se declara admisible el recurso extraordinario y se deja sin efecto la sentencia con el alcance indicado. Con costas. Vuelvan los autos al tribunal de origen a fin que, por medio de quien corresponda, proceda a dictar un nuevo fallo con arreglo a lo expressado.

Asimismo, se declara inoficioso el recurso interpuesto por la actora.

Agréguense ambas quejas al principal, las que se acumulan en este acto. Notifíquese y remítase. (Names of judges follow)

VOTO DEL SEÑOR PRESIDENTE DOCTOR DON RICARDO LUIS LORENZETTI

Considerando:

Que contra la sentencia de la Sala C de la Cámara Nacional de Apelaciones en lo Comercial que revocó la sentencia de primera instancia y condenó al Banco de la Provincia de Buenos Aires a pagar a Previfort S.A. la suma de $ 524.351,30 con más intereses, por los perjuicios ocasionados por el incumplimiento de un contrato de sindicatión de acciones de mando y bloqueo concertado entre todos los accionistas de "La Fortuna S.A. de Seguros de Retiro", tanto la parte actora como la demanda interpusieron sus respectivos recursos extraordinarios cuyas denegationes motivaron sendas quejas.

Que para así decidir, el a quo sostuvo que la magistrada de grado había resuelto la cuestión desde una óptica societaria, en lugar de considerarlo como un incumplimiento contractual del que derivaría el derecho indemnizatorio pretendido. En este sentido, agregó que los pactos de sindicación de acciones, como contratos parasociales, presentaban perfiles que solamente concernían a quienes son parte en ellos y que, en tal contexto, las impugnaciones debían dirigerse contra las singulares actuaciones de los sindicados, sin que las decisiones adoptadas en el marco del sindicato adquieran relevancia en el plano societario en tanto no persiguiera un objeto ilícito, se agravie la causa societaria o el interés social o se constituya en un mero instrumento para el abuso del derecho o el fraude...

Por ello, y habiendo dictaminado la señora Procuradora Fiscal, se declara procedente la queja deducida por la demanda, admisible el recurso extraordinario interpuesto con los alcances indicados, y se deja sin efecto la sentencia apelada. Con costas. Asimismo, se declara inoficioso el recurso interpuesto por la actora. Vuelvan los autos al tribunal del origen a fin de que, por intermedio de quien corresponda, se dicte una nueva sentencia con arreglo a lo expressado. Agréguense ambas quejas al principal, las que se acumulan en este acto. Reintégrense los depósitos. RICARDO LUIS LORENZETTI

(38) Composition of German court decisions

In Germany, the so-called juridic style is cultivated in the academia and in juridical institutions. It is perceived by the jurists as being two-fold. It consists of the style of legal opinions, (D) *Gutachtenstil,* and the style of court decisions, (D) *Urteilsstil.* The (D) *Urteilsstil* is accomplished through the reversal of the (D) *Gutachtenstil.* The difference between both varieties of the juridic style, however, seems to be not that much one of style but of the form of reasoning. Whereas (D) *Gutachtenstil,* which is used mostly by law students in their written exams, proceeds in an interogative mood, (D) *Urteilsstil,* in which court decisions are written, is of assertive nature. The (D) *Gutachtenstil*-opinion may read, e.g.: *A could have a claim against B for payment of the price according to Art. 433BGB. This requires a valid sale contract between the parties. The parties may have concluded a sale contract in that they exchanged e-mails.* In turn, the same text written in (D) *Urteilsstil* would read: *A has a claim against B for payment of the price according to Art. 433 BGB as there is a valid sale contract between the parties. Through the exchange of successive and mutually related e-mails the parties agreed upon the sale of a good.* The form of reasoning of the 'juridic style' has its basis in medieval rhetoric of disputation. Meanwhile, it is also particularly gratifying to apply Toulmin's argumentation model upon such legal-argumentative constructs. Toulmin's model, which has been prepared for the description of daily argumentation, fits perfectly the legal reasoning in court opinions. In the model, the data that leads to a conclusion is subject to a modifier. The modifier is subject to a warrant that may be backed by additional arguments as well as to a possible argumentative rebuttal.

The (D) *Urteilsstil* is illustrated by the following court opinion.

OLG Hamburg 3.3.2006–5 U 1/05

Excerpts from the motives of the judgment: Die Parteien streiten darum, ob die Klägerinnen berechtigt sind, Wein unter der Bezeichnung REVIAN's zu vertreiben. Die Klägerinnen gehören zu der Steiner-Racke-Dujardin Getränkegruppe, die Beklagte ist eine französische Aktiengesellschaft mit Sitz in dem Kurort Evian-les-Bains in den französischen Alpen. Die Beklagte ist u. a. Inhaberin einer deutschen Wortmarke EVIAN mit Priorität vom 11.11.1985 für Mineralwasser. Sie vertreibt seit ca. 40 Jahren unter dieser Bezeichnung ein stilles Mineralwasser auch in Deutschland. Dabei verwendet sie auf den Flaschen eine Schreibweise in kleinen Buchstaben und mit einer Bergkulisse als Hintergrund.

Gestützt auf ihre deutsche Marke EVIAN hat die Beklagte in einem vorangegangenem, rechtskräftig abgeschlossenen Rechtsstreit gegen die Klägerinnen u. a. ein Verbot erwirkt, die Bezeichnungen REVIAN zur Kennzeichnung von Wein zu verwenden und außerdem in die Löschung weiterer für die Klägerin zu 1 eingetragener Marken einzuwilligen, nämlich REWIAN und REVAN.

Bereits während des noch laufenden Rechtsstreits, nämlich jedenfalls seit September 1999, haben die Klägerinnen die Kennzeichnung ihrer Weine auf REVIAN's umgestellt. Für diese Bezeichnung haben die Klägerinnen zwei deutsche Wort/Bildmarken mit Priorität vom 1.10.98 und 14.7.98 eintragen lassen. Ferner haben die Klägerinnen am 21.9.1998 eine der letzteren Marke entsprechende Gemeinschaftsbildmarke angemeldet. Der gegen diese Marke von der Beklagten erhobene Widerspruch ist von der Widerspruchsabteilung des Harmonisierungsamtes am 23. 11. 2001 zurückgewiesen worden.

Die von der Beklagten eingelegte Beschwerde hat die Beschwerdekammer des Harmonisierungsamtes am 22. 7. 2005 zurückgewiesen. Über die hiergegen von der Beklagten eingereichte Klage hat das Europäische Gericht erster Instanz bislang nicht entschieden. Mit Schreiben vom 13. 2. 2003 forderte die Beklagte die Klägerinnen auf, die Benutzung der Bezeichnung REVIAN's für Weine zu unterlassen, da dies gegen das Urteil des Landgerichts Hamburg vom 19.3.1997 verstoße. Außerdem verlangte sie Auskunft über den Umfang der Benutzungshandlungen. Daraufhin erhoben die Klägerinnen gegen die Beklagte Klage auf Feststellung, dass die Beklagte aus dem Urteil vom 19.3.1997 keine Ansprüche wegen der Verwendung der Bezeichnung REVIAN's herleiten könne. Die Beklagte erhob Hilfswiderklage mit folgenden Anträgen:

1. die Klägerinnen zu verurteilen, es bei Meidung der gesetzlichen Ordnungsmittel zu unterlassen, die Bezeichnung "REVIAN's" zur Kennzeichnung eines Weines im geschäftlichen Verkehr zu verwenden, so gekennzeichneten Wein anzubieten, in den Verkehr zu bringen oder zu den genannten Zwecken zu besitzen, unter der Marke „REVIAN's" ein- und auszuführen, die Bezeichnung „REVIAN's" in Geschäftspapieren oder in der Werbung zu benutzen;
2. festzustellen, dass die Klägerinnen als Gesamtschuldner verpflichtet sind, der Beklagten allen Schaden zu ersetzen, der der Beklagten aus der unter Ziffer 1. bezeichneten Zuwiderhandlung entstanden ist und/oder noch entstehen wird;
3. die Klägerinnen als Gesamtschuldner zu verurteilen, der Beklagten Auskunft zu erteilen über den Umfang der unter Ziffer 1. beschriebenen Zuwiderhandlungen in Form einer zeitlich geordneten Aufstellung, insbesondere der Verkaufsmenge, der erzielten Verkaufspreise, der Gestehungskosten und des Gewinns des unter der Bezeichnung „REVIAN's" verkauften Weins und der dafür geschalteten Werbung, geordnet nach Werbeträgern und Verbreitungsdatum.

Mit seit dem 30.5.2004 rechtskräftigen Teilurteil vom 21.4.2004 hat das Landgericht der Feststellungsklage stattgegeben. Mit Schlussurteil vom 25.11.2004 hat es auch der Widerklage weitgehend stattgegeben, allerdings alle Ansprüche auf Auskunft und Schadensersatzfeststellung auf die Zeit ab dem 30.5.2001 beschränkt. Wegen der Einzelheiten des erstinstanzlichen Partei- vortrags wird auf den Tatbestand des Schlussurteils Bezug genommen...

(39) Samples of Japanese court decisions

Some samples of Japanese court decisions may indicate differences in the legal argumentation there. However, as long as systematic research into this issue is missing, it is difficult to generalize this first impression. The impression of a cultural difference may also result from the English translations, here quoted after Upham (1990: 625).

(A divorce case) Inoue v. Inoue (Japan's Supreme Court Third Petty Bench Feb. 19, 1952 6 Minshuu 110)

Reasons: As found by the High Court, the Appellee's conduct in pouring water on the Appellant and beating him with a broomstick is truly vulgar and improper. It is obvious however, that the reason for this behavior was the Appellant's sexual relation with "S" resulting in her pregnancy. The Appellant reaped what he sowed, as it were the Appellee's behavior as found by the High Court was all excusable and does not constitute a conduct so cruel and humiliating that cohabitation is intolerable as set forth in Art. 813 of the former Civil Code.

Another case concerns the so-called Minamata-disease (mercury poisoning caused by eating fish which was contaminated by effluents from a chemical plant) and state agencies responsibility for injuries. The court argumentation in it seems to differ to a degree from the Western patterns:

Re. Kawamoto Teruo (Tokyo High Court 1977, June 14):

Whether or not this case constitutes an abuse of the right of public prosecution and should therefore be dismissed will be discussed below. What is distinctive about this case is that the claim of bias which constitutes the essential part of the appeal does not rest on the comparison of the suspects in this case with suspects in another case of the same kind. Instead, the discrimination lies in the manner of dealing with the two parties involved. In other words, there is a so-called assailant's side and a victim's side in a pollution incident. The discrimination in this case is further complicated by the fact that pollution can be called a fatal contradiction in present day society.

(40) Plessy v. Fergusson (U.S.)

Excerpts from the U.S. Supreme Court decision Plessy v. Ferguson (163 U.S. 537 1896).

(...) The petitioner was a citizen of the United States and a resident of the state of Louisiana, of mixed descent, in the proportion of seven-eighths Caucasian and one-eighth

African blood; that the mixture of colored blood was not discernible in him, and that he was entitled to every recognition, right, privilege, and immunity secured to the citizens of the United States of the white race by its constitution and laws; that on June 7, 1892, he engaged and paid for a first-class passage on the East Louisiana Railway, from New Orleans to Covington, in the same state, and thereupon entered a passenger train, and took possession of a vacant seat in a coach where passengers of the white race were accommodated; that such railroad company was incorporated by the laws of Louisiana as a common carrier, and was not authorized to distinguish between citizens according to their race, but, notwithstanding this, petitioner was required by the conductor, under penalty of ejection from said train and imprisonment, to vacate the said coach, and occupy another seat, in a coach assigned by said company for persons not of white race, and for no other reason than that petitioner was of a colored race; that, upon petitioner's refusal to comply with such order, he was, with the aid of a police officer, forcibly ejected from said coach, and hurried off to, and imprisoned in, the parish jail of New Orleans, and there held to answer a charge made by such officer to the effect that he was guilty of having criminally violated an act of the general assembly of the state, approved July 10, 1890, in such case made and provided...

By the fourteenth amendment, all persons born or naturalized in the United States, and subject to the jurisdiction thereof, are made citizens of the United States and of the state wherein they reside; and the states are forbidden from making or enforcing any law which shall abridge the privileges or immunities of citizens of the United States, or shall deprive any person of life, liberty, or property without due process of law, or deny to any person within their jurisdiction the equal protection of the laws...

The object of the amendment was undoubtedly to enforce the absolute equality of the two races before the law, but, in the nature of things, it could not have been intended to abolish distinctions based upon color, or to enforce social, as distinguished from political, equality, or a commingling of the two races upon terms unsatisfactory to either. Laws permitting, and even requiring, their separation, in places where they are liable to be brought into contact, do not necessarily imply the inferiority of either race to the other, and have been generally, if not universally, recognized as within the competency of the state legislatures in the exercise of their police power. The most common instance of this is connected with the establishment of separate schools for white and colored children, which have been held to be a valid exercise of the legislative power even by courts of states where the political rights of the colored race have been longest and most earnestly enforced...

In his dissenting opinion Justice Harlan wrote:

It was said in argument that the statute of Louisiana does not discriminate against either race, but prescribes a rule applicable alike to white and colored citizens. But this argument does not meet the difficulty. Every one knows that the statute in question has its origin in the purpose, not so much to exclude white persons from railroad cars occupied by blacks, as to exclude colored people from coaches occupied by or assigned to white persons. Railroad corporations of Louisiana did not make discrimination among whites in the matter of accommodation for travellers. The thing to accomplish was, under the guise of giving equal accommodation for whites and blacks, to compel the latter to keep to themselves while traveling in railroad passenger coaches. No one would be so wanting in candor as to assert the contrary. The fundamental objection, therefore, to the statute, is that it interferes with the personal freedom of citizens. 'Personal liberty,' it has been well said, 'consists in the power of locomotion, of changing situation, or removing one's person to whatsoever places one's own inclination may direct, without imprisonment or restraint, unless by due course of law.' If a white man and a black man choose to occupy the same public conveyance on a public highway, it is their right to do so; and no government, proceeding alone on grounds of race, can prevent it without infringing the personal liberty of each.

(41) Brown v. Board of Education (U.S.)

Excerpts from the U.S. Supreme Court decision Brown v. Board of Education (347 U.S. 483 1954):

> In each of the cases, minors of the Negro race, through their legal representatives, seek the aid of the courts in obtaining admission to the public schools of their community on a nonsegregated basis. In each instance, they had been denied admission to schools attended by white children under laws requiring or permitting segregation according to race. This segregation was alleged to deprive the plaintiffs of the equal protection of the laws under the Fourteenth Amendment. In each of the cases other than the Delaware case, a three-judge federal district court denied relief to the plaintiffs on the so-called "separate but equal" doctrine announced by this Court in Plessy v. Ferguson, 163 U.S. 537. Under that doctrine, equality of treatment is accorded when the races are provided substantially equal facilities, even though these facilities be separate...
>
> Segregation of white and colored children in public schools has a detrimental effect upon the colored children. The impact is greater when it has the sanction of the law, for the policy of separating the races is usually interpreted as denoting the inferiority of the negro group. A sense of inferiority affects the motivation of a child to learn. Segregation with the sanction of law, therefore, has a tendency to retard the educational and mental development of negro children and to deprive them of some of the benefits they would receive in a racially integrated school system...
>
> We conclude that, in the field of public education, the doctrine of "separate but equal" has no place. Separate educational facilities are inherently unequal. Therefore, we hold that the plaintiffs and others similarly situated for whom the actions have been brought are, by reason of the segregation complained of, deprived of the equal protection of the laws guaranteed by the Fourteenth Amendment.

Likewise, the *Declaration of Independence* (1776) provided the linguistic pattern for the doctrine of *separate but equal* through its reference to the *separate and equal station* that has to be assumed by prospective Americans. The elevated diction that characterizes the doctrine has its rhetoric roots in the coinage of the overly sentimental style of the Declaration. Thomas Jefferson drafted 1775 the *Declaration of Independence* that includes an example of intertextuality of *separate but equal*:

> When we decided that we would dissolve the political bands that connected us with Britain and that we would assume among the powers of the earth the *separate but equal* station that we claim through the Laws of Nature and of Nature's God, then since we decently respect the opinions of mankind, we decided that we would declare why we do so. These truths are self-evident – we are all equal in our creation, we derive from God certain Rights that we intend to keep, and among those rights, we include Life, Liberty and the opportunity to make ourselves Happy.

(42) Supreme Court's order in Brown v. Board of Education (U.S)

The court order in Brown v. Board of Education reads as follows:

> Supreme Court of the United States
> No. 1 --, October Term, 1954
>
> Oliver Brown, Mrs. Richard Lawton, Mrs. Sadie Emmanuel et al., Appellants
>
> vs. Board of Education of Topeka, Shawnee County, Kansas, et.al
>
> Appeal from the United States District Court for the District of Kansas.
>
> This cause came to be heard on the transcript of the record from the United States District Court for the District of Kansas, and was argued by counsel.
>
> On consideration whereof, it is ordered and adjudged by this court that the judgment of the said District Court in this cause be, and by the same is hereby, reversed with costs; and that this cause be, and the same is hereby, remanded to the said District Court to take such proceedings and enter such orders and decrees consistent with the opinion of this Court as are necessary and proper to admit to public schools on a racially non-discriminatory basis with all deliberate speed the parties to this case.
>
> Per Mr. Chief Justice Warren, May 31, 1955 (signature)

J. Rosen (2013: 33) mentions that when the U.S. Supreme Court in 1954 handed down its opinion Brown v. Board of Education, Chief Justice Warren "insisted that it be written as plainly as possible, so that it could be printed in newspapers and understood by all American citizens."

(43) Racist ordinances (U.S.)

(US) Greenville city ordinance requiring separation of the races in restaurants (Code of Greenville, 1953, § 31–8, as amended in 1958, and still in force 1960:

"It shall be unlawful for any person owning, managing or controlling any hotel, restaurant, café, eating house, boarding-house or similar establishment to furnish meals to white persons and colored persons in the same room, or at the same table, or at the same counter; provided however, that meals may be served to white persons and colored persons in the same room where separate facilities are furnished. Separate facilities shall be interpreted to mean:

(a) Separate eating utensils and separate dishes for the serving of food, all of which shall be distinctly marked by some appropriate color scheme or otherwise;
(b) Separate tables, counters or booths;
(c) A distance of at least thirty-five feet shall be maintained between the area where white and colored persons are served;
(d) The area referred to in subsection (c) above shall not be vacant but shall be occupied by the usual display counters and merchandise found in a business concern of a similar nature;
(e) A separate facility shall be maintained and used for the cleaning of eating utensils and dishes furnished the two races."

(US) Code of Durham (1947), c. 13, § 42:

"In all licensed restaurants, public eating places and 'weenie shops' where persons of the white and colored races are permitted to be served with, and eat food, and are allowed to congregate, there shall be provided separate rooms for the separate accommodation of each race. The partition between such rooms shall be constructed of wood, plaster or brick or like material, and shall reach from floor to the ceiling. Any person violating this section shall, upon conviction pay a fine of ten dollars and each day's violation thereof shall constitute a separate and distinct offense."

(44) Nazi-Germany Racist law

Inhuman law, of which the following text is a specimen, is designed textually in a classical linguistic shape of a *statute*, (D) *Gesetz*. It tends to strengthen its legal appearance also through the use of legislative techniques such as regulatory precision, to be seen particularly in sec. 4 of the statute below (cf. Galdia 2014: 203–208). Particularly informative about the language of the Nazi regime in Germany remains the classical work by Viktor Klemperer (1969). Jurists' involvement in the application of inhuman law is documented in works by Ingo Müller (2014) and Richard Weisberg (1992: 127–175). For discursive mechanisms responsible for the emergence of evil in society cf. Hannah Arendt (1968). Traditional legal theory perceives every piece of legislation as law as long as it has been enacted in appropriate procedures. In the discursively oriented legal linguistics it would be pertinent to ask whether the concepts of law and of statute discovered by the critical discourse theory are compatible with this sort of regulation.

Reichsgesetzblatt, Jahrgang 1935, Part I

Gesetz zum Schutze des deutschen Blutes und der deutschen Ehre (dated September 15, 1935)

Durchdrungen von der Erkenntnis, dass die Reinheit des deutschen Blutes die Voraussetzung für den Fortbestand des Deutschen Volkes ist, und beseelt von dem unbeugsamen Willen, die Deutsche Nation für alle Zukunft zu sichern, hat der Reichstag einstimmig das folgende Gesetz beschlossen, das hiermit verkündet wird:

§1 (1) Eheschließungen zwischen Juden und Staatsangehörigen deutschen oder artverwandten Blutes sind verboten. Trotzdem geschlossene Ehen sind nichtig, auch wenn sie zur Umgehung dieses Gesetzes im Ausland geschlossen sind. (2) Die Nichtigkeitsklage kann nur der Staatsanwalt erheben.

§2 Außerehelicher Verkehr zwischen Juden und Staatsangehörigen deutschen oder artverwandten Blutes ist verboten.

§3 Juden dürfen weibliche Staatsangehörige deutschen oder artverwandten Blutes unter 45 Jahren in ihrem Haushalt nicht beschäftigen.

§4 (1) Juden ist das Hissen der Reichs- und Nationalflagge und das Zeigen der Reichsfarben verboten. (2) Dagegen ist ihnen das Zeigen der jüdischen Farben gestattet. Die Ausübung dieser Befugnis steht unter staatlichem Schutz.

§5 (1) Wer dem Verbot des §1 zuwiderhandelt, wird mit Zuchthaus bestraft. (2) Der Mann, der dem Verbot des §2 zuwiderhandelt, wird mit Gefängnis oder Zuchthaus bestraft. (3) Wer den Bestimmungen des §§ 3 oder 4 zuwiderhandelt, wird mit Gefängnis bis zu einem Jahr und mit Geldstrafe oder mit einer dieser Strafen bestrafft.

§6 Der Reichsminister des Innern erlässt im Einvernehmen mit dem Stellvertreter des Führers und dem Reichsminister der Justiz die zur Durchführung und Ergänzung des Gesetzes erforderlichen Rechts- und Verwaltungsvorschriften.

§7 Das Gesetz tritt am Tage nach der Verkündung, §3 jedoch erst am 1. Januar 1936 in Kraft.

Nürnberg, den 15. September 1935, am Reichsparteitag der Freiheit.

Der Führer und Reichkanzler (signature)

(45) Frigaliment v. B.N.S. (U.S.)

Frigaliment Importing Co. v. B.N.S. International Sales Corp.
190 F. Supp. 116 (S.D.N.Y. 1960):

Friendly, Circuit Judge. Plaintiff says 'chicken' means a young chicken, suitable for broiling and frying. Defendant says 'chicken' means any bird of the genus that meets contract specification on weight and quality, including what it calls 'stewing chickens' and plaintiff pejoratively terms 'fowl'. To support its claim, plaintiff sends a number of volleys over the net; defendant essays to return them and adds a few serves of its own. Assuming that both parties were acting in good faith, the case nicely illustrates Oliver Wendell Holmes's remark "that the making of a contract depends not on the agreement of two minds in one intention, but on the agreement of two sets of external signs – not on the parties' having meant the same thing but on having said the same thing." Since the word 'chicken' standing alone is ambiguous, I turn first to see whether the contract itself offers any aid to its interpretation.

Plaintiff's first contention hinges on an exchange of cablegrams which preceded the formal contracts. After testing the market price, plaintiff accepted, and sent defendant a confirmation. These and subsequent cables between plaintiff and defendant, which laid the basis for the additional quantities under the first and for all of the second contract, were predominantly in German, although they used the English word 'chicken'. Defendant's agent testified that when asked plaintiff's agent what kind of chicken were wanted, received the answer "any kind of chicken". Defendant relies on conduct by the plaintiff after the first shipment had been received. Defendant argues that if plaintiff was sincere in thinking it was entitled to young chickens, plaintiff would not have allowed the shipment under the second contract to go forward.

Plaintiff's next contention is that there was a definite trade usage that 'chicken' meant 'young chicken'. Here there was no proof of actual knowledge of the alleged usage; indeed it is quite plain that defendant's belief was to the contrary. Plaintiff endeavored to establish such a usage by the testimony of witnesses. However, one witness stated that a careful businessman protected himself by using 'broiler' when that was what he wanted and 'fowl' when he wished older birds. An employee of a company that publishes a daily market report on the poultry trade gave his view that the trade meaning of chicken was "broilers and fryers." Defendant provided a witness that said that in the trade, 'chicken' would encompass all the various classifications of chicken. Defendant also provided a regulation of the Department of Agriculture that defined 'chicken' as various classes including "Broiler or Fryer, Roaster, Capon, Stag, Hen or Stewing chicken or Fowl".

When all the evidence is reviewed, it is clear defendant believed it could comply with the contracts by delivering stewing chickens. Plaintiff asserts that it is equally plain that plaintiff's own subjective intent was to obtain broilers and fryers. Because plaintiff has the burden of showing that 'chicken' was used in the narrower rather than in the broader sense, and this it has not sustained, judgment shall be entered dismissing the complaint.

(46) OHG v. Kolodny (U.S.)

OHG v. Kolodny (NY County, Supreme Court 1st Jud. Dept., IA Part II, 1992):

Baer, Justice Plaintiff is an auction house dealing in works of art. Defendant is an art dealer. His gallery has purchased fine art from the plaintiff over the years, presumably with happier results than in this case. In 1988, defendant received, in New York, a catalogue sent by the plaintiff that described works of art that would be put for auction by plaintiff. Among these, defendant says, was a "bronze sculpture produced by Hilaire Germain Edgar Degas before 1990," to wit, the "Dancer Gazing". Plaintiff phoned defendant in New York during the auction and solicited a bid for the "Dancer". Without ever having set eyes on the right foot or any other part of the sculpture, plaintiff offered a bid of DM 220,000 and triumphed. Defendant was never told the identity of the consignor of the Degas. Defendant wired to plaintiff the purchase price and a commission.

The "Dancer" arrived shortly thereafter in New York, where she immediately did a pirouette and departed for London. Defendant wished to let no grass grow under either of his feet; he would put the Degas up for resale at Christie's and would, he was confident, earn a great deal of not bronze, but sterling. Eagle eyes at Christie's surveyed the work. Defendant was told, to his horror, that Christie's suspected that the statue was ersatz, in a word, a fake. Defendant contacted Herr Hanstein and advised that his heart was heavy and his wallet, he was afraid, too light. Defendant sought a refund.

Defendant allegedly secured the agreement of plaintiff that the "Dancer" would be given the once or twice over by the world's foremost expert of Degas Bronzes, whose determination would be binding. The statue was brought to New York, where an expert, like many other world's foremost experts, resides. His conclusion unfortunately was that the work was not genuine.

A German court decided in favor of plaintiff, rejected defendant's contention that he was entitled to an offset for the purchase price of the pseudo-Degas. The court held that plaintiff had disclaimed any warranty as to the authenticity of the "Dancer"; that since the job of an auction house is to sell as a commission agent many items owned by others, the authenticity of which the auctioneer cannot readily confirm, disclaimers do not violate the law; and that defendant in his letter on the Riopelle has disavowed any offset.

After plaintiff launched its "Blitzkrieg" here in New York, defendant responded with a lawsuit of his own. Defendant seeks to recover the purchase price for the ill-fated Degas. Defendant, relying inter alia upon Article 15 of the New York Arts and Cultural Affairs Law (the "Art Law"), contends that plaintiff is liable for having provided inaccurate information about the Degas and that the German judgment contravenes New York public policy, as a consequence of which its enforcement in favor of plaintiff is *verboten*. This argument, while creative and well presented, must fail.

CPLR Sec. 5304(b)(4) provides that a monetary judgment of a foreign country need not be recognized by New York if the cause of action on which the judgment is based is "repugnant to the public policy of the state". Normally, the judgment of a foreign nation will be given effect. Differences between the laws of New York and those of many sovereign nations of the world are likely to arise often, but such differences alone cannot constitute a violation of public policy. As Judge Cardozo said, "We are not so provincial as to say that every solution of a problem is wrong because we deal with it otherwise at home". Were we New Yorkers to be overly provincial, we might well inspire foreign nations to reject enforcement of New York judgments, precisely the opposite of the purpose Article 53 was created to achieve and an outcome particularly undesirable as the economy of this country grows every day more intertwined with those of other nations.

The German court applied German law in this case. This is not unreasonable since the auction occurred in Germany and defendant placed his bid during a telephone call with the auction house in Germany. In addition, plaintiff's conditions of sale stated that legal relations between plaintiff and the bidder would be governed by German law. Defendant appeared in the German action, defended, and lost. There is, of course, no claim that German law and procedures are unfair and unworthy of respect here.

The Germans are less Bismarckian than defendant contends. German law, as exemplified by the decision of the Cologne court in this case, is not indifferent to the general sale of fakes by art merchants. The court relied upon the warranty exclusion that formed a condition of sale. Enforcement of the German judgment would not undermine the public interest, public confidence in law or security for individual rights, nor violate fundamental notions of what is decent and fair. The German judgment is enforceable.

(47) U.S. v. Haggar Apparel (U.S.)

U.S. v. Haggar Apparel Company (526 U.S. 380 1999):

Kennedy, J. The case concerns regulations relating to the customs classification of certain imported goods issued by the United States Customs Service. The question is whether these regulations are entitled to judicial deference in a refund suit brought in the Court of International Trade. Contrary to the position of that Court and the Court of Appeals for the Federal Circuit, we hold the regulation in question is subject to the analysis required by Chevron U.S.A. Inc. v. Natural Resources Defense Council, Inc., and that if it is a reasonable interpretation and implementation of an ambiguous statutory provision, it must be given judicial deference.

Respondent Haggar Apparel Co. designs, manufactures and markets apparel for men. This matter arises from a refund proceeding for duties imposed on men's trousers shipped by respondent to this country from an assembly plant it controlled in Mexico. The fabric had been cut in the United States and then shipped to Mexico, along with the thread, buttons and zippers necessary to complete the garments. There the trousers were sewn and reshipped to the United States. If that had been the full extent of it, there would be no dispute, for if there were mere assembly without other steps, all agree that imported garments would have been eligible for the duty exemption which respondent claims.

Respondent, however, in the Government's view, added one another step at the Mexican plant: permapressing. Permapressing is designed to maintain the garment's crease in the desired place and to avoid other creases or wrinkles that detract from its proper appearance. The Customs Service claimed the baking was an added process in addition to assembly, and denied a duty exemption; respondent claimed the baking was simply part of the assembly process, or, in the words of the controlling statute, an "operation incidental to the assembly process". After being denied the exemption it sought for the permapressed articles, respondent brought suit for refund in the Court of International Trade. The court declined to treat the regulation as controlling. The court ruled in favor of respondent. On review, the Court of Appeals for the Federal Circuit declined to analyze the regulation under Chevron, and affirmed.

The statute on which respondent relies, Section 9802, provides importers a partial exemption from duties otherwise imposed. The relevant regulation interpreting the statute with respect to permapressed articles provides as follows:

Any significant process, operation, or treatment other than assembly whose primary purpose is the fabrication, completion, physical or chemical improvement of a component, or which is not related to the assembly process, whether, or not it effects a substantial transformation of the article, shall not be regarded as incidental to the assembly and shall preclude the application of the exemption to such article. The following are examples of operations not considered incidental to the assembly:

(4) Chemical treatment of components or assembled articles to impart new characteristics, such as a showerproofing, permapressing, sanforizing, dying or bleaching of textiles.

The Customs Service (which is within the Treasury Department) is charged with the classification of imported goods under the proper provision of the tariff schedules in the first instance. In addition, the Secretary is directed by statute to "establish and promulgate such rules and regulations not inconsistent with the law...as may be necessary to secure a just, impartial and uniform appraisement of imported merchandise and the classification and assessment of duties thereon at the various ports of entry."

For the reasons we have given, the statutes authorizing customs classification regulations of an administering agency warrant judicial deference. We turn to respondent's second major contention, that the statutes governing the reviewing authority of the Court of International Trade in classification cases displace this customary framework. The Court of Appeals held in this case, and in previous cases presenting the issue, that these regulations were not entitled to deference because the Court of International Trade is charged to "reach the correct decision" in determining the proper classification of goods. The whole point of regulations such as these, however, is to ensure that the statute is applied in a consistent and proper manner. Deference to an agency's expertise in construing a statutory command is not inconsistent with reaching a correct decision. If the agency's statutory interpretation fills a gap or defines a term in a way that is reasonable in light of the legislature's revealed design, we give that judgment controlling weight.

The customs regulations may not be disregarded. Application of the Chevron framework is the beginning of the legal analysis. Like other courts, the Court of International Trade must, when appropriate, give customs regulations Chevron deference.

The judgment is vacated and the case is remanded for further proceedings consistent with this opinion.

The U.S. Court of Appeals for the Federal Circuit affirmed the above decision (U.S. v. Haggar Apparel Company, 222 F.3d 1337 Fed.Cir. 2000). The U.S. Supreme Court refused to grant certiorari in this case, so that the decision is final. The difference between *incidental* and *substantive* has been discussed and solved in the U.S. Supreme Court decision McCullough v. Maryland from 1819. In it, the Chief Justice John Marshall posed the famous question whether the Congress had the power to incorporate a bank. The part of the decision interesting here reads as follows: "The power of creating a corporation, though appertaining to sovereignty, is not, like the power of making war, or levying taxes, or of regulating commerce, a great substantive and independent power, which cannot be implied *as incidental to* other powers, or used as a means of executing them. It is never the end for which other powers are exercised, but a means by which other objects are accomplished. No contributions are made to charity for the sake of an incorporation, but a corporation is created to administer the charity; no seminary of learning is instituted in order to be incorporated, but the corporate character is conferred to subserve the purposes of education. No city was ever built with the sole object of being incorporated, but is incorporated as affording the best means of being well governed. The power of creating a corporation is never used for its own sake, but for the purpose of effecting something else. No sufficient reason is, therefore, perceived, why it may not pass *as incidental to* those powers which are expressly given, if it be a direct mode of executing them." (emphasis added) As can be seen from the following text sample, *'incidental'* is used as a catch all word: "The Act...empowers the Home Secretary to regulate the procedures on application for admission into a retreat, the medial treatment, and other matters *incidental* to the due execution of the Act."

(48) Rollerblade v. U.S. (U.S.)

Rollerblade, Inc. v. U.S. (282 F.3d 1349 Fed.Cir. 2002):

Rader, Circuit Judge. Rollerbade, Inc. (Rollerblade) appeals from a summary judgment of the United States Court of International Trade affirming the United States Customs Service (Customs) classification of imported in-line roller skating protective gear under subheading 9506.99.6080 (99.6080) of the Harmonized Tariff Schedules of the United States (HTSUS). Because Customs correctly classified the imports, this court affirms. The imports in this case are in-line roller skating protective gear, such as knee pads, elbow pads, and wrist guards. Customs classified the imported protective gear as residual "other" sports equipment under subheading 99.6080 of the HTSUS, which carries a duty rate of 4% ad valorem. Rollerblade appealed to the Court of International Trade, arguing that Customs should have classified the protective gear as "accessories" under subheading 9506.70.2090. HTSUS subheading 70.2090 carries a 0% duty rate. Rollerblade sought this "accessory" classification because the protected gear was designed, tested, manufactured and marketed solely for use with in-line roller skates.

The Court of International Trade affirmed the Customs classification based primarily on its interpretation of the dictionary meaning of the term "accessory". According to the trail court, an accessory under subheading 70.2090 must be "of" or "to" the article (roller skates) listed in the heading, not "of" or "to" the activity (roller skating) for which the article is used. The trial court found that the protective gear had a direct relationship to the activity of roller skating, but not to the HTSUS heading, namely roller skates. Hence, the trial court affirmed Custom's refusal to classify Rollerblade's protective gear under subheading 70.2090 as an "accessory" to roller skates. Moreover, on summary judgment, the Court of International Trade concluded that Customs properly classified the protective gear under the residual "other" (sports equipment) subheading 99.6080.

Classification of goods under the HTSUS entails both ascertaining the proper meaning of specific terms in the tariff provision and determining whether the merchandise subject to tariffs comes within the description of those HTSUS terms. When reviewing whether the imports fit within those terms, this court uses a clear error standard. Universal Elecs., Inc. v. United States, 112 F.3d 488, 491 (Fed. Cir. 1997). When the HTSUS does not define a tariff term, the term receives its "common and popular meaning." E.M. Chems. v. United States, 920 F.2d 910,913 (Fed.Cir.1990). To determine a term's common meaning, a court may consult "dictionaries, scientific authorities, and other reliable information sources." C.J. Tower & Sons v. United States, 69 C.C.P.A. 128, 673 F.2d 1268, 1271 (CCPA 1982). Like the trial court, this court also observes that HTSUS offers no definition for the term "accessory". Thus, the trial court correctly consulted the common (dictionary) meaning of the term. As the Court of International Trade found, dictionary definitions indicate that an "accessory" must bear a direct relationship to the primary article that it accessorizes. In this case, under subheading 70.2090, the article accessorized is roller skates, not the general activity of roller skating. Moreover, as found by the trial court, the protective gear lacks a direct relationship to the roller skates. The protective gear does not directly act on the roller skates at all. Unlike a roller skate part or accessory, the protective gear does not directly affect the skates' operation. Thus, based on the common meaning of "accessory" and the language of subheading 70.2090, this court sustains the trial court's conclusion that Rollerblade's imported protective gear is not a roller skate accessory. Rollerblade argues that the protective gear is, alternatively, "parts" of the roller skates. Rollerblade would classify the protective gear as roller skate parts because it contributes to the safe and effective operation of the skates and functions by design solely with the skates. A "part" is "an essential element or constituent; integral portion which can be separated, replaced, etc." Webster's New World Dictionary 984 (3d College Ed. 1988). Thus, based on the common meaning, the term "part," like the term "accessory," must have a direct relationship to the primary article, rather than to the general activity in which the primary article is used. Again, the protective gear in this case has a relationship to the activity of roller skating, and not directly to the roller skates. Rollerblade's imported protective gear protects the wearer from injuries related to an activity using the article. The imports are not necessary to make the skates themselves work, nor are they necessary to make the skates themselves work efficiently or safely. At best, the protective gear adds to the comfort and convenience of the wearer while roller skating. In other words, the roller skates work in the same manner whether the skater wears the protective gear or not. Concurrent use of the protective gear with the roller skates no doubt reduces injuries to the skater from the activity of roller skating, but this observation does not make the protective gear "parts" of the roller skates.

In this case, the most applicable heading is 9506, entitled "articles and equipment for general physical exercise...gymnastics, athletics, other sports." Subheading 99.6080, entitled "other," is the so-called catch-all for this provision. The definition offered for "equipment" includes those articles that are necessary and specifically designed for use in athletics and other sports. Rollerblade's imported protective gear fits within this category because it is "equipment" specifically designed for use in the sport of roller skating. In sum, the Court of International Trade did not err in its determination that Customs properly classified Rollerblade's imported protective gear under the residual subheading 99.6080. Affirmed.

(49) Mark Realty v. Rogness (U.S.)

Mark Realty, Inc., (Appellant) v. Tilman A. Rogness (Appellee)

No. 81–1605 1982, FL. 1379, District Court of Appeal of Florida, Fifth Circuit

Appeal from the Circuit Court for Brevard County, Roger F. Dykes, Judge

Appellate Panel

Decision of the Court delivered by the Honorable Judge Cowart.

The case involves whether a particular brokerage transaction was "an offer for a unilateral contract subject to revocation by the owner at any time before performance by the broker" or whether the transaction constituted a bilateral contract not subject to revocation during the time provided and, if it was a bilateral contract, whether it created as "exclusive agency to sell" or an "exclusive right to sell."

Appellee, owner, entered into four separate agreements with appellant real estate broker. The agreements were identical in form and substance except for the dates and time periods and property involved. They were entitled "exclusive right of sale" and gave the broker, for a stated period of time, the exclusive right to sell the property for a certain stated price and on certain terms. The broker sued on the four agreements for brokerage commissions, alleging that during the time provided in the agreements the owner had conveyed the four properties. The owner's answer contained denials of some of the allegations of the broker's amended complaint and also alleged affirmative defenses to the effect that the owner had "cancelled, revoked and terminated" the brokerage agreements before the properties were sold and that the broker had never performed under the agreements. It is not clear whether the last defense was meant to allege that under the agreements the broker was not entitled to commissions unless the broker procured the purchasers and that the broker did not, or whether the defense was an inartful allegation that the broker had not performed obligations under the agreement thereby breaching them before the sales by the owner.

Following a non-jury trial, the trial judge found that the deed relied on by the broker as a sale of one of the properties (Lot 4, Ocean Residence North, William C. Irvin, et ux, et al) was, notwithstanding its form, a security agreement and not a sale within the meaning of the brokerage agreement. Appellant having failed to demonstrate that this finding of fact is not supported by competent substantial evidence, that portion of the final judgment is affirmed.

However, rather than deciding appellant's claims for commissions as to the other three transactions on the evidence, the trial judge construed the brokerage agreements to constitute mere offers to enter into unilateral contracts under which the broker would be entitled to a commission only if he performed by "finding a purchaser of the above property."

The trial court was concerned about the fact that the brokerage agreements were stated in the first person, that the owner was "doing all of the agreeing" and that the broker had signed only under words stating "accepted by." The trial court (1) noted "there is no covenant or promise by the broker to do anything," (2) concluded that, since the owner's agreement was "not supported by a consideration in the form of a promise" by the broker, the document was only a promise of the owner to pay in exchange for performance by the broker finding a purchaser, (3) construed the documents as unilateral contracts, or more particularly, as offers for unilateral contracts subject to withdrawal or revocation by the owner at any time before the performance by the broker and (4) found, as a matter of fact, that "the offers were revoked by the owner-defendant prior to performance by the plaintiff."

If the documents in question are merely "offers limited to acceptance by performance only" the trial judge's analysis and conclusion would be correct. Because of the one-sidedness of this type of contract, we may agree that such a construction might reach a more fair result, but we cannot agree that the documents were only offers for a unilateral contract. The documents illustrate what has been termed "the usual practice" in the making of bargains. One party first indicates what he will do and what he requires in exchange and the other then agrees. These documents, when first executed by the owner and tendered to the broker, constituted offers which, when accepted by the broker by his execution, constituted contracts. While the fact that the document was first prepared by the broker may cause any ambiguities therein to be construed against the drafting broker, the form of the instrument is an offer by the owner which was accepted by the broker. The contract is bilateral because it contains mutual promises made in exchange for each other by each of the contracting parties.

The most common recurring brokerage transaction is one in which the owner employs a broker to find a purchaser able and willing to buy, on terms stated in advance by the owner, and in which the owner promises to pay a specific commission for the service. Such a transaction as this is an offer by the owner of a unilateral contract, an offered promise to pay by the owner, creating in the broker a power of accepting the offer by actual rendition of requested services. Here the only contemplated contract between the owner and broker is a unilateral contract – a promise to pay a commission for services rendered. Such an offer of a promise to pay a commission for services rendered is revocable by the owner by notice before the broker has rendered any part of the requested service. The owner's promise to the broker to pay a commission may itself be conditional, as where he promises to pay "on closing of the deal," etc. The broker's right to payment is thus made subject to such an additional express condition.

On the other hand, the transaction between the owner and the broker can be a bilateral contract. An owner who puts his land in the hands of a broker for sale usually clearly promises to pay a commission but the broker rarely promises in return that he will produce a purchaser, although he often promises, expressly or impliedly, that he will make certain efforts to do so. If the parties have thus made mutual promises, the transaction no longer has the status of an unaccepted offer – there is an existing bilateral contract and neither party has the power of revocation. During the term of such a contract the owner may withdraw any power the owner has given the broker to contract with a third party in the owner's name, but this is not a revocation of the contract between the owner and the broker and normally such action constitutes a breach of the brokerage contract unless the owner reserved a power of termination either by notice or by effecting a sale through other channels. In this case, the broker promised to inspect the property, to list the property with a multiple listing service, to advertise the property in the local newspaper or other media, to furnish information to inquiring cooperating brokers and prospective purchasers, to show the property, to make efforts to find a purchaser, to "make an earnest and continued effort to sell" and to direct the concentrated efforts of his organization in bringing about a sale. The Florida Supreme Court in Flynn v. McGinty, 61 So.2nd 318 (Fla. 1952), held that, in a contract similar to the instant contract, a clause that required the broker to "endeavor to procure a purchaser" was sufficient consideration for the brokerage agreement.

On the other hand, the transaction between the owner and the broker can be a bilateral contract. An owner who puts his land in the hands of a broker for sale usually clearly promises to pay a commission but the broker rarely promises in return that he will produce a purchaser, although he often promises, expressly or impliedly, that he will make certain efforts to do so. If the parties have thus made mutual promises, the transaction no longer has the status of an unaccepted offer – there is an existing bilateral contract and neither party has the power of revocation. During the term of such a contract the owner may withdraw any power the owner has given the broker to contract with a third party in the owner's name, but this is not a revocation of the contract between the owner and the broker and normally such action constitutes a breach of the brokerage contract unless the owner reserved a power of termination either by notice or by effecting a sale through other channels. In this case, the broker promised to inspect the property, to list the property with a multiple listing service, to advertise the property in the local newspaper or other media, to furnish information to inquiring commitment of a broker as an 'exclusive agent to sell; and the granting to him the 'exclusive right to sell.' In the former contract, the owner does not surrender his own right to sell the property and in the event he does so, is under no obligation to pay a commission to the broker. In the latter case, the broker is entitled to his commission if owner makes sale during the life of the contract. This distinction seems to be valid, based on sound reasoning and is abundantly supported by the authorities. In fact we find no case asserting a contrary rule. 61 So.2nd at 320

Since the contract before the Flynn court "plainly and unequivocally stated that commission will be earned whether the property was sold 'by myself, or through your instrumentality or any other person.'" the court held the contract plainly granted an exclusive right to sell. Flynn v. McGinty has been consistently followed by Florida appellate courts and where the contract clearly gives up the owner's right to sell without paying a commission, a broker has been held entitled to his brokerage commission upon sale of the property no matter who procures the purchaser. In the instant case, the contract clearly provided that the brokerage commission would be paid "whether the purchaser would be secured by you or by me, or by any other person..." Thus the contract granted the broker an exclusive right of sale and the trial court erred in construing the agreement as an offer of a unilateral contract revocable at will at any time prior to performance.

Since the trial court ruled that the contracts were unilateral and therefore revocable at will, the trial court never reached the issue of whether appellant broker had breached the brokerage contracts prior to the sale by the owner. The owner should be given an opportunity to have the trial court consider that issue; therefore the final judgment is reversed and this cause is remanded for the trial court to consider that issue as a defense to the broker's claim for a commission under the three contracts. The trial court may take further testimony as it deems necessary for a fair and proper determination of that issue.

Affirmed in part; reversed in part; and remanded for further proceedings consistent with this opinion.

The Honorable Judge Orfinger and Cobb, J., concur.

(50) Ashcroft v. Free Speech Coalition (U.S.)

(535 U.S. 234 2002)

Syllabus (Headnote)

Supreme Court of the United States

Ashcroft, Attorney General, et al., v. Free Speech Coalition et al.

Certiorari to the United States Court of Appeals for the Ninth Circuit

No. 00–795. Argued October 30, 2001 – Decided April 16, 2002

The Child Pornography Prevention Act of 1996 (CPPA) expands the federal prohibition on child pornography to include not only pornographic images made using actual children, U.S.C. § 2256(8)(A), but also "any visual depiction, including any photograph, film, video, picture, or computer-generated image or picture" that "is, or appears to be, of a minor engaging in sexually explicit conduct," §2256(8)(B), and any sexually explicit child pornography. Fearing that the CPPA threatened their activities, respondents, an adult-entertainment trade association and others, filed this suit alleging that the "appears to be" and "conveys the impression" provisions are overbroad and vague, chilling production of works protected by the First Amendment. The District Court disagreed and granted the Government summary judgment, but the Ninth Circuit reversed. Generally, pornography can be banned only if it is obscene under Miller v. California, 413 U.S. 15, but pornography depicting actual children can be proscribed whether or not the images are obscene because of the State's interest in protecting the children exploited by the production process, New York v. Ferber, 458 U.S. 747, 758, and in prosecuting those who promote such sexual exploitation, id., at 761.

Held: Section 2256 (8)(B) covers materials beyond the categories recognized in Ferber and Miller, and the reasons the Government offers in support of limiting the freedom of speech have no justification in the Court's precedents or First Amendment Law.

The CPPA is inconsistent with Miller. It extends to images that are not obscene under the Miller standard, which requires the Government to prove that the work in question, taken as a whole, appeals to the prurient interest, is patently offensive in light of community standards, and lacks serious literary, artistic, political, or scientific value, 413 U.S., at 24. Materials need not appeal to the prurient interest under the CPPA, which proscribes any depiction of sexually explicit activity, no matter how it is presented. It is not necessary, moreover, that the image be patently offensive. Pictures of what appear to be 17-year-olds engaging in sexually explicit activity do not in every case contravene community standards. The CPPA also prohibits speech having serious redeeming value, proscribing the visual depiction of an idea – that of teenagers engaging in sexual activity – that is a matter of modern society and has been a theme in art and literature for centuries.

The CPPA finds no support in Ferber. The Court rejects the Government's argument that speech prohibited by the CPPA is virtually indistinguishable from material that may be banned under Ferber. That case upheld a prohibition on the distribution and sale of child pornography, as well as its production, because these acts were "intrinsically related" to the sexual abuse of children in two ways, 458 U.S., at 759. First, as a permanent record of child's abuse, the continued circulation itself would harm the child who had participated. See id., at 759, and n. 10. Second, because the traffic in child pornography was an economic motive for its production, the State had an interest in closing the distribution network. Id., at 760. Under either rationale, the speech had what the Court in effect held was a proximate link to the crime from which it came. In contrast to the speech in Ferber, speech that is itself the record of sexual abuse, the CPPA prohibits speech that records no crime and creates no victims by its production. Virtual child pornography is not "intrinsically related" to the sexual abuse of children. While the Government asserts that the images can lead to actual instances of child abuse, the causal link is contingent and indirect. The harm does not necessarily follow from the speech, but depends upon some unquantified potential for subsequent criminal acts.

The Court rejects other arguments offered by the Government to justify the CPPA's prohibitions. The contention that the CPPA is necessary because paedophiles may use virtual child pornography to seduce children runs afoul of the principle that speech within the right of adults to hear may not be silenced completely in an attempt to shield children from it. The argument that virtual child pornography whets paedophiles' appetites and encourages them to engage in illegal conduct is unavailing because the mere tendency of speech to encourage unlawful acts is not a sufficient reason for banning it, absent some showing of a direct connection between the speech and imminent legal conduct. The argument that eliminating the market for pornography using real children necessitates a prohibition on virtual images as well is somewhat implausible because few pornographers would risk prosecution for abusing real children if fictional, computerized images would suffice. Moreover, even if the market deterrence theory were persuasive, the argument cannot justify the CPPA because, here, there is no underlying crime at all. Finally, the First Amendment is turned upside down by the argument that, because it is difficult to distinguish between images made using real children and those produced by computer imaging, both kinds of images must be prohibited. The overbreadth doctrine prohibits the Government from banning unprotected speech if a substantial amount of protected speech is prohibited or chilled in the process.

Thus, the CPPA does more than prohibiting pandering. It bans possession of material pandered as child pornography by someone earlier in the distribution chain, as well as sexually explicit film that contains no youthful actors but has been packaged to suggest a prohibitive movie. The First Amendment requires a more precise restriction.

The prohibitions of §§ 2256(8)(b) and 2256(8)(d) are overbroad and unconstitutional.

(51) Aslam Khaki v. Syed Mohammad Hashim (Pakistan)

This case has been decided by the Supreme Court of Pakistan (Shariah Appellate Bench PLD 2000 SC 225) in 2000. In 1991 the Federal Shariah Court of Pakistan declared the payment of interest (*riba*) on loans and deposits to be contrary to Islamic law. The government of Pakistan together with several banks appealed against this decision to the Supreme Court. The decision was described in 2002 by the same court as erroneous and impracticable (cf. United Bank Limited v. Farooq Brothers et al., PLD 2002 SC 800). The whole Supreme Court decision is ca. one thousand pages long. Below some of its most relevant arguments are quoted (cf. also Mattila 2013: 341–342 on legal English in Pakistan).

(40) Imam Abubakr Al-Jassas (d. 380 AH) in his famous work Ahkamul Qur'an has explained *riba* in the following words: "And the *riba* which was known to and practiced by the Arabs was that they used to advance loan in the form of *Dirham* (silver coin) for a certain term with an agreed increase on the amount of the principal advanced."

(133) Although the Holy Qur'an has itself decided what is injustice in a transaction of loan, and it is not necessary that everybody finds out all the elements of injustice in a *riba* transaction, yet the evil consequences of interest were never so evident in the past

than they are today. Injustice in a personal consumption loan was restricted to a debtor only, while the injustice brought by the modern interest affects the economy as a whole.

(140) Imam Al-Ghazzali (d. 505 A.H.) the renowned jurist and philosopher of the Islamic history has discussed the nature of money in an early period when the Western theories of money were non-existent...He says: "...And whoever effects the transactions on interest on money is, in fact, discarding the blessing of Allah and is committing injustice, because money is created for some other things, not for itself. So, the one who has started trading in money itself has made it an objective contrary to the original wisdom behind its creation..."

(151) This is exactly what Imam Al-Ghazali had pointed out nine hundred years ago. The evil results of such an unnatural trade have been further explained by him at another place, in the following words: "*Riba* is prohibited because it prevents people from undertaking real economic activities. This is because when a person having money is allowed to earn more money on the basis of interest, either in spot or in deferred transactions, it becomes easy for him to earn without bothering himself to take pains in real economic activities. This leads to hampering the real interests of the humanity, because the interests of the humanity cannot be safeguarded without real trade skills, industry and construction."

(158) Thus, financing a business on the basis of interest creates an unbalanced atmosphere which has the potential of bringing injustice to either of the two parties in different situations. That is the wisdom for which the *Sha'riah* did not approve an interest-based loan as a form of financing...

(52) Wood v. Duff-Gordon (U.S.)

Overcoming formalism in law (cf. also Galdia 2014: 150) is a task addressed by B. Cardozo in the following decision Wood v. Duff-Gordon (222 NY 88). The case has been decided in the New York court according to the private law of this state. In order to better understand the formalities of the case, that are concededly a minor issue for us, it is good to bear in mind the structure of New York courts. The trial court in New York is named *Supreme Court.* Within the Supreme Court, trials are conducted by courts called *Special Term.* Intermediate appeals from Special Term trial courts are heard by the *Appellate Division.* Appeals from the Appellate Division go to the top court, the *Court of Appeals.* The above labels differ from the U.S. federal court system and that of many other U.S. states.

Otis F. Wood (Appelant) v. Lucy, Lady Duff-Gordon (Respondent)

Defendant is a "creator of fashions" whose favor helps a sale, and manufacturers of feminine apparel are willing to pay for a certificate of her approval. She entered into an agreement with plaintiff employing him to turn this vogue into money. He was to have, for the term of one year, and thereafter unless terminated by a written notice, the exclusive right, subject to her approval, to place her indorsements on the designs of others and in return she was to have one-half of all profits and revenues derived from any contract he might make. Plaintiff claims that he kept the contract and that the defendant broke it, by placing her indorsement on articles without his knowledge and withholding the profits, and sues her for the damages. Defendant demurs to the complaint on the ground that the agreement lacks the elements of a contract in that plaintiff does not promise in express terms, such a promise is fairly implied. Defendant gave an exclusive privilege and plaintiff's promise to pay one-half of the profits and revenues resulting from the exclusive agency and to render accounts monthly, was a promise to use reasonable efforts to bring profits and revenues into existence, and, hence, the demurrer cannot be sustained.

Wood v. Duff-Gordon, 177 App. Div. 624, reversed.

(Argued November 14, 1917; decided December 4, 1917.)

Appeal from a judgment entered April 24, 1917 upon an order of the Appellate Division of the Supreme Court in the first judicial department, which reversed an order of Special Term denying a motion by defendant for judgment in her favor upon the pleadings and granted said motion.

The nature of the action and the facts, so far as material, are stated in the opinion.

John Jerome Rooney for appellant. Assuming that the contract does not contain an express covenant and agreement on the part of the plaintiff to use his best endeavors and efforts to place indorsements, make sales or grant licenses to manufacture, nevertheless such a covenant must necessarily be implied from the terms of the contract itself and all the circumstances. (Booth v. Cleveland Mill. Co. 74 N.Y. 15; Wells v. Alexandre, 130 N.Y. 642, Jacquin v. Boutard, 89 Hun, 437; 157 N.Y. 686; Wilson v. Mechanical Orguinette Co., 170 N.Y. 542; Horton v. Hall & Clarke Mfg. Co., 94 App. Div. 404; Hearn v. Stevens & Bros., 111 App. Div. 101; Baker Transfer Co. v. Merchants R.I. Mfg. Co., 1 App. Div.; Wildman Mfg. Co. v. Adams T.C.M. Co., 149 Fed. Rep. 201.)

Edward E. Hoenig and William M. Sullivan for respondent. The motion for judgment on the pleadings was properly granted and the demurrer properly sustained by the appellate court, as the agreement upon which the action is based is nudum pactum and not binding upon the defendant for lack of mutuality and consideration. (Elliott on Cont. §231 ; Grossman v. Schenker, 206 N.Y. 468; Levin v. Dietz, 194 N.Y. 376; Commercial W. & C. Co. v. Northhampton P.C. Co., 115 App. Div. 393; 190 N.Y. 1; Wood v. G.F. Inc. Co. 174 App. Div. 834 ; White v. K.M.C. Co., 69 Misc. Rep. 628; Cook v. Casler, 87 App. Div. 8; Vogel v. Pekoe, 30 L.R.A. 491; Moran v. Standard Oil Co., 211 N.Y. 189; City of New York v. Poali, 202 N.Y. 18; Barrel S.S. Co. v. Mexican Hotchkiss, 97 N.Y. 395; Marie v. Garrison, 43 N.Y. 14; Chicago & G.E.R. Co. v. Dane, 43 N.Y. 240; Jermyn v. Searing, 170 App. Div. 720, Rafolovitz v. Amer. Tobacco Co., 73 Hun, 87; Pollock v. Shubert, 146 App. Div. 628.) The order of the Appellate Division should be affirmed, for under the contract the appellant assumes no obligation and there is no provision therein enforceable against him. (Commercial W. & C. Co. v. Northampton P.C. Co., 115 App. Div. 393;

190 N.Y. 1; Pollock v. Shubert Theatrical Co., 146 App. Div. 629; Arnot v. P.&E. Coal Co., 68 N.Y. 565; Booth v. Milliken, 127 App. Div. 525; Vogel v. Pekoe, 30 L.R.A. 491.)

Cardozo, J.

The defendant styles herself « a creator of fashions ». Her favor helps a sale. Manufacturers of dresses, millinery and like articles are glad to pay for a certificate of her approval. The things which she designs, fabrics, parasols and what not, have a new value in the public mind when issued in her name. She employed the plaintiff to help her to turn this vogue into money. He was to have the exclusive right, subject always to her approval, to place her indorsements on the designs of others. He was also to have the exclusive right to place her own designs on sale, or to license others to market them. In return, she was to have one-half of "all profits and revenues" derived from any contracts he might make. The exclusive right was to last one year from April 1, 1915, and thereafter from year to year unless terminated by notice of ninety days. The plaintiff says that he kept the contract on his part, and that the defendant broke it. She placed her indorsement on fabrics, dresses and millinery without his knowledge, and withheld the profits. He sues her for the damages, and the case comes here on demurrer.

The agreement of employment is signed by both parties. It has a wealth of recitals. The defendant insists, however, that it lacks the elements of a contract. She says that the plaintiff does not bind himself to anything. It is true that he does not promise in so many words that he will use reasonable efforts to place the defendant's indorsements and market up her designs. We think, however, that such a promise is fairly to be implied. The law has outgrown its primitive stage of formalism when the precise word was the sovereign talisman, and every slip was fatal. It takes a broader view to-day. A promise may be lacking, and yet the whole writing may be "instinct with an obligation," imperfectly expressed (Scott, J., in McCall Co. v. Wright, 133 App. Div. 62; Moran v. Standard Oil Co., 211 N.Y. 187, 198). If that is so, there is a contract.

The implication of a promise here finds support in many circumstances. The defendant gave exclusive privilege. She was to have no right for at least a year to place her own indorsements or market her own design except through the agency of the plaintiff. The acceptance of the exclusive agency was an assumption of its duties (Phoenix Hermetic Co. v. Filtrine Mfg. Co., 164 App. Div. 424; W.G. Taylor Co. v. Bannerman, 120 Wis. 189; Mueller v. Bethesda Mineral Spring Co., 88 Mich. 390). We are not to suppose that one party was to be placed at the mercy of the other (Hearn v. Stevens & Bro., 111 App. Div. 101, 106; Russell v. Allerton, 108 N.Y. 288). Many other terms of the agreement point the same way. We are told at the outset by way of recital that "the said Otis F. Wood possesses a business organization adapted to the placing of such indorsements as the said Lucy, Lady Duff-Gordon has approved." The implication is that the plaintiff's business organization will be used for the purpose for which it is adapted. But the terms of the defendant's compensation are even more significant. Her sole compensation for the grant of an exclusive agency is to be one-half of all the profits resulting from the plaintiff's efforts. Unless he gave his efforts, she could never get anything. Without an implied promise, the transaction cannot have such business "efficacy as both parties must have intended that at all events it should have" (Bowen, L.J. in The Moorrock, 14 P.D. 64, 68). But the contract does not stop there. The plaintiff goes on to promise that he will account monthly for all money received by him, and that he will take out all such patents and copyrights and trademarks as may in his judgment be necessary to protect the rights and articles affected by the agreement. It is true, of course, as the Appellate Division has said that if he was under no duty to try to market designs or to place certificates of indorsement, his promise to account for profits or to take out copyrights would be valueless. But in determining the intention of the parties, the promise has a value. It helps to enforce the conclusion that the plaintiff had some duties. His promise to pay the defendant one-half of the profits and revenues resulting from the exclusive agency and to render accounts monthly, was a promise to use reasonable efforts to bring profits and revenues into existence. For this conclusion, the authorities are ample (Wilson v. Mechanical Orguinette Co., 170 N.Y. 542; Phoenix Hermetic Co. v. Filtrine Mfg. Co., supra, Jacquin v. Boutard, 89 Hun, 437; 157 N.Y. 686; Moran v. Standard Oil Co., supra; City of N.Y. v. Paoli, 202 N.Y. 18; M'Intyre v. Belcher, 14 C.B. (N.S.) 654; Devonald v. Rosser & Sons, 1906, 2 K.B. 728; W.G. Taylor v. Bannerman, supra; Mueller v. Bethesda Mineral Spring Co., supra; Baker Transfer Co. v. Merchants' R. & I. Mfg. Co., App. Div. 507).

The judgment of the Appellate Division should be reversed, and the order of the Special Term affirmed, with costs in the Appellate Division and in this court.

Cuddeback, McLaughlin and Andrews, JJ., concur; Hiscock, Ch.J., Chase and Crane, JJ., dissent.

Judgment reversed, etc.

(53) Palsgraf v. Long Island Railroad (U.S.)

Justice B. Cardozo created in the following decision Palsgraf v. Long Island Railroad an imagery consisting of cases in a case. The hypothetical cases are used in the narration to clarify the legal notion of the proximate cause. Cardozo's principal professional goal is to show why the main case which has been brought by the plaintiff does not fulfill the requirements developed within the proximate cause doctrine. The part of the case that interests here is its story, therefore it would be more correct to speak about stories in a story rather than about cases in a case. Cases reflect stories within the legal framework of professional argumentation; stories have a role to play in cases but they do not interfere directly with doctrinal issues. Cardozo did not experiment with legal references nor did he reformulate them in his opinion. Therefore, his cases in the case remain within the framework of the classical legal argumentation of his time. His particular innovations within the argumentation are the stories that position the plaintiff's case and her story in a specific perspective which is relevant to his final decision. Writing stories based on facts is a particularly intricate task. Next to introducing stories as a strategy for deciding cases, Cardozo develops also linguistic tests which are based on the specific features of the legal language. Cardozo stresses the instability of meanings which evolve in law. He has also demonstrated how the plaintiff should use the legal language in order to comply with the juridical test that evaluates the wrong which might have occurred to her.

Palsgraf v. Long Island Railroad, Co. (248 N.Y. 339, 172 N.E., 1928)

Cardozo, C.J. Plaintiff was standing on a platform of defendant's railroad after buying a ticket to go to Rockaway beach. A train stopped at the station, bound for another place. Two men ran forward to catch it. One of the men reached the platform of the car, without mishap, though the train was already moving. The other man, carrying a package, jumped aboard the car, but seemed unsteady as if about to fall. A guard on the car, who had held the door open, reached forward to help him in, and another guard of the platform pushed him from behind. In this act, the package was dislodged, and fell upon the rails. It was a package of small size, about fifteen inches long, and was covered by a newspaper. In fact it contained fireworks, but there was nothing in its appearance to give notice of its contents. The shock of the explosion threw down some scales at the other end of the platform, many feet away. The scales struck the plaintiff, causing injuries for which she sues.

The conduct of the defendant's guard, if a wrong in its relation to the holder of the package, was not a wrong in its relation to the plaintiff, standing far away. Relatively to her it was not negligence at all. Nothing in the situation gave notice that the falling package had in it the potency of peril to persons thus removed. Negligence is not actionable unless it involves the invasion of a legally protected interest, the violation of a right. "Proof of negligence in the air, so to speak, will not do" (Pollock, Torts, 11th ed., p. 455). "Negligence is the absence of care, according to the circumstances" (Willes, J., in Vaughan v. Taff Vale, Ry. Co., 5 H.&N. 679, 688; Adams v. Bullock, 227 N.Y. 298, 211; Parott v. Wells-Fargo Co. (the Nitro-Glycerine case, 15 Wall. (U.S.) 524). The plaintiff as she stood upon the platform of the station might claim to be protected against unintentional invasion of her bodily security. Such invasion is not charged. She might claim to be protected against unintentional invasion by conduct involving in the thought of reasonable men an unreasonable hazard that such invasion would ensue. These, from the point of view of the law, were the bounds of her immunity, with perhaps some rare exceptions, survivals for the most part of ancient forms of liability, where conduct is held to be at the peril of the actor (Sullivan v. Dunham, 161 N.Y. 290). If no hazard was apparent to the eye of ordinary vigilance, an act innocent and harmless, at least to outward seeming, with reference to her, did not take to itself the quality of a tort because it happened to be a wrong, though apparently not one involving the risk of bodily insecurity, with reference to someone else. "In every instance, before negligence can be predicated of a given act, back of the act must be sought and found a duty to the individual complaining, the observance of which would have averted or avoided the injury" (McSherry, C.J., in W. Va. Central RR. Co. v. State, 96 Md. 652, 666). "The ideas of negligence and duty are strictly correlative" (Bowen, L.J., in Thomas v. Quartermaine, 18 Q.B.D. 685, 694). The plaintiff sues in her own right for a wrong personal to her, and not as the vicarious beneficiary of a breach of duty to another.

A different conclusion will involve us, and swiftly too, in a maze of contradictions. A guard stumbles over a package which has been left upon a platform. It seems to be a bundle of newspaper. It turns out to be a can of dynamite. To the eye of ordinary vigilance, the bundle is abandoned waste, which may be kicked or trod on with impunity. Is a passenger at the other end of the platform protected by the law against unsuspected hazard concealed beneath the waste? If not, is the result to be any different, so far as the distant passenger is concerned, when the guard stumbles over a valise which a truckman or a porter has left upon the walk? The passenger far away, if the victim of a wrong at all, has a cause of action, not derivative, but original and primary. His claim to be protected against invasion of his bodily security is neither greater nor less because the act resulting in the invasion is a wrong to another far removed. In this case, the rights that are said to have been violated, the interest said to have been invaded, are not even of the same order. The man was not injured in his person nor even put in danger. The purpose of the act, as well as its effect, was to make his person safe. If there was a wrong to a property interest only, the safety of his package. Out of this wrong to property, which threatened injury to nothing else, there has passed, we are told, to the plaintiff by derivation or succession a right of action for the invasion of an interest of another order, the right to bodily security. The diversity of interests emphasizes the futility of the effort to build the plaintiff's right upon the basis of a wrong to someone else. The gain is one of emphasis, for a like result would follow if the interests were the same. Even then, the orbit of the danger as disclosed to the eye of reasonable vigilance would be the orbit of the duty. One who jostles one's nighbor in a crowd does not invade the right of others standing at the outer fringe when the unintended contact casts a bomb upon the ground. The wrongdoer as to them is the man who carries the bomb, not the one who explodes it without suspicion of the danger. Life will have to be made over, and human nature transformed, before provisions so extravagant can be accepted as the norm of conduct, the customary standard to which behavior must conform.

The argument for the plaintiff is built upon the shifting meanings of such words as "wrong" and "wrongful", and shares their instability. What the plaintiff must show is "a wrong" to herself, i.e. a violation of her own right, and not merely a wrong to someone else, nor conduct "wrongful" because unsocial, but not "a wrong" to any one. We are told that one who drives at reckless speed through a crowded city street is guilty of a negligent act and, therefore, of a wrongful one irrespective of the consequences. Negligent the act is, and wrongful in the sense that it is unsocial, but wrongful and unsocial to other travellers, only because the eye of vigilance perceives the risk of damage. If the same act were to be committed on a speedway or a race course, it would lose its wrongful quality. The risk reasonably to be perceived defines the duty to be obeyed, and risk imports relation; it is risk to another or to others within the range of apprehension. This does not mean, of course, that one who launches a destructive force is always relieved of liability if the force, though known to be destructive, pursues an unexpected path. "It was not necessary that the defendant should have had notice of their particular method in which an accident would occur, if the possibility of an accident was clear to the ordinarily prudent eye" (Munsey v. Webb, 231 U.S. 150,156). Some acts, such as shooting, are so imminently dangerous to anyone who may come within reach of the missile, however unexpectedly, as to impose a duty of prevision not far from that of an insurer. Even today, and much oftener in earlier stages of the law, one acts sometimes at one's peril. Under this head, it may be, fall certain cases of what is known as transferred intent, an act willfully dangerous to A resulting by misadventure in injury to B (Talmage v. Smith, 101 Mich. 370, 374). These cases aside, wrong is defined in terms of the natural or probable, at least when unintentional (Talmage v. Wells-Fargo Co., 15 Wall. (U.S.) 542). The range of reasonable apprehensions is at times a question for the court, and at times, if varying inferences are possible, a question for the jury. Here by concession, there was nothing in the situation to suggest to the most cautious mind that the parcel wrapped in newspaper would spread wreckage through the station. If the guard had thrown it down knowingly and willfully, he would not have threatened the plaintiff's safety, so far as appearances could warn him. His conduct would not have involved, even then, an unreasonable probability of invasion of her bodily security. Liability can be no greater where the act is inadvertent.

Negligence, like risk, is thus a term of relation. Negligence in the abstract, apart from things related, is surely not a tort, if indeed it is understandable at all...

The law of causation, remote or proximate, is thus foreign to the case before us. The question of liability is always anterior to the question of the measure of the consequences that go with liability. If there is no tort to be redressed, there is no occasion to consider what damage might be recovered if there were a finding of a tort. We may assume, without deciding, that negligence, not at large or in the abstract, but in relation to the plaintiff, would entail liability for any and all consequences, however novel or extraordinary. There is room for argument that a distinction is to be drawn according to the diversity of interests invaded by the act, as where conduct negligent in that it threatens an insignificant invasion of an interest in property results in an unforeseeable invasion of an interest of another order, as e.g. one of bodily security. Perhaps other distinctions may be necessary. We do not go into the question now. The consequences to be followed must first be rooted in a wrong.

Case dismissed.

(54) Hynes v. New York Central Railroad (U.S.)

Hynes v. New York Cent. R. Co.

May 31, 1921

Action by Florence Hynes, as administratrix of James Harvey Hynes, deceased, against the New York Central Railroad Company. From the judgment of the Appellate Division (190 App.Div. 915, 179 N.Y. Supp. 927) affirming by a divided court a judgment of the Trial Term dismissing the complaint, plaintiff appeals.

Reversed, and new trial granted.

See, also, 188 App. Div. 178, 176 N.Y. Supp. 795.

Hiscock, C.J. and Chase and McLaughlin, JJ., dissenting.

CARDOZO, J.

On July 8, 1916, Harvey Hynes, a lad of 16, swam with two companions from the Manhattan to the Bronx side of the Harlem River, or United States Ship Canal, a navigable stream. Along the Bronx side of the river was the right of way of the defendant, the New York Central Railroad, which operated its trains at that point by high-tension wires, strung on poles and cross-arms. Projecting from defendant's bulkhead above the waters of the river was a plank or springboard, from which boys of the nighborhood used to dive. One end of the board had been placed under a rock on the defendant's land, and nails had been driven at its point of contact with the bulkhead. Measured from this point of contact the length behind was 5 feet; the length in front 11. The bulkhead itself was about 3 ½ feet back of the pier line as located by the government. From this it follows that for 7 ½ feet the springboard was beyond the line of the defendant's property and above the public waterway. Its height measured from the stream was 3 feet at the bulkhead, and 5 feet at its outermost extremity. For more than five years swimmers had used it as a diving board without protest or obstruction.

On this day Harvey Hynes and his companions climbed on the top of the bulkhead, intending to leap into the water. One of them made the plunge in safety. Hynes followed to the front of the springboard, and stood poised for his dive. At that moment a cross-arm with electric wires fell from the defendant's pole. The wires struck the diver, flung him from the shattered board, and plunged him to his death below. His mother, suing as administratrix, brings this action for her damages. Thus far the courts have held that Hynes at the end of the springboard above the public waters was a trespasser on the defendant's land. They have thought it immaterial that the board itself was a trespass, an encroachment on the public ways. They have thought it of no significance that Hynes would have met the same fate if he had been below the board and not above it. The board, they have said, was annexed to the defendant's bulkhead. By force of such annexation, it was to be reckoned as a fixture, and thus constructively, if not actually, an extension of the land. The defendant was under a duty to use reasonable care that bathers swimming or standing in the water should not be electrocuted by wires falling from its right of way. But to bathers diving from the springboard, there was no duty, we are told, unless the injury was the product of mere willfulness or wantonness – no duty of active vigilance to safeguard the impending structure. Without wrong to them, cross-arms might be left to rot; wires highly charged with electricity might sweep them from their stand and bury them in the subjacent waters. In climbing on the board, they became trespassers and outlaws. The conclusion is defended with much subtlety of reasoning, with much insistence upon its inevitableness as a merely logical deduction. A majority of the court are unable to accept it as the conclusion of the law.

We assume, without deciding, that the springboard was a fixture, a permanent improvement of the defendant's right of way. Much might be said in favor of another view. We do not press the inquiry for we are persuaded that the rights of bathers do not depend upon these nice distinctions. Liability would be doubtful, we are told, had the boy been diving from a pole, if the pole had been vertical. The diver in such situation would have been separated from the defendant's freehold. Liability, it is said has been escaped because the pole was horizontal. The plank when projected lengthwise was an extension of the soil. We are to concentrate our gaze on the private ownership of the board. We are to ignore the public ownership of the circumambient spaces of water and of air. Jumping from a boat or a barrel, the boy would have been a bather in the river. Jumping from the end of a springboard, he was no longer, it is said, a bather, but a trespasser on the right of way.

Rights and duties in systems of living law are not built upon such quicksands.

Bathers in the Harlem River on the day of this disaster were in the enjoyment of a public highway, entitled to reasonable protection while they were diving from encroaching objects or engaging in the sports that are common among swimmers. Such acts were not equivalent to an abandonment of the highway, a departure from its proper uses, a withdrawal from the waters, and an entry upon land. A plane of private right had been interposed between the river and the air, but public ownership was unchanged in the space below it and above it. The defendant does not deny that it would have owed a duty to this boy if he had been leaning against the springboard with his feet upon the ground. He is said forfeited protection as he put his feet upon the plank. Presumably the same result would follow if the plank had been a few inches above the surface of the water instead of a few feet. Duties are supposed to arise and to be extinguished in alternate zones or strata. Two boys walking in the country or swimming in a river stop to rest for a moment along the side of the road or the margin of the stream. One of them throws himself beneath the overhanging branches of a tree. The other perches himself on a bough a foot or so above the ground. Hoffman v. Armstrong, 48 N.Y. 201, 8 Am. Rep. 537. Both are killed by falling wires. The defendant would have us say that there is a remedy for the representatives of one and none for the representatives of the other. We may be permitted to distrust the logics that leads to such conclusions.

The truth is that every act of Hynes from his first plunge into the river until the moment of his death was in the enjoyment of the public waters, and under cover of the protection which his presence in those waters gave him. The use of the springboard was not an abandonment of his rights as bather. It was a mere by-play, an incident, subordinate and ancillary to the execution of his primary purpose, the enjoyment of the highway. The by-play, the incident, was not the cause of the disaster. Hynes would have gone to his death if he had been below the springboard or beside it. Laidlaw v. Sage, 158 N.Y. 73, 97, 52 N.E. 679, 44 L.R.A. 216. The wires were not stayed by the presence of the plank. They followed the boy in his fall, and overwhelmed him in the waters.

The defendant assumes that the identification of ownership of a fixture with ownership of land is complete in every incident. But there are important elements of difference. Title to the fixture, unlike title to the land, does not carry with it rights of ownership usque ad coelum. There will hardly be denial that a cause of action would have arisen if the wires have fallen on an aeroplane proceeding above the river, though the location of the impact could be identified as the space above the springboard. The most that the defendant can fairly ask is exemption from liability where the use of the fixture is itself the efficient peril. That would be the situation, for example, if the weight of the boy upon the board had caused it to break and thereby throw him into the river. There is no such causal connection here between his position and his injuries. We think there was no moment when he was beyond the pale of the defendant's duty – the duty of care and vigilance in the storage of destructive forces.

This case is a striking instance of the dangers of 'a jurisprudence of conceptions' (Pound, Mechanical Jurisprudence (Columbia Law Review, 605, 808, 610), the extension of a maxim or a definition with relentless disregard of consequences to 'a dryly logical extreme'. The approximate and relative become the definite and absolute. Landowners are not bound to regulate their conduct in contemplation of the presence of trespassers intruding into private structures. Landowners are bound to regulate their conduct in contemplation of the presence of travelers upon the adjacent public ways. There are times when there is little trouble in marking off the field of exemption and immunity from liability and duty. Here structures and ways are so united and commingled, superimposed upon each other that the fields are brought together. In such circumstances, there is little help in pursuing general maxims to ultimate conclusions. They have been framed alio intuitu. They must be reformulated and readapted to meet exceptional conditions. Rules appropriate to spheres which are conceived of as separate and distinct cannot both be enforced when the spheres become concentric. There must then be readjustment or collision. In one sense, and that a highly technical and artificial one, the diver at the end of the springboard is an intruder on the adjoining lands. In another sense, and one that realists will accept more readily, he is on public waters in the exercise of public rights. The law must say whether it will subject him to the rule of the one field or of the other, of this sphere or of that. We think that considerations of analogy, of convenience, of policy, and of justice, exclude him from the field of the defendant's immunity and exemption, and place him in the field of liability and duty. Beck v. Carter N.Y. 283, 23 Am. Rep. 175; Jewhurst v. City of Syracuse, 108 N.Y. 303, 15 N.E. 409; McCloskey v. Buckley, 223 N.Y. 187, 192, 119 N.E. 395.

The judgment of the Appellate Division and that of the Trial Term should be reversed, and a new trail granted, with costs to abide the event.

HOGAN, POUND; and CRANE, JJ., concur.

HISCOCK, C.J., and CHASE and McLAUGHLIN, JJ. dissent.

Judgment reversed, etc.

(55) Torres v. Reardon (U.S.)

Excerpts from Jose Torres v. Michael Reardon et al. (Court of Appeal of California, 3 Cal. App. 4th 831; 1992 Cal. App.):

Croskey, J. Plaintiff and appellant Jose Torres (Torres) appeals from the summary judgment against him and in favor of defendants Michael and Ona Reardon (the Reardons). Because there is no evidence that Torres's injuries resulted from any act of negligence by, or attributable to, the Reardons, or that any circumstances existed that would impose upon them liability for Torres's injuries under the peculiar risk doctrine, the trial court properly granted summary judgment.

Factual and procedural background

During the years of 1980 to 1988, Jose Torres was a self-employed gardener, doing business under the name of Jose Torres Gardening Service. From approximately 1984 until June of 1988, as part of his gardening business, Torres performed weekly general gardening services at several homes on Cricklewood Street in the City of Torrance, California, including the home of the Reardons.

Early in 1988, the Reardons began discussing with Torres the possibility of employing him to trim a 65- to 70-foot-tall tree located in their front yard. In mid-June of that year, it was agreed that Torres would trim the tree for a price of USD 350. Final arrangements for the trimming were made between Torres and Ona Reardon. The Reardon's next door neighbor, David Boice, was also present at the conversation in which the arrangements were made. Boice expressed concern at that time that care be taken in the cutting of a large branch that overhung Boice's house to assure that the branch did not fall onto his roof.

At 11 a.m., on the morning of June 20, 1988, four days after agreeing to trim the Reardons' tree, Torres arrived at the Reardons' home with one helper, prepared to do the job. The Reardons were not at home when Torres arrived, or at any time while he was working. David Boice, the next door neighbor, was at home in his garage-workshop, building an electrical panel. (Boice was an electrical contractor by trade and had done electrical work on the Reardons' home.) Boice reminded Torres to take care that the large branch overhanging his house did not fall onto the roof, and he occasionally left his garage to observe Torres's work. Torres used a chain saw to cut the larger branches of the tree. At one point, Boice observed that Torres was not using safety lines, and asked why. Torres answered that he did not need them.

The branch that extended over Boice's house left the tree's trunk at a point approximately 25 feet from the ground and had a diameter of approximately 20 inches. When Torres was ready to cut it, Boice came outside to hold a rope that was tied to the branch, apparently with the intention of pulling the branch away from Boice's roof as it fell. Torres positioned himself on the branch next to the trunk and began to cut at a point just beyond where he was standing. Torres was wearing a safety belt around his waist, but it was not attached to the tree, as he did not have a line long enough to reach the branch strong enough to hold him. According to Torres, Boice pulled on the rope when Torres was not expecting a pull. As a result, Torres's chain saw "kicked back", and Torres fell from the tree, landing on his back. Torres was rendered paraplegic as a result of his fall.

On April 12, 1989, Torres filed suit against the Reardons and against the manufacturer and seller of the chain saw that he was using when he fell from the tree. On December 7, 1990, the trial court granted the Reardons' motion for summary judgment. Judgment was entered thereon, and this appeal followed.

Contentions on appeal:

Torres contends that: (1) a triable issue of fact existed as to whether he was an employee of the Reardons at the time of the accident that caused his injuries; (2) if Torres was engaged by the Reardons as an independent contractor, rather than an employee, the Reardons are liable for his injuries under the doctrine of "peculiar risk"; (3) a triable issue of fact existed as to whether the Reardons were negligent in the hiring and supervision of Torres, and whether such negligence was the cause of his injuries; (4) a triable issue of fact existed as to whether Torres reasonably assumed the risks involved in trimming a 70-foot tree. (...)

(56) Bronston v. U.S. (U.S.)

Distinguishing true from false depositions which are provided as evidence in courts is a professional task that judges have to master. The decision which follows illustrates the specific problem of distinguishing whether the answer which is on its face truthful may be perceived as perjury because it negatively implies another result. In the case syllabus, the U.S. Supreme Court provided the following holding: *Federal perjury statute, 18 U.S.C. 1621, does not reach a witness' answer that is literally true, but unresponsive, even assuming the witness intends to mislead his questioner by the answer, and even assuming the answer is arguably "false by negative implication". A perjury prosecution is not, in our adversary system, the primary safeguard against errant testimony; given the incongruity of an unresponsive answer, it is questioner's burden to frame his interrogation acutely to elicit the precise information he seeks.* The text of sec. 1621 is rendered in this book in the paragraph 4.3.2 as an example of a culturally valuable achievement in law. The U.S. Supreme Court realizes that "*(T) here is, indeed, an implication in the answer to the second question that there was never a personal bank account; in casual conversation this interpretation might reasonably be drawn.*" The court recognizes that the language is used here in a specific legal framework and that speech acts which come about under such conditions cannot be evaluated with means applied for the appraisal of speech acts made in colloquial speech. Therefore, what may be perceived as a lie in ordinary language will not automatically be converted into a perjury in law? The reason for this is that language use requirements in these different speech acts differ. Ordinary language provides for very vague and simplified requirements for the distinguishing between true and false statements whereas the legal language provides an institutionally established catalogue of prerequisites, in casu sec. 1621, which enables the interpretation of the speech act in terms of law.

U.S. Supreme Court

Bronston v. United States, 409 U.S. 352 (1973)

Certiorari to the United States Court of Appeals for the Second Circuit

Mr. Chief Justice Burger delivered the opinion of the Court.

We granted the writ in this case to consider a narrow but important question in the application of the federal perjury statute, 18 U.S.C. 1621: whether a witness (409 U.S. 352, 353) may be convicted of perjury for an answer, under oath, that is literally true but not responsive to the question asked and arguably misleading by negative implication.

Petitioner is the sole owner of Samuel Bronston Productions, Inc., a company that between 1958 and 1964, produced motion pictures in various European locations. For these enterprises, Bronston Productions opened bank accounts in a number of foreign countries; in 1962, for example, it had 37 accounts in five countries. As president of Bronston Productions, petitioner supervised transactions involving the foreign bank accounts.

In June 1964, Bronston Productions petitioned for an arrangement with creditors under Chapter XI of the Bankruptcy Act, 11 U.S.C. 701 et seq. On June 10, 1966, a referee in bankruptcy held a 21(a) hearing to determine, for the benefit of creditors, the extent and location of the company's assets. Petitioner's perjury (409 U.S. 352, 354) conviction was founded on the answers given by him as a witness at the bankruptcy hearing, and in particular on the following colloquy with a lawyer for a creditor of Bronston Productions:

"Q. Do you have any bank accounts in Swiss banks, Mr. Bronston?

"A. No, sir.

"Q. Have you ever?

"A. The company had an account there for about six months, in Zurich.

"Q. Have you any nominees who have bank accounts in Swiss banks?

"A. No, sir.

"Q. Have you ever?

"A. No, sir.

It is undisputed that for a period of nearly five years, between October 1959 and June 1964, petitioner had a personal bank account at the International Credit Bank in Geneva, Switzerland, into which he made deposits and upon which he drew checks totaling more than $ 180,000. It is likewise undisputed that petitioner's answers were literally truthful. (a) Petitioner did not in the time of questioning have a Swiss bank account. (b) Bronston Productions, Inc., did have the account in Zurich described by petitioner. (c) Neither at the time (409 U.S. 352, 355) of questioning nor before did petitioner have nominees who had Swiss bank accounts. The Government's prosecution for perjury went forward on the theory that in order to mislead his questioner, petitioner answered the second question with literal truthfulness but unresponsively addressed his answer to the company's assets and not to his own – thereby implying that he had no personal Swiss bank account at the relevant time.

At petitioner's trial, the District Court instructed the jury that the "basic issue" was whether petitioner "spoke his true belief." Perjury, the court stated, "necessarily involves the state of mind of the accused" and "essentially consists of willfully testifying to the truth of a fact which the defendant does not believe to be true", petitioner's testimony could not be found "willfully" false unless at the time his testimony was given petitioner "fully understood the questions put to him but nevertheless gave false answers knowing the same to be false." The court further instructed the jury that if petitioner did not understand the question put to him and for that reason gave an unresponsive answer, he could not be convicted of perjury. Petitioner could, however, be convicted if he gave an answer "not literally false but when considered in the context in which it was given, nevertheless constitute (d) a false statement." (409 U.S. 352, 356). The jury began its deliberations at 11:30 a.m. Several times it requested exhibits or additional instructions from the court, and at one point, at the request of the jury, the District Court repeated its instructions in full. At 6:10 p.m., the jury returned its verdict, finding petitioner guilty on the count of perjury before us today and not guilty on another charge not here relevant.

In the Court of Appeals, petitioner contended, as he had in post-trial motions before the District Court, that the key question was imprecise and suggestive of various interpretations. In addition, petitioner contended that he could not be convicted of perjury on the basis of testimony that was concededly truthful, however unresponsive. A divided Court of Appeals held that the question was readily susceptible of a responsive reply and that it adequately tested the defendant's belief in the veracity of his answer. The Court of Appeals further held that, "(f)or the purposes of 18 U.S.C. 1621, an answer containing half of the truth which also constitutes a lie by negative implication, when the answer is intentionally given in place of the responsive answer called for by a proper question, is perjury." 453 F.2d 555, 559. In this Court, petitioner renews his attack on the specificity of the question asked him and the legal sufficiency of his answer to support a conviction for perjury. The problem of the ambiguity of the question asked him and the legal sufficiency of his answer to support a conviction for perjury. This problem of the ambiguity of the question is not free from doubt, but we need not reach that issue. (409 U.S. 352, 357) Even assuming, as we do, that the question asked petitioner specifically focused on petitioner's personal bank accounts, we conclude that the federal perjury statute cannot be construed to sustain a conviction based on petitioner's answer.

The statute, 18 U.S.C. 1621, substantially identical in its relevant language to its predecessors for nearly a century, is "a federal statute enacted in an effort to keep the course of justice free from the pollution of perjury." United States v. Williams, 341 U.S. 58, 68 (1951). We have held that the general federal perjury provision is applicable to federal bankruptcy proceedings. Hammer v. United States, 271 U.S. 620 (1926). The need for truthful testimony in a 21 (a) bankruptcy proceeding is great, since the proceeding is "a searching inquiry into the conditions of the estate of the bankrupt, to assist in discovering and collecting the assets, and to develop facts and circumstances which bear upon the question of discharge." Travis v. United States, 123 F. 2d 268, 271 (CA10 1941). Here, as elsewhere, the perpetration of perjury "well may affect the dearest concerns of the parties before a tribunal..." United States v. Norris, 300 U.S. 564, 574 (1937).

There is, at the outset, a serious problem in applying 1621 to petitioner's answer. The words of the statute confine the offence to the witness who "willfully...states...any material matter which he does not believe to be true." Beyond question, petitioner's answer to the crucial question was not responsive if we assume, as we do, that the first question was directed at personal bank accounts. There is, indeed, an implication in the answer to the second question that there was never a personal account; in casual conversation this interpretation might reasonably be drawn. But we are not dealing with casual conversation and the statute does not make it a criminal act for a witness to willfully (409 U.S. 352, 358) state any material matter that implies any material matter that he does not believe to be true.

The Government urges that the perjury statute be construed broadly to reach petitioner's answer and thereby fulfill its historic purpose of reinforcing our adversary factfinding process. We might go beyond the precise words of the statute if we thought they did not adequately express the intention of Congress, but we perceive no reason why Congress would intend the drastic sanction of a perjury prosecution to cure a testimonial mishap that could readily have been reached with a single additional question by counsel alert – as every examiner ought to be – to the incongruity of petitioner's unresponsive answer. Under the pressures and tensions of interrogation, it is not uncommon for the most earnest witness to give answers that are not entirely responsive. Sometimes the witness does not understand the question, or may in an excess of caution or apprehension read too much or too little into it. It should come as no surprise that a participant in a bankruptcy proceeding may have something to conceal and consciously tries to do so, or that a debtor may be embarrassed at his plight and yield information reluctantly. It is the responsibility of the lawyer to probe; testimonial interrogation, and cross-examination in particular, is a probing, prying, pressing form of inquiry. If a witness evades, it is the lawyer's responsibility to recognize the evasion and to bring the witness back to (409 U.S. 352, 359) the mark, to flush out the whole truth with the tools of adversary examination.

It is no answer to say that here the jury found that petitioner intended to mislead his examiner. A jury should not be permitted to engage in conjecture whether an unresponsive answer, true and complete on its face, was intended to mislead or divert the examiner; the state of mind of the witness is relevant only to the extent that it bears on whether "he does not believe (his answer) to be true". To hold otherwise would be to inject a new and confusing element into the adversary testimonial system we know. Witnesses would be unsure of the extent of their responsibility for the misunderstandings and inadequacies of examiners, and might well fear having that responsibility tested by a jury under the vague rubric of "intent to mislead" or "perjury by implication". The seminal modern treatment of the history of the offense concludes that one consideration of policy overshadowed all others during the years when perjury first emerged as a common-law offense; "that the measures taken against the offense must not be so severe as to discourage witness from appearing or testifying." Study of Perjury, reprinted in Report of New York Law Revision Commission, Legis. Doc. No. 60, p. 249 (1935). A leading 19th century commentator, quoted by Dean Wigmore, noted that the English law "throws every fence round a person accused of perjury," for "the obligation of protecting witnesses from oppression, or annoyance, by charges, or threats of charges, of having borne false testimony, is far paramount to that of giving every perjury its deserts. To repress that crime, prevention is better than cure: and the law of England relies, for this purpose, on the means provided for detecting and exposing the crime at the moment of commission, – such as publicity, (409 U.S. 352, 360) cross-examination, the aid of jury etc.; and on the infliction of a severe, though not excessive punishment, wherever the commission of the crime has been clearly proved." W. Best, Principles of the Law of Evidence 606 (C. Chamberlayne ed. 1883). See J. Wigmore, Evidence 275–276 (3d ed. 1940). Addressing the same problem, Montesquieu took as his starting point the French tradition of capital punishment for perjury and the relatively mild English punishment of the pillory. He thought the disparity between the punishments could be explained because the French did not permit the accused to present his own witnesses, while in England "they admit of witnesses on both sides, and the affair is discussed in some measure between them; consequently false witness is there less dangerous, the accused having a remedy against the false witnesses, which he has not in France." Montesquieu, The Spirit of the Laws, quoted in Study of Perjury, supra, p. 253.

Thus, we must read 1621 in light of our own and the traditional Anglo-American judgment that a prosecution for perjury is not the sole, or even the primary, safeguard against errant testimony. While "the lower federal courts have not dealt with the question often," and while their expressions do not deal with the unresponsive testimony and are not precisely in point, "it may be said that they preponderate against the respondent's contention." United States v. Norris, 300 U.S., at 576. The cases support petitioner's position that the perjury statute is not to be loosely construed, nor the statute invoked simply because a wily witness succeeds in derailing the questioner – so long as the witness speaks the literal truth. The burden is on the questioner to pin the witness down to the specific object of the questioner's inquiry. United States v. Wall, 371 F.2d 398 (CA6 1967); United State v. Slutzky, 79 F.2d 504 (CA3 (409 U.S. 352, 361) 1935); Galanos v. United States, 49 F.2d 898 (CA6 1931); United States v. Cobert, 227 F. Supp. 915 (SD Cal. 1964).

The Government does not contend that any misleading or incomplete response must be sent to the jury to determine whether a witness committed perjury because he intended to sidetrack his questioner. As the Government recognizes, the effect of so unlimited an interpretation of 1621 would be broadly unsettling. It is said, rather, that petitioner's testimony falls within a more limited category of intentionally misleading responses with an especially strong tendency to mislead the questioner. In the federal cases cited above, the Government tells us the defendants gave simple negative answers "that were both entirely responsive and entirely truthful...In neither case did the defendant – as did the petitioner here – make affirmative statements of one fact that in context constituted denials by negative implication of a related fact." Thus the Government isolates two factors which are said to require application of the perjury statute in the circumstances of the case: the unresponsiveness of petitioner's answer and the affirmative cast of that answer, with its accompanying negative implications.

The analysis succeeds in confirming the Government's position, but it does not persuade us that Congress intended to extend the coverage of 1621 to answers unresponsive on their face but untrue only by "negative implication". Though perhaps a plausible argument can be made that unresponsive answers are especially likely to mislead, any such argument must (409 U.WS. 352, 362) we think, be predicate upon the questioner's being aware of the unresponsiveness of the relevant answer. Yet, if the questioner is aware of the unresponsiveness of the answer, with equal force it can be argued that the very unresponsiveness of the answer should alert counsel to press on for the information he desires. It does not matter that the unresponsive answer is stated in the affirmative, thereby implying the negative of the question actually posed; for again, by hypothesis, the examiner's awareness of unresponsiveness should lead him to press another question or reframe his initial question with greater precision. Precise questioning is imperative as a predicate for the offense of perjury.

It may well be that petitioner's answers were not guileless but were shrewdly calculated to evade. Nevertheless, we are constrained to agree with Judge Lumbard, who dissented from the judgment of the Court of Appeals, that any special problems arising from the literally true but unresponsive answer are to be remedied through the "questioner's acuity" and not by a federal perjury prosecution.

Reversed.

(57) Northeast Iowa v. Global Syndicate (U.S.)

Court opinions are parts of a textual succession on a hierarchical ladder of instances. More often than not, they are understandable only toward the background of foregoing decisions of lower courts. In court opinions, legal intertextuality is also manifest in the reference to statutory provisions, mostly through use of numbers, rarely by direct quotations of provisions. This is another aspect of their legal intertextuality. Legal intertextuality is illustrated by the following case:

United States Court of Appeals

For the Eighth Circuit (No. 06–1833)

Northeast Iowa Ethanol, L.L.C., an Iowa Limited Liability Company, Appellee,

v.

Global Syndicate International, Inc.; Martin Ubani; Peter B. Topol; Defendants,

Jerry Drizin; Appellant,

Michelle Arsenault; William G. Davenport; Dorchester Enterprises, Inc.; Don Walls; Jesse W. Erwin, Defendants

Appeal from the United States District Court for the Northern District of Iowa.

Submitted: August 31, 2007

Filed: September 10, 2007.

Before Wollman, Colloton, and Benton, Circuit Judges.

PER CURIAM.

Following a bench trial, Jerry Drizin appeals the district court's (1) order and judgment in favor of Northeast Iowa Ethanol, L.L.C. (NIE), holding him liable for $3.8 million in compensatory damages and $7.6 million in punitive damages for misappropriating funds. Having carefully reviewed the parties' arguments and the record on appeal, we affirm.

To begin, we hold that the court did not err in exercising personal jurisdiction over Drizin. See Bowman v. Koch Transfer Co., 862 F. 2d 1257, 1258 (6th Cir. 1988) (by answering complaint, defendants waived any personal jurisdiction defense); Gilmore v. Shearson/Am.Express Inc., 811 F.2d 108, 112 (2d Cir. 1987) (if personal jurisdiction defense has been waived by failure to raise it in response to original complaint, it may not be resurrected merely because amended complaint was filed); cf. Dever v. Hentzen Coatings, Inc., 380 F.3d 1070, 1072 (8th Cir. 2004) (personal jurisdiction questions are reviewed de novo).

We further hold that the district court's credibility determinations and inferences are permissible, and that none of its findings are based on an erroneous view of the law or are clearly erroneous. See Fed. R.Civ.P. 52(a) (findings of fact, whether based on oral or documentary evidence, shall not be set aside unless clearly erroneous, and due regard shall be given to opportunity of trial court to judge credibility of witnesses), Richardson v. Sugg, 448 F.3d 1046, 1052 (8th Cir. 2006) (following bench trial, trial court's factual findings are reviewed for clear error; court will overturn factual findings only if they are not supported by substantial evidence in record, if they are based on erroneous view of law, or if appellate court is left with definite and firm conviction that error was made; due regard is given to district court's judgment of witness credibility, and choice between two permissible views of evidence is not clearly erroneous).

Given the district court's factual findings, we conclude that the court did not err in holding Drizin liable for conversion of $3.8 million belonging to NIE. See Bearbower v. Bearbower (In re Estate of Bearbower), 426 N.W.2 392, 394 n.1 (Iowa 1988) (essential elements of conversion are (1) ownership by plaintiff or other possessory right in plaintiff greater than that of defendant; (2) exercise of dominion or control over chattels by defendant inconsistent with, and in derogation of, plaintiff's possessory rights thereto, and (3) damage to plaintiff). We also conclude that the court was warranted in awarding $7.6 million in punitive damages. See McClure v. Walgreen Co., 613 N.W.2d 225, 230 (Iowa 2000) (en banc) (standard for awarding punitive damages requires showing that, by "a preponderance of clear, convincing, and satisfactory evidence, the conduct of the defendant from which the claim arose constituted willful and wanton disregard for the rights or safety of another"; "willful and wanton disregard" includes intentional act in disregard of known or obvious risk creating high probability of harm, usually accompanied by conscious indifference to consequences); cf. Heslinga v. Bollman, 482 N.W.2d 921, 922 (Iowa 1992) (affirming judgment for compensatory and punitive damages in action for conversion). We thus find it unnecessary to address the merits of the district court's additional liability determinations. See Simmons v. Cook, 154 F.3d 805, 808–09 (8th Cir. 1998) (appellate court may affirm on any basis supported by record).

Finally, we reject as meritless Drizin's suggestion that reversal is appropriate because of improper conduct by the district court or by NIE's counsel.

The judgment is affirmed. See 8th Cir. R. 47B.

The Honorable John A. Jarvey, then a United States Magistrate Judge for the Northern District of Iowa, now a United States District Judge for the Southern District of Iowa, to whom the case was referred for final disposition by consent of the parties pursuant to 28 U.S.C. § 636(c).

(58) PGA Tour, Inc. v. Martin

(532 U.S. 661, 121 S.Ct. 1879, 2001 U.S. Lexis 4115)

The Martin-case concerns the application of the Americans with Disabilities Act (ADA). In its pertaining part the ADA prescribes as a general rule:

> No individual shall be discriminated against on the basis of disability in the full and equal enjoyment of the goods, services, facilities, privileges, advantages, or accommodations of any place of public accommodation by any person who owns, leases (or leases to), or operates a place of public accommodation. 42 U.S.C. § 12182(a)

According to the ADA, the term 'discrimination' includes:

> "a failure to make reasonable modifications in policies, practices, or procedures, when such modifications are necessary to afford such goods, services, facilities, privileges,

advantages, or accommodations to individuals with disabilities, unless the entity can demonstrate that making such modifications would fundamentally alter the nature of such goods, services, facilities, privileges, advantages or accommodations." 42 U.S.C. §12182(b)(2)(A)(ii).

Excerpts from the case:

Steven, Justice. This case raises two questions concerning the application of the Americans with Disabilities Act of 1990 (42 U.S.C. § 12101 et seq.) to a gifted athlete: first, whether the Act protects access to professional golf tournaments by a qualified entrant with a disability, and second, whether a disabled contestant may be denied the use of a golf cart because it would "fundamentally alter the nature" of the tournaments to allow him to ride when all other contestants must walk.

Petitioner PGA Tour, Inc., a non-profit entity formed in 1968, sponsors and cosponsors professional golf tournaments conducted on three annual tours. About 200 golfers participate in the PGA Tour; about 170 in the Nike Tour; and about 100 in the Senior PGA Tour. PGA Tour and Nike Tour tournaments typically are four-day events, played on courses leased and operated by petitioner. The revenues generated by television, admissions, concessions, and contributions from cosponsors amount to about $ 300 million a year, much of which is distributed in prize money. The "Conditions of Competition and Local Rules," often described as the "hard card," apply specifically to petitioner's professional tours. The hard cards for the PGA Tour and Nike Tour required players to walk the golf course during tournaments, but not during open qualifying rounds. On the Senior PGA Tour, which is limited to golfers age 50 and older, the contestants can use golf carts. Most seniors, however, prefer to walk.

Casey Martin is a talented golfer. As an amateur, he won 17 Oregon Golf Association junior events before he was 15, and he won the state championship as a high school senior. He played on the Stanford University golf team that won the 1994 National Collegiate Athletic Association (NCAA) championship. As a professional, Martin qualified for the Nike Tour in 1998 and 1999, and based on his 1999 performance, qualified for the PGA Tour in 2000. In the 1999 season, he entered 24 events, made the cut 13 times, and had six top-10 finishes, coming in second twice and third once.

Martin is also an individual with a disability, as defined in the Americans with Disabilities Act of 1990 (ADA or Act). Since birth he has been afflicted with Klippel-Trenaunay-Weber Syndrome, a degenerative circulatory disorder that obstructs the flow of blood from his right leg back to his heart. The disease is progressive; it causes severe pain and has atrophied his right leg. During the latter part of his college career, because of the progress of the disease, Martin could no longer walk an 18-hole golf course. Walking not only caused him pain, fatigue, and anxiety, but also created a significant risk of haemorrhaging, developing blood clots, and fracturing his tibia so badly that an amputation might be required.

When Martin turned pro and entered petitioner's Qualifying-School, the hard card permitted him to use a cart during his successful progress through the first two stages.

He made a request, supported by detailed medical records, for permission to use a golf cart during the third stage. Petitioner refused to review those records or to waive its walking rule for the third stage. Martin therefore filed this action.

At trial, petitioner PGA Tour did not contest the conclusion that Martin has a disability covered by the ADA, or the fact "that his disability prevents him from walking the course during a round of golf." Rather, petitioner asserted that the condition of walking is a substantive rule of competition and that waiving it as to any individual for any reason would fundamentally alter the nature of the competition. Petitioner's evidence included the testimony of a number of experts, among them some of the greatest golfers in history. Arnold Palmer, Jack Nicklaus, and Ken Venturi explained that fatigue can be a critical factor in a tournament, particularly on the last day, when psychological pressure is at a maximum. Their testimony makes it clear that, in their views, permission to use a cart might well give some players a competitive advantage over other players who must walk. They did not, however, express any opinion on whether a cart would give Martin such an advantage.

Rejecting petitioner's argument that an individualized inquiry into the necessity of the walking rule in Martin's case would be inappropriate, the District Court stated that it had "the independent duty to inquire into the purpose of the rule at issue, and to ascertain whether there can be a reasonable modification made to accommodate plaintiff without frustrating the purpose of the rule" and thereby fundamentally altering the nature of petitioner's tournaments. The judge found that the purpose of the rule was to inject fatigue into the skill of shot-making, but that the fatigue injected "by walking the course cannot be deemed significant under normal circumstances." Furthermore, Martin presented evidence, and the judge found, that even with the use of a cart, Martin must walk over a mile during an 18-hole round, and that the fatigue he suffers from coping with his disability is "undeniably greater" than the fatigue his able-bodied competitors endure from walking the course. As a result, the judge concluded that it would "not fundamentally alter the nature of the PGA Tour's game to accommodate him with a cart." The judge accordingly entered a permanent injunction requiring petitioner to permit Martin to use a cart in tour and qualifying events.

The Court of Appeals concluded that golf courses remain places of public accommodation during PGA tournaments. On the merits, because there was no serious dispute about the fact that permitting Martin to use a golf cart was both a reasonable and a necessary solution to the problem of providing him access to the tournaments, the Court of Appeals regarded the central dispute as whether such permission would "fundamentally alter" the nature of the PGA Tour or Nike Tour. Like the District Court, the Court of Appeals viewed the issue not as "whether use of carts generally would fundamentally alter the competition, but whether the use of a cart by Martin would do so." That issue turned on "an intensively fact-based inquiry," and, the court concluded, had been correctly resolved by the trial judge. In its words, "all that the cart does is permit Martin access to a type of competition in which he otherwise could not engage because of his disability."

Congress enacted the ADA in 1990 to remedy widespread discrimination against disabled individuals. In studying the need for such legislation, Congress found that "historically, society has tended to isolate and segregate individuals with disabilities, and despite some improvements, such forms of discrimination against individuals with disabilities continue to be a serious and pervasive social problem." After thoroughly investigating the problem, Congress concluded that there was a "compelling" need to a "clear and comprehensive national mandate" to eliminate discrimination against disabled individuals, and to integrate them into the economic and social mainstream of American life." To effectuate its sweeping purpose, the ADA forbids discrimination against disabled individuals in major areas of public life, among them employment (Title I of the Act), public services (Title II), and public accommodations (Title III). At issue now is the applicability of Title III to petitioner's golf tours and qualifying rounds, in particular to petitioner's treatment of a qualified disabled golfer wishing to compete in those events.

It seems apparent, from both the general rule and the comprehensive definition of "public accommodation," that petitioner's golf tours and their qualifying rounds are comfortably within the coverage of Title III, and Martin within its protection. The events occur on "golf courses," a type of place specifically identified by the Act as a public accommodation (Section 12181 (7) (l)). In this case, the narrow dispute is whether allowing Martin to use a golf cart, despite the walking requirement that applies to the PGA Tour, the Nike Tour, and the third stage of the Qualifying-School, is a modification that would "fundamentally alter the nature" of these events.

As an initial matter, we observe that the use of carts is not itself inconsistent with the fundamental character of the game of golf. From early on, the essence of the game has been shot-making – using clubs to cause a ball to progress from the teeing ground to a hole some distance away with as few strokes as possible. That essential aspect of the game is still reflected in the very first of the Rules of Golf, which declares: "The Game of Golf consists in playing a ball from the teeing ground into the hole by a stroke or successive strokes in accordance with the rules." Over the years, there have been many changes in the players' equipment, in golf course design, in the Rules of Golf, and in the method of transporting clubs from hole to hole. Originally, so few clubs were used that each player could carry them without a bag. Golf carts started appearing with increasing regularity on American golf courses in the 1950s. Today they are everywhere. And they are encouraged. For one thing, they often speed up play, and for another, they are great revenue producers. There is nothing in the rules of golf that either forbids the use of carts or penalizes a player for using a cart.

Petitioner, however, distinguishes the game of golf as it is generally played from the game that it sponsors in the PGA Tour, Nike Tour, and the last stage of the Qualifying School – golf at the "highest level." According to petitioner, "the goal of the highest-level competitive athletics is to assess and compare the performance of different competitors, a task that is meaningful only if the competitors are subject to identical substantive rules." The waiver of any possibly "outcome-affecting" rule for a contestant would violate this principle and therefore, in petitioner's view, fundamentally alter the nature of the highest-level athletic event. The walking rule is one such rule, petitioner submits, because its purpose is "to inject the element of fatigue into the skill of shot-making," and thus its effect may be the critical loss of a stroke. As a consequence, the reasonable modification Martin seeks would fundamentally alter the nature of petitioner's highest-level tournaments.

The force of petitioner's argument is, first of all, mitigated by the fact that golf is a game in which it is impossible to guarantee that all competitors will play under exactly the same conditions or that an individual's ability will be the sole determinant of the outcome. For example, changes in the weather may produce harder greens and more head winds for the tournament leader than for his closest pursuers. A lucky bounce may have a shot or two. Whether such happenstance events are more or less probable than the likelihood that a golfer afflicted with Klippel-Trenaunay-Weber Syndrome would one day qualify for the Nike Tour and PGA Tour, they at least demonstrate that pure chance may have a greater impact on the outcome of elite golf tournaments than the fatigue resulting from the enforcement of the walking rule.

Further, the factual basis of petitioner's argument is undermined by the District Court's findings that the fatigue from walking during one of petitioner's 4-day tournaments cannot be deemed significant. The District Court credited the testimony of a professor in physiology and expert on fatigue, who calculated the calories expended in walking a golf course (about five miles) to be approximately 500 calories – "nutritionally less than a Big Mac." What is more, that energy is expended over a 5-hour period, during which golfers have numerous intervals for rest and refreshment. In fact, the expert concluded, because golf is a low-intensity activity, fatigue from the game is primarily a psychological phenomenon in which stress and motivation are the key ingredients. And even under conditions of sever heat and humidity, the critical factor in fatigue is fluid loss rather than exercise from walking. Moreover, when given the option of using a cart, the majority of golfers in petitioner's tournaments have chosen to walk, often to relieve stress or for other strategic reasons. As Nike Tour member Eric Johnson testified, walking allows him to keep in rhythm, stay warmer when it is chilly, and develop a better sense of elements and the course than riding a cart.

Even if we accept the factual predicate for petitioner's argument – that the walking rule is "outcome affecting" because fatigue may adversely affect performance – its legal position is fatally flawed. Petitioner's refusal to consider Martin's personal circumstances in deciding whether to accommodate his disability runs counter to the clear languages and purpose of the ADA. As previously stated, the ADA was enacted to eliminate discrimination against "individuals" with disabilities, and to that end Title III of the Act requires without exception that any "policies, practices, or procedures" of a public accommodation be reasonably modified for disabled "individuals" as necessary to afford access unless doing so would fundamentally alter what is offered. To be sure, the waiver of an essential rule of competition for anyone would fundamentally alter the nature of petitioner's tournaments. As we have demonstrated, the walking rule is at best peripheral to the nature of petitioner's athletic events, and thus might be waived in individual cases without working a fundamental alteration.

Under the ADA's basic requirements that the need of a disabled person be evaluated on an individual basis, we have no doubt that allowing Martin to use a golf cart would not fundamentally alter the nature of petitioner's tournaments. As we have discussed, the purpose of the walking rule is to subject players to fatigue, which in turn may influence the outcome of tournaments. Even if the rule does serve that purpose, it is an uncontested finding of the District Court that Martin "easily endures greater fatigue even with a cart that his able-bodied competitors do by walking." The purpose of the walking rule is therefore not compromised in the slightest by allowing Martin to use a cart. A modification that provides an exception to a peripheral tournament rule without impairing its purpose cannot be said to "fundamentally alter the tournament". What it can be said to do, on the other hand, is to allow Martin the chance to qualify for and compete in the athletic events petitioner offers to those members of the public who have the skill and the desire to enter. That is exactly what the ADA requires. As a result, Martin's request for a waiver of the walking rule should have been granted. The judgment of the Court of Appeals is affirmed. It is so ordered.

Dissenting opinion, Scalia, Justice: In my view today's opinion exercises a benevolent compassion that the law does not place it within our power to impose. The judgment distorts the text of Title III, the structure of the ADA, and the common sense. I respectfully dissent. In the Court's world, there is one set of rules that is "fair with respect to the able-bodied" but "individualized" rules, mandated by the ADA, for "talented but disabled athletes." The ADA mandates no such ridiculous thing. Agility, strength, speed, balance, quickness of mind, steadiness of nerves, intensity of concentration – these talents are not evenly distributed. No wild-eyed dreamer has ever suggested that the managing bodies of the competitive sports that test precisely these qualities should try to take account of the uneven distribution of God-given gifts when writing and enforcing the rules of competition. And I have no doubt Congress did not authorize misty-eyed judicial supervision of such a revolution.

(59) Falcoal, Inc. v. Kurumu (U.S.)

(660 F. Supp 1536 (S.D. Tex. 1987):

David Hittner, District Judge. Plaintiff Falcoal, Inc. is an American Corporation having its principal place of business in Houston, Texas. Defendant Kurumu (TKI) is a commercial entity, owned and controlled by the Turkish government. TKI decided to import a portion of Turkey's coal supply. In an attempt to solicit bids, TKI issued a notice announcing a "şartname" (terms and conditions). This announcement was made in local Turkish-language publications. The şartname distributed by TKI was issued in Turkish and provided by its terms that any conflicts as to its terms would be settled by reference to the original Turkish language version. Falcoal submitted the bid that was ultimately accepted by TKI. Falcoal's bid was signed and submitted by its authorized agent, Zihni, a Turkish company. The negotiation of the contract took place entirely in Ankara, Turkey.

After the parties had agreed to the terms, Zihni prepared two copies of the contract, an English version and a Turkish version. Although the parties assert that they believed the content of the two versions to be identical, the English contract and the Turkish contract contain forum selection clauses which directly contradict each other. The Turkish-language version provides that "the final jurisdiction for the settlement of any disputes, in the case of the purchaser (TKI) submitting a claim, lies within the jurisdiction of the Houston commercial courts and, in the case of the supplier (Falcoal) submitting a claim lies within the jurisdiction of the Ankara commercial courts." The English-language contract, by contrast, provides that any dispute "shall be finally settled in Houston and submitted to the jurisdiction of the Courts of the U.S.A. if the claim is put forward by supplier (Falcoal) and in Ankara, Turkey, and submitted to the Turkish Courts if the claim is put forward by buyer (TKI)."

Pursuant to the contract, Falcoal was to deliver 100,000 tons of coal to a shipper of TKI's choice. Falcoal agreed to post a performance bond in an amount equal to 10 percent of the contract price and, pursuant to this agreement, Citibank International-Ankara issued a performance bond in favor of TKI in the amount of $400,000. This bond was secured by a letter of credit opened by Falcoal at Citibank International-Dallas. The contract further provided that, to secure payment for the coal, TKI was to open a letter of credit in New York forty-five days before shipment. TKI failed to open this letter of credit. When the coal was not shipped, TKI, allegedly wrongfully and without authorization, drew on Falcoal's performance bond. Falcoal subsequently brought this suit against TKI alleging breach of contract for failing to open the New York letter of credit in Falcoal's favor, conversion and fraud for wrongfully drawing on Falcoal's performance bond, and injury to Falcoal's business reputation. TKI has moved to dismiss, alleging lack of subject matter jurisdiction and lack of personal jurisdiction.

TKI asserts that this court lacks subject matter jurisdiction because TKI, as an entity of the Turkish government, has sovereign immunity under the Foreign Sovereign Immunities Act of 1976 (FISA), 28 U.S.C. § 1602 et seq. However, Falcoal contends that TKI waived sovereign immunity by agreeing to a forum selection clause and falls within the commercial exception of the FSIA. The waiver provision and commercial exception are found in section 1605(a):

A foreign state shall not be immune from the jurisdiction of courts of the United States or of the States in any case-

(1) in which the foreign state has waived its immunity either explicitly or by implication, notwithstanding any withdrawal of the waiver which the foreign state may purport to effect except in accordance with the terms of the waiver;
(2) in which the action is based upon a commercial activity carried on in the United States by the foreign state; or upon an act performed in the United States in connection with a commercial activity of the foreign state elsewhere; or upon an act outside the territory of the United States in connection with a commercial activity of the foreign state elsewhere and that act causes a direct effect in the United States.

This Court would find merit to Falcoal's "waiver" argument, were the English version forum clause the only clause at issue. However, the Court cannot ignore the existence of the Turkish contract, whose forum clause provides for suit in Houston when TKI is the plaintiff. That contract expressly provides for suit against TKI in Turkey. Clearly, under the facts of this case, as here, there are two contradictory forum clauses and where the issue of which forum clause should control is vigorously contested, the English-language clause cannot be said to constitute a waiver of sovereign immunity.

The Court next reviews Falcoal's argument that TKI's actions place it within the exceptions to sovereign immunity set forth in section 1605(a)(2). Clearly this action is not one "based upon commercial activity carried on (by TKI) in the United States." The FSIA defines such commercial activity as activity "having substantial contact with the United States." The mere provision for payment in the United States, however, is not a "substantial contact" meeting the test for commercial activity under the FSIA. It remains for this Court to determine whether TKI's conduct falls within the third clause of section 1605 (a)(2) as to whether the conduct alleged against TKI constitutes "an act outside the territory of the United States in connection with the commercial activity of the foreign state elsewhere" which "causes a direct effect in the United States:" At issue is the definition of "direct effect".

TKI asserts, and Falcoal has not shown otherwise, that it has had no contacts with the Texas forum, nor in fact with the United States, other than its involvement in the contract which is the subject of this suit. That contract was solicited, negotiated, drafted, and executed in Turkey and in the Turkish language. The contract itself does not establish minimum contacts with the Texas forum. Nor does TKI's agreement to pay through a letter of credit in New York create personal jurisdiction. Thus, in the instant case the constitutional requirements for exercise of in personam jurisdiction are lacking.

In an effort to resolve the tension between 28 U.S.C. § 1605 (a) (2) and 28 U.S.C. § 1330 (b), courts have taken two approaches. Some have held that an effect cannot reach the level of "direct" effects described in the statute and thus sovereign immunity cannot be overcome, unless the effect fulfills the "minimum contacts" requirement. Other courts have given "direct effect" its literal meaning and found such an effect when an American corporation has suffered a direct financial injury due to a foreign sovereign's conduct. This court finds the latter approach to be most reasonable. The Court holds that the conduct of TKI in drawing on Falcoal's performance bond was an action which caused a direct effect in the United States, and thus TKI cannot claim sovereign immunity from this suit. Subject matter jurisdiction, therefore, exists.

Constitutionally, this court cannot exercise personal jurisdiction over TKI unless TKI has taken some action that may be construed as an expression of waiver or implied consent to the exercise of such jurisdiction. Falcoal contends that such an implied consent is found in the forum selection clause of the English version contract. This Court could find waiver, however, only if it were found that the Turkish-language clause is unenforceable and the English version valid. The Court thus faced with the existence of two contradictory clauses, must look to the law of the appropriate forum to determine which clause to enforce. Because the contract was solicited, negotiated and executed in Turkey, Turkish law must apply. Both parties agree that, were Texas law to apply, the existence of contradictory clauses would evidence a lack of meeting of the minds on the issue of forum for suit, and the clause should be dropped from both contracts. However, in the absence of a determination of similar Turkish law, the clauses cannot be eliminated from the contract. Although this Court finds that TKI has been divested of its sovereign immunity to this suit by its actions in Turkey having a direct effect in the United States and, thus, subject matter jurisdiction exists, the Court finds that it lacks personal jurisdiction over TKI. Motion to dismiss is granted.

(60) Ramirez v. Plough, Inc. (U.S.)

(15 Cal. App. 4th 1110, 12 Cal. Rptr. 2d 423, 1992):

Court of Appeal of California

Thaxer, Judge Jorge Ramirez, a minor, by his guardian ad litem, Rosa Rivera, appeals from a summary judgment in favor of Plough, Inc. Appellant action sought damages for injuries sustained in March 1986 when Jorge, who was then four months old, contracted Reye's Syndrome after ingesting St. Joseph Aspirin for Children (SJAC). Plough marketed and distributed SJAC.

Reye's Syndrome is a serious disease of unknown cause characterized by severe vomiting, lethargy, or irritability which may progress to delirium or coma. The disease generally strikes children or teenagers who are recovering from a mild respiratory tract infection, influenza, chicken pox, or other viral illnesses. The mortality rate of the disease is high, and permanent brain damage occurs in many cases. As a result of contracting Reye's Syndrome, appellant suffered catastrophic injuries including quadriplegia, blindness, and profound mental retardation.

In the early 1980s, there was significant scientific debate concerning the cause of Reye's Syndrome. Several state studies suggested a statistical association between the ingestion of aspirin and the disease. In December 1982, the federal government acknowledged the debate. After considering the state studies and their critics, the federal government rejected a proposal which would require a warning label and instead, undertook an independent study. Apparently, Plough participated in efforts to influence government officials and agencies to reject the label proposal which Plough considered premature.

In December 1985, the Food and Drug Administration (FDA) requested that aspirin manufacturers voluntarily place a label on aspirin products warning consumers of the possible association between aspirin and Reye's Syndrome. Plough voluntarily complied and began including a warning and insert in SJAC packaging. On June 5, 1986, the Reye's Syndrome warning became mandatory.

In March 1986, SJAC labeling bore the following warning: "Warning: Reye's Syndrome is a rare but serious disease which can follow flu or chicken pox in children and teenagers. While the cause of Reye's Syndrome in unknown, some reports claim aspirin may increase the risk of developing this disease. Consult a doctor before use in children or teenagers with flu or chicken pox." In addition, the SJAC package insert included the following statement: "The symptoms of Reye's Syndrome can include persistent vomiting, sleepiness and lethargy, violent headaches, unusual behavior, including disorientation, combativeness, and delirium. If any of these symptoms occur, especially following chicken pox or flu, call your doctor immediately, even if your child has not taken any medication. Reye's Syndrome is Serious, so Early Detection and Treatment are Vital."

Rosa Rivera purchased SJAC on March 12, 1986, and administered it to appellant who was suffering from what appeared to be a cold or upper respiratory infection. She gave appellant the aspirin without reading the directions or warnings appearing on the SJAC packaging. The packaging was in English and Ms. Rivera can speak and understand only Spanish. She did not seek to have the directions or warnings translated from English to Spanish, even though members of her household spoke English.

The trial court granted Plough's motion for summary judgment on the grounds that "there is no duty to warn in a foreign language and there is no causal relationship between plaintiff's injury and defendant's activities."

It is undisputed SJAC was marketed and intended for the treatment of minor aches and pains associated with colds, flu, and minor viral illness. The SJAC box promised "fast, effective relief of fever and minor aches and pains of colds." Both parties accept the premise that Plough had a duty to warn consumers that the use of SJAC after a viral infection or chicken pox could lead to Reye's Syndrome, an illness with serious, possibly fatal, consequences. In March 1986, federal regulations requiring a Reye's Syndrome warning had been promulgated and were final, although not yet effective. The FDA had previously solicited voluntary labeling. In response to the request for voluntary labeling, Plough started packaging SJAC with explicit warnings of the risks of Reye's Syndrome and the use of aspirin after a viral illness. There is no doubt Plough had a duty to warn of the Reye's Syndrome risk.

The question thus is whether the warning given only in English was adequate under the circumstances. Respondent argues that as a matter of law it has no duty to place foreign-language warnings on products manufactured to be sold in the United States and that holding manufacturers liable for failing to do so would violate public policy. While the constitutional, statutory, regulatory, and judicial authorities relied on by respondent may reflect a public policy recognizing the status of English as an official language, nothing compels the conclusion that a manufacturer of a dangerous or defective product is immunized from liability when an English-only warning does not adequately inform non-English literate persons likely to use the product. Plough's evidence showed that over 148 foreign languages are spoken in the United States and over 23 million Americans speak a language other than English in their homes. The evidence plainly does not prove that Plough used reasonable care in giving an English-only warning. Plough, then, resorts to arguing that the burden on manufacturers and society of requiring additional warnings is so "staggering" that the courts should preclude liability as a matter of law. We are not persuaded.

Certainly the burden and costs of giving foreign-language warnings is one factor for consideration in determining whether a manufacturer acted reasonably in using only English. The importance of that factor may vary from case to case depending upon other circumstances, such as the nature of the product, marketing efforts directed to segments of the population unlikely to be English-literate, and the actual and relative size of the consumer market which could reasonably be expected to speak or read only a certain foreign language. Plough presented no evidence from which we can gauge the extent of the burden under the facts of this case.

Ramirez submitted evidence that Plough knew Hispanics were an important part of the market for SJAC and that Hispanics often maintain their first language rather than learn English. SJAC was advertised in the Spanish media, both radio and television. That evidence raises material questions of fact concerning the foreseeability of purchase by a Hispanic not literate in English and the reasonableness of not giving a Spanish-language warning. If Plough has evidence conclusively showing that it would have been unreasonable to give its label warning in Spanish because of the burden, it did not present that evidence below.

Given the triable issues of material fact, if we accepted Plough's arguments in this case in effect we would be holding that failure to warn in a foreign language is not negligence, regardless of the circumstances. Such a sweeping grant of immunity should come from the legislative branch of government, not the judicial. In deciding that Plough did not establish its right to judgment as a matter of law, we do not hold that manufacturers are required to warn in languages other than English simply because it may be foreseeable that non-English literate persons are likely to use their products. Our decision merely recognizes that under some circumstances the standard of due care may require such warning.

Because evidence shows triable issues of material fact and because Plough did not establish its immunity from liability as a matter of law, its motion for summary judgment should have been denied.

(61) In re Maldonado (UK)

The following English court decision is known among jurists as the Maldonado-case. It is particularly complex in its linguistic and juridical structure. Although some of its paragraphs have been quoted in the main text, it seems expedient to quote here also the entire text. It perfectly illustrates many issues discussed in the theoretical part of this book. In the English private international law, the Maldonado-case concerns the problem of characterization (FR *qualification*) of legal notions and especially the issue of perspective in which this characterization should be undertaken. Here, the legal-linguistic perspective dominates the analysis. Issues relevant to this case as one of the leading cases of the English private international law of characterization are therefore mentioned only in the margin. In the main text, the Maldonado-case has been dealt with because it addresses or rather touches upon some principal legal-linguistic questions such as whether a judicial decision may be viewed as "a mere matter of words", or a "distinction without difference". In the decision there is a direct reference to such proceedings where the foreign State is perceived as one which "can constitute itself successor" (cf. p. 1585 of the decision in All E. R.). This makes plain that the legal language and the underlying legal reality are created and not simply found and that they are created with linguistic means. The Maldonado-case may not be the best available source for the analysis of processes in which the legal language is created. It shows, however, in a unique way how this specific language is used and how it functions in a judicial decision. It functions in this case as a piece of argumentation where a unanimous legal decision reached by a collegial body should appeal to readers in a controversial case. All three judges delivered their opinions in which despite the reference to views contrary to the result reached in the case, the same main line of justification is maintained. This subliminal argument on which the whole opinion is based is that the result reached is overwhelmingly better justified than the thinkable opposite result. The fact that three concurring opinions are delivered, strengthens the impression that the decision is right or at least that it is much better than the thinkable opposite decision. Intertextual references as legal arguments are abundantly used to this effect. References to the precedents and to the legal literature are frequent; the quotation from Dicey's *Conflict of Laws* is even literally quoted twice in the same decision (cf. pp. 1582 and 1584), which as such seems to be already a legal-linguistic rarity. Passages from the legal literature are perceived as "incorporated in this judgment" (cf. p. 1585) and the numerous quotes which could also be used to support the opposite view to the one reached in the unanimous decision are repeated several times in the concurring opinions as well. For the contrary view, there are apparently no convincing arguments; the third judge, therefore, concludes assertively "I can see no warrant for acceding to, nor authority to support, it." (cf. p. 1587). The final formulas repeated three times: "I think the appeal fails and should be dismissed" (cf. p. 1584), "I agree that this appeal fails and should be dismissed" (cf. p. 1587), and "I think that this appeal fails." (cf. p. 1587), let no room for doubts, especially when repeated almost literally. The juridical text type underlying the judgment is called *seriatim opinion*. The term *domicile* is spelled *domicil* in the court opinion (cf. 2.3.2.1).

Re Maldonado (deceased)

State of Spain v. Treasury Solicitor

(All England Report 1953 vol. 2, pp. 1579–1587)

Court of Appeal (Sir Raymond Evershed, M.R., Jenkins and Morris, L.JJ.) November 26, 27, 30, 1953.

Conflict of Laws – Succession to estate of intestate – Foreign domicil of intestate – Personal property in England – Claim by foreign State as sole and universal heir

On Oct. 11, 1924, the deceased, a Spanish citizen domiciled in Spain died there a widow and intestate, leaving movable property in England. On June 4, 1930, the State of Spain obtained in Spain a declaration of heirship on failure of heirs on intestacy, and now claimed a grant of letters of administration of the English property. On the evidence, the State of Spain was "a true heir just as any individual heir according to Spanish law", but it was contended by the Crown that the maxim "mobilia sequuntur personam" stopped short of recognition of a State as successor.

Held: assuming that there was a valid distinction between the case where a foreign State claimed property in England of a person dying intestate and domiciled in the territory of the foreign State on the footing that it was ownerless and bona vacantia and the case where the foreign State claimed to be the successor by virtue of its own laws, in the latter case there was no rule of the English law which confined such succession to individuals having a particular quality or characteristic or had the effect of excluding a State from entertaining the capacity of an heir, and therefore, the State of Spain as true heir was entitled to a grant.

Decision of Barnard, J. (ante, p. 300), affirmed.

As to Intestate Succession to Movables see Halsbury, Hailsham Edn., Vol. 6, p. 245, para. 299; and for cases see Digest, Replacement Vol. 11, pp. 397, 398, Nos. 525–550. Cases referred to:

(1) Re Barnett's Trusts, (1902) 1 Ch. 847; 71 L.J.Ch. 408; 86 L-T. 346; 11 Digest, Replacement, 398, 548.
(2) In the Estate of Musurus, (1936) 2 All E.R. 1666; Digest Supp.

Appeal by the defendant, The Treasury Solicitor, from a decision of Barnard, J., dated May 22, 1953, and reported ante, p. 300.

Eloisa Hernandez Maldonado, a Spanish subject domiciled in Spain, died there on Oct. 11, 1924, a widow and intestate, with no ascendant, descendant or collateral relative entitled to succeed to her estate on her death under the law of Spain. She left movable property in England valued at the time of her death at the sum of £ 31,515 5s. 4d. but now said to be worth some £ 27,000. Article 956 of the Spanish Civil Code, as translated for the purposes of this case, and in the form in which it stood at the death of the intestate, was in these terms:

"In default of persons having the right to inherit in accordance with the provisions of the foregoing sections (which is the present case) the State shall inherit, the assets being devoted to institutions of charity and free instruction in the following order: (i) municipal charitable establishments and free schools of the place of residence of the deceased, (ii) establishments of both classes of the province to which the deceased belonged, (iii) charitable establishments and educational establishments of a general character."

On June 4, 1930, the State of Spain obtained in Spain a declaration of heirship in accordance with art. 958 of the Spanish Civil Code "to enable the State to take physical possession of the estate". The State of Spain brought proceedings in this country claiming that letters of administration to the estate of the intestate in this country should issue to the duly constituted attorney of the Spanish State as the sole and universal heir to her estate by Spanish law. The defendant in the action was the Treasury Solicitor, who claimed that a grant should issue for the benefit of the Crown as bona vacantia. On May 22, 1953, Barnard, J., held that on the evidence before him the State of Spain was a true heir just as any other individual heir according to Spanish law; that there was nothing contrary to English policy or repugnant to English law in a foreign State being permitted to take possession of the movables of one of its citizens in this country, and that, therefore, the State of Spain was entitled to a grant of letters of administration of the English estate. The Treasury Solicitor appealed.

Sir Lynn Ungoed-Thomas, Q.C., and Victor Russell for the Treasury Solicitor. Russell, Q.C. and Lindner, Q.C., for the State of Spain.

Sir Raymond Evershed, M.R., stated the facts and continued: It was agreed in the court below, and it has been conceded in this court, that the question is, as between the plaintiff, the State of Spain, and the defendant, the Treasury Solicitor: Who is entitled to the property? – since it is conceded that the right to the grant depends on the right to the property. The claim of the State of Spain is that by the law of Spain the State is entitled, in the circumstances of the case, as "successor" to inherit all the property of the intestate, and, accordingly, that the English courts will apply the principle mobilia sequuntur personam and accept the State of Spain as entitled to the property in question. On the other side, the Treasury Solicitor argues that the claim of the State of Spain is in truth not by way of a succession, but by the exercise of a paramount right of a sovereign State to take property of its nationals which has become ownerless on their deaths, and that the corresponding right of the English Crown to ownerless property is the only right that the English courts will recognise, having regard to the fact that the property in question is in England.

Barnard, J., had first to determine what was the relevant Spanish law. The material article of the Spanish Civil Code which was in force on Oct. 11 1924 (the date of the death) is art. 956. On this article there was a sharp conflict of expert testmony. Two witnesses called for the State of Spain said that the effect of the article was, as is stated by its terms, that the intestate having left no issue, parents or grandparents, surviving spouse, or collaterals within the sixth degree (for the purpose of art. 955 in force in October, 1924), the State of Spain was entitled as ultimus heres. On the other side, Dr. Colas, for the Treasury Solicitor said that, notwithstanding the language of the article, the State of Spain was not a true heir or successor but had become entitled to this property as bona vacantia. Between these two views the learned judge decided clearly in favour of the witnesses for the State of Spain. He said (ante, p. 305): "I am satisfied on the evidence before me that the State of Spain is a true heir just as any individual heir according to Spanish law". This finding has not been challenged in this court.

The Crown's argument before us may fairly be stated in the form of four propositions. (i) Prima facie, movable property situate within the limits and jurisdiction of any State is subject to the laws of the State, and if such property be found to be ownerless it will pass to and become the property of the State. This, at least, is the law of England, and in the case supposed the property in England is assumed by the Crown as bona vacantia. (ii) To the above general rule there is an exception, being a rule of private international law generally accepted by and forming part of the law of civilised States, including England. The exception is expressed by the formula mobilia sequuntur personam. Thus in the case of movables belonging, for example, to a deceased national of another country who died domiciled in that other country (as in the present case), the courts of this country will treat as entitled to the movables the person or persons who are by the law of that other country entitled to succeed thereto either under a testamentary disposition valid by the law of that other country or on an intestacy, as the case may be. But, (iii) the extent and scope of the exception expressed by the formula mobilia sequuntur personam is a matter in the case of each State for its own municipal law. And, (iv) in the case of a national of another State dying domiciled in the other State, and dying, according to its laws, intestate (as in the present case) the English courts will not recognise as having a title in this country to the movables of the intestate any persons who are not "successors" in accordance with some generally recognised nexus of personal relationship with the intestate, or, at least, will not recognise as a successor the foreign State itself which has made itself such by its own laws; for; notwithstanding the language used in those laws, the truth is that the State is exercising the equivalent of our jus regale as regards ownerless property. In further support of his fourth proposition counsel for the Crown has argued that since the rules of private international law apply to the relations inter se of individuals or, at least of subjects of States and not to the relations inter se of States themselves, the scope of the exception necessarily and logically stops short of recognition of a State as successor.

Counsel for the State of Spain has not, at any rate for the purpose of this appeal, been concerned to contest the first three of the propositions submitted by the Crown. His challenge has been directed to the fourth and last. According to this argument the successors of the foreign intestate are those persons, whether natural persons or personae fictae (including the foreign State itself) who, by the laws of the foreign State, are constituted successors. There can, according to counsel, be no justification for a requirement by our courts that the successors should have a particular quality, for example, that they should be blood relations of the deceased in some degree. Thus, to take the example used during the course of the argument, if the Spanish law decreed that, in default of any relations of the degree stated in the Code, the Archbishop of Toledo should be the next successor, the English courts must recognise the title of the archbishop to the movables here of a Spanish intestate. It follows thence that no line can be drawn to exclude a persona ficta, whether a corporation, a municipality, or the State itself, so long as, by the Spanish law, such personae are in truth made successors and do not claim their title otherwise, for example, by a right of appropriation of the property as bona vacantia.

In confining his argument to this single question, counsel accepted as good law the decision by Kekewich, J., in Re Barnett's Trusts (1) the English Crown claimed as bona vacantia movables belonging to a former Austrian citizen. But there was joined as a party for the purpose of the argument a representative of the then Austrian government who also claimed the property. The relevant art. 760 of the General Civil Code of Austria, unlike the article with which we are concerned of the Spanish Code, used this language:

"If the spouse is no longer alive, the succession is confiscated as heirless property either by the fiscus or by those persons who according to the political ordinances are justified in confiscating heirless estates"; and, having regard to the terms of that article, Kekewich, J., held that the claim of the Austrian government or its representative did not depend on his being in the guise or clothing of a successor, his claim was a claim to ownerless property, and, as between similar claims on the part of the British Crown and on the part of the Austrian government, that of the former must prevail. The argument for the Crown is set out at length (1902 1 Ch. 849), and it was observed pertinently by counsel for the State of Spain that there was no argument put forward on the part of the English Crown that no claim to "ownerless" movables by a foreign State as a successor, or in any other capacity, could, in any event, be successfully put forward in these courts. The argument of the representatives of the Crown was based on the terms of the article which I have read, and was to the effect that the right asserted by the Austrian government rested on a confiscation in the terms of art. 760 of the property as heirless (that is, ownerless) property. At the end of the argument it was said (1902 1 Ch. 852): "If in one of the countries a different principle prevailed (that is, if the State took not as on confiscation of heirless property, but as being a successor), a more difficult question might arise, because international law depends on reciprocity. But as in this country, so in Austria the State takes, not as 'ultimus heres' but 'jure regali'. It being clear that goods of this kind are taken by the Crown in both countries as bona vacantia, the law of England must apply to the English goods as the law of Austria would to goods in Austria".

The representative of the Crown cited Bar's Private International Law, Gillespie's translation, 2nd ed., p. 843, para. 387, which reads: "The question to which State property is to fall where there is no heir, whether to that in which it is situated, or to that to which the last possessor belonged, is dependent upon whether the right of the State to succeed is to be considered to be a right occupatione or a right of consolidation belonging to the feudal superior, or as a true right of succession. In either the first or the second case, the property will go to the State where the property is situated; in the last case it will fall to that of the domicil of the deceased, in so far as both States hold the theory of a universal succession, or as the estate is made up of movables. The theory which is in conformity with modern ideas of law, which is more deserving of our respect, and which undoubtedly now prevails as the theory of the law in Germany, is that, if there is no nearer in blood to be called to the succession, a man's fellow-countrymen must be regarded as his heirs. This view is supported by the fact that it is the State to which a man belongs that fixes the circle of those who are entitled to succeed to him as heirs, drawing it more or less wide, as it pleases; while, on the other hand, it has more or less of the air of robbery for a State to seize on the movable estate of a deceased person, who was by mere accident resident there at the moment of his death. Thus the State whose subject and citizen the deceased was, will be entitled to succeed him. But, beyond Germany, the other rule still prevails, and each State seizes the movables which happen to be within its borders."

In the course of his judgment Barnard, J., also referred to a passage in Wolff on Private International Law, 2nd ed., p. 579, which is as follows: "In default of the next of kin, the universal rule is that the property goes to the State or the Crown or a township or some other public body – in Germany, Italy, and Switzerland as ultimate 'heir', in England, Austria and Turkey by virtue of jus regale over bona vacantia. In the latter case the conflict rule on succession is not applicable because there is no 'succession' (inheritance)… the right to 'heirless' property is governed by the lex situs."

Other examples of a recognition of the distinction in the character in which a sovereign State may take is to be found in other text-books to which we were also referred during the course of the argument. For example, in Dicey's Conflict of Laws, 6th ed., the statement of r. 178 (p. 817): "The succession to the movables of an intestate is governed by the law of his domicil at the time of his death…" is followed by this passage (ibid., p. 818): "Where a person dies, e.g., intestate and a bastard, and under the law of the country where he is domiciled there is no succession to his movables, but they are bona vacantia, and leaves movables situate in a country, e.g., England, in which he is not domiciled, the title to such movables is governed by the lex situs, i.e., under English law the movables being situate in England, the Crown is entitled thereto. In such a case the foreign Treasury claims not by way of succession but because there is no succession. It does not follow that the decision would be the same if the law of the domicil was such that the foreign Treasury claimed as ultimus heres. That would be a true case of succession and would, it is submitted, be governed by the law of the domicil."

As will be observed in that work, the distinction, or the result, in the case of a foreign State claiming by way of succession is put as a submission. It is stated more positively in Cheshire's Private International Law, 4th ed., p. 59. But assuming that there is a valid distinction between the case where a Sovereign State claims the property on the footing that it is ownerless and bona vacantia, and the case where the State claims as being successor by virtue of its own laws, there is, at any rate, no statement, in any of the cases or the text-books, that I have been able to find, or to which our attention was drawn, that there is in England a rule which confines successors to individuals having a particular quality or characteristic, or which has the effect of excluding a State from ever entertaining the capacity.

In my judgment the real question is: What is the right or title by virtue of which the Spanish State now makes its claim? And, in my judgment, this point has been decided adversely to the Crown. That decision, the validity of which has not been challenged, I regard as conclusive against the appeal. I am unable to accept that, notwithstanding the finding of the learned judge, who said (ante, p. 305): "I am satisfied on the evidence before me that the State of Spain is a true heir just as any individual heir according to Spanish law," these courts will reject the result on an apriori view of the necessary qualifications for succession. If by the law of Spain it is possible to limit or define the individuals who can claim to be successors, that is, individuals having some connection by blood or marriage with the deceased, I can see no reason why the law of Spain should not nominate or constitute as heir, in default of such individual, any person or corporation, including the State itself. The idea of succession no doubt imports some notion of continuity of, for example, title. But, I see no reason why this conception is inapplicable to the State which is constituted successor by the laws of the State. It is, indeed, as I understand it, conceded that if under a valid will property of the deceased were given to the State of Spain, the State of Spain would be then treated as being a successor, although in that case as the result of the testamentary disposition. Nor does the Latin word "heres" from which the word "inherit" is derived necessarily involve any notion of some blood connection. To quote a sentence from Cicero, me nemo nisi amicus heredem fecit. I add that, in my judgment, there is no question of the law of Spain amounting to such a confiscation as would be regarded as repugnant to our own laws, and therefore, not enforceable in these courts. Finally, I refer again to the passage at the end of the reported argument in Re Barnett's Trusts where the matter is put (1902 1 Ch. 852): "If in one of the countries a different principle prevailed, a more difficult question might arise, because international law depends upon reciprocity." There is before us no evidence of what the law of Spain would be in the controversial case of an English national dying domiciled in England intestate without next of kin under the English law and leaving movables in Spain. I am, however, not able to reject the argument of counsel of the State of Spain on the ground that there is no evidence that the law, as I think it should held in this country, might not be reciprocal in Spain. I think the appeal fails and should be dismissed.

Jenkins, L.J., stated the facts as set out above and continued: The general rule to be applied in a case such as this is summed up in the maxim mobilia sequuntur personam, and is thus stated in Dicey's Conflict of Laws, 6th ed., p. 814: "Rule 177. The distribution of the distributable residue of the movables of the deceased is (in general) governed by the law of the deceased's domicil (lex domicilii) at the time of his death." Thus, in the present case the personality in question should, prima facie, devolve in accordance with the provisions of art. 956. There is, however, an admitted exception to the general rule to the effect that if, according to the law of the foreign State in which the deceased is domiciled, there is no one entitled to succeed to the movable property of the deceased owing, for example, to the bastardy of the deceased, or to the failure of kin near enough in degree to qualify for succession under the law of the domicil, and, by the law of the foreign State, the State itself is, in such circumstances, entitled to appropriate the property of the diseased as ownerless property, by virtue of some jus regale corresponding to our own law of bona vacantia, English law will not recognise the claim of the foreign State as part of the law of succession of the domicil, but will treat it merely as to the assertion by the foreign State of a prerogative right which has no extra-territorial validity and must yield to the corresponding prerogative right of the Crown. That appears from Dicey's Conflict of Laws, 6th ed., p. 818, to which Sir Raymond Evershed, M.R., has already referred: " Where a person dies, e.g., intestate and a bastard, and under the law of the country where he is domiciled there is no succession to his movables, but they are bona vacantia, and leaves movables situate in a country, e.g., England, in which he is not domiciled, the title to such movables is governed by the lex situs, i.e. under English law the movables being situate in England, the Crown is entitled thereto. In such a case the foreign Treasury claims not by way of succession but because there is no succession."

But the law of the relevant foreign country may be such as to constitute the State itself the successor to the deceased in the absence of any individual with a prior right of succession under that law, and the question then arises whether the claim of the foreign State should be recognised under the general rule as the claim of a person entitled to succeed according to the law of domicil, or should be treated as falling within the exception on the ground that the claim of the foreign State as self-constituted successor does not differ in substance or in principle from a claim by a foreign State by virtue of its paramount right to ownerless property within its dominions as bona vacantia or the equivalent.

Accordingly, two questions were debated in the court below: First, whether under the Spanish Civil Code the State takes as a true heir or successor in the eye of Spanish law, or takes by virtue of a jus regale; and, secondly, if it takes in the former capacity, whether English law will recognise the State of Spain as a true heir or successor for the purpose of the maxim mobilia sequuntur personam. Barnard, J., having heard evidence on both sides in regard of the Spanish law, answered the first question in the former sense, and the second question in the affirmative, holding in effect that the answer to the second followed from the answer to the first. The decision of Barnard, J., on the first question has not been challenged by the Crown in this court. The sole issue before us, therefore, is whether or not the State of Spain, being admittedly according to its own law the true heir of, or successor to, the intestate, should be recognised as such by English law in its application of the maxim mobilia sequuntur personam. This question has not been the subject of any direct decision, but the distinction between the sovereign State claiming "jure regali" and as true heir or successor was recognised in Re Barnett's Trusts (1) and In the Estate of Musurus (2). Inasmuch as the foreign law in each of those cases was held to give the foreign State concerned a jus regale as distinct from a true right of succession, there was no actual decision on the present question, but, as I have said, the distinction was recognised. Indeed, as Sir Raymond Evershed, M.R., has pointed out, both those cases would have been susceptible of a short and simple answer if the view then taken of the law had been that in no circumstances could a foreign State claim the assets situated in this country of a deceased intestate, whether the claim was founded on jus regale or on a true right of succession. The question has also been discussed in various text-books on this branch of the law. For example, in Dicey's Conflict of Laws, 6th ed., p. 818, the page which I have quoted continues: "It does not follow that the decision would be the same if the law of the domicil was such that the foreign Treasury claimed as ultimus heres. That would be a true case of succession and would, it is submitted, be governed by the law of domicil".

There are also passages referred to by Sir Raymond Evershed, M.R., in Wolff on Private International Law, 2nd ed., p. 579, in Bar's Private International Law (Gillespie's Translation), 2nd ed., p. 843, para. 387, and Cheshire's Private International Law, 4th ed., p. 59, all of which I treat as incorporated in this judgment.

The conclusion of Barnard, J., therefore, has the support of no inconsiderable weight of learned opinion, and although, for my part, I find it difficult to embrace with enthusiasm either side of this highly technical question, his conclusion also commends itself to me on the ground of consistency. In cases such as the present, English law professes to apply the law of the domicil to the devolution of the intestate's movables situated in this country. If the law of the domicil is that of a foreign State under whose law of intestacy the State itself is the successor, why should English law not give effect to that provision as part of the law of succession which it professes to apply? The reasons why, it is claimed, English law does not do so are expressed in a variety of ways. First, the distinction between succession by a sovereign State is said to be a mere matter of words. This argument is not without persuasive force, but I do not think the question can truly be said to be one of distinction without difference. The foreign State can only succeed under its own law of succession where the succession is governed by that law. On the other hand, where the case is not one of succession but of appropriation of ownerless property, the right applies to any ownerless property which may be reached by the law of the foreign State concerned, irrespective of the law by which its devolution is governed, provided only that by the relevant law it is in fact ownerless. Then it is said that the foreign State, being omnipotent so far as its own law of succession is concerned, can constitute itself successor in circumstances in which it could equally well rely on a claim based on jus regale. But in accepting the foreign State's law of succession, English law recognises the foreign State as arbiter of what the succession is to be. The foreign State could, for instance, enact that older relatives should be preferred to younger, or that male relatives should be preferred to female, or vice versa, or even that fair-haired relatives should be preferred to dark-haired. And to such distinctions, unreasonable as they might seem, English law would, as I understand the matter, have no objection. Why, then, should English law stop short of recognising the foreign State itself as a successor where, according to its own law, it is indeed such? The answer that English law recognises it to be the function of the relevant foreign law to regulate succession as between individual subjects or citizens, but declines to recognise rights conferred by the foreign State on itself in exercise of that function does not commend itself to me. It involves distinctions at least as arbitrary and artificial as those discerned by the Crown in the distinction between jus regale and true inheritance by the State. For example, it was, I think, conceded in argument that if the Spanish law of succession provided that in circumstances such as those of the present case the estate of the intestate was to go to some person, or body, or corporation, other than the State itself, for application to charitable purposes such as those stated in art. 956 of the

Spanish Civil Code, there would be no reason why the English courts, in applying the general rule to the inheritance, should not recognise and allow effect to be given to that provision. Why, then, should not the same result ensue where, as in the present case, the estate goes by Spanish law to the Spanish State itself for application to those same charitable purposes?

Then it is said that private international law is concerned only with the rights of individuals and not with the competing rights of sovereign States. That may well be so. But it is clear that English law recognises the legitimate proprietary rights of foreign sovereign States, and I see no reason why a right of succession to an intestate's estate should not be held to answer that description. Then it is said that English law should not recognise as "heir" or "successor" any person not bound by some personal nexus with the deceased. I cannot follow this. The heir or successor is surely the person, whether related to the deceased or not, who under the relevant law is entitled to inherit or to succeed. Then it is said that there is no reciprocity, because Spanish law would not give effect to a claim by the Crown in respect of bona vacantia. But non constat that Spanish law would not recognise a right to succession belonging to the Crown if any such right existed, and it could easily be made to exist by Act of Parliament if that were thought expedient.

There might be a case where a so-called right of succession claimed by a foreign State could be shown to be in truth no more than a claim to bona vacantia. If so, then, no doubt, it would be right to apply the recognised exception to the general rule, but this has not been shown to be such a case. On the contrary, it has been found (and the Crown has accepted the finding) that the State of Spain is, in the eye of Spanish law, the true heir, and I would add that, to my mind, notwithstanding what was said (1936 2 All E.R. 1667) by Sir Boyd Meriman, P., In the Estate of Musurus (2), the conclusion that this is a case of genuine succession is reinforced by the circumstance that the State of Spain is by art. 856 of the Spansh Civil Code enjoined to apply the property of the intestate to the charitable purposes therein mentioned. Accordingly, for the reasons given by Sir Raymond Evershed, M.R., and for such additional reasons as I have been able to offer, I agree that this appeal fails and should be dismissed.

Morris, L.J.: It is, I think, well settled that where a person dies domiciled in a foreign country our courts will follow and apply the law of that country when dealing with the succession, using that word in a strict sense, to the ownership of movables in this country. The property will go to the person who becomes heir to it according to the law of the domicil. One result is that the English court will, as a rule, make a grant of administration to the person who is constituted the personal representative of the deceased in the country where he was domiciled at his death. It is unnecessary to consider the basis of the recognised principle; it has been said to imply a fiction which deems movables to exist in the place of the domicil of the deceased. Re Barnett's Trusts (1) was a case where, according to the General Civil Code of Austria, there was no one to whom distribution of the property could be made, so that it became liable under the Code to be confiscated as ownerless. The provision to this effect was held by Kekewich, J., to be precisely on the lines of the English law as to bona vacantia. As Kekewich, J., said (1902 1 Ch. 859): "Where there is no heir, some paramount authority steps in and claims it, not against any one, but because there is no one to claim it at all." As the ownerless property was in England he held that the paramount authority was the English Crown.

The State of Spain has not found it necessary to challenge the decision in Re Barnett's Trusts (1) which has stood since 1902. It has in its favour the finding of Barnard., J., not assailed in this court, that the State of Spain is a true heir just as any individual heir according to Spanish law. Counsel for the Crown, while acknowledging that he must accept that this is the position under Spanish law, submits that the substance of the matter is that the Spanish State is to take in default of there being kindred of the deceased, and he submits that our adoption of the law of the deceased's domicil need not go beyond the stage when it legitimates to distribute among those with some personal nexus with the deceased, and, in any event, can stop short of any stage at which the State is decreed to take. Though the submission is reasonable and clearly formulated, I can see no warrant for acceding to, nor authority to support, it. It invites the court to lay down new doctrine in one of two alternative forms. It requires partial non-acceptance of the law of succession of the domicil, and the existence of the alternative submissions points to the fact that the court is really being asked to fix in arbitrary manner some limit to the extent of the adoption of the law of the domicil relating to succession. No question arises for consideration whether there might be provisions in a foreign law of such a nature that, either on grounds of public policy or of repugnance to English principles, our courts would not recognise rights to succession given by the foreign law.

I can see no reason why either this or another country should not by law provide that on intestacy the Crown or the State should in certain circumstances inherit. The line in such a case between becoming owner as heir or inheritor by a law dealing with inheritance on intestacy and acquiring movables because there is no one who is made their owner as heir or inheritor may be a fine one, but it is, I think, a real one. If in regard to the foreign law dealing with succession as such, partial non-acceptance is embarked upon, the line of such non-acceptance must be arbitrarily drawn. I can see no warrant for differentiating between a provision of the foreign law which on intestacy might, for example, give to remote relatives and a provision which, for example, might give to some public body whose activities might be generally welcome. As it is established and not in this court challenged, that the State of Spain is under Spanish law the heir of the deceased, and is as truly the heir as any individual heir would be, I can see no reason why the English courts should decline to recognise this particular heir. The substance of the matter, as it seems to me, is that by the law to which reference is made, the property in England is not left ownerless, but is to pass to an heir, that heir being the State of Spain. I think that this appeal fails.

Appeal dismissed.

(62) Statutory pardon for A.M. Turing (U.K.)

The text below represents a text type of *personal pardon*. The pardon meant is the remission of legal consequences of an offence or criminal conviction. The personal pardon does not quash the initial decision (cf. 1(2) of the Act). As a legal text type the pardon follows the general text pattern for British legal acts (cf. esp. the formula "To be enacted ..." and the short title). In the Act A. Turing is not simply pardoned but is "to be taken for pardoned". This semantic balancing act enables pardoning and simultaneous maintenance of the judgment against the convicted person.

A Bill to give a statutory pardon to Alan Mathison Turing for offences under section 11 of the Criminal law Amendment Act 1885 of which he was convicted on 31 March 1952:

Be it enacted by the Queen's most Excellent Majesty, by and with the advice and consent of the Lords Spiritual and Temporal, and Commons, in this present Parliament assembled, and by the authority of the same, as follows:

1 Statutory Pardon to Alan Mathison Turing

(1) Alan Mathison Turing, who was born on 23 June 1912 and died on June 1954, and who was convicted of offences under section 11 of the Criminal Law Amendment Act 1885 (gross indecency between men) at the Quarter Sessions at Knutsford in Cheshire on 31 March 1952, is to be taken for pardoned for those offences.

(2) This Act does not affect any conviction or sentence or give rise to any right, entitlement or liability, and does not affect the prerogative of mercy.

2 Short title and extent

(1) This Act may be cited as the Alan Turing (Statutory Pardon) Act 2012.

(2) This Act extends to England and Wales.

(63) Regina v. Jackson (CAN)

R. *v.* Jackson, [2007] 3 S.C.R. 514, 2007

SUPREME COURT OF CANADA

Miguel Arias Jackson, Appellant and **Her Majesty The Queen,** Respondent

OFFICIAL ENGLISH TRANSLATION: Reasons of Deschamps J.

CORAM: Bastarache, Binnie, LeBel, Deschamps, Fish, Abella and Rothstein JJ.

REASONS FOR JUDGMENT: (paras. 1 to 11)	Fish J. (Bastarache, Binnie, Abella and Rothstein JJ. concurring)
DISSENTING REASONS: (paras. 12 to 22)	Deschamps J. (LeBel J. concurring)

The accused was arrested with four others on the site of a secluded marijuana plantation in a remote area of the forest and was convicted of illegal production of marijuana. The majority of the Court of Appeal upheld the conviction; the dissenting judge would have substituted an acquittal on the basis that the verdict was unreasonable within the meaning of s. 686(1) (*a*)(i) of the *Criminal Code*.

Held (LeBel and Deschamps JJ. dissenting): The appeal should be dismissed and the accused's conviction affirmed.

Per Bastarache, Binnie, Fish, Abella and Rothstein JJ.: The mere presence of an accused at the scene of a crime does not prove culpable participation in its commission; here, however, the accused's conviction does not rest merely on his presence at the scene. It rests, rather, on the cumulative effect of his apprehension at the scene, the rejection of his explanation for being there, the particular nature of the offence, the context in which it was committed, and other circumstantial evidence of his guilt. In view of the circumstances and facts of this case, it was open to the trial judge to conclude that the accused's presence was consistent only with his culpable involvement in the illegal production of marijuana.

Per LeBel and Deschamps JJ. (dissenting): The accused is charged not with being present at a cannabis production site but, rather, with producing cannabis. Yet it can be seen from the trial judge's reasons that his decision to convict the accused was based solely on the presence of the accused at the scene. No evidence establishing his participation in the alleged crime was adduced. Had the judge analysed the elements of the offence, he would have had to conclude that the unexplained presence of the accused on the plantation was not in itself evidence of his participation in the production of cannabis, and enter an acquittal.

The judgment of Bastarache, Binnie, Fish, Abella and Rothstein JJ. was delivered by FISH J.

The appellant was convicted at trial for having illegally produced marijuana and his conviction was affirmed by a majority in the Quebec Court of Appeal (2007 Q.J. No. 285 (QL), 2007 QCCA 67). The dissenting judge would have set aside the appellant's conviction and entered an acquittal on the ground that the verdict at trial was unreasonable. The present appeal to this Court, as of right, is based entirely on the dissent in the Court of Appeal and the only issue, therefore, is whether the appellant's conviction amounts to an unreasonable verdict within the meaning of s. 686(1) (*a*)(i) of the *Criminal Code*, R.S.C. 1985, c. C-46. To succeed under that provision, the appellant was bound to persuade us that no properly instructed jury acting judicially could reasonably have found him guilty – as the trial judge did in this case. He has failed to do so, and I would therefore dismiss the appeal.

The appellant relies for the success of his appeal on the proposition that mere presence at the scene of a crime does not prove culpable participation in its commission. That proposition is entirely sound. As we shall see, however, it is of little assistance to the appellant, whose conviction does not rest on his *mere presence* at the scene of the crime. It rests, rather, on the cumulative effect of his apprehension at the scene, the rejection of his explanation for being there, the particular nature of the offence, the context in which it was committed, and other circumstantial evidence of his guilt. A brief overview of the facts will suffice to explain this conclusion.

The appellant and four others were arrested on the site of a secluded marijuana plantation in a remote area of the forest. The entire site was dedicated to the production of marijuana on a commercial scale. It bore no evidence of any legitimate business enterprise, wilderness camping or other recreational activities. As indicated by its dimensions and equipment, this operation engaged more than one participant, or even two. At the time, the appellant had been there for at least two days. Of the four others present, two were previous acquaintances. At least one is admitted to have been actively engaged in the production of marijuana on that plantation during that time. The equipment found there – [TRANSLATION] "as if by chance", in the trial judge's words – indicated that five persons were involved. As I have mentioned, five persons were in fact present when the police arrived. The appellant was one of the five. When the police appeared, the appellant was sleeping in a camouflaged tent on the site. The tent contained fertilizer and the trial judge found as a fact that [TRANSLATION] "[t]here was. . . growing equipment in the tent he was staying in and where he was arrested" (emphasis added). The appellant emerged from that tent wearing rubber boots, not the running shoes he claimed to have been wearing on his arrival. The boots, he said, were his size – but belonged to someone else.

The appellant did not contradict any of this evidence in his testimony at trial; nor, in appealing his conviction, did he challenge any findings of fact by the trial judge. Moreover, the appellant's implausible explanation of his presence on the marijuana plantation was rejected, understandably, by the trial judge. This rejection of his explanation precluded any reasonable inference that the appellant in fact had a "better" – or *exculpatory* – reason for being there. As the Court made clear in *Dunlop v. The Queen*, [1979] 2 S.C.R. 881, an accused's mere presence at the scene of a crime in circumstances consistent with innocence will not support a conviction. But that is not our case. Here, the accused's prolonged and unexplained presence on the marijuana plantation was a cornerstone of the Crown's case against him, but not its entire evidentiary edifice.

In the circumstances and on the facts I have outlined, it was open to the trial judge to conclude, as he did, that the appellant's presence at the scene of the crime was consistent only with his culpable involvement in the production of marijuana with which he was charged. For all of these reasons and those given by the majority in the Court of Appeal, I would dismiss the present appeal and affirm the appellant's conviction at trial.

English version of the reasons of LeBel and Deschamps JJ. delivered by

DESCHAMPS J. (dissenting) – The state benefits from broad investigative powers. This is necessary for the prevention and suppression of crime. The police investigation is essential to the work of prosecutors, who must prove beyond a reasonable doubt that alleged crimes have been committed. They cannot do so by means of vague allusions or associations; not even the cumulative effect of many such allusions or associations can turn a lack of evidence into evidence that a properly instructed judge, acting judicially, might rely on to convict the appellant. In my opinion, there is a lack of evidence in the case at bar.

It is the majority's view that the appellant was convicted on the basis of his presence on the plantation, the rejection of his explanation, the nature of the offence he is charged with, the context, and other circumstantial evidence. With respect, it can be seen from the judge's reasons that his decision to convict the appellant was based solely on the appellant's presence at the scene. No evidence establishing his participation in the alleged crime was adduced. Moreover, the discredit thrown on his testimony does not turn an unexplained presence into a culpable one.

The trial was short. Two police officers testified briefly, and a map and 46 photographs were produced. The appellant also testified. The testimony is reproduced in its entirety. The oral judgment is brief. It consists primarily of an explanation of the judge's reasons for rejecting the appellant's testimony. The judge does not address the elements of the offence. The most relevant passage of the judgment reads as follows:

[TRANSLATION] From the moment the accused gave testimony that was not credible, it must also be asked whether that testimony raises a doubt. I have already answered this question. However, it must be asked whether, on the basis of the evidence, of all the evidence, that includes his testimony. It must of course be asked whether, on the basis of all the evidence accepted by the Court, whether there is proof beyond a reasonable doubt. I am absolutely convinced that there is such proof, and I am absolutely convinced, beyond a reasonable doubt, of the guilt of the accused and of his culpable presence at the scene.

This conclusion follows a series of comments that show clearly the importance the judge attaches to the appellant's presence on the plantation:

[TRANSLATION] So here, the location must be considered. The location here, it was in the woods, and there was rudimentary equipment, camouflaged, evidently to conceal what was going on at this location. There were five (5) people there and, as if by chance, the equipment was consistent with the presence of five (5) people. It was in the woods, in an out-of-the-way place, where there is no doubt that illegal activities, namely the growing of cannabis, were taking place. It is clear that, given the circumstances, the location of the place, and the activities going on there, it is clear that the accused, who was under no obligation to testify, nevertheless had a certain *de facto* obligation to explain his presence at the scene. Furthermore, there was growing equipment in the tent he was staying in and where he was arrested. He therefore testified in an attempt to explain his presence at the scene. . . .

. . . It was clear that, from that moment, the accused, who says that he did not want to get involved in what was going on at the scene, should have left — that much is sure. He was so certain that he should not get involved in this type of activity that he should have left the scene. He did not do so. . . .

. . . [] given the place where the events in question took place, given the activities that went on there, and given the presence of equipment in the tent of the accused, the accused had, at a minimum, to raise a reasonable doubt for the Court in his testimony. . . . [Emphasis added.]

The problem is that the appellant is charged not with being present at a cannabis production site but, rather, with producing cannabis. As the dissenting judge in the Court of Appeal pointed out, the evidence is quite limited:

[TRANSLATION] When he was arrested, the appellant was asleep in the tent, in the middle of the plantation. There is no direct evidence establishing that he took part in any way whatsoever in the production of cannabis. There were no visual observations by the police, the appellant's fingerprints were not found on any of the objects used to grow, propagate or harvest the cannabis plants, and neither the accused nor anyone else gave testimony or made statements to the effect that he had taken part. The appellant's testimony, which the judge did not find to be credible, cannot be used to prove, *a contrario*, the acts that the appellant denies having committed; in other words, not believing the appellant's denial that he handled any object whatsoever used to produce cannabis does not justify a conclusion that, contrary to what he says, he did handle the objects in question. The presence of a bag of manure in the tent where the appellant was sleeping and the fact that he slipped on a pair of rubber boots before exiting the tent when he was arrested are not sufficient, in my view, to establish beyond a reasonable doubt that the appellant was producing cannabis or was aiding and abetting, within the meaning of s. 21 *Cr.C.*, any other persons to do so.

These excerpts suffice to demonstrate a lack of evidence of the essential elements of the offence charged against the appellant. It is not open to the Court to reinterpret the evidence. Unfortunately, that is what the majority are doing, and I would accordingly like to stress two points.

The majority refer (at para. 5) to the trial judge's comment that, [TRANSLATION] "as if by chance, the equipment [on the plantation] was consistent with the presence of five (5) people". However, this comment is not supported by the evidence. What can be seen from the evidence is that the following items were found there: three tents, an unspecified number of mattresses and sleeping bags, a few pieces of clothing, a flashlight, an air pistol, three pairs of scissors used in the production of marihuana, bags of fertilizer, some pots, tubs of water, a pumping system, pesticide application equipment, and a dryer. There is no doubt that this is all the equipment needed to grow cannabis, but there is absolutely nothing in the evidence to justify the conclusion that "the equipment was consistent with the presence of five (5) people". In my opinion, this assertion should be disregarded, as should the judge's association of the appellant with [TRANSLATION] "a longtime friend, a fellow countryman, [who] was at the scene, who was unquestionably involved in the business". The fact that the appellant was found in the company of a fellow Dominican who was growing cannabis does not make him a party to the offence. No one, in Canada, is guilty by association.

The majority also appear to attach probative value to the fact that, when the appellant was arrested, he came out of his tent wearing someone else's boots. The appellant commented on the incident of the boots, stating that he had slipped on the boots of his tent-mate, who had rushed out of the tent without putting them on. The trial judge did not say that he considered this incident to be relevant. I have great difficulty inferring anything from the fact that the appellant was not wearing his own shoes, given the commotion described both by the appellant and by the police officer involved in the operation.

In *R. v. Beaudry*, [2007] 1 S.C.R. 190, 2007 SCC 5, Fish J. distinguished the approach to be taken by an appellate court in respect of a jury's verdict from the one to be taken in respect of reasons given by a judge. It is the judge's reasons that the appellate court must review to determine whether the verdict is unreasonable or is not supported by the evidence. If the facts on which the judge relies are not in the record, the judge's reasons cannot serve as a basis for the verdict.

In the case at bar, the judge focused on the fact that the appellant was present at the scene. There is no evidence to support his comment on the correlation between the number of people and the equipment. He did not analyse the elements of the offence. Had he done so, he would have had to conclude that the appellant's unexplained presence was not evidence of his participation in the alleged crime. Many valid judgments are rendered by trial courts. But when trial courts err, appellate courts have the authority and a duty to intervene.

For these reasons, I would allow the appeal. Given the lack of evidence, I would have entered an acquittal.

Appeal dismissed, LEBEL *and* DESCHAMPS JJ. *dissenting.*

(64) Declan O'Byrne v. Sanofi Pasteur (E.U.)

Discursive elements may correspond strictly to each other in composed discourses that are results of claims in courts where claims and court reactions to them are recorded. That it can be done very formalistically can be illustrated on the following excerpts of a court decision:

ECJ (February 2006 –C-127/04)

The High Court of Justice of England and Wales, Queen's Bench Division referred in the matter Declan O'Byrne v. Sanofi Pasteur MSD Ltd (C-127/04 9, February 2006) following questions to the European Court of Justice for preliminary ruling:

1. On the true interpretation of Art. 11 of the Directive 85/374, when a product is supplied pursuant to a contract of sale by a French manufacturer to its wholly-owned English subsidiary, and then by the English company to another entity, is the product put into circulation:
   a) when it leaves the French company; b) when it reaches the English company; or c) when it leaves the English company; or d) when it reaches the entity receiving the product from the English company?
2. Where proceedings asserting rights conferred on the claimant pursuant to Directive 85/374 in respect of an allegedly defective product are instituted against one company (A) in the mistaken belief that A was the producer of the product when in fact the producer of the product was not A but another company (B), is it permissible for a Member State to confer a discretionary power on its courts to treat such proceedings as "proceedings against the producer" within the meaning of Art. 11 of Directive 85/374?
3. Does Art. 11 of the Directive 85/374, correctly interpreted, permit a Member State to confer a discretionary power on a court to allow B to be substituted for A as a defendant to proceedings of the kind referred to in Question 2 above ("the relevant proceedings") in circumstances where: a) the period of 10 years referred to in Art. 11 has expired; b) the relevant proceedings were instituted against A before the 10-year period expired; and c) no proceedings were instituted against B before the expiry of the 10 year period in respect of the product which caused the damage alleged by the claimant?

...By its first question the referring court asks essentially whether, in the case where a product is transferred by a producer company to a distribution subsidiary and sold by that subsidiary to third party, Art. 11 of the Directive 85/374 is to be interpreted as meaning that the putting into circulation of the product occurs at the time of the transfer of the product from the production company to the subsidiary, or instead when that product is transferred by the subsidiary to the third party...By its second and third question, which it is appropriate to examine together, the referring court asks essentially whether, when an action is brought against the company mistakenly considered to be the producer of a product, whereas, in reality, it was manufactured by another company, it is open to the national courts to view such an action as being brought against that production company and to substitute the latter, as defendant to the action, for the company initially proceeded against...Therefore the reply to the second and the third questions must be that, when an action is brought against a company mistakenly considered to be the producer of a product whereas, in reality, the product was manufactured by another party, it is as a rule for national law to determine the conditions in accordance with which one party may be substituted for another in the context of such an action. A national court examining the conditions governing such a substitution must, however, ensure that due regard is had to the personal scope of Directive 85/374, as determined by Articles 1 and 3 thereof...

(65) In re Standesamt Stadt Niebüll (E.U.)

Decision of the European Court of Justice, C-96/04, 27 April 2006:

The case that follows concerns the application of Art. 234 EC Treaty that states:

The Court of Justice shall have jurisdiction to give preliminary rulings concerning:

(a) The interpretation of this Treaty;
(b) The validity and interpretation of acts of the institutions of the Community and of the ECB:...

Facts: In accordance with a certificate issued by the competent Danish authority to that name, the child was given, in accordance with Danish law, the surname Grunkin-Paul, which was entered on his birth certificate drawn up in Denmark. The Registrar's Office (Standesamt) in Germany refused to recognize the surname of the child of Ms Paul and Mr Grunkin as it had been determined in Denmark on the ground that, under Para. 10 of the German Law introducing the Civil Code (EGBGB), the name of a person falls to be decided under the law of the country of his nationality, and that German law does not allow a child to bear a double-barrelled name composed of his father and mother's surnames. The actions brought by Ms Paul and Mr Grunkin against that refusal were dismissed at final instance by the judgment of the Kammergericht (Higher Regional Court) in Berlin. The Bundesverfassungsgericht (Federal Constitutional Court) refused to examine the constitutional complaint brought in the child's name.

Ms Paul and Mr Grunkin, who had divorced in the meantime, did not use a common married name and refused to determine the name of their child in accordance with Para. 1617(1) of the German Civil Code (BGB). The Registrar's Office in Niebüll brought the matter before the Amtsgericht (Local Court) in Niebüll, as Family Court, in order to transfer the right to determine the child's surname to one of his parents in accordance with Para. 1617(2) and (3) BGB. Taking the view that, if Community law requires that the name which is valid under Danish law be recognized under the German legal system, the proceedings pending before it would have no purpose, the Amtsgericht Niebüll decided to stay the proceedings before it and to refer the matter to the Court of Justice for a preliminary ruling.

Extract from the court decision:

(10) The Amtsgericht Niebüll referred the following question to the court for preliminary ruling: In light of the prohibition of discrimination set out in Art. 12 EC and having regard to the right to the freedom of movement for every citizen of the Union laid down by Art. 18 EC, is the provision on the conflict of laws contained in Art. 10 of the EGBGB valid, in so far as it provides that the right to bear a name is governed by nationality alone?

(11) Under the first paragraph of Art. 234 EC, the Court of Justice has jurisdiction to give preliminary rulings concerning, inter alia, the interpretation of the EC Treaty and of the acts of the institutions of the European Community. The second paragraph of

that article adds that 'where such a question is raised before any court or tribunal of a Member State, that court or tribunal may, if it considers that a decision on the question is necessary to enable it to give judgment, request the Court of Justice to give a ruling thereon'. The third paragraph of Art. 234 EC states that 'where any such question is raised in a case pending before a court or tribunal of a Member State against whose decisions there is no judicial remedy under national law, that court or tribunal shall bring the matter before the Court of Justice.'

(12) In order to determine whether a body making a reference is a court or tribunal for the purposes of Art. 234 EC, which is a question governed by Community law alone, the Court takes account of a number of factors, such as whether the body is established by law, whether it is permanent, whether its jurisdiction is compulsory, whether its procedure is inter partes, whether it applies rules of law and whether it is independent.

(13) Furthermore, whilst Art. 234 EC does not make a reference to the Court subject to there having been an inter partes hearing in the proceedings in the course of which the national court refers a question for a preliminary ruling, it follows none the less from that article that a national court may refer a question to the Court only if there is a case pending before it and if it is called upon to give judgment in proceedings intended to lead to a decision of a judicial nature.

(14) Therefore, when it exercises administrative authority, without the same time being called on to decide a dispute, the referring body, even if it satisfies the other conditions mentioned in para. 12 of the present judgment, cannot be regarded as exercising a judicial function.

(15) In that connection it must be observed that where parents who do not use a married name but who jointly exercise custody of a child have not chosen, by declaration before a Registry Office official, either the father's or the mother's name as the birth name of that child, German law provides that the Familiengericht is competent to transfer the right to determine the child's surname to one of the parents.

(16) It follows that the Familiengericht is required to adopt a decision without a Registry Office official having taken, or been able to take, an earlier decision on the matter. Thus, it is apparent from the file that, in the case in the main proceedings, the Standesamt merely brought the matter before the Amtsgericht Niebüll.

(17) In those circumstances it must be held that the Amtsgericht Niebüll exercises administrative authority, without at the same time being called on to decide a dispute.

(18) It is true that there was a dispute between the parents and the administration as to the possibility of registering the double-barrelled name 'Grunkin-Paul' in Germany. However, that dispute was settled at last instance by the Kammergericht Berlin and is not the subject of the proceedings before the Amtsgericht Niebüll.

(19) Furthermore, there is no dispute, in the case in the main proceedings, between the parents, since they are in agreement about the name they wish to give to their child, namely the double-barrelled name composed of their respective surnames.

(20) It is clear from all of the foregoing that, in those proceedings, the Amtsgericht Niebüll cannot be regarded as exercising a judicial function. Therefore, the Court has no jurisdiction to answer the question referred by the Amtsgericht Niebüll in its decision of 2 June 2003.

(66) Petro Ecuador v. Shell Oil Company (U.S. – CISG)

Court of Appeal of California (15 Cal. App. 4th 1110, 12 Cal. Rptr. 2d 423, 1992)
A case demonstrating an error in the application of law committed by a judge:

PetroEcuador (incorporated under the laws of Ecuador) sent Oil International Ltd. (an American corporation incorporated in Texas) an invitation to bid for supplying 140,000 barrels of unleaded gasoline deliverable CFR to Ecuador. Oil International responded favorably to the invitation, and PetroEcuador confirmed the sale on its contract form. The final agreement required that the oil be sent "CFR La Liberdad-Ecuador". A separate provision, paragraph 10, states: "Jurisdiction: Laws of the Republic of Ecuador". The contract further specifies that the gasoline have a gum content of less than three milligrams per one hundred milliliters, to be determined at the port of departure. PetroEcuador appointed Saybolt Inc., a company specialized in quality control services, to ensure this requirement was met. To fulfill the contract, Oil International purchased gasoline from Shell Oil Company and, following testing at Saybolt, loaded it on board the M/T TIBER at Shell's Deer Park, Texas, refinery. The TIBER sailed to La Liberdad, Ecuador, where the gasoline was again tested for gum content. On learning that the gum content now exceeded the contractual limit, PetroEcuador refused to accept delivery. Eventually, International Oil resold the gasoline to Shell at a loss of approximately two million dollars. Oil International sued PetroEcuador for breach of contract. Oil International argued that the term CFR demonstrated the parties' intent to pass the risk of loss to PetroEcuador once the goods were delivered on board the TIBER. The district court disagreed and held that under Ecuadorian law, the seller must deliver conforming goods to the agreed destination, in this case, Ecuador. CISG has not been applied by the district court. An appeal followed.

(67) MCC-Marble Ceramic Center, Inc. v. Ceramica Nuova D'Agostino (U.S. – CISG)

The following case is interesting within linguistic legislation:

The plaintiff, a Florida corporation, is a retailer of tiles and the defendant is an Italian manufacturer of tiles. The parties arrived at an oral agreement about the sale of tiles and also entered into a requirements contract in February 1991. Thereafter, the plaintiff completed a number of orders pursuant to the requirements contract but defaulted on payment for previous shipments. The defendant failed to satisfy the additional order; the plaintiff then brought a suit against defendant claiming a breach of contract. The defendant responded that there was no obligation to fill plaintiff's order because plaintiff's default on payment according to certain clauses printed on the reverse of defendant's pre-printed order forms. Especially, clause 4 on the reverse side of the purchase order form required that all complaints for defects must be made in writing not later than 10 days after receipt of merchandise and this had not been done by MCC. MCC contended that the parties never intended the term and conditions printed on the reverse of the order form to apply to their agreement.

Birch, Circuit Judge. Article 8 of the CISG provides: "For purposes of this Convention statements made by and other conduct of a party are to be interpreted according to his intent where the other party knew or should have been aware what that intent was. Due consideration is to be given to all relevant circumstances of the case including negotiations." The plain language of the Convention, therefore, requires an inquiry into a party's subjective intent as long as the other party to the contract was aware of that intent. MCC argues that it did not intend to be bound by the terms on the manufacturer's form since it was entirely in Italian. We find it nothing short of astounding that an individual, purportedly experienced in commercial matters, would sign a contract in a foreign language and expect not to be bound simply because he could not comprehend its terms. The general proposition is that they will bind parties who sign contracts regardless of whether they have read them or understand them. Nonetheless, Article 8(1) of the CISG requires a court to consider evidence of the parties' subjective intent. Affidavits of agents of MCC acknowledged that D'Agostino's representatives were aware of MCC's subjective intent not to be bound by the fine print terms.

The issue of whether the parol evidence rule applies to the CISG is a question of first impression in this circuit. It is important to whether the testimony of MCC's subjective intent and D'Agostino's awareness of it will be admitted to contradict or vary the terms of the written contract. We begin by observing that the parol evidence rule, contrary to its title, is a substantive rule of law, not a rule of evidence. The Uniform Commercial Code includes a version of the parol evidence rule that states that: "a writing intended by the partes as a final expression of their agreement may not be contradicted by evidence of any prior agreement or contemporaneous oral agreement." The CISG contains no express statement on the role of parol evidence. Moreover, Article 8(3) expressly directs the courts to give "due consideration to all relevant circumstances of the case including the negotiations." It is a clear instruction to admit and consider parol evidence regarding the negotiations to the extent they reveal the parties' subjective intents.

What a judge or jury does with the parol evidence once it is entered into evidence is within their discretion as the weighers of the evidence. A reasonable finder of fact is free to disregard the parol evidence that conflicts with the written contract. Thus, it may disregard testimony that sophisticated international merchants signed a contract without intending to be bound as simply too incredible to believe and hold MCC to the conditions printed on the reverse side of the contract. However, this is for the trier of fact to determine. Moreover, because Article 8 requires a court to consider any "practices which the parties have established between themselves, usage, and the subsequent conduct of the parties" in interpreting contracts, whether the parties intended to adhere to the ten day limit for complaints of defects, as stated on the reverse of the contract, will have an impact on whether MCC was bound to adhere to the limit in order to preserve its warranty claims.

The CISG precludes the application of the parol evidence rule, which would otherwise bar the consideration of evidence concerning a prior or contemporaneously negotiated oral agreement. Since material issues of fact remain, we cannot affirm the district court's summary judgment in D'Agostino's favor.

(68) V. Rydberg's *Juris Prudentia*

The Swedish poet Victor Rydberg (1828–1895) included in one of his lyrical cycles the poem *Juris Prudentia,* which is followed by *Medicina* (cf. V. Rydberg, *Dikter,* Göteborg 1882).

Juris Prudentia (Exod. 19)

Som för heta ökenvinden hvirfla moln af stoft och dam,/ så dref Israel från Horeb än i lösa skaror fram./ Kan det tåget nå Jordanen, när ej ordning är deri?/Se, då reser sig mot himlen blixtomstråladt Sinai! /Berg och dälder återskalla åskans dån och lagens röst,/och ett genljud svarar amen ur de häpna menskobröst,/och de lösa skaror växa, sedan rätten fått en tolk,/växa till ett härligt rike, växa till ett heligt folk.

Bibliography

The following bibliography includes only works quoted in the main text of this book. A general bibliography of legal linguistics is included in Mattila (2006) and Mattila (2012a, 2013a). Some of the works quoted in the main text include only marginal remarks on legal-linguistic issues or are dealing with doctrinal aspects of law that are transformed in this book into explicit legal-linguistic knowledge. Some others can be called explicitly legal-linguistic. The difference between these two types of sources is not marked in the bibliography. Furthermore, some works related to fundamental issues of social sciences may be relevant to our topic only in terms of its theoretical frame of reference. This circumstance notwithstanding, they are listed in this bibliography. Works of classics such as Cicero's Topica, Boethius' De differentiis topicis or the Roman Corpus Iuris Civilis that belong to the universal history of thought are not included in my bibliography. Works from which only textual examples have been borrowed are mentioned in the main text. Likewise, works commented in the main text that are provided bibliographic information there are not listed in this bibliography.

Aarnio, A., Alexy, R., Peczenik, A. (1983): Grundlagen der juristischen Argumentation, in: Krawietz, W., Alexy, R. (eds.): Metatheorie juristischer Argumentation (Berlin: Duncker & Humblot).

Aarnio, A. (1987): The Rational as Reasonable: a Treatise on Legal Justification (Dordrecht: Reidel).

Aarnio, A. (1989): Laintulkinnan teoria (Porvoo, Helsinki: W. Söderström).

Aarnio, A. (2011): Essays on the Doctrinal Study of Law (New York: Springer).

Aarnio, A. (2014): Oikeutta etsimässä. Erään matkan kuvaus (Helsinki: Talentum).

Adamolekun, L. (ed.) (1999): Public Administration in Africa: Main Issues and Selected Country Studies (Boulder: Westview Press).

Adams, K.A. (2005): A lesson in drafting contracts, in: Business Law Today, vol. 15, no. 2, pp. 1–3.

Agard, W.R. (1942): What Democracy Meant to the Greeks (Chapel Hills: University of North Carolina Press).

Ahlström, A. (1912): Våra medeltidslagar. Studier i fornsvensk stilistik och prosarytmik (Lund: Håkan Ohlssons Boktryckeri).

Ahonen, P. (1988): The Semiotics of Finnish Constitutional Law on Government Finance, in: Kevelson, R. (ed.): Law and Semiotics, vol. 2 (New York/London: Plenum Press) pp. 13–30.

Ahrens, W. (2002): Der Unfallort hat sich bereits entfernt. Neue juristische Stilblüten (München: Beck).

Ahrens, W. (2005): Der Geschädigte liegt dem Vorgang bei oder die besten juristischen Stilblüten (München: Beck).

Ahrens, W. (2008): Der Polizist rettete sich durch einen Seztensprund. Neue juristische Stilblüten (München: Beck).

Ahrens, W. (2009): Der Angeklagte erschien in Bekleidung seiner Frau. Die neuesten juristischen Stilblüten (München: Beck).

Ahrens, W. (2010): Der Angeklagte trägt die Kisten des Verfahrens. Die neuesten juristischen Stilblüten (München: Beck).

Ahrens, W. (2015): In dubio torero. Neue juristische Stilblüten (München: Beck).

Aichison, J. (1978): Linguistics (London: Wodder & Stoughton).

Aikhenvald, A.Y., Dixon, R.M.W. (eds.) (2015): Possession and Ownership. A Cross-Linguistic Typology (Oxford: Oxford University Press).

Ajani, G. (2005): Sistemi Giuridici Comparati. Lezioni e Materiali (Torino: G. Giappichelli Ed.).

Akmajian, A. et al. (2001): Linguistics. An Introduction to Language and Communication, 5th ed. (Cambridge: MIT Press).

Alaux, J. (2003): Introduction to Eschyle, Les Suppliantes (Paris: Les Belles Lettres).

Alchourrón, C., Bulygin, E. (1971): Normative Systems (Vienna/New York: Springer).

Alderman, T. (2005): Forensic Speaker Identification. A Likelihood Ratio-based Approach Using Vowel Formants (München: Lincom).

Aldrich, H.E. (1979): Organizations and Environments (Upper Saddle River: Prentice Hall).

Aleksandrov, A.S. (2003): Vvedenije v sudebnuju lingvistiku (Nizhnyi Novgorod).

Alexy, R. (1983): Theorie der juristischen Argumentation (Frankfurt/M: Suhrkamp).

Allen, C.K. (1939): Law in the Making (Oxford: Clarendon Press).

Altehenger, B. (1983): Die richterliche Entscheidung als Texttyp, in: Petöfi, (ed.) Texte und Sachverhalte. Aspekte der Wort- und Textbedeutung (Hamburg: H. Buske) pp. 185–227.

Altehenger, B. (1996): Forensische Texte. Aspekte einer Explikation der im forensischen Diskurs vorkommenden Texte und ihrer Verarbeitung am Beispiel des Zivilprozesses (Hildesheim: G. Olms).

Amira, von, K. (1882/1895): Nordgermanisches Obligationsrecht, vol. I Altschwedisches Obligationsrecht, vol. II Westnordisches Obligationsrecht (Berlin: W. de Gruyter).

Amira, von, K. (1905): Die Handgebärden in den Bilderhandschriften des Sachsenspiegels (München: Abhandlungen der Königlichen Akademie der Wissenschaften).

Amossy, R. (2010): L'argumentation dans le discours, 3rd ed. (Paris: Colin).

Anderson, K., Okuda,Y. (2007): Translation of Japan's Private International Law: Act on the General Rules of the Application of Laws, in: Yearbook of Private International Law 8/2007.

Andersson, J., Furberg, M. (1977): Språk och påverkan. Om argumentationens semantik, 6th ed. (Bonniers/Aldus: Stockholm).

Ando, C. (2005): Interpretatio Romana, in: Classical Philology, vol. 100 (1), pp. 41–51.

André-Salvini, B. (2008): Le Code de Hammurabi (Paris: Musée du Louvre Editions).

Anesa, P. (2009): Courtroom Discourses: An Analysis of the Westerfield Jury Trial (University of Verona).

Anesa, P. (2012): Jury Trials and the Popularization of Legal Language. A Discourse-Analytical Approach (Bern/Berlin: P. Lang)

Apter, E. (2013): Against World Literature: On the Politics of Untranslatability (London: Verso).

Arendt, H. (1968): Eichmann in Jerusalem: A Report on the Banality of Evil (New York: Viking).

Arntz, R. (2002): The Roman Heritage in German Legal Language, in: Mattila (ed.) (2002a) pp. 33–54.

Aroui, J.-L. (1993): Linguistique et sciences cognitives: Aristote ou Platon? D'un adepte confronté à l'avocat du diable, in: Recherches linguistiques de Vincennes, vol. 22 Francs-tireurs de la linguistique (Saint-Denis: Université Paris VIII), pp. 125–136.

Arsova-Nikolić, L. (1999): Preveduvanje. Teorija i praktika (Skopje: Univerzitet Sv. Kiril i Metodij).

Arutjunova, N.D., Rjabceva, N.K. (eds.) (1993): Logicheskij analiz jazyka (Moskva: Nauka).

Asher, N., Lascarides, A. (2003): Logics of Conversation (Cambridge: Cambridge University Press).

Ashley, K.D. (1990): Modeling Legal Argument: Reasoning with Cases and Hypotheticals (Cambridge: Bradford Books/MIT Press).

Atiah, P.S., Summers, R.S. (1987): Form and Substance in Anglo-American Law: A Comparative Study of Legal Reasoning, Legal Theory, and Legal Institutions (Oxford: Clarendon Press).

Atias, C. (1986): Épistémologie juridique (Paris: puf).

Atias, C. (1994): Épistémologie du droit (Paris: puf).

Atienza, M., Ruiz Manero, J. (1996): Las piezas del derecho: Theoría de los enunciados jurídicos (Barcelona: Ariel).

Atienza, M. (1999): El derecho como argumentación, in: Isegoría 21, pp. 37–47.

Atienza, M. (2006): El derecho como argumentación (Barcelona: Ariel).

Atria, F., MacCormick, D.N. (eds.) (2003): Law and Legal Interpretation (Burlington, Vermont: Ashgate).

Auerbach, E. (1992): Philologie der Weltliteratur. Sechs Versuche über Stil und Wirklichkeitswahrnehmung (Frankfurt a. M.: Fischer).

Austin, J.L. (1956/7): A Plea for Excuses, in: Proceedings of the Aristotelian Society, vol. LVII, pp. 1–29.

Austin, J.L. (1962): How to Do Things with Words (Oxford: Oxford University Press).

Avotins, I. (1989): On the Greek of the Code of Justinian. A supplement to Liddell-Scott-Jones together with observations on the influence of Latin on legal Greek (Hildesheim/Zürich: Olms-Weidmann).

Ayer, A.J. (1966): Can There Be a Private Language?, in: Wittgenstein. The Philosophical Investigations. Pitcher, G. (ed.) (New York: Doubleday Anchor) pp. 251–266.

Ayub, M. (2010): Language Policy and Planning in Urban Kenya (Saarbrücken: VDM Publishers).

Baaij, C.J.W. (2012): The Role of Legal Translation in Legal Harmonization (Alphen a.d. Rijn: Wolters Kluwer).

Babić, J. (ed.) (2013): Jezik u pravu. Okrugli stol ordžan 8. svibnja 2013 u palači Akademije u Zagrebu (Zagreb: Hrvatska akademija znanosti i umjetnosti).

Badura, B. (2007): Mathematische und soziologische Theorie der Kommunikation, in: Burkart, R., Hömberg, W. (eds.): Kommunikationstheorien. Ein Textbuch zur Einführung, 4th ed. (Wien: Braumüller).

Bacewicz, T. (2003): Milczenie w prawie, in: Stelmach, J. (ed.) Studia z filozofii prawa (Kraków: Wydawnictwo Uniwersytetu Jagielońskiego).

Bäcker, C. (2012): Begründen und Entscheiden: Kritik und Rekonstruktion der Alexyschen Diskurstheorie des Rechts, 2nd ed. (Baden-Baden: Nomos).

Baker, M.C. (2002): The Atoms of Language (Oxford: Oxford University Press).

Balkema, J., de Groot, G.R. (eds.) (1987): Recht en vertalen (Deventer: Kluwer).

Bańczerowski, J., Pogonowski, J., Zgółka, T. (1982): Wstęp do językoznawstwa (Poznań: Wydawnictwo Naukowe Universytetu im. A. Mickiewicza).

Bańczerowski, J. (1996): A Formal Approach to a General Theory of Language, in: Sackmann, R. (ed.) Theoretical Linguistics and Grammatical Description. Papers in honour of Hans-Heinrich Lieb (Amsterdam/Philadelphia: J. Benjamins) pp. 13–30.

Bańkowski, Z. (1981): The Value of Truth: Fact Scepticism Revisited, in: Legal Studies, vol. 257/68.

Barak, A. (2005): Purposive Interpretation in Law (Princeton/Oxford: Princeton University).

Baranov, A.N. (2011): Lingvističeskaja ekspertiza teksta. Teoretičeskije osnovanija i praktika (Moskva: Flinta).

Barenot, P.N. (2014): A View of French Legal Lexicography – Tradition and Change from a Doctrinal Genre to the Modern Era, in: Mac Aodha, M. (ed.) Legal Lexicography. A Comparative Perspective (Farnham/Burlington: Ashgate).

Bařinka, C. (ed.) (1933): Uporedna slavenska pravnička terminologia (Bratislava: Gen. Sek. sastanka pravnika slavenskih država).

Barnett, H. (1999): Constitutional and Administrative Law, 2nd ed. (London: Cavendish Publishing).

Bartin, E. (1897): De l'impossibilité d'arriver à une solution définitive de conflicts de lois, in : Journal de droit international, vol. 24.

Bartoszewicz, A. (1979): Istoria russkogo literaturnogo jazyka (Warszawa: PWN).

Bartsch, S. (2016): Roman Literature: Translation, Metaphor & Empire, in: Daedalus, vol. 145, no. 2, pp. 30–39.

Baum, B. (1986): Der Stabreim im Recht. Vorkommen und Bedeutung in Antike und Mittelalter (Frankfurt a. M.: P. Lang).

Bauman, Z. (2004): Wasted Lives. Modernity and its Outcasts (Cambridge/Malden: polity).

Bautro, E. (1933): Idea antytetyki prawniczej (Szkic pragmatyczny) (Lwów).

Bautro, E. (1934): De iurisprudentia symbolica, vol. I Prolegomena do logistyki prawniczej (Lwów).

Bautro, E. (1935): Idea lingwistyki i semantyki prawniczej (Lwów: Dom Książki Polskiej).

Bayer, T.I. (2008): Vico's Principle of Sensus Communis and Forensic Eloquence, Kent Law Review, vol. 83/3, pp. 1–26.

Baylis, J., Smith, S. (eds.) (2005): The Globalization of World Politics, 3rd ed. (Oxford: Oxford University Press).

Baylon, Ch. (1991): Sociolinguistique. Société, langue et discours (Paris: Nathan Université).

Beaudoin, L. (2002): Legal Translation in Canada, in: Mattila (ed.) (2002a) pp. 115–130.

Beaugrande, de, R.A., Dressler, W.U. (1981): Introduction to Text Linguistics (London : Longman).

Beck, H., (ed.) (1983): Verbwörterbuch zur altisländischen Grágás (Konungsbók) 2 vols. (Frankfurt a. M.: P. Lang).

Beck, A. (2014): Die Straßburger Eide in der Frühen Neuzeit. Modellstudie zu vor- und frühgermanischen Diskursstrategien (Wiesbaden: Harrassowitz).

Becker, W., Seidel, H. (1953): Gesetz über die Verbreitung jugendgefährdender Schriften (Münster: Aschendorffsche Verlagsbuchhandlung).

Becker, S. (1972): Untersuchungen zur Redaktion der Strassburger Eide (Bern: P. Lang).

Becker, J.M. (2013): Sprachattitüden in Uganda. Sprachpolitik und interethnische Beziehungen (Frankfurt a. M.: P. Lang).

Behrends, O. (1978): Institutionelles und prinzipielles Denken im römischen Privatrecht, in: Zeitschrift der Savigny-Stiftung für Rechtsgeschichte. Romanistische Abteilung, vol. 95, pp. 187–231.

Bench-Capon, T.J.M., Coenen, F.P. (1992): Isomorphism and Legal Knowledge Based Systems, in: Artificial Intelligence and Law, vol. 1, pp. 65–86.

Benedetti, G. (1999): Diritto e linguaggio. Variazioni sul 'diritto muto', in: Europa e diritto privato, vol. 1, pp. 137–152.

Benson, S. (1994): Danskt lagspråk 1561. Studier i Frederik II:s sjörätt (Göteborg: Kungl. Vetenskaps- och Vitterhets-Samhället).

Berman, D.H., Hafner, C.D. (1987): Indeterminacy: A Challenge to Logic-based Models of Legal Reasoning, in: Yearbook of Law Computers and Technology, vol. 3, pp. 1–35.

Berman, D.H., Hafner, C.D. (1993): Representing Teleological Structure in Case-Based Legal Reasoning: The Missing Link, in: Proceedings of the 4th International Conference on Artificial Intelligence and Law, pp. 50–60 (New York: ACM Press).

Berman, H.J. (1977): The Origins of Western Legal Science, in: Harvard Law Review, vol. 90/ 894.

Berman, H.J. (1983): Law and Revolution. The Transformation of Western Legal Tradition (Cambridge/London: Harvard University Press).

Berman, H.J. (1995): World Law, in: Fordham International Law Journal, vol. 18.

Berman, H. (2013): Law and Language (Cambridge: Cambridge University Press).

Berring, R. (2000): Legal Information and the Search for Cognitive Authority, in: California Law Review, vol. 88, pp. 1673–1708.

Berteloot, P. (2002): Legal French in France and in the European Communities, in: Mattila, H. (ed.) (2002): The Development of Legal Language (Helsinki: Kauppakaari) pp. 81–99.

Berwick, R.C., Chomsky, N. (2016): Why Only Us. Language and Evolution (Cambridge: The MIT Press).

Beveridge, B. (2002): Legal English. How it Developed and Why it is not Appropriate for International Commercial Contracts, in: Mattila (ed.) (2002a) pp. 81–99.

Bianchi, A. (2010): Textual Interpretation and (International) Law Reading: The Myth of (In)Determinacy and the Genealogy of Meaning, in: Bekker, P. et al. (eds.) Making Transnational Law Work in the Global Economy (Cambridge: Cambridge University Press) pp. 34–55.

Biel, L. (2014): Lost in Eurofog: The Textual Fit of Translated Law (Frankfurt/Berlin: P. Lang).

Biscardi, A. (1982): Diritto greco antico (Milano: Giuffré).

Bittar, E.C.B. (2009): Linguagem Jurídica, 4th ed. (São Paolo: Saraiva).

Bix, B. (1993): Law, Language and Legal Determinacy (Oxford: Clarendon Press).

Bix, B.H. (2012): Legal Interpretation and the Philosophy of Language, in: Tiersma, P.M., Solan, L.M. (eds.) The Oxford Handbook of Language and Law (Oxford: Oxford University Press) pp. 145–155.

Black, E.A., Bell, G.F. (2011): Law and Legal Institutions of Asia. Traditions, Adaptations and Innovations (Cambridge: Cambridge University Press).

Bloomfield, L. (1914): An Introduction to the Study of Language (London: G.Bell & Sons/New York: Henry Holt & Co.).

Blumenberg, H. (1968): Wirklichkeitsbegriff und Staatstheorie, in: Schweizer Monatshefte, vol. 2, pp. 121–146.

Boghossian, P. (1992): Externalism and Inference, in: Villanueva, E. (ed.) Information, Semantics and Epistemology (Oxford: B. Blackwell) pp. 11–28.

Bonsdorff, von, P. (1984): Om det svenska lagspråket i Finland, in: Tidskrift utgiven av Juridiska Föreningen i Finland, pp. 403 sqq.

Borja Albi, A. (2004): La investigación en traducción jurídica, in: García Peinado, M.A., Ortega Arjonilla, E. (eds.): Panorama actual de la investigación en traducción (Granada: Atrio).

Borja Albi, A., Prieto Ramos, F. (2013): Legal Translation in Context. Professional Issues and Prospects (Oxford: P. Lang).

Börjesson, K. (2014): The Semantics-Pragmatics Controversy (Berlin/Boston: De Gruyter).

Bos, J.T.K. (1986): Stelselmatige rechtsspraak. Een theorie over de beschrijving van rechtsspraak, uitgewerkt voor de jurisprudentie op art. 29 Sv (Arnhem: Gouda Quint).

Bouglé-Le Roux, C. (2013): La litterature française et le droit. Anthologie illustrée (Paris: LexisNexis).

Boutet, J. (2008): La vie verbale au travail – Des manufactures aux centres d'appels (Toulouse: Octares).

Brand-Ballard, J. (2010): Limits of Legality. The Ethics of Lawless Judging (Oxford: Oxford University Press).

Brandom, R.B. (2000): Articulating Reasons (Boston: Boston University Press).

Branting, K. (1991): Reasoning with Portions of Precedents, in: Proceedings of the 3rd International Conference on Artificial Intelligence and Law (New York: ACM Press) pp. 145–154.

Brodziak, K. (2004): O lingwistycznym statusie języka prawnego, in: Studia Prawnicze vol.1, pp. 110–124.

Broekman, J.M. (1984): Text als Institution, in: Rechtstheorie, Beiheft 4: Recht als Sinn und Institution, pp. 145–167.

Broekman, J.M. (2011): Introduction, in: Broekman, J.M., Mootz, III, F.J. (eds.): The Semiotics of Law in Legal Education (Heidelberg: Springer) pp. 2–4.

Brooks, P. (1996): The Law as Narrative and Rhetoric, in: Brooks, P., Gewirtz, P., (eds.) Law's Stories: Narrative and Rhetoric in the Law (New Haven: Yale University Press) pp. 14–22.

Brooks, P. (2005): Narrative in and of the Law, in: Phelan, J., Rabinowitz, P.J. (eds.) A Companion to Narrative Theory (Oxford: Blackwell) pp. 415–426.

Brown, J., Cappelen, H. (2014): Assertion. New Philosophical Essays (Oxford: Oxford University Press).

Brueckner, A.L. (2003): Contents just aren't in the head, in: Erkenntnis, vol. 58 (1), pp. 1–6.

Bülow, E. (1981): Materialien zu einer Bibliographie der Rechtslinguistik (Ein Versuch), in: Studium Sprachwissenschaft, vol. 5 (Münster: WWU).

Bülow, E. (1985): Interdisziplinarität, Legitimität und Finalisierbarkeit der angewandten Sprachwissenschaft, in: Peuser, G., Winter, S. (eds.) Angewandte Sprachwissenschaft: Grundfragen Bereiche Methoden (Bonn: Bouvier) pp. 17–40.

Bülow, E. (1986): Strafdrohungen und ihr magisches Potential, in: Lange-Seidl, A. (ed.) Zeichen und Magie (Tübingen: Stauffenburg Verlag).

Bülow, E. (1990): „Der war's! Wer sonst?" Fiktionen im Rechtsbewußtsein von Laien, in: Zeitschrift für Semiotik, vol. 12/3, pp. 237–242.

Bülow, E. (2013): Zurück zur Sprache. Eine Dokumentation des Übens (Berlin: LIT Verlag).

Bülow, L., Bung, J., Harnisch, R., Wernsmann, R. (eds.) (2016): Performativität in Sprache und Recht (Berlin: W. de Gruyter).

Bulygin, E. (ed.) (1983): El lenguaje del derecho: homenaje a Genaro R. Carrió (Buenos Aires: Abaledo-Perrot).

Burge, T. (1979): Individualism and the Mental, in French, P.A., Uehling, T.E., Wettstein, H.K. (eds.) Midwest Studies in Philosophy, vol. IV, (Minneapolis: University of Minnesota Press) pp. 73–121.

Burge, T. (1986): Individualism and Psychology, in: Philosophcal Review, vol. 95, pp. 3–45.

Burge, T. (2010): Origins of Objectivity (Oxford: Oxford University Press).

Burge, T. (2013): Cognition through Understanding: Self-Knowledge, Interlocution, Reasoning, Reflection (Oxford: Oxford University Press).

Burkart, R., Hömberg, W. (eds.): Kommunikationstheorien. Ein Textbuch zur Einführung, 4th ed. (Wien: Braumüller).

Busse, D. (1992): Recht als Text (Tübingen: Niemeyer).

Busse, D. (1993): Juristische Semantik: Grundlagen der juristischen Interpretationslehre in sprachwissenschaftliucher Sicht (Berlin: Duncker & Humblot).

Cacciaguidi-Fahy, S., Wagner, A. (eds.) (2008): Obscurity and Clarity in the Law. Prospects and Challenges (Aldershot: Ashgate).

Cagliero, R., Jenkins, J. (eds.) (2010): Discourses, Communities, and Global Englishes (Bern/Berlin: P. Lang).

Caiden, G.E. (1994): Globalizing the Theory and the Practice of Public Administration, in: Garcia-Zamor, J.C., Khator, R. (eds.) Public Administration in the Global Village (Westport: Praeger Publishers) pp. 45–59.

Canale, D., Tuzet, G. (2007): On Legal Inferentialism. Towards a Pragmatics of Semantic Content in Legal Interpretation?, in: ratio juris, vol. 20, no. 1, pp. 32–44.

Canale, D. (2015): What Inferentialism Tells Us about Combinatory Vagueness in Law, in: Bocconi Legal Studies Research paper no. 2627120 (available online).

Cao, D. (2005): Chinese Law. A Language Perspective (Aldershot: Ashgate).

Cao, D. (2007): Translating Law (Clevedon/Buffalo/Toronto: Multilingual Matters).

Cao, D. (2008): Is the Chinese Legal Language More Ambiguous and Vaguer?, in: Wagner, A.,

Capone, A., Poggi, F. (eds.) (2016): Pragmatics and Law. Philosophical Perspectives (Basel: Springer).

Capotorti, F. (1991): Study on the Rights of Persons Belonging to Ethnic, Religious or Linguistic Minorities (New York: United Nations).

Carcassonne, G. (2005): La Constitution, 7th ed. (Paris: Éditions du Seuil).

Cardozo, B.N. (1928): The Nature of the Judicial Process (New Haven: Yale University Press).

Carrión Wam, R. (1982) Panorama de la Semiótica Jurídica, in: Investigationes Semióticas 2/3 1982–83, pp. 116–190.

Carson, A., (2012): Antigonick (Sophokles) (New York: New Directions).

Carval, S. (1995): La responsabilité civile dans sa fonction de peine privée (Paris: LGDJ).

Casertano, L. (2008): Il linguaggio giuridico russo, in: Pozzo, B., Timoteo, M. (eds.) Europa e linguaggi giuridici (Milano: Giuffrè) pp. 209–258.

Cassese, A. (2005): International Law, 2nd ed. (Oxford: Oxford University Press).

Chan, Ho-yan (2012): Bridging the gap between language and law. Translational issues in creating legal Chinese in Hong Kong, in: Babel, vol. 58/2, pp. 127–144.

Chan, Ho-yan (2014): Liang An San Di. Heyuefa Zhongyao Cihui. Key Terms in Contract Law of Hong Kong, Mainland China and Taiwan (Hong Kong: City University of Hong Kong Press).

Chan, Ho-yan (2015): Liang An San Di. Qinquanfa Zhongyao Cihui. Key Terms in Tort Law of Hong Kong, Mainland China and Taiwan (Hong Kong: City University of Hong Kong Press).

Chaniotis, A. (2016): Memory, Commemoration & Identity in an Ancient City: The Case of Aphrodisias, in: Daedalus, vol. 145, no. 2, pp. 88–100.

Charpin, D. (2008): Hammu-Rabi de Babylone (Paris: puf).

Chernyh, P. Ya. (1953): Jazyk "Ulozhenija 1649 g." (Moskva: Izdatelstvo AN SSSR).

Chomsky, N. (1981): Lectures on Government and Binding (Dordrecht: Foris).

Chomsky, N. (2000): New Horizons in the Study of Language and Mind (Cambridge: Cambridge University Press).

Christmann, H.H. (1983): Das Französische der Gegenwart, in: Hausmann, F.J. (ed.) Die französische Sprache von heute (Darmstadt: Wissenschaftliche Buchgesellschaft) pp. 411–440.

Christiansen, T. (2011): Cohesion: A Discourse Perspective (Bern/Berlin: P. Lang).

Chroma, M. (2004): Legal Translation and the Dictionary (Tübingen: Niemeyer).

Clancy, J.J. (1989): The Invisible Powers. The Language of Business (Lexington: Lexington Press).

Clark, B. (2013): Relevance Theory (Cambridge: Cambridge University Press).

Clegg, A. (2010): A Matter of Interpretation (in: Financial Times, February 2, 2010).

Coates, J. (1983): The Semantics of the Modal Auxiliaries (London: Croom).

Collier, C.W. (2009): Meaning in Law: a Theory of Speech (New York/Oxford: Oxford University Press).

Conclin, W.E. (1998): The Phenomenology of Modern Discourse: the Juridical Production and the Disclosure of Suffering (Aldershot/Brookfield: Ashgate).

Conley, J., O'Barr, W. (2005): Just Words: Law, language and power, 2nd ed. (Chicago: Chicago University Press).

Constantino Martínez, F., Rivera León, M.A. (2010): Elementos de lingüística jurídica. Deconstrucción conceptual: Herramientas hacia la interpretación normativa (México: Fontamara-Universidad de Sonora).

Cooter, R., Ulen, T. (2004): Law and Economics, 4th ed. (Boston: Pearson).

Cordeiro, A.M. (2004): Vernáculo jurídico: directrizes ou directivas, in: Revista Ordem dos Advogados, an. 64/vol. I/II.

Cornu, G. (2005): Linguistique juridique, 3rd ed. (Paris: Montchrestien).

Corten, O., Klein, P. (2011): The Vienna Convention on the Law of Treaties (Oxford: Oxford University Press).

Cotterrell, R. (2006): Law, Culture and Society: Legal Ideas in the Mirror of Social Theory (Aldershot: Ashgate).

Coulthard, M., Johnson, A. (2007): An Introduction to Forensic Linguistics: Language in Evidence (Abingdon/Oxon: Routledge).

Coulthard, M., Johnson, A. (eds.) (2010): The Routledge Handbook of Forensic Linguistics (Abingdon/Oxon: Routledge).

Cover, R.M. (1983): The Supreme Court, 1982 Term – Foreward: Nomos and Narrative, in: Faculty Scholarship Series, paper 2705, pp. 4–68.

Cox, J., Hillman, R., Langevoort, D. (2006): Securities Regulation, 5th ed. (New York: Aspen).

Craig, H. (2011): Using discourse analysis methodology to teach 'Legal English', in: International Journal of Law, Language and Discourse, vol. 1/2, pp. 1–19.

Craig, B. (2013): Cyberlaw. The Law of the Internet and Information Technology (Boston/Columbus/Indianapolis: Pearson).

Cruse, A. (2010): Meaning in Language. An Introduction to Semantics and Pragmatics, 3rd ed. (Oxford: Oxford University Press).

Crystal, D. (1997): English as a Global Language (Cambridge: Cambridge University Press).

Curtius, E.R. (1996): Evropska književnost i latinski sredni vek, (orig. Europäische Literatur und lateinisches Mittelalter) (Beograd: Srbska Književna Zadruga).

Dantès Nascimento, E. et al. (1980): Linguagem forense. A língua portuguesa aplicada à linguagem do foro, 4th ed. (São Paulo: Saraiva).

David, R. (1978): Les grands systèmes de droit contemporains, 7th ed. (Paris: Dalloz).

Davidson, D. (2001): Inquiries into Truth and Interpretation, 2nd ed. (Oxford: Clarendon Press).

De Groot, R.G., Schulze, R. (eds.) (1999): Recht und Übersetzen (Baden-Baden: Nomos).

Deleuze, G., Guattari, F. (1991): Qu'est-ce que la philosophie? (Paris: puf).

Dell'Anna, M.V. (2013): In nome del popolo italiano. Linguaggio giuridico e lingua della sentenza in Italia (Roma: Bonacci).

Delmas-Marty, M. (1998): Trois défis pour un droit mondial (Paris: Seuil).

Den Boer, M.: The Legal Art of Unambiguous Storytelling (unpublished conference paper).

Diakofotakis, Y. (2002): Expanding Conceptual Boundaries (Athens: Sakkoulas / Brussels: Bruylant).

Dijk, van, T. (1980): Textwissenschaft. Eine interdisziplinäre Einführung (Tübingen: Niemeyer).

Dilcher, G. (1961): Paarformeln in der Rechtssprache des frühen Mittelalters (Darmstadt: Rinck).

DiMatteo, L. (2005): A Theory of Interpretation in the Realm of Idealism, bepress Legal Series, working paper 872.

Dölle, H. (1949): Vom Stil der Rechtssprache (Tübingen: Mohr).

Dominicy, M. (1993): De Toulmin à Perelman. Analyse d'un réseau argumentatif, in: Verbum 1–2-3/ 1993.

Domingo, R. (2010): The New Global Law (Cambridge: Cambridge University Press).

Dorato, J.A. (2013): A Jurilinguistic Approach in Legal Education, in: International Journal for the Semiotics of Law, vol. 26/3, pp. 635–650.

Đorđević, M. (2002): Pravo u hermeneutičkom krugu (Beograd: Službeni list SRJ).

Douglas, D.M. (2001): The Jeffersonian Vision of Legal Education, in: Journal of Legal Education vol. 51, no. 2, pp. 185–211.

Dreier, T., Ohly, A. (eds.) (2013): Plagiate. Wissenschaftsethik und Recht (Tübingen: Mohr Siebeck).

Dreißigacker, M. (2002): Sprachenfreiheit im Verbrauchervertragsrecht (Frankfurt/M.: P. Lang).

Drolshammer, J., Vogt, N.P. (2003): English as the language of law? An essay on the legal lingua franca of a shrinking world (Zürich: Schultheiss).

Drooghenbroeck, van, S. (2000): La nozione di "beni" ai sensi dell'articolo 1 del Primo protocollo addizionale, in: The European Legal Forum, vol.7 , pp. 437–444.

Du, J. (2004): Forensic Linguistics (Shanghai: Foreign Language Education Press).

Duarte i Monserrat, C. (1985): El vocabulari jurídic del llibre de les costums de Tortosa (Ms. de 1272) (Barcelona: Generalitat de Catalunya).

Duarte i Montserrat, C., Martinez, A. (1995): El Lenguaje Jurídico (Buenos Aires: A-Z Editora).

Duarte i Montserrat, C. (1998): Lenguaje administrativo y lenguaje jurídico, in: J. Bayo Delgado (ed.), Lenguage judicial (Madrid: Consejo general del poder judicial).

Dubois, J. (1983): Le "Néo-Français". Réalité ou illusion?, in: Hausmann, F.J. (ed.) Die französische Sprache von heute (Darmstadt: Wissenschaftliche Buchgesellschaft) pp. 145–166.

Du Bois, J.W. (2002): Discourse and Grammar, in: Tomasello, M. (ed.) The New Psychology of Language. Cognitive and Functional Approaches to Language Structure, vol. 2 (Mahwah/New York: Lawrence Erlbaum Associates).

Dubouchet, P. (1990): Sémiotique juridique. Introduction à une science du droit (Paris: puf).

Dubrovskaya, T. (2010): Sudjebnyi diskurs: rechevoe povedenije sud'i (Moscow: MNEPU).

Dubrovskaya, T.V. (2014): Sudebnyj diskurs kak kulturnyj fenomen: nacionalno-kulturnyje osobennosti rechi sudej, in: Voprosy Jazykoznanija, no. 2, pp. 76–88.

Durant, A., Leung, J.H.C. (2016): Language and Law. A Resource Book for Students (London: Routledge, Taylor & Francis Group).

Dworkin, R. (1977): Taking Rights Seriously (London: Duckworth).

Dworkin, R. (1991): Law's Empire (London: Fontana Press).

Ebel, U. (1994): Von der Zwiespältigkeit des Rechts in der Droplaugar sona saga, in: Uecker, H. (ed.) Studien zum Altgermanischen. Festschrift für Heinrich Beck (Berlin/New York: de Gruyter) pp. 101–115.

Eckmann, H. (1969): Rechtspositivismus und Sprachanalytische Philosophie. Der Begriff des Rechts in der Rechtstheorie H.L.A. Harts (Berlin: Duncker & Humblot).

Eco, U. (2006): Sémiotique et philosophie du langage, 2nd ed. (Paris: puf).

Edzard, L. (1998): Language as a medium of legal norms. Implications of the use of Arabic as a language in the United Nations System (Berlin: Duncker & Humblot).

Eemeren, F.H. van, Grootendorst, R., (2004): A Systematic Theory of Argumentation. The Pragma-Dialectic Approach (Cambridge: Cambridge University Press).

Ehrhardt, S. (ed.) (2014): Europäische Mehrsprachigkeit in Bewegung: Treffpunkt Luxemburg. Des plurilinguismes en dialogue: rencontres luxembourgeoises (Bern/Berlin/Bruxelles: P. Lang).

Enbuske, M. (2008): Vanhan Lapin valtamailla. Asutus ja maankäyttö historiallisen Kemin Lapin ja Enontekiön alueella 1500-luvulta 1900-luvun alkuun (Helsinki: Suomalaisen Kirjallisuuden Seura).

Endicott, T. (2000): Vagueness in Law (Oxford: Oxford University Press).

Engberg, J. (1997): Konventionen von Fachtexten. Kontrastive Analysen zu deutschen und dänischen Gerichtsurteilen (Tübingen: G. Narr).

Engberg, J. (2001): Entwicklungslinien in der Verwendung von sollen in deutschen Gesetzestexten, in: Gotti, M., Dossena, M. (eds.), Modality in Specialized Texts (Bern: P. Lang) pp. 193–212.

Engberg, J. (2007): Vom Vorgriff auf das Ungreifbare – (Schein?-)Präzision, unvermeidliche und erstrebte Vagheit in der Gesetzesredaktion, in: Lötscher, A., Nussbaumer, M. (eds.) Denken wie ein Philosoph und schreiben wie ein Bauer. Sprache, mit der der Staat zu machen ist (Zürich: Schulthess) pp. 67–82.

Engberg, J., Kjaer, A. L. (2011): Approaches to Language and the Law – Some Introductory Notes, in: Hermes – Journal of Language and Communication Studies, vol. 46, pp. 7–10.

Engberg, J. (2013a): Comparative Law for Translation: the Key to Successful Mediation between Legal Systems, in: Borja Albi, A, Prieto Ramos, F. (eds.) Legal Translation in Context. Professional Issues and Prospects (Oxford: P. Lang).

Engberg, J. (2013b): Legal linguistics as a mutual arena for cooperation. Recent developments in the field of applied linguistics and law, in: AILA Review, vol. 26, pp. 24–41.

Engel, D. (2002): Die sprachenrechtliche Situation der Angehörigen von Minderheiten im Völkerrecht (Berlin: Berlin Verlag).

Engel., P. (1994): Introduction à la philosophie de l'esprit (Paris: Editions de la découverte).

Engel, P. (ed.) (2000): Précis de philosophie analytique (Paris: puf).

Enos, T. (ed.) (1996): Encyclopedia of Rhetoric and Composition (New York/London: Garland Publishing).

Eriksson, L.D. (1997): Att förstå och att tolka, in: Kangas, U., Timonen, P. (eds.): Juhlajulkaisu A. Aarnio, pp. 13–25 (Helsinki: Suomalainen Lakimiesyhdistys).

Escarra, J. (1936): Le droit chinois. Conception générale, aperçu historique (Beijing: Henri Vetch)

Ewers, J.P.G., (1826): Das älteste Recht der Russen in seiner geschichtlichen Entwicklung (Dorpat: A. Sticinsky/Hamburg: F. Perthes).

Falcone, G. (1991): Per una datazione del "De verborum quae ad ius pertinent significatione" di Elio Gallo, in: Ann. Sem. giur. Univ. di Palermo, vol. 41, pp. 223–226.

Falkenberg, G. (1982): Lügen. Grundzüge einer Theorie der sprachlichen Täuschung (Tübingen: Niemeyer).

Fedotov, M.R. (1996): Etimologicheskij slovar' chuvashskogo jazyka, vol. I–II (Cheboksary: Chuvashskij gosudarstviennyi institut gumanitarnych nauk).

Feigenson, N. (2006): Digital Visual and Multimedia Software and the Reshaping of Legal Knowledge, in: Wagner, A., Pencak, W. (eds.) Images in Law, (Aldershot: Ashgate) pp. 89–116.

Felder, E. (2003): Juristische Textarbeit im Spiegel der Öffentlichkeit (Berlin/New York: W. de Gruyter).

Felder, E. (2012): Unendliche Semiose im Recht als Garant der Rechtssicherheit, in: Bäcker, C., Klatt, C., Zucca-Soest, S. (eds.) Sprache – Recht – Gesellschaft (Tübingen: Mohr) pp. 141–162.

Felder, E. (2013a): Normtext und Bedeutung – Der sprachwissenschaftliche Blick auf ein schwieriges Verhältnis, in: Zeitschrift für Vergleichende Rechtswissenschaft, vol. 4/2013, pp. 482–490.

Felder, E. (2013b): Juristische Fachsprache oder wie Bedeutung im Recht entsteht, in: Deutsch, A. (ed.) Historische Rechtssprache des Deutschen (Heidelberg: Winter) pp. 75–93.

Felder, E., Luth, J., Vogel, F. (2016): ‚Patientenautonomie' und ‚Lebensschutz': Eine empirische Studie zu agonalen Zentren im Rechtsdiskurs über Sterbehilfe, in: Zeitschrift für germanistische Linguistik, vol. 44/2016, pp. 1–36.

Feltham, R.G. (1998): Diplomatic Handbook, 7th ed. (London/New York: Longman).

Felton Rosulek, L. (2015): Dueling Discourses. The Construction of Reality in Closing Arguments (Oxford: Oxford University Press).

Feng, H. (2011): Discourses and Tales of Grant-Seeking Activity. Academic Writing and Professional Expertise (Bern/Berlin: P. Lang).

Fenrich, J., Galizzi, P., Higgins, P. (eds.) (2011): The Future of African Customary Law (Cambridge: Cambridge University Press).

Féral-Schuhl, Ch. (2010): Cyberdroit. Le droit à l'épreuve de l'internet, 6 ed. (Paris: Dalloz).

Ferraz Júnior, T.S. (1997): Direito, Retórica e Comunicação, 2nd ed. (São Paolo: Saraiva).

Ferretti, F. (2001): Jerry A. Fodor: Mente e Linguaggio (Roma: Laterza).

Filippova, E.I. (2013): Jazyki menshinstv: juridicheskij status i povsednievnye praktiki (Moskva: Rosinformagroteh).

Finnemore, M. (2000): Are Legal Norms Distinctive?, in: Harvard Law Review, vol. 32, pp. 699–705.

Fischer, F., Forester, J. (1993): Editor's Introduction, in: Fischer, F., Forester, J. (eds.) The Argumentative Turn in Policy Analysis and Planning (London: UCL Press) pp. 1–20.

Fish, S. (1989): Doing What Comes Naturally: Change, Rhetoric, and the Practice of Theory in Literary and Legal Studies (Oxford: Clarendon Press).

Fisher, H.D. (2009): The German Legal System and Legal Language, 4th ed. (Abingdon/New York: Routledge/Cavendish).

Fletcher, G.P. (2007): The Grammar of Criminal Law. American, Comparative, and International, vol. 1: Foundations (Oxford: Oxford University Press).

Fodor, J. (1975): The Language of Thought (Cambridge: Harvard University Press).

Fodor; J. (1990): A Theory of Content and other Essays (Boston: MIT Press).

Fodor, J. (2008): LOT 2: The Language of Thought Revisited (Oxford: Oxford University Press).

Foley, R., Salmi-Tolonen, T., Tukiainen, I., Vehmas, B. (eds.) (2008): Kielen ja oikeuden kohtaamisia. Heikki E.S. Mattilan juhlakirja (Helsinki: Talentum).

Fonsén, T. (2011): Saksan vaikutuksesta suomen oikeuskieleen, in: Virittäjä, vol. 115/2, pp. 239–250.

Forget, P. (2014): La phraséologie chez des jurilexicographes: les examples linguistiques dans la deuxième édition du Dictionnaire de droit privé et lexiques bilingues, in: Mac Aodha, M. (ed.) Legal Lexicography. A Comparative Perspective (Farnham/Burlington: Ashgate) pp. 223–264.

Forsthoff, E. (1940): Recht und Sprache. Prolegomena zu einer richterlichen Hermeneutik (Halle: M. Niemeyer).

Foucault, M. (1966): Les mots et les choses. Une archéologie des sciences humaines (Paris: Gallimard).

Foucault, M. (1969): L'archéologie du savoir (Paris: Gallimard).

Frändberg, Å. (2001): Rättsordningen och rättstillämpningen, in: Strömholm, S. (ed.) Svensk rätt – en översikt (Uppsala: Iustus Förlag).

Freidhof, G. (1995): Der Schauprozess als Exemplum forensischer Linguistik. Teil 1. Einführung und Typologie von charakteristischen Sprechhandlungen, in: Freidhof, G., Kusse, H., Schindler, F. (eds.) Slawische Sprachwissenschaft und Interdisziplinarität (München: Sagner) pp. 7–36.

Freidhof. G. (1996): Der Schauprozess als Exemplum forensischer Linguistik. Teil 2. Metakommunikation, Metadialog und Master Speech Act, in: Freidhof, G., Kusse, H., Schindler, F. (eds.) Slawische Sprachwissenschaft und Interdisziplinarität, (München: Sagner) pp. 95–131.

Frijda, N., Mesquita, B. (2000): Beliefs through Emotions, in Frijda, N. et al. (eds.) Emotions and Beliefs: How Feelings Influence Thoughts (Cambridge: Cambridge University Press).

Frisch, D., Bhala, R. (1999): Global Business Law. Principles and Practice (Durham: Carolina Academic Press).

Fuchs-Khakhar, C. (1987): Die Verwaltungssprache zwischen dem Anspruch auf Fachsprachlichkeit und Verständlichkeit. Ein Vergleich der Darstellungen dieses Konflikts in der deutschen Verwaltungssprache und der Vorschläge zu seiner Bewältigung seit 1958 (Tübingen: Stauffenberg).

Fuller, L. (1958): Positivism and Fidelity to Law – A Reply to Professor Hart, in: Harvard Law Review, 71/630.

Gadamer, H.G. (1965): Wahrheit und Methode (Tübingen: Mohr).

Gagarin, M., Cohen, D. (eds.) (2005): The Cambridge Companion to Ancient Greek Law (Cambridge: Cambridge University Press).

Gagarin, M. (2011): Writing Greek Law (Cambridge: Cambridge University Press).

Gagarin, M., Perlman, P. (2015): The Laws of Ancient Crete, ca. 650–400 BC (Oxford: Oxford University Press).

Galdia, M. (1989): Länsisaksalaisen oikeustieteen umpikujat ja oikotieet, in: Oikeus, vol. 4, pp. 328–331.

Galdia, M., Höpp, K, (1993): Aspekte der Zweisprachigkeit bei den Finnougriern am Beispiel der Mari und der Komi, in: Berliner Beiträge zur Hungarologie, vol. 6, pp. 185–194.

Galdia, M. (1995): Der Paradigmenwechsel in der finnischen Rechtswissenschaft (Frankfurt/ New York: P. Lang).

Galdia, M. (1999): Lakisaksa, in: Encyclopaedia Iuridica Fennica, vol. VII., (Helsinki: Suomalainen Lakimiesyhdistys), pp. 550–555.

Galdia, M. (2003a): Juridisten tekstien kääntäminen erityisesti suomalais-saksalaisen vertailun näkökulmasta, in: Lakimies 2003, pp. 3–22.

Galdia, M. (2003b): Flerspråkiga juridiska ordböcker, in: LexicoNordica, vol. 10, pp. 119–131.

Galdia, M., Voronina, N. (2004a): Pravo i etnichnost v subjektah Rossijskoj Federacji (Moskva: EU-Russia Cooperation Programme).

Galdia, M., Voronina, N. (2004b): Problemy pravovogo regulirovaniya mezhetnicheskih otnosheniji i antidiskriminacjonnogo zakonodatelstva v Rossijskoj Federacji (Moskva: Tacis).

Galdia, M. (2006): Review of H. Mattila, Comparative Legal Linguistics, in: European Legal Forum (I), vol. 5/6, p. 271.

Galdia, M. (2008): Oikeuskielen pragmaattiset aspektit, in: Foley, R. et al. (eds.), Kielen ja oikeuden kohtaamisia, pp. 13–29.

Galdia, M. (2013): Strategies and Tools for Legal Translation, in: Comparative Legilinguistics, vol.16, pp. 77–94.

Galdia, M. (2014): Legal Discourses (Frankfurt aM: Peter Lang).

Galdia, M., Liaci, A. (2016): Fairness as Interpretive Device in Law? (An Analysis of Discursive Practices in the Recent Conflict about Voting Rights in Hong Kong and their Anchorage in Argumentative Practices of East Asia), in: Comparative Legilinguistics. International Journal for Legal Communication, vol. 26, pp. 125–150.

Galgano, F. (2005): La globalizzazione nello specchio del diritto (Bologna: Mulino).

Gandasegui, J. (1998): Historia del lenguage judicial, in: Lenguaje judicial, Bayo Delgado, J. (ed.)(Madrid: Consejo general del poder judicial).

Gardiner, R. (2010): Treaty Interpretation (Oxford: Oxford University Press).

Garrett, M.L. (2010): Trademarks as a System of Signs: A Semiotic Look at Trademark Law, in: International Journal for the Semiotics of Law, vol. 23, pp. 70–75.

Garzone, G. (2001): Deontic Modality and Performativity in English Legal Texts, in: Gotti, M., Dossena, M. (eds.) Modality in Specialized Texts (Bern: P. Lang) pp. 153–173.

Garzone, G. (2013): Variation in the use of modality in legislative texts: Focus on shall, in: Journal of Pragmatics, vol. 57, pp. 68–81.

Gast, W. (2015): Juristische Rhetorik, 5th ed. (Heidelberg/München: C.F. Müller).

Gaudemet, J. (1986): Tentatives de systématisation du droit à Rome, in: Archives de philosphie du droit, vol 31.

Gaudemet, J. (2001): Les naissances du droit, 3rd ed. (Paris: Montchrestien).

Gauker, C. (2011): Words and Images. An Essay on the Origin of Ideas (Oxford: Oxford University Press).

Gebhardt von, U.C.J. (2009): Sermo iuris: Rechtssprache und Recht in der augusteischen Dichtung (Leiden: Brill).

Geer, de Louis (1853): Om den juridiska stilen (Christianstad: Schmidt & Comp.)

Geertz, C. (1983): Dichte Beschreibung. Beiträge zum Verstehen kultureller Système (Frankfurt: stw).

Gémar, J.C (2004): Traduire le language du droit, in: Übersetzung Translation Traduction, Kittel, H. et al. (eds), vol. 1 (Berlin: Walter de Gruyter).

Gémar, J.-C., Kasirer, N. (eds.) (2005): Jurilinguistique: entre langues et droits – Jurilinguistics: Between Law and Language (Montréal/Brussel:Bruylant/Thémis).

Gernet, L. (1964): Droit et société dans la Grèce ancienne, 2nd ed. (Paris: Sirey).

Gibbons, J. (2003): Forensic Linguistics: An Introduction to Language in the Justice System (Oxford: Blackwell).

Gillespie, J., Nicholson, P. (2012): Law and Development and the Global Discourses of Legal Transfers (Cambridge: Cambridge University Press).

Gilmer, H.W. (1975): The if-you form in Israelite law (Missoula: Scholars Press).

Giordan, H. (ed.) (1992): Les minorités en Europe (Paris: Éditions Kimé).

Girard, P. (1929): Manuel élémentaire du droit romain, 8th ed. (Paris : Rousseau).

Girard, P. (1923): Textes du droit romain, 5th ed. (Paris: Rousseau).

Giraudeau, M. (1984): Les notions juridique et sociales chez Hérodote. Etudes sur le vocabulaire (Paris: De Boccard).

Gizbert-Studnicki, T. (1979): Czy istnieje język prawny?, in: Państwo i Prawo, vol. 3, pp. 49–60.

Gizbert-Studnicki, T. (1986): Język prawny z perspektywy socjolingwistycznej (Warszawa/Kraków: PWN).

Gizbert-Studnicki, T. (1987): Der Vorverständnisbegriff in der juristischen Hermeneutik, in: Archiv für Rechts- und Staatsphilosophie 1987, pp. 476–493.

Gizbert-Studnicki, T. (2004): Sytuacyjne uwarunkowanie językowych właściwości tekstów prawnych, in: Malinowska, E. (ed.) Język – Prawo – Społeczeństwo (Opole: Wydawnictwo Uniwersytetu Opolskiego) pp. 37–48.

Gizbert-Studnicki, T. (2009): Postulat jasności i zrozumiałości tekstów prawnych a dostęp do prawa, in: Mróz, A., Niewiadomski, A., Pawelec, M. (eds.) Prawo i język (Warszawa: Uniwersytet Warszawski) pp. 9–18.

Glass, A. (1988): Fish and Legal Practice, in: Rechtstheorie, vol. 19, pp. 443–460.

Glendon, M., Gordon, M., Carozza, P. (1999): Comparative Legal Traditions, 2nd ed. (Hong Kong: Thomson).

Glenn, H.P. (2004): Legal Traditions of the World, 2nd ed. (Oxford: Oxford University Press).

Glenn, H.P. (2013): Cosmopolitan State (Oxford: Oxford University Press).

Glötzner, V. (1967): Die strafrechtliche Terminologie des Uloženie 1649. Untersuchungen zur russischen Rechtsgeschichte und Gesetzessprache (Wiesbaden: Harrassowitz).

Goddard, C. (2010a): Legal Linguists: As (In)substantial as Ghosts and True Love?, in: Giannoni, D.S., Frade, C. (eds.) Researching Language and the Law. Textual Features and Translation Issues (Bern: P. Lang).

Goddard, C. (2010b): Legal Linguistics as an Academic and Professional Discipline: Identifying Clients, Customers, Stakeholders, in: Heine, C., Engberg, J. (eds.). Reconceptualizing LSP. Online proceedings of the XVII European LSP Symposium 2009 (Aarhus).

Goetz, L.K. (1916): Deutsch-Russische Handelsverträge (Hamburg: Kolonialinstitut).

Goldberg, S.C. (2015): Assertion. On the Philosophical Significance of Assertoric Speech (Oxford: Oxford University Press).

Goletiani, L. (2011): O razvitii juridicheskoi lingvistiki v Rossii i Ukraine, in: Studi Slavistici VIII, pp. 241–262.

Goletiani, L. (2016): Vyrazhenie deonticheskoy modalnosti ‚objazatelstvo': Russkije i ukrainskije glagolnyje konstrukcii, in: Comparative Legilinguistics, vol. 26, pp. 7–30.

Golev, N.D. (2004): Juridičeskije aspekty jazyka i lingvističeskije aspekty prava. Mežvuzovskij sbornik naučnych statej (Barnaul: Izdatelstvo Altajskogo Universiteta).

Goodman, N. (1978): Ways of Worldmaking (Indianapolis: Hackett Publ.).

Goodrich, P. (1984): Law and Language: An Historical and Critical Introduction, in: Journal of Law & Society, vol. 11, no. 2, pp. 173–206.

Goodrich, P. (1987): Legal Discourse. Studies in Linguistics, Rhetoric and Legal Analyses (Basingstoke: Macmillan).

Goodrich, P. (1990): Language of Law. From Logics of Memory to Nomadic Masks (London: Weidenfeld and Nicolson).

Gorelov, B.I. (1989): Teoreticheskaja grammatika kitajskogo iazyka (Moskva: Prosvjeshtchenje).

Gortych, K. (2009): The Function of Ancient Greek in Modern Greek – Polish Legal Translation Training, in: Comparative Legilinguistics. International Journal for Legal Communication, vol. 1/2009, pp. 190–206.

Gortych-Michalak, K. (2013): Struktura polskich, greckich i cypryjskich aktów normatywnych. Studium porównawcze w aspekcie translatologicznym (Poznań: Wydawnictwo Naukowe Contact).

Gotti, M. (2011): Investigating Specialized Discourse, 3d ed. (Bern/Berlin: P. Lang).

Goulemot, J.M. (1991): Ces livres qu'on ne lit que d'une main. Lecture et lecteurs de livres pornographiques au XVIIIe siècle (Aix-en-Provence: Alinea).

Goźdź-Roszkowski, S. (2011): Patterns in Linguistic Variation in American Legal English. A Corpus-Based Study (Frankfurt aM/Berlin: P. Lang).

Grabarek, J. (1984): Die Sprache des Schöffenbuches der alten Stadt Toruń (Rzeszów: Wydawnictwo WSP).

Grabowski, A. (1999): Judicial Argumentation and Pragmatics (Kraków: Księgarnia Akademicka).

Granet, M. (1934): La pensée chinoise (Paris: Alban Michel).

Grasnich, W. (2001): Entscheidungsgründe als Textcollage, in: Müller, F., Wimmer, R. (eds.) Neue Studien zur Rechtslinguistik (Berlin: Duncker & Humblot).

Graziani, S. (1986): I testi mesopotamici datati al regno di Serse (485–465 a.C.) (Roma: Herder).

Greene, T. (1991): The language of the Constitution. A resourcebook and guide to the ideas, terms and vocabulary used by the framers of the United States Constitution (New York: Greenwood Press).

Greenhouse, L. (2012): Public Opinion & the Supreme Court: The Puzzling Case of Abortion, in: Daedalus, vol. 141, no. 4, pp. 69–82.

Greenwalt, K. (2010): Legal Interpretation: Perspectives from other Dissciplines and Private Texts (Oxford : Oxford University Press).

Greenwood, E. (2016): Reception Studies: The Cultural Mobility of Classics, in: Daedalus, vol. 145, no. 2, pp. 41–49.

Greimas, A.J. (1976): Analyse sémiotique d'un discours juridique. La loi commerciale sur les societés, in: Sémiotique et sciences sociales, pp. 79–128.

Grodzieński, E. (1980): Wypowiedzi performatywne o doniosłości prawnej lub quasiprawnej, in: Schaff, A. (ed.) Zagadnienia socjo- i psycholingwistyki (Wrocław: Zakład Narodowy im. Ossolińskich).

Grossfeld, B. (1986): Das Elend des Jurastudiums, in: Juristenzeitung, pp. 357 sqq.

Grossfeld, B. (1989):.....Rechtsausbildung und Rechtskontrolle, in: Neue Juristische Woche 1989, pp. 875–881.

Grossfeld, B. (1990): The Strength and Weakncss of Comparative Law (London: Clarendon Press).

Grossfeld, B., Winship, P. (1992): The Law Professor Refugee, in: Syracuse Journal of International Law and Commerce, vo. 18, pp. 1–20.

Grossfeld, B. (2005): Poesie und Recht. Rechtsvergleichende Zeichenkunde (Paderborn: F. Schöningh).

Gruber, M.C. (2014): I'm Sorry for What I've Done. The Language of Courtroom Apologies (Oxford: Oxford University Press).

Grzybek, J. (2013): Alternatywne metody rozwiązywania sporów w przekładzie chińsko-polskim i polsko-chińskim (Poznań: Wydawnictwo Naukowe Contact).

Gu, S. (2006): The Boundaries of Meaning and the Formation of Law. Legal Concepts and Reasoning in the English, Arabic and Chinese Traditions (Montreal: McGill-Queen's University Press).

Guimezanes, N. (1995): Introduction au droit français (Baden-Baden: Nomos).

Gunnarsson, B.L. (1982): Lagtexters begriplighet. En språkfunktionell studie av medbestämmandelagen (Lund: Liber Förlag).

Gustafsson, M. (1975): Some Syntactic Properties of English Law Language (Turku: University of Turku).

Haarmann, H. (2013): Mythos Demokratie. Antike Herrschaftsmodelle im Spannungsfeld von Egalitätsprinzip und Eliteprinzip (Frankfurt a.M.: P. Lang).

Habermas, J. (1988): Theorie des kommunikativen Handelns, vol. 1 and 2 (Frankfurt/M: Suhrkamp).

Habermas, J. (1996): Die Einbeziehung des Anderen (Frankfurt a.M.: Suhrkamp).

Hadryan, M. (2015): Demokratyzacja języka urzędowego. Współczesne tendencje polityki językowej w Szwecji i w Polsce (Poznań: Contact).

Hage, J. (2005): Studies in Legal Logic (Dordrecht: Springer).

Halpérin, J.L. (2009): Profils des mondialisations du droit (Paris: Dalloz).

Halpérin, J.L. (2014): Five Legal Revolutions since the 17th Century: An Analysis of the Global Legal History (Heidelberg/Berlin: Springer).

Hałas, B. (1995): Terminologia języka prawnego (Zielona Góra: WSP).

Hare, R.M. (1952): The Language of Morals (Oxford: Clarendon Press).

Hargitt, S. (2013): What Could be Gained in Translation: Legal Language and Lawyer-Linguists in Globalized World, in: Indiana Journal of Global Legal Studies, vol. 20, pp. 425–447.

Harju, V. (ed.) (2013): Oikeuden näyttämöt. Kuvallisuus lainkäytössä (Helsinki: Valtion Taidemuseo/Suomen Lakimiesliitto).

Harmer, L.C. (1983): Der Zustand des heutigen Französisch, in: Hausmann, F.J. (ed.) Die französische Sprache von heute (Darmstadt: Wissenschaftliche Buchgesellschaft) pp. 216–258.

Hart, H.L.A. (1958): Positivism and the Separation of Law and Morals, in: Harvard Law Review 71/593.

Hart, H.L.A. (1961): The Concept of Law (Oxford: Clarendon Press).

Hartig, M (1997): Erfolgsorientierte Kommunikation (Tübingen/Basel: Francke).

Hartkamp, A.S., Hesselink, M.W., Hondius, E.H. (1994): Towards a European Civil Code (Dordrecht: M. Nijhoff).

Hattenhauer, H. (1987): Zur Geschichte der deutschen Rechts- und Gesetzessprache (Göttingen: Vandenhoeck Ruprecht).

Heitsch, E. (1980): Recht und Argumentation in Antiphons 6. Rede. Philologische Erläuterungen zu einem attischen Strafprozess (Mainz: Akademie der Wissenschaft und der Literatur).

Held, D. (2005): Principles of Cosmopolitan Order, in: Brock, G., Brighouse, H. (eds.) The Political Philosophy of Cosmopolitanism (Cambridge/New York: Cambridge University Press).

Helin, M. (1990): Kielitekojen teoriasta institutionaaliseen oikeusteoriaan, in: Hirvonen, A., Tuori, K. (eds.) Oikeus, kieli ja kritiikki (Helsinki: Itakapaino) pp. 141–157.

Heller, D., Ehlich, K. (eds.) (2007): Studien zur Rechtskommunikation (Bern/Berlin: P. Lang)

Heller, M. (1992): Reform der deutschen Rechtssprache im 18. Jahrhundert (Frankfurt/M.: P. Lang).

Henderson, G. (2015): Creating Legal Worlds. Story and Style in Culture of Argument (Toronto: University of Toronto Press).

Herbots, J.B. (1987): La traduction juridique. Un point de vue belge, in: Cahiers de Droit, vol. 28, pp. 813–844.

Heunen, C., Sadrzadeh, M, Grefenstette, E. (2013): Quantum Physics and Linguistics. A Compositional, Diagrammatic Discourse (Oxford: Oxford University Press).

Hiltunen, R. (1990): Chapters on Legal English. Aspects Past and Present of the Language of the Law (Helsinki: Suomalainen Tiedeakademia).

Hiltunen, R. (2001): Some Syntactic Properties of English Law Language, in: Hiltunen, R. Battarbee, K. et al. (eds.): English in Zigs and Zags: A Festschrift for Marita Gustafsson (Turku: University of Turku).

Hirvonen, A., Tuori, K. (eds.) (1990): Oikeus, kieli ja kritiikki (Helsinki: Helsingin yliopiston julkisoikeuden laitoksen julkaisuja).

Hlouch, L. (2007/8): Teorie a realita právní interpretace (unpublished PhD-thesis, University of Brno).

Hoecke van, M. (2002): Law as Communication (Oxford/Portland: Hart).

Hoffmann, L. (1983): Kommunikation vor Gericht (Tübingen: Narr).

Hoffmann, C. (1991): Introduction into Bilingualism (London/New York: Longman).

Hofstede, G. (1991): Cultures and Organizations: Software of the Mind (New York: McGraw-Hill).

Hohfeld, W.N. (1913): Fundamental Legal Conceptions as Applied in Judicial Reasoning, in: Yale Law Journal 23/16.

Hohmann, H. (1998): Logic and Rhetoric in Legal Argumentation: Some Medieval Perspectives, in: Argumentation, vol. 12, pp. 39–55.

Holmes, B. (2016): Tragedy in the Crosshairs of the Present, in: Daedalus, vol. 145., no. 2, pp. 20–29.

Hölscher, T. (2004): The Language of Images in Roman Art: Art as a Semantic System in the Roman World (Cambridge: Cambridge University Press).

Holtgraves, T. M. (2002): Language as Social Action. Social Psychology and Language Use. (Mahwah/London: LEA Lawrence Erlbaum Associates).

Honig, B. (2013): Antigone, Interrupted (Cambridge: Cambridge University Press).

Honkatukia, P. (2001): Ilmoitti tulleensa raiskatuksi. Tutkimus poliisin tietoon vuonna 1998 tulleista raiskausrikoksista (Helsinki: Tilastokeskus).

Honoré, A.M. (1962): Gaius (Oxford: Clarendon Press).

Horie, Y. (2010a): The Roots of Japanese Legal Terminology, in: Comparative Legilinguistics. International Journal for Legal Communication, vol. 4, pp. 79–90.

Horie, Y. (2010b): Divorce Proceedings Differences in Polish and Japanese Law for Purposes of Legal Translation, in: Legilingwistyka Porównawcza, vol. 3, pp. 23–35.

Horie, Y., Trzaskawka, P. (2015): Cechy japońskiego i polskiego języka prawa, in: Comparative Legilinguistics, vol. 22, pp. 7–24.

Hotta, S. (2009): Saiban to koṭoba to tikara (Tokyo: Hituzi Syoboo).

Hotta, S. (2010): Hoo kontekusuto nokeru gengo-siyoo no rironteki-zissyooteki kenkyuu (Tokyo: Hituzi Syoboo).

Huang, Y. (2007): Pragmatics (Oxford: Oxford University Press).

Husa, J. (1998): Johdatus oikeusvertailuun (Helsinki: Kauppakaari).

Husa, J. (2007): Kreikan oikeus ja oikeuskieli (Helsinki: Suomalainen Lakimiesyhdistys).

Husa, J. (2011): Comparative Law, Legal Linguistics and Methodology of Legal Doctrine, in: Hoecke, van, M. (ed.) Methodologies of Legal Research. Which Kind of Method for What Kind of Discipline (Oxford: Hart) pp. 209–228.

Husa, J. (2013): Bysantin oikeushistoria. Johdatus itäroomalaiseen oikeuskultuuriin (Helsinki: Suomalainen Lakimiesyhdistys).

Husa, J. (2015a): A New Introduction to Comparative Law (Oxford/Portland: Hart Publishing).

Husa, J. (2015b): Exploring Imaginative Legal Theory: The Legalism of the House Stark in the Game of Thrones, in: Media & Arts Law Review, vol. 20, pp. 181–197.

Husa, J. (2016a): Varieties of Fairness and Procedural Cultures: A Comparative Discussion, in: Global Journal of Comparative Law, vol. 5, pp. 208–225.

Husa, J. (2016b): Translating Legal Language and Comparative Law, in: International Journal for the Semiotics of Law, vol. 29, no. 2, pp. 473–493.

Hutton, C. (2014): Defining Ordinary Words for Mundane Objects: Legal Lexicography, Ordinary Language and the Word Vehicle, in: Mac Aodha, M. (ed.) Legal Lexicography. A Comparative Perspective (Farnham/Burlington: Ashgate) pp. 178–200.

Igarashi, K. (1990): Einführung in das japanische Recht (Darmstadt: Wissenschaftliche Buchgesellschaft).

Ikobwa, J.M. (2008): Language Politics and Policies in Postcolonial Africa (Nairobi: University of Nairobi).

Ilie, C. (1995): The Validity of Rhetorical Questions as Arguments in the Courtroom, in: van Eemeren, F.H., Grootendorst, J.A. et al. (eds.): Special Fields and Cases. Proceedings of the Third International ISSA Conference on Argumentation (Amsterdam: SICSAT) pp. 73–88.

Iluk, J. (ed.) (2014): Beiträge zur Linguistik. Grammatik, Pragmatik, Lexikologie, Rechtssprache (Katowice: Wydawnictwo Uniwersytetu Śląskiego).

Innis, R.E. (ed.) (1985): Semiotics. An Introductory Anthology (Bloominigton: Indiana University Press).

Jackendorff, R. (2002): Foundations of Language (Oxford: Oxford University Press).

Jacobs, S. (1989): Some Problems of Communication for Argumentation Theory, in: Newsletter ISSA, no. 5, pp. 2–10.

Jackson, B. (1985): Semiotics and Legal Theory (London: Routledge).

Jackson, B. (1988): Narrative Models in Legal Proof, in: International Journal for the Semiotics of Law 1/3, pp. 226–246.

Jackson, B.S. (1990): Narrative Theories and Legal Discourse, in: Nash, C (ed.) Narrative in Culture (London: Routledge) pp. 23–50.

Jackson, B. (1995): Making Sense in Law. Linguistic, Psychological, and Semiotic Perspectives (Liverpool: Deborah Charles Publications).

Jagić, I.V (1910): Istoria Slavianskoj Filologii (St. Petersburg: Tipografia Imperatorskoj Akademii Nauk).

Jareborg, N. (1972): Vilseledande genom antydningar, in: Festskrift till P.O. Ekelöf (Stockholm: Kungl. Boktr.).

Jaszczolt, K. (2016): Meaning in Linguistic Interaction – Semantics, Metasemantics, Philosophy of Language (Oxford: Oxford University Press).

Jayme, E. (2012): Zugehörigkeit und kulturelle Identität. Die Sicht des Internationalen Privatrechts (München: Walstein).

Jeand'Heur, B. (1988): Sprachliches Referenzverhalten bei der juristischen Entscheidungstätigkeit (Berlin: Duncker & Humblot).

Jestaedt, M. (2012): Wissenschaftliches Recht, in: Kirchhof, G., Magen, S., Schneider, K. (eds.): Was heißt Dogmatik? (Tübingen: Mohr Siebeck) pp. 117–149.

Jopek-Bosiacka, A. (2006): Przekład prawny i sądowy (Warszawa: Wydawnictwo Naukowe PWN).

Jopek-Bosiacka, A. (2011): Legal Communication: A Cross-Cultural Perspective (Warsaw: University Press).

Jörgensen, N. (1987): Studier över syntax och textstruktur i nordiska medeltidslagar (Lund: Lund University Press).

Jori, M. (1985): Saggi di Metagiurisprudenza (Milano: Giuffrè).

Joxe, P. (2009): Cas de conscience (Paris: Labor et Fides).

Juhl, P.D. (1980): Interpretation. An Essay in the Philosophy of Literary Criticism (Princeton: Princeton University Press).

Jyränki, A. (ed.) (1999): Oikeuden kielet (Turku: Turun yliopiston oikeustieteellisen tiedekunnan julkaisuja B: 71).

Kaag, J.J. (2009): Pragmatism and the Lessons of Experience, in: Daedalus, vol. 138/2, pp. 63–72.

Kaczmarek, K. (2011): Lingua Legis w aspekcie translatologicznym węgiersko-polskim i polsko-węgierskim, in: Legilingwistyka Porównawcza/Comparative Legilinguistics, vol. 6.

Kaiser, F. B. (1965): Der europäische Anteil an der russischen Rechtsterminologie der petrinischen Zeit, in: Forschungen zur osteuropäischen Geschichte, vol. 10, pp. 75–333.

Kalinowski, M. (2011): Introduction to Wang Chong, Lun Heng/Balance de Discours (Paris: Les Bellles Lettres).

Kangas, U. (1991): Ihmisen nimi. Nimenmääräytymisen oikeudelliset rajat (Helsinki: Lakimiesliiton kustannus).

Kaser, M. (1983): Römisches Privatrecht (München: Beck).

Katzenmeier, C. (2013): Der Behandlungsvertrag – Neuer Vertragstypus im BGB, in: Neue Juristische Wochenschrift, vol. 12., pp. 817–823.

Kellaway, L. (2016): My ambition to look more like Theresa May in meetings, in: Financial Times, July 18, 2016.

Kelsen, H. (1960): Reine Rechtslehre, 2nd ed. (Wien: F. Deuticke).

Kelsen, H. (1991): General Theory of Norms (Oxford: Clarendon Press).

Kemp, W. (ed.) (2001): Quiet Diplomacy in Action: The OSCE High Commissioner on National Minorities (The Hague: Kluwer).

Kennedy, D. (1982): The Stages of the Decline of the Public/Private Distinction, in: Univ. of Pennsylvania Law Review, vol. 130, pp. 1349–1357.

Kesola, E. (2007): Valtiosopimusten termistö ja sen käyttö (unpublished thesis, Tampere University, Finland).

Kevelson, R. (1990): Peirce, Paradox, Praxis: the Image, the Conflict and the Law (Berlin/New York: Mouton de Gruyter).

Khurana, R. (2007): From Higher Aims to Hired Hands. The Social Transformation of American Business Schools and the Unfulfilled Promise of Management as a Profession (Princeton/Oxford: Princeton University Press).

Kielar, B. (1977): Language of the Law in the Aspect of Translation (Warszawa: Wydawnictwo UW).

Kielar, B. (1979): W obronie koncepcji "języka prawnego" jako rejestru języka naturalnego, in: Państwo i Prawo, no. 8–9, p. 172 sqq.

Kilscher, U. (2015): Rechtsvergleichung (München: C.H. Beck).

Kinnunen, T. (2006): Käännös oikeudenkäyntiaineistona. Lakitekstien tulkinta oikeuskäsitteiden kääntämisen näkökulmasta (Tampere: Tampereen yliopisto).

Kirchhof, P. (1987): Die Bestimmtheit und Offenheit der Rechtssprache (Berlin/New York: W. de Gruyter).

Kirchhof, G., Magen, S., Schneider, K. (eds.) (2012): Was heißt Dogmatik? (Tübingen: Mohr Siebeck).

Kirchmann, von, J. (1938): Die Wertlosigkeit der Jurisprudenz als Wissenschaft (Stuttgart/ Berlin: Kohlhammer).

Kirchner, H., Pannier, D. (2008): Abkürzungsverzeichnis der Rechtssprache, 6th ed. (Berlin: De Gruyter).

Kissinger, H. (1994): Diplomacy (New York: Simon and Schuster).

Kjaer, A.L. (1990): Normbetingede ordforbindelser i tysk juridisk sprog (København: Copenhagen Business School Press).

Klatt, M. (2008): Making the Law Explicit: the Normativity of Legal Argumentation (Oxford/New York: Hart).

Klava, K. (1989): Die Sprache der lettischen Dokumente vom Ende des 17. Jahrhunderts. Ein Beitrag zur lettischen Sprachgeschichte (Stockholm: Almqvist & Wiksell International).

Kleiber, G. (1990): La sémantique du prototype. Catégories et sens lexical (Paris: Presses Universitaires de France).

Klemperer, V. (1969): LTI (Lingua Tertii Imperii). Die unbewältigte Sprache, 3rd ed. (München: dtv).

Klimov, G.A., Halilov, M. Sh. (2003): Slovar' kavkazkih jazykov. Sopostavlenije osnovnoj leksiki (Moskva: Vostochnaja Literatura RAN).

Koch, H.J. (ed.) (1976): Juristische Methodenlehre und analytische Philosophie (Kronberg Ts.: Athenäum Verlag).

Kocher, G. (1992): Zeichen und Symbole des Rechts. Eine historische Ikonographie (München: C.H. Beck).

Kolańczyk, K. (1986): Prawo Rzymskie (Warszawa: PIW).

Kořenský, F., Cvrček, F., Novák, F. (1999): Juridická a lingvistická analýza pravných tekstů (právněinformatický přistup) (Praha: Academia).

Korolev, S. (2010): Procedural Misfires of Cross-Cultural Legal Communication in the Perspective of J. Austin and J. Langshaw Austin, in: Comparative Legilinguistics. International Journal for Legal Communication vol. 4/2004, pp. 27–35.

Korte, D. (1974): Untersuchungen zu Inhalt, Stil und Technik angelsächsischer Gesetze und Rechtsbücher des 6.-12. Jahrhunderts (Meisenheim a.G.: A. Hain).

Koshkin, I.S. (2008): Russko-germanskije jazykovyje kontakty v gramotah severozapada Rusi XII–XV vv (St.Petersburg: Izdatelstvo St. Peterburskogo Universiteta).

Koskenniemi, M. (1999): The Effect of Rights on Political Culture, in: Alston, P. (ed.) The EU and Human Rights, pp. 99–116 (Oxford: Oxford University Press).

Koskensalo, A. (2002): The Functionality of Business Letters in the Face of Globalisation, in: Satzger, A. Poncini, G. International Perspectives on Business Communication. From Past Approaches to Future Trends, pp. 55–64 (Frankfurt/M: P. Lang).

Kotarbiński, T. (1955): Kurs logiki dla prawników (Warszawa: PIW).

Kotarbiński, T. (1965): Praxiology. An Introduction to the Science of Efficient Action (New York: Pergamon Press).

Kotarbiński, T. (1986): Drogi dociekań własnych. Fragmenty filozoficzne (Warszawa: PWN).

Kovačević, Z. (2004): Međunarodno pregovaranje (Beograd: Diplomatska akademija MSP SCG).

Kraakman, R., Davies, P. et al. (2004): The Anatomy of Corporate Law. A Comparative and Functional Approach (Oxford: Oxford University Press).

Krasilnikova, K. (2006): Problem stworzenia klasyfikacji argumentów (na podstawie rosyjskich i polskich badań), in: Rozprawy Komisji Językowej ŁTN, vol. LI.

Krefeld, T. (1985): Das französische Gerichtsurteil in linguistischer Sicht: zwischen Fach- und Standessprache (Frankfurt a. M.: P. Lang).

Kredens, K., Goźdź-Roszkowski, S. (eds.) (2007): Law and the Language: International Outlooks. Lodz studies in Language series, vol. 16. (Frankfurt/M.: Lang).

Krugman, P. (2017): Facts are enemies of the people, in: The New York Times International Edition, March 14, 2017, p. 13.

Kryk-Kastowski, B. (2006): Legal Pragmatics, in: Brown, K. (ed.) Encyclopedia of Languages and Linguistics (New York: Elsevier) pp. 14–20.

Kuchar, R. (1998): Právo a slovenčina v dejinách (Budmerice: RAK).

Kusov, G. V. (2004): Oskorblenie kak illokutivnyi lingvokulturnyi concept (University of Volgograd).

Kuzmins, A. (2015): Daži normatīvie un politikas plānošanas akti valodu politikas jomā (1918–1992) in: Buzajevs, V. (ed.): Mazākumtautību tiesiskais un faktiskais stāvoklis Latvijā. Pēc viņu aizstāvju datiem (Riga: Latvijas Cilvēktiesību komiteja) pp. 134–159.

Kwarciński, W. (2002): A Speech Act Approach to Legal Discourse (unpublished PhD-thesis, University of Poznań).

Kwarciński, W. (2004): Recipient Design of Statutes and Judgments, in: Studia Anglica Poznanensia, vol. 40, pp. 209–225.

Kwarciński, W. (2005): Some Parallels between Pragmalinguistic and Legal Models of Interpretation (unpublished presentation at the 7th IAFL Conference – Cardiff University).

Kwarciński, W. (2006): A Diachronic Speech Act Analysis of Sworn Testimonies in Polish Criminal Trials, in: Kryk-Kastorsky, B. (ed.) Historical Courtroom Discourse, pp. 293–314.

Kymlicka, W. (1995) Multicultural Citizenship (Oxford: Oxford University Press).

Lachmayer, F. (1979): Präkonstitutionelles Gewohnheitsrecht, In: Juristische Blätter 99, pp. 411–415.

Ladjili-Mouchette, J. (1990): Histoire juridique de la Méditerranée. Droit romain, droit musulman (Tunis: Imprimerie Officielle de la République Tunisienne).

Laffi, U. (2013): In greco per i Greci. Ricerche sul lessico greco del processo civile e criminale romano nelle attestazioni di fonti documentarie romane (Pavia: IUSS Press).

Lambert Jr., R.G. (1997): Emily Dickinson's use of Anglo-American legal concepts and vocabulary in her poetry (Lewiston: Edwin Mellen Press).

Lampe, E.J. (1970): Rechtsanthropologie I. Individualstrukturen in der Rechtsordnung (Berlin : Duncker & Humblot).

Landqvist, H. (2003): Abolition, militärmål, rusdryck och kåkfarare. Studier i ett svenskt juridiskt ordförråd 1800–2000, ORDAT 20 (Göteborg: Göteborgs universitet).

Landquist, H. (2008): Spår i SAOB: David Ehrenståle Nehrman och Svenska Akademiens ordbok, in: Foley, R. et al., Oikeuden ja kielen kohtaamisia, pp. 157–171.

Lang, A. (2011): World Trade Law after Neoliberalism – Re-imagining the Global Economic Order (Oxford: Oxford University Press).

Langevoort, D. (1999): Half-Truths: Protecting Mistaken Inferences by Investors and Others, in: Stanford Law Review, vol. 52.

Lasarte, C. (2006): Curso de derecho civil patrimonial, 12 ed. (Madrid: Tecnos).

Lauersdorf, M.R. (1996): The question of "Cultural Language" and interdialectical norm in 16th century Slovakia. A phonological analysis of 16th century Slovak legal texts (München: Sagner).

Laurén, Ch. (2002): Iconism as Special Language, in: Mattila (2002a) pp. 11–20.

Leech. G. (2014): The Pragmatics of Politeness (Oxford: Oxford University Press).

Lee, D.S., Hall.,C, Barone, S. M. (2007): American Legal Language: Using Language in Legal Contexts, 2nd ed. (Ann Arbor: Michigan University Press).

Lehman, J., Phelps, S. (eds.) (2005): West's Encyclopedia of American Law, 2nd ed. (Detroit, San Diego: Thomson).

Lehmann, V. (2013): Linguistik des Russischen. Grundlagen der formal-funktionalen Beschreibung (München/Berlin/Washington: Otto Sagner).

Lentano, M. (2014): Retorica e diritto. Per una lettura giuridica della declamazione latina (Lecce: Grifo).

Leodolter, R. (1975): Das Sprachverhalten von Angeklagten bei Gericht (Kronberg: Scriptor).

Lepper, M. (2012): Philologie zur Einführung (Hamburg: Junius).

Lerch, K.D. (2004): Verständlichkeit als Pflicht? Zur Intransparenz des Transparenzgebotes, in: Lerch, K.D. (ed.) Recht verstehen. Verständlichkeit, Missverständlichkeit und Unverständlichkeit von Recht (Berlin/New York: de Gruyter) pp. 239–283.

Letto-Vanamo, P. (2002): Legal Systems and Legal Languages, in: H. Mattila (ed.) The Development of Legal Language, pp. 21–30 (Helsinki: Kauppakaari).

Leveneur, L. (ed.) (2016): Dossier spécial Code civil. Projet de réforme du droit des contracts, du régime général et de la preuve des obligations (Paris: LexisNexis).

Levinson, S. (1983): Pragmatics (Cambridge: Cambrigde University Press).

Liebman, B.L. (2014): Legal Reform: China's Law-Stability Paradox, in: Daedalus, vol. 143 (2), pp. 96–109.

Lindahl, L. (1977): Position and Change: a Study in Law and Logic (Dordrecht/Boston: D. Reidel Pub.).

Lindroos, E. (2015): Im Namen des Gesetzes. Eine vergleichende rechtslinguistische Untersuchung zur Formelhaftigkeit in deutschen und finnischen Strafurteilen (Rovaniemi: Acta Universitatis Lapponiensis).

Linhart, K. (2005): Internationales Einheitsrecht und einheitliche Auslegung (Mohr Siebeck: Tübingen).

Lippert, S.L. (2004): Ein demotisches juristisches Lehrbuch. Untersuchungen zu Papyrus Berlin P 23757 rto, Ägyptologische Abhandlungen 66 (Wiesbaden: Harrassowitz Verlag).

Liu, W. (2005): Illocutionary and Perlocutionary Acts in Chinese Judge's Attached Discourse (unpublished presentation at 7th IAFL Conference, Cardiff University).

Liu, H. (2007): Falü Yuyanxue (Beijing: Beijing Daxue Chubanshe).

Liu, H. (2016): Name, don't shame, in: China Daily Oct 14–20, p. 23.

Lizisowa, M.T. (2004): Literackie przekodowanie tekstu prawnego w "Panu Tadeuszu", in: Annales Universitatis Paedagogicae Cracoviensis, Studia Historicolitteraria, vol. 4, pp. 21–34.

Lizisowa, M.T. (2013): Metody badań języka prawnego wobec ontologicznej natury prawa, in: Comparative Legilinguistics vol. 14, pp. 21–46.

Lizisowa, M.T. (2017, in print): Komunikacyjna teoria języka prawnego (Poznań: Wydawnictwo Naukowe Contact).

Loewe, R. (1989): Internationales Kaufrecht (Wien: Manzsche Verlags- und Universitätsbuch- handlung).

Loewe, M. (2004): The Men who Governed Han China. A Companion to a Biographical Dictionary of the Qin, Former Han and Xin Periods (Leyden: Brill).

Löfstedt, B.M. (1961): Studien über die Sprache der langobardischen Gesetze. Beiträge zur frühmittelalterlichen Latinität (Stockholm/Göteborg/Uppsala: Almquist &Wiksell).

Lucas, S.E. (1976): Portents of Rebellion: Rhetoric and Revolution in Philadelphia 1765–1776 (Philadelphia: Temple University Press).

Lucas, S.E. (1998): The Stylistic Artistry of the Declaration of Independence, in: Prologue. Quarterly of the National Archives, vol. 74, pp. 241–260.

Lukashuk, I. (1996): Mezhdunarodnoje pravo, Obshchaja chast (Moskva: Beck).

Lundmark, T. (1999): Über die grundlegende Unmöglichkeit ein juristisches Wörterbuch mit der Zielsprache Englisch zu erstellen. Plädoyer für eine Rechtsenzyklopädie, in: de Groot, R., Schulze, R. (eds.): Recht und Übersetzen (Baden-Baden: Nomos) pp. 59–65.

Lundmark, T. (2005): Talking Law Dictionary (Münster: LexisNexis).

Lundmark, T. (2006): How (Not) to Write a Bilingual Law Dictionary, in: Lundmark, Th., Wallow, A. (eds.): Law and Language – Recht und Sprache (Berlin: LIT Verlag) pp. 57–65.

Lundmark, T. (2012): Charting the Divide between Common and Civil Law (Oxford: Oxford University Press).

Lüscher, C. (2012): Zum Verhältnis von Sprache und Recht, dargestellt an einer (Re-) konstruktion der wörtlich-grammatikalischen Interpretationsmethode, in: Rechtstheorie, vol. 43, pp. 45–84.

Lutz, E. (1998): Language as a Medium of Legal Norms (Berlin: Duncker & Humblot).

Luzzati, C. (1990): La vaghezza delle norme. Un'analisi del linguaggio giuridico (Milano: Giuffrè).

Lyons, J. (1968): Introduction to Theoretical Linguistics (Cambridge: Cambridge University Press).

Mac Aodha, M. (ed.) (2014): Legal Lexicography. A Comparative Perspective (Farnham/Burlington: Ashgate).

Maccoby, H. (1989): Judaism in the First Century (London: Sheldon Press).

MacCormick, N. (1984): Coherence in Legal Justification, in: Theorie der Normen. Festgabe für Ota Weinberger zum 65. Geburtstag (Berlin: Duncker & Humblot).

MacCormick, N. & Bańkowski, Z. (1986): Speech Acts, Legal Institutions and Real Laws, in: The Legal Mind. Essays for Tony Honoré, in: MacCormick, N. & Birks, P. (eds.) (Oxford: Clarendon Press) pp. 120–133.

MacCormick, N., Weisberger, O. (1986): An Institutional Theory of Law. New Approaches to Legal Positivism (Dordrecht/Boston: D. Reidel Publishing).

MacCormick, N., Summers, R. (eds.) (1991): Interpreting Statutes. A Comparative Study (Aldershot: Dartmouth).

MacCormick, N., Summers, R. (eds.) (1997): Interpreting Precedents. A Comparative Study (Aldershot/Ashgate: Dartmouth).

Macías Otón, E. (2015): Los problemas conceptuales y socioculturales de la traducción jurídica (inglés/francés-español), in: Revista de Llengua i Dret, vol. 63, pp. 49–62.

Mack. P. (2011): A History of Renaissance Rhetoric 1380–1620 (Oxford: Oxford University Press).

Mackie, J.L. (1977): Ethics. Inventing Right and Wrong (New York: Viking Press).

Madsen, D. (1997): Towards a Description of Communication in the Legal Universe. Translation of Legal Texts and the Skopos Theory, in: Fachsprache, vol. 1, pp. 17–27.

Malinowska, E. (2012): Konstytucja jako gatunek tekstu prawnego (Opole: Wydawnictwo Uniwersytetu Opolskiego).

Malinowski, A. (2006): Polski język prawny. Wybrane zagadnienia (Warszawa: LexisNexis).

Mallat, C. (2007): Introduction to Middle Eastern Law (Oxford: Oxford University Press).

Mandela, N. (1994): Long Walk to Freedom (Boston: Little, Brown and Co.).

Mannoni, M. (2015): Fondamenti di Linguistica Forense Cinese. Traduzione Giuridica e Semiotica (Pisa: Il Campano).

Mannoni, M. (2016): Challenging the Existence of Legal Translation: A Comprehensive Translation Theory, in: Comparative Legilinguistics, vol. 26, pp. 99–124.

Mansfeld, J. (1964): Die Offenbarung des Parmenides und die menschliche Welt (Assen).

Mariani Marini, A., Bambi, F. (eds.) (2013): Lingua e diritto. Scritto e parlato nelle professioni legali (Pisa: Pisa University Press).

Marion, M. (2000): Philosophie de la logique et des matématiques, in: Engel, P. (ed.) Précis de philosophie analytique (Paris: puf) pp. 141–155.

Markhardt, H. (2006): Wörterbuch der österreichischen Rechts-, Wirtschafts- und Verwaltungsterminologie (Frankfurt a. M.: P. Lang).

Marmor, A. (2005): Interpretation and Legal Theory, 2nd ed. (Oxford/Portland: Hart).

Marmor, A. (2008): The Pragmatics of Legal Language, in: Ratio Juris, vol. 21, pp. 423–452.

Marmor, A. Soames, S. (eds.) (2011): Philosophical Foundations of Language in the Law (Oxford: Oxford University Press).

Marmor, A. (2014): The Language of Law (Oxford: Oxford University Press).

Martineau, F. (2008): Petit traité d'argumentation judiciaire, 3. ed. (Paris: Dalloz).

Maspero, H. (1950): Le taoïsme et les religions chinoises (Paris: Gallimard).

Matias Camargo, S.R. (2012): Tendencias y enfoques de la investigación en derecho, in: Diálogos de Sabres, vol. 36, pp. 9–15.

Matoesian, G.M. (1993): Reproducing Rape: Domination through Talk in the Courtroom (Cambridge: Polity Press).

Mattila, H.E.S. (1992): Juridiset tieto- ja määritelmäsanakirjat latinalaisissa maissa, in: Lakimies vol. 1, pp. 19–43.

Mattila, H.E.S. (ed.) (2002a): The Development of Legal Language (Helsinki: Kauppakaari).

Mattila, H.E.S. (2002b): Vertaileva oikeuslingvistiikka (Helsinki: Kauppakaari).

Mattila, H.E.S. (2002c): De aequalitate Latinitatis jurisperitorum. Le latin juridique dans les grandes familles de droit contemporaines à la lumière des dictionnaires spécialisés, in: Revue du droit comparé, pp. 717–758.

Mattila, H.E.S. (2002d): Review of R. Pitkäranta's Finnish-Latin-Finnish Dictionary, in: LexicoNordica vol. 9, pp. 271–283.

Mattila, H. (2002e): Les materiaux non finnois dans l'interprétation juridique en Finlande, in: Sacco, R. (ed): L'interprétation de texts juridiques redigés dans plus d'une langue (Turin: Isaidat Harmattan Italia) pp. 151–182.

Mattila, H.E.S., Jussila, A, Kaltio, O. (2004): Oikeuselämän lyhennesanakirja. Juridisk förkortningsbok (Helsinki: Talentum).

Mattila, H.E.S. (2005): Språket och den nordiska rättsfamiljen, in: Tidskrift utgiven av Juridiska Föreningen i Finland, vol. 1, pp. 43–57.

Mattila, H.E.S. (2006): Comparative Legal Linguistics (Aldershot: Ashgate).

Mattila, H.E.S. (2008): Oikeuskielen muutokset nykymaailmassa, in: Lakimies, vol. 7–8, pp. 1149–1165.

Mattila, H.E.S. (2009): Oikeusleksikologisista tutkimustarpeista, in: Lakimies, vol. 7–8, pp. 1175–1180.

Mattila, H.E.S. (2010a): Oikeuslingvistiikka ja oikeusvertailu, in: Lakimies, vol. 5, pp. 719–730.

Mattila, H.E.S., Piehl, A., Pajula, S. (eds.) (2010b): Oikeuskieli ja säädöstieto. Suomenkielinen lakikirja 250 vuotta. Rättsspråk och författningsinformation. Den finskspråkiga lagboken 250 år. (Helsinki: Lakimiesyhdistys).

Mattila, H.E.S. (2012a): Jurilinguistique comparée: Langage du droit, latin et langues modernes (Montréal: Yvon Blais).

Mattila, H.E.S. (2012b): Legal Vocabulary, in: Tiersma, P.M., Solan, L.M. (eds.) The Oxford Handbook of Language and Law (Oxford: Oxford University Press) pp. 27–38.

Mattila, H.E.S. (2013a): Comparative Legal Linguistics, 2nd ed. (Aldershot: Ashgate).

Mattila, H.E.S. (2013b): Tuomarinviitasta banianpuun lehviin. Oikeuden kuvallisuus historiallisesti ja kansainvälisesti, in: Harju, V. (ed.) Oikeuden näyttämöt. Kuvallisuus lainkäytössä (Helsinki: Valtion Taidemuseo/Suomen Lakimiesliitto) pp. 20–45.

Mattila, H.E.S. (2014): Oikeudellis-kielellisen dominanssin jatkuvuudesta. Alankomaiden Itä-Intian ja itsenäisen Indonesian oikeus- ja kieliolojen tarkastelua, in: Oikeuden historiasta tulevaisuuden Eurooppaan. Pia Letto-Vanamo 60 vuotta (Helsinki: Suomalainen Lakimiesyhdistys) pp. 181–200.

Matulewska, A. (2007): Lingua Legis in Translation (Frankfurt: P. Lang).

Matulewska, A. (2009): Methods of expressing deontic modality in English and Polish statutory instruments, in: Comparative Legilinguistics, vol. 1, pp. 133–146.

Matulewska, A. (2010): Deontic modality and modals in the language of contracts, in: Comparative Legilinguistics, vol. 2, pp. 75–92.

Matulewska, A. (2013): Legilinguistic Translatology. A Parametric Approach to Legal Translation (Bern/Berlin: P. Lang).

May, R. (1980): Problematik chinesischen Rechtsverständnisses, in: Archiv für Rechts- und Staatsphilosophie, vol. LXVI/2, pp. 193–205.

McAdams, R.H. (2015): The Expressive Powers of Law: Theories and Limits (Cambridge: Harvard University Press).

McCormick, J. (1997): Habermas' Discourse Theory of Law: Bridging Anglo-American and Continental Legal Traditions?, in: The Modern Law Review Limited, pp. 734–743.

McLaughlin, S., Powell, E.J. (2011): Domestic Law Goes Global (Cambridge: Cambridge University Press).

McWhorter, J. (2014): The Language Hoax: Why the World Looks the Same in Any Language (Oxford: Oxford University Press).

Mellinkoff, D. (1963): The Language of the Law (Boston/Toronto: Little).

Menski, W. (2006): Comparative Law in a Global Context. The Legal Systems of Asia and Africa, 2nd ed. (Cambridge: Cambridge University Press).

Mešanović-Meša, E. (2011): Kontrastivna analiza bosanskog, hrvatskog i srpskog jezika u zakonima Federacje Bosne i Hercegovine (Sarajevo: Slavistički komitet).

Milgram, S. (1983): Obedience to Authority: An Experimental View (New York: Harper & Row).

Milov, L.V. 1999: Vizantijskaja Ekloga i "Pravda Jaroslava" (K rekonstrukcji vizantijskogo prava na Rusi), in: Gennadios. K 70-letiju akademika G.G. Litavrina (Moskva: Indrik) pp. 129–142.

Minda, G. (1995): Postmodern Legal Movements (New York: New York University Press).

Mittman, S. (2003): Notas do Tradutor e Processo Tradutório. Análise e reflexão sob a perspectiva discursiva (Porto Alegre: Ed. da UFRGS).

Modéer, K.A., Sunnqvist, M. (eds.) (2012): Legal Stagings. The Visualization, Medialization and Ritualization of Law in Language, Literature, Media, Art and Architecture (Copenhagen: University of Copenhagen/Museum Tusculanum Press).

Moeketsi, R. (1999): Discourse in a Multilingual and Multicultural Courtroom: A Court Interpreter's Guide (Pretoria: J.L. van Schalk).

Moens, G., Gillies, P. (2006): International Trade and Business: Law, Policy and Ethics, 2nd ed. (Abingdon: Routledge/Cavendish).

Mohammed, A. (1987): Development of Scientific and Technical Terminology with Special Reference to African Languages (Addis Ababa: Academy of Ethiopian Languages).

Mooney, A. (2014): Language and Law (Basingstoke: Palsgrave Macmillan).

Moraldo, S. M. (ed.) (2012): Sprachenpolitik und Rechtssprache. Methodische Ansätze und Einzelanalysen (Frankfurt a.M.: P. Lang).

Morawetz, T. (1992): Epistemology of Judging. Wittgenstein and Deliberative Practices, in: Patterson, D.M. (ed.): Wittgenstein and Legal Theory (Boulder/S. Francisco: Westlaw Press) pp. 3–27.

Morello, R. (2012): Uma política pública e participativa para as línguas brasileiras: sobre a regulamentação e a implementação do Inventário Nacional da Diversidade Linguística (INDL), in: Revista Gragoatá, vol. 2, pp. 1–11.

Moréteau, O. (2009): Les frontièrs de la langue et du droit: vers une méthodologie de la traduction juridique, in: Revue international de droit compare, vol. 61, pp. 695–713.

Mörsdorf, K. (1937): Die Rechtssprache des Codex juris canonici. Eine kritische Untersuchung (Paderborn: Schöningh).

Most, G.W. (2003): Violets in Crucibles: Translating, Traducing, Transmuting, in: Transactions of the American Philological Association, vol. 133 (2), pp. 381–390.

Mounin, G. (1963): Les problèmes theoriques de la traduction (Paris: puf).

Mukhwana, A. (2010): Language Policy and Planning in Urban Kenya (VDM Publishers: Saarbrücken).

Mukhwana, A. (2013): A New Language Policy but Old Language Practices: the Case of Kenya after 2010 Constitution, in: International Journal of Innovative Research and Development, vol. 2, issue 9 (available online).

Müller, F. (1975): Recht – Sprache –Gewalt. Elemente einer Verfassungstheorie (Berlin: Duncker & Humblot).

Müller, F. (ed.) (1989): Untersuchungen zur Rechtslinguistik (Berlin: Duncker & Humblot).

Müller, F. (1997): Methodik, Theorie, Linguistik des Rechts. (Berlin: Duncker & Humblot).

Müller, I. (2014): Furchtbare Juristen. Die unbewältigte Vergangenheit unserer Justiz, 7th ed. (München: Kindler).

Munday, R. (1983): The Common Lawyer's Philosophy of Legislation, in: Rechtstheorie, vol. 2, pp. 191–203.

Mushchinina M. (2009): Rechtsterminologie – ein Beschreibungsmodell: das Russische Recht des geistigen Eigentums (Berlin: Frank & Timme)

Mutius, von, H.G. (2003/2004): Rechtsentscheide von Moses Nachmanides aus Gerona, vols. 1–3 (Frankfurt a.M: P. Lang).

Mwangi, P.W. (2003): Description of Non-Cooperatives in Legal English in Kenya, based on Grice's Principle of Cooperation (MA-thesis, Repository: University of Nairobi).

Napierski, K. (1868): Russisch-livländische Urkunden (St. Petersburg).

Neumann-Duesberg, H. (1949): Sprache im Recht (Münster: Regensberg).

Nerhot, P. (1992): Law, Writing, Meaning. An Essay in Legal Hermeneutics (Edinburgh: Edinburgh University Press).

Nettle, D., Romaine, S. (2000): Vanishing Voices: the Extinction of the World's Languages (New York: Oxford University Press).

Ng, Kwai Hang (2009): The Common Law in Two Voices. Language, Law and the Postcolonia Dilemma in Hong Kong (Stanford: Stanford University Press).

Ngugi, W. W. (1994): Legal Illiteracy in Kenya: a Case for the Right to Legal Literacy (LLM-thesis, Repository: University of Nairobi).

Niemi-Kiesiläinen, J., Honkatukia, P., Karma, H., Ruuskanen, M. (eds.) (2006): Oikeuden tekstit diskursseina (Helsinki: Suomalainen Lakimiesyhdistys).

Niemi-Kiesiläinen, J., Honkatukia, P., Ruuskanen, M. (2007): Legal Texts as Discourses, in: Svensson, Å., Gunnarsson E.M., Davies, M. (eds.) Exploiting the Limits of Law: Swedish Feminism and the Challenge to Pessimism (Aldershot: Ashgate) pp. 69–88.

Nilsson, P.E. (1976): Juridiskt språk, in: Molde, B. (ed.) Fackspråk (Lund: Esselte) pp. 49–54.

Nordbäck-Linder, H. (1972): Att vara tolk. Teknik, utbildning, arbetsmöjligheter (Stockholm: Natur och Kultur).

Nowak, J. (2010): Lunfardo Lexical Units Related to Law, in: Comparative Legilinguistics. International Journal for Legal Communication, vol. 2, pp. 93–103.

Nowak-Michalska, J. (2012): Modalność deontyczna w języku prawnym na przykładzie polskiego i hiszpańskiego kodeksu cywilnego (Poznań: Wydawnictwo Rys).

Obronovskij, S.P. (1934): "Russkaja Pravda" kak pamjatnik russkogo literaturnogo jazyka, in: Izviestja AN SSSR, p. 776 sqq.

Oduor, J., Xu, J. (2016): The Status of Mother Tongues in Kenya and China. Lessons the Two Countries Can Learn from Each Other, in: The University of Nairobi Journal of Language and Linguistics, vol. 5, pp. 14–32.

Ohlin, G. (1976): Ekonomins språk, in: Molde, B. (ed.) Fackspråk (Lund: Esselte) pp. 41–48.

Okawara, M.H. (1998): The Comprehensibility of Japanese Legal Language: the Penal Code in: Chiiki Seisaku Kenkyu, vol. 1/2, pp. 197–206.

Okawara, M.H. (2006): A Linguistic Analysis of Some Japanese Trademark Cases (unpublished PhD- thesis, University of Sidney).

Olanrewaju, F. R. (2009): Forensic Linguistics. An Introduction to the Study of Language and the Law (Munich: Lincom).

Oliveira, G.M. (ed.) (2004): Declaração Universal dos Direitos Linguísticos – Novas Perspectivas em Política Lingüística (São Paolo: Mercado de Letras).

Olivekrona, K. (1969): Det rättsliga språket och verkligheten (Lund: Ekstrands Tryckeri).

Olsson, J. (2008) Forensic Linguistics: Second Edition (London/New York: Continuum).

Olsson, J., Luchjenbroers, J. (2014): Forensic Linguistics, 4th ed. (London: Bloomsbury).

Omondi, L.N. (1989): Language, Gender and the Law, in: Mbeo, M.A., Ooko-Ombaka, O. (eds.) Women and Law in Kenya (Nairobi: Initiatives).

Onsongo Bush, O.R. (2010): Effectiveness of Language Interpretation in Case Management at the Chief Magistrate's Court at Kisumu (MBA-thesis, Repository: University of Nairobi).

Opeibi, O. (2008): Between Obscurity and Clarity in Nigerian Legal Discourse: Aspects of Language Use in Selected Written Texts, in: Wagner, A., Cacciaguidi-Fahy, S. (eds.), Obscurity and Clarity in the Law. Prospects and Challenges (Aldershot: Ashgate).

Örücü, E. (2004): The Enigma of Comparative Law. Variations on a Theme for the Twenty-first Century (Leiden: Nijhoff).

Ost, F. (2009): Le droit comme traduction (Québec: Presses de l'Université de Laval).

Oxburgh, G., Myklebust, T., Grant, T., Milne, R.R. (eds.) (2015): Communication in Investigative and Legal Contexts. Integrated Approaches from Forensic Psychology, Linguistics and Law Enforcement (London: Wiley).

Pajula, P. (1960): Suomalaisen oikeuskielen historia pääpiirteittäin (Porvoo/Helsinki: WSOY).

Palmgren, S. (2002): Legal Swedish and Legal Finnish, in: Mattila. H. (ed.) (2002): The Development of Legal Language, pp. 153–161.

Panaretou, E. (2005): Nomi kai kanones dikeu: glossika kai kimenika xaraktiristika (Athens: Parousia).

Panaretou, E. (2009): Nomikos logos. Glossa kai domi ton nomon (Athens: Ekdoseis Papazis).

Pardo, M.L. (1996): Derecho y Lingüistíca: Como se Juzga con Palabras (Buenos Aires: Ediciones Nueva Vista).

Parijs, van, P. (2011): Linguistic Justice for Europe and the World (Oxford: Oxford University Press).

Paroussis, M. (1995): Theorie des juristischen Diskurses. Eine institutionelle Epistemologie des Rechts (Berlin: Duncker & Humblot).

Pasternak, V. (1996): Chinesisch als Rechtssprache in Hongkong (Frankfurt a.M./ Bern: P. Lang).

Paunio, E., Lindroos-Hovinheimo, S. (2010): Taking Language Seriously: An Analysis of Linguistic Reasoning and Its Implications in EU Law, in: European Law Journal, vol. 16, no. 4, pp. 395–416.

Peczenik, A. (1986): Rätten och förnuftet (Lund: Nordstedts).

Peczenik, A. (1995): Vad är rätt? Om demokrati, rättssäkerhet, etik och juridisk argumentation (Stockholm: Fritzes Förlag).

Peczenik, A. (2005): Kinds of Legal Argumentation – Draft 2005 (available online).

Peerenboom, R.P. (2002): China's Long March toward Rule of Law (Cambridge: Cambridge University Press).

Pellegrino, P. (2014): Miti, favole, fiabe. Modelli alternativi di comunicazione giuridica tra prosa e poesia: lezioni di narratologia del diritto (Roma: Aracne).

Peotta, L. (1998): Kontrastive Fachtextpragmatik. Deutsche und italienische Gerichtsurteile im Vergleich (Frankfurt a.M./Bern: P. Lang).

Perelman, C., Olbrechts-Tyteca, L. (1983): Traité de l'argumentation, 4th ed. (Bruxelles: Editions de l'Université).

Perillo, J. M. (2003): Calamari and Perillo on Contracts, 5th ed. (St. Paul: Momsen West).

Perry, E.J. (2002): Challenging the Mandate of Heaven: Social Protest and State Power in China (Armonk: Sharpe).

Perry, E.J. (2008): Chinese Conceptions of Rights: From Mencius to Mao – and Now, in: Perspectives of Politics, vol. 6, pp. 37–50.

Petrażycki, L. (1955): Law and Morality (Cambridge: Harvard University Press).

Petzel, J. (2006): Język prawny w świetle lingwistycznej teorii rejestru językowego, in: Studia Juridica XLV, pp. 153–163.

Peursen, van, C.A., Bertels, K., Nauta, D. (1984): Informatie, 3rd ed.(Utrecht/Antwerpen: Het Spectrum).

Phillips, A. (2003): Lawyers' Language. How and Why Legal Language is Different (London/New York: Routledge).

Piehl, A. (2002): The Influence of EC Legislation on Finnish Legal Language: How to Assess it?, in: Mattila (H.) (ed.): The Development of Legal Language, pp. 101–112.

Pieńkos, J. (1999): Podstawy juryslingwistyki. Język w prawie – prawo w języku (Warszawa: Muza).

Pigolkin, A.S. (ed.) (1990): Iazyk zakona (Moskva: Juridicheskaya literatura).

Piller, I. (2016): Linguistic Diversity and Social Justice (Oxford: Oxford University Press).

Pintore, A. (1995): Law and Language: The Italian Analytical Tradition, in: Jackson, B.S. (ed.), Making Sense in Law. Linguistic, Psychological and Semiotic Perspectives (Liverpool: Deborah Charles Publications)

Plantin, C. (1996): L'argumentation (Paris: Seuil).

Plotnikova, N.S. (ed.) (2010): Pravda. Diskursy spraviedlivosti v russkoj intelektualnoj istorii (Moskva: Biblioteka instituta spraviedlivyj mir).

Podlech, A. (1976): Rechtslinguistik, in: Grimm, D. (ed.) Rechtswissenschaft und Nachbar- wissenschaften, vol. 2 (München: Beck) pp. 106–116.

Pohl, I. (ed.) (2008): Semantik und Pragmatik – Schnittstellen (Frankfurt/M: P. Lang).

Pollak, W. (1983): Entwicklungstendenzen im neuesten Französisch, in: Hausmann, F.J. (ed.) Die französische Sprache von heute (Darmstadt: Wissenschftliche Buchgesellschaft) pp. 127–144.

Ponsoda Sanmartín, J.J. (1996): El català i l'aragonés en els inicis del Regne de València segons el Llibre de Cort de Justícia dc Cocentina (1269–1295) (Alcoi: Marfil).

Posner, R. (1987): The Decline of Law as an Autonomous Discipline: 1962–1987, in: 100 Harvard Law Review 761.

Pozzo, B. (ed.) (2005): Ordinary Language and Legal Language (Milano: Giuffrè).

Pradid, J. F. (2002): Vstup do juridichnoi lingvistiki. Navchalskij posibnik (Simferopol: Dolya).

Preite, C. (2013): Des années 1970 au nouveau millénaire: essor de la jurilinguistique ou linguistique juridique, in: Parallèles, vol. 25, pp. 43–50.

Prieto de Pedro, J. (1991): Lenguas, lenguaje y derecho (Madrid: Civitas).

Prieto Ramos, F. (2011): Developing Legal Translation Competence: An Integrative Process-Oriented Approach, in: Comparative Legilinguistics. International Journal for Legal Communication, vol. 5, pp. 7–21.

Primus, R.A. (1999): The American Language of Rights (Cambridge: Cambridge University Press).

Puig, R. (2002): Ciencia y arte de la traducción (Montevideo: Universidad de la República).

Putnam, H. (1975): The Meaning of Meaning (Cambridge: Cambridge University Press).

Quine, W. (1983): Wort und Gegenstand (orig. Word and Object) (Stuttgart: Ph. Reclam).

Raadschelders, J.C.N. (2011): Public Administration. The Interdisciplinary Study of Government (Oxford: Oxford University Press).

Rabel, E. (1956): Das Problem der Qualifikation (Darmstadt: Wissenschaftliche Buchgesellschaft).

Raffman, D. (2014): Unruly Words. The Study of Vague Language (Oxford: Oxford University Press).

Rajah, J. (2012): Authoritarian Rule of Law. Legislation, Discourse and Legitimacy in Singapore (Cambridge: Cambridge University Press).

Ramić, Š. (2003): Language and the Interpretation of Islamic Law (Cambridge: Islamic Texts Society).

Rathert, M. (2006): Sprache und Recht (Heidelberg: Winter).

Rawls, J. (1971): A Theory of Justice (Cambridge: Harvard University Press).

Rawls, J. (1993): The Law of Peoples, in: Collected Papers, Freeman, S. (ed.) (Cambridge: Harvard University Press) pp. 529–564.

Rawls, J. (1999): The Law of Peoples, with the Idea of Public Reason Revisited (Cambridge: Harvard University Press).

Rawls, J. (2005): Political Liberalism (New York: Columbia University Press).

Reboul, A., Moeschler, J. (1998): Pragmatique du discours. De l'interprétation de l'énoncé à l'interprétation du discours (Paris: A. Colin).

Recanati, F. (2008): Philosophie du language (et de l'esprit) (Paris: Gallimard).

Redaktion der ÖJZ (eds.) (2014): Sprache und Recht (Wien: Manz).

Reed, C. (ed.) (2011): Computer Law, 7th ed. (Oxford: Oxford University Press).

Reiss,.K.,Vermeer, H.J. (1984): Grundlegung einer allgemeinen Translationstheorie (Tübingen: Max Niemeyer).

Resnik, J. (2014): Reinventing Courts as Democratic Institutions, in: Daedalus, vol. 143, no. 3, pp. 9–27.

Reus-Smit, C. (2005): International Law, in: Baylis, J., Smith, S. (eds.) (2005).

Rimmon-Kenan, S. (1989): Narrative Fiction: Contemporary Poetics (Routledge: London and New York).

Rhees, R. (1966): Can There Be a Private Language?, in: Pitcher, G. (ed.) Wittgenstein. The Philosophical Investigations (New York: Doubleday Anchor) pp. 267–285.

Robertshaw, P. (1998): Summary Justice. Judges Address Juries (London/Washington: Cassell).

Rodingen, H. (1977): Pragmatik der juristischen Argumentation (Freiburg/München: Alber).

Roehl, K. F. (2003): Das Recht nach der visuellen Zeitenwende, in: Juristenzeitung vol. 7.

Rorty, R. (1992) (ed.): The Linguistic Turn (Chicago/London: University of Chicago Press).

Rorty, R. (1993): Human Rights, Rationality, and Sentimentality, in: Shute, S., Hurley, S. (eds.) On Human Rights, The Oxford Amnesty Lectures (London: BasisBooks) pp. 112–134.

Rosen, J. (2013): Can the Judicial Branch be a Steward in a Polarized Democracy, in: Daedalus, vol. 142 (2), pp. 25–35.

Rosenberg, A. (2000): Philosophy of Science. A Contemporary Introduction (London/New York: Routledge).

Ross, A. (1957): Tû Tû, in: Harvard Law Review 70/5, pp. 812–825.

Ross, A. (1966): Om ret og retfærdighed. En indførelse i den analytiske retsfilosofi (København: Nyt Nordisk Forlag A. Busck).

Rottleuthner, H. (1973): Richterliches Handeln. Zur Kritik der juristischen Dogmatik (Frankfurt/M: Athenäum Fischer).

Rovere, G. (2005): Capitoli di linguistica giuridica. Ricerche su corpora elettronici (Alessandria: Ed. Dell'Orso).

Rumfitt, I. (2015): The Boundary Stones of Thought. As Essay in the Philosophy of Logic (Oxford: Oxford University Press).

Ruthström, B. (2003): Land och Fæ. Strukturellt-rättsfilologiska studier in fornnorsk lagspråk (Lund: Bloms i Lund Tryckeri).

Rydzewska-Siemiątkowska, J. (2016): Linguistic Analysis of Necessity Expressions in Finnish and Polish Legal Texts in Terms of Deontic Strength, in: Comparative Legilinguistics, vol. 26, pp. 47–69.

Rzeszutko, M. (2003): Rozprawa sądowa w świetle lingwistyki tekstu (Lublin: Wydawnictwo Uniwersytetu Marii Curie-Skłodowskiej).

Saarenpää, A. (1980): Rutiinijuttu (Helsinki: Helsingin Yliopisto).

Sacco, R. (2010): Mute law, in: Legal Theory and the Social Sciences, vol. II, eds. DelMar, M., Giudice, M. (Farnham: Ashgate).

Sager, J. (1990): A Practical Course in Terminology Processing (Amsterdam: Benjamins).

Said, E. (1979): Orientalism (New York: Vintage Books).

Saïd, S., Trédé, M., Le Boulluec, A. (2013): Histoire de la littérature grecque, 3rd ed. (Paris: puf).

Salas, M. E. (2001): ¿Que pasa actualmente en la teoría del derecho alemana?, in: Doxa, vol. 24, pp. 203–234.

Salmi-Tolonen, T. et al. (eds.) (2001): Law and Language – Prospect and Retrospect (Rovaniemi: Lapin yliopisto).

Salmi-Tolonen, T. (2008a): Forensista lingvistiikkaa – kielentutkimuksen juridisia sovellutuksia, in: Foley, R. et al. (2008), pp. 375–393.

Salmi-Tolonen, T. (2008b): Language and the Functions of Law (Rovaniemi: University of Lapland).

Samuel, G. (2014): An Introduction to Comparative Law Theory and Method (Oxford: Hart).

Santirocco, M.S. (2016): Introduction: Reassessing Greece & Rome, in: Daedalus, vol. 145, no. 2, pp. 5–19.

Saramandu, M (1986): Terminologia juridic-administrativă românească în perioda 1780–1850 (Bucureşti: Universitatea din Bucureşti).

Sarangi, A. (ed.) (2010): Language and Politics in India (Oxford: Oxford University Press).

Šarčević, S. (1997): New Approach to Legal Translation (The Hague: Kluwer).

Savigny, von, E. (1973): Grundkurs im wissenschaftlichen Definieren, 3.rd ed. (München: dtv).

Savigny, von, E. (1981): Inwiefern ist die Umgangssprache grundlegend für die Fachsprachen?, in: Hahn, v.,W. (ed.), Fachsprachen. Wege der Forschung (Darmstadt: Wissenschaftliche Buchgesellschaft).

Savigny, von, E. (1983): Zum Begriff der Sprache. Konvention, Bedeutung, Zeichen (Stuttgart: Reclam).

Savigny, von, F.C. (1840): System des heutigen Römischen Rechts, vol. I, (Berlin).

Scarpelli, U. (1953): Filosofia analitica e giurisprudenza (Milano: Nuvoletti).

Schaff, A. (1962): Introduction to Semantics (New York: Springer).

Schauer, F. (ed.) (1993): Law and Language (Aldershot/Hong Kong: Dartmouth).

Schauer, F., Wise, V.J. (1997): Legal Positivism as Legal Information, in: Cornell Law Review vol. 82, pp. 1080–1110.

Schauer, F., Wise, V.J. (2000): Nonlegal Information and the Delegalization of Law, in: Journal of Legal Studies, vol. 29, pp. 495–515.

Schauer, F. (2014): Our Informationally Disabled Courts, in: Daedalus, vol. 143, no. 3, pp. 105–114.

Schiff-Berman, P. (2012): Global Legal Pluralism. A Jurisprudence of Law beyond Borders (Cambridge: Cambridge University Press).

Schirren, T., Zinsmaier, T. (eds.) (2003): Die Sophisten. Ausgewählte Texte (Stuttgart: Reclam).

Schmidt, J. (1972): Einige Bemerkungen zur Präzision der Rechtssprache, in: Jahrbuch für Rechtssoziologie und Rechtstheorie, vol. II, pp. 390–437.

Schmidt-König, C. (2005): Die Problematik der Übersetzung juristischer Terminologie. Eine systematische Darstellung am Beispiel der deutschen und der französischen Rechtssprache (Münster/Hamburg/Oxford: LIT Verlag).

Schönherr, F. (1985): Sprache und Recht. Aufsätze und Vorträge (Wien: Manzsche Verlags- und Universitätsbuchhandlung).

Schwintowski, H.P. (2003): Die Bedeutung interdisziplinären Arbeitens von Rechts- und Sprachwissenschaft, in: Neue Juristische Wochenschrift, vol. 9, pp. 632–638.

Schwyter, J.R. (1996): Old English Legal Language (Odense: Odense University Press).

Scotto di Carlo, G. (2015): Diachronic and Synchronic Aspects of Legal English: Past, Present, and Possible Future of Legal English (Newcastle upon Tyne: Cambridge Scholars Publishing).

Searle, J. (1969): Speech Acts. An Essay in the Philosophy of Language (Cambridge: Cambridge University Press).

Searle, J. (1999): Mind, Language and Society. Doing Philosophy in the Real World (London: Weidenfield & Nicolson).

Searle, J. (ed.) (2004): Filosofija iazyka (Moskva: URSS), (Engl. orig.: The Philosophy of Language, Oxford: Oxford University Press).

Searle, J. (2011): Die Konstruktion der gesellschaftlichen Wirklichkeit. Zur Ontologie sozialer Tatsachen (Frankfurt: Suhrkamp) (Engl. Orig.: The Construction of Social Reality, 2005).

See, von, K. (1964): Altnordische Rechtswörter. Philologische Studien zur Rechtsauffassung und Rechtsgesinnung der Germanen (Tübingen: Niemeyer).

Seibert, T.M. (1981): Aktenanalyse. Zur Schriftform juristischer Deutungen (Tübingen: G. Narr).

Seibert, T.M. (1989): Schriftform und Mündlichkeitsprinzip im Rechtsdiskurs, in: Hoffmann, L. (ed.) Rechtsdiskurse. Untersuchungen zur Kommunikation in Gerichtsverfahren (Tübingen: G. Narr) pp. 217–250.

Selishchev, A.M. (1957): O jazykie "Russkoj pravdy" v svjazi s voprosom o drevniejshem tipie russkogo literaturnogo jazyka, in: Voprosy Jazykoznanija, no. 4.

Sen, A. (2005): The Argumentative Indian. Writings on Indian History, Culture and Identity (New York: Picador).

Serpe, A. (2006): Analysis of language and legal rights within the Scandinavian debate. Human rights: a "hidden essence"?, in: Frónesis 13/3.

Shahmatov, A. (1886): Issledovanije o jazykie novgorodskih gramot XIII i XIV vieka (St. Petersburg).

Shapiro, S. (2014): Varieties of Logic (Oxford: Oxford University Press).

Shaw, M. (2000): Theory of the Global State (Cambridge/NewYork: Cambridge University Press).

Sheriff, J. (1989): The Fate of Meaning: Charles Peirce, Structuralism and Literature (Princeton: Princeton University Press).

Shuy, R. W. (2006): Linguistics in the Courtroom: A Practical Guide (Oxford: Oxford University Press).

Shuy, R. W. (2012): The Language of Perjury Cases (Oxford: Oxford University Press).

Shuy, R.W. (2014): The Language of Murder Cases. Intentionality, Predisposition and Voluntariness (Oxford: Oxford University Press).

Siems, M. (2014): Comparative Law (Cambridge: Cambridge University Press).

Siitonen, A. (1989): Problems of Aporetics (Helsinki: Suomalainen Tiedeakademia).

Simonnaes, I. (2012): Rechtskommunikation national und international im Spannungsfeld von Hermeneutik, Kognition und Pragmatik (Berlin: Frank & Timme).

Skinner, Q. (2014): Forensic Shakespeare (Oxford: Oxford University Press).

Skutnabb-Kangas, T., Phillipson, R. (eds.) (1995): Linguistic Human Rights (Berlin/New York: Mouton/de Gruyter).

Skutnabb-Kangas, T. (2000): Linguistic Genocide in Education – or Worldwide Diversity and Human Rights? (Mahwah: Lawrence Erlbaum Associates).

Sloane, T.O. (ed.) (2001): Encyclopedia of Rhetoric (Oxford: Oxford University Press).

Slocum, B.G. (2012): Linguistics and 'Ordinary Meaning' Determinations, in: Statute Law Review, vol. 33(1), pp. 39–83.

Slocum, B.G. (2016): Ordinary Meaning: A Theory of the Most Fundamental Principle of Legal Interpretation (Chicago: University of Chicago Press).

Smirnov, A.V., Manukyan, A.G. (2008): Tolkovanije norm prava (Moskva: Prospekt).

Smith, C.S., McWilliams, J.P., Bloomfield, M. (1983): Law and American literature. A collection of essays (New York: Knopf).

Smits, J.M. (2005): The Principles of European Contract Law and the Harmonisation of Private Law in Europe, in: Vacquer, A. (ed.): La Tercera Parte de Los Principios de Derecho Contractual Europeo (Valencia: Tirant) pp. 567–590.

Smolka, J., Pirker, B. (2016): International Law and Pragmatics – An Account of Interpretation in International Law, in: International Journal of Language & Law, JLL 5, pp. 1–40.

Snell-Hornby, M. (1986): Übersetzungswissenschaft. Eine Neuorientierung. (Tübingen: UTB).

Sohoudé, K.M. (2010): Rechtsstaatlichkeit und Verantwortlichkeit bei Heinrich von Kleist (Frankfurt/Berlin/Bern: P. Lang).

Sokol, B.J., Sokol, M. (2000): Shakespeare's Legal Language. A Dictionary (London: The Athlone Press).

Solan, L.M. (1993): The Language of Judges (Chicago: University of Chicago Press).

Solan, L.M. (2010): The Language of Statutes. Laws and their Interpretation (Chicago: University of Chicago Press).

Sonderegger, S. (1965): Die ältesten Schichten einer germanischen Rechtssprache. Ein Betrag zur Quellensystematik, in: Festschrift K.S. Bader (Zürich: Schultheiss) pp. 419–438.

Sonsino, R. (1980): Motive clauses in Hebrew law. Biblical forms and Near Eastern parallels (Chico: Scholars Press).

Sørlie, M. (1965): En færøysk-norsk lovbok fra omkring 1310. En studie i færøysk språkhistorie (Tórshavn: Mentunargrunnor Føroya Løgtings/Bergen/Oslo: Universitetsforlaget).

Souza, de, A.A. (2005): Linguagem jurídica e poder (Recife: Nossa Livraria).

Sowinski, B. (1983): Textlinguistik. Eine Einführung (Stuttgart/Berlin: Kohlhammer).

Sperber, D. (1984): A dictionary of Greek and Latin legal terms in Rabbinical literature (Ramat-Gan: Bar Ilan University Press).

Sperber, D., Wilson, D. (1995): Relevance (Cambridge: Cambridge University Press).

Spiegelberg, W. (1892): Studien und Materialien zum Rechtswesen des Pharaonenreiches (Leipzig: Vereinigung wissenschaftlicher Verleger).

Spiegelberg, W. (1907): Die Schrift und Sprache der alten Ägypter (Leipzig: Vereinigung wissenschaftlicher Verleger).

Spiegelberg, W. (1922): Das Verhältnis der griechischen und ägyptischen Texte in den zweisprachigen Dekreten von Rosette und Kanopus (Berlin/Leipzig: Vereinigung wissenschaftlicher Verleger/ W. de Gruyter).

Spitzmüller, J., Warnke, I. (2011): Diskurslinguistik: Eine Einführung in Theorien und Methoden der transtextuellen Sprachanalyse (Berlin: De Gruyter).

Ståhle, C. I. (1958): Syntaktiska och stilistiska studier i fornnordiskt lagspråk (Lund).

Stalnaker, R. (2014): Context (Oxford: Oxford University Press).

Stang, C. (1935) Die westrussische Kanzleisprache des Großfürstentums Litauen (Oslo: Norske Videnskaps Akademi).

Stang, C. (1939): Die altrussische Urkundensprache der Stadt Polock, (Oslo: Norske Videnskaps Akademi).

Stein, D., Olsen, F., Lorz, R.A. (2008): Law and Language. Theory and Society (Düsseldorf: Düsseldorf University Press).

Stein, D, Olsen, F., Lorz, R.A. (2009): Translation Issues in Law (London: Palgrave/ Macmillan).

Stein, D. (2010): Vom Bedeuten in der Sprach- und Rechtswissenschaft, in: Krüper, J. Merten, H., Morlok, M. (eds.): An den Grenzen der Rechtsdogmatik (Tübingen: Mohr Siebeck) pp. 139–145.

Steiner, G. (1984): Antigones: The Antigone Myth in Western Literature, Art, and Thought (Oxford: Oxford University Press).

Steinbauer, B. (1989): Rechtsakt und Sprechakt. Pragmalinguistische Untersuchung zu deutschsprachigen Urkunden des 13. Jahrhunderts (Innsbruck: Institut für Germanistik).

Steinvorth, U. (1990): Klassische und moderne Ethik (Hamburg: dtv).

Stephens, M., Boyce, M. (2014): The Struggle for Civic Space between a Minority Legal Language and a Dominant Legal Language: The Case of Māori and English, in: Mac Aodha, M. (ed.) Legal Lexicography. A Comparative Perspective (Farnham/Burlington: Ashgate) pp. 289–319.

Stolze, R. (2005): Übersetzungstheorien. Eine Einführung, 4th ed. (Tübingen: Narr).

Strawson, P. (1992): Analysis and Metaphysics (Oxford: Oxford University Press).

Stygall, G. (2012): Discourse in the US Courtroom, in: Tiersma, P.M., Solan, L.M. (eds.): The Oxford Handbook of Language and Law (Oxford: Oxford University Press) pp. 369–380.

Supiot, A. (2005): Homo juridicus. Essai sur la function anthropologique du Droit (Paris: Seuil).

Swales, J.M. (2005): Genre Analysis. English in Academic and Research Setting (Cambridge: Cambridge University Press).

Szabó, M. (2001): Jog és nyelv. Trivium, gramatika, logika, retorika joghallgatók számára (Miskolc: Miskolci Egyetem).

Szabó, M. (2002): A jogi kommunikació. Kommunikació általában és a jogban (Miskolc: Bibor).

Tammelo, I. (1978): Modern Logic in the Service of Law (Wien/New York: Springer).

Tannen, D. (2013): The Argument Culture, in: Daedalus, vol. 142. no. 2, pp. 177–184.

Tanquerey, A. (1909): Synopsis theologiae dogmaticae fundamentalis ad mentem S. Thomae Aquinatis hodiernis moribus accommodata, 13th ed. (Rome/Paris: Desclée).

Tiersma, P. M. (1999): Legal Language (Chicago/London: University of Chicago Press).

Tiersma, P.M. (2010): Parchment, Paper, Pixel: Law and the Technologies of Communication (Chicago: Chicago University Press).

Timoteo, M. (2014): Il diritto per immagini. Aspetti del linguaggio giuridico cinese contemporaneo, in: Pozzo, B. (ed.) Lingua e diritto: Oltre l'Europa (Milano: Giuffrè).

Timoteo, M., Pozzo, B. (eds.) (2008): Europa e linguaggi giuridici (Milano: Giuffrè).

Timsit, G. (1991): Les noms de la loi (Paris: puf).

Thornton, G. C. (1996): Legislative Drafting, 4th ed. (London: Butterworths).

Thür, G. (2003): Recht im antiken Griechenland, in: Manthe, U. (ed.), Rechtskulturen der Antike. Vom Alten Orient bis zum Römischen Reich (München: Beck).

Todorov, T. (1992): The Conquest of America. The Question of the Other (New York: HarperPerennial).

Todorov, T. (2007): La littérature en péril (Paris: Flammarion).

Toprakyaran, E. (2007): Das osmanische Petitionswesen (mezalim) seit dem 18. Jahrhundert am Beispiel von Stadt und Provinz Trabzon (Frankfurt a. M.: P. Lang).

Torop, P. (1992): Tartuskaja shkola kak shkola, in: Bezprozvannyi, V. et al. (eds.): V chest 70-letija professora J. M. Lotmana. To honour professor Yu. M. Lotman (Tartu: Eidos).

Torop, P. (1998): Granicy perevoda, in: Sign Systems Studies, vol. 26, pp. 136–150.

Toulmin, E.S. (1958): The Uses of Argument (Cambridge: Cambridge University Press).

Tribe, L.H. (2000): American Constitutional Law, vol. I, (New York: Foundation Press).

Trimmel, F. (1993): Igazságügyi retorika (Pécs: JPTE).

Tronskij, I.M. (2001): Istoricheskaja grammatika latinskogo jazyka. Obshcheindoevropejskoje yazykovoje sostoyanie (voprosy rekonstrukcji) (Moskva: Indrik).

Trosborg, A. (1997): Rhetorical strategies in legal language. Discourse analysis of statutes and contracts (Tübingen: Narr).

Turell, M.T. (ed.) (2005): Lingüística Forense, Lengua y Derecho: Conceptos, Métodos y Aplicaciones (Barcelona: IULA).

Turi, J. (1995): Typology of Language Legislation, in: Skutnabb-Kangas, T., Phillipson, R. (eds.) Linguistic Human Rights. Overcoming Linguistic Discrimination (Berlin, New York: Mouton/de Gruyter) pp. 111–119.

Tzadua, A.P. (trans.), Strauss, P.L. (ed.) (1968): The Fetha Nagast: The Law of the Kings (Addis Ababa: Haile Selassie I University/Faculty of Law).

Udvari, L. (2013): I verbi modali "müssen" e "sollen" nel diritto privato svizzero. Frequenze e problemi di traduzione, in: Egger, J.L., Ferrari, A., Lala, L. (eds.) Le forme linguistiche dell'ufficialità (Bellinzona: Casagrande) pp. 151–212.

Unbegaun, B.O. (1969): Iazyk russkogo prava. Selected Papers on Russian and Slavonic Philology (Oxford: Oxford University Press).

Upham, F.K. (1990): Introduction into East Asian Legal Systems (Boston: Boston College Law School).

Urmson, J.O. (1992): J.L. Austin, in: Rorty, R.M. (ed.) The Linguistic Turn. Essays in Philosophical Method (Chicago/London: University of Chicago Press) pp. 232–238.

Urofsky, M.I. (2015): Dissent and the Supreme Court. Its Role in the Court's History and the Nation's Constitutional Dialogue (New York: Pantheon Books).

Uus, U. (1994): Blindness of Modern Science (Tartu: Tartu Observatory).

Vaidhyanathan, S. (2001): Copyrights and Copywrongs. The Rise of Intellectual Property and How it Threatens Creativity: NewYork/London: New York University Press).

Varennes, de, F. (1996): Language Minorities and Human Rights (The Hague/New York: Martinus Nijhoff).

Vasmer, V. (2003): Etymologicheskij slovar russkogo jazyka (vols. I–IV) (Moskva: Astrel'/Ast).

Vernant, J.P., Vidal-Naquet, P. (1988): Myth and Tragedy in Ancient Greece (New York: Zone Books).

Veronesi, D. (2000): Linguistica giuridica italiana e tedesca (Padova: Unipress).

Verschueren, J., Östman, J.-O. et al. (eds.) (1995): Handbook of Pragmatics (Amsterdam/Philadelphia: John Benjamins Publishing).

Viehweg, T. (1954): Topik und Jurisprudenz (München: C.H. Beck).

Vilar Sánches, K. (ed.) (2007): Mikrofunktionen in Arbeitsverträgen deutsch-spanisch (Bern, Berlin: P. Lang).

Villa-Real, R., del Arco Torres, M.A. (1999): Diccionario de términos jurídicos (Granada: Comares).

Vinnai, E. (2010): A jogi nyelv nyelvészeti megközelítése, in: Publicationes Universitatis Miskolciensis. Sectio Juridica et Politica, vol. 28, pp. 145–171.

Vinnai, E. (2011): Nyelvhasználat a jogi eljárásban (unpublished PhD-thesis at the University of Miskolc, available online).

Visconti, J. (2016): La lingua del giudice, in: Romboli, R. et al (eds.) VIII Giornate di diritto costituzionale (Pisa: Pisa University Press) pp. 32–41.

Vlasenko, N.A. (1997): Iazyk prava (Irkutsk: Vostochno-Sibirskoe knizhnoe izdatelstvo).

Vogel, H.J. (1988): Juridiska översättningar (Lund: Juristförlaget).

Wagner, A. (2002): La Langue de la Common Law (Paris: L'Harmattan).

Wagner, A. (2006): The Rules of the Road: A Universal Visual Semiotics, in: International Journal for the Semiotics of Law, vol. 19, pp. 311–324.

Wagner, A., Cacciaguidi-Fahy, S. (eds.) (2008): Obscurity and Clarity in Law. Prospects and Challenges (Aldershot: Ashgate).

Wagner, A., Bhatia, V. K. (eds.) (2009): Diversity and Tolerance in Socio-Legal Contexts: Explorations in the Semiotics of Law (Farnham/Burlington: Ashgate).

Wandruszka, M. (1979): Die Mehrsprachigkeit des Menschen (München/Zürich: Piper).

Wangui, R.B. (2015): Training as a Minimum Requirement to Improve Court Interpretation in Kenya: a Case of Milimani Chief Magistrate's Courts (Thesis, Repository: University of Nairobi).

Wank, R. (2015): Die Auslegung von Gesetzen, 5th ed. (München: Vahlen).

Ward, I. (1995): Law and Literature. Possibilities and Perspectives (Cambridge: Cambridge University Press).

Warda-Radys, L. (2006): O polszczyźnie urzędowej w Gdańsku w dobie średniopolskiej, in: Rozprawy Komisji Językowej ŁTN, vol. LI.

Watzlawick, P, Beavin, J.H., Jackson, D.D. (1969): Menschliche Kommunikation. Formen, Störungen, Paradoxien, 4th ed. (Bern: Huber).

Wedberg, B. (1928): Lagstil. Några citat och reflektioner (Stockholm: Norsted & Söners Förlag).

Wee, L. (2011): Language without Rights (Oxford: Oxford University Press).

Weerts, S. (2015): La langue de l'Etat. Proposition d'un modèle de pluralisme linguistique à partir de l'étude comparée des droits belge et suisse (Bruxelles: Bruylant).

Wegmann, P.F. (2016): Vermutung und Fiktion. Widerstände einer im Recht verwendeten Denkfigur (Schulthess: Zürich).

Weinberger, O., Weinberger, C. (1979): Logik, Semantik, Hermeneutik (München: Beck).

Weinrich, H. (1966): Linguistik der Lüge (München: C.H. Beck).

Weisberg, R. (1992): Poethics and Other Strategies of Law and Literature (New York: Columbia University Press).

Weisgerber, O. (1961): Übersetzungsfehler im Südtirol-Konflikt (Innsbruck: Leopold-Franzens-Universität).

Weiss, B. (1978): Interpretation in Islamic Law: The Theory of Ijtihād, in: The American Journal of Comparative Law, vol. 26/2, pp. 199–212.

Wennström, B. (1996): The Lawyer and Language (Uppsala: Justus Förlag).

Wennström, T. (1946): Lagspråk och lagtexter. Rättsfilologiska studier över medeltida svenska lagar (Lund: Gleerupska Universitetsbokhandeln).

Wessén, E. (1965): Svenskt lagspråk (Lund: Gleerups).

White, J.B. (1990): Justice as Translation: An Essay in Cultural and Legal Criticism (Chicago: Chicago University Press).

White, J.B. (1994): Acts of Hope: Creating Authority in Literature, Law and Politics (Chicago: Chicago University Press).

Wierzbicka, A. (1987): Boys will be boys: Radical semantics vs. radical pragmatics, in: Language, vol. 63, pp. 95–114.

Wierzbicka, A. (2013): Imprisoned in English. The Hazards of English as a Default Language (Oxford: Oxford University Press).

Wigoder, G. (ed.) (1996): Dictionnaire encyclopédique du judaïsme (Paris: Cerf/R. Lafont).

Wiktorsson, P.A. (1981): Avskrifter och skrivare. Studier i fornsvenska lagtexter (Stockholm: Almqvist & Wicksell).

Wildhaber, L. (2002): Protection against Discrimination under the European Convention on Human Rights – a Second-Class Guarantee? in: Zemele, I. (ed.), Baltic Yearbook of International Law, vol. 2.

Williams, C. (2005): Tradition and Change in Legal English (Bern: P. Lang).

Wilmer, S.E., Zakauskaite, A. (eds.) (2010): Interrogating Antigone in Postmodern Philosophy and Criticism (Oxford: Oxford University Press).

Witczak-Plisiecka, I. (2004): Linguistic Aspects of Deontic Shall in the Legal Context, in: Goźdź-Roszkowski, S., Kredens, K. (eds.) Language and the Law: International Outlooks (Frankfurt a. M.: P. Lang) pp. 181–199.

Wittgenstein, L. (1984): Philosophische Untersuchungen (Frankfurt/M: suhrkamp).

Wohlrapp, H. (ed.) (1995): Wege der Argumentationsforschung (Stuttgart: problemata fromann-holzboog).

Wolf, E. (1950–1957): Griechisches Rechtsdenken, vol. I–V (Frankfur/M: V. Klostermann).

Wolff, H.-J. (1961): Beiträge zur Rechtsgeschichte Altgriechenlands und des hellenistisch-römischen Ägypten (Weimar: Böhlau).

Wolff, L. (2011): Legal Translation, in: Malmkjær, K., Wandle, K. (eds.) The Oxford Handbook of Translation Studies (Oxford: Oxford University Press), pp. 228–242.

Woo, M.Y.K., Gallagher, M.E. (2011): Chinese Justice: Civil Dispute Resolution in Contemporary China (Cambridge: Cambridge University Press).

Woodruff, P. (2011): The Ajax Dilemma: Justice, Fairness and Rewards (Oxford: Oxford University Press).

Working Group, (2001): Tuomioistuinsanasto (Helsinki: Edita).

Working Group, Cabinet Secretariat (2006): Hôrei yôgo nichi-ei hyôjun taiyaku jisho. Japanese-English Legal Terms Standard Bilingual Dictionary (www.cas.go.jp).

Wright, von, G.H. (1951): Deontic Logics, in: Mind, vol. 60, pp. 1–15.

Wróblewski, J. (1988): Sądowne stosowanie prawa (Warszawa: PWN).

Wu, R. (2003): Xianggang shuangyu tingshen zhong de ruogan wenti, in: Zhou, Q., Wang, J., Su, J., Yuyan yu falü yanjiu de xin shijie. Language and Law in a New Perspective (Beijing: Law Press China) pp. 213–224.

Wydra, D. (2008): Autonomie auf der Halbinsel Krim. Eine völker- und verfassungsrechtliche Analyse (Wien: Braumüller).

Wydra, D., Galdia, M. (2010): Rechtliche Grundlagen interethnischer Beziehungen in der Russischen Föderation, in: Osteuropa-Recht, vol. 3, pp. 283–302.

Xirinachs, M. (2002): Promoting Legal Catalan, in: Mattila, H.E.S. (ed.) The Development of Legal English (Helsinki: Kauppakaari) pp. 131–149.

Xu, W.Y. (1998): The Court Records of O.J. Simpson Trial (Beijing: Publishing House of Law).

Yacoub, J. (1998): Les minorités dans le monde (Paris: Desclée De Brower).

Yankova, D. (2004): Statutory Provisions in English and Bulgarian (Sofia: Tip-Top Press).

Yankova, D. (2008): The Text and Context of European Directives. Translation Issues in Approximating Legislation (Sofia: Sofia University Press).

Youn, Y.J. (2016): Recht und Rechtssprache in Korea und Deutschland. Probleme bei der Übertragung juristischer Texte aus übersetzungswissenschaftlicher Sicht unter besonderer Berücksichtigung des Ehe- und Familienrechts (Frankfurt a. M.: P. Lang).

Yu, S. (2010): Fayuan Yu Yanjiu (Beijing: Beijing Daxue Chubanshe).

Zabłocka, M. (2010): Rzymskie korzenie współczesnego języka prawnego, in: Mróz, A., Niewiadomski, A., Pawelec, M. (eds.) Prawo, język, etyka (Warszawa: Lingua Iuris) pp. 9–16.

Zaccaria, G. (ed.) (2000): Übersetzung im Recht. Translation in Law (Münster: LIT Verlag).

Zamyatin, K. (2014): An Official Status for Minority Languages? A Study of State Languages in Russia's Finno-Ugric Republics (Helsinki: University of Helsinki)

Zgółka, T., Zieliński, M. (2003): Perswazja w języku prawnym i prawniczym, in: Mosiołek-Kłosińska, K., Zgółka, T. (eds.): Język perswazji publicznej (Poznań: Wydawnictwo Poznańskie).

Zgusta, L. (1971): Manual of Lexicography (Praha/The Hague: Academia/Mouton).

Zhang, N. (2002): Guoji fa yuanli (The Theory of International Law) (Beijing: Zhongguo Zheng Fa Daxue).

Zhang, Q. (2004): Traditional Chinese Culture (Beijing: Foreign Languages Press).

Zhao, Y. (2001): Drafting Policy on Bilingual Legislation. Comments on the Hong Kong Securities and Futures Act, published as LC Paper No. CB (2) 1136/00–01 (01).

Zhou, Q., Wang, J., Su, J. (eds.) (2003): Yuyan yu falü yanjiu de xin shiye. Language and Law in a New Perspective (Beijing: Law Press China).

Ziccardi Capaldo, G. (2008): The Pillars of Global Law (Aldershot: Ashgate).

Zieliński, M. (1972): Interpretacja jako proces dekodowania tekstu prawnego (Poznań: UAM Prace Wydziału Prawa).

Zitelmann, E. (1888): Die Möglichkeit eines Weltrechts (München/Leipzig: Duncker & Humblot).

Znamenáčková, K. (2007): Fachsprachliche Wortgruppen in Textsorten des deutschen Zivilrechts (Frankfurt/M: P. Lang).

Index of Issues

Bold numbers refer to pages in the main text where the issues have been treated with particular attention. Regular numbers refer to pages in the main text where the issues have been mentioned in a specific context.

V

W

Index of Names

In this index the names of persons mentioned in the main text are listed. Names of researchers whose contributions are constantly quoted in the main text such as H.E.S. Mattila, G. Cornu or J. Searle are referred to with the page number indicating the central part of the argument that was developed in this book. Names of classics, e.g. Aristotle or Boethius, are not included.

T

V

W

Y

Z